ALEXANDER TCHEREPNIN:
A COMPENDIUM

by

BENJAMIN FOLKMAN

Including a newly annotated first English-language edition of
ALEXANDER TCHEREPNIN by WILLI REICH

translated from the German by

Mosco Carner, Marjorie Glock and Benjamin Folkman

and

extensive supplementary biographical and analytical
material, with numerous extracts from the
composer's own published and unpublished writings.

Inks and Bindings
888-290-5218
www.inksandbindings.com
orders@inksandbindings.com

IN MEMORIAM

HSIEN MING TCHEREPNIN
(1911–1991)

GEORGE E. HESSE III
(1947–1991)

Alexander Tcherepnin in his Monte Carlo *pied à terre*, 1925

FOREWORD BY SIR YEHUDI MENUHIN

Alexander Tcherepnin belonged to that wonderful period of the twenties which brought such a wealth of cross-fertilization to music, to dance, to painting and sculpture, largely accomplished in Paris, where Russian and French painters and composers (the famous Six) found refuge and allowed their overwhelming genius to flower in partnership. Contributing cultures to Russia from Asia, the Mohammedan world, Georgia, Gypsies and Jews had already brought Russian art to a high level of universal expression, but the Revolution squeezed out some of the most visionary and gifted of them. They explored the complexities of the western world of France together with contributing cultures from Africa, from Bali and the Pacific islands.

Tcherepnin went one step beyond and married his wonderful and devoted Ming, a pure Chinese lady, thus expanding his sources of inspiration and impressions even further.

I was so thrilled to broadcast and record the Tcherepnin Violin Sonata with the composer. It is a beautiful and expressive work, and, of course, to play it with Tcherepnin himself was a real privilege.

I always knew him to be a perfectly balanced human being, a gentleman in every sense of the word—not only in Paris but also in New York, at home everywhere. His mind, gentle and probing, original and stimulating, compassionate and wise, was never dogmatic or self-willed. He was in every way a civilized human being, and as two "Russians" we embraced each other with love, devotion and understanding.

Surely this book, in which many of Tcherepnin's own writings appear for the first time, will do its hero, this unique man, the justice he so richly deserves.

London, 15 July, 1991

Edited by Bejamin Folkman

TABLE OF CONTENTS

BOOK I: BIOGRAPHICAL

PART I. ALEXANDER TCHERPNIN by Willi Reich

(* This Chapter written by Benjamin Folkman)

PART II: THREE AUTOBIOTRAPHICAL ACCOUNTS

PART III. EPISODES AND EPILOGUE

INTERMEZZI: TCHEREPNIN AND HIS COLLEAGUES

BOOK II ANALYTICAL

SEVENTEEN TCHEREPNIN MASTERPIECES
by Benjamin Folkman

PART I (1922-1932)

PART II (1942-1965)

BOOK III: PERSONAL

TCHEREPNIN SPEAKS

Front cover: Alexander Tcherepnin in Chicago, ca. 1955.

Back cover: Laboriously prepared as a birthday card for his first wife Louisine in 1931, this circular design is a thematic catalogue of the works Tcherepnin had composed during the course of their relationship. The inmost of the 36 nested circles encloses the date 14 XI 1931. The four circles immediately surrounding the center contain birthday wishes and endearments:2. Tous voeux de bonheur 3. Eternel devo[u]ement 4. Toute toute tendresse 5. Tout amour tout amour. The catalogue itself (circles 6 through 30) reads radially from "out" to "in" rather than circularly. Circles 10 through 6 give the titles of eleven instrumental scores, the names of nineteen operatic characters, and the names of five characters and the setting from the never performed (and possibly never finished) ballet *Sodom's Miracle*. (Thirty-six names in all). Lined up with these titles and names in circles 30 through 11 are thirty-six musical themes associated with them. Gridlines serve as staves; filled-in spaces are musical notes, appropriately stemmed. Circles 35 through 31 contain birthday wishes in English, French, German and Russian, penned left to right (no longer radially) five letters per line into the 36 five-square-by-five-square arrays that abut the 36 musical themes (some of the wishes continue through two or three arrays).

INTRODUCTION BY THE EDITOR

This large volume is the end product of what began as a small initiative: an attempt to issue an English translation of Willy Reich's German-language monograph *Alexander Tcherepnin*, the first biography of the composer ever published. Long regarded as required reading for anyone interested in Tcherepnin's life and works, Reich's brief, elegantly written book on his composer-friend (seventy-one pages in its first edition) had appeared in 1961. A French translation followed a year later.

Although a classic of its kind, Reich's effort was, as we shall see, very much an authorized biography of an artist in mid-career, with all the virtues and flaws of that genre. Its authorized nature is particularly relevant because Tcherepnin was a consummate careerist, amazingly adroit in controlling much of what was printed about him. For each new score, he would supply reporters with an effective "hook"—a provocative technical, artistic or circumstantial description-which they often incorporated into their reviews and stories. The "Tcherepnin party-line" was a comprehensive ideology, polished to a high gloss through many years of trial and error.

Reich's book hewed to every tenet of that line. While replete with invaluable information supplied and carefully vetted by the composer, it was, at the same time, noticeably hagiographic in tone, reticent in independent critical perspective and occasionally either silent or outright misleading about biographical details-even about the chronology of some Tcherepnin works (notably, the recycled scores that the composer offered as new when establishing himself in America in the 1950s). Tcherepnin himself found a drawback in the author's attempt to combine comprehensiveness and brevity. "Willi Reich," he wrote "did a very good job and I appreciate it; yet he tried to cover too much ground and therefore there are no highspots." Despite these flaws, however, the biography's appearance in English in the 1960s or 70s would have filled a useful gap, as no comparable account of the composer's life and work existed in our language.

Plans for an English translation, however, ran into difficulties (which will later be discussed in detail). Although the void in Tcherepniana in English was partly filled in 1989 by Enrique Alberto Arias's bio-bibliography of the composer, that effort was primarily a source study, meant chiefly for the shelves of music libraries, and merely reproduced, moreover, from a typewritten original—quite unlike the opulent Reich book with its many illustrations and musical examples. The composer's widow Hsien Ming Tcherepnin still cherished the notion of issuing the Reich, a genuine biography by a prestige author, in English; and in 1991, she brought in the present editor.

Yet by then it was obvious that issuing Reich's biography merely as he had left it would have been a disservice to readers seeking an accurate perspective on Tcherepnin. At the same time, that book had been available in German and French for decades, and offering a heavily edited version as Reich's work could not be countenanced.

It thus seemed best to present his text as the opening section of a much larger publication, one in which Reich's biography serves as a kind of center around which a comprehensive portrait of the composer, his work and his philosophy gradually takes shape, a portrait produced with the aid of hundreds of pages of the composer's own published and unpublished writings.

The result, *Alexander Tcherepnin: A Compendium*, incorporates three books, designated "Biographical," "Analytical" and "Personal" (categories offered as guidelines rather than hard and fast divisions). A section entitled "Intermezzi: Tcherepnin and his Colleagues" appears between Books I and II. Three large sections of photographs separate the compendium's various parts, and in the Reich biography, photos are interspersed with the text, emulating the layout of the book's two German editions.

Book I: Biographical

Alexander Tcherepnin by Willi Reich stands as Part I of Book I. Produced, as noted, with the full and active cooperation of the composer beginning in 1959, Reich's text draws heavily upon Tcherepnin's own unpublished autobiography, a single-spaced fifty-six-page typescript written in French, originally commissioned by Flammarion Press, Paris and completed on August 26, 1947. Flammarion had presumably expected Tcherepnin, a charming raconteur, to provide an anecdotal account of his event-crammed life: a narrative replete with Revolutionary perils and exotic travel vistas, highlighted by the romance of Tcherpnin's storybook round-the-world courtship of his second wife, Ming, and spiced with inside information about high-jinks at those watering places of the rich to which Tcherepnin had once had entree through his wealthy first wife, Louisine—a book much like Arthur Rubinstein's subsequent best-sellers. When the composer submitted instead a narrative almost completely devoid of references to his personal life—an analytical, year-by-year, score-by-score discussion of his development as an artist and the impact of his creative work upon his external career—the publisher had declined to issue it.

Happily, the academic judiciousness and thoroughness that made Tcherepnin's book useless to Flammarion in 1947 were precisely the qualities that made it indispensable to Reich a decade later. Often, Tcherepnin, in describing the genesis or the technical content of a score, had done the job so well that Reich, in his biography, properly contented himself with merely paraphrasing the French account.

The composer's hand is evident elsewhere in the shaping of Reich's book. Tcherepnin made it clear that there were personal matters he did not wish discussed or elaborated upon in print (accordingly, his first marriage, a twelve-year union, is mentioned only in one oblique reference to its dissolution). On the other hand, in information that Tcherepnin supplied off the record, he concealed little or nothing from Reich—indeed, in the accounts he sent his biographer (written in articulate and idiomatic if at times wrong-gendered German) he showed unusual candor, feeling, apparently, that the better Reich understood him, the better the book would be. Presumably, Tcherepnin even selected and annotated the thirty-odd musical examples that enrich Reich's account. (Many years later, Arias discovered a collection of Tcherepnin papers labeled *Beispiele* [*i. e.*, "Examples"] and the first page of these, as Arias describes it, is identical in music and commentary to Example 1 in Reich's study.) The final chapter of Reich is also dominated by the composer's influence: in its discussion of Tcherepnin's work in different countries, it follows a scheme that Tcherepnin himself devised in one of his letters.

In November 1961, several months after the biography appeared, translators approved by the composer were commissioned to produce French and English versions, respectively, Harry Halbreich and Mosco Carner. Reading their work in the spring of 1962, Tcherepnin noted that he "found the French translation fair and, with few exceptions, fit to print"; but he had serious reservations about the English rendering. A British publisher concurred and postponed plans for an edition. Halbreich's French version went to the printer immediately and appeared later the same year, published by *La Revue Musicale* in its *Musiciens du Vingtième Siècle* series. In this translation, the text had been updated (almost certainly in accordance with Tcherepnin's instructions) to cover the composer's activities between 1959 and 1962.

At the end of the decade, Reich expanded his biography, using additional information supplied by the composer to extend the chronicle of Tcherepnin's life up to June of 1968—an addition that has documentary value but rather spoils the shape of Reich's original narrative plan, designed to climax with the magisterial *Symphonic Prayer*. This second edition appeared in 1970, and it seemed likely that an English version would soon follow. Tcherepnin's reputation in America had declined only a little from the peak it had attained in the 1950s, a time when virtually every year saw the premiere of a new Tcherepnin symphonic work by a major conductor and orchestra, while his career in England, after decades in the doldrums, was at last flourishing, largely due to the promotional efforts of the BBC's Sir William Glock.

Another translator was procured in 1970 to provide an English version of Reich's additions, but his work proved unusable, partly because he was ignorant of German musical terminology. So it happened that the English translation did not get back on track until the mid-1970s, when Tcherepnin began working over the Carner text with Sir William's sister, Marjorie Glock. Again, Tcherepnin treated a biographical collaborator as a confessor, supplying details not meant for publication in a series of memos which also identified inaccuracies and infelicities in the original translation, corrected errors in Reich's account and provided personal and analytical information that Tcherepnin considered crucial.

Unfortunately, by the time Ms. Glock had finished her revision of Carner, the publishing climate had become less favorable for a book of this sort. Moreover, Tcherepnin—who for most of his life had been able to claim his own special niche in the modernist pantheon—suddenly seemed, in his last years, to belong to the past, if only because he had not completed a large orchestral work since 1965. After his death in 1977, his music went into temporary eclipse. In the 1980s, at the behest of Ming Tcherepnin, Guy Wuellner, a Tcherepnin scholar, and Lily Chou, corresponding secretary of the Tcherepnin Society, prepared an amplified version of the Carner-Glock English translation.

For the present compendium, however, the Editor elected to bring the much-amended typescript back into accord with Reich. A good deal of information and opinion that had been added during revisions was either removed entirely or transferred to footnotes, a process that involved the re-translation of numerous passages. Since Reich had used no footnotes, the Editor risked no confusion by introducing some, primarily where it seemed obligatory to correct errors immediately, or to provide essential information. A few longer Editor's notes surrounded by curly brackets —{ }—also appear, at junctures where necessary explanations seemed too long for footnotes. The Editor, however, deemed one major interpolation necessary, producing a supplementary piece on Tcherepnin's last years (1968-1977) which has been designated Chapter 7A and inserted into the chronological sequence of Reich's book between his last two chapters (7 and 8).

The first book of the Compendium concludes with some eighty additional pages of biographical material. Book I, Part II - contains three separate autobiographical accounts, all formal presentations by the composer. The first, the only one of the three to reach print during his lifetime, is a short autobiography intended for general audiences. Tcherepnin wrote the second, more specialized in approach, to supply comprehensive information about his development as a composer to Nicolas Slonimsky, who was preparing an entry about Tcherepnin for *Baker's Musical Dictionary*. The third, and surely the most important of these autobiographical pieces, is Tcherepnin's "Basic Elements of My Musical Language," a detailed disquisition upon his personal compositional theories and techniques illustrated with more than thirty musical examples, to which he appends pithy observations summing up his artistic odyssey and philosophy.

The third and final section of Book I draws on Tcherepnin's copious autobiographical writings. The nature of these makes the following, somewhat lengthy digression necessary.

During a life rich in travel, the composer—in effect—went everywhere, did everything, and knew everybody, and his memoirs on his experiences were voluminous, to say the least. He had a lifelong habit of keeping diaries, and although some of those dealing with the Petersburg-Petrograd period (*i.e.*, up to 1918) were left in a trunk in that city and have undoubtedly disappeared forever, those from age nineteen on remained in his possession, ready to be drawn upon to supplement his retentive memory and keen eye for detail.

Tcherepnin's autobiographical writings were more extensive, in fact, than the listing in Arias' bio-bibliography indicates. Arias missed some important documents altogether; moreover, the documents that Arias mentioned were sometimes inaccurately described. For example, Arias identified two separate autobiographies: the aforementioned fifty-six-page account in French, completed in 1947, and an English narrative, ending on page 158 and completed on May 27, 1962. What Arias was unaware of, however, is that these two typescripts are actually the beginning and the ending of a *single* autobiography. Tcherepnin himself wrote about the macaronic nature of this curious assembly of papers on June 12, 1959:

> The first part of [my autobiography], written in French, was completed in 1947 in Chene Rogneux. To this, I have added two addenda, the second one bringing the Autobiography up to February 1953; page 71 is the last page of the text completed in February 1953 in Chicago.
>
> Last month...when I started to plan the continuation, I found that my French [had become] much worse than it was, while my English, although also no good, is easier for me to use. Also, I wanted to give more emphasis to the change in my life that occurred after our settling in Chicago. So I resumed the writing of the Autobiography in English: and marked falsely the first page of continuation as 69-it should follow the page 70.
>
> To have the full picture, one has to combine the pages 57-70 of the French text with the pages of the English text covering the same period and then, after 1953, there is only English text.
>
> I admit it looks like a mess, but it is the best I could do.

Not all of this hybrid account could be located when the Compendium was being prepared: the Editor was able to peruse only the original French autobiography, a few additional French pages dealing with the early 1950s and two English continuations, one covering the period September 1957-June 1959 and marked as pages 105-118, and the other (typed on a different machine) extending from June 1959 to May 1962 and bearing the page numbers 116-158.

Even more material is available, however; for at some time in subsequent years, probably in the late 1960s, Tcherepnin began another autobiography, this time entirely in English (not mentioned by Arias, presumably because Ming Tcherepnin did not make it available to him). Far more detailed in treatment than its bilingual predecessor, and laden with intimate, sometimes embarrassing personal revelations (particularly about his treatment of his first wife), this account begins in the composer's earliest years and breaks off in 1937 after 190 pages, many typed single-spaced with the stingiest of margins. Apparently, this was designed not for publication, but, rather, for later use in the preparation of an autobiography or biography. Indeed, Tcherepnin later typed the thirty-seven-page opening of yet *another* autobiography—which was perhaps at last intended as a definitive version, for here Tcherepnin made a conscious attempt to employ a more "literary" narrative style.

Returning to the Compendium: these voluminous materials figure significantly in Part III of Book I, entitled "Episodes and Epilogue." This section consists of six biographical sketches. Five of these, recast from the composer's narratives by Lily Chou working under Ming Tcherepnin's supervision, and later somewhat revised by the Editor, deal, respectively, with the Russian years, the journey west, the composer's first London successes, his first experiences of America and his musical life in China and Japan. It is hoped that these will give the reader more humanized pictures of Tcherepnin's experiences than Reich could attempt in his limited space. The Epilogue of Book I, Part III is a survey of Tcherepnin's life and works by the composer Phillip Ramey—a former Tcherepnin student and an expert on his music—who also provides an overall critical appraisal.

Intermezzi: Tcherepnin and his Colleagues

The title of this intermediary section is self-explanatory. Its first portion contains a collection of tributes to Tcherepnin the man and Tcherepnin the artist, furnished by composers, conductors and performers of his era. Part II presents Tcherepnin's own descriptions of his encounters with, or impressions of, many legendary musicians, mostly composers; these, except where otherwise noted, are drawn from his writings and from interviews.

Book II: Analytical Seventeen Tcherepnin Masterpieces

Book II was prepared by the Editor as a sort of counterweight to Reich's monograph. Where Reich presented a general overview of Tcherepnin against the background of his total oeuvre, the Editor has undertaken a specialized study of the composer, formed around separate essays on seventeen significant Tcherepnin scores, which are discussed in analytical and biographical detail. Of inestimable help here were various analyses by Tcherepnin himself, some of them exhaustive, others cursory. Moreover, Tcherepnin's memoirs made it possible to include a good deal of biographical information that does not appear in Book I. While such a study can make no pretense to completeness, it can examine important qualities in the individual works, perhaps prompting new insights.

Book III: Personal Tcherepnin Speaks

In the final book, the composer again speaks for himself. Part I is a series of observations and anecdotes, culled from Tcherepnin's autobiographies, notes, letters and interviews, and arranged according to topic. These begin with comments on composing and performing but later range farther afield and ultimately touch on questions of personal and national philosophies. Part II is dominated by writings that Tcherepnin intended for publication; these are accompanied by some private writings that are especially characteristic.

Each section of *Alexander Tcherepnin, A Compendium* is introduced by a "Tcherepnin Prelude," an observation penned by the composer or given by him in interviews.

The volume concludes with several catalogues and a bibliography. The two catalogues of Tcherepnin's scores, one chronological, one generic, were prepared by Lily Chou, who updated the standard Tcherepnin work-list compiled by Christopher Chang and Phillip Ramey, and also included information found in Enrique Arias' *Alexander Tcherepnin—A Bio-Bibliography* along with other material supplied by Serge Tcherepnin.

A discography of Tcherepnin's music follows, amplified from the discography of LPs and 78 recordings prepared by Phillip Ramey and made available to Arias for his book. Although the LPs that form the bulk of these listings have long been out of circulation, some may still be found in the larger libraries or on E-bay. The Editor has also provided a second discography of Tcherepnin's work *as a pianist*, along with a selected list of unpublished broadcast recordings in which the composer played or conducted his own works.

Although *Alexander Tcherepnin: A Compendium* was substantially completed in 1992, it remained unpublished for various reasons. A print-out was made available, however, to the Russian musicologist Liudmila Korabelnikova, who included extracts from it in her Russia-language book on Tcherepnin, published in Moscow in 1999. As translated into English by Anna Winestein, Dr. Korabelnikova's volume reached print in 2007, issued by Indiana University Press under the title *Alexander Tcherepnin: The Saga of a Russian Émigré Composer*. This book has the distinction of being both the first Russian-language and the first English-language biography of the composer.

In her book, Dr. Korabelnikova felt impelled to examine Tcherepnin in the context of a milieu deliberately neglected by Soviet scholars: the rich culture established in the West by Russian emigre artists. While such a specialized approach gives the book a singular value, it also leaves room for the more general biographical treatment provided in the present Compendium.

No one can fail to notice the "themes" that recur again and again in the Alexander Tcherepnin's observations—for, indeed, with Tcherepnin integrity was not a mere obligation but an inner trait stemming from a devotion to humanism. He firmly believed that music must have moral integrity: that a composer must strive to express himself without self-aggrandizement or crowd-pleasing compromise. Ethics, however, are no substitute for original artistic vision, and in the final stage beyond analysis it is the primal creative power in Tcherepnin's best music, inborn, mysterious and indomitable, that continues to compel.

A great many people have worked to make this volume possible. Thanks are due to: The late Sir William Glock, who gave much valuable advice about the translation;

Guy Wuellner, who, with his knowledge and understanding of Tcherepnin's music, provided a treasure-trove of important information;

Lily Chou, archivist for Ming Tcherepnin, who responded to the Editor's incessant requests for material with unfailing resourcefulness and good humort;

Jane Hohfeld Galante, whose excellent translation of Tcherepnin's French autobiography was of use to the Editor in emending the portions translated for this compendium.

Steven Cerf, who patiently vetted the German translation sentence by sentence and also made astute suggestions about the rest of the volume;

Serge Tcherepnin, the composer's second son, most knowledgeable of all authorities on Tcherepnin's writings, who unearthed hidden jewels from pounds and pounds of documents, and otherwise provided the Editor with salutary guidance.

The late Ivan Tcherepnin, the composer's third son, who enabled to Editor to examine the contents of key manuscripts and responded to inquiries with encouragement.

Peter Tcherepnine, the composer's first son and now Chairman of the Tcherepnin Society, for his extraordinary understanding and generosity in volunteering to accommodate family affairs to the requirements of this project. The Editor wishes to acknowledge, also, the great personal kindness shown him by all three of the composer's sons.

The Editor also owes an inestimable debt to Phillip Ramey. It was he who introduced me to Tcherepnin personally and brought me into contact with him on the several subsequent occasions that I met him. Ramey has also been an inexhaustible source of Tcherepnin lore, and his numerous observations about the composer to me, stemming from his special perspective as a Tcherepnin-trained composer and close friend of the family, have had an overwhelming influence upon the tenor of this book. Moreover it is impossible to overestimate the worth of the extraordinary source material with which Ramey so enthusiastically and so copiously furnished me: his letters from Alexander and Ming Tcherepnin and his private tapes of Tcherepnin lectures and radio interviews yielded fascinating information that often-filled major gaps in the composer's own accounts.

Unfortunately, the most valuable and unstinting assistance of all—that provided by the composer's widow, Hsien Ming Tcherepnin—can only be acknowledged posthumously. It was one of Ming's cherished wishes to see this volume in print, and the Editor has the consolation that she had, at least, the opportunity to examine much of it in progress before her death in 1991. In every aspect of this undertaking, she lent the Editor the kind of assistance that no one else could have given. Even as she battled the ravages of cancer (the malady that would claim her son Ivan eight years later), she proved able, until the end, to draw touching reserves of energy in service of her beloved husband's work and memory. Ultimately, it is to the unrelenting fervor of her vision that this book owes its existence.

New York
February 2008

Benjamin Folkman
President, The Tcherepnin Society

❀ ❀ ❀

SPELLING AND PRONUNCIATION: A NOTE

This is as good a place as any to discuss the four different spellings of Alexander Tcherepnin's surname that are in common use. Partly because of the imperfect interface between the Cirillic and Latin alphabets, partly because of the idiosyncrasies of the various Western European languages, Tcherepnin was one of those unfortunate expatriates Russians whose name had to be spelled in at least three different ways if speakers of French, German and English were all to pronounce it with reasonable correctness.

When the composer first came West to live in France, he used the spelling Tcherepnine. The final "e" was necessary to keep the French from applying a nasal vowel to the last syllable and pronouncing it as "na" (with the short a of "hat"). The opening T prevented a mispronunciation such as "Sherepnin."

For German exposure, however, two changes had to be made. First, to avoid confusion of the "ch" sound with the guttural heard in "Bach," the "Tch" combination was changed to "Tsch"; further, a German reading "nine" will pronounce it "neena," so the final e was dropped. Accordingly, German publishers spelled his name Tscherepnin.

In English, the final e was unnecessary, and even misleading (inviting readers to rhyme the name with "fine"); and when the composer moved to America, he adopted the spelling Tcherepnin—his own pronunciation of the last syllable was somewhere between "nin" and "neen," and in speech he reportedly syllabified the name as Tcher-ep-nin. (The composer's eldest son, Peter, retains the spelling Tcherepnine, which was on his passport as a child and didn't seem to be worth the trouble of removing.)

To make the situation even more chaotic, the New York Public Library insists on spelling the name Cherepnin, on the grounds that the opening T is supererogatory in English (although it is needed in both French and German to make the equivalent of our English "ch" sound).

Just how did the composer pronounce his name? Nicolas Slonimsky said that the accent came on the last syllable (TcherepNIN)—but this description is not perfectly accurate. It is best to imagine the first and last syllables as having equal stresses (TCHE-repNIN)—indeed, a reiterated musical figure in the first of the composer's celebrated *Bagatelles* can be used as a guide to stresses:

As if all this were not confusing enough, yet another pronunciation is preferred among some of the composer's grandchildren—Tche-REP-nin—one that Alexander Tcherepnin himself always considered an annoyingly inaccurate rendering of his name.

❀　❀　❀

Forewords to Previous Editions of

ALEXANDER TCHEREPNIN BY WILLI REICH

Foreword to the First Edition

Only once in his life, and then only by chance, did Alexander Tcherepnin consult a professional fortune-teller. The meeting took place at the home of friends in St. Petersburg in 1918. Gazing intently into her crystal ball, the soothsayer predicted travel, world-wide travel for him. The nineteen-year-old Tcherepnin laughed at the idea. At that time St. Petersburg and its environs were caught up in the confusion and chaos of war and revolution, sealed off from the outside world. Under these circumstances, the young musician could hardly have visualized himself in the role of an indefatigable globe-trotter. Nevertheless, the prophecy came true. The following pages are an attempt to record the different stations of Tcherepnin's voyages, and to discover their significance in the internal and external evolution of the artist.

Willi Reich, Zurich, Autumn 1960

Foreword to the Second Edition

This new edition of Alexander Tcherepnin's biography has been brought up to date with additional material and musical illustrations. It is primarily concerned with continuing the attention given to the composer's search for new paths of musical creativity that marks the more recent period of his life up to 1968. The list of recordings of his works has also been extended. Moreover, the inclusion of important bibliographical data connected with both his personal life and his compositions affords a rich source for those who may be interested in pursuing a closer study of the totality of Alexander Tcherepnin's accomplishments in the world of music.

Willi Reich, Zurich, Autumn 1969

TCHEREPNIN PRELUDE

Petersburg. Pel's house on the ninth line of the Basil Island. Number of the house, 44. The apartment, on the second floor. The year of 1904, January. At the window of the nursery, a little blond boy moved the chiffon curtain. His eyes are directed to the yard covered by the snow and the adjoining house with a small garden. "What a big boy I am," he thinks, "I am five years old!" I am this boy. And this is one of the first impressions which stayed strongly in my memory, maybe even the first realization of my "being me."

Whatever existed before, I found out later...

ALEXANDER TCHEREPNIN

by

Willi Reich

1. Youth in Old Russia   (1899-1921)

Alexander, age 6, with his mother Maria, St. Petersburg, 1905.

Alexander Nicolayevich Tcherepnin was born in St. Petersburg on January 21, 1899. His father, the composer and conductor Nicolai Tcherepnin (1873-1945), was of wholly Russian ancestry; by contrast, his mother Marie was the daughter of Albert Benois, a painter of French descent, and Maria Kind, a German pianist. Among the boy's other maternal forebears were the Venetian composer Catterino Cavos (1770–1840) and the German poet Johann Friedrich Kind (1768–1843), who wrote the libretto of Weber's opera *Der Freischütz*. Young Alexander's cousins on his mother's side would later include the painter Nicolas Benois and the playwright and actor Peter Ustinov.

As an only child, Alexander was drawn more consistently into the life of grown-ups than might have been the case under other family circumstances. His close acquaintance with the artists who frequented his parents' and grandparents' homes was to have a major impact upon his intellectual development.

Nicolai Tcherepnin was a conductor at the Imperial Opera (Mariinsky Theatre) and taught the conducting class at the St. Petersburg Conservatory. His opera and concert rehearsals and performances provided young Alexander with his first impressions of the world of music. Between 1909 and 1912, the boy had the opportunity to watch his father conduct Serge Diaghilev's magnificent Russian Ballet and Opera productions on tour in Paris, Rome, Berlin and London,[1] and to see celebrated performers such as Chaliapin, Nijin-sky, Karsavina and Pavlova in action.

Nicolai Tcherepnin had been a pupil of Rimsky-Korsakov (1844-1908) and remained in close contact with Rimsky's circle, which included Alexander Glazunov (1865–1936), Anatole Liadov (1855–1914) and Igor Stravinsky (1882–1971) among its most notable figures. Cesar Cui (1835–1914) and Sergei Liapunov (1855–1924), the last representatives of the old Russian school, were also frequent guests at Nicolai's home. Another regular visitor was Sergei Prokofiev (1891–1953), who, as a former member of Tcherepnin's conducting class, remained devoted to his teacher, and played over all of his early compositions to him. Prokofiev's First Piano Concerto and his Sinfonietta, Op. 5 are dedicated to the elder Tcherepnin.[2] Alexander heard many of these works in his father's house, and also attended the premiere of Prokofiev's *Scythian Suite* (St. Petersburg, 1916) at a Siloti concert. The youth was equally impressed by his father's numerous discussions with his painter-uncle Alexander Benois, the set-designer Leon Bakst, the choreographer Michel Fokine, and the impresario Serge Diaghilev, as they planned their European *Ballets Russes* tours. Indeed, music and the arts—as Alexander Tcherepnin later once observed—were regarded with almost religious reverence in his boyhood household; so it is scarcely surprising that the desire to be a creative artist—a composer—germinated in his earliest youth. He received his first instruction in singing and piano from his mother as a five-year-old, learning to read and write music at the same time he learned the alphabet.[3] His greatest joy was improvise freely on the piano, but he could indulge in this activity only during the few hours when his father was away from the house.

Nicolai Tcherepnin did not learn about his son's musical inclinations until several years later, and would not, in fact, have been at all pleased by the boy's intensive music making. For he firmly believed that a creative musician's son should not follow in his father's footsteps under any circumstances, and it is difficult to imagine what he would have said or done had he any inkling of Alexander's veritably professional commitment to composition.

For the boy's early efforts were not the modest juvenilia one might expect—the usual small-scaled piano preludes, songs without words, marches, dances and other salon pieces—but, instead, "grown-up" operas on grand philosophical texts, the themes of which attracted the budding master all the more strongly for what he did not understand in them. In his solitary hours at the piano, he set the texts just as they stood, embroidering them with special sound effects, much to the discomfiture of his neighbors.

His mother, trying to direct the boy's musical furor into more orderly channels, arranged for him to have piano lessons from a series of frail, elderly lady piano teachers. Alexander made little real progress in these studies, however; for, during the precious moments when his father's piano was available, he much preferred improvising to technical drudgery. He seldom practiced the pieces assigned to him for "finger development" because he was too busy attempting to orchestrate them.

---

1 For a more detailed account of Nicolai Tcherepnin's work with Diaghilev, see Episodes and Epilogue: "The Tcherepnins of Russia," p. 110.

2 A youthful scherzo was also dedicated to Nicolai. See "Tcherepnin on Prokofiev," p. 145.

3 Tcherepnin himself stated, however, that he could read music *before* he knew the alphabet. See "A Short Autobiography," p. 81.

Nicolai Tcherepnin

Alexander at age 11

{*Editor's Note:* Tcherepnin's somewhat different account of these early events, contained in a typewritten letter to Mrs. H. P. Krause dated February 15, 1964, deserves to be included here (with some minor copy-editing of the composer's not-always-idiomatic English):

…my father, Nicolai Tcherepnin, was an outstanding composer. He also was a brilliant conductor and a great pedagogue. I loved him dearly. He was a nervous man, lived under the pressure of an extremely heavy schedule of conducting operas, concerts, of teaching and of composing. When he was at home (and it was not often) I never dared to touch the piano. He knew that I was studying piano, but never heard me perform, [because he] lacked the time. [Although] my father was extremely successful, he felt that the career of a musician is a nerve-wracking one and hoped it would be spared to me.

His love was for the countryside, and when speaking with me about my future, he [fancied that I would] become a gentleman-farmer—a typically Russian ideal. Of course, we had no estate, no farm, no property of such kind, but probably it was his own dream, that he wished for his son to materialize. Each time he spoke to me or in my presence to his friends about such prospects for my future, I was ready to cry—because from my earliest youth I wished to become a composer, and each morning and each evening when praying, facing the old darkened icon with a burning lampade [sic] under it at the right corner of my room in St. Petersburg, I asked God to help me to become a composer.}

One evening, however, at a party in his grandfather's house, Alexander played a J. S. Bach sarabande with such insight that his astonished father then and there changed his mind, soon afterward presenting his son with a piano of his own on which to continue his pianistic experiments, and also withdrawing his objections to the boy's pursuit of a musical career. He stipulated only that Alexander should not undertake the Conservatory's demanding professional training until he had completed secondary school. These academic studies between 1908 to 1917, were interrupted by numerous childhood illnesses, and the boy was obliged to spend long periods of convalescence in the Crimea, where his aunt owned an estate on the Black Sea shore near the ancient city of Sudak.

While pursuing his high school ("Gymnasium") studies—which he completed with no special difficulties, graduating in the spring of 1917— Alexander continued to take private music lessons. He had occasional instruction in traditional harmony from some of his father's colleagues at the Conservatory, but this made little impression on him, scarcely influencing his youthful style. Similarly, the cello lessons that he undertook at his mother's wish and continued with several teachers bore little fruit, although they did familiarize the young composer with the characteristics of stringed instruments. Far more important were regular piano lessons throughout his school years with Leocadia Kashperova, a pupil of Anton Rubinstein. His steady progress at the keyboard enabled him to perform successfully at student and charity concerts, and also aroused his compositional interest in the smaller forms of chamber music, where he achieved (within the scope of his capabilities at that time) far better results than he did with his large operas and symphonies. Of the many works Tcherepnin composed during that period, virtually the only ones he ever published were short piano pieces written for festive family gatherings—pieces that his father (while recognizing their artistic quality) jokingly called *bloshki*, meaning "little fleas" in Russian.[4]

In assessing Tcherepnin's creative evolution, the *bloshki* are of special significance as a starting point. They display a style that the young composer developed quite unselfconsciously by embracing the aims of the Russian avant-garde, most vividly represented by Prokofiev. This young generation of musicians no longer reacted against either the Westernized Russian school of composers, which included Rubinstein, Tchaikovsky, Taneyev, Arensky and Rachmaninoff, or the Slavophile group originating with Glinka and continuing with Mussorgsky and his circle. Instead, they directed their attacks against the vague and blurred outlines of French Impressionism. In the *bloshki*, the young Tcherepnin showed his preference for rhythmically clear-cut, firmly accentuated lines, and sharply contoured, though at times primitive, forms. His melodies and textures indicate a partiality for wide intervals and extreme registers and his sense of tonality, always

---

4   A name surely suggested by the small size and odd melodic leaps of these pieces.

firmly anchored, tends towards modality rather than the major-minor system. Vertical combinations are determined by the young composer's personal ear for sound, and in no way reflect the traditional distinction between self-sufficient consonance and dissonance requiring resolution. At fourteen, Tcherepnin gained an inkling that the musical establishment would not accept his approach to the art of composition when, at his father's request, he played one of his *bloshki* for a few conservatory professors and had to endure dismissive mockery.

{*Editor's Note:* In the 1964 letter already cited, Tcherepnin describes this humiliation in vivid and charming detail, connecting it to his first performance for his father noted earlier by Reich:

Example R1A

Pièces sans titres, Op. 7, No. 4
© 1925 by Durand & Cie., Paris
With the kind permission of the publisher

One of the *Bloshki*, composed at age 14.

Quite unusual here is the theme's appearance a semitone lower in the recapitulation, while the accompaniment remains in the same key as in the exposition.

After...the *Sarabande* from the A minor English Suite by Bach...found the approval of the guests, including that of my father (who for the first time heard me playing—I must have been 13 or so)—I was asked to perform one of my own compositions. So I performed one or two of my short piano pieces. My father seemed agreeably surprised, told me, "It looks as if you really are a musician." You can imagine how happy and excited I was. What's more, my father suggested that I prepare some of my piano pieces to perform at a party at our home, to which he would invite some of his Conservatory colleagues.

The great day came. After the dinner at our home the guests—St. Petersburg['s] outstanding musicians—were invited to the living room to hear me play.

At that time, we had no electric light in our home. We used petroleum lamps and candles. At the grand piano on which I was to perform, the candles were lit and I was to get loose. At that occasion, I decided to start by performing the piece that later became *Bagatelle* No. 7. The musical friends and colleagues of my father were seated around me in comfortable armchairs or on sofas; the rest of the room was rather dark, but I could see the faces surrounding me. I played the piece to the best of my abilities, and at the end paused and looked around to read on the faces of the guests the impression that my composition and my playing gave them.

I remember, just as if it were yesterday, the face of a great musical Petersburg authority, the bearded composer and pedagogue A. Petroff. He was red in the face and could not hold back his laughter. "If this is music, I will be darned,"[5] exclaimed he, still loudly laughing. "It is not music but a caricature [of] music! The funniest thing I ever heard"—and

---

5   In other accounts, Tcherepnin had Petroff saying "I will be damned." Presumably Tcherepnin, old world gentleman that he was, refrained here from using such language because his letter was intended for a lady.

so on, and so on. I felt embarrassed, played no more, timidly retiring. I felt that all is lost and that I will not be permitted to continue with my music.

But after the departure of the guests my dear father umarmed me[6] [*i. e.*, "embraced me"] and said: "I see that you are a musician, I realize you have original ideas. From now on, one of the grand pianos will be brought to your room so that you can use it at your discretion. I have faith in you." So what I thought was a failure was my greatest blessing, and from then on, my aim to become a composer became legal and approved by my father.}

Example R1b

Bagatelle No. 7 (from Op. 5)

Presumably it was young Tcherepnin's blithe major second "consonances" that led
Professor Petroff to deride this Bagatelle's original version as "a caricature of music."

Tcherepnin's first "serious" attempts at writing for the stage also date from his years at the Gymnasium. He wrote little plays in collaboration with his cousin Nicolas Benois, and set them to music, producing them for family and friends in his own puppet theater. When his school mounted a student production of *Oedipus the King* the sixteen-year-old composer provided the play with incidental music for strings, harp and several woodwinds and conducted it himself.

Tcherepnin's last three years at the Gymnasium coincided with the First World War, the horrors of which affected the sensitive youth deeply. To be sure, only one composition reflects the war: the first movement of a piano suite depicting the sufferings of a wounded soldier abandoned on the battlefield. Nevertheless, more personal and subjective elements now began to appear in the adolescent's music.

This new artistic attitude may have been partly caused by his experiences of the revolution in St. Petersburg during the spring and autumn of 1917, which led to the Czarist downfall. Alexander frequently witnessed bloody demonstrations and street fighting, and such experiences weighed heavily upon his spirits, just as cold and lack of food caused him physical suffering. Yet despite all inner and outer tribulations, his musical development was constant. After graduating from the Gymnasium in the spring of 1917, he enrolled both at St. Petersburg University (as a law student) and at the Conservatory—where, after presenting some of his compositions, including ten piano sonatas, some smaller piano pieces and several orchestral scores, and also demonstrating his pianistic abilities, he was awarded the Borodin scholarship and admitted to classes in harmony (Sokolov) and piano (Kobiliansky). Tcherepnin found these strictly conservative lessons less pleasurable and stimulating than the lectures on musical history and aesthetics given by the more progressive Professor Karatiguin. More provocative still were his exchanges of ideas with like-minded fellow-students, such as the future composers Schillinger, Shaporin, Yudina, Vinogradova, and Richard Bick. He also took a lively interest in the city's musical life, which was still intensely active despite the war.

During this period Tcherepnin concentrated almost entirely on piano music. The four new sonatas (Nos. 11-14) not only reveal the compositional and pianistic advances he had made during the previous few years, but also exhibit dramatic features reflecting the emotional and physical turmoil of his life. This is particularly evident in Sonata No. 13, composed during Holy Week in 1918 when Tcherepnin was suffering from scurvy brought on by malnutrition. The work pulsates with the sense of physical suffering and the presentiment of the composer's imminent separation from his homeland.

The autobiographical elements in Sonata No. 13 troubled the composer so deeply that for several years he was psychologically incapable of practicing it regularly to prepare a public performance. It was not until the autumn of 1926, during a piano recital at the Salle Érard in Paris, that he gave the score its premiere; it had been published shortly before under its present title, *Sonatine Romantique* (Op. 4, 1925).

Other works dating from those last St. Petersburg years include several pieces from *Episodes* and *Pièces sans titres*, and an operatic aria expressing the grief of a Finnish maiden forsaken by her lover, which Tcherepnin later transformed

---

6   A quaint teutonicism. Tcherepnin here applied English conjugation to the German verb *umarmen* (to embrace).

into the fourth *Bagatelle*. The last music he wrote in St. Petersburg was the first movement of the Piano Sonata No. 14, a score that he completed a year later in Tbilisi and published in 1924 as his First Piano Sonata, Opus 22.

Example R2

Main Theme of *Sonata Romantique, Op. 4*
(originally Piano Sonata No. 13, composed 1918, Petrograd)
© 1925 by Durand & Cie., Paris
With the kind permission of the publisher

Compare this theme with the Medieval Russian Requiem-theme (also based on three notes) used by Tcherepnin as the *cantus firmus* of the Fourth Symphony's finale (Ex. R32b, p. 62).

In the summer of 1918, Nicolai Tcherepnin became the director of the Conservatory in Tiflis (today Tbilisi), the capital of Georgia, which had declared itself an independent Socialist Republic after the revolution. The family arrived there in the early autumn, after a long and adventurous journey through a country that was still in the grip of civil war and occupied, in places, by the Germans. Long afterwards, Tcherepnin discovered in an American library some lines by the Russian poet Vladimir Mayakovsky that perfectly expressed the emotion he felt at this separation from his homeland:

You blithely
        forget
              the place and the day
Where you idly
        feasted
              to bursting,
But never
        the land
              that was next
                    on your way,
With its hard years
        of hungering
            and thirsting!
(From "Very Good! Poem of the October Revolution"
by Vladimir Mayakovsky.)[7]

The Tcherepnins found living conditions in Tiflis deplorably primitive, and life very hard. Shortly after their arrival, Alexander fell ill with typhus and Spanish influenza, and for a long time he was hardly able to work at all. When he finally recovered, he resumed his education, at the University (history and philosophy) and at the Tiflis Conservatory, where he studied the piano with Tamara Ter Stepanova and counterpoint with Thomas de Hartmann. He undertook practical activities as well, writing music reviews for several daily papers, giving concerts throughout Georgia and Armenia, and becoming musical director of the Kamerni Theatre, where he produced incidental music for several classical and modern plays. With other young musicians and actors, he founded the GATIEN group, whose regular gatherings were enlivened by spirited discussions, readings, and music-making.[8] Through his father, who was now conductor of the Tiflis Opera, Alexander came to know the most important Georgian composers. He found a source of inspiration in the richly diverse melodies and forms of Georgian folk and church music (the latter, in fact, is marked by a tradition of elaborate three-part singing that dates all the way back to the fourth century A. D.).

---

7   Translated from the German rendering by Hugo Heppert, as quoted by Reich.

8   Liudmila Korabelnikova's biography *Alexander Tcherepnin: The Saga of a Russian Émigré Composer* provides a detailed account of Tcherepnin's extensive activities in Georgia's flourishing musical and theatrical milieux. It also includes substantial quotations from the young composer's reviews of numerous concerts and operas, which sometimes bore the pseudonymous bylines "Fuldan," "Platon Valanchal" or "Es" (for Sascha).

Indeed, Georgia, and above all Tiflis, with its mix of various peoples (Armenians, Persians, Russians, etc.) provided the stimulation of a wide range of folklores, but these ethnic elements were not to bear fruit in Tcherepnin's work until later.

The music Tcherepnin composed in Tiflis between 1919 and 1921 was important to his artistic development in two respects: in the wake of his intensive concertizing, his new piano works exhibited an increasing measure of virtuosity, and a decided gain in immediate expressive power. These qualities, representing what the composer with gentle irony once described as his *Sturm und Drang* period,[9] are especially evident in the *Nocturne*, Op. 2, the *Danse*, Op. 8, the *Petite Suite*, Op. 6, and several unpublished *Poèmes* and *Etudes*, but above all in the Piano Concerto No. 1 in F Major, Op. 12. Also belonging to this category are the chamber works written for the GATIEN group, a number of which remain unpublished.

More important than this emergence of *Sturm und Drang*, however, was the clarity Tcherepnin was gradually achieving in the theoretical foundations of his musical language. Analysis of his early works reveals a predilection for the simultaneous sounding of major and minor triads with the same root. From this chordal mixture, Tcherepnin derived two six-step scales in ascending and descending order:

The twenty-two-year-old Tcherepnin in Tiflis

ascending:

descending:

The interlocking of these two scales yields a nine-step scale consisting of three tetrachords, all identical in interval-structure:

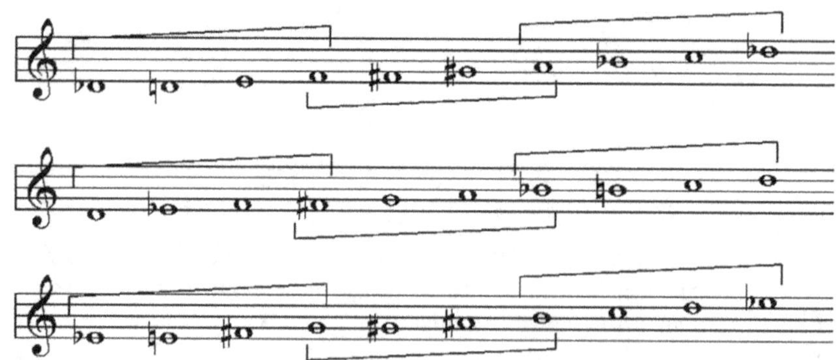

Each tetrachord has only three transpositions:

This nine-step scale,[10] which combines major and minor (and may thus be called a major-minor scale) is capable of eight permutations, according to the positions of the tetrachords: the first tetrachord may come second or third in the series, the second tetrachord, first or third, and the third tetrachord, first or second. As with major and minor keys, modulations are also possible in Tcherepnin's tonal system. He used the six-note scales deliberately for the first time in

---

9   Tcherepnin often used *Sturm und Drang* as a term of self-reproach; he applied it not only to these youthful works, but also to some of his 1940s scores that he thought stylistically questionable. See "Letter to Slonimsky," p. 88.

10   These technical features of the nine-step scale are discussed in somewhat more detail by Tcherepnin himself in "Basic Elements of My Musical Language," p. 89.

Nos. 2 and 3 of his *Feuilles libres*, Op. 10, composed in Tiflis in 1920. In his subsequent Paris period, however, he adopted the nine-step scale, with its far richer possibilities, as the tonal basis of his music.

❋   ❋   ❋   ❋   ❋   ❋

{*Editor's Note:* For an account of the difficulties surrounding the Tcherepnins' journey to Paris, a subject not covered by Reich, readers may wish to consult "The Long Journey West," page 114.}

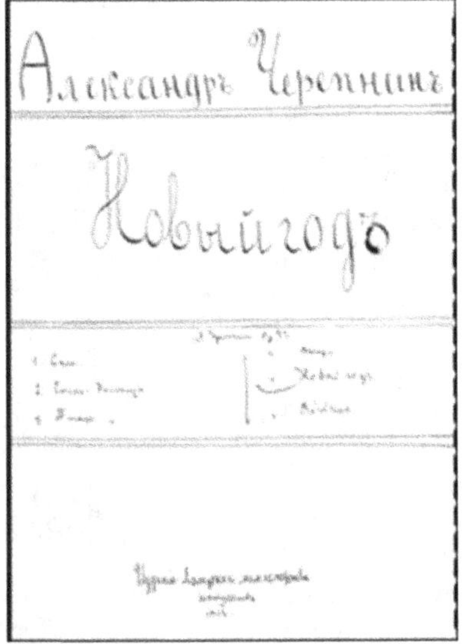

Young Alexander drew "professional" title pages, complete with publisher's imprint and date. On the 1913 example above, he has even made a music-store-like pencil mark to indicate that this is No. 5 of his six pieces, "Op. 33."

A year later, the fifteen-year-old made this watercolor cover for a piano piece. By now he had reached Op. 64.

Tcherepnin in Tiflis (*ca.* 1920) with his friends in the GATIEN group

2. In the Aura of Paris   (1921-1925)

From what has been said about Tcherepnin's harmonic explorations, it should be understood that by the time the 22-year-old moved with his parents to Paris (second half of 1921), his artistic individuality was already so sharply defined that the French Capital's distinctive musical atmosphere—stimulating though he found it—could not influence him in essentials or in any way re-orient him. This point should be stressed, because several of Tcherepnin's early critical commentators ascribed his so-called "Parisian style" to works composed *before* the Paris period. Their error arose because the pieces that Tcherepnin took to Paris, notably the *Bagatelles*, Op. 5, and the *Inventions*, Op. 13, showed remarkable similarities to piano works by Francis Poulenc and Georges Auric, which struck out in the same anti-Impressionist direction. Since Tcherepnin had then had no contact with the Poulenc-Auric group of *Les Six*, the best explanation of this stylistic kinship is that composers of the same generation tend to reflect the same ideals.

In Paris, Tcherepnin enrolled in the counterpoint class of Paul Vidal at the Paris Conservatory, and in Isidore Philipp's piano class at the *École Normale de Musique*, but remained at both institutions only a few months, after which Philipp gave him free private lessons[1]. Philipp, as noted earlier, arranged for the publication of Tcherepnin's piano works by the Parisian firms of Durand, Heugel, Eschig, and Hamelle. However, the Leipzig firm of Belaieff was Tcherepnin's first publisher, issuing his *Toccata in D minor*, Op. 1 (1921) and *Nocturne and Danse*, Op. 2 (1919), both of which appeared in 1922 and were printed in the composer's revised versions in 1957.

Tcherepnin (*l.*) and Victor Young with their teacher Isidore Philipp, on the balcony of Philipp's Paris apartment.

Among the works produced during Tcherepnin's first months in Paris were three collections of songs on Russian poems by Gorodezky, Opp. 15-17 (published, however, only in French translation) and several piano and chamber compositions. In the latter, which are based largely on the nine-step scale, Tcherepnin developed a distinctive polyphonic technique which he named "Interpoint," and which he brought to a high degree of perfection in the late 1920s, especially in the First Symphony, Op. 42, and the Piano Quintet, Op. 44. The musical examples that follow illustrate the technique.

Tcherepnin's evolution towards strict polyphony is also clear in his ballet *Training* (1922), written for small orchestra and cast in the form of a prelude and fugue. Unfortunately, the production, for which Leon Bakst had sketched scenery, had to be abandoned because the Paris theater that was sponsoring it unexpectedly went bankrupt. It was not until 1934 that the ballet was first staged, in Vienna, where the score had been published by Universal Edition in 1931 under the title *Praeludium zu einem Boxtraining* (literally, *"Prelude to a Training Bout"*), Op. 37, No. 3.

Example R3

Prelude for Cello and Piano, Op. 38, No. 2
from *The Well-Tempered Violoncello*:
Twelve preludes for violoncello and piano in the nine-step scale

© 1927 by Durand & Cie., Paris
With the kind permission of the publisher

a) (measures 1-2)

---

1   Reich is mistaken about Tcherepnin's departure from the Conservatory. Tcherepnin said that on his arrival, "my knowledge of counter-point... was, of course, insufficient. I could not even write four-voice counterpoint in clefs. I spent a good year at the Conservatory, and the teacher saw that I was working well so in one year I passed counterpoint and fugue. The next year I started to concertize and there were no more lessons."

b) (measures 29-30)

Notes:
a) Theme in cello accompanied by a rhythmic figure in piano.
b) Development of cello theme, as piano right hand provides a rhythmic-melodic figuration Interpuntally related to the rhythm of a). Piano left hand dovetails an additional Interpoint.
c) Further development of cello theme, accompanied by figures a) and b) in vertical Interpoint.
NB. The title *Well-Tempered Violoncello* indicates that the cellist is to adopt the equal temperament of the piano, ignoring theoretical differences in tuning between such notes as d-sharp and e-flat.

Example R4

Piano Quintet, Op. 44
© 1930 by Universal Edition, Vienna
With the kind permission of the publisher

Second movement
a) measures 1-4: Example of vertical Interpoint

b) measures 26-29: Example of horizontal Interpoint: the two-voice pairs, each in vertical Interpoint, are assembled to form a quadruple (eight-voice) canon in horizontal Interpoint.

Another work that Tcherepnin had written in 1922 for the same theater was a pocket opera called the *Idylle Astrale* (*Idyll of the Stars*) for voice, narrator, and string quartet, on a libretto by Maria Star (also known as Ernesta Stern). Shortly after the theater's demise, he reworked the music into his First-String Quartet, Op. 36, a one-movement score premiered in Paris in 1925, and published by Schott of Mainz with the subtitle *Liebesopfer der Heiligen Therese vom Kinde Jesu* (*The Love-offering by Saint Theresa of the Infant Jesus*).

Anna Pavlova in Tcherepnin's first international success: *Ajanta's Frescoes*, London, 1923.

The ballet *Ajanta's Frescoes*, written for Anna Pavlova in the summer of 1923, turned out to be a more fortunate theatrical venture. During a world tour, the famous ballerina had visited India, where she assembled a collection of valuable ethnological and folkloric materials: rare reproductions of temple art, costume designs, and phonograph recordings of Indian music. She wanted to use these in a stage work, and Tcherepnin was given a completely free hand in employing them. He chose as his subject the story of Buddha's renunciation of the world, finding a parallel in the frescoes of the Ajanta Temple. The ballet, which was completed in only a few weeks, received its first performance in London at the Royal Opera House, Covent Garden, in September 1923, with Pavlova and Novikov in the leading roles. It was subsequently produced in many European theaters.

Tcherepnin's career as a concert pianist in Western and Central Europe had been launched somewhat earlier in London (in November 1922, with a concert of his own works). {*Editor's note:* This debut was actually a joint appearance by Tcherepnin with violinists Adila Faschiri and Jelly d'Aranyi. These sisters, grandnieces of Joachim, had sponsored Tcherepnin's visit. The program included Milhaud chamber music along with works by Tcherepnin, who was billed as "Alex Tcherepnin." See also: "Encountering the English," p. 117.} During his first stay in London he wrote four piano pieces, to which he gave the collective title *Préludes nostalgiques*, Op. 23; the "nostalgia" of these—as he observed—was not for his old Russian fatherland but rather for his newly-adopted home of France.

Shortly afterward (in the spring of 1923) he made his continental debut in Western Europe as a piano virtuoso, playing his Piano Concerto No. 1, Op. 12 (composed 1919-20) in Monte Carlo, with his father conducting. The performance was a double triumph for him as composer and performer. The friends he made and the beauty of the Riviera induced him to rent a *pied-à-terre* in Monaco. Over the next decade the tiny apartment proved to be not only an ideal place to rest after his strenuous concert tours, but also his favorite place for writing music.

{*Editor's Note:* Among the "friends he made" in Monte Carlo was a wealthy American socialite, Louisine Weekes, nee Peters (conceivably named after her aunt-by-marriage, Louisine Havemeyer), whom Tcherepnin met in 1924 and, with considerable trepidation, married in 1926 after she divorced her husband. At that time, she was forty-one years old (fourteen years her new husband's senior) and had an eleven-year-old daughter named Hathaway—always called "Happy." On his subsequent tours to the U. S., Tcherepnin would find Louisine's home in Islip, Long Island another congenial place for composition. She and Tcherepnin were not, however, well suited to each other: neither was comfortable in the social milieu the other preferred, and Tcherepnin was almost constantly oppressed by the feeling of being trapped.}

During the 1922-23 season, Tcherepnin wrote two of his most important instrumental works of the early twenties: the *Rhapsodie Géorgienne* (*Georgian Rhapsody*), Op. 25, for cello and orchestra, and the Piano Concerto No. 2 in A, Op. 26 (in one movement). Although actual Georgian folk melodies are absent from the *Rhapsodie*, the music makes extensive use of Georgian folk rhythms and is harmonically organized around a chord widely used in Georgian folk-music—the first inversion of a three-voiced chord in fourths:

Tcherepnin (*r.*) and Prokofiev, Monte Carlo, 1925.

 first inversion: 

The *Rhapsodie Géorgienne* was performed first in Bordeaux and then at the *Concerts Colonne* in Paris, early in 1924, with Andre Hekking as soloist, and soon became part of the permanent violoncello repertory. To this day, the work, in its orchestral form and in the version for cello and piano, remains one of Tcherepnin's most frequently played compositions.

In contrast to the Piano Concerto No. 1, which was written four years earlier with pianistic virtuosity in mind, the Piano Concerto No. 2 shows a much stricter approach to construction (particularly in its development-variations) and greater rhythmic complexity. This Concerto was first performed by Nadia Boulanger and the composer in a reduction for two pianos, at a concert of the *Société Nationale* in Paris in January 1924. The original piano and orchestra version was premiered a year later in Brest, France with Tcherepnin at the piano.[2]

The *Transcriptions Slaves* (*Slavic Transcriptions*), Op. 27, for piano, owe their origin to a suggestion made by Isidore Philipp in 1924. Authentic and pseudo-Slavonic folk melodies are used here as a pretext for pianistic flamboyance rather than as a basis for ethnically representative transcription. (The first piece is a paraphrase on the popular Volga Boat Song.)

In this period, however, Tcherepnin's creative interests focused less on folklore than on the forging of aesthetically resourceful compositional techniques, and above all, on the problems of opera. Here, he was attracted neither by grand themes of classical tragedy nor by modern heroic or pathetic materials. He wanted, instead, a subject springing from the lives of ordinary people, with simple everyday joys and sorrows that could be set to music of an equally simple and immediate character. He found one in *The Days of Our Life*, a play by the Russian poet Leonid Andreyev, which deals with normal, realistic incidents in the lives of Russian students, something quite familiar to Tcherepnin from his university days. In fashioning his own libretto, the composer reduced the five acts of Andreyev's play to three scenes, and used the name of the play's heroine, Ol-Ol, as the title of the opera. which deals with normal, realistic incidents in the lives of Russian students, something quite familiar to Tcherepnin from his university days. In

Tcherepnin around the time of *Ol-Ol*

2　See also the analytical essay on Concerto No. 2, in *Seventeen Masterpieces*, p. 159.

fashioning his own libretto, the composer reduced the five acts of Andreyev's play to three scenes, and used the name of the play's heroine, Ol-Ol, as the title of the opera. In fashioning his own libretto, the composer reduced the five acts of Andreyev's play to three scenes, and used the name of the play's heroine, Ol-Ol, as the title of the opera.[3] He started the music in August 1924, and wrote the first scene in a few weeks, but it took him more than a year to finish the opera in its entirety. The premiere took place in Weimar in 1928, and the work was subsequently produced in theaters in several other German cities, as well as in Vienna, Prague, Bratislava, Ljublana, and New York.

Tcherepnin interrupted his work on the opera to compose several major pieces of chamber music, a genre to which he was then much attracted. Among these were two sonatas for cello and piano (Op. 29 and Op. 30, No. 1), which are sharply contrasted. The first displays an evenly balanced polyphonic texture, while the second exhibits the sort of rich, glowing melody that is normally associated with the character of stringed instruments. The two themes of the Op. 29 finale are modelled on blackbird-songs that Tcherepnin heard in Monte Carlo.

There were other important works in that period, such as the Piano Trio, Op. 34, and the *Concerto da Camera*, Op. 35, for flute, violin and chamber orchestra, with which Tcherepnin won the first prize in a competition sponsored by the music publishing firm of Schott's in Mainz. The concerto was first performed, with great success, at the Donaueschingen Music Festival in July 1925, under the direction of Hermann Scherchen. Almost overnight, it made Tcherepnin's name well-known in Central Europe,[4] and led him into a new epoch, in which the creative impulses nurtured in the aura of Paris were to reach an even higher stage of fulfillment; at the same time, his activities as a virtuoso pianist were to extend still further.

Nicolai and Alexander Tcherepnin at
St. Malo, 1923.

---

3   Actually, Tcherepnin had been considering this play for an opera ever since seeing it in Tiflis. He remarked that it pleased him as a subject because-unlike so many operatic stories-it was "without murders or corpses." See also the analytical essay on *Ol-Ol, Seventeen Master-pieces*, p. 170.

4   See also the analytical essay on the *Concerto da Camera*, in *Seventeen Masterpieces*, p. 165.

3. Composing and Concertizing Around the World   (1925-1933)

It is impossible to go into detail here about the extensive concert tours that took Tcherepnin all across Europe for several months each year and, starting in 1926, to many American cities as well. These tours not only brought him world fame as a pianist; they were instrumental in making his works known to the public, since Tcherepnin's programs consisted almost entirely of his own music. Mention should be made, however, of his first brief visit to America (in the fall of 1926) during which Tcherepnin gave his New York debut recital and recorded a few of his pieces on Ampico piano rolls,[1] and of a tour through the Balkans in February 1932, during which he spent several memorable evenings with Maurice Ravel and Marguerite Long in Bucharest, deepening his long-standing friendship with both.

More important for Tcherepnin's work was a vacation trip to Egypt, Palestine, Crete and Greece in the spring of 1931, which provided him with new musical stimulation. In these years of concertizing and travel, his creative philosophy was undergoing a change which was to lead him away from his preoccupation with complex musical techniques and back to the folk sources of Russian music—and, eventually, on to the Far East, where wholly new realms of music would open for him.

A characteristic example of Tcherepnin's style at the beginning of this period—his methods of intertwining of complex procedures—can be found in *Message*, for piano, Op. 39, written in the summer of 1926 and cast as a single movement in free sonata form. Here the nine-tone-scale-based harmony, the totally free rhythms and the sonically relentless polyphony (which proceeds wholly according to the rules of Interpoint) all interact to give the piece a unique musical imprint, as can be seen in the following examples.

Example R5

Message for Piano, Op. 39
© 1926 by Universal Edition, Vienna
With the kind permission of the publisher

a) Page 1, Measures 10-14

b) Page 2, Measures 4-7

---

c) Page 2, Measures 12-15

Notes:
a) Theme and vertical interpoint.
b) Theme in three-part canon in vertical interpoint (accents indicate the rhythmic displacement).
c) Theme in vertical interpoint. Rhythmic figures provide the interpuntal voice with its own vertical interpoint.

The recapitulation of *Message* is compressed into three bars of music, and the work ends dramatically with the first rhythmic cell of the main theme (the "message") tapped with the knuckles on the wood of the piano[2]. At this time, Tcherepnin's tendency to strip a theme down to its rhythmic skeleton over the course of a composition was also present in his works for large orchestra, a medium to which he now turned for the first time. The specific examples are *Magna Mater*, Op. 41, and the Symphony No. 1, Op. 42, both completed in 1927.

In *Magna Mater* the composer took his theme from the incantatory epigraph with which the poet Issarlo prefaced his poem of the same name:

> *Magna Mater*, Mother Earth, Mighty Creatrix!
> All originates in Thee! All returns to Thee!

The music parallels this motto, after the exposition of a laconic theme, in a single crescendo, with chordal and melodic elements eventually withdrawn little by little until only the rhythm of the theme remains, played by the percussion alone. In effect, the terrestrial circle of events evoked by the poet completes itself, so that it can begin anew.

At this time, Tcherepnin conceived the orchestra as a means to achieve a greater clarity and dynamic range in the architectural expression of his musical ideas, and not merely as a means to achieve color for its own sake. If the application of this principle is already apparent in *Magna Mater*, it is in full view in the Symphony No. 1.

{*Editor's Note:* Tcherepnin's own view of his instrumentation in these works, as expressed in his French autobiography, is at once more critical and more revealing of his artistic aims:

"In both their ideology and their writing, *Magna Mater* and the Symphony were an outgrowth of my chamber orchestra works. As my musical materials grew denser, I felt it impossible to continue limiting myself to a reduced ensemble, and I turned to the symphony orchestra. I was not seeking enrichment of my palette at the time, but instead an augmentation of volume and number. And I treated my symphony orchestra not as a thing in itself but as an enlarged chamber orchestra.

"To be frank, I did not like the orchestra at this time, rejected the idea of treating it *al fresco*, and obstinately ignored the fundamental laws of acoustics."}

---

2   See also the analytical essay on *Message* in *Seventeen Masterpieces*, p. 179.

The four movements of the Symphony No. 1 reveal Tcherepnin's mastery of his own highly evolved musical language, a language capable of such succinctly organized passages as the one at the conclusion of the Symphony's third movement, the *Andante*. Here, the three principal themes of the movement finally commingle Interpuntally to form a six-part polyphonic coda, which Tcherepnin calls "Formula"—a thematic and dynamic climax that grows out of all that has gone before.

Example R6

Symphony No. 1, Op. 42
© 1929 by Durand & Cie., Paris
With the kind permission of the publisher

Third Movement

a) Page 38, Measures 1-4

b) Page 38, Measures 21-24

c) Page 42, Measures 4-7

d) Page 49, Measures 1-4

Formula

a) First interpuntal pair.
b) Second interpuntal pair.
c) Third interpuntal pair.
d) The three pairs are combined in a six-part "formula" which
    constitutesthe core of the movement and serves as its coda.

The premiere of the Symphony No. 1 took place on October 29, 1927, at one of the Colonne Concerts at the Theatre du Chatelet in Paris, under the direction of Gabriel Pierne. The reaction of the audience was tumultuous: after the second movement (scored for percussion only), the mixture of boos, hisses and applause was punctuated by calls of "Bravo!" "Back to Moscow!" and "Barbarian!" along with cries of approval. It took police intervention in the gallery before a semblance of order was restored and Pierné could continue with the third movement.

The critics were likewise divided: "The apotheosis of rhythm" (*Le Temps*), "cacophony" (*Le Ménestral*), "indescribable noise" (*Le Matin*), "Youthfully fresh and blooming view of the future," (*Le Figaro*), "Demonstration of Bolshevist inroads in music" (*Le Journal*), "Very beautiful themes, powerful, stirring effect" (*Le Courier Musical*).

At the time no one perceived that the controversial second movement was a logical continuation and conclusion of the first movement, reducing the latter's original thematic and harmonic materials to their elementary rhythmic basis.[3]

Tcherepnin's constructive skill reaches its peak in the Piano Quintet, Op. 44, a three-movement masterpiece of polyphonic and Interpuntal textures which was also written in 1927. Soon after Tcherepnin completed that piece, a growing suspicion that he had arrived at a creative turning point was reinforced by his decision to write an opera on a drama he had long admired: *Die Hochzeit der Sobeide* (*The Wedding of Sobeide*) by the Viennese poet Hugo von Hofmannsthal, whose acquaintance he had made in Vienna in January 1928. Work on the opera, which occupied him until 1930, presented genuine practical difficulties at first: for Tcherepnin was setting the libretto in the original German, and although his conversational command of the language was fluent, the text's profound literary subtleties required unhurried study.[4] Moreover, Hofmannsthal's text, with its rarefied intimacy and spirituality, could not register properly in opera without mimetic simplification and sharpened dramatic contrasts. Tcherepnin achieved contrast by introducing a large dance scene in the second act, the music of which he subsequently adapted into a four-movement orchestral suite, *Festmusik* (*Festival*

---

3   See also the analytical essay on Symphony No. 1 in *Seventeen Masterpieces*, p. 183.

4   Tcherepnin wrote: "German, not being my mother tongue, did not evoke the same automatic, instinctive musical reactions within me that Russian does."

Music), which was published as his Op. 45b and received numerous performances. The opera was first produced at the Vienna Volksoper in March 1933.[5]

Shortly after the premiere, the composer started a new opera, *Die Orgel von St. Veit* (*St. Veit's Organ*) from a text by the Austrian poet Hermann Heinz Ortner. He soon gave up this project, however, as he found it increasingly difficult to reconcile the Germanic atmosphere of the libretto with his own very different spiritual orientation, one which he saw as becoming increasingly "Eurasian." This was about the only project that Tcherepnin ever consciously abandoned.[6]

The oriental milieu of *Die Hochzeit der Sobeide* and certain poetic details of Hofmannsthal's text prompted Tcherepnin to take a critical view of the music he had written to date and to meditate upon the nature of his musical roots. He now saw that in every thought and every feeling, he was Russian, and the significance of this perception for his art became ever clearer as he renewed his studies of Russian poetry, philosophy and history: to be Russian meant to occupy a geographical and spiritual position astride the East and the West, Asia and Europe; the central task of a Russian artist, he concluded, was to bring the two together in a convincing synthesis, a Eurasian synthesis.

The first production of *Die Hochzeit der Sobeide*, premiered March 17, 1933.
Left: Desider Kovacs as the rich merchant. Right: Sobeide (Jolanthe Garde)
pleads with the scheming Ganem (Kurt Preger).

The immediate consequences of this decision were: renunciation of his purely constructivistic approach to polyphonic elaboration—without, however, withdrawing from the sound world this had opened to him—and extensive derivation of thematic materials from primordial folklore.

---

5   See also the analytical essay on *The Wedding of Sobeide* in *Seventeen Masterpieces*, p. 195.

6   Quite untrue-Reich was misled here by a statement in Tcherepnin's French autobiography.

Rudiments of these new tendencies are already present in the two works which followed the Hofmannsthal opera: the ten short piano pieces *Entretiens* (*Conversations*), Op. 46, and the Concertino, Op. 47, for violin, 'cello, piano and string orchestra. In the *Entretiens* it is predominantly the spoken inflections of everyday conversational Russian which give certain of the pieces their "Eurasian" character. In the four-movement Concertino the mathematically complex rhythms of the first movement are supplanted in the Finale by the rhythms—not the melodic elements!—of a Georgian song.[7] There is a further advance towards Tcherepnin's new style in the Piano Concerto No. 3, Op. 48, composed in 1932, especially in the first movement, *Wanderung* (*Wandering*); here, the three-measure motif that pervades the whole movement like a "motto":

Example R7

Piano Concerto No. 3, Op. 48

was patterned on a rhythmically uniform Egyptian boatmen's song, which Tcherepnin heard as he sailed up the Nile from Aswan to Philae, and adopted as an archetype for the use of repetition in shaping the concerto movement.[8] The song's melodic profile, however, has nothing in common with the harsh intervals created by the lower line of the motto. Essentially the first movement is a Prelude to a wholly "non-Eurasian" second movement Fugue in very complex Interpoint.

The high point of "Eurasian" tendencies was reached in the Duo for Violin and Cello, Op. 49, composed in 1932 as one of the commissions given by the American League of Composers in New York to mark the tenth anniversary of its foundation. Here, strict nine- step language is replaced by freely developed harmonic and melodic formations in all five of the Duo's movements, and the approach to Interpuntal combination is simplified. The highly unusual fourth movement is built upon the rhythmic noises of insects.[9]

Tcherepnin thought of beginning a series of *Eurasian Notebooks* with the Duo—the second volume to consist of the five *Russian Dances*, Op. 50, for orchestra, written in 1933 at the suggestion of a publisher friend. Work on the *Dances*, however, clearly showed him the impossibility of a synthesis between thematic ideas taken from folklore and the subtle, complex language (the nine-step scale, Interpoint, etc.) that he had developed over the last decade. Until now, when Tcherepnin had employed centuries-old melodies sprung from the people as his basic material, his entire aim had been to use them as a basis for complex artistic manipulation, rather in the spirit in which de Falla, Stravinsky, Bartók and many other contemporary composers had developed such musical ideas. But with the *Russian Dances* he was confronted for the first time with the problem of using folk material not merely as a source of inspiration but as the immanent musical

---

7 Tcherepnin noted: "It is a pity that Willi Reich does not give more details about this work, [which] has a long story." Tcherepnin's many versions of this piece—which was ultimately retitled Triple Concertino—are discussed in the analytical essay on the Triple Concertino in *Seventeen Masterpieces*, p. 212.

8 Reich here missed an important point that Tcherepnin made about this motto in his French autobiography—that the "continual repetitions" of the "short, monotonous song intoned by the boatmen" were "separated by brief intervals of silence." The composer continued: "It is these repetitions of the same (very brief) song and the intervals of silence (not merely the song itself) that gave me the idea of using this 'process' in a work."

9 See also the analytical essay on the Duo, *Seventeen Masterpieces*, p. 217.

basis of the composition, a basis that had to remain essentially unaltered. He soon realized that the predominantly modal (diatonic) character of Russian themes—indeed, their entire melodic and rhythmic outline—made them incompatible with the highly chromatic style he had cultivated in his recent works. As he faced grave decisions at this creative impasse, an unforeseen change in the outward circumstances of his life allowed him to resolve his artistic crisis in entirely new surroundings.

❅　❅　❅　❅　❅　❅

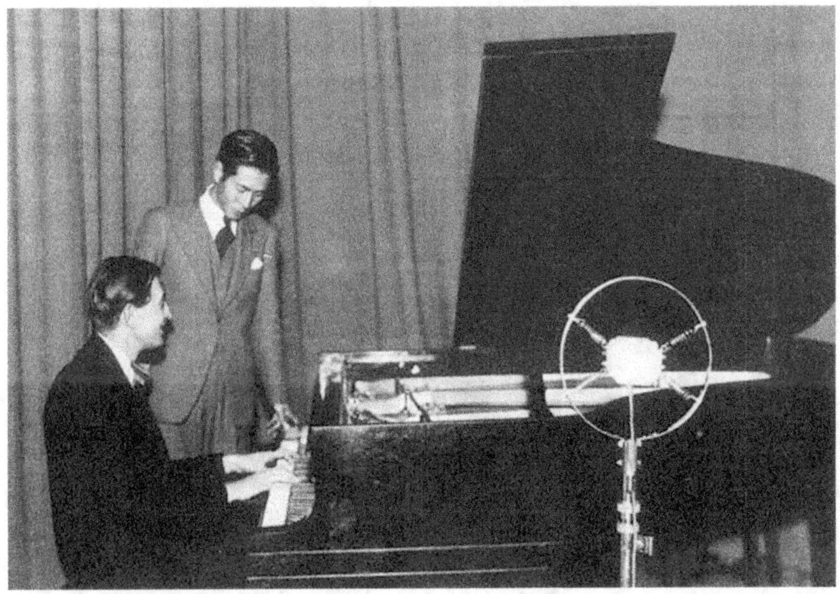

Tcherepnin at the Victor studios in Tokyo, preparing to record a 78 RPM disc of Japanese music as the composer Akiro Ikufube looks on.

4. The Experience of the Far East (1934-1937)

It was external happenstance rather than internal compulsion that first drew Tcherepnin to the Far East: the American impresario A. Strok booked him for a world-wide concert tour in the spring and summer of 1934, scheduled to begin in China in April. The rest of the itinerary covered Japan, the Philippines, Singapore, Egypt and Palestine; for the following season, he already had commitments in Europe and America. But everything was to turn out quite differently. After his first concert in Shanghai, Tcherepnin encountered a pianist friend, Boris Zakharov, who taught at the local conservatory. Among the pupils to whom Zakharov introduced him was a highly gifted young Chinese pianist, Lee Hsien Ming, to whom he at once felt a strong attraction.

During that first meeting, he formed a firm resolve to make Lee Hsien Ming his wife. So that he could stay near her, he freed himself from his commitments for the rest of the tour and instead accepted new engagements in China and Japan, along with an honorary professorship at the Shanghai Conservatory and a post as musical advisor to the Chinese Ministry of Education. His disappointment was all the greater when Miss Lee, having been awarded a fellowship for her outstanding piano playing, left China in the autumn of 1934 to further her musical studies in Europe. The two would not see each other again until three years later[1]. As the first musical token of his affection, Tcherepnin inscribed in her album the opening bars of a piano piece on which he had been working.

Example R8

Hommage à la Chine, Op. 52, No. 3
© 1936 by B Schott's Söhne, Mainz
With the kind permission of the publisher

---

1   This is incorrect. The two saw each other in Europe the following spring. See "China and Japan," p. 126.

The pentatonic scale is derived from a sequence of four successive fifths:

{*Editor's Note:* Chinese tuning			*Equal Temperament*	
(*pure fifths*)			(*flatted fifths*)	
88	=	F	=	88
132	=	C	=	131.85
198	=	G	=	197.55
297	=	D	=	295.996
445.5	=	A	=	443.49 }

Bringing these notes within the confines of one octave and arranging them in ascending order:

yields the pentatonic scale, which is equally euphonious in its melodic and harmonic combinations. Five different "modes" are possible, depending on which of the five notes comes first:

1. FGACD 2. GACDF 3. ACDFG 4. CDFGA 5. DFGAC

In Chinese music, semitones are used only in descending motion, and then only when they have the function of "guide tones" in the transition from one mode to another as, for example, in the transition from the first to the fifth mode:

In the tuning of Chinese instruments, the third and the sixth are slightly lower [*sic*] in pitch than in the tempered scale of Western music.

{*Editor's Note:* Reich is confused here. The third and sixth (first mode) are distinctly higher to western ears, as the frequency chart on the previous page indicates.}

The design of the Japanese pentatonic scale is analogous to that of the Chinese, but the third and sixth are noticeably lower in pitch, so that a European ear hears the following scale:

(F — G — A flat — C — D flat)

The two semitonal steps have the general effect of making Japanese music sound more astringent than Chinese; an analogy may be drawn between these pentatonic archetypes, Chinese and Japanese, and the European major and minor.

After the austere discipline of working with Interpoint and the nine-step scale, Tcherepnin found the folk-based pentatonic system of the Far East a source of artistic liberation. At the same time, strangely enough, his explorations of this alien yet curiously familiar world of sound freed him as well from the fetters of Western art music's traditional meters and rhythms. This stylistic change became apparent in his completion of Mussorgsky's unfinished opera *The Marriage*, published for the first time in the composer's original piano-score manuscript version by the Russian State Press in 1933. Through a close study of Gogol sources, Tcherepnin was able to establish that the libretto, of which Mussorgsky had set only the first of the three scenes, combined several Gogol concepts.[2] After pruning away subsidiary action, Tcherepnin was able to bring the central story to completion in a single scene, whose proportions perfectly complemented those of the scene composed by Mussorgsky. The newly devised text was set to music in Shanghai and Myanoshita (Japan) in 1934, and the orchestration of the whole was completed in the following year. This double-work of Mussorgsky and Tcherepnin was first produced in German at Essen in 1937, and was given in Paris in Russian in 1939. On both occasions, it was received with great acclaim.

Example R9

The Marriage (Mussorgsky-Tcherepnin)
© 1938 by Universal Edition, Vienna
With the kind permission of the publisher

(Second scene, A. Tcherepnin)

N.B. The stepwise legato descent of the vocal line is characteristic of singing in the Chinese theater, which is influenced by the phonetic modulations of Chinese pronunciation. Compare this melody with that of *Bagatelle Chinoise* No. 4 (Example R12).

Following Mussorgsky's example, but without imitating his style, Tcherepnin treated Gogol's text in a rhythmically free manner, mirroring the melodic curves of speech, and foreshadowing the free melodic style he was to develop in later instrumental works.

In a sense, Tcherepnin's new scene for *The Marriage* forms an organic link between his "Eurasian" works of 1932-33 and the "Far Eastern" compositions of the subsequent period.

In order to steep himself in the sound-world of the Far East—to which he felt himself drawn in veritably "magical" fashion—Tcherepnin made a close study of the peculiarities of Chinese stringed and wind instruments, the stage craft of the popular Chinese theater, the traditional shadow and puppet plays and the surviving examples of ancient Imperial court music.

However, as he got into closer touch with music students in all the great Chinese cities (through his activities as concert artist, teacher and musical advisor to the Chinese Ministry of Education) he was somewhat disappointed to find their compositions studded with "westernisms" that compromised their originality and naturalness. To try and change the situation, he organized a competition with the help of the director of Shanghai Conservatory, for a piano work of genuine Chinese character. The winner was the young composer He Luting (Rodin Ho) with *Buffalo Boy's Flute*.[3] (Later, in Japan, Tcherepnin promoted a similar competition for symphonic works by Japanese composers.) To secure publication for this piece and other works by young Chinese and Japanese musicians, he founded a publishing firm in Tokyo, which issued over fifty works between 1935 and 1937, including ten orchestral scores, under the imprint "Collection Tcherepnine." To young Western-seeking musicians who came to him for advice, he would stress that he himself had drawn powerful inspiration from Far Eastern culture, especially its music and literature.

{*Editor's Note:* Tcherepnin also championed Oriental music in the West. During the 1935-36 concert tours that separated his two visits to the Far East, he performed piano pieces by young Chinese and Japanese composers on an NBC

---

2 This statement is a bit misleading. Gogol himself had embedded one of his early comedies into *The Marriage* as a sub-plot, and Mussorgsky's libretto faithfully reflected this.

3 He Luting later became the director of the Shanghai Conservatory and one of the most important composers in China.

broadcast in New York and repeated them in recitals and lecture-recitals in some dozen European cities. In April 1936, he recorded four Japanese pieces for Victor in Tokyo (see "The Early Yamaha," p. 455).

Most interesting, perhaps, was the reaction in Nazi Germany. When commentators there pooh-poohed the Oriental selections in Tcherepnin's programs as culturally inappropriate for concert use, he publically defended his proteges and insisted that Chinese and Japanese composers had enormous value and potential. This defense became a legend among Eastern musicians—sometimes with a legend's questionable relationship to fact. By the 1960s, He Luting was boasting that Tcherepnin had told him of playing *Buffalo Boy's Flute* for Adolf Hitler during his German visit. It is extremely unlikely that Tcherepnin said or did anything of the sort. (*Reichskanzler* Hitler can scarcely ever have attended a Tcherepnin concert, nor can one imagine him inviting Tcherepnin to perform his modernist music in private.) Chinese officials, however, took he is accounted all too seriously during the Cultural Revolution, and made considerable trouble for him because of his supposed friendship with Hitler!}[4]

4   A more detailed account of Tcherepnin's comings and goings between Europe and the Far East—drawn largely from the composer's Personal Autobiography—can be found in "China and Japan," p. 168. See also Tcherepnin's own article, "Music in Modern China," p. 472.

In 1936 Tcherepnin published a pedagogical work, his *Technical Studies on the Pentatonic Scale*, Op. 53, in which he translated Western piano exercises into their pentatonic equivalents, thus enabling his piano students to practice exercises written in an idiom that was familiar to their ears. The following example illustrates the unusual pianistic agenda of this volume.

Example R10

Technical Studies for Piano in the Five-Note Scale, Op. 53
© 1935 by C. F. Peters, Leipzig
With the kind permission of the publisher

These studies specify the following fingerings for the scales and arpeggios of the five pentatonic modes. Note that the thumb passes under the fifth finger in moving from octave to octave.

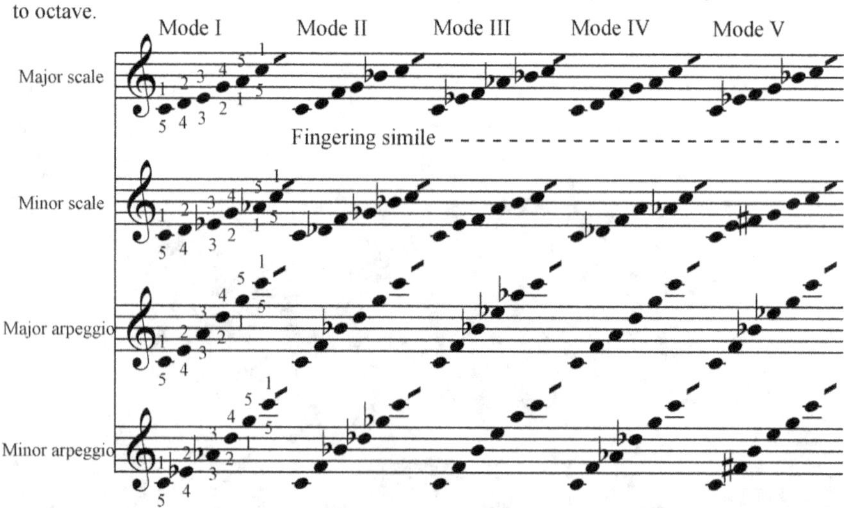

In addition to the purely technical *Studies*, Tcherepnin composed a series of piano pieces belonging to the same pedagogical category but also designed for performance, which were published under the title *Étude de Piano sur la Gamme Pentatonique* (*Piano Study on the Pentatonic Scale*), Op. 51. The collection comprises two suites, and a set of twelve *Bagatelles chinoises* in which, as if to prove the universality of the pentatonic system, Tcherepnin intersperses typically European dance rhythms and Chinese folk melodies.

Example R11

Étude de Piano sur la Gamme pentatonique, Op. 51
© 1935 by Heugel, Paris
With the kind permission of the publisher

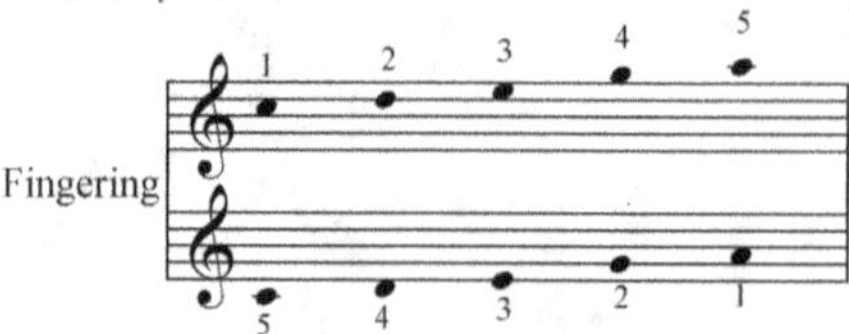

"Chanson des marins" (Sailors' Song), Op. 51, No. 1

Example R12

Bagatelles chinoises, Op. 51, No. 3
Bagatelle IV

Cf. the melody from *The Marriage* (Example R9)

Finally, in the *Cinq Études de Concert* (*Five Concert Studies*), Op. 52, Tcherepnin demonstrates that pentatonic materials can sustain demanding pieces for the concert stage. Three of the *Études* are inspired by images of life in the Far East. A fourth, *The Lute*, mirrors an ancient Chinese legend while attempting, through special effects of touch and pedal, to reproduce the sonorities of an aboriginal lute-like instrument {the *gu-ging*} on the modern Western piano.

Example R13

The Lute, Op. 52, No. 2
© 1935 by B. Schott's Söhne, Mainz
With the kind permission of the publisher

The entire piece, which lasts about four minutes, is based on the pentatonic scale beginning on F and the pedal is held from beginning to end, lending a timeless immanence to the pentatonic sound-world.

At the center of this cycle stands the previously cited *Hommage à la Chine*, with which Tcherepnin had begun working as a pentatonic composer in 1934, and which, with its dedication to Lee Hsien Ming, was of fateful importance in his personal, as well his professional life.

Although some musical dictionaries maintain that Tcherepnin spent three whole years in the Far East, his sojourn in China and Japan was actually interrupted by a year's stay in Europe. When he returned to the West for good in the autumn in 1937, he was confronted with new and entirely different musical challenges. Nevertheless, the musical language that he had developed while immersing himself in the experience of the Far East would continue to echo in his later works, and represented a permanent and significant extension of his artistic resources.

❀ ❀ ❀ ❀ ❀ ❀

5. Europe Again   (1937-1948)

Tcherepnin's return to Europe—in the summer of 1937—was largely motivated by his desire to marry Lee Hsien Ming.[1] After a short stay with his parents in Paris, he went to Brussels, where he supported himself by composing various commissions and giving concerts on the Belgian radio. The most important of these commissions was the ballet *Trepak*, written for the American dancer Lucia Chase. As a subject, Tcherepnin chose an ancient Russian legend about a young girl obsessed with dancing. He sketched the scenario in collaboration with a friend, the painter Sergei Sudeikin. The composition occupied him until January 1938.[2] He then made an extended tour of the U. S., and it was in Richmond that the premiere took place in October.

The singular musical feature of this ballet—which is one of Tcherepnin's major stage works—is that each individual scenic element is associated with its own particular sound-world: the peasants are represented by balalaika music, a religious sect by mystical choruses, the demons by an accordion, the voice of nature by a soprano, the whole richly enveloped in the symphonic sound of a large orchestra.

Example 14

Trepak (Ballet), Op. 55
© 1938 by Universal Edition, Vienna
With the kind permission of the publisher

a) "Round Dance," measure 1

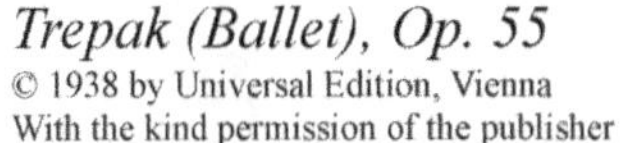

Russian pentatonic theme in free harmonization

b) "Round Dance," measure 20

The same theme freely harmonized with a rhythmic ostinato accompaniment

c) "Round Dance," measure 25

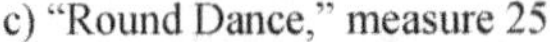

The same theme, pentatonic harmonization and accompaniment

---

1   The increasing seriousness of the war between China and Japan was also a significant factor in Tcherepnin's decision to leave.

2   This is incorrect. The ballet was not completed until August 1938.

d) "Round Dance," measures 29-30

Coda:
Measure 29,
quasi-Chinese
theme
Measure 30,
free conclusion

Musically, *Trepak* is an attempt to represent a stylized world of Russian folklore, using the compositional insights and vocabulary that the composer had just developed in the Far East. To quote Tcherepnin from a conversation, the ballet "displays the Eurasian under Asian light." It is from this viewpoint that the preceding examples should be understood.

Tcherepnin composed another ballet in the same period, inspired this time by German folklore, *Der Fahrend Schüler mit dem Teufelbannen)* (*The Wandering Scholar Who Exorcised the Devil*), Op. 54, based on the Hans Sachs Mardi Gras play of the same name. Its first performance, however, did not take place until 1965 in Kiel (in a new orchestration, because the original score had been lost during the War).

The piano pieces that Tcherepnin now wrote on commission from his publishers included 12 transcriptions of Russian masters (mostly opera extracts), and a piece entitled *Autour des Montagnes Russes* for an Eschig album commemorating

A gathering at the *Café de la Muette* after a contemporary music concert just before the war. Left to right: Suzanne Roche, Tibor Harsanyi, Georges Auric, Pierre Bernac, Marcel Mihalovici, Francis Poulenc, Ming Tcherepnin, Bohuslav Martinu, Alexander Tansman, Charlotte Martinu, Alexander Tcherepnin, Christiane Senart.

the 1937 Paris *Exposition Universelle*. Other contributors to this album were Tcherepnin's composer friends Arthur Honegger, Tibor Harsanyi, Marcel Mihalovici, Federico Mompou, Ernesto Halffter, Vittorio Rieti and Alexandre Tansman.

{*Editor's Note:* Each piece in this volume evoked a different composer's favorite spectacle at the exposition's fair-grounds. The Russian Tcherepnin appropriately chose the *Montagnes Russes* (roller coaster—literally "Russian mountains" in French), which had gained notoriety because of a few accidents, and charmingly evoked its ups and downs in a four-movement suite. Reich's list of names should have also included Bohuslav Martinu.}

Shortly before the outbreak of World War II, Tcherepnin received a divorce from his first wife and married Lee Hsien Ming,[3] with whom he would live in a most happy marriage blessed by three fine sons. The couple initially lived in the Paris suburb of Vanves, but soon moved into the "heart" of the capital: the Latin Quarter on the left bank of the Seine.

Responding to an odd commission from an American publisher, Tcherepnin produced a series of teaching pieces for unusual instrumental combinations, mostly involving winds (Opp. 58-64).[4] Even in this pedagogical province, he found it possible to glean valuable experience. At this time, he also completed his Anthology of Russian Music, subtitled "80 Examples from the Origins to the Beginning of the 19th Century," and submitted it to Belaieff.[5]

The most important orchestral work of these years was the *Suite Géorgienne (Georgian Suite)*, Op. 57, for piano and string orchestra, composed in 1938, which received great acclaim at a concert in Paris in 1940, shortly before the German invasion; the soloist was Ina Marika and the conductor, Charles Munch . This four-movement work, in which a

---

3   Isidore Philipp was best man at their wedding.

4   See also Tcherepnin's essay "Let Underprivileged Instruments Play," p. 334.

5   Tcherepnin's own account of the genesis and subsequent history of this volume, a pet project since his student days, appears on p. 336.

closely interwoven interplay between soloist and orchestra is sustained almost continuously, is one of Tcherepnin's most frequently played compositions.

Examples R15 and R16

Suite Géorgienne for Piano and String Orchestra, Op. 57
© 1940 by Max Eschig, Paris
With the kind permission of the publisher

a) First movement (Overture) measures 1-4

b) First movement (Overture), measures 25-28

a) Opening theme (a Georgian folk song).
b) The same theme in a "transposed" version, treated on the basis of the nine-step scale.

As the armies of the invasion approached Paris, Tcherepnin attempted to escape to the south with his family and parents, but they were overtaken by German troops and had to return to Paris, where they remained for the duration of the Occupation in living conditions of considerable privation.[6] At this time, he wrote a good deal of commercial dance music (usually pseudonymous), arranged or "ghost-composed" film music for other composers and gave occasional private lessons in composition. Early on in the war, he had written several original scores for a company of Russian ballet dancers, but the troupe was dissolved by the German authorities upon the outbreak of hostilities between Germany and Russia. Tcherepnin withdrew some other short works from this period, intending to rework them later.

{*Editor's Note:* In his French autobiography, Tcherepnin gave the following description of the atmosphere in the capital during wartime:

"This first year in occupied Paris was the most difficult year I have ever known in my life. Like Sleeping Beauty, Paris seemed to be dead, drained of all its vital forces, of its reason for being. It seemed as if we were living in a bad dream. And yet we had to live, to muddle through, to look for work, to feed ourselves and our relatives, to work at survival until the day we woke up.

---

6   The Tcherepnins attempted to escape by car, but ran out of gasoline and could get no more owing to shortages. At this point, they realized that they were surrounded by invading forces, and there was nowhere to go.

"[After] the *Ballets Russes de Paris* company was dispersed[7]…some particularly black months followed. Bowled over, crushed, baffled by the development of events, I could not compose. Reading Tolstoy's *War and Peace* was the only thing that saved me from atrophying completely."}

The joy that he felt when France was liberated was an emotion that compared, in his experience, only to his youthful euphoria at the collapse of the Czarist regime, and it roused him from the creative numbness that had gripped him during the years of physical and spiritual hardship. He now produced in quick succession a series of works which, though still clearly echoing his experiences in the Far East, show an increased striving to blend folk and exotic elements into the language of Western art-music in a more stylistically unified manner.

The Seven Songs on Chinese Poems, Op. 71, written in 1945 to ancient Chinese texts and only later translated into English and Russian for publication, still belong wholly to the Far East. But Tcherepnin's next three works, all composed in 1945, reflect completely different cultural climates: the ballet *Le Déjeuner sur L'Herbe* (*Picnic on the Grass*) on themes by Joseph Lanner; *Les Douze* (*The Twelve*), Op. 73, for narrator and small orchestra, on the poem by Alexander Blok; and the cantata *Le Jeu de la Nativité* (*Nativity Play*), Op. 74 for two sopranos, tenor, bass, strings and percussion, based on ancient and modern French and Russian texts.

Five short piano pieces that Tcherepnin dedicated to the French patroness of the arts Mathilde Amos and published in 1946 under the title *Le Monde en Vitrine* (*Showcase*), Op. 75, may be considered virtuoso curios.[8]

Meanwhile, in 1945, Tcherepnin had been charged with the interesting task of composing music in collaboration with Arthur Honegger for the ballet *Chota Rostaveli* based on a scenario by the poet Evreinov and choreographed by Serge Lifar.[9] The project proved so extensive that the collaborators were able to meet the 1946 deadline only by enlisting the aid of a third composer, the Hungarian Tibor Harsan-yi, who wrote the entire third act. The second act is by Tcherepnin and probably represents the peak of his "folkloristic period," for here he successfully combined exotic procedures and folk music with great consistency and economy of means.

Tcherepnin with his sons (*l.* to *r.*) Serge, Ivan and Peter. Chene Rogneux, 1946.

Example R17

Fantasie (Concerto No. 4) for Piano and Orchestra, Op. 78

© 1949 by Hinrichsen Edition Ltd., London
With the kind permission of the publisher

First movement (piano cadenza, page 5)

Bitonal pentatonic writing (C and A-flat)

---

7   The ban on the company ended their series of performances of Tcherepnin's ballet *The Legend of Razin*. The composer later expressed an intention to revise this folk-inspired work but never did so.

8   See also the analytical essay on *Showcase*, in *Seventeen Masterpieces*, p. 226.

9   According to an old legend, the knight and poet Chota Rostaveli was the founder of the Georgian Nation in the 12th Century.

A sort of farewell to the musical world of the Far East can be found in a ballet composed in America in 1948, *La Femme et son Ombre* (*The Woman and her Shadow*), Op. 79, based on a Paul Claudel scenario set in Japan. Similar nostalgia marks the three-movement Concerto No. 4 (*Fantaisie*), Op. 78, for piano and orchestra (1947), a programmatic work inspired by Chinese impressions.

During these years Tcherepnin's new works and his increasingly frequent concert tours brought a revival of his pre-war international activities. In 1946, he received an American commission for a symphony; the result was the Symphony No. 2, Op. 77, composed in 1947, orchestrated in 1951. This was the start of another new period of composition in Tcherepnin's career, one characterized by a synthesis of all of his previous experiences.

The Symphony No. 2 was premiered in 1952 by Rafael Kubelik and the Chicago Symphony. Quite complex in its tonal language, this four-movement work ranges beyond the nine-step and pentatonic scales, employing other synthetic scales and chromatic series, both horizontally and vertically. These technical means, however, are placed at the service of a dynamic expressivity that pervades the entire score and endows the music with unimpeded directness and communicative power.

Examples R18 and R19

Symphony No. 2, Op. 77
© 1957 by Associated Music Publishers, Inc., New York
With the kind permission of the publisher

The pentatonic scale is used as a five-note chord treated as a consonance, and the theme is stated in five-part harmony. The note G, on the viola, is alien to this major-pentatonic scale, and thus represents a dissonance, which, however, will not be resolved but simply eliminated.

The 25-measure main theme of the Rondo Finale is freely based on the nine-step scale.

With the Symphony No. 2, Tcherepnin advanced into a new world of musical sound and structure, one he would continue to explore in his following works. At the same time, changes in his outward circumstances were to contribute appreciably to the opening of a new phase in his creative life.[10]

❋ ❋ ❋ ❋ ❋ ❋

---

10   See also the analytical essay on Symphony No. 2, *Seventeen Masterpieces*, p. 230.

6. Culmination in America   (1949-1958)

Tcherepnin's Symphony No. 2—whose compositional technique we briefly discussed in the previous chapter—had special significance in the composer's life and work. It represented an energetic effort to dispel the artistic dissatisfaction that had afflicted him during the war and its immediate aftermath. He felt that most of his output from those years was scarcely better than adroit *Gebrauchsmusik*, produced merely to earn a living, and he cared little whether it even appeared under his own name. Far more valuable to him were certain "personal" sketches which revealed their importance only much later. It is noteworthy, for instance, that although the Symphony No. 2 was composed in 1947, it was not orchestrated—and thus not genuinely completed—until four years later in America.

Given these circumstances, it seems possible that Tcherepnin—long guided by a sense of artistic mission-now believed that with the approach of his fiftieth birthday (1949) the mission had been essentially accomplished. Indeed, he at first saw only temporary possibilities in his appointment that year as professor at DePaul University in Chicago with an accompanying post in musical theory and piano for Lee Hsien Ming. The Tcherepnins planned to stay for a single school year (1949-50), but the composer developed such enthusiasm about his pedagogical experience that in 1950 he and Ming became full-fledged faculty members and made a permanent home in Chicago.

Tcherepnin felt that in America—far more than in Europe—music was an organic part of general cultural life, and that a music teacher's noblest duty was to teach his students accordingly: his aim was to make them aware of music's cultural function and not merely to give specialized training in composition or in any one instrument. His University instruction in composition, counterpoint, orchestration, music history and the piano and his lecture and concert tours throughout the U. S. A. not only brought him great satisfaction, as he noted the progress of his pupils and their personal devotion to him, but also expanded his horizons in his own creative work and brought his art to full fruition. Art now appeared to him more and more as a "service" to mankind, not in the sense of an easy accommodation to public taste, but as a sacerdotal transmission of spiritual values. This new attitude seems to have renewed creative stimuli that had lain fallow for years and that now invested even music written on commission with an aura of urgent personal confession.

At work in Chicago

The first test of these new concepts came with the Symphony No. 3, Op. 83, commissioned by an American patron, Patricia Gordon, in 1952. The formal concept of this four-movement work parallels the structure of a novel; unfolding without repetition, it develops from the initial thematic material, material that "lives out its destiny," so to speak, by undergoing transformations that lead to an ultimate climax where every dimension of the composition is brought into play. The work was given its first performance in 1955 in Indianapolis under the direction of Fabien Sevitzky, and was later well received in New York.

{*Editor's Note:* The foregoing observations on the Symphony No. 3 and the upcoming comments on the opera *The Farmer and the Fairy* and the Suite for Orchestra, Op. 87, require a word. Reich writes of all of these works as if they were newly composed; actually, they belong largely to the 1940s. Tcherepnin recycled much of Symphony No. 3 from three ballets, drawing on *Dyonis* (1940) in the first and last movements, *Atlantide* (1943) in the second movement and *Vendeur des Papillons* (1942) in the third movement. *The Farmer and the Fairy* was merely Tcherepnin's 1945 cantata *Pan Kéou* rescored for small orchestra, provided with stage directions and librettistically altered to conceal the Chinese origins of the material. For the Suite, Tcherepnin used three scenes (unchanged) from his ballet *Le Gouffre* (*The Abyss*, 1949), appended an orchestration of his Rondo for two pianos (1952) as a finale, and gave the whole a new programmatic integument (it is amusing to note that "Conflict," a mugging-rape scene in the ballet, became a depiction of Chicago gangs in the Suite).

The patrons and organizations that commissioned these three scores were subsidizing new music. They had no interest in re-cycled works and would have been displeased had they known the music was not fresh from Tcherepnin's pen, a fact the composer sedulously concealed. This deception, not to mince words, was ethically questionable. It should at least be noted, however, that in the case of the opera and the Suite, Tcherepnin unquestionably gave his patrons value for money: the former was an immediate hit and a prize-winner, the latter was taken up by several orchestras and enjoyed notably warm reception. Reich continues:}

Another highly successful orchestral work from these first American years was the Symphonic March, Op. 80, composed in 1951 for large orchestra, and arranged in 1954 for wind band.

In the spring of 1952, Tcherepnin completed the lyric opera *The Farmer and the Fairy*, Op. 72 (later published under the title *The Nymph and the Farmer*) for the Aspen Institute. The music is largely based on the pentatonic scale, but contains expressive elements that go beyond the pentatonic framework, as for example a significant chord that had fact, tragic personal associations for Tcherepnin. He had heard it in an oratorio-sketch played by his father on the eve of his death: and even then, he had felt the fateful power of its sound.

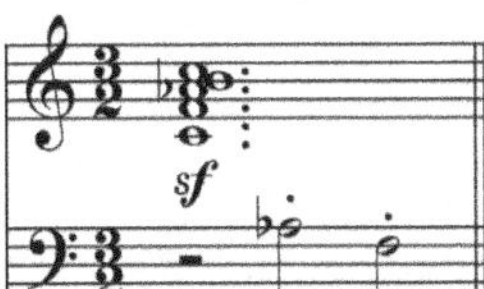

The opera was an enormous success at its first production in 1952 at the Aspen Festival in Colorado under Joseph Rosenstock.[1]

Tcherepnin now turned to new formal and technical experiments in the more intimate medium of the piano. The ten miniatures, *Expressions*, Op. 81 (1951), and the five *Songs Without Words*, Op. 82, (1949-51) were followed by works of larger and more complex formal design, the *12 Preludes*, Op. 85 (1952-53), and the *Eight Pieces for Piano*, Op. 88 (1955), which demonstrate Tcherepnin's mastery of the piano. Common to all these pieces is a formally free manner of construction in which all types of repetition are avoided; as a result, the initial themes often lead to consequences that seem totally unexpected, given their original nature.

In analogy with the "novelistic" form of the Symphony No. 3, the piano pieces, with their terser forms may be likened to short stories. The unity of each piece is achieved by organic growth from a thematic cell or by reference to a tonal center, a feature which does not necessarily lead to diatonic, modal or pentatonic harmony. (The, Op. 85, for example, cover the entire twelve-note cycle of the chromatic scale.)

The Farmer and the Fairy at Aspen, 1952

The following examples illustrate some of these new technical devices:

▸ Enrichment of harmonic palette through the use of chordal appoggiaturas:

Example R20

From *12 Preludes, Op. 85 (Piano)*
New Edition
© 1972 by M. P. Belaieff
With the kind permission of the publisher

Prelude I, measures 22-23

▸ Extension of the method of Interpoint, no longer exclusively "note-against-note" but now extended to "phrase-against-phrase" and "rhythm-against-rhythm":

---

1   After further performances in New York and Chicago, the opera was given the David Bispham Award in 1960 by the American Opera Society.

Example R21

From *Expressions for Piano, Op. 81*
© 1951 by Leeds Music Corp., New York
With the kind permission of the publisher

Expression No. 10

While the right hand melody is in free rhythm, the left hand plays six figures in 5/8 meter, one in 4/8 and then another two in 5/8. This procedure can be considered a kind of horizontal interpoint in which the simultaneous notes are asynchronous in phrasing.

▸ Various piano registers set systematically against one another:

Example R22

From *12 Preludes, Op. 85*
Prelude XI, Measures 26-29

Juxtaposition of piano registers.

▸ New ornamental patterns:

Example R23

From *12 Preludes, Op. 85*
Prelude III, measures 1-4

Example R23

► Dissolution of thematic complexes into smaller entities:

Example R24

From *12 Preludes, Op. 85*
Prelude XI, measures 26-29

▸ Use of the asymmetrical "prose" rhythms of speech:

Example R25

8 Pieces for Piano, Op. 88
© 1957 by Theodore Presser Company, Bryn Mawr, Pennsylvania
With the kind permission of the publisher

II. Intermezzo

Prose rhythms

Each of these piano collections, Opp. 81, 82, 85 and 88, forms a cycle in the Romantic sense; that is, the individual pieces bear an emotional and musical relationship to one another. This is most clearly evident in the *12 Preludes,* in which the last piece serves as a kind of epilogue to the whole, providing, as it were, a retrospective view of the preceding music from a higher vantage point.

Before we discuss Tcherepnin's later work in America, it should be pointed out that this new creative period, starting at the end of 1950, was richly "Interpointed" with concert tours in which the composer was able to realize his new creative achievements in lively personal interpretations.

Tcherepnin furnished proof of his newly-won creative freedom in 1953 with several pieces for violoncello and piano, commissioned by the famous cellist Gregor Piatigorsky. In this collection (*Songs and Dances* for Violoncello and Piano, Op. 84) Tcherepnin used folkloric material but subjected it to extensive manipulation utilizing the new techniques described above. The result was a closed cycle of four interrelated pieces, innovative in its string writing, based on the alternation of Georgian and Russian melodies with Tartar and Cossack dance motifs.

Meanwhile, in the spring of 1952, the harmonica virtuoso John Sebastian had commissioned Tcherepnin to write a concerto for that instrument with orchestra. The technical peculiarities of the harmonica and the balance problems it posed were more or less unknown to the composer, and writing the score proved to be a challenge to his imagination that absorbed all his creative attention.

The language of this work has its basis in the following four chords, which are "native" to the instrument:

Example R26

The harmonica's four chords encompass a complete chromatic scale, which can be played by exhaling and inhaling in proper alternation.

Bearing this practical consideration in mind, Tcherepnin composed a four-movement concerto in which the outer movements are in C major and the two inner ones in D-flat major. Given the somewhat primitive character of the harmonica, he resorted to traditional classical forms to a considerable extent, designing the first movement in textbook sonata form, while the last—which is prefaced by an extensive harmonica cadenza—is a Rondo. The three themes of this finale are melodies invented by Tcherepnin's three sons as children.

John Sebastian found the concerto thoroughly idiomatic for the harmonica, and premiered it with great success at the Venice Biennale Music Festival in the autumn of 1956 (Fabien Sevitzky conducting).

Example R27

Concerto for Harmonica and Orchestra, Op. 86
© 1956 by Associated Music Publishers, New York
With the kind permission of the publisher

a) Third movement

b) Fourth movement

a) the harmonica in combination with solo instruments
b) harmonica and full orchestra

Example R28

The main theme of the rondo, which was "composed" by Tcherepnin's son Serge in 1948 at age seven. Serge performed it by whistling the opening and playing the answering chords on a small harmonica.

Tcherepnin's son Peter found this theme at the piano at age four in 1943. It leads to the second subject of the rondo and also appears at that episode's climax.

This idea, which serves as the second theme of the rondo, was composed by Tcherepnin's son Ivan in 1949 at age six. He would begin it in the top octave of the piano and continue repeating it, descending octave by octave until he had reached the bottom of the keyboard.

Example R29

The Lost Flute, Op. 89, for narrator and orchestra
© 1956 by Templeton Publishing Co., Inc., New York
With the kind permission of the publisher

a) "The poet rises late," measures 176-181   Example for orchestra alone

The theme (woodwinds) and its answer (brass) are in 2/4. The accompaniment is given to the strings pizzicato. The divided first violins play a rhythmic figure in 5/8 against its vertical Interpoint. Against this are set the divided second violins in horizontal Interpoint, both parts also playing a 5/8 figure, but at the distance of a single eighth rest (1/8), in vertical Interpoint. The violas continually repeat a 4/8 figure, each repetition interrupted by a quarter-note rest. Their part evolves as arhythmic Interpoint set against the other parts. The cellos play a 3/4 figure which is imitated in vertical Interpoint by the double basses. The whole passage shows four-fold horizontal Interpoint combined with a free line plus theme and answer.

Before describing the stages by which Tcherepnin's later orchestral works evolved, some discussion must be devoted to a unique score within his oeuvre: *The Lost Flute*, Op. 89, a six-part cycle for narrator and orchestra. This work was suggested to Tcherepnin by the conductor Thor Johnson, who, at the end of 1953, sent the composer a collection of Chinese poems of that title, in English translation by Gertrude Laughlin Joerissen. Johnson asked for a piece based on these verses and featuring Tcherepnin's wife as narrator, to be premiered at the 1954 Peninsula Summer Festival in Fish Creek, Wisconsin. Tcherepnin studied the poems for many months before he succeeded in making a selection and arranging them in an order that suited his artistic and musical needs. Finished early in July 1954, the work took this form:

I.   As a kind of motto, the title of Chang Wou-Kien's poem *The Lost Flute* is recited against a gently subdued orchestral background.

II.   1st Interlude: An ancient Chinese poem is recited without music.

III.   The Poet's Day: Several ancient Chinese poems are recited to an orchestral accompaniment. 2nd Interlude: Recitation without music.

IV.   After an orchestral prelude, accompanied recitation of several contemporary Chinese poems on the theme of "Childhood."

V.   3rd Interlude: Unaccompanied recitation of the ancient Chinese poem, "Faithfulness."

VI.   Accompanied recitation of three ancient Chinese poems on "Love." 4th Interlude: An ancient Chinese poem without music.

VII.   Recitation of two ancient Chinese poems on "War," accompanied only by percussion. 5th Interlude: Unaccompanied recitation of an ancient Chinese poem.

VIII.   Recitation of two ancient Chinese poems on "Death," with orchestral accompaniment.

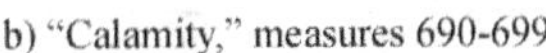

b) "Calamity," measures 690-699   Example for narrator and ensemble

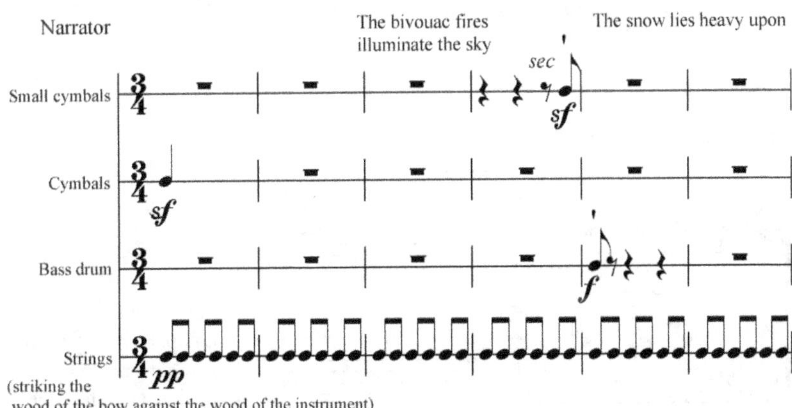

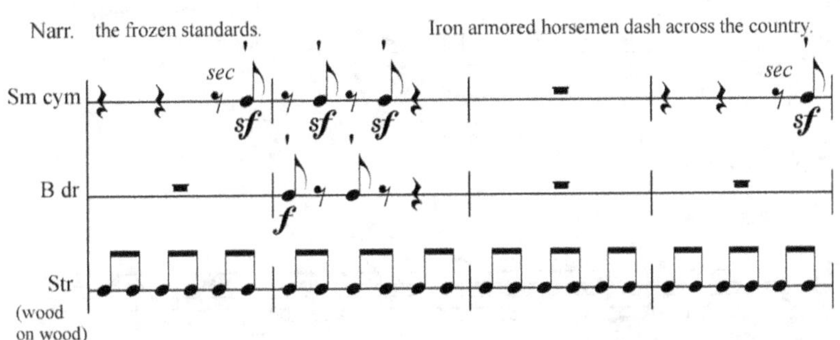

The scoring is for strings, double woodwinds, two horns, two trumpets, trombone, harp, timpani and percussion (including some original Chinese percussion instruments). Among all of Tcherepnin's creations, it is surely *The Lost Flute*, with its highly individual spiritual traits, that most accurately and intimately reflects the totality of his essential artistic being. The two preceding examples may suggest the unique quality of its musical construction.

Tcherepnin's wife took special elocution lessons for her part as the narrator and gave a deeply moving performance of the work at its premiere at the Peninsula Festival on August 4, 1954: as is evidenced by the live-concert recording of the work made in San Francisco in 1955 in a version for narrator (Lee Hsien Ming), piano (the composer) and percussion (Tcherepnin's son Ivan).

Decisive, however, in Tcherepnin's full realization of his genius was his determination to immerse himself in the world of the orchestra, to which he was led by a Louisville Orchestra commission in the Spring of 1953. The work was originally to be a symphony; but Tcherepnin's growing identification with American city life inspired him instead to write four pieces on "The City": mood pictures without any specific programmatic tendencies, which reflected his impressions of Chicago—and did not lend themselves to any genuine symphonic layout. The result was the Suite for Orchestra, Op. 87, completed at the end of 1953, the four movements of which evoke the moods, respectively, of an early morning urban *Idyll*, underworld *Conflicts*, the loneliness of the individual surrounded by multitudes, and the bustle of traffic.

Example R30

Suite for Orchestra, Op. 87
© 1954 by C. F. Peters, New York
With the kind permission of the publisher

A) "Conflicts" (movement II)
a) (measure 161)

Allegro risoluto

b) (measure 174)

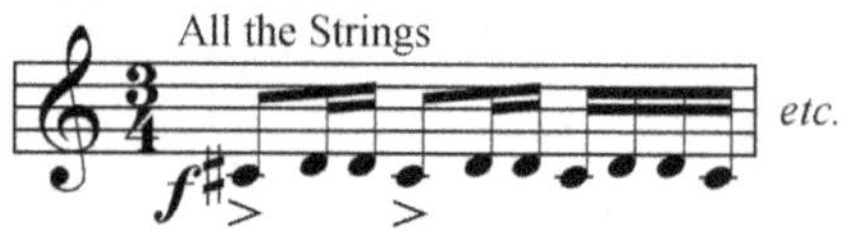

B) "Nostalgia" (movement III)

Lento (measures 372-373)

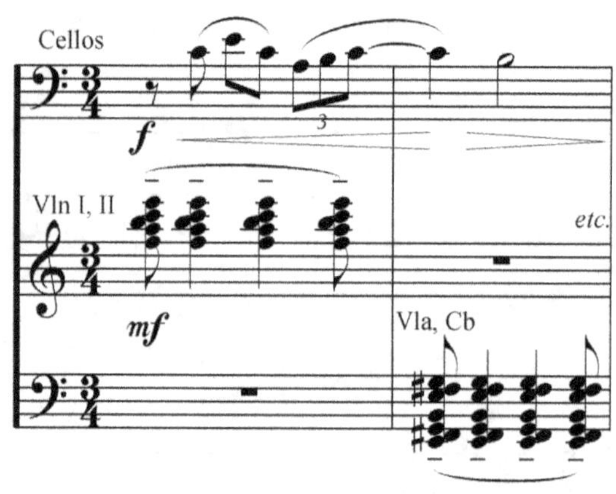

The cantabile theme for all the cellos is accompanied by chords alternating between extreme registers. Note that these chords telescope the minor mode of the pentatonic scale. This is but a brief excerpt from a 30-measure-long melody.

C) Rondo (movement IV)

a) Russian folk song (main theme of the Rondo)
b) Russian folk song (first subsidiary theme)
c) Quasi-Chinese pentatonic melody (second subsidiary theme)

Almost a year after the completion of the Suite for Orchestra, Tcherepnin was again invited to produce a symphony. This was a commission from the conductor Charles Munch, a commission that gave the composer total freedom to determine the form of the work and to choose its completion date. But it was exactly this total freedom, along with the feeling of responsibility toward the generous colleague and patron who would perform the work with his celebrated Boston Symphony Orchestra, that prompted Tcherepnin to subject his ideas to the most merciless scrutiny before he felt that he had found a worthy starting point for the new large work.[2] Also to blame for this "fermata" in his creativity was the increasingly vulnerable state of the overworked composer's health. At the end of November 1955, just after he had finished sketching the first movement of the new symphony and found the main theme of the second, he suffered a severe heart attack in Chicago, necessitating another long hiatus in his work on the Symphony.

The first months after his convalescence were devoted to concert tours in America. In early 1956 he was roused from the doldrums of tormenting creative sterility by two magnificent performances of Classical-period music: a Mozart Serenade performed by Fritz Reiner, and Beethoven's Fourth Symphony conducted by Charles Munch. The Mozart gave him the idea of a divertimento for orchestra,[3] while the Beethoven Symphony threw new light on his own symphony, leading him to abandon his earlier drafts and to begin again from scratch with the sketching of new ideas.

Tcherepnin and his wife Ming converse with Boston Symphony conductor Charles Munch over drinks at Tanglewood, the orchestra's summer home.

As he wanted to let the symphony ripen further within him, he next completed the last (third) movement of the Divertimento, and reworked his earlier symphony-materials as the Divertimento's first two movements, the complete score (Op. 90) being premiered by Fritz Reiner and the Chicago Symphony Orchestra in November 1957.

---

2   Reich is embroidering here. Tcherepnin's reasons for postponing work on the Symphony were far less artistic than practical: he had two commissions that he had to finish first. For a completely accurate account of the genesis of his Divertimento, Op. 90 and Symphony No. 4, Op. 91, See: "Tcherepnin on Munch and Reiner," pp. 149-151.

3   Reiner, in fact, had requested an orchestral piece, but specified that he did not want a symphony. In the Divertimento, Tcherepnin in effect gave the conductor a symphony under another name.

Formally speaking, the Divertimento represents a renewed confrontation with the classical symphonic model. The first movement is in sonata form and culminates in a violently dramatic coda; the middle movement is an expressive five-part song form; and the finale is a brilliant rondo with a fast and regular tempo.[4]

Example R31

Divertimento, Op. 90
© 1966 by Boosey and Hawkes, Ltd., London
With the kind permission of the publisher

a) First movement

The main theme is freely chromatic, with a tendency towards the nine-step scale; the chordal interjections are in vertical Interpoint.

b) Second movement, measures 421-425

---

4   See also the analytical essay on the Divertimento, *Seventeen Masterpieces*, p. 338.

c) Third movement

Beginning of the main theme of the last movement.

The Symphony No. 4, Op. 91 (1957) and the Divertimento, Op. 90 assumed their final shape almost simultaneously, and although both works make use of the nine-step scale and of a concentrated and perfected form of Interpoint, they are very different, almost opposites. It is true that both works begin with a sonata movement. Nevertheless, the Symphony's first movement is serene and measured in mood, Apollonian in character, while the opening movement of the Divertimento is agitated and dramatic. The Symphony's middle movement is an *Allegro* in *Tempo di Valse*, perhaps suggested by illustrious Russian precedents. The contrast is strongest in the concluding movements. Where the Divertimento ends with a brilliant and fast Rondo, the Symphony No. 4 closes with a deeply meditative *Andante*, which finds its inevitable resolution in the old Russian liturgical melody for the *Requiescat in Pace*, intoned in the long-held notes of a *cantus firmus* like a dignified funeral eulogy.[5]

Example R32

Symphony No. 4, Op. 91
© 1959 by Boosey and Hawkes Ltd., London
With the kind permission of the publisher

a) Second movement

The main theme of the second movement, introduced by solo piccolo without accompaniment.

b) Third movement

Cantus firmus (*Requiescat in pace*) from medieval Russian church music.

This cantus firmus theme occurs near the end of the third movement (see measure 941ff.). Compare it to the theme from the Sonatine Romantique, Op. 4 (example R2), also based on three notes.

This somber, pious conclusion proved the harbinger of the tragic blow that was to strike Tcherepnin at the end of December 1958: the death of his mother, who had shared nearly her entire existence with the composer and his family.

---

5   See also the analytical essay on Symphony No. 4, *Seventeen Masterpieces*, p. 354.

The close of the Symphony No. 4, which was premiered in December 1958 in Boston by Charles Munch with great success, seems to announce a progression toward the new religious sphere to which Tcherepnin's next composition, the *Symphonic Prayer*, Op. 93, for orchestra, clearly belongs. Completed in July 1959, this work was commissioned to open the Chicago Festival of Pan-American Music that August, where it was conducted by Eleazar de Carvalho. The piece is composed in an immediately comprehensible lapidary style which, in its combination of Russian Church music with modern technique, not only reveals the universality of Tcherepnin's compositional technique and the sovereignty of his musical powers of expression, but also demonstrates the sense of "spiritual mission" that imbues the entirety of his work with a passionate urgency that no unprejudiced listener can ignore.[6]

Example R33

Symphonic Prayer, Op. 93
© 1960 by M. P. Belaieff, Frankfurt
With the kind permission of the publisher

a) (measures 1-9)

(a) The theme is a nine-step series and generates, as it unfolds, a nine-part chord. In the ninth measure, this chord undergoes a threefold change, the last permutation resulting in a ten-part chord. Up to the first quarter of the ninth measure, the series is in mode III of the nine-step scale. The three subsequent chords encapsulate, respectively, (1) mode II of (nine-step) A, (2) mode I of (nine-step) B, and (3) mode III of (nine-step) E.

b) The melody is harmonized in "hard" chords (*i. e.* chords from which thirds are omitted). The accents indicate the displacement of the strong beats of the measure.

---

6   See also the analytical essay on *Symphonic Prayer, Seventeen Masterpieces*, p. 372.

c) (measures 84-85)

c) Rhythmic interlocking of the "hard" chords.

d)

d) The theme derives from the responsorial chant in the Russian liturgy, in which the first part is sung by the priest and the second by the choir.

Vladimir Dokudovsky, Ted Shawn, Nina Stroganova, Alexander Tcherepnin and a group of dancers after the premiere of Tcherepnin's ballet *Le Gouffre* (*The Abyss*, alias Suite for Orchestra, Op. 87) at Jacob's Pillow in 1956.

Tcherepnin and Paul Claudel discuss their ballet *La Femme et son Ombre* with Janine Charrat, Paris, 1948.

7. Later Developments[1]   (1959-1968)

Although Tcherepnin maintained close artistic and personal ties to America after 1958[2]—as the discussion of the Fourth Symphony and the Symphonic Prayer has already shown—that year also marked the point of departure for a notable expansion of his field of activity.

This new phase in his career began in June 1958 with a journey to Europe, his first after an unbroken stay of eight years in North America. Among Tcherepnin's most moving personal experiences abroad were his reunions with many old friends in major English and continental cities, particularly with Paul Grlimmer in Zurich.[3] During a visit to Hermann Scherchen's studio in Gravesano, near Lugano, he acquired some basic practical knowledge in the field of electronic music. In Zurich, he began a significant friendship with Karl Weber and his wife Margrit, the noted pianist. Indeed, this splendid performer played the *Bagatelles*, Op. 5, for Tcherepnin with such brilliance that he decided to provide the work with an instrumental accompaniment. Two versions resulted—one for piano and strings, the other for piano and orchestra—and both were premiered by Margrit Weber, the first in 1960 in Lucerne, the second in 1961 in Vienna.

With Margrit Weber

At the end of the year, the Symphony No. 4 was awarded the Glinka Prize, and the beginning of 1959 was marked by numerous celebrations in honor of Tcherepnin's 60th birthday, at which the composer often took part as conductor or pianist. In January alone, broadcast or public concerts featuring Tcherepnin's music took place in Milan, Hamburg, Hannover, Berlin, Stuttgart, Baden-Baden and Basel; private celebrations occurred in Zurich and Paris.

That spring, he resumed teaching in Chicago, and in July he taught at the *Académie Internationale d'été* in Nice. Works composed during this hectic year include not only the *Symphonic Prayer*, Op. 93, but also a suite for orchestra, which Tcherepnin formed out of his portion (the second act) of the 1945 ballet *Chota Rostaveli* and published under the title *Georgiana*, Op. 92.

Between January 1960 and May 1964, Tcherepnin ostensibly divided his life between two professions, alternating long periods of teaching as a professor in Chicago with short, but intensive bursts of concertizing and teaching in Europe. Common to both pursuits, however, was Tcherepnin's steadily continuing creative work, which underwent stylistic evolutions that will be examined more specifically in the upcoming discussions of individual pieces.

First came two charming occasional works: the Trio for flute, violin and cello (intended as a present for the Webers' three children, each of whom played one of the instruments) and the Fanfare for brass and percussion, commissioned and performed as the opening piece of the February 1961 International Music Festival in Miami, Florida. In the Fanfare, the musical letters of the name of the conductor Fabien Sevitzky (Fa-B-E) and of his wife Marus (Mi-A-Re-Ut-Es) were woven into the thematic material as *soggetti cavati* ("hidden subjects"). The harmony contains many pentatonic elements, alluding to compositions by Chinese and Japanese composers which were also scheduled for the festival.

Shortly after completing the Fanfare, Tcherepnin became absorbed in compositional problems remarkably similar to those presented by the Concerto for Harmonica commissioned by John Sebastian in 1952. This time the commission came from the American Accordion Association, which wanted a piece for their instrument, then very popular in America. Once again, Tcherepnin was fascinated by the challenge of adapting his music's sounds and sentence structure to the peculiarities of a device that had rarely received solo exposure in "serious" music—an instrument whose exciting musical and technical possibilities could be exploited quite effectively, as long as certain limitations in its vocabulary were taken into account.

With Hermann Scherchen at Gravesano, 1959

---

1   Reich's original title to this chapter was "Latest Developments."

2   The Tcherepnins became American citizens on April 1, 1958.

3   for whom he had written the 3rd Cello Sonata and the Concertino.

Preparation for this task involved several months of continued study, but the reward was a most substantial success: completed in 1961, the Partita for solo accordion was enthusiastically received by the public and the critical community all over the nation, and later brought the composer two more commissions from the Accordion Association: one for a solo work, the other for a Capriccio for accordion and orchestra.[4]

Although not finished until 1959, the *Symphonic Prayer* was surely the crowning achievement of the period referred to as Tcherepnin's "culmination in America." The succeeding years were marked by a continual search for new paths, and the creative results of this quest would not become fully evident until considerably later. During this period of exploration, Tcherepnin, as we have seen, composed only occasional works: arrangements of earlier pieces and smaller commissioned works such as the Fanfare and the Partita. At first glance, his next work, the Piano Sonata No. 2, Op. 94, completed in ten days in September 1961, appears to belong to this category. The Sonata was commissioned by the Berlin Festival, to be performed there by the composer himself. To say that it took ten days to write, an incredibly short time for Tcherepnin, is deceptive: in reality, the musical language of the sonata was the result of a year-long preparation which Tcherepnin had spent creating a singular chromatic world of sound based on new formal and tonal principles, including the elaboration of a system of interlocking tetrachords. These innovations, which will be further discussed, show the Sonata to be at the threshold of a new phase in Tcherepnin's musical evolution.

The character of the Piano Sonata No. 2 was strongly influenced by terrifying personal circumstances. Upon returning to Chicago from Europe in February 1959, the composer suddenly noticed disquieting changes in his hearing. The initial symptom was a penetrating note sounding almost uninterruptedly in his left ear; shortly afterward, a second note appeared, a whole tone higher in pitch, and the two notes continued to sound, either in alternation or both together. A second symptom was that music played at a distance sounded to him as if it had been transposed up a semitone. [5] Tcherepnin was deeply disturbed by these symptoms, as he knew that his father and his grandfather had both suffered from increasing deafness in their old age. None of the many doctors he consulted could help him. Then suddenly, after two and a half years of torment, complete recovery came "by itself." The regaining of the inviolate silence of his inner ear and the return of accurate musical hearing even at the "critical distance" were the immediate events that inspired the creation of the Second Piano Sonata—in which a few aspects of the

Example R34

Second Piano Sonata, Op. 94

© 1962 by Boosey and Hawkes Ltd., London
With the kind permission of the publisher

From the second part of the first movement:
(Here only as D-E)

From the close of the third movement
(Here in the forms D-E and E-flat-F)

---

4   This last piece was never written.

5   Tinnitus, the hearing of "phantom" sounds is a common affliction, but was especially bothersome to composers such as Schumann (tormented by an A) and Smetana (an Ab). The notes that rang in Tcherepnin's ears were F and G.

composer's "aural tragedy" was artistically represented. The symptom most graphically reproduced was the major-second ostinato, which appears as an *idée fixe* throughout the sonata.

It was in the Sonata and the Partita that Tcherepnin's "novella-like" formal principle, as it might be appropriately called, was first consistently used.[6] Here, all the developments move the work as a whole toward a conclusion as a plot moves toward its denouement. No single musical movement or section by itself provides a definitive resolution. A movement is to be grasped in much the same way as a single chapter in a novella is read, as part and parcel within a dynamic progression.

In the three-movement Sonata, novella-like development occurs throughout. Thus the first movement concludes with melodic motifs dominated by the descending fourth, the same interval which marks the beginning of the second movement, as can be seen in the following example:

First movement:
fourth measure from the end

Second movement:
first measure

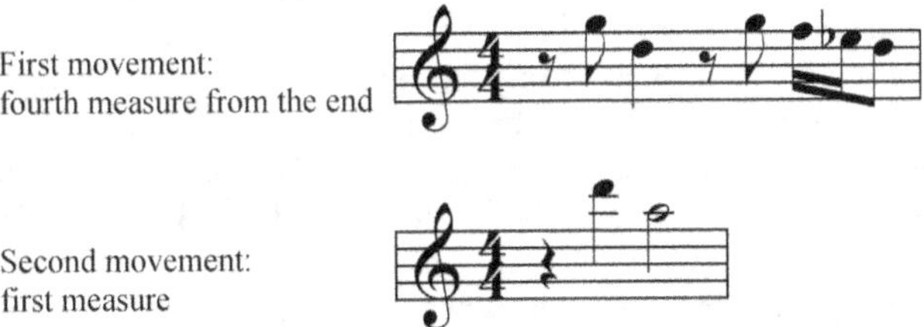

Similarly, the close of the Sonata's second movement can be seen as a thematic preparation for the third movement, whose coda, with the addition of entirely new thematic material, brings a conclusion to the "novella".

So far as the individual movements are concerned, the first consists of five parts—the first, third and fifth marked *Lento*—with thematic material deriving from the harmony of the first two measures:

The second part, marked *Animato*, is dominated by the aforementioned *idée fixe*, whereas the essential thematic figure of the fourth part (*Agitato*) is a descending chromatic figure:

It should be noted that parts 1, 3 and 5 originate from the same harmonic basis, and in no way stand in the traditional relationship of exposition, development and reprise. They may be considered "further developments" of a single nucleus. The Sonata's second movement (*Andantino*) can likewise be interpreted as a continuing development of the basic ideas presented in the opening measures, steadily progressing toward a close that prepares the way for the third movement, of which this is the main theme:

The structure develops from two chromatic tetrachords along with the four-note melodic line which Tcherepnin describes as "the hard tetrachord."

---

6   This should not be confused with the "novelistic" form discussed earlier. Here, Reich invokes the literary genre of the novella, where novelistic scope is allied to an unusually concentrated expositional style in a perfectly balanced narrative of moderate length.

This movement bears a genuine kinship with traditional rondo form, yet the reprises of what would be the rondo theme are not fully carried through: its last repetition "trickles away" as it were, in a *diminuendo* that culminates in a long coda. Here, the mood is distinctly similar to that of the first movement's slower passages, but the themes provide something quite new, namely the completion of the "novella."

The Piano Sonata No. 2 was followed in Tcherepnin's output by more "occasional" music: his *Processional* and *Recessional*, two organ pieces written for the double-wedding of his two nephews. They were first performed at the joint ceremony in Honolulu in September 1962.

In the list of Tcherepnin's works, the Seven Chinese Folksongs appear as Op. 95. Five of them were written in December 1962, commissioned by the Chinese bass Yi-Kwei Sze, who sang them for the first time that month at Town Hall in New York. The other two songs had been composed for the same singer in 1956. Each of the seven folksongs were left intact, sung by the bass voice as a kind of *cantus firmus*, not "harmonized" or "arranged" so much as "enveloped" in freely polyphonic instrumental parts.

Although the Piano Concerto No. 5, Op. 96 (composed at several locales in Switzerland between April and September 1963) was commissioned by the Berlin Festival, it was inspired by the composer's personal experiences at that time. In the spring of 1963, Tcherepnin's wife received news that her sister was gravely ill, and immediately rushed to her bedside in Honolulu. Anxious about his absent wife and his ailing sister-in-law, as well as his sick friend Paul Grlimmer (in whose house at Zollikon he was now living alone), Tcherepnin sensed the influence of nature around him in a way that he had never experienced before. The feeling seemed to emanate, above all, from the woods surrounding the house, where he took long, solitary walks. In the forest stillness, he was filled with diverse, often highly contradictory attitudes toward nature. Often, she seemed to him disquieting, cruel, misanthropic and frightening; just as often, he found her comforting, a feeling induced by the cheerful polyphony of bird calls, the clear sound of church bells, the splendor of giant trees and distant mountains. A dawning sense of admiration for the ingenious and yet mysterious order of the cosmos brought him calm and inner peace.

Alexander and Ming Tcherepnin, 1960

These contradictions were reflected in the first movement of Piano Concerto No. 5 as it slowly matured that summer: the musical form, in fact, arose from exactly such contrasts. The feeling of expectation created by contradictions also lends a strangely mystical tone to the short second movement, which is best understood as a transition to the finale. Yet this expectation is not, after all, resolved by a finale of glowing fulfillment: the movement concerns itself instead with the stormily pulsating continuation of onward-streaming life. This conclusion can quite justly be interpreted as another kind of "fulfillment" of what has gone before, and was probably so considered by the composer. There is no question of vague romanticizing: Tcherepnin's Piano Concerto No. 5 can be exactly defined in all its details. But before going on to technical considerations, I should like to quote what Tcherepnin, two years after completing the Piano Concerto, said about the manner in which he sets out to compose:

"First, I 'feel' the work inside myself without 'hearing' any actual sound. Only gradually does that inner feeling shape itself into tonal ideas which at first, however, are not 'tempered,' and should be called, rather, free, 'untempered' rhythms and formations of intervals. The next stage of development brings the ordering of these free formations into a tempered musical language. Only then is the work finally formed and completed in all its details. The composer's main task is to remain true to the original idea in its final formulation. This task leaves him no peace while he is writing. He finds rest only after a long period of gestation, when the clearly written score lies before him like a new-born child in its cradle. And then one asks oneself: Why did it take so long to find the solution? Why all the doubts, all the testing, all the sleepless nights, when everything is so obvious and simply cannot be otherwise?"

The technical basis of Piano Concerto No. 5 is a special modal type of chromaticism, which Tcherepnin innovatively developed from two tetrachords and "the hard tetrachord." The example overleaf diagrams the first mode of the two tetrachords with "the hard tetrachord" filling in the scale-intervals.

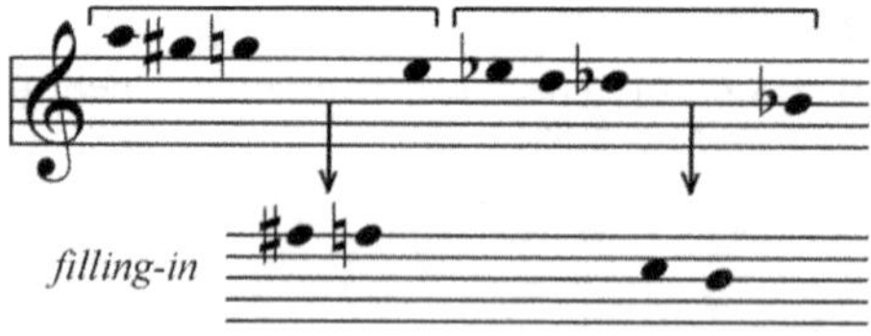

Example R35 shows the derivation of four separate thematic forms from a single rhythmic model, demonstrating the fundamental importance of rhythm in the shaping of the Piano Concerto's thematic material.

Example R35

Piano Concerto No. 5, Op. 96
© 1964 by M. P. Belaieff, Frankfurt
With the kind permission of the publisher

The converse also occurs frequently, with themes remaining unaltered while their rhythms are varied:

Rhythmic and thematic contrasts are decisive in shaping the Concerto's form, which can justly be termed "dialectic," proceeding as it does from thesis to antithesis. The Fifth Concerto was premiered on October 13, 1963, at the Berlin Festival, performed by the Philharmonia Hungarica under Miltiades Caridis, with the composer at the piano.[7]

The year 1964 marked a turning point in Tcherepnin's life. He relinquished his professorship at DePaul University in May, giving up teaching in order to devote himself entirely to writing music and presenting concerts. This newly won

---

7   See also the analytical essay on Concerto No. 5, *Seventeen Masterpieces*, p. 271, and Tcherepnin's discussion of his tetrachord system in "Basic Elements of My Musical Language," p. 99.

creative freedom allowed him to speed the completion of two important commissions: the Serenade for string orchestra, Op. 97, finished in May 1964 while Tcherepnin was still in Chicago, and the cantata *Of Things Light and Earnest*, completed in June 1964, in New York. The Serenade, commissioned by the Zurich Chamber Orchestra and its conductor, Edmond de Stoutz, consists of five movements which flow into one another without a break. These individual movements are not, however, bound together through thematic relationships, but cohere instead by reflecting a single formal archetype: their meditative and unstructured beginnings find resolution in passages of ever clearer definition and steadily increasing intensity. The first movement, a *Mesto*, has a prefatory character and culminates, after various solo interjections, with the appearance of the entire string choir. Upon this pedestal, a second movement *Allegretto* is built, in which various elements are played off against one another on multiple levels (Principal of Contrasts). The third movement is a rapid and transparent *Vivace* interlude; its conflicts are resolved in the fourth movement (*Lento*), which begins pensively but concludes with a massive dramatic outburst. In the Finale, an *Allegro moderato* rich in rhythmic as well as dynamic contrasts, overall consolidation is attained at a climax of structural culmination (the "novella's" resolution).[8]

Example R36

Serenade, Op. 97
© 1966 by Edition Eulenberg, Zürich
With the kind permission of the publisher

a) **Allegretto** (mm. 6-10)

b) measures 16-18

a) Cello-bass figures based on three pitches are juxtaposed with violin II-viola figures based on four pitches. The E major *pizzicato* of the lower strings is contrasted to the B-flat major of the bowed violin melody.

b) Robust rhythmic figures provide further contrast to the skittishness of a).

---

8   See also the analytical essay on the Serenade, *Seventeen Masterpieces*, p. 282.

c) **Lento** (measures 21-25)

A quiet interplay for two violins from which a *tutti* climax gradually builds.

The Zurich Chamber Orchestra, under Edmond de Stoutz, gave the highly acclaimed first performance of the Serenade at the XXVIII International Music Festival of the Venice Biennale, on September 11, 1965 in the presence of the composer.

The Cantata *Of Things Light and Earnest*, Op. 98, for female voice and string orchestra, commissioned by the Festival Strings of Lucerne and their conductor Rudolf Baumgartner, was inspired by the collection of farces called *Fun and Earnestness*[9] written in 1519 by the Franciscan monk, Johannes Pauli. It was above all the contrast between gaiety and earnestness that inspired Tcherepnin in sketching out the composition. With his assured grasp of folklore, it was not difficult for him to group the folk songs he chose according to the principle of "contrasting moods" shown in the very titles of the five songs:

> Of Things Earnest: The Mystery of Dreams
> Of Things Light: The Cossack Seeks a Bride
> Of Things Earnest: The Lover's Parting
> Of Things Light: The Maiden Meets a Shepherd in the Spring
> Of Things Earnest: The Meaning of Life.

Tcherepnin wanted to create a "Eurasian cantata": that is, to treat Asiatic folksongs in a European manner. The work's first performance took place in the composer's presence on September 5, 1964, at a *Musica Nova* concert of the Lucerne Festival. Rudolf Baumgartner conducted the Lucerne Festival Strings with the Swiss contralto Nata Tlischer.

After the first performance, Tcherepnin decided to expand the work, a task completed in June 1965: he connected the individual songs with orchestral intermezzi, also adding a purely instrumental piece based on another folk melody and scored for

Example R37

Of Things Light and Earnest, Op. 98
© 1966 by Gerig Edition, Cologne
With the kind permission of the publisher

a) Folksong in Three Keys (measures 278-281)

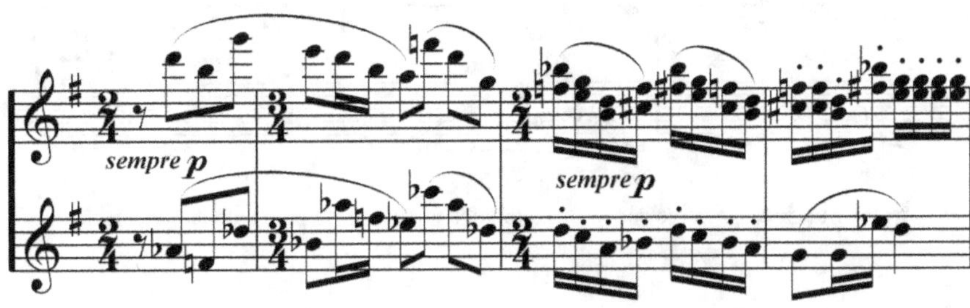

---

9   *Spaß* ("fun") in this title is a bowdlerization. The more Rabelaisian original, *Schimpf und Ernst*, might be translated "Jeers and Meditations."

b) IV. Of Things Light: The Maiden meets a Shepherd in the Spring (measures 313-317)

two violins and viola, which he called *Folksong à 3.*[10] This new version of the Folksong Cantata, now to be performed without pauses, reveals Tcherepnin's continuing interest "novella-like" musical forms.

Amid his extended European and American concert tours between September 1964 and May 1965, Tcherepnin still found time to make a new orchestration of the ballet *The Wandering Scholar Who Exorcised the Devil*, Op. 54, the original full score having disappeared during the war. The premiere of this new version took place in January 1965, in Kiel, Germany.

He also began to write another large work in January 1965, the Piano Concerto No. 6, Op. 99. The tiny village of Bach in the Swiss canton of Schwyz, twenty miles from Zurich, took on a many-sided significance in the composition of the Concerto. For one thing, the Concerto was completed there in August 1965, in a villa lent to him by his close friends Karl and Margrit Weber. (Tcherepnin's admiration for Margrit Weber's piano playing had led him to write the concerto for her, and also influenced the nature of the demanding piano part.)

It was a foregone conclusion that name of the village (B-AE-C-H) would find its way into the Concerto (in the finale as a *soggetto cavato*, spelled musically Bb-A-E-C-B), given the many well-known manipulations of the B-A-C-H motif. The principle of thesis- antithesis, of which Tcherepnin had recently made frequent use, also applies to the relationship between Piano Concertos Nos. 5 and 6. The Fifth is a veritable poem, inspired by deep personal experiences, and written according to new general principles of composition. The Sixth, on the other hand, may be viewed as an apotheosis of piano sound, in which the virtuosic piano part is only loosely dependent on orchestral support.[11]

Example R38

Piano Concerto No. 6, Op. 99
© 1970 by M. P. Belaieff, Frankfurt
With the kind permission of the publisher

a) **Allegro** (measures 98-100)

The wide virtuoso leaps in the concerto's animated portions also permeate its lyrical sections.

---

10   Actually, "Folksong in 3 keys."

11   See also the analytical essay on Concerto No. 6, *Seventeen Masterpieces*, p. 291.

b) measures 185-186

In the opening movement Tcherepnin employs these episodes of quasi-Romantic virtuoso rhetoric as a foil to the prevailing *moto perpetuo* repeated-note style.

c) **Finale: Animato** (measures 391-393)

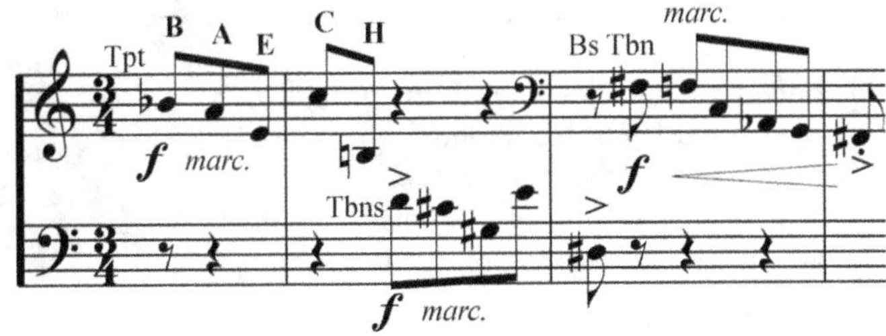

After the September 1965 premiere of the Serenade, Tcherepnin returned to Bach, where, in October, he completed a new version of the Concertino, Op. 47, originally composed in 1930. The Concertino was left basically unaltered, except for a richer elaboration of the three solo parts (violin, cello, and piano), and the addition of woodwinds, brass, and timpani to the original string orchestra. Tcherepnin was the piano soloist at the first performance of the new version, now named Triple Concertino, a year and a half later, in 1967, with the Orchestre de Chambre de Paris under Fernand Quatrocchi.

Example R39

Suite for Harpsichord, Op. 100

Third movement (*Explorations*) measures 9-15

At the beginning of December 1965, Tcherepnin conducted his First Symphony in Berlin with the RIAS Orchestra, and played his Concertino (old version) at the Braunschweig Festival. Spending a serene Christmas with a former pupil, Sister Vivian, at a Phoenix, Arizona convent, he returned to New York in early 1966, and immediately began a short harpsichord piece commissioned several months before[12] by the noted Swiss cembalist Antoinette Vischer. Upon completing this score, entitled *Interlude*, he felt that he had by no means exhausted this instrument's capabilities, and still had more that he wanted to say.[13] So it was that his Op. 100 evolved, a suite for harpsichord consisting of five movements: *Introduction, Sequences, Explorations, Interlude* and *Conclusion*, whose musical functions are explained by their titles. The first and fourth pieces were later recorded by Mme. Vischer, to whom the Suite was dedicated.

After another extended concert tour, which took him through the American Midwest during February-March 1966, Tcherepnin began work in New York on a piece for viola da gamba and organ, the *Sonata da Chiesa*, Op. 101. For years he had wanted to write such a piece, inspired by his friend Paul Grlimmer, who in his later years had planned to stage a viola da gamba festival in Switzerland. Grlimmer did

Tcherepnin with his longtime friend and recital partner Paul Grlimmer

Example R40

---

12   Tcherepnin mentioned this commission in a radio interview the previous April; he probably received it in January 1965.

13   To a former student of whom he was fond, the composer Phillip Ramey, Tcherepnin whimsically wrote: "The Harpsichord piece [was] finally delivered by Cesarian. Yet my womb contained more than one. Might become triplets or even quadruplets."

not live to see the realization of his plan.[14] He died in Zug, in October 1965, lovingly tended till the end by his daughter Sylvia (herself an outstanding gamba player). The festival was held in May 1966, in his memory. The three-movement *Sonata da Chiesa* served as a memorial as well. The first movement expresses the grief of final parting; the second movement (for gamba alone) is filled with the distress felt at his passing; the third movement, however, asserts Tcherepnin's faith in the transfiguration of the immortal soul. The work is dedicated to Sylvia Grlimmer, who premiered it at the Gamba Festival in Zug. Tcherepnin attended the festival, where he honored his friend in the only manner suitable for him—through creative art.

In America, Tcherepnin had a project of a different sort waiting for him—another commission from the American Accordion Association, this time for a concert etude for solo accordion. He produced a piece called *Tzigane*, based on Gypsy melodies that he had heard in Rumania many years before.[15] Completing yet another concert tour of the Midwest, Tcherepnin and his wife came to Duluth, Minnesota, where he stayed for a month as "composer in residence" at the College of St. Scholastica (the appointment had been arranged by a local convent). A charming little house on the perimeter of the cloister was placed at the couple's disposal and Tcherepnin spent his time teaching, lecturing and performing. He already knew several of the Sisters who taught at the College, [16] and repeatedly engaged them in discussions about the then-recent Papal decree on singing the Mass in the vernacular. After frequent attendance at divine services and other experiences in this spiritual milieu, Tcherepnin felt moved to write a Roman Catholic Mass for three female voices (one alto and two soprano), his Op. 102.

Learning the accordion

Deeply religious in inspiration, the work is fully intended for liturgical use. To his great regret, Tcherepnin was obliged to leave Duluth before the first performance of the Mass, sung by the nuns of the Cloister of St. Scholastica during a celebration of a Catholic Mass.

Example R41

Mass for three equal voices, Op. 102
© 1968 by C. F. Peters, New York
With the kind permission of the publisher

from *Gloria*

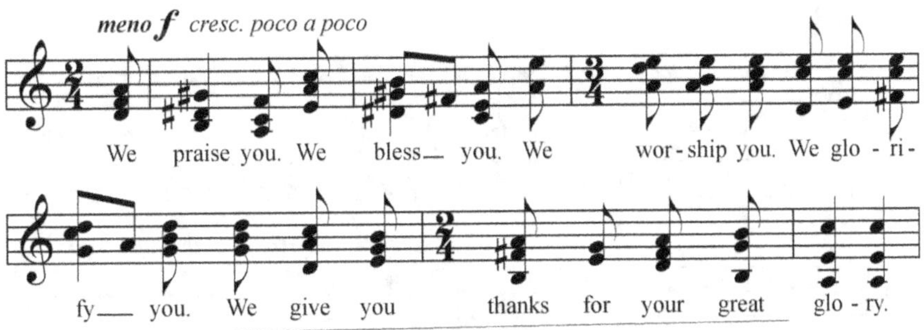

After more concerts in the Midwest, the Tcherepnins were able to pass a restful August in Bach, where the composer's thoughts turned to a new work, his Symphony No. 5, commissioned by the Koussevitzky Foundation. He was delighted

---

14   Information supplied by Ramey and Ming Tcherepnin indicates that the composer planned a two-gamba concerto in late 1964. The eventual result was presumably the less ambitious *Sonata da Chiesa*.

15   Tcherepnin had used much of this material in the *Tzigane* of his unpublished 1941 ballet *The Legend of Razin*. The slow introduction, however, was newly written for the accordion version.

16   Some of them had been his students at DePaul.

once again to face the challenge of composing in a large orchestral form and thereby, as he used to say, to "enjoy life to the full"; but shortness of his Bach stay and the press of other engagements were to hamper the realization of his plans.[17]

Tcherepnin spent the greater part of September in Munich, where he was a member of the jury in the International Competition for Pianists, and then conducted a broadcast performance of his 1953 orchestral Suite, Op. 87, given by the Bavarian Radio Symphony Orchestra. The following month found him in Paris, where he accompanied Boris Christoff in a recording for His Master's Voice of the complete songs of Borodin. He also played his Piano Concerto No. 5 at a gala concert of the *Semaines Musicales Internationales de Paris*, with the Paris Philharmonic Orchestra conducted by Charles Bruck. Concerts and lecture tours in London, Vienna and Germany followed, and it was only after his return to Paris at the end of December that he could at last work on the symphony again. But in February 1967, he had to break off composing. After the aforementioned Paris premiere of the Triple Concertino came an extended German tour followed by more recording in Paris (a group of his own piano pieces from various stylistic periods and an HMV record of Balakirev Songs with Boris Christoff).

In May 1967, at last, came an experience for which Tcherepnin had long yearned: a return to the homeland he had not seen since his departure 49 years before. Indeed, a formal invitation to visit Russia had been extended to the composer and his wife by the Union of Composers of the USSR. The joy which Tcherepnin felt at being reunited with his homeland, and the enthusiastic welcome he received from the Russian musical world, are evident in the account of the journey that the composer wrote for the quarterly of the International Music Council of UNESCO (No. 4/1967), issued in German, English and French by the International Institute for Comparative Music Studies and Documentation in *The World of Music* (Verlag Barenreiter, Kassel).[18] Tcherepnin gave concerts and lectures in Moscow, Tbilisi and Leningrad, always attracting large and enthusiastic audiences. Especially moving for Tcherepnin was his appearance at the Leningrad Conservatory, where he had enrolled as a student half a century before.

During October and November 1967, as an echo of his Russian journey, Tcherepnin wrote several choral compositions on Russian texts, which were later published with English translations: the Six Liturgical Chants, Op. 103, based on the Russian liturgy, and the Four Russian Folksongs, Op. 104, both for mixed chorus *a capella*, published by C. F. Peters.

Example R42

Six Liturgical Chants, Op. 103
for mixed chorus a cappella

© 1969 by C. F. Peters, New York
With the kind permission of the publisher

No. 4: Prayer to the Holy Spirit (incipit)

---

17   The Koussevitzky commission, which dated back about a decade, had originally specified an opera. Try as he might, however, Tcherepnin could never find a satisfactory subject for a libretto, and at last renegotiated the commission as a symphony.

18   This article, "A Trip to the Soviet Union," appears on p. 347.

In January 1968, Tcherepnin went on a concert tour of England, during which, at a Promenade Concert by the BBC Northern Orchestra in Manchester, he conducted a program that included his own Divertimento, Op. 90, along with works by Haydn, Tchaikovsky, Borodin and Rimsky-Korsakov.

After recording sessions as piano soloist in his Second and Fifth Concertos with Rafael Kubelik in Munich, he returned to New York in April, where a new commission from the American Accordion Association awaited him. He found time, however, to complete only one of the requested pieces: an Invention for solo accordion; the second, a Capriccio for accordion and orchestra, remained unfinished.

Tcherepnin then undertook a short tour in Scandinavia, planning to journey directly on to Paris. The student uprising there, however, prevented him from doing so; instead he flew from Copenhagen to Switzerland, and subsequently took part in the Second Gamba Festival in Zug. There his new version of the *Sonata da Chiesa*, with the accompaniment arranged for flute, strings and harpsichord, was well received at its first performance; Sylvia Grlimmer again played the solo gamba part.

A commission from the BBC took Tcherepnin back to England for the summer of 1968. He was to compose the music for a radio play, *The Story of Ivan the Fool*, based on a fairy tale by Tolstoy. This work was of particular artistic importance to him as he could now fulfill a long-standing wish: to bring electronic sounds into his creative vocabulary.

Tcherepnin's idea, suggested by the special nature of the story, was to illustrate the realistic part of the play with traditional means (orchestra, chorus, vocal soloists and narrator) and the fantastic part with electronic music. The BBC placed its electronic studio at Maida Vale at his disposal. And at his request his son Serge, a specialist in electronics, was enlisted as a collaborator. With his son's indispensable assistance, Tcherepnin succeeded in producing a five- minute tape that fully realized the sounds he had conceived in his inner ear. This success encouraged him to speculate about the use of electronic sounds more extensively in later works.

But before he could think seriously about creative plans, he again had to take up the burden of touring engagements in Europe and America. He sadly referred to these commitments, which dominated the 1968-69 season, as "the never-ending." But above the "never-ending" stood "the eternal"—that musical art to whose service Alexander Tcherepnin had devoted his creative energies with so selfless a dedication for so many decades.

(1969)

❋　❋　❋　❋　❋　❋

Berlin Festival 1961.Alexander and Ming
Tcherepnin with Igor Stravinsky and Aribert
Reimann

Piano Sonata No. 2, Op. 94, composed in a mere ten days during September 1961: manuscript of the first page.

7A. Full Circle—The Last Years　　(1968-1977)

by Benjamin Folkman

{*Note:* The editor has elected to insert this supplementary chapter here—before Reich's final chapter—because it continues the chronicle of Tcherepnin's life and works where Reich left off, in mid-1968. Much of the following material is based on the researches of Lily Chou and Guy Wuellner. The Reich biography, as published in 1970, resumes on p. 119 with concluding remarks about Tcherepnin's achievement.}

Tcherepnin began composing the music to *The Story of Ivan the Fool* at the BBC Studios in late June 1968. The orchestral portion was written very quickly. The electronic material, on the other hand, proved more time consuming than Tcherepnin had expected, but in early August he was at last able to report, in a letter to Phillip Ramey, that the thirty-minute score was complete. "No cheating this time: all new!" he wrote, evidently proud that this piece, unlike some of his other recent efforts, contained no recycled material. The composer was scheduled to conduct the BBC recording sessions for *Ivan the Fool* in September; in the interim he appeared with the cellist Christopher Bunting in a performance of his *Twelve Preludes*, Op. 38, at the Summer School of Music at Dartington Hall, also giving a number of lectures, and then left for the continent to fulfill a concert engagement in Lucerne and to attend several festivals.

Had it ever occurred to Tcherepnin to list the musical events of 1968 that influenced him most deeply, he would undoubtedly have placed two experiences at the top of his list. One of these has already been discussed: the completion of *Ivan the Fool*, which marked his first creative use of electronic sound, a medium he believed to have inordinate potential. The other, also involving unusual musical timbres, was a concert at the Montreux Festival that summer by the Strasbourg Percussion Ensemble. Tcherepnin's enthusiasm for pure rhythm as a means of expression was kindled anew, and when this group asked him for a composition, he eagerly agreed. As he thought over percussion possibilities during the next few weeks, ideas came so easily and so abundantly that he realized the piece could be a sizable one.

Tcherepnin with his son Serge, working on the electronic portions of *Ivan the Fool*
BBC Studios, 1968

Tcherepnin returned to America just in time to begin his fall season in Pittsburgh, where he played his Piano Quintet, Op. 44, with the Carnegie-Mellon Fine Arts Quartet on October 8. Back in New York, he set to work composing. By now, an ambitious plan had crystallized in his mind. He would put aside the sketches for a symphony he had made in 1966 and 1967. His Symphony No. 5 would, instead, be something far more unusual than he had originally envisioned: a work of full classical dimensions for percussion alone. Though written for the Strasbourg ensemble, this piece would be substantial enough to meet the requirements of the Koussevitzky Foundation commission as well. Sustaining such a structure would present compositional problems far more delicate and complex than those posed long ago by the brief unpitched-percussion movement of the First Symphony, itself already an impressive tour-de-force.

To be sure, Tcherepnin did not plan to limit himself to unpitched percussion in this score. His sketches, as his son Ivan reported to the author, indicate an extensive use of xylophone, marimba, vibraphone and pitched tom-toms along with the more traditional percussion paraphernalia. In deploying these in a manner that would support an argument of symphonic weight, however, Tcherepnin found himself required to break new technical and aesthetic ground. Nevertheless, he made steady progress on the score during the autumn.

These electronic and percussion projects indicate that the composer, although now approaching his seventieth birthday, still saw himself—and still hoped to be regarded—as a musical futurist. To the general public, of course, he remained a modernist; but the modernist elite tended to view him as a maverick. Never the leader of an avant-garde movement, he was not even a follower of the 1960s acknowledged leaders. His exploitation of avant-garde devices had always been singular and selective, and marked by a stylistic equanimity that his colleagues may well have found disconcerting. For, rather than being extensively reoriented by new techniques, he succeeded in integrating them into a personal style that preserved classical conceptions of melody and accompaniment which the Impressionists and their successors had sought to obliterate.

For example, his nine-step scale, a product of the serial impulse, had paralleled Schoenberg's twelve-tone system while, at the same time, looking back to proto-serial Russian devices such as the "mystic chord" of Scriabin and the octatonic scale explored by Rimsky-Korsakov, the pre-World War I Stravinsky, Maximilian Steinberg and, of course,

Nicolai Tcherepnin. Where Schoenberg had abolished the tonic triad, Tcherepnin had expanded it into the major-minor triad. Tcherepnin's Interpoint, akin to the "lean, athletic style" of Hindemith and other 1920s composers, also provided his own private pathway for the then-popular journey "back to Bach." Later, Tcherepnin embraced folklore just as a wave of populism and nationalism was about to sweep a musical and political world ravaged by the great Depression—but did so in a large-minded fashion that ignored borders, at the same time that aggressive nationalism was creeping into the work of other important creative artists. Even Tcherepnin's melodic and harmonic manipulation of tetrachords in the 1950s had an equivalent among his colleagues, for it resembled the permutations that Webernites applied to their serial subsets.

Now, in the late 1960s, Tcherepnin's electronic interests prefigured the vast increase in electronic exploration soon to be undertaken by composers of all generations, just as his percussion symphony foreshadowed the "color-effects" movement that would shortly sweep through the universities and concert halls. Characteristically, in both of these avant-garde areas his aims were quite atypical. Where others created increasingly "instrumental" or "imaginary instrumental" effects from synthesizers, Tcherepnin prized the unexplored vocabulary of anti-orchestral sounds; and while the colorists, with their string glissandos, vibraphone flourishes and consciously "exquisite" timbre mixes, wrote post-impressionistic scores featuring floating, viscous rhythms incompatible with dance and folk-song patterns, Tcherepnin's exotic percussion unabashedly radiated primitivistic energy. Indeed, the appearance at this time of the projected Tcherepnin percussion symphony—unfortunately never completed—could well have had a salutary effect on those composers that Aaron Copland reportedly dubbed, rather sourly, "the sound-effects boys."

Late in the fall of 1968, Tcherepnin appeared before French television cameras in New York with Charles Munch, who was touring with the newly formed *Orchestre de Paris*. Munch planned to record Tcherepnin's Fourth Symphony upon his return to Europe, but this project never came to fruition, owing to his untimely death during the tour.

The editor of the Philharmonic Hall program booklet now decided to run an article on Tcherepnin early the following year in honor of the composer's seventieth birthday, and, accordingly, Tcherepnin was interviewed in November by Phillip Ramey. Tcherepnin was articulate in his answers to a wide range of questions, but was not about to let anyone get wind of his singular plans for the fifth symphony. To Ramey's inquiries, he merely responded that work on the piece was "going well," adding, with demure understatement, that the score would "contain a few surprises." The article also discussed Tcherepnin's recording of his Second and Fifth Piano Concertos with Rafael Kubelik and the Bavarian Radio Symphony, completed in 1968, and the upcoming American premiere of the Fifth Piano Concerto, which Tcherepnin was to play in Kansas City in December.

During the premiere, Tcherepnin was frightened by persistent chest pains, and an examination confirmed his suspicion that he had suffered another heart attack. He was scheduled to begin a European tour shortly, and refused at first, despite the urging of his doctor, to cancel it. Ming was unable to change his mind through gentle suasion, and as she could never bear to give her husband a really severe scolding, she turned in desperation to his friends: thus it fell to Ramey to maintain a diplomatic tone while reading Tcherepnin the riot act. Tcherepnin, though touched, initially shrugged off Ramey's admonitions, but the next day, much to Ming's relief, he called off the tour.

The world-wide celebrations for Tcherepnin's 70th birthday in 1969 began a few days early with the BBC broadcast of *Ivan the Fool* on Christmas Eve 1968. As noted in the previous chapter, Tcherepnin had enlisted the help of his son Serge for the electronic passages, and the presentation became even more of a "family affair" when Peter Ustinov, Tcherepnin's cousin, was selected to do the narration.

Tcherepnin made a good recovery during January 1969. On the 24th and 26th of the month, the Pittsburgh Symphony commemorated the composer's 70th year with two performances of his Divertimento, Op. 90, conducted by James Levine. Ramey's article "Tcherepnin at Seventy" duly appeared in the Philharmonic Hall pro-grams throughout February. By the middle of that month Tcherepnin, well enough to resume his activities, was back in France, appearing in a concert of his cello works on February

Tcherepnin with his composer son Ivan and his actor cousin Peter Ustinov

26. Ming, apprehensive about a repetition of the Kansas City attack, took care to have Tcherepnin's doctor in the audience, but the composer sailed through the concert without stress or fatigue. Plans were now finalized for a disc of six Tcherepnin

chamber works with the composer at the piano and several leading French string players, including the cellist Paul Tortelier and his violinist son, Yan Pascal Tortelier; Tcherepnin was advised that recording sessions for the Piano Quintet and the Piano Trio would begin on May 22.

Returning to America, Tcherepnin went to the Midwest for a series of solo recitals, and an all-Tcherepnin orchestral program in Elkhart, Indiana, where he conducted his Suite for Orchestra and *Georgiana*, and took the solo part in his Piano Concerto No. 2.

In the spring, Tcherepnin recorded a concert for the BBC (eventually broadcast in September). During that visit to England, he told an interviewer that he had completed three and a half movements of his Fifth Symphony the previous fall, but hadn't resumed work on the piece since his heart attack. During the summer in the Pyrenees, however, he felt equal to a less demanding task-a short piano piece commissioned for a French teaching anthology. "Somehow," he wrote, "it was impossible for me to compose just one piece for children, so I wrote a dozen or so in a medium that would introduce young players to the contemporary idiom. I chose one of them for the album, and called it *Ascension* because it starts in the lowest register of the piano and ends on the highest note." As will be seen, the piano miniature, a genre mastered by Tcherepnin so long before in his boyhood *bloshki*, was to assume increased importance in the composer's later years.

Pianist Ozan Marsh (L.), Tcherepnin and Robert Muczynski, Tucson, 1969

Anniversary tributes later in 1969 included a celebration in November in Tucson, Arizona, organized by another former Tcherepnin pupil, the composer Robert Muczynski, who appeared as pianist in a concert of Tcherepnin's music together with a number of his fellow University of Arizona faculty members, several students and guest artists also participating.

One of the tributes that had failed to materialize during the year was the projected performance of Tcherepnin's First Symphony on the subscription concerts of what was now his home town orchestra, the New York Philharmonic. Tcherepnin had some correspondence with the orchestra's administration about the piece, and Leonard Bernstein tentatively selected it for scheduling. The composer would have been especially gratified by this presentation: he always thought it fitting that the Symphony, written in New York, be given a hearing there. Unfortunately, plans to play the piece were ultimately shelved. The Philharmonic remained, in fact, the only leading American orchestra that never programmed Tcherepnin's work during his lifetime.

In January 1970, at a reception given in Tcherepnin's honor at the French Embassy in New York, the composer was presented with the decoration of *Chevalier de l'ordre des Arts et des Lettres*, awarded by the French government. No sooner was Tcherepnin back in Paris than he had to set out for Dijon, where, in ceremonies that included a performance of his Cello Sonata No. 3, the director of the Conservatory presented him with the Rameau medal.

Having added to his long series of triumphs in France, Tcherepnin now began to receive unwonted adulation from the British. In the years following his initial success as a pianist in 1922 and with *Ajanta's Frescoes* in 1923, England had proved an increasingly tough nut for Tcherepnin to crack—the reviews of *Message* and the Piano Trio at a 1931 concert had been particularly brutal, and during the subsequent three decades, he had been almost completely absent from British concert life.

However, with the success of Tcherepnin's BBC work in 1968 and 1969, interest in the composer's work at last burgeoned, and Tcherepnin's visit in early 1970 was an unqualified triumph. The weeks between February 22 and March 18 saw a veritable Tcherepnin festival in England and Ireland: his name appeared almost daily in all the major newspapers, including the *London Times*, the *Guardian*, the *Daily Telegraph*, the *Irish Press*, the *Irish Independent* and the *Irish Times*. Glowing reviews greeted Tcherepnin's first appearance, a broadcast on Radio 3 in which he conducted the BBC Symphony in Haydn's Symphony No. 88, Tchaikovsky's symphonic poem *Fate*, and his own Symphony No. 1, also performing as soloist in his Piano Concerto No. 2. A Queen Elizabeth Hall concert a week later by the Alberni Quartet, featuring Tcherepnin's Second String Quartet and the Piano Quintet with the composer at the keyboard was received no less enthusiastically.

One somber note was sounded during the visit by Tcherepnin himself, when he informed an interviewer that he had abandoned his Fifth Symphony owing to dissatisfaction with its form. "It is like losing a child," he said. Later, however, he provided another explanation, writing that after illness had "interrupted [his] line of argument," he had not been able to make progress on the score. Other remarks of his indicate that he still thought it possible that one day he would finish it.

On March 8, after being held up at the London airport all day as flight after flight was canceled as a result of strikes and bad weather, the Tcherepnins finally reached Dublin at 6 A. M. The 71-year-old veteran took a short nap at his hotel and then went off to Francis Xavier Hall to conduct the Radio Telefis Eireann Orchestra in a morning rehearsal for an all-Russian program (Tchaikovsky, Borodin and his own Piano Concerto No. 5 with Charles Lynch as soloist). The actual concert was held at the Gaiety Theatre, Dublin, and repeated in the Cork City Hall the following evening to unanimously favorable reviews.

During the summer of 1970—which Tcherepnin spent partly in Elmen, Austria, and partly in Bach, Switzerland—he began writing the Brass Quintet, Op. 105. That work had been suggested to him by Walter Hinrichsen, president of C. F. Peters and was produced as a memorial to this personal friend, who had died of a heart attack the year before. Composition of the Quintet was interrupted by trips to Paris and London, and by a concert tour of East Germany—German territory in which Tcherepnin had not appeared since before World War II. In Leipzig, he recorded several of his pieces for a radio broadcast and appeared as soloist in a Collegium Musicum concert at the Rathaus, the program including his Serenade for Strings, Concertino for violin, cello, piano and strings, and *Bagatelles* (piano and string orchestra version). Subsequently, he gave piano recitals of his own compositions in Gera and Bad Kostritz.

Of the Brass Quintet, which was completed in Paris, Tcherepnin wrote: "In the first movement, I aimed at using five-part writing with no doubling, while the second movement is slow and lyric. The third movement is purely rhythmical. I completed these three movements in Elmen in the Austrian Tyrol, and originally felt this would be all. But while in Bach, I added to this a fourth movement in which each of the instruments gets a solo, and then in Paris I added the finale, thus bringing the number of movements to five."

Example R43

Early in 1970, Tcherepnin attended the French National Radio recording of his opera *Ol-Ol*, with Pierre Michel Leconte conducting the Lyric Orchestra. Nadia Boulanger listened to the broadcast with great pleasure. Although now almost blind, she went to the trouble of personally penning the following note of appreciation, in an almost illegible scrawl: "Dear Sasha, Your opera (Ol-Ol) Wednesday evening on the Radio. Thanks! It seemed to me the performance was good, the ensemble striking. Suddenly you were present! A real joy! With all my heart. Nadia."

Tcherepnin was one of the few composers who could boast of having composed a body of cello music large enough to fill an entire concert, and on February 24, 1971, he partnered the cellist Paul Olefsky in an Alice Tully Hall retrospective

With Nadia Boulanger,
Fontainebleau, 1970

program of his works for the instrument. Interspersed with the three cello and piano sonatas were the Suite for Solo Cello and the *Twelve Preludes* for Cello and Piano. When one reviewer commented that the composer was still an elegant pianist at age 72, Tcherepnin was somewhat upset, seeing no reason why any deterioration should be expected in him.

Early that spring, however, the ravages of age made themselves felt in full force. Tcherepnin suffered another heart attack, this one quite severe, and was confined to the hospital for a lengthy stay. This illness interrupted his work on a score commissioned the previous summer by the Kansas City Youth Orchestra; nevertheless, the piece was ready in time for its premiere on May 16, 1971, in Kansas City. It was scarcely one of Tcherepnin's most strenuous creative undertakings, for the composer here utilized a good deal of folkloric material, thinking this ideal fodder for young players; the work was entitled *Russian Sketches* and published as Op. 106.

As Tcherepnin recuperated in Bach that summer, he was strong enough to compose another brief work, the *Baptism Cantata* for children's choir, solo voice, recorders, flutes, organ and strings, based on a poem by Irene Vogel-Sulzer. This piece is ecumenical in design—suitable for any religion that practices baptism.

By the fall, Tcherepnin was able to resume a full concert schedule. On September 21, he appeared as soloist in his Piano Concerto No. 2 under Herbert Kegel in Leipzig; on November 15, he participated in a chamber music concert in Munich with the Seitz Quartet, playing Borodin's Piano Quintet and his own Piano Quintet (the program also included Tcherepnin's String Quartet No. 2). And to round off the year, he performed his Piano Concerto No. 5 with the Vienna Symphony Orchestra under Horst Stein in a broadcast public concert on December 19. Back in Switzerland at the beginning of 1972, Tcherepnin attended the first performance of his *Baptism Cantata* at a christening service in a church in Zumikon. Deciding that communal singing was essential in a work commemorating a child's entrance into the Christian community, Tcherepnin had written a simple melody to be sung by the congregation in antiphony with the soloist and children's choir. At the premiere, the composer had copies of this melody together with the words distributed to the congregation, who participated with evident relish.

Tcherepnin seemed to have rebounded strongly from his most recent heart attack. His endurance was again equal to the "never-ending" grind of concertizing. But something still impeded his creative work. Tcherepnin confided to Phillip Ramey that he was now unable to muster the concentration needed to sustain large-scale musical arguments. His thematic ideas were as promising as ever; his facility in Interpuntal elaboration was unimpaired; yet every piece he undertook either remained fragmentary or was rounded off as a miniature.

The missing element, strange to say, was the perpetual cigarette that for decades had dangled from Tcherepnin's lips as he composed. Now, in the wake of his heart attack, he had given up smoking on the orders of his doctors; and he was unable to rid himself of the notion that, for him, the steady consumption of tobacco had become an integral part of the composing process[1]. To be sure, other factors may have been in play. The act of composition, with the intense concentration it entails, requires far more physical strength and stamina than generally realized, and a severe illness can leave a composer too depleted to do his best work. Haydn had to give up composing at the height of his powers because his physical constitution could no longer stand the strain; Charles Ives, after his serious heart attack found that, when beginning a new piece he was unable to keep it "up and sailing"; Prokofiev's last works reveal the tragically diminished musical endurance of a semi-invalid. Whether through illness, or, as Tcherepnin was inclined to think, through a truly physiological or merely psychological dependence on smoking, the result was the same: Tcherepnin's composing life had become a struggle against a block. The Fifth Symphony had long lain untouched, even though he had already completed the first three movements in sketch form and had begun the fourth; and now the prospects of his ever finishing the score seemed bleak. To Ramey, Tcherepnin frequently expressed the conviction that if only he could take up cigarettes again, his creative fluency would return.

When the Brass Quintet was printed, Tcherepnin presented Ramey with a copy, and began the written salutation preceding his signature with the words "swan song." He then clumsily drew something on the page which Ramey could not recognize, eventually explaining, "It's a swan." Tcherepnin, of course, was being unduly pessimistic; in fact, he never abandoned the idea of completing another Symphony, and continued to write music all through his last years. Still, the composer who had begun so long before with *bloshki* must have found it disheartening that, after a lifetime of development, he was again a specialist in little piano pieces.

---

1   In fact, Tcherepnin had had a similar experience after his previous heart attack. See Tcherepnin on Munch and Reiner, pp. 149-151.

Perhaps Tcherepnin found some consolation in the warm reception his works continued to receive throughout the world. On September 5, 1972, his Piano Concerto No. 6 was at last premiered—some seven years after its completion—at the Lucerne International Festival with Margrit Weber as soloist and the Amsterdam Concertgebouw Orchestra directed by Rafael Kubelik. The performance was televised by the Swiss Television Network and rebroadcast several times. Both the Concerto and Margrit Weber's playing were unanimously praised in the press.

At a reception afterwards, a huge portrait of Tcherepnin by the Swiss painter Hans Erni was unveiled. This work had been commissioned by Karl Weber as a souvenir of the many happy hours the composer had spent, composing and relaxing, at their villa in Bach, and was intended to be hung there. However, the framed painting was of such enormous dimensions that it could not be brought into the house. It later reached the walls of the Lucerne Conservatory of Music.

Meanwhile, during the spring and summer, Sir Yehudi Menuhin had been making efforts to arrange a BBC tribute to Tcherepnin commemorating the composer's first London appearance fifty years earlier. This anniversary presentation was aired on December 28 at 9:55 P.M. Third Programme listeners heard Tcherepnin reminiscing about his London debut in 1922 and performing his *Préludes Nostalgiques*, written during that original visit, along with several pieces from the debut program, including the *Bagatelles* and the Sonata for Violin and Piano. The violinist in this performance (later issued on a BBC Archive recording) was Menuhin, who played with compelling warmth and affection—and for a minute fraction of his usual fee.

The anxiety that Tcherepnin presumably felt in these years about his creative work in no way diminished his zest for the joys of everyday living. His manner was as kindly and urbane as ever, and he continued to take special pleasure in

Rehearsing his Violin Sonata with Yehudi Menuhin

stimulating company, frequently hosting splendid parties and lively gatherings of internationally celebrated musicians in his apartments on Manhattan's West Side and the left bank in Paris. (Typically, the Tcherepnins felt no attraction to "fashionable" neighborhoods such as Manhattan's East Side or Paris's sixteenth arrondissement, preferring areas where artists could be found in abundance.)

One such evening was a memorable dinner party for composers, with, so to speak, the crowning glory of American music in attendance: the guests included Aaron Copland, Virgil Thomson, Mr. and Mrs. Elliott Carter and Leonard Bernstein, along with two suitably impressed members of the younger generation, Phillip Ramey and Benjamin Folkman. Ming served one of her specialties, a chicken orientale, accompanied by copious supplies of Beaujolais, and the sparkling conversation ranged through such subjects as Charles Rosen's book *The Classical Style* (much admired by all present) and aleatory devices in "high entropy" music. On another occasion, the flutist Jean-Pierre Rampal, whom the Tcherepnins had known for many years, came with Julius Baker, principal flutist of the New York Philharmonic and Carleton Sprague Smith. As a surprise for Tcherepnin, they pulled out their instruments and played his Flute Trio, Op. 59, to the delight of their hosts and the numerous guests.

Tcherepnin's success continued undiminished in 1973. On March 14, the composer attended a BBC Orchestra performance of his First Symphony under Colin Davis and received the warmest possible ovation. Tcherepnin never ceased to wonder at the difference between the symphony's present reception and the hostile reactions of 1927. "I didn't change a note!" he would say, in a puzzled tone. The composer subsequently journeyed to the continent where, with the collaboration of Kurt Redel, he made a string orchestra version of his String Quartet No. 1. Under the new title *Musica Sacra*, this transcription was premiered on April 28 at the Lourdes Easter Festival in France, with the Munich Pro Arte String Orchestra conducted by Redel, who also directed the score later that year in Lausanne and Brussels.

Tcherepnin had long enjoyed the challenge of composing for what he termed "underprivileged instruments," as his earlier works for timpani, tuba, saxophone, harmonica and accordion indicate[2]. Arriving at Bach after again giving early summer lectures at the Dartington School, the composer explored the peculiarities of a truly arcane instrument, the Celtic harp, in a short, four-movement suite entitled *Caprices Diatoniques*. As modulations are impossible on the Celtic harp without stopping to retune, Tcherepnin did not use the standard major and minor keys, but, instead, set each of the movements in a different one of the old Renaissance modes.

---

2   See Tcherepnin's essay "Let Underprivileged Instruments Play," p. 334.

In Paris that December, Tcherepnin recorded a group of his songs for the HMV label, accompanying the internationally famous operatic tenor Nicolai Gedda.

Tcherepnin began his 75th birthday on January 21, 1974, with a morning visit to the *New York Times* radio station WQXR, where, for two hours, he was Robert Sherman's guest on "The Listening Room," discussing his career and commenting on recorded selections from his works. Over the course of this year, he performed his violin and piano sonata on six different concert programs: with Erick Freedman in Miami and New York, with Yan Pascal Tortelier in London, with Yehudi Menuhin in Gstaad and with Sandor Vegh in Dartington. He also conducted his Sixth Concerto for Margrit Weber in Winterthur, Nuremberg, Koblenz, Cologne and Esch, Luxemburg.

With Nicolai Gedda, Paris, 1977

Among the many organizations that feted Tcherepnin during this anniversary year was the National Arts Club of New York, which presented a concert of his works performed by Aldo Parisot, cellist, the Blue Hill String Quartet and soprano Judith Blegen, the latter accompanied by the composer. Another concert was held at the Bohemian Club in New York, where, the composer accompanied Nicolai Gedda in several of his songs, and the distinguished pianist Grant Johannesen played *Showcase*. Tcherepnin was also named a member of the National Institute of Arts and Letters, having been nominated by Elliott Carter and seconded by both Aaron Copland and Virgil Thomson.

That June in London, Tcherepnin played a concert of his chamber works in Queen Elizabeth Hall with his old friends Tortelier *père* and *fils*, the program including the Sonata for Violin and Piano, *Twelve Preludes* for Cello and Piano, Suite for Solo Cello, Piano Trio, Duo for Violin and Cello and Sonata No. 2 for Cello and Piano. BBC broadcast a recording of this concert on December 30.

During their visits to London in the 1960s and 1970s, the Tcherepnins had at first been guests of Sir William Glock, music director of the BBC, and his wife Lady Anne. But as their affection for England grew, he and Ming preferred to set up a home there, however temporary, each time they visited. One day when they were out walking, Ming intuitively stopped a stranger with a dog and inquired if he knew of any simple cottage they might rent. As luck would have it, the stranger's father-in-law was just then attempting to lease his semi-detached house in Marlow-on-the-Thames. So it was that the Tcherepnins were soon installed in a cottage just beyond White City. There in mid-1975 having planned only a very light concert schedule that year,[3] Tcherepnin grappled with his long-standing commissions for symphonies: one for the Koussevitzky Foundation, the other for George Solti and the Chicago Symphony.

Yet although he found conditions at Marlow "ideal for concentration," sustained musical argument continued to elude him. On May 26, he sketched the opening of "A Merry 'Pickwick' Symphony," but could not find a continuation. A theme in a different vein on June 4 seemed more promising, and this found its way into a score labeled "Symphony No. 5," begun on June 20. But many of the ideas jotted down during July and early August—at least eighteen separate sketches in varying styles—fitted neither project. At this point, he decided to round off all of these efforts into brief piano pieces, penning them into a single continuous manuscript, which he dubbed *Opivochki*. The translations of this word offered by commentators—"little leftovers" or "little remnants" are euphemisms. The most accurate rendering, sadly, is "little dregs," Tcherepnin's implication being that the wine of his creativity had been drunk, leaving in the glass only a few drops of liquid clouded by flakes of sediment.

On August 14 , he wrote out five *opivochki*, commencing with the Fifth Symphony idea; the Pickwick sketch was the first of four pieces brought to completion the following day. He unfailingly headed each entry with a specific metronome marking and noted its exact duration over the closing double bar line. By the end of September the number of finished pieces had risen to twenty-five. Five more were added to the manuscript on October 9, with another pair following on the 16th. Tcherepnin then put the collection aside, but would return to it intermittently.

Over the next ten months, Tcherepnin did more work on the Fifth Symphony, completing the first movement in short score (twenty pages) along with the first two pages of a second movement, the rest of which is only sketched.

Another project claimed Tcherepnin's attention in early 1976 in New York, his Quintet for Woodwinds, Opus 107, written in honor of his friend Robert Wiesedanger, the outgoing president of Zug Conservatory in Switzerland. This and two small piano pieces for a pedagogical album proved to be his last compositions in America. The Quintet was premiered on April 3 in Zug.

---

3   Worried about Tcherepnin's non-stop activity in 1974 and its effect on his heart, Ming noted with some satisfaction, "I have made a deal with my husband. No concertizing in 1975-at least for 6-8 months."

The Woodwind Quintet is a tartly good-humored work cast in three tiny movements and lasting about seven minutes. In the score it is indicated that each or all of the movements may be repeated—a melancholy indication that Tcherepnin was self-conscious about the extreme brevity of the piece.

A puckish four-note motif (E-D-C-C) is heard at the outset in octave-displacement statements that jostle one another, and this is revealed, in the last movement, to be the opening (transposed) of a *soggetto cavato* capriciously derived from Robert Wiesedanger's name (the letters R and O are not generally thought of as musical, but Tcherepnin finds notes in them through the following process: R=*re*=D; O=*do*=C; similarly Wi=E, etc.). The *Allegro marciale* first movement is a veritable toy-soldier march: following the beginning described above, a jaunty tune in thirds is heard, which is later re-harmonized in "hard" intervals.

The second movement (mostly in 6/8 and 9/8 meter) begins glumly, but waxes lyrical, even romantic, until a mocking outburst in faster tempo occurs near the end, dispelling any aura of sentiment. The finale is cast in a compressed sonata form, the mood here restoring the bustle of the first movement. Its second subject is a D-major tune that fits to Russian words meaning "Many many years, many many years," a traditional toast that Tcherepnin penned into the score.

With progress on Symphony No. 5 fitful at best that winter, Tcherepnin in March 1976 entertained the idea of salvaging the abandoned percussion symphony—three-and-a-half movements of which already existed in rough score. After making seven pages of additional sketches for the piece, however, he put it aside. Back in Marlow for the summer, he returned to the Fifth Symphony, but apparently ceased work on it after July 21.

At an impasse with his symphonic projects, the composer in August again turned to *Opivochki*, adding three pieces that may have been specifically designed to conclude the collection. Tellingly, the second of these, No. 36, is marked "comme une marche funebre," and over the doleful No. 37 Tcherepnin placed an even more revealing observation in Russian. It translates: "Sad at heart, am I really incapable of large forms, in old age only fit for little dregs (*opivochki*)?"

Opivochki ultimately grew to thirty-nine pieces. The last, begun on July 21, 1977 and added to the manuscript August 16, was evidently a discarded sketch for the Flute Duo, Op. 108. Beneath the title on the first page of the collection he penned the words "close to the heart." An alternative title to the right reads: "Slivers" with the comment "but sometimes also windfalls!," and beneath this Tcherepnin penned yet another description: "aphorisms."

In a New Year's Day 1976 diary entry, Tcherepnin had indicated he might consider combining the *Opivochki* and some pieces composed in 1969 into "one grand work, perhaps some kind of modern *Gradus ad Parnassum*." He took no such steps, however, and it is unfortunate that collection was titled *Gradus ad Parnassum* in the catalogue of Tcherepnin's works prepared under Ming's supervision (with *Opivochki* given only as a subtitle). Equally misleading is a catalogue description suggesting that the pieces systematically survey "problems modern piano playing" involving "rhythm, polyphony, aleatory devices, free choice in the ordering of sections, polyrhythms, mathematically constructed forms, etc."

In fact, no vestige of aleatory practice or mathematical construction is discernible in *Opivochki*. Far from being a pedagogical method of any sort, the set is a grab-bag of ideas, some promising, some not. It contains tiny modernist gems (Nos. 3 and 17) along with more conservative episodes, some of which are delightful (Nos. 19, 9, 38) some poignant (Nos. 11, 23, 37), some lugubrious in the extreme (Nos. 8, 32, 36). The most consistently successful pieces reflect Tcherepnin's Russian heritage, whether in liturgical solemnity (Nos. 14 and 18) or exuberance (Nos. 16, 28, 29). Others are arid and labored- Interpuntal exercises at best. Only two pieces are as much as two minutes long (in one of these, No. 25, Tcherepnin attempts fascinating mosaic-like juxtapositions of highly diverse materials), some last only twenty or thirty seconds, and in all, these thirty-nine pieces add up to less than thirty-five minutes of music. As yet unpublished, *Opivochki* has been assigned the opus number 109.

Tcherepnin spent the first two months of 1977 in New York. He then went to Chicago, where he lectured before the Illinois State Music Teachers Association, conducted a master class, spoke on his music at the Cliff Dwellers Club and appeared on radio station WFMT as Studs Terkel's guest. Shortly afterward he received an honorary doctorate from the San Francisco Music and Arts Institute.

Arriving at Marlow on June 12, Tcherepnin immediately began work on his Flute Duo, Op. 108, which had been commissioned the year before by the Swiss flutist Dominique Hunziger and his Japanese partner Anne Utagawa, and was heartened to find that some of his creative fluency had returned. He completed the draft on September 2, and after finishing the final copy six days later, he told his wife that he "liked [the piece] very much" and that he had "given much time and thought to it."

Characterized by biographer Enrique Arias as "one of [Tcherepnin's] most important compositions," (one suspects that Ming Tcherepnin urged this encomium on him) the Duo is, in fact, a lovely little work of considerable technical interest. Nine-step materials are particularly prominent in the first three of the five movements: all three conclude with flourishes harmonized in thirds and based on either the "minor-third" form of arpeggiation (in the pattern C-Eb-F-Ab-B-C#-E etc.) or the hexachord form (C-Eb-E-G-Ab-B). By contrast, the last two movements end with flourishes built mostly from fourths. Indeed, through the course of the composition, materials featuring thirds often yield to materials featuring fourths (usually, fourths alternating with half-steps or whole steps, with the intervals often unexpectedly changing directions).

Also present are the two-rising series of alternating minor and major thirds (beginning with the minor third produces the notes of the Dorian mode; beginning with the major third, those of the Lydian mode). Tcherepnin superimposes these as follows:

```
Lydian-----    E- (M)-G#- (m) -B- (M) -D#- (m) -F#- (M)-A#- (m) -C#
Dorian-----    C- (m) -Eb- (M)-G- (m) -Bb- (M)-D - (m) -F - (M)-A- (m) -C
```

Striking an effective balance between homophonic writing (often in thirds) and polyphonic-Interpuntal interplay, Tcherepnin takes full advantage of the equal instrumental timbres (a feature denied him in the brass and woodwind quintets), devising part-crossings that pass-through unisons in *trompe-l'oreille* fashion.

Example R44

Duo for Two Flutes, Op. 108
© 1978 by M. P. Belaieff, Frankfurt
With the kind permission of the publisher

Movement II, measures 17-23

The first movement begins with a rather stately, basically homophonic *Moderato*. After a witty and virtuosic central portion, the original tempo returns, the materials now presented in reverse order and polyphonically treated; and there is a brief concluding *arpeggio* flourish. The second movement opens plaintively with a songful, homophonic *Lento* and proceeds to a *Vivo* in shifting irregular rhythms: in this section, a folk-like motif that starts with three repeated notes is introduced and bandied about Interpuntally between the two flutes.

To commence the third movement, the first flute provides a cadenza in which reminiscences of the folk-motif appear. The second flute soon enters and, so to speak, cajoles the first flute into echoing its material. A *Sostenuto* in most lyrical Interpoint follows, the second flute taking the upper part throughout. The slow opening of the fourth movement precedes a roistering and primitivistic polka-like episode, where the repeated-note folk-motif is given a new continuation and obsessive rhythmic cells are employed, some outlining the Georgian chord in descending figuration (F-Eb-Bb). There is an austere closing in which fourths are prominent. The final movement is a whirlwind gigue beginning in thirds. In the *Maestoso* opening of the coda, the folk motif (inverted) is transformed into a grandiose chorale in trills; then a delicate *Vivo* reaches an unexpectedly emphatic conclusion.

Gardening in Marlow, September 3, 1977, the last photograph of Tcherepnin

Apparently Tcherepnin removed a movement intended for the Duo from the score, preserving it, however, as the final piece in the *Opivochki* collection (No. 39).

As mid-September approached in Marlow, the Tcherepnins received the disturbing news that their Paris apartment had been broken into. Since they had been planning to go to Paris anyway (Tcherepnin was scheduled for a radio program there) they advanced their travel plans and left Marlow early. In France they found papers and manuscripts strewn all over their apartment, but nothing had been taken.

The radio program was taped as planned—two hours of recorded selections interspersed with commentary by Tcherepnin—and the composer turned to a modest project for *Piano Quarterly* magazine. The editor had requested a short, easy piano piece, either newly composed or selected from unpublished material. Tcherepnin copied out one of the *bloshki* from his sixteenth year, gave it the title *Sunny Day—bagatelle oubliée*, placed it in an envelope together with a cover letter and took it to the post office. It was the last manuscript he completed: with this return to his *bloshki*, the composer had come full circle.

There is a small mystery connected with this piece. Phillip Ramey was given the manuscript by Ming, who told him that it had been copied on the day the composer died. So said Ramey to Enrique Arias, and Arias in his book on Tcherepnin accordingly assigned the date September 29 to the manuscript. Ramey now sees reason for doubt, however. For, in fact, Tcherepnin's cover letter is clearly dated the previous day, September 28. Tcherepnin may have written the letter first and prepared the score the next day, but it seems more likely that the letter and the manuscript share the same date—and that Tcherepnin devoted his last day to other music.

On the evening of September 29, Tcherepnin arranged his desk in preparation for the next day's work, and then set out with his wife for their dinner engagement as guests of Jean Fournet, the French conductor, and his wife. At the restaurant, *Le Port St. Germain* on the Boulevard St. Germain near the Rue de Rennes and within easy walking distance from their home, they had an extremely pleasant visit with the Fournets. After a light fish dinner of *dorade*, the Tcherepnins were walking home when, halfway there, the composer quietly exclaimed, "Ming, I'm falling," as he slowly collapsed. He died in the arms of his wife in the doorway of 12 rue de l'Abbeye, across the street from the church of St. Germain-des-Pres, the victim of a final heart attack.

Condolences and tributes arrived from friends and colleagues all over the world. *Sunny Day* reached the offices of *Piano Quarterly* almost simultaneously with the news of the composer's death, and the piece appeared in the magazine's Winter 1977 as a memorial feature. Tcherepnin's radio program was aired posthumously. Upon hearing it, Olivier Messiaen sent the following letter of condolence to the widow:

> Chere Madame,
>
> It was with deep-felt emotion that I just heard the program in the *"Concert égoiste"* series devoted to Alexander Tcherepnin. I was overcome to hear his voice again. and I marvelled at the admirable writing for strings in his Serenade, where trilled chords and pizzicati mingle with moto perpetuos in such a persuasive and effective way.
>
> I embrace you very affectionately, in memory of our very great friend.
>
> With deep emotion!
>
> (Signed) Olivier Messiaen[4]

The premiere of Tcherepnin's band arrangement of *Russian Sketches* had long been scheduled for October 9, 1977, at the International Band Music Festival in Uster, Switzerland, with the Bulgarian Sofia Orchestra directed by Sasha Mihailov. This performance turned out to be one of the first *in memoriam* concerts. The Flute Duo was premiered in Tokyo on April 14, 1978, by the flutists who had commissioned it.

Tcherepnin had given careful thought to the disposal of his legacy and remains. On November 25, 1976, he wrote out twelve pages of informal notes aimed at putting his affairs in order. He began by specifying necessary revisions in his music (he wished, for example, to double certain woodwind lines in the First Symphony's opening movement, either at the octave or another interval-he also wished to suppress a few "Tchaikovskyisms" in the Second and Third Symphonies). He then cited published scores in his catalogue that especially needed vetting for misprints, even noting impractical page-turns that he wanted eliminated in future editions. He identified books of special rarity in his compendious library. Fearing, apparently, that performances of his music might decrease after his death-the case with so many composers-he made a list of "works of mine that I think are worth playing," which included the Duo for Violin and Cello, the Triple Concertino (final version), the Serenade, the 2nd and 4th Symphonies, the 2nd, 5th and 6th Piano Concertos, the *Mouvement perpetuel* for violin and piano, three operas (*Ol-Ol*, *The Wedding of Sobeide* and *The Nymph and the Farmer*), the Divertimento, the *Symphonic Prayer*, the Second Piano Sonata and *Showcase*.

---

4   A tribute to Tcherepnin by Messiaen's wife Yvonne Loriod appears on p. 142.

Unflinchingly avoiding euphemisms, he also made specific requests about memorial arrangements: "Would prefer to be burnt after my death, the ashes not to be kept, but thrown in a river or garbage can[.] no popes, no requiem, no receptions, no flowers, no donations, present the bill to Mutuality of SACEM[5] for reimbursement."

Tcherepnin's remains were cremated; some of his ashes were strewn upon the waters of the Thames near his beloved Marlow, the remainder were interred with his father Nicolai in the Russian cemetery at Ste. Genevieve-des-Bois, a few miles south of Paris. In accordance with the composer's obvious desire for simplicity, the family discouraged public tributes. An exception was made, however, in the case of the Lucerne Festival, perhaps the one performance venue at which Tcherepnin's chamber, vocal and orchestral works had been unfailingly welcome during his last years. Tcherepnin appearances there were always treated by performers and public alike as major events, and, in fact, he had long since accepted an engagement to perform at the 1978 Festival. To all concerned, it seemed superbly appropriate to reschedule this appearance as a program commemorating his death.

So it was that on August 25, 1978, the Lucerne Festival presented a Tcherepnin Memorial Concert played by the Basel Radio Symphony Orchestra and consisting of orchestral works by three generations of Tcherepnins- Nicolai, Alexander and Ivan. Ivan Tcherepnin conducted his recent orchestral piece *Le va et le vient*, a musical meditation on the death of his father and the almost simultaneous birth of his son; Gennady Rozhdestvensky took the podium for Nicolai Tcherepnin's *La Princesse Lointaine* (1899) and three compositions by Alexander Tcherepnin: *Mystère* for Cello and Orchestra, Triple Concertino for Violin, Cello, Piano and String Orchestra, and Symphony No. 4. The soloists were violinist Hanzheinz Schneeberger (a last-minute replacement for Yehudi Menuhin, who was ill), cellist Maurice Gendron and pianist Margrit Weber. For many who loved the composer and his work, the elegiac third movement of the Symphony, with its roots deep in Tcherepnin's beloved Russian church-music tradition, served as the most moving possible reminder of what the world had lost.

{The concluding chapter of Willi Reich's biography follows.}

---

5   The Societe des auteurs, compositeurs et editeurs de musique, a French organization similar to the American ASCAP.

8. In Retrospect

It is to the idea of "mission," mentioned earlier in our study of the *Symphonic Prayer*, that we must turn for an appreciation of the central themes that ring out in the life and work of Alexander Tcherepnin.

The ideas that had guided the first Russian school were very much alive in the milieu of his youth ("Youth in Old Russia"). Through Rimsky-Korsakov, his father's teacher, whom he got to know personally,[1] along with other Russian masters Balakirev, Cui, Liadov and Glazunov, Tcherepnin became intimately acquainted with the spiritual atmosphere in which the greatest accomplishments of the first Russian school had been achieved. From this, he proceeded to a great admiration for the art of Tchaikovsky, which he absorbed following his father's example, and which brought important elements to his first conceptions as a young composer. He also experienced the advent of the new Russian school as an eyewitness, since Prokofiev regarded his father as his mentor, and bonds of personal and professional friendship linked his family with the Diaghilev circle. An intimate knowledge of Russian-and later Georgian-folk music was perfectly natural for an artist brought up as he had been, and many compositions from every period of his career indicate how deeply rooted he was in this inexhaustibly nourishing soil. Tcherepnin must therefore be considered a "Russian" composer par excellence, not only in his youth, but also throughout his entire career.

Tcherepnin's stay in Paris during the most impressionable years of his youth ("In the Aura of Paris") served to add some typically French traits to his musical personality. His teachers, Paul Vidal and Isidore Philipp, inspired him with pedagogical ideals that he later pursued in his own teaching career. Within the circle of friends gathered under the banner of the *École de Paris*, he experienced a human and intellectual camaraderie that enriched the lives of all, offering as it did a climate of friendship favorable to the free exchange of ideas, though not diminishing in any way the innate originality of each of the young musicians. Indeed, one of Paris's principal merits is that it seems to provide all alert and open-minded artists with significant intellectual and artistic inspirations, which remain vital throughout their later careers-and which, far from compromising their originality, actually enhance it through an indefinable *cachet*, a *cachet* that may justly be said to mark Tcherepnin as a "French composer," along with the other members of the *École de Paris*. During this period, the Parisian influence expressed itself most palpably in the heightened brilliance of his creative and interpretive work, and especially in the development of expressive technical resources; it was also of decisive importance in his years of "Composing and Concertizing Around the World" that immediately followed.

From this artistic situation, very dangerous for his development in some respects, Tcherepnin rescued himself during the years 1934-37 by engrossing himself more and more deeply in "The Experience of the Far East." Intimate acquaintance with ancient traditions and techniques of Chinese and Japanese music suddenly put all he had previously experienced, studied and created in a new light. The folklore of the Far East fertilized his work in quite a different way

Tcherepnin in Beijing with Professor Tsong-Chi Yan and five young Chinese music students

from previous folk music influences. His Far Eastern activity as a teacher evolved from one-sided exchange into a mutual dialogue beneficial to both teacher and pupil, and the deep personal intimacy of his marriage with Lee Hsien Ming, the Chinese pianist, also infused his creative work with a new spirit that boldly united what is often perceived as Oriental exoticism with Western culture. While Tcherepnin is sometimes described as a "Chinese composer" on the strength of a few works written for special national occasions, it must be borne in mind that this label applies to him only in the narrowest sense and that his Far Eastern experiences led above all to the enrichment of a wholly individual creative personality.

This enrichment helped him to endure the difficult years of the Second World War, which, apart from material hardships, were especially oppressive to him because he was forced to produce pieces that were mostly alien to his nature, suppressing his genuine creative instincts. That Tcherepnin safely survived this crisis is testimony not only to his spiritual resilience, but also to the consummate mastery that he had gained over his art. Indeed, these crises appear in retrospect as a necessary prerequisite for his development into an "American composer," a description frequently applied to him after he acquired U. S. citizenship in 1958. Yet here too this description is far too narrow. The chapter entitled "Culmination in America" does not show a Tcherepnin forced to adjust to any special limitations of musical life in America, but, rather, chronicles

---

1   Tcherepnin's personal impressions of Rimsky, however, were those of a young boy, and had no significant effect on his artistic development.

the growth of Tcherepnin's art beyond all local and temporal limitations, toward an all-encompassing humanism allied to a clear awareness of high artistic "mission"-insights that he again began to share all over the musical world after 1959. {And the editor will add at this point that even if the ubiquitous hospitality Tcherepnin later enjoyed in Switzerland and his acquisition of a beloved third home in Marlow did not transform him into a "Swiss composer" or an "English composer," the privileged position he attained in both nations during his last years unquestionably reflected an artistic universality in his work that had endeared him again and again to new audiences in new nations throughout the course of his creative life.} Among the "Later Developments," it is exactly this international return, understood in its deeper implications, that allows us to choose an epithet for Alexander Tcherepnin that most justly reflects the full scope of his human and artistic aspirations: "Musical Citizen of the World."

The front entrance to the Tcherepnin third floor Paris apartment at 2 Rue de Furstenberg, near the corner of Rue Jacob. Plaque top left.

Alexander Tcherepnin works on *Tzigane* during his stay at the College of St. Scholastica in Duluth, Minnesota, 1966.

Tcherepnin's last completed manuscript, prepared either on the afternoon of his death, September 29, 1977, or the day before.

ALEXANDER TCHEREPNIN:
A COMPENDIUM

PART II:

THREE AUTOBIOGRAPHICAL ACCOUNTS

BOOK I: BIOGRAPHICAL

PART II: THREE AUTOBIOTRAPHICAL ACCOUNTS

INTRODUCTION

The three autobiographical accounts in Part II of Book I are complementary. Each gives an overview of Tcherepnin's musical life from a different standpoint.

The *Short Autobiography* (1964) deals with Tcherepnin's public life as a composer. It bears signs of editing-probably with the composer's approval-and has appeared in print in *Tempo* magazine.

The second piece is an extract from a lengthy letter to Nicolas Slonimsky, intended to furnish information for Baker's Dictionary. It is undated, but certain events referred to on the last pages place its origin at the end of 1950, perhaps November. (Enrique Arias' date of 1967 is quite wrong.) The first pages of this letter have been omitted here, because Tcherepnin later covered the same ground in his *Short Autobiography*. In the remainder, however, Tcherepnin discussed his stylistic evolution in a pithy and technically sophisticated manner, pin-pointing aesthetic and organizational problems that he felt impelled to tackle and solve at various stages of his creative odyssey.

Presenting this letter-extract involved some difficult editorial decisions. Of all Tcherepnin's writings in English, this is the most wayward in grammar and syntax. At the time he sent it, he had been in America no longer than fifteen months; in later years, his English prose would become more idiomatic.

Although Enrique Arias and Lily Chou had both found it necessary to devise shortened and substantially edited versions of this letter, the present editor originally hoped to supply a scholarly reproduction of Tcherepnin's original text, with all necessary editorial emendations clearly identified. An attempt to do this, however, produced a nine-page thicket so formidably fraught with ellipsis dots and square brackets that only the hardiest scholar would dream of plowing through it. In this case-if the document is to be printed at all-a polished-up version seemed to be unavoidable. Accordingly, the editor elected, although not without trepidation, to take Lily Chou's version as a basic text, altering it in a few cases to bring it into closer conformity sometimes to what Tcherepnin wrote, at other times to what he apparently meant. The editor attempted to avoid any license greater than that allowed a scrupulous translator-indeed, the version here may be considered a "translation from the English by Lily Chou and Benjamin Folkman."

The third account, "Basic Elements of My Musical Language," does not-strictly speaking-belong to the category of autobiography at all. Yet, of the three pieces, it is this one, painstakingly handwritten on twenty-four pages of music paper in January 1961, that surely gives the deepest insight into Tcherepnin's life as an artist. Indeed this essay is the obligatory starting point for any serious study of the composer's music, for here Tcherepnin discusses his technical procedures in pithy detail, covering aspects of nine-step and pentatonic harmony that are usually ignored. Much of this piece was quoted or summarized by Arias, but some details were omitted. Particularly valuable among the latter are Tcherepnin's illustrations of arpeggio-derivations, and his explanations of nine-step grammar's notational singularities (in nine-step, for example, a D major triad will sometimes appear in the nominally "illiterate" spelling D-Gb-A; moreover, in some nine-step contexts, an interval such as the major-second Eb-F is categorized as a minor-third).

Tcherepnin also summarizes his folk-explorations, and closes with twenty-four biographical and aesthetic "observations." Published previously by Arias (under the rather unfortunate title "Alexander Tcherepnin's Thoughts on Music"), these deceptively casual and even avuncular remarks add up to an incisive philosophical self-portrait.

Numerous corrections in the "Basic Elements" manuscript indicate that Tcherepnin hoped to make its English as cogent and idiomatic as possible. The editor has not hesitated to go even beyond these emendations, the paramount concern being a clear and unambiguous presentation of Tcherepnin's technical points.

❋ ❋ ❋ ❋ ❋ ❋

TCHEREPNIN PRELUDE

R ussian composer
Georgian composer
Composer of the School of Paris
Chinese composer
American composer.

Is this a handicap or an advantage?

I once calculated that in the 21 years between the two World Wars, I spent two on board ship, on trains, planes and in cars. My home was where my table and my sheet music was. Another full year of travel could be added for the period after the Second World War. I wandered around in 40 countries, was at home everywhere and really felt at home nowhere. My only home is in my inner self, which remains the same and follows its own development.

It is an unusual fate.

The *Wandering Jew* or *Peter Schlemihl* by Chamisso could be my model.

A man without a shadow, without a home. Is it a handicap or an advantage?

I. A SHORT AUTOBIOGRAPHY (1964)

My father, Nicolai Tcherepnin, was an outstanding Russian composer, brilliant conductor, enlightened pedagogue. My mother had a beautiful mezzo-soprano voice, but because she was extremely timid, she became a *soprano domestica*, and I was the only one to accompany her singing of the German *Lieder*, Russian romances and French songs, which of course, I treasured.

Music in our home was a religion. I was the only child, and as a result I was admitted to all musical reunions (thus remembering Rimsky, Liadov, Cui, Glazunov, Stravinsky, Prokofiev, Diaghilev, Benois, Fokine, Pavlova, Chaliapin etc.) and rehearsals at home and at the concert halls when my father, his friends, or his students were conducting, as well as to concerts, to operas, and to ballets. Admissions also included home discussions of the Russian Ballet (Diaghilev, my father, Benois, Fokine, Bakst, Nouvel, Nurok and *tutti quanti*) during the time of its conception and formative years. I was also permitted to associate via the Benois family (that of my mother) with contemporary painters and sculptors, attended their exhibitions, and met with writers and poets the stature of Gorodezky, Kamensky, Gumilev, etc.

My father believed in God and loved the church-he was Greek Orthodox-so I went with him to church services and attended discussions about religion at home with bishops and priests (the late Mitropolitan Evloogi an was intimate and dear friend of my father's). I was equally at home in the Roman Catholic church (my mother was Catholic) and with Roman Catholic priests, Moslem priests, Moslem mullahs, Shintoists, Confucianists and Taoists-also with various branches of the Christian church-Georgian, Armenian, Syrian, Constantinopolitan, Jerusalemian and Coptic.

This was my background and it is no wonder that since my earliest childhood, music became my religion, my life, my goal, in fact, the very reason for my existence. According to my parents, I was hardly out of my cradle, when I took to singing motifs, I heard (such as the principal theme of Borodin's B minor Symphony) or motifs freely invented by me. There were two baby grand pianos in our home, and no sooner would my parents leave than I would be at one of them exploring the sounds, trying to find the sounds that I heard going on within me. (As a matter of fact to this day, when I listen within me, I can hear sounds-melodies, motifs, harmonies, various sound combinations: music never stops working within me; it is as if music were part of my blood circulation, a part of my system.)

I never dared to improvise or to touch the piano in the presence of my father for fear of disturbing him, but I was less shy with my mother who soon realized what music meant to me. There was plenty of music paper lying around in our home. I observed how my father was writing his scores and tried to do the same while alone. Noticing this, my mother taught me the secrets of music notation when I was 5 years old, so it happened that I learned how to write music and how to notate my musical ideas before I learned how to write words-before I learned the alphabet. So it is that even now the most direct expression of my thoughts is by music rather than by words. Yet, strangely enough, no regular music instruction in theory was given to me until the age of 19, at which time I was graduated from high school and had entered the Petrograd Conservatory. The only music instruction I had was piano study and even this was done casually. Instruction was initially given me by my mother, then by some old ladies, and finally by Leocadia Kashperovaan elderly woman who studied in her youth with Anton Rubinstein, and who composed and taught privately in her home, having no affiliation with any of the numerous Petrograd music schools. She used to tell me that I am running and that all she can do for me is to move my feet in order that I do not break them by running too fast and indeed I was running: outside of the pieces she would assign me, I was busy studying classical and modern music of my choice and even had the nerve to perform them [sic] in public without my teacher's control or my parents' knowledge.

The fact is that music having been my natural language I always wanted to converse in this language with my fellow human beings. When on the stage, I felt as natural and happy as in my home and never experienced stage fright-just the contrary. There was always a longing to be on the stage-a delight in performing at any occasion. This was a feeling begun in my early age and one that has continued until now at age 65! I cannot separate myself from music. It is through music that I communicate with people. The stage is like a church for me-the exact place where I can serve my religion which is music, thus accomplishing my mission towards human beings.

As mentioned, during the first 14 years of my "creative life" in the field of composition, I was left entirely to myself with no instruction, no supervision, no other way of learning the reactions of people and musicians than by performing my compositions on the stage. I must admit that after nearly every concert that I played up to the age of 15 or 16, I would return home and go to bed weeping. Whether it was a reaction after the excitement of playing in public or whether it was because I felt the inadequacy of my abilities or a combination of both I cannot say; yet, it is a fact that after each performance I would hide myself under the bed cover and cry until the fatigue would close my eyes and put me to sleep.

Being very shy when I was young, even with my parents whom I loved dearly, I never confessed my troubles. The idea of shocking or troubling my parents was unbearable to me, so I never admitted my troubles to them and proceeded alone in my artistic development.

It was my wish to see my family happy, in fact I wished for all humans to be happy. Even in my earliest childhood I realized that happiness and unhappiness, joy and sorrow [are always] coexisting and cannot be separated from each other. As childish as it seems, it brought me in music, to the idea of the combination of major and minor. I had always felt that the major-minor triad of C, E flat, E natural and G is a "fundamental," "final" chord-therefore, "consonant," "stable" and not in search of resolution like a dissonance in the classical concept of this term. I felt attracted to this major-minor chord. I heard it constantly sounding in me, and somehow, even in the early instinctive period of my composing, I used this chord as a final "consonant" chord. Later I realized that one of the reasons my ear protested against this well-tempered pitch in which the intervals are different from the natural intervals, was because my ear was still hearing the traditional pitch with its traditional intervals rather than the Major-Minor Triad. There was conflict between what I heard within me and what I would be able to reproduce by the conventional medium of the so called "musical" sounds.

{*Editor's Note:* An amplification of this point may help some readers:

	NATURAL			WELL-TEMPERED
	440 =	A	=	440
MAJOR	550 =	C#	=	554
	660 =	E	=	659.26
	440 =	A	=	440
MINOR	528 =	C	=	523.25
	660 =	E	=	659.26

Compared to natural thirds, the well-tempered major third is sharp; the minor third is flat. Playing both well-tempered thirds simultaneously creates the illusion that the "in-between" natural frequencies are heard.}

Had I been born in 1949, I most certainly would have turned to electronic music in search of exact reproduction of what I heard in me, but being born in 1899-at the first decade of our century, there was no other way for me than to try by combinations of intervals to give the impression of natural intervals. Instead of searching for new means of reproducing the correct sounds that my ear heard, I had to adapt my ear to the convention of established music sounds. Of course in my early teens I had no idea about the difference between natural and well-tempered pitch and blamed my ear instead of blaming the well-tempered tuning.

The acceptance of the Major-Minor Triad resulted in further acceptance of many unorthodox chords. So it came that already in my earliest composition the function of "dissonance" was lost, modes replaced the tonalities, and the self-made musical language, resulting from what was instinctive in me, was the tool which enabled me to materialize my musical thoughts and ideas. For the entrance exam of the Petrograd Conservatory for which I applied at the age of 19, I produced orchestra and choral works, operas, ballets, 5 piano concerti, 12 piano sonatas, chamber music and vocal compositions that were passed among members of the jury, Glazunov, Liadov, Sokolov, Petrov, Ossovsky etc. The jury scanned the manuscripts and I have often wondered what the jury would really have thought if they had thoroughly read them, but such was not the case. I had a good ear and played well and so was admitted to the harmony class of Nicolai Sokolov and for the first time in my life had instruction in traditional harmony. Only then did I realize how different and unorthodox my own way of facing the harmony problem was. I did the required assignments with ease and this study gave me the idea to analyze my own way of musical methods which until this time was chiefly instinctive.

The 1917-1918 season was that of Revolution. In August 1918, my parents and I left Petrograd and settled in Tbilisi, capital of the then independent republic of Georgia in the Caucasus. We stayed there for three years. While studying piano and concertizing there, I was again left alone as a composer.

I studied the Classics, especially Beethoven, his musical language and form, and was attracted by Georgian popular and liturgical music. This together with the self-analysis that started in Petrograd, crystallized my own musical language.

Superimposing two Major-Minor Triads I discovered that they would fit into a hexachord that reads: C, E flat, E natural, G, A flat, B, (C); the same hexachord reversed and read from the top down would be C, A, A flat, F, E, D flat, (C). Added together they produce a nine-step synthetic scale that reads: C, D flat, E flat, E, F, G, A flat, A natural, B, (C). The major-minor triad is the fundamental triad of this scale. Due to the fact that the 2 tetrachords forming this scale are joined and identical, there could be only 4 nine-step scales as to actual sound, each having 3 modes-which brings the number of 9-step tonalities (or 9 step modes) to twelve as to sound. I found that my instinctively composed music leaned towards this nine-step synthetic scale, is based on it, and is explained through it. From then on, what had previously been done instinctively was now done through theory and conscious application.

Meditating about the progress in music and rejecting the traditionalism from my early youth and the vagueness associated with it, I found in my mind that progress would be achieved via clear part-writing and therefore by polyphony. Here again, through analysis of instinctively acquired part-writing technique, I found that I ha[d] been naturally following certain polyphonic rules, a procedure I named "Interpoint." The name of this device is self-explanatory: punctus- inter-punctum, (as opposed to punctus-contra-punctum). It can be vertical if taken in the strict sense of the word or it can be horizontal when each of the parts acts as if having its own bar line, its own time; it can be polyrhythmic if each of the parts has its own meter in the form of a rhythmic pattern. It can also be a combination of both or of all three forms. Derived from my instinctively-composed works, the nine-step scale and the Interpoint now became devices that I was able to use consciously, and which were particular to my musical language.

During World War I, Russia was completely isolated from the Western world. There was no radio. The only news that one would have was through the newspapers which were strictly censored. There were no airplanes. The entire western border of Russia was a line of battlefields; the only directly accessible Western neighbors were Germany and Austria. In the south the Black Sea was dominated by Turkey, who was also in the war against Russia. To travel from Russia to France, one would have to go to Finland, then further via Sweden and Denmark or Norway by ship through the North Sea under the menace of German submarines, to England and from there cross the Channel under the same menace, to France. This was the only route of communication with the West. The Southern route was too close to Turkey, while the lengthy route via Siberia, Japan and the U. S. A. was complicated by the necessity of crossing two oceans before reaching Western Europe.

[Thus] cultural exchanges ceased. There was no knowledge in Petrograd about the progress of musical trends in the West, and vice-versa. Even worse than the occupation of greater Russia by the Armies of the German-Austro-Hungarian Empires was the Civil War from within Russia itself. No less isolated was Georgia and the Caucasus during the three years of my stay in Tbilisi, and even more isolated since early in 1921, [when] Georgia was besieged by Communist armies coming from Azerbaijan. So it happened (in my case so small compared with the great events around me) that from the age of 15 until the age of 22 I had no communications with the West. In Georgia, I had not a single friend with whom I could discuss my musical ideas; whatever I thought about music and its progress, I did in my own private meditations.

When I came to Paris in the fall of 1921, with a suitcase of my manuscripts and a small dog named Touchkan, whom I picked up on the street of Tiflis, I found that my way of thinking about the progress in music was somehow identical with the views of the Western composers of my generation. The Western trend towards polyphony, towards organization of chromatic writing, towards using the medieval polyphonic devices, with or without classical form, corresponded precisely to my idea of organization of chromaticism via 2 hexachords (that could also serve to organize the 12-tone scale) or via varieties of the nine-step scales, to the search of a new approach to the polyphony that I saw in Interpoint. So I felt more at home in Paris than I felt in Russia or in Georgia, and this is probably why I settled in Paris.

If one looks through the score of my First Symphony (1927) one will find the practice of serial thematic construction of the theme and all the medieval polyphonic artifices associated with the use of Interpoint. And if one examines the Finale of my First Cello Sonata (1924) one will find bird calls used as motifs and, above all, the urge to be clear in texture and concise in form. In fact, the urge to get away from the conventional pitch resulted in scoring the 2nd movement of the 1st Symphony for percussion instruments only, which produced considerable controversy at the time of the premiere of the First Symphony conducted by Gabriel Pierné, at the *Concerts Colonne* in Paris, 1927.

All of this happened before the birth of dodecaphonic music, before Messiaen's looking for bird calls for thematic material, before the esoteric use of rhythmic patterns by many a Western composer, and long before the liberation of music from a conventional pitch that became dear to post-Second-World-War composers. The fact is that progress in music, the development of new means of sound-making, new techniques in sound organization and sound production is never due to a single man; rather, the "what next" comes as a continuation of what was before. Whether as an amplification of the "old climate" or an opposition to it, the "new climate" is the logical reaction mostly brought on by a new generation. It is not important who was the first, but more important who was the best. He who succeeds in being congenial with his time, who in Art expresses most strongly the "present," will be the one who will survive by representing the "present" to the "future." In my case, notwithstanding the differences that might exist due to personality, to the way of life, to the belonging to one or another community or country, I feel the affiliation to my generation which came after the First World War: a generation which opposed impressionism in music. Most of the composers of my generation had the same problems, which each of us tried to face and solve to the best of his abilities.

The ideas that were previously mentioned as being instinctively mine, then consciously used, might have been my own personal ideas as I saw them, but they were also the ideas of my generation. They were "in the air," I felt them, faced them, and tried to use appropriate means to materialize them. I was not alone, and who of us was "first" is of no importance. The essential thing is to be honest and to compose music that one feels to be right. The ultimate value of a composition is the complete balance of the "what" with the "how." The "how" can and should be analyzed. The "what" is extemporaneous and can only be felt, and escapes every cerebral investigation.

I believe that the creation originates in what we call the instinct. How much the instinct is instinctive, I do not know. It might be that a composer is sensitive to non-audible sounds and then further expresses them into sounds that we call "musical." The composer's work consists of expressing the instinctively-chosen sounds which are approved by his ear for the construction of a musical composition by adequate technical means.

In the late twenties, I started to become tired of my own "technicality" of the nine-step scale, of Interpoint, of polyphonic devices, and even of the instinctively found musical material. The life of a composer is a continued drive towards progress, so I looked for a new means, for a deeper meaning of art. I began to reconsider values in order to get nearer to people and to get away from a *deus ex machina* kind of production.

Born and educated in Russia, I meditated about Russian music, about Russian people, about Russian World concept (*Weltanschauung*) and Russian mission in art. This meditation brought me to the Eurasian theory about the Russian race. Old Russia-around 1,000 years ago-was geographically situated in feudalistic states not always friendly towards one another. The Mongolian invasion put all these states under the domination of Mongols, so Russia became part of the great Mongolian State extending from [the] Vis[tu]la to the Pacific Ocean. After many centuries, the Russians succeeded in defeating the Mongols-the Mongols were never driven away-instead of Mongols dominating the Russians, the Russians dominated the Mongols, and inherited the great Mongolian Empire from [the] Vis[tu]la to the Pacific. There is a French proverb which reads, "Scratch a Russian, and you will find a Tatar." Indeed the Mongols merged with the Russians, and the actual Russian race is in many ways the result of this assimilation.

Hence, Russia is as much a European country as she is an Asiatic one-a true "Eurasian" empire-both geographically and ethnically. Russia is as much at home in the West as in the East; but while in relation to the West, Russia has an inferiority complex due to the superiority of the Western Culture-in relation to the East, she feels an equal. What is more, Russia has a message to bring to the East, while it has a message to receive from the West. To a Russian, the East is not exotic; it is familiar, a part of the Russian nature. Western influence on Russia might be materially important but it is spiritually destructive, while Eastern influence is of great artistic and spiritual value. The influence of Tibetan sacred painting on the Russian icon is obvious and important; the influence of Eastern Music is manifest in such masterpieces as *Prince Igor* or *Steppes of Central Asia* of Borodin or *Scheherezade* of Rimsky Korsakov, just to mention but a few of many examples.

When it came time to "scratch" myself, I recognized my affiliation with the East, natural for me as a Russian, and I found in the Eurasian *Weltanschauung* a stimulation, both philosophically and musically. To get away from my own musical formulas, I began to look into musical folklore. I came to the conclusion that what the knowledge of the anatomy of the human body is to the painter, the folklore of the people is to the musician. The lines of the human body are the lines of life, the lines of survival. Michaelangelo, Leonardo, Delacroix, each for his own purpose, studied the anatomy of the human body, and this helped each of them to operate with eternal lines in the production of their masterpieces. So did Picasso-only instead of recreating the image of a human, he used the same eternal lines of the body for abstract constructions, which gave life to his abstract paintings.

The musical lines of folk music are the lines of musical survival, for the folklore of all nations shares the common quality of having lasted through the centuries. In operating with material from folklore, the composer operates with eternal lines-lines for him to use in whichever way he feels appropriate.

I felt that the use of folklore in my compositions would be the right way to get away from the self-imposed technical formulas. I started the search for folklore in Egypt and in Palestine. I returned to the Georgian, Armenian, Persian, Azerbaijan, Russian folk melodies that I had known and collected before.

It happened that shortly after the start of this "search," I went on my first concert tour to China and Japan in 1934. The concert tour was to last a few weeks in each country; but, entranced by what I saw and heard, I stayed in Japan and China for an entire year; then after my return to Europe I once again returned to the Orient for another year of concerts, of teaching and of learning. In the many compositions that I did between 1933-1939 I used various folklores as material which helped me to find a new way. Perhaps the most important among them are the ballet *Trepak*, that I composed in 1937[1] for Lucia Chase[-]in which I used Russian folklore in a Chinese way, and the ballet *La Femme et son Ombre* that I composed on a libretto by Paul Claudel for Roland Petit's *Ballet de Paris*, in which Japanese folklore was used.

---

1 Actually, in 1938.

The War came, and what I-like most of humanity-lived through could not help but influence my art. Everything seemed so small in comparison to the tragedy and suffering that the War brought to everyone. It was no longer possible to think of art for art's sake, nor to seek refuge in operating with folklore. The most important goal for the composer seemed now to serve humanity, to help unite people by works of art, to try to bring understanding, beauty and balance to shaken minds.

The first of my composition that was composed after the war with this idea was my 2nd, Symphony. Here I have tried to express my deep feelings of love for and affiliation to humanity, to produce a score in which every note would be "composed," not manufactured, by technique. I consider it as providential that precisely at that moment of my life, I was engaged to teach at DePaul University in Chicago, that I came to the U. S. A., settled in Chicago, and became associated with the American community.

Now, more than ever before, I realized the responsibility of the composer's mission towards humanity. The high standard of living in the United States provides many millions of people access to cultural values. The composer can converse with humanity through radio, television, and records. Concerts also expose the composer to a direct association with humanity, since music unites people around a work of art. Thus, the work of art must be worthy, must bring a positive message to the people via music. The composer absorbs what humanity gives him and gives it back to his community in the form of a work of art.

I feel happy that I have been able to contribute to the life of American music as a composer, performer, lecturer, and pedagogue, and to serve the American community in every way I can to the best of my ability. I love people, I love to associate with people, and I love the American people. It is in this spirit that I have composed during the past 15 years.

As to the "technical" means I feel that I came to synthesize the dreams of my youth: the range of what we today consider as "musical" sounds is wider and richer. The unpitched-percussion movement of my First Symphony is no more a problem, and non-pitch music is cultivated by the post Second World War generation of composers. The electronic medium gives the chance to reproduce the sounds that one hears in himself, exactly as one hears them with no concessions-thus realizing the urge that I had since I first listened inside myself, (an urge which is no longer contested by others). All the species of Interpoint as I conceived them in my youth are now audible and present in avant- garde compositions of the new generation, while the chromaticism, for which I fought in the early twenties-whether it be in a serial way or in the way of arbitrary scale combination-has become integrated in dodecaphonic musical speech. The aleatory approach that I tried to materialize in the *Sonatine Sportive* for Saxophone and Piano in 1939 is one of the many approaches of the music making of today. What is most important, music becomes more and more a religion in that it serves to unite people by way of participating in the production of a musical composition-an ideal in which I have always believed, an ideal which makes the life of a composer worth living.

I feel fortunate to have survived until the time when music became truly universal, and to be able to discard the multi-secular conventions; to create the true art of sound.

II. FROM A LETTER TO NICOLAS SLONIMSKY (1950)

...Instead of formal, theoretical Conservatory education, I received so to speak "object-lesson" training-one like that of the apprentice learning at the house of his master. My teacher or teaching was not what I was told to learn, but what I heard; and as most of what I heard and listened to was from my father, I can consider him my teacher, though he never gave me a single "lesson."

Some of my father's remarks, as I remember them were, "this music has much innovation" (which meant it was good, because it was new). Or, censuring: "this composer picks up what is on the floor" (which meant, bad)....

My father's esthetics between 1910 and 1920 involved "getting free from technics" (his words)-of course, he meant a liberation from school technique of the Glazunov type, and not the rejection of technical composing skill. It is quite possible that that was the reason why he left my composing endeavors unsupervised, and did not hurry to give me formal training. About good composers, father used to say, "he is a composer by the grace of God." He considered me thus blessed by the "grace of God" and left me alone to prove it.

All my first compositions were done under the sign of this freedom and intuition. I remember clearly that the composing process was like the actions of a blind person who gropes and touches objects until, gradually, after many contacts with the separate parts, he has built the image of the whole. My process of composing at this time definitely resembled such a "searching in the dark"-and even now I would not deny completely that this is true. The *Bagatelles*, *Episode* and Little Suites, the *Romantic Sonatina* and the First Sonata, as well as an innumerable quantity of manuscripts left in Russia, are the results of that period.

After we moved to Tbilisi, the situation changed. My enthusiasm for piano playing brought on the acceptance of a conventional pianistic idiom, which handicapped my clear intuitive approach and resulted in the search for sound effects. Added to it was my enthusiasm for music of the classical period, which resulted in form that was broader in scope but, at the same time, less natural as an issue of the original idea. The First Piano Concerto, both Nocturnes and both Dances, the Concert Etude in B major/minor are the most typical works of this transitional period, which proved useful to me, as it made me think and not rely solely on instinct.

At the same time, however, my creative power was asserting itself, and, together with those conventional works, there were others such as *Arabesques*, Eight Preludes, Ten Etudes in which the pianism was subordinated to the creative conception and served as the medium for refined harmonic, formal and rhythmic explorations. The six- and nine-tone scales, that resulted from my searchings' were found *intuitively, without my noticing*.

Also in Tbilisi, at the end of 1920, I "arrived" at polyphony. "Long live Polyphony!" I wrote down in my diary. My first steps in this direction, together with the wished-for simplification and liberation from Impressionism and its adherents-as well as from everything second-rate-were the Inventions, later published by Eschig under the title of *Nine Inventions*. Of them, eight are two-voiced and one three-voiced. Six-step scales and chromaticism provided their bases. My first Violin Sonata, written in Tbilisi in 1921, continued in this direction. A slight deviation, under the influence of my pianism, was the First toccata (later released in Paris as toccata and novelette). When I left Tbilisi for Paris in the summer of 1921, I was an ardent advocate of the denial of Impressionism, the curtailing of harmony, and the proliferation of polyphony and linear writing. I was a neoclassic in form, believing in my "scales" and in the renovation of music by self-restriction and a return to the pre-Bach forms.

I arrived at all this by myself, as in Tbilisi, cut off from Western Europe in 1914, [where] a Ravel Sonatina was considered the peak of novelty, Debussy, a decadent, Scriabin, the prophet-and I did not have any contemporaries with whom I could agree, as I saw the modern in a completely different light.

But when I arrived in Paris, I found that the whole of my generation of composers was pursuing a direction similar to mine-those composers in various countries, independently of each other, were arriving at similar conclusions. In the light of this discovery, my convictions became even stronger and more pointed. My scale, then analytically realized, helped me to become a neo-classic in form but not in expression (language). My Interpoint, vertical (*punctus inter punctum*) and horizontal (the transfer of accents in different voices), became the individual development of my linear polyphonic thinking. At first, I took the road of simplification (First and Second Cello Sonatas, the Songs and Preludes for Piano, the Violin Sonata, the *Concerto da Camera*). The climax of this approach was reached in the Piano Trio (1925), after which I realized that if I went on simplifying, nothing would be left. Beginning with this Piano Trio, I began to introduce complications which resulted in the Symphony No. 1, the Piano Quintet, and *The Wedding of Sobeide* After which, once again, I realized I could not go on like this. So, if I had been a Soviet composer, I would have repented in 1925 for too much simplification and, in 1930, for too much complication-and in both cases I would have been sincere, even if my repentance happened to correspond with the Party ideology. Moreover, the nine-step scale on which the two-hour-long opera *Sobeide* was based, likewise the Piano Quintet, the Quartet No. 2 and the Symphony No. 1, no longer satisfied me completely. I started looking for vertical correlation of intervals, divided them and their chords into "firm" ones (without thirds) and "soft" ones (based on thirds) and saw in this a useful contrast for building the form.[1]

In addition, the conception of Russia's world mission being based on its Eurasian character fascinated me and won my complete acceptance. I found myself interested in Folklore, which I saw as a means of getting out of the abstract, in the same way as a painter sees in the anatomy of the human body the eternal source of absolute lines, truth and beauty. Already in *The Wedding of Sobeide* there had been a certain leaning towards the Eurasian, though the element of folklore there was nine-step in character. It was even more evident in the Concertino for Violin, Cello, Piano and Orchestra, in whose last movement the Georgian folk theme underwent the nine-step treatment.

The trip to Egypt and Palestine made me even more attracted to folklore, though it was not the Oriental species for which I was looking. Both my Piano Concerto No. 3 (partly) and the Duo (in greater degree)-though they do not have any folkloric themes-were the result of this psychology and use some of the principles of folk-music. And in the Duo, those of "natural" music-the fourth movement being a musical representation of the insects ("katy did, katy didn't") I listened to one summer night on Long Island. However, the 3rd Piano Concerto, with its second movement fugue based on three pairs of subjects and employing all kinds of polyphonic manipulations, belongs more to the preceding period.

A complete revolution and revelation occurred in 1933, when my friend, the publisher Benno Balan, asked me to write a Suite of Russian Dances. I composed this in Stroble, Austria, and used partly folk melodies I had heard in Russia and partly folk music taken from collections. I designed it so that one theme directly developed into another, or was repeated in variation, so as to eliminate any element of pressure on the themes or their technical elaboration. It added up to a suite of five short numbers, which I started to orchestrate. When at the beginning of January 1934, I heard my suite in Philadelphia at the "trial" readings for young composers instituted by Stokowski and conducted by Smallens, I was appalled by my orchestration-everything was so thin, and nothing "sounded." The reason was that my concept of the orchestra had been derived from chamber music-and when I came to the symphony orchestra in my Symphony No. 1 and *Magna Mater*, I did not treat it as an "instrument," with its own naturally rich palette, but as a chamber orchestra, merely augmented to accommodate complicated material. Of course, it was not acoustically correct, but it did not annihilate the music completely because the extremely developed polyphony stood its ground and automatically brought forth interesting and full sounds.

But it was different with the *Russian Dances*, which had a thin structural texture and needed both coloring and acoustically correct distribution and doublings. The rehearsal in Philadelphia served as a practical lesson which I accepted completely. I totally reorchestrated the score, and when I later heard it in Baden I saw that I had not worked in vain-and that the change in the style of the work demanded also a change in the approach to the orchestra.

The *Russian Dances* were my first folkloric work, as a previous folk- named score, the *Georgian Rhapsody* for Cello and Orchestra, had used not folk themes, but only folk rhythms or the rhythms of folksongs adapted to free melodic designs. The *Russian Dances*, however, was the piece that started my "cure" from the formalistic abstract by means of folklore.

And then, as if by design, my first tour of China and Japan took place, which brought me into contact with the rich tradition of instrumental and theatrical music of these nations with their wealth of folklore. This became my passion. Just at the time when I became indifferent to my nine-step scale, I "found" its replacement in the Chinese and Japanese pentatonic. And my Eurasian conception received at last a realistic direction. Like the slogan "Proletarians of all countries unite," I used to say at that time, "Folklores of all countries unite."

When I returned from my second Far Eastern tour in 1937. I received from M. Mordkin and Lucia Chase the commission to write for them a ballet. Together with Sudeikin, we made a libretto based on the old Russian legend about a maiden possessed by dancing. The ballet was called *Trepak* and was a typical folkloric creation. I found the thematic material in a collection of Palchikiv where, to my joy, a number of wonderful pentatonic Russian folk themes were present. Thus a new Russian folk style was created in which I treated these Russian pentatonic themes in "Chinese style," and it resulted in the Eurasian creation for which I had been searching. Sorry to say, I have never heard this ballet, as it was performed in New York and through the U. S. A. when I was in Europe. I continued on the road of folklore and the liberation from everything artificial in my *Georgian Suite* for Piano and String Orchestra (1938-39) and especially in the ballet *The Legend of Razin*, which I imagined as a real folk show. But my "cure" was beginning to fade, and after *The Legend of Razin* (which was the climax of this period) I was looking for something different. The "different" expressed itself in two orchestral works written during the Occupation. During my folkloring period I had mastered orchestration, and therefore wished to do orchestration for its own sake. But my "material," freed from folklore, could not find immediately a free expression. And I found myself in my so-to-speak *Sturm und Drang* period, especially in the first of the two works,

---

1   Elsewhere Tcherepnin described these as "hard" and "soft" intervals: later, he thought "severe" might be a better description than either firm or hard-apparently, he never came to a final decision.

The Nevsky Prospect (or *The Return of the Coach Driver*)[2], in which there was a mixture of styles-the evil characteristic of most of my Russian generation. In the second, *Evocation*, I at least stuck to the Georgian chord and from this achieved a good sound harmonically.

I returned to folklore, though this time completely re-adjusting my way of thinking, in the commissioned ballet *Chota Rostaveli*, the Fantasy for Piano and Orchestra[3] (China) and the ballet *The Woman and her Shadow* (Japan). Beginning with *Perpetuum mobile* for Violin and Piano, I looked for broader forms, rhythmic development, and free application of everything I had obtained and experienced.

The most significant work resulting from this thinking was my Symphony No. 2, written in 1947 for AMP but not orchestrated yet. Here I tried to create everything and "fabricate" nothing. I was looking for the uninterrupted, for pure creation put into a broad, intentional form. And I will try to continue in this direction as long as my life will permit....

As a resume, dear Kolia, here is a schematic summary of the periods of my development, as I just described them to you:

From Childhood until the Departure from Russia (*i. e.*, 1918)—
instinctive composing. Most characteristic and well-known
works: *Bagatelles.*
1918-1920—engrossment in pianism—1st Piano Concerto, harmonic and scale-like searchings—*Arabesques.*
1921-1930—Polyphony-Counterpoint-the Nine-step scale.
The Primitive: *Inventions*—Violin and Cello Sonatas, Trio.
Development: 2nd Quartet, Quintet, Symphony, *Sobeide's Wedding.*
The orchestra—from chamber music gradually to the symphony as developed chamber orchestra.
1930-1933—Introduction of the idea of firm and soft intervals, increasing of rhythmic principle, Eurasianism: Concertino, 3rd Piano Concerto, Duo.
1933-1941—The healing by folklore. From *Russian Dances* through *Trepak*—Chinese etudes to *Georgian Suite* and the *Legend of Razin.*
1941-1944—*Sturm und Drang*-blending of styles, search of unoriginal instead of original which was caused by writing so much conventional *Gebrauchsmusik.*
1945 up till now—The seeking of pure creation and broad form.

---

2   At this date, Tcherepnin had not yet produced the revised version of this score, which he published under the name *Romantic* Overture-a curious choice of title since, in fact, he had removed the most musically "Romantic" episodes from the piece in shortening it by about one third.

3   Later designated Tcherepnin's Piano Concerto No. 4.

III. BASIC ELEMENTS OF MY MUSICAL LANGUAGE

A. Tcherepnin

New York, January 1962

---

1   Tcherepnin's original table of contents has been adapted to the present pagination.

I. Nine-step scale

Major-minor tetrachords are constructed within the interval of a major third using two half-steps and one whole-step:

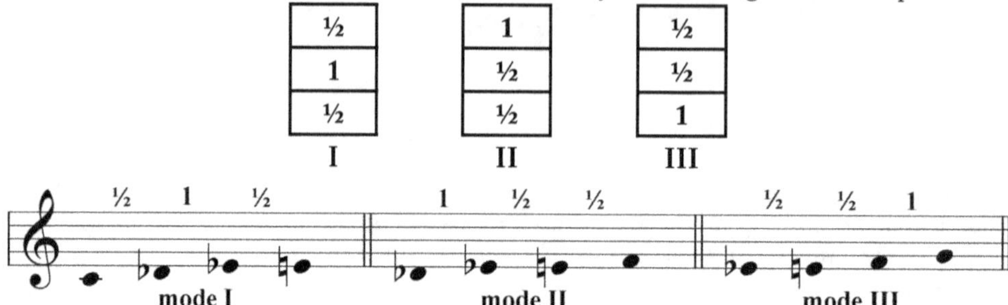

Major-minor hexachords are constructed within the interval of a major seventh using alternations of half-step and one-and-a-half-step intervals:

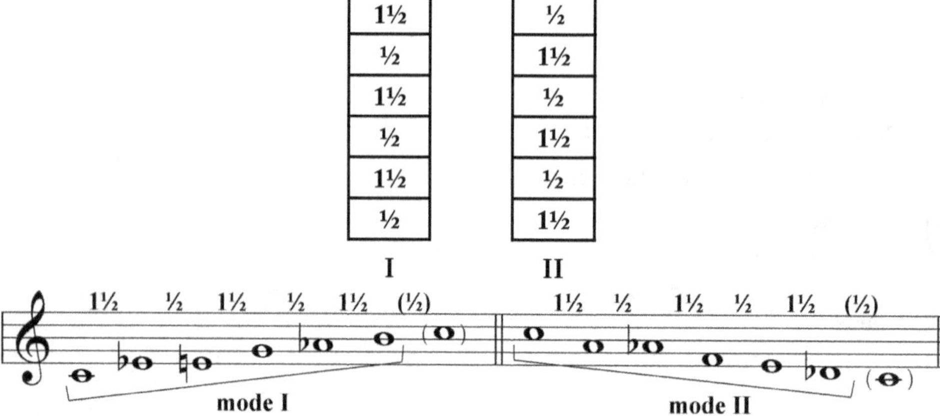

with one octave added to complete the row:

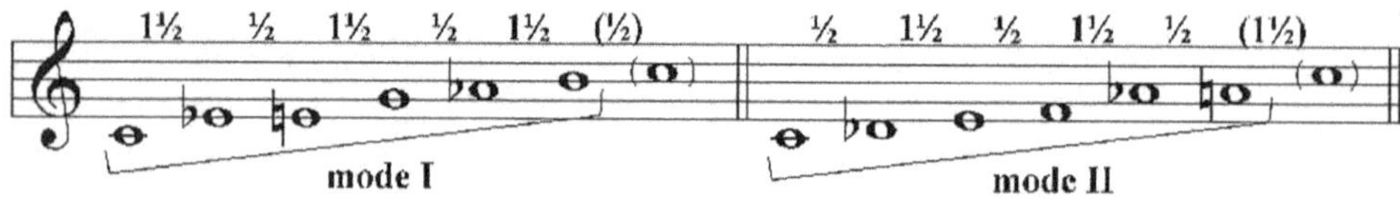

As shown in the example, mode II is the inversion of mode I.

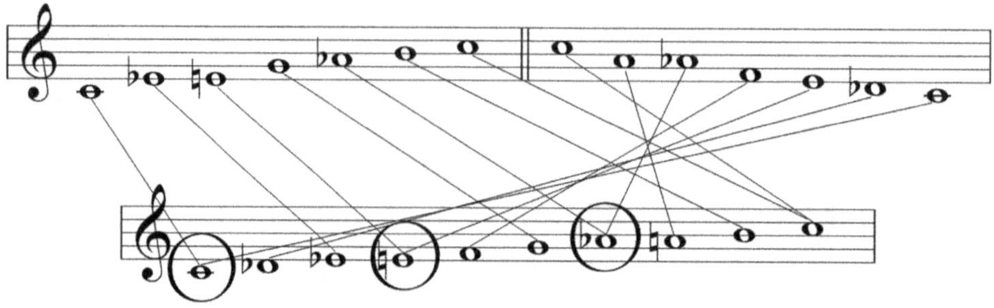

Note that **C, E** and **Ab** are common to both hexachords and that the major third interval between them is the same distance covered by the tetrachord of Mode I.

The nine-step scale, which results from the addition of two major-minor hexachords is therefore based on three interlocking major-minor tetrachords and can have three modes:

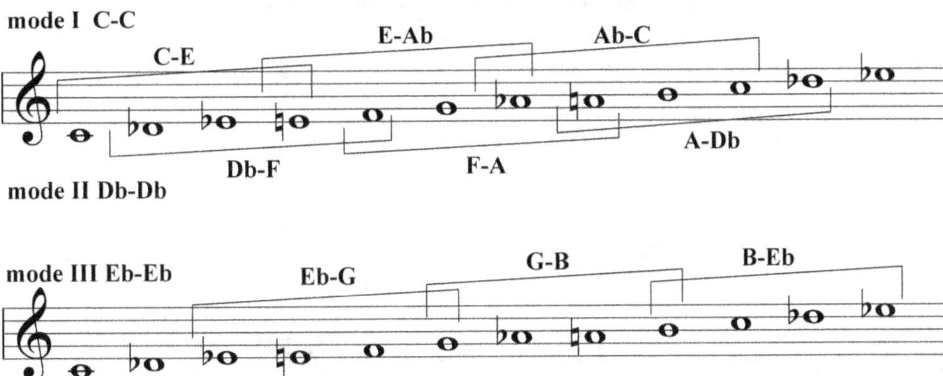

Because the interlocked tetrachords have identical intervals, the nine step major-minor scale can have three points of departure (three tonics) in the same row, which are indicated by changes in notation (not by transposition).

As each nine-step row can have three modes and three tonics for *each* of the modes (differing by notation), this results in a total of 9 nine-step scales for each row: 3 fundamental and 6 derivatives (through change of notation).

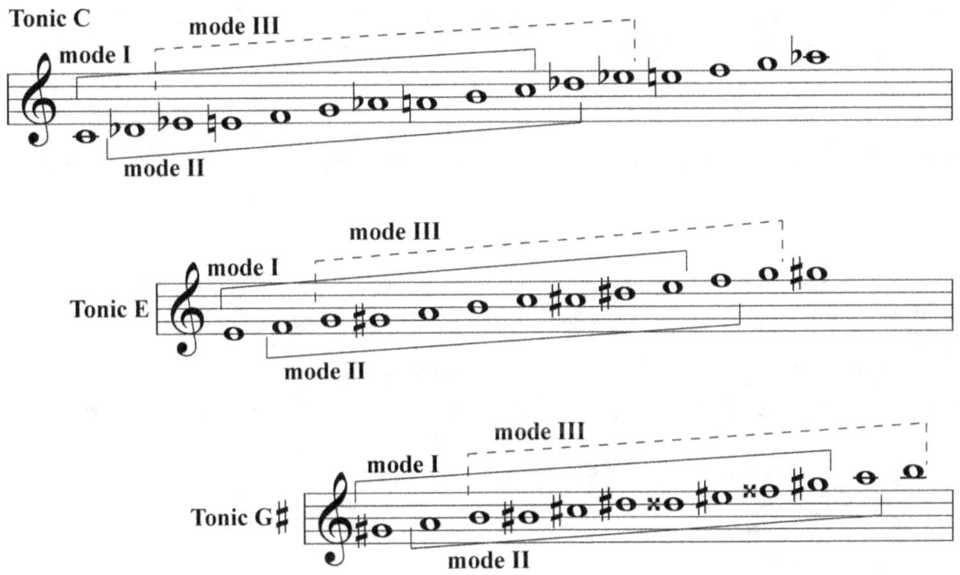

Each nine-step row can be transposed [only] three times in "fixed Doh" terms, [*i. e.*, by a half-step, a whole step, or a step-and-a-half], since any further transposition merely yields a one of the four fundamental rows (or scales), with the tonic (fundamental tone of the start) placed a major third above or below.

There can therefore be 4 fundamental nine-step scales, each with three modes (12 scales altogether) and 8 derivative nine-step scales (obtained by change of notation), each with 3 modes each (24 altogether).

This brings the number of nine-step-scale "tonalities" or modes to 36.

The four fundamental nine-step scales are as follows:
(notation in ascending fifths)

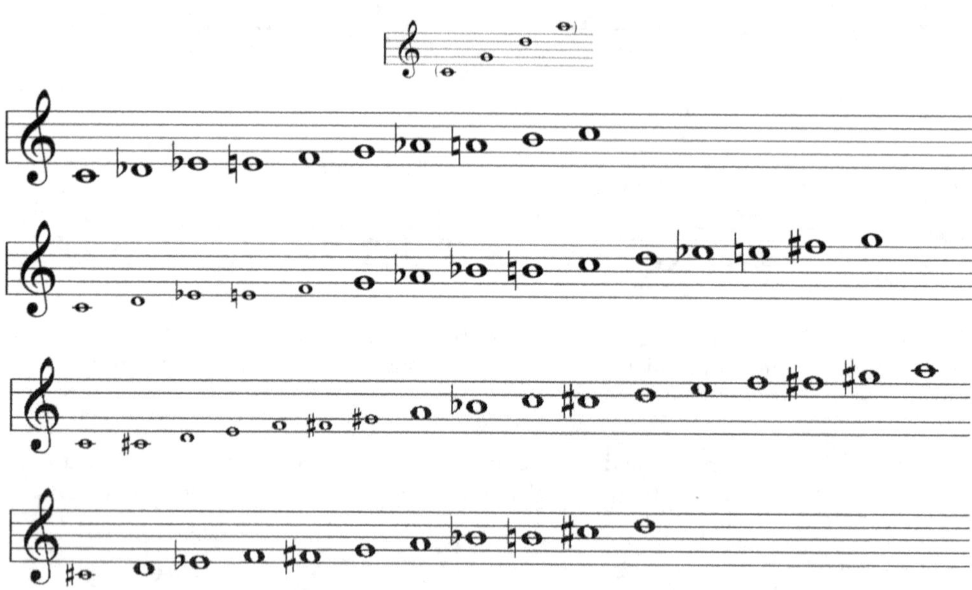

The notation will indicate the position of the point of departure (the tonic) and can be said to indicate the position of the tonal center.

If used in major thirds or minor sixths the scale will keep those intervals *audibly* intact (although some of the thirds will be written as diminished fourths, and some of the sixths will be written as augmented fifths):

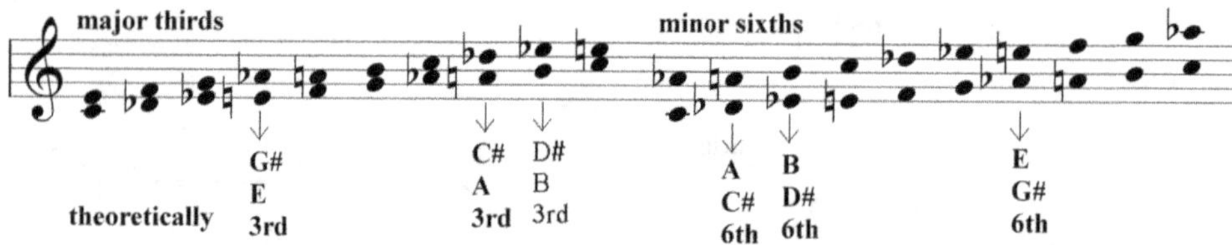

If used in minor thirds or in major sixths, the intervals will *audibly vary* between minor thirds and major seconds (when in thirds) or between major sixths and minor sevenths (when in sixths):

If used in fourths or fifths the intervals will audibly vary between perfect and augmented fourths (when in fourths) or between perfect and diminished fifths (when in fifths).

If used in minor seconds or major sevenths the intervals will vary audibly between major and minor seconds (when in seconds) or major and minor sevenths (when in sevenths).

In arpeggiated form, the nine-step scale can be presented in the following ways:

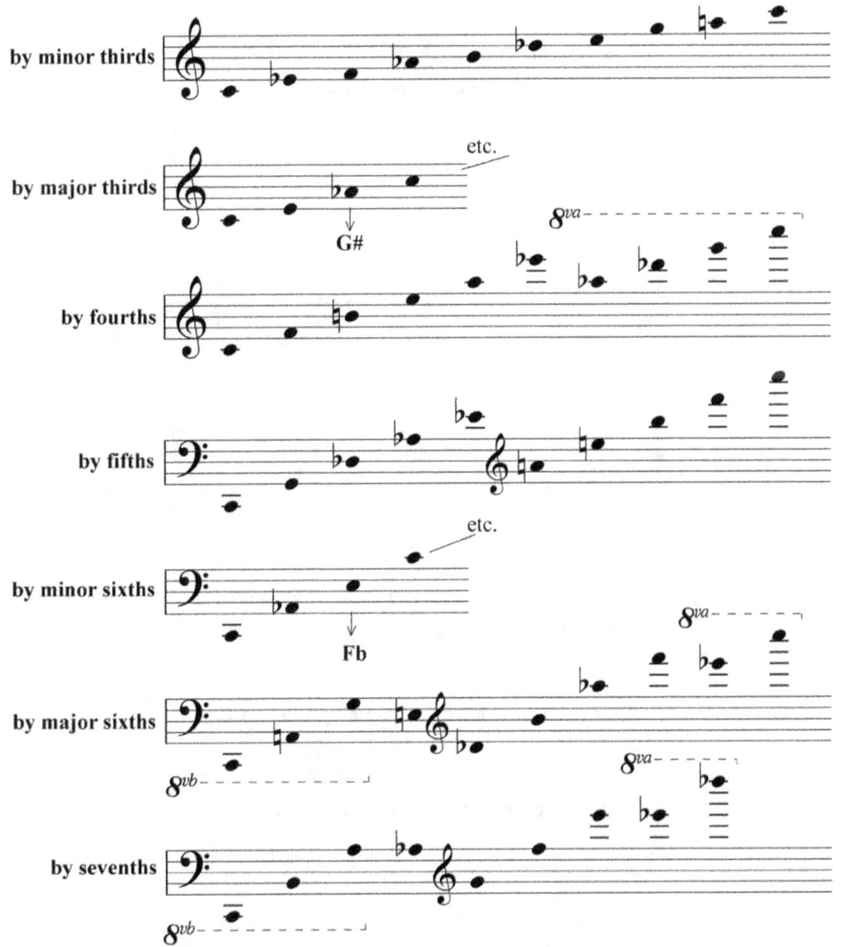

The three-voice nine-step triads
and their inversions

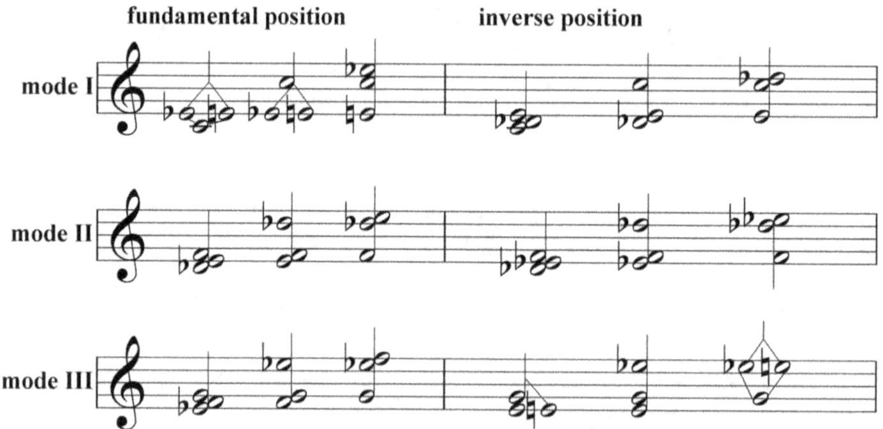

The fundamental perfect chord of nine-step scale harmony is the major-minor tetrachord.

The major-minor tetra/chord
and its inversions:

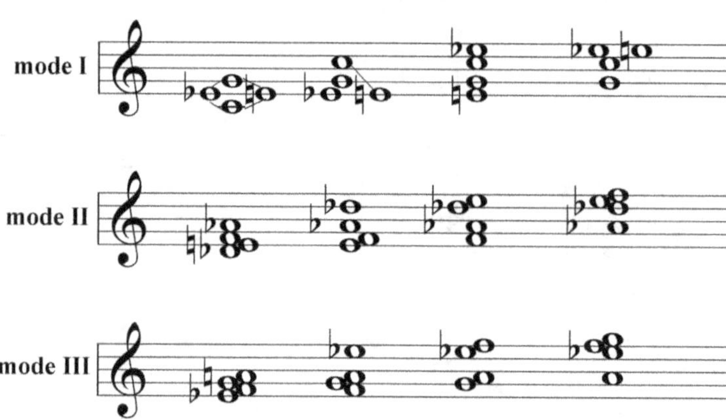

In five-part settings in which the fundamental tetra/chord is considered as stable (and final) any note of the fundamental tetra/chord can be doubled; the penta/chord introduces the element of instability.

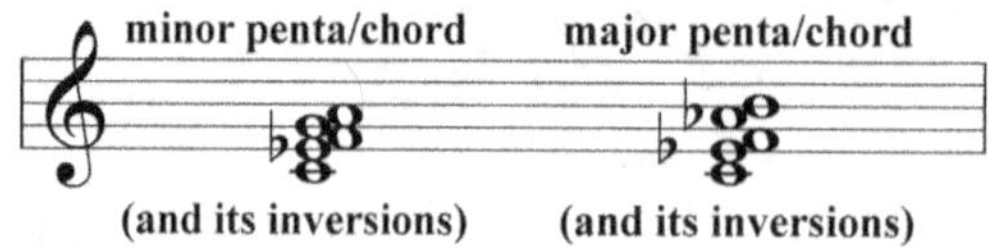

The minor penta/chord is tonal in its "resolution":

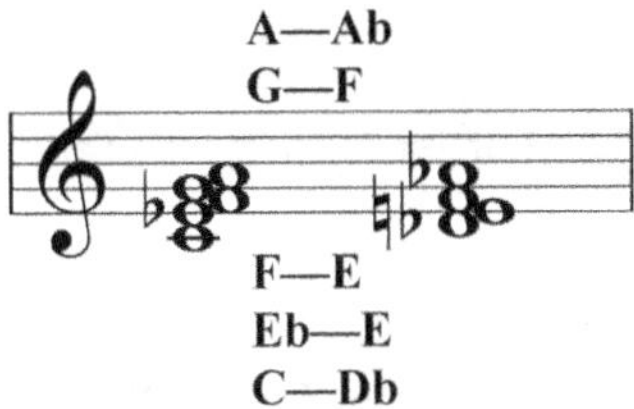

The major penta/chord can effect modulation by nine-step resolutions that arrive at a new tonal center:

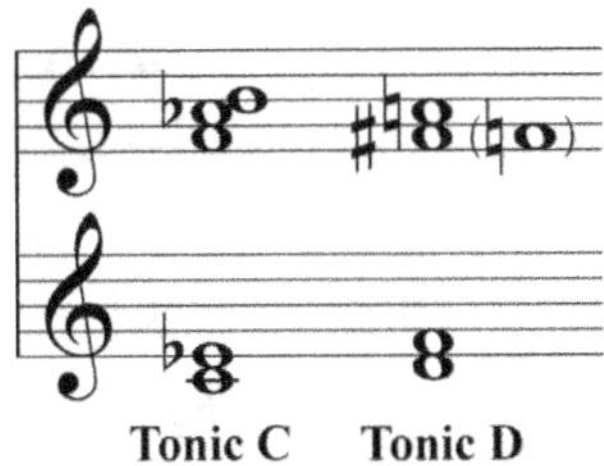

In six-part settings the penta/chord (major or minor) is considered as stable, while the hexa/chord is unstable, finding resolution in a penta/chord, and so on, up to the point at which-in ten-part harmony-the entire nine-step scale becomes a stable chord, with instability provided by an extra tonal appoggiatura (in ten-part settings), two extra appoggiaturas (eleven-part) or three appoggiaturas (twelve-part).

Examples of the hexachord conception of musical speech:

Feuilles libres, Op. 10, No. 2
Nine Inventions, Op. 13
Sonata for Violin and Piano, Op. 14
Six melodies, Op. 15, No. 5
Six études de travail, Op. 21

Nine-step as exclusive tonal basis:

Four Preludes, Op. 24
Canzona, Op. 28
Sonata for Cello and Piano, Op. 29
Sonata for Cello and Piano, Op. 30, No. 1
Four Romances, Op. 31
Concerto da Camera, Op. 33
Trio, Op. 34
Mystere for Cello and Orchestra, Op. 37, No. 2
Training, Op. 37, No. 3
Violoncelle bien tempere (Twelve Preludes for Cello and Piano), Op. 38
Message, Op. 39
Voeux, Op. 39bis
Second Quartet, Op. 40

Magna Mater for Orchestra, Op. 41
Symphony No. 1, Op. 42
Piano Quintet, Op. 44
Hochzeit der Sobeide, opera, Op. 45
Piano Concerto No. 3, Op. 48 (subordinate theme of 1st movement, entire second movement)

**Example of employing the entire nine-step scale as a chord,
and the use of nine tone rows with appoggiatura resolution:**
Symphonic Prayer, Op. 93 (measures 1-43)

II. Interpoint
(punctus inter punctum)

Interpoint can be *vertical* (which is self-explanatory):

Example: Symphony No. 1, third movement

can be *horizontal*:

Example: Symphony No. 1, first movement

N. B. The accented string rhythms coincide with the strong beats of the measure. Woodwinds establish their rhythm on the second 8th-note (horizontal displacement by the value of 1/8). Horns start on the third 8th-note (horizontal displacement by the value of 1/4).

can be *metrical*:

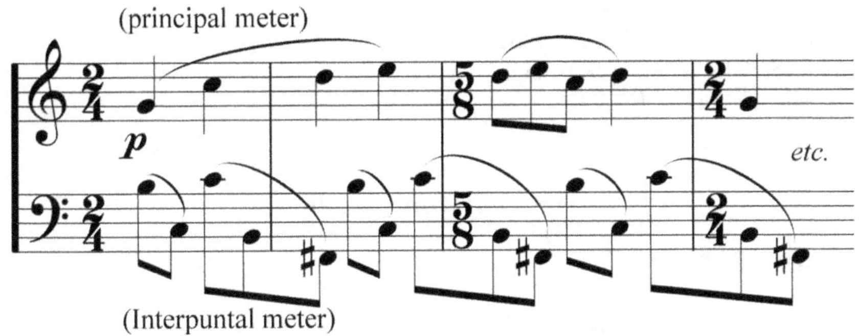

Example: Expressions, Op. 81, No. 10 (Exit)

N. B. Although the patterns coincide vertically, they are of different meters and different lengths.

can consist of various combinations of the three essential trends:

Example: Showcase, Op. 75

Combination of metrical and vertical Interpoint

More complex combinations:

- ▸ 6-part "Formula" (3rd movement of Symphony No. 1, Op. 42)
- ▸ 8-part vertical/horizontal Interpoint (Quintet Op. 44, 2nd movement)[2]

Examples of Interpoint

Twelve Preludes for Cello and Piano, Op. 38 (especially Nos. 2, 4, 7, 10)
Message, Op. 39
Second String Quartet, Op. 40 Quintet, Op. 44
Piano Concerto No. 3, Op. 48
Duo, Op. 49
Chant et refrain, Op. 66 ("refrain")

---

2   Both of these passages are included in Reich. The Symphony is Example R6 a through d, pp. 17-18; the Quintet is Example R4b, p. 12.

Showcase, Op. 75 (especially Nos. 1 and 3)
Expressions, Op. 81
Eight Pieces, Op. 88 (No. 2, Intermezzo, No. 7, Etude)
The Lost Flute, Op. 89 (especially II. The poet's day)
Symphony No. 4 (especially movement II)

III. Pentatonic Scales

a.) Major pentatonic scale and its modes:

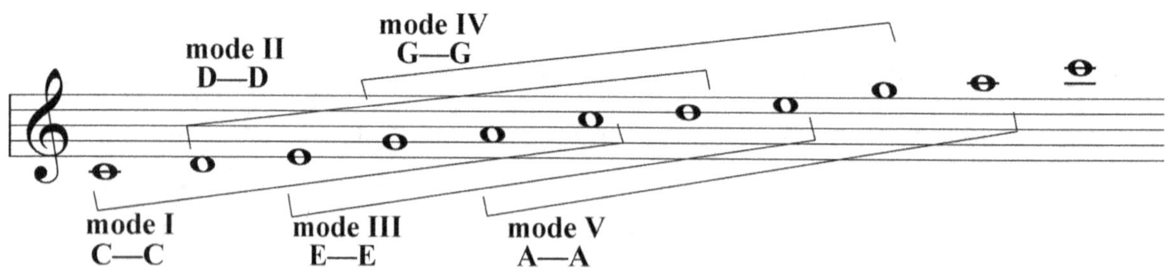

or, if taken from the same tonal center,

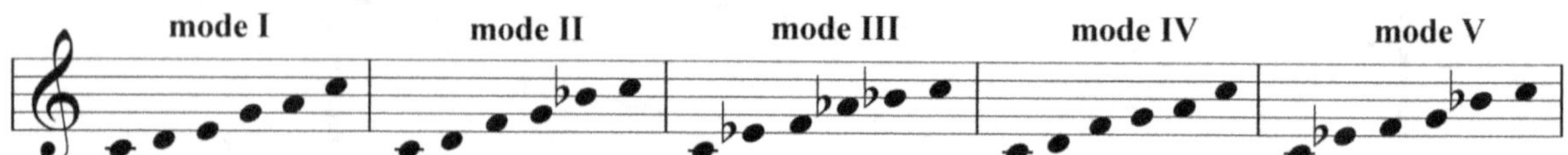

b.) Minor pentatonic scale:

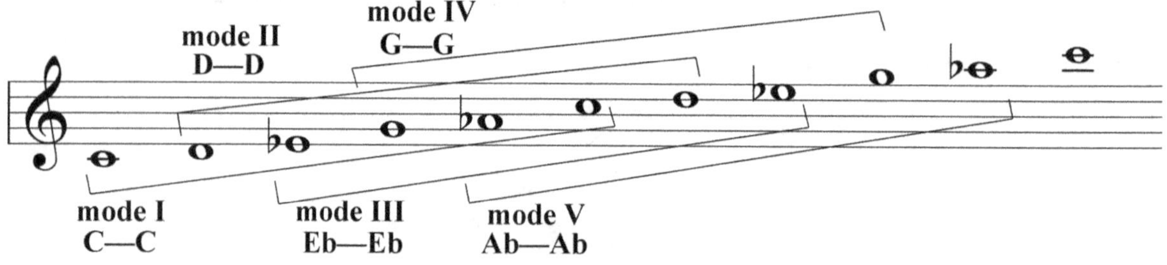

or, if taken from the same tonal center,

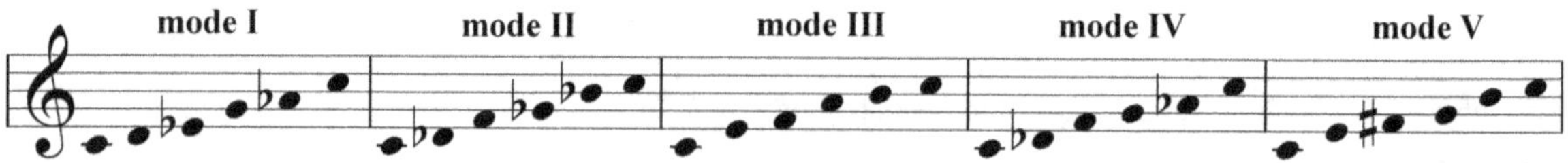

Major pentatonic as chord (constructed by using every second step).

of course, also in 3rd, 4th, 5th and 9 step construction.

Minor pentatonic as chord (constructed by using every second step).

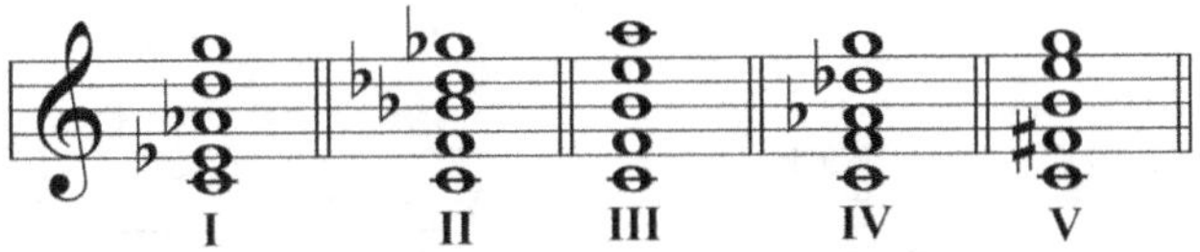

of course, also in 3rd, 4th, 5th and 9 step construction.

Examples of Major Pentatonic

Etude de Piano sur la gamme pentatonique, Op. 51
    No. 1 Premiere Suite
    No. 2 Deuxieme Suite
    No. 3 Bagatelles Chinoises
Five Concert Studies, Op. 52
    Ombres Chinoises
    Luth
    Hommage a la Chine
    Guignol
    Cantique
Techniche Studien auf der pentatonischer Tonleiter, Op. 53
Deux mélodies, Op. 68
Seven Songs on Chinese Poems, Op. 71

Major and Minor Pentatonic

Trepak, Op. 55
Etude No. 7, Op. 56
Flute Trio, Op. 59
The Farmer and the Fairy, Op. 72 (also scale as chord)
Suite for Solo Cello, Op. 76
Fantaisie for Piano and Orchestra, Op. 78
La femme et son ombre, Op. 79
Suite for Orchestra, Op. 87 (third movement)
Symphony No. 3, Op. 83 (beginning of first movement)
The Lost Flute, Op. 89 (beginning)
Elegy Op. 82, No. 1 (stated as chord)

IV. Chromatic Tetrachords

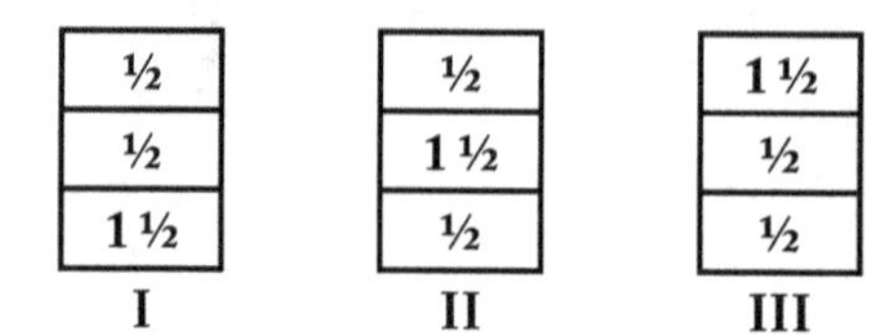

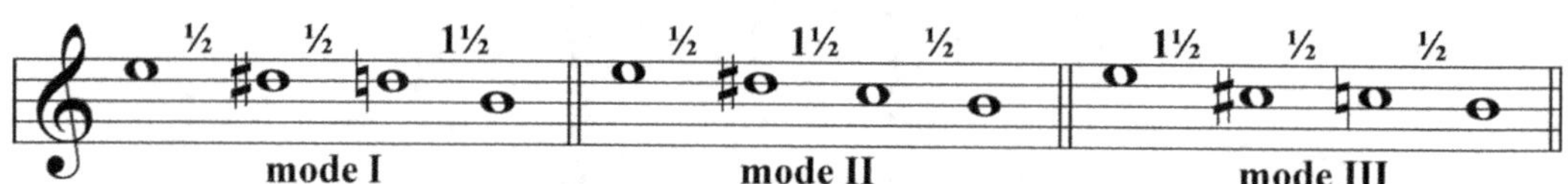

Eight-step scale
constructed from two non-interlocking tetrachords

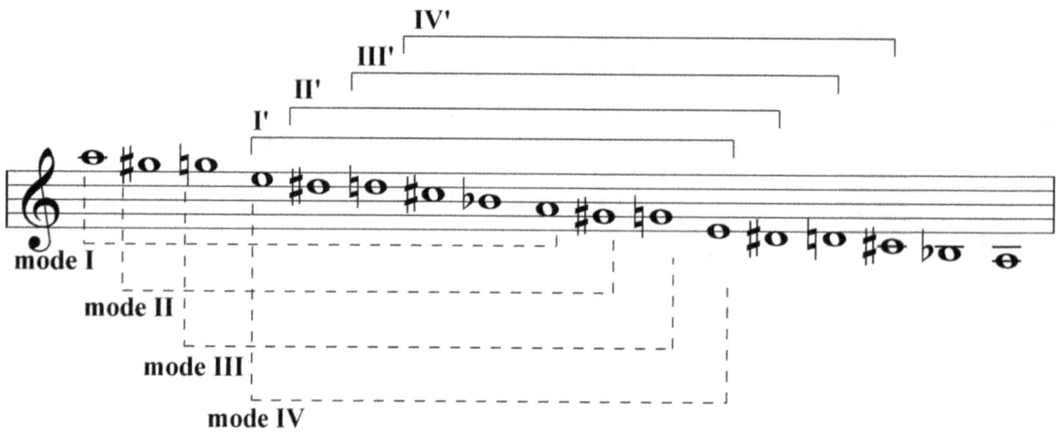

Modes I, II, III and IV differ through the construction (modes) of the tetrachords.
Modes I', II', III' and IV' differ from fundamental modes I, II, III, IV only through pitch.
It is possible to produce a variety of scale construction by combining different modes of the tetrachords.
The fundamental chord would be one of the four tetrachords taken as a chord, and its inversions.

Examples of Tetrachord Construction

Symphony No. 4, Op. 91 (middle section of third movement-taken as a chord)
Partita for Accordion (third movement)
Piano Sonata No. 2, Op. 94 (eight-step scale)

V. Georgian Harmony

Fundamental Georgian triad and its inversions:

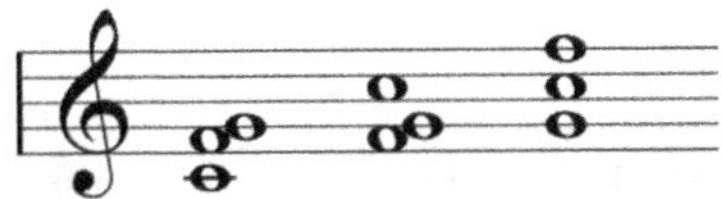

Examples of its use as a tonal basis

Rhapsodie Georgienne for Cello and Orchestra, Op. 25
Suite Georgienne for Piano and Orchestra, Op. 57
Enfance de Sainte Nino, Op. 69
Georgiana, Op. 92

VI. Hard and Soft Intervals, Hard and Soft Harmony

Hard intervals are major and minor sevenths and seconds, also perfect and augmented fourths and perfect and diminished fifths. Soft intervals are major and minor thirds and sixths.

Hard-interval triad and its inversions:

a) Georgian triad

b) hard-triad

Harmony in hard intervals is limited to four parts:

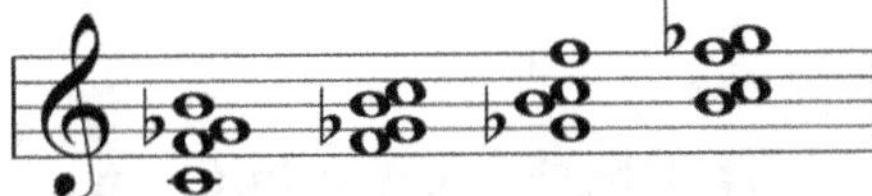

Examples of hard-interval harmony

Piano Concerto No. 3, Op. 48 (exposition of the principal theme)
Suite, Op. 87 (beginning and end of the second movement)
Symphonic Prayer, Op. 93 (second section; also appoggiaturas in hard-interval setting)
Piano Etude Op. 56, No. 4

Alternation of hard- and soft-interval writing

Piano Concerto No. 3, Op. 48

Principal theme of the first movement (hard intervals):

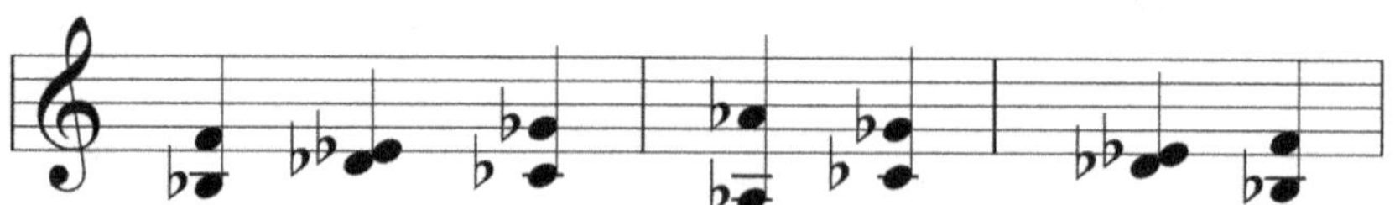

Subordinate theme of the first movement:

Chords built by thirds in nine-step setting

VII. Rhythmic Modulation

Rhythmic modulation: consists of "transposing" one theme into the meter of another theme or vice versa.

Example of rhythmic modulation: Cello Sonata No. 2, Op. 30, No 1, first movement recapitulation. The principal theme is transposed into the meter of the subordinate theme, the subordinate theme into the meter of the principal theme.

Rhythmic stretto: consists of gradually shortening the length of the measure.

Examples:
String Quartet No. 2, Op. 40, first movement—4/4, 3/4, 2/4, 3/8
Quintet, Op. 44, (at the end of the last movement preceding Coda) 4/4, 3/4, 2/4, 3/8, 1/8
Concertino, Op. 47, (first movement, second section)—7/4, 5/4, 3/4, 2/4, 1/4
Symphony No. 1, Op. 42, from 19 —4/4, 3/4, 2/4, 3/8

VIII. Rhythm in its pure form liberated from pitch

Examples:
Message, Op. 39, last measure-the principal motif reduced to its purely rhythmic value
Magna Mater, Op. 41, coda-pure unpitched rhythm (percussion alone)
Symphony No 1, Op. 42-the thematic material of the first movement reduced to its purely rhythmic value and developed on that basis
The Farmer and the Fairy, Op. 72-introduction for unpitched metallic percussion instruments only
The Lost Flute, Op. 89, movement Va) Calamity-pure rhythm for unpitched percussion only

IX. Use of Folklore as musical material

I a) Russian Folklore

Transcriptions Slaves, Op. 27, Nos. 1, 2, 3, 4
Russian Dances for Orchestra, Op. 50 (Russian and Ukrainian themes)
The Legend of Razin, ballet (Russian and Ukrainian themes)
Flute Quartet, Op. 60, third movement (Ukrainian theme)
The Twelve, Op. 75, for Narrator and Chamber Orchestra (quotation of Russian themes)
Ol-Ol, opera, Op. 35 (two themes of Russian student songs)
Suite Populaire Russe [for small orchestra, 1941]
Songs and Dances for Cello and Piano, Op. 84, (No. 3, Ukrainian song; No. 4, Kazakh song)
Suite, Op. 87, last movement Rondo (Russian songs)

b) Russian liturgical chants

Symphony No. 4, Op. 91 (Requiem theme as cantus firmus in last movement).
Symphonic Prayer, Op. 93 (liturgical psalmody in third section)

II a) Georgian Folklore

Rhapsodie Georgienne for Cello and Orchestra, Op. 25
Suite Georgienne for Piano and Orchestra, Op. 57 (themes "transposed" in nine-step setting)
Concertino, Op. 47, last movement (rhythm of Georgian theme used as rhythm for freely invented theme)
Songs and Dances, Op. 84, No. 1
Chota Rostaveli, ballet, Act II
Georgiana, Suite for Orchestra, Op. 92

b) Georgian liturgical chants

> Enfance de Sainte Nino, Op. 69, middle section (psalmody from Georgian liturgy)
> Shamkhaz Venache (Hymn to our Lady) [piano], Op. 82, No. 5 (Georgian medieval chant)

III Armenian Folklore

> Duduki, from the Episodes
> The Legend of Razin, end of Scene 2

IV Tatar Folklore

> Songs and Dances, Op. 84, No. 2

V Czech Folklore

> Chanson tcheque, Op. 27, No. 5

VI Chinese Folklore

> Punch and Judy, Op. 52, No. 4 Chant (liturgical), Op. 52, No. 5

VII Japanese Folklore

> Flute Trio, Op. 61, last movement (theme of Tokyo Ondo)
> La Femme et son ombre, Op. 74 (theme of Etentuku, theme of Tokyo Ondo)

VIII Birdcalls used as material

> Sonata No. 1 for Cello and Piano, Op. 29, (1924) last movement
> Entretiens, Op. 46, No. 10
> Expressions, Op. 81, No. 9

IX Insect rhythms and calls

> Duo, Op. 49, fourth movement

X Rhythm of the spoken word used as foundation for thematic material

> Entretiens, Op. 46, No. 4
> Enfance de Sainte Nino, Op. 69, middle section
> Sonatina for Timpani and Piano, Op. 58, third movement Expressions, Op. 81, No. 2

X. Some observations

1. The origins of the nine-step scale.
   Since my early youth I had the tendency and the urge to combine major and minor chords. Only a major-minor tetra/ chord gave me the sensation of finality and of stability. Then gradually I extended the 1½-tone ½-tone 1½-tone row further to reach the octave. By adding the ascending hexachord with the descending one I found the nine-step scale which evidently guided me instinctively before I started to theorize it (the first appearance of the nine-step scale is in the Romantic Sonatine, Op. 4, composed in 1918, while the conscious theorization of it came only in 1922 after the theorizing of hexachords that started around 1920.

2. Twelve Preludes for Cello and Piano, Op. 38 (1925-1926) are written in the complete circle of the 12 nine-step [tonalities]. I called it "Violoncelle bien tempere" to underline the equality of flats and sharps which is characteristic of the nine-step scale.

3. Quite early in my life I had the urge to use pure rhythm liberated from any pitch. The first application of it was the reduction of the principal theme (motif) to its purely rhythmic value at the end of *Message*, Op. 39: the pianist has to beat it on the wood of the piano. A far more elaborate application of this urge for pure rhythm is in the second movement of the First Symphony (1927) which is for percussion alone. Here the thematic material of the first movement is reduced to its purely rhythmic value.

4. The "folklore" of bird calls, of insects ("Katy did Katy didn't" etc.)— the sounds of nature, the rhythm of the spoken word-always had fascination for me. I started to use bird calls as musical material as early as 1924-the two themes of the last movement of my First Cello Sonata, Op. 29 (1924) are the calls of a "merle des roches" that I heard in Monte Carlo and "transposed" into the nine-step scale.
    The insects (fourth movement of the Duo) I heard during early autumn nights in Islip, Long Island, in the twenties. I have used the rhythm of the spoken word on many occasions. The third movement of the Sonatina for Timpani and Piano uses the prosody of the "Pater Noster" recited in Russian.

5. At the end of the twenties I embraced the so-called "Eurasian" ideology, which is based on the idea that the Russian "Empire" inherited the empire founded by the Mongols, [with the result] that Mongols became assimilated with Russians (or vice versa). The opera *Hochzeit der Sobeide* and the Concertino, Op. 47, [reflected] this ideology. Then, after a visit to Egypt and Palestine where I looked for the familiar Orient came the Third Piano Concerto, [along with] the Duo that I baptized as No. 1 of *Cahiers Eurasiens*.

6. Eurasian ideology helped me [to escape from] the technicalities of my musical thinking which [had] culminate[d] in the Quintet, Op. 44 (1927). Yet [my approach] was still quite complex [in the period when] I was looking for simplification and renewal of my technical vocabulary.

7. Such simplification and renewal came via Folklore. I felt that, what the anatomy of the human body is for a painter-folklore is for a composer. The anatomy of the human body gives the lines of "life survival." Every great painter has studied it-Michelangelo, Leonardo, Delacroix, Picasso-each one used it for his purposes (Picasso for abstract construction). [Similarly], Folklore gives us the lines of "musical survival." Operating with themes from Folklore, composers work with eternal material which they can use for any purpose.

8. My "cure" by Folklore started with the Russian Dances, Op. 50; then continued in China and Japan, where I became fascinated by the instrumental, theatrical and vocal heritage of the Orient; then returned to Georgian Folklore: as there is a saying "proletarians of the world, unite!"-I would say that the Folklore of all countries and all races have the same eternal value.
    In my ballet *Trepak*, which I composed in 1937 on my return from China, I used musical themes from Russian Folklore that are pentatonic and treated them in a Chinese way.

9. There was a great decline in the quality of my production during the war years. To live through the occupation was not easy and I had to compose lots of trash-for dancers, for music halls, etc.- which had to be signed [with a *nom de plume*] because I was Russian. This helped *me* survive, but little of this war production of mine survived.

10. Immediately after the end of the occupation, even before the end of the war, my fertility returned. In one single summer (1945) I composed the cantata *Pan Kéou* in the Chinese idiom (which was produced at the Paris Opera for the celebration of the Chinese Double X), *The Twelve*, and the ballet *Déjeuner sur l'herbe*; then during the autumn and winter-*Jeu de la Nativité*, *Showcase*, and the ballet *Chota Rostaveli*.

11. The great change in my life occurred in 1949 when I came to live in the USA in Chicago; especially during the time between 1950-1958 during which I did not leave the USA. Numerous commissions gave birth to orchestral compositions. I orchestrated the Second Symphony, produced the Third using some older materials, then- Divertimento; Fourth Symphony.

12. The new musical language which I now used to express myself in larger orchestral forms synthesized all the technical devices of the past-which I outlined in [the previous pages]-and became combined with new research in form.

13. I see the profession of composer as a mission: a mission to serve the community to which he belongs, which stimulates him, in the first place, to give back to human beings what he receives from them, shaping it in the form of a work of art. When I say "serve" I do not mean to play down; on the contrary, to serve the community by art is to guide the community, just as a priest guides his congregation.

14. A work of art (a composition) as I see it must directly project the message it contains. Only if it communicates is it worth examining later on to [determine its principles of] "order," which are the technical means that the composer has used.

15. The technical devices employed by the composer can never be a goal in themselves, but only the means to express the message.

16. Above all is the imagination. Then comes personal taste that chooses among the products of imagination and after this the technical means that put in order the things imagined.

17. There are no "neutral" technical means. Each new idea needs new means, or extension of means.

18. So it is like building a house, extending it in all directions. Never reject what one had, but always add.

19. The greater the ideas-the larger the form.
A large form cannot be filled up by extension of small ideas.

20. It is the Form and not the musical language that makes a composition long living. Every musical language becomes outdated sooner or later, but the message expressed by it in adequate form survives.

21. I do not believe in the so-called music of "tomorrow." The music that fully expresses "today"-which can be identified with the aims and with the cultural state of human beings in the community to which the composer belongs-is the music that may survive, by "fixing" a "memento" of the life of humanity.

22. Music is a construction in time: so many minutes of time put in order and "fixed" by the composer.

23. The reason why people like to listen to pieces of music heard before that projected [meaning to] them is a kind of "nostalgia" for the past.

24. Music is [a] uniting [of] people; [that] is its ultimate goal: its ultimate raison d'etre is to make people feel united by contributing-[either] actively, in performing, or emotionally, in attending a performance of a work of art.

New York, January 10, 1962

❀　❀　❀　❀　❀

ALEXANDER TCHEREPNIN:
A COMPENDIUM

PART III:

EPISODES
AND
EPILOGUE

BOOK I: BIOGRAPHICAL

PART THREE: EPISODES AND EPILOGUE

INTRODUCTION

The five biographical "episodes" included here, drawn from a series of longer essays by Lily Chou, have a special authority. Large portions of them closely paraphrase the composer's own narrative accounts. All statements in which attitudes, frames of mind or emotions are described are founded in Tcherepnin's own words. For these revised versions, the editor examined Tcherepnin's autobiographical accounts, adding direct quotations where appropriate, and also providing amplifications-notably the passages involving Tcherepnin's first marriage (a subject Ms. Chou had not broached in her essays).

The epilogue is an essay by Phillip Ramey, which originally appeared in the May 1984 edition of *Ovation* magazine. It is perhaps the best balanced of all the short pieces on Tcherepnin, giving requisite attention to both biographical and artistic details. His overview of Tcherepnin's output is informed by valuable historical insights and a notably original critical perspective.

❀　❀　❀　❀　❀

TCHEREPNIN PRELUDE

Any composer is influenced by his place of birth. If I had been born in, say, Timbuktu, or in the South Seas, I probably would have composed music for drums or howling. But it so happened that I was born in the town that was called at my birth St. Petersburg, and I was surrounded by the musicians and the people there....

My father was Greek Orthodox, my mother the daughter of a French emigré— she was Catholic but her mother was Protestant—and as a child I went to three churches: to the Russian church with papa, to the Catholic church with mama, and to the Protestant church to please my grandmama. Similarly, I was exposed to the three Russian composers: I heard Rimsky, Glazunov and Prokofiev, and, as you can guess, my choice was Prokofiev.

I. THE TCHEREPNINS OF RUSSIA

The Tcherepnin family originated in Isborsk, an old Russian town in the administrative district of Pskov. Sometime in the early nineteenth century, Pyotr Tcherepnin—Alexander's great-grandfather—left his home town and established himself in St. Petersburg, former capital of the Russian Empire. As far as can be ascertained, he was in State service. His son, Nicolai Petrovitch Tcherepnin, the grandfather of Alexander, was born in St. Petersburg and became a prominent doctor of medicine. His specialty was skin diseases, and he was the inventor of a soap which had a milk base. This much-touted "Soap of Dr. Tcherepnin," was believed by experts to be genuinely beneficial to the skin. Alexander later wrote, "I still remember that it was packed in a rather thick paper with a picture of a brown cow and a background of green prairie and trees." He also remembered that "the clients of my grandfather belonged mostly to the capital's 'intelligentsia.' Dostoevsky was one of them, and my grandfather had the sorrow to [attend] the dying writer till his last moments." Through one of his colleagues, a Dr. Golovin, Dr. Tcherepnin was introduced to Mussorgsky. He recounted to his family that he remembered well having heard Mussorgsky playing and singing scenes from *Boris Godounov* at the home of Dr. Golovin.

Alexander Tcherepnin remembered his grandfather, who died when he was five or six, as being white-bearded, nearly deaf, and infinitely kind.

The first wife of his grandfather (and mother of his father) was Zinaida Rataieff. The Rataieff family came from Yaroslavl, one of the oldest Russian towns on the Volga. While giving birth to Alexander's father, Nicolai Tcherepnin, on May 3rd, 1873, Zinaida died from gynecological complications. His grandfather later married Olga Sergeovna Ivanchinzova, who came of a prominent family from Pskov; she was related to Field Marshal Souvoroff and was close to the Imperial Court. This marriage was blessed with five children. Olga tried to be as loving to Nicolai as if he were her own son, yet his super-sensitive nature made him feel that the other children had more right to her motherly affection.

Nicolai was initiated into the world of music by an aunt on his father's side, Olympiada Petrovna Tcherepnin. A competent amateur musician, she owned a Schroeder grand piano and gave the boy regular lessons. Later, at St. Petersburg's Sixth Gymnasium, an institution which was both grammar and high school, Nicolai was taught piano by Professors Schischkin and Demiansky and introduced to Wagner's operas and Liszt's symphonic poems by the gifted German maestro Zikke, conductor at the city's Imperial Opera Theater.

In compliance with his father's wishes, Nicolai completed a law degree at St. Petersburg University in 1895. By that time, however, he was also studying composition at the city's Conservatory with Rimsky-Korsakov. In those days a single teacher led the student from the beginning to the end of his studies: one year was spent on harmony, one year on counterpoint, one year on fugue, and at least one year on so-called "free composition." Alexander Tcherepnin wrote, "Rimsky-Korsakov was an inspiration for his students and responsible for the formation of more than one generation of Russian composers. While the self-imposed academicism of his teaching gave [his] students a solid basis, his own compositions opened… new ways and new horizons [for them]. Some of his students-like A. K. Glazunov—[chose] academicism, some others—like Stravinsky—embraced the new way. My father, at first 'tamed' by the academic approach, [decided] to reject it later on. If his early compositions were somehow under the influence of Rimsky as a teacher, his later compositions were influenced by Rimsky as a composer, until he... found his own way."

Nicolai became a favorite of Rimsky-Korsakov's and conducted the first performance of Rimsky's opera *Coq d'Or* in St. Petersburg.

Alexander was an impressionable nine-year-old when, in 1908, he saw the bearded figure of Rimsky for the last time. It was just a few months before the great man's death, when he came to bid a fond farewell to Nicolai Tcherepnin at the railway station in St. Petersburg. Nicolai was on his way to Paris to supervise a performance of Rimsky's *Snegurotchka* (*The Snow-maiden*) at the Opéra Comique.

During the first decade of the twentieth century, musical life in Russia was dynamic. The influence that Mussorgsky and, to a certain extent, Rimsky, had exercised on Debussy and on the "debussyists" was now ricocheting back to Russia, and making Impressionism a medium particularly dear to progressive Russian composers. At the same time, untouched by the French influence, Arensky and Rachmaninoff continued the traditions of Tchaikovsky, while Scriabin appealed to the musical intelligentsia with his metaphysical theories and obsessive harmonic research. After the death of Rimsky-Korsakov, the composer's other favorite student, Glazunov, was generally looked upon as his successor and the guardian of his principles. Nicolai Tcherepnin, and later on Stravinsky, sought the continuation of their master's ideas along more progressive lines.

Nicolai and Glazunov generally disagreed about policy at the Conservatory, but Nicolai persevered in several innovations. He founded and taught a conducting class, and here students such as Sergei Prokofiev and Nicolai Malko gained practical experience by conducting a conservatory orchestra whose members included, at one time or another, Jascha Heifetz, Mischa Elman and Nathan Milstein. When Alexander finally entered the conservatory, he would sometimes play timpani in this orchestra.

In 1909, Nicolai Tcherepnin was engaged by Sergei Diaghilev to conduct the celebrated season of Russian Opera and Ballet in Paris that was to make such a deep impact on artistic developments in Western Europe. Young Alexander accompanied his parents abroad on this and other Diaghilev tours. Later, he would recollect with nostalgic affection his attendance in 1909 of the first "Russian Season" in Paris which included Rimsky's *Pskovitanka* (with Chaliapin) under his father's baton, and Nicolai's ballet *Pavillon d'Armide* (with Karsavina and Nijinsky). It was in fact the enormous success of this ballet that launched the *Ballets Russes* into international fame and won it return Paris engagements. Another Nicolai Tcherepnin ballet, *Narcisse*, enjoyed comparable success when Diaghilev produced it at Monte Carlo in 1911. Returning to Russia after his numerous tours, Nicolai discovered that the French direction of his compositions had earned him the sobriquet of "Ravelevich."

On Alexander's maternal side, the family was anything but Russian. His mother, Marie Benois, was the daughter of the famous water-color painter Albert Benois, who painted the portraits of the last Tsar and the Imperial family, and the celebrated concert pianist Maria Kind, a favorite student of Leschetizky. The Benois family emigrated to Russia from France after the French Revolution and Napoleonic Wars. Many of the Benois became famous in Russia as architects and painters. Among these was Nicolai Benois, who designed the main terminal of the first great railway in Russia which linked St. Petersburg to Moscow.

Albert Benois, the maternal grandfather of Alexander, had several distinguished brothers. One of them was Louis, the director of the Imperial Fine Arts Academy; another, Nicolai, a general in the Russian Army; yet another, Alexander, the celebrated painter and scholar, who, during his association with Diaghilev, designed the scenery for Stravinsky's *Petrushka* and Nicolai Tcherepnin's *Pavillon d'Armide*.

Alexander Tcherepnin always retained vivid memories of his boyhood years at No. 15 Torgovaya Street, where the Tcherepnins occupied a spacious third floor apartment between 1907 and 1918. After decades abroad, he was still able to pen a detailed description of his native city as he had known it in his formative years:

> The town in which I was born was called, at that time, St. Petersburg. It was not an old town. Peter the Great had founded it in 1703. It is situated on the delta of the Neva, a river that flows from Lake Ladoga to the Finnish Bay. The river, deep and wide, is about 50 miles long. It flows majestically, and where it nears the bay, it divides into two wide branches, the actual Neva and the Nevka (little Neva), and a smaller, third branch, Fontanka. Many canals are built along these branches.
>
> The city is built mostly on islands between these waterways, with only a small part standing on the mainland. Most of the ground is of a swampy nature, but there are some rocks of granite here and there. Early foreign travellers nicknamed the capital the "Northern Venice" and the "New Amsterdam." Peter the Great called it "A Window into Europe" and turned to the West for progress in his country. Like a child who believes that his mother is the most beautiful woman in the world, I felt that St. Petersburg was the most beautiful town on earth. And even after decades of absence, after having traveled the world and seen places of renown and beauty, it still gives me infinite pleasure to recollect the different aspects of St. Petersburg that have stayed engraved in my memory.
>
> What comes to my mind first? Perhaps the large Nikolaievsky Bridge, with a chapel in the middle. How nice it was to look from this bridge during the summer months on the flowing river and to see the small passenger steamboats busily crossing the water in all directions, and to wonder at the large white Swedish steamships moored alongside the piers, or the wheel-steamships sailing to the fortress of Kronstadt, and the cruisers and torpedo boats of the Imperial Navy anchored in the middle of the river.
>
> It was equally pleasant to look from the bridge during the winter months when the Neva was frozen solid for half the year. The large space, a tremendous white field, looked like a playground. An electric tramcar line was built from one side of the river to the other. Many wide roads crossed this expanse where one could either ride on a slide-chair pushed by a driver on skates or, alternatively, ski or skate.
>
> Then in the late spring, a few weeks after the sun had melted away the Neva ice, it became a gateway for the frozen waters of Lake Ladoga, driven by the current towards the Finnish Bay. They came in ice-blocks of all dimensions, and sometimes one could see animals travelling on such blocks-bears, deer, foxes-jumping from one block to another, moving or sitting half-frozen and looking sternly ahead.

The principal thoroughfare of the town was Nevsky Prospect. It was a large avenue, many miles long, running from the Nikolaievsky Railway Station towards the Neva. Gogol has described the life and animation on this avenue in his novel[la] *Nevsky Prospect*. Business, officialdom, romance could all be found here, and it was certainly the principal melting-pot for all elements of the population.

When I think of the Russian crowd, as I recall from the experience of my youth, the most particular expression it seemed to wear was one of humility. Whenever men of all classes approached a church, be it on foot, or in a coach or streetcar, they would take their hats off and cross themselves out of respect to God.

The soldiers saluted not only military officials but anyone in uniform. It appeared to me as if everybody in the street felt inferior to the next person. The motto was: "Excuse me for living." This humility was not only reserved for the underprivileged. Just as a peasant walking in the streets of the capital assumed an expression which seemed to say, "excuse me for being a peasant," a rich, well-dressed person seemed to say, "excuse me for being rich," and a nobleman, "excuse me for being noble." Is it that my memory paints it all in Utopian colors? Or is it that the people of my country, through centuries of enslavement, whether by the Mongols or the Tsars, or by religion, were brought up and educated to feel unworthy and inferior?

It was in the house on Torgovaya Street that Alexander's musical and artistic character was formed. A number of the short pieces that he composed there (the *bloshki*) were later published. Although he was receiving no formal training as a composer, he was able to learn much by emulating his father. Alexander may, indeed, have been "a composer by the grace of God," as his father termed him, but there is no doubt that he was deeply influenced by the daily musical environment in his boyhood household. He watched how Nicolai composed, heard the incubation of creativity through improvisation at the piano: how, from the uncertain and disconnected musical material at the beginning, came the formation of a cohesive musical composition. He saw him writing it all down. He saw how, as a result of many attempts at the piano, an orchestral score was created. At night he would often fall asleep to the sounds of the operas of Rimsky-Korsakov, such as *The Snow-maiden* (which he loved), *Sadko* and *Coq d'Or*, or perhaps it might be Borodin's *Prince Igor* or the ballets of his father, not to mention the orchestral works of the Russian composers which his father studied at the piano or played for the guests.

The first opera he ever saw was Glinka's *A Life for the Tsar*. At that early stage, his favorite pastime was composing operas: the first of them was written to a text by Kozma Prutkoff and bore the unlikely title *Discussion of Ancient Greek Philosophers on Beauty*. Soon after this came a five-act opera, *The Death of Ivan the Terrible*, based on a drama by Alexei Tolstoi. For dramatic effect, at the moment of the Tsar's death, the boy threw a large metal plate on the floor which produced the most infernal sound. Of course his parents, being absent, were not aware of the racket, but one day he received a personal note from the retired admiral who lived in the flat below. This neighbor-none other than Ippolit Tchaikovsky, the brother of the famous composer-wrote as follows: "Dear Sasha, I am ill and bed-ridden. Have pity on an old, sick man and stop your improvisations for a while. Your piano practicing, however, I am able to stand."

It was only after receiving a note of thanks from I. I. Tchaikovsky expressing appreciation for the silence, announcing his restoration to health, and inviting the budding composer to resume his improvisations that Sasha dared to continue-shyly at first-his research at the piano. Next, he composed a very long opera based on Maikoff's drama *Two Worlds*, which depicted the sufferings and martyrdom of the early Christians in Rome. When this was finished, his mother bound it in a large volume, and he was quite proud of the sheer dimension of it. The last and (as he remembered it) perhaps the most elaborate of these operas was *Tsarevitch Malish*, for which he also fashioned the libretto from a fairy tale of Sergei Gorodezky, a contemporary Russian poet whom he greatly admired.

Then came the ballets. Tales by E. T. A. Hoffmann, by Anatole France, by Edgar Allan Poe served as plots which exalted his imagination. Those were followed by symphonies, one after another, fully composed and orchestrated-and none of them intended for performance.

Even as Sasha was finishing his secondary education and preparing to enter the conservatory, momentous events were afoot. One morning, in the last days of February 1917, he took his usual stroll from Torgovaya Street along the English Prospect to Pokrov Square and caught the number 14 streetcar, getting off at Tchernyshev Pereulok in order to walk to the Gymnasium via the Tchernyshev Bridge. But after only a few classes, officials closed school and told the mystified students to go home. The sun was shining, so Sasha decided walk past the Alexander Theatre towards the Finnish Station, crossing the Neva. Before the theater he saw a great gathering of people clustered around a group of agitators, who had decapitated a policeman and were displaying the bloody head on a spear. Suddenly, shouts were heard: "The Cossacks!" And indeed a detachment of mounted Cossacks was approaching. Everyone went into hiding. There were whispered rumors that the revolution had started. An exhilarating feeling of solidarity and fraternity was in the air.

A few days later these "absurd" rumors proved to be true. The Tsar had abdicated, along with his son, handing over the throne to his brother Michael, who in turn, abdicated for the benefit of the people. A temporary government was formed, then a council of delegates of the workers and soldiers was convoked. The Tsarist regime tumbled like a house of cards. What generations of Russians had hoped for, fought for all their lives, had finally become a reality. Russia was free. Young Tcherepnin's joy was unbounded… to live in a free Russia whose yoke of centuries, created by autocracy, was at long last broken. The fate of Russia was now in the hands of the liberated Russian people.

Alexander and his family spent that summer at Sudak in the Crimea-their annual vacation spot since 1913-in his Aunt Camille's home. Nicolai's hospitable composer-friend Spendiarov had a nearby dacha, and frequently invited the Tcherepnins over for music making. Spendiarov had grown more and more interested in young Alexander's music and was encouraging his performing and composing pursuits.

Sudak was an extremely favorable composing site for the two Tcherepnins. Here, in the course of two years, Nicolai wrote one of his most important works, the Sinfonietta, and in the summer of 1917 he worked on his ballet *The Tale of the Tsarevna Ulyba* along with such songs as "The Far-away Worlds." In Sudak Alexander composed a ballet, *Daucus Morkov* (*Carrots*), and several piano pieces including, in the summer of 1917, a Scherzo for two pianos that was later published by Durand in Paris in a version for piano solo. In August 1917, after taking leave of the Spendiarovs "until next summer," they left Sudak-never to see it again.

The winter of 1917-18 was one of severe privation in Petrograd. Surrounded by foreign and White Russian armies, the city was deprived of its food supply. Alexander fell ill with scurvy. That spring, totally unexpectedly, his father received an invitation to be director of the Tiflis Conservatory on a three-year contract. During the summer, the family hastily disposed of their belongings for a mere trifle. All this was quite inexplicable to the young Tcherepnin. His father, at 45, was at the peak of his fame. His compositions were widely performed, especially his songs. During the Revolution of 1905 his choral work "Do not weep over the corpses of the slain fighters," to the words of Palma, had become a kind of hymn, performed on occasions of commemoration or burial of the heroes of the revolution. This made him a person near and dear to the masses. His position at the Conservatory was excellent and, on Glazunov's imminent retirement, Nicolai had every chance of being elected the Conservatory's next director. Why then, under all these conditions, did Nicolai choose to leave Petrograd? The famine? But who could guarantee that it would be better in Tiflis, remote capital of the impoverished Georgian province? His irrevocable decision to leave the metropolis was seen in the relentless liquidating of his most-prized earthly possessions, collected over a lifetime.

Owing to the difficulties in travelling through German-occupied Ukraine, it was impossible to take along any heavy luggage. Nicolai packed some of his most cherished manuscripts; his wife brought some letters from her friends; Alexander took the manuscripts of most of his sonatas, hundreds of "fleas," some songs, and a score that Prokofiev had liked long ago. All these, together with clothes for the entire family and, for some inexplicable reason, bed linen, were crammed into just two medium-sized suitcases. And so it was, on July 19, 1918, that the Tcherepnin family departed from famine-stricken, cholera-ridden Petrograd. Years later, Alexander could still remember buying a newspaper at the train station and learning of the fatal shooting of the Imperial family at Ekaterinburg. Meanwhile they made their way to Tiflis by train and military transport boat, along the route of which their eyes would occasionally light upon the scattered carcasses of horses and the still-visible traces of recent battles. Little did Nicolai and Maria realize that nearly half a century would pass before Alexander returned to Russia—that they themselves would never see their homeland again.

II. THE LONG JOURNEY WEST

Between the years 1918 and 1922, Russia was torn apart by civil war. Soon after the fall of Tiflis in February 1921, Georgia was taken over by the Red Army. Faced with uncertainty of ever again being appointed as director of the Georgia Conservatory, threatened with insubordination in the opera theater where he was conductor, confounded by economic chaos and famine, Nicolai Tcherepnin yearned for Paris. He had received a letter of invitation from a composer-banker friend, Alexander Wyschnegradsky, who had himself emigrated to Paris. Enclosed with the letter was a check for 600 francs, which would partly cover transportation costs for the family. Another of Nicolai's friends also wrote from Paris, promising to publish Nicolai's works. Diaghilev, too, had stayed abroad. Nicolai's long-time admirer, Anna Pavlova, who had commissioned several ballets from him, had also emigrated to Paris, as had Fokine. Not surprisingly, Nicolai anticipated a pleasurable artistic collaboration with his former colleagues, remembering with keen joy his pre-war successes in Western Europe with Diaghilev's *Ballets Russes*, and looking forward to reunions with his numerous friends abroad.

And so, on the day of the Annunciation on March 25, 1921, Tcherepnin's father went to see Meliton Balanchivadze-Commissar of Art of the Georgian Republic and father of George Balanchine—and said: "According to a Russian tradition, on this day people release birds and set them free. Please let me and my family go to Paris." Balanchivadze promised his help, and from that moment their departure for Paris was assured.

This decision, however, did not appeal to young Alexander, who was graduating from the Conservatory-to which he was devoted-in the spring. He believed in the revolution and wanted to take an active part in it, not just for the time being in Tiflis but ultimately in his hometown of St. Petersburg. At the same time, he could not see himself breaking his parents' hearts by refusing to go. They tried to convince him that in Paris he would at last fulfill his dream of a complete musical education with the best professors, and that he would eventually return to his homeland as an accomplished artist. Neither his parents nor he thought at that time that their journey to Paris would be final or that they themselves would become émigrés.

So, in June, having completed his studies at the Tiflis Conservatory and Tiflis University, he filled a small suitcase-largely out of sentiment-with manuscripts including the *bloshki* and the Toccata that he had completed just prior to departure. Above the title of the Toccata he had inscribed the slogan *vive la polyphonie*, and between its pages he had placed a white rose that had been given him at his farewell concert. Altogether, then, with father, mother, himself and Touchkan (a stray mongrel that had adopted them some time ago), they embarked on that great journey.

Tcherepnin wrote: "Much later on in my life, in 1938 in Paris, I... expressed how I felt in the Coda of the last movement of the *Suite géorgienne*, [which is] *pianissimo* all through, as if fading away; [but] then ends abruptly, like [the] falling of the guillotine-knife-the knife of the irrevocable reality."

On June 16th, 1921, they boarded an Italian steamer, S. S. Mongibello, which was packed to overflowing with Armenian refugees bound for Constantinople (now Istanbul). The arduous voyage took two weeks-for a passage that would normally have required no more than three or four days. Sanitary conditions on board were deplorable; food was scarce. The waterline was high because there was no cargo, which made the rickety ship even more unstable. Repairs had to be carried out on the high seas as none of the Turkish ports would accept the steamer. Little provision boats would approach it whenever it stopped, only to be gunned away. No bread, no food, were to be sold to the Armenian refugees. Only by the good fortune of having a Muslim, one Mahmud, on board, who dared to go ashore at one of the ports to forage for food, were the people saved from starvation.

Finally, on June 27th, after a passage through the scenic Bosporus, the steamer landed in Constantinople. Never did a *lull kebab* taste more delicious than on that first evening. Touchkan, the dog, was terrified by the highly belligerent cats in the streets of the Galata district, where the Tcherepnins had found an inexpensive hotel, and more than once Alexander had to carry the animal in his arms. The family's immediate concern was to establish contact with Nicolai's friends in Paris, for Georgia had been totally cut off from the western world. In the meantime they provided for survival by giving concerts, one at the YMCA and another at a club called "The Russian Lighthouse."

They received funds from their faithful friend Wyschnegradsky, and after waiting six weeks for red tape to be cut, they finally procured a French visa. This period, though nerve-wracking, gave the receptive mind of the young Tcherepnin a chance to savor Constantinople, which he later considered one of the most entrancing cities he had ever visited. The lore of its Byzantine past, the fantastic large Orthodox cathedral-the Aya Sofia, the little Aya Sofia, the ruins of Rumelia Hissar—left an indelible impression on him. The visit of the Patriarch of Constantinople-so modest, so human, so kind-also touched him; the whole climate of the Patriarchate was unpretentious, non-aggressive and unceremonious. The liturgy in the Greek Orthodox churches intrigued him greatly: formally, it was like that of the Russian Orthodox churches, but the hymns, the singing, the psalmody of the priest, were quite different and much more Oriental.

No less interesting was his discovery of the Turkish past of Constantinople, with its palaces, cemeteries, and ancient buildings. A visit to Skadar, on that side of the Bosporus opposite Constantinople, stirred Alexander's historical imagination: here the old Turkey was still intact and reminded him of the Tartars' settlement in the Crimea that he used to visit in his teens.

At the beginning of August the Tcherepnins finally received their French visa and, on August 4th, they embarked on a small Spanish freighter, the San Jose, with Marseilles as their destination. As on board the Mongibello, they were deck passengers; but this time they traveled in relative comfort, camping beneath the open sky in the stern. They even had a table at their disposal, and both father and son joyously wrote music at it. The trip took them through the Marmara Sea, the Dardanelles (upon which the remnants of Russian White Army camps were easily visible) and the Aegean and Mediterranean Seas. The Greek islands Messina, brightly lit at night, and the Strait of St. Bonifacio between Sardinia and Corsica, were by no means the only picturesque features of this voyage.

The steamer reached Marseilles during the night, and the passengers awoke on August 13th to the sight of the French landscape and its islands, with the many ships in and around port, and the hustle and bustle of traffic on shore even at that early hour: trains speeding in and out of short tunnels, cars and trucks, smoke streaming from tall factory chimneys, planes buzzing noisily overhead.

After so many years of austerity, it was overwhelming to see such abundance: the *Cannebière* was swarming with people, large department stores were stocked with goods, food shops were overflowing with products. There were numerous *boulangeries* with the enticing smell of good French bread, many tempting candy shops. It must have been a relief to hear a tongue that was reasonably familiar to them, and to see well-dressed, well-fed, contented and busy people milling around under the sunny skies. Nicolai, like many Russians a great lover of fish, treated them to a bouillabaisse luncheon.

Then came time to board the night-train to Paris. With the help of a porter, they squeezed their luggage into a crowded third-class compartment. Young Tcherepnin was fascinated by the speed of the train and stayed in the corridor late into the night looking through the window: Avignon, Valence, Lyon, Dijon and then-early in the morning-Paris! Tcherepnin wrote that he wished he had had a camera to photograph their arrival at the Gare de Lyon: his father, mother, himself all strangely dressed, Touchkan sniffing the scent of his French colleagues at every street corner, and their battered luggage. "I was dressed in a suit too small for me, given by an American YMCA, had a strange round hat on my head and Georgian (Caucasian) national slippers." The first item on their agenda was to find a roof. A short walk around the Gare de Lyon brought them to the City Hotel on the Rue de Lyon, and this small, old-fashioned establishment condescended to accept them. Their room on the third floor, with a large bed for the parents and a small one for Alexander, had no running water; but the hotel was clean, the price reasonable, and they considered themselves fortunate to have so quickly found adequate living quarters "for the duration." Not for a moment did they suspect that their emigration was final. Alexander's father felt that his stay in Paris would be similar in some way to his prewar tours: that he would be asked to conduct and to compose for the Diaghilev ballet, that in the meantime the international situation would somehow clear up, and that he would be asked to return to his homeland.

The manuscripts in Alexander's suitcase soon found welcome markets, not with one, but four Paris publishers-thanks to the recommendation of Isidore Philipp, his piano teacher. These sentimental souvenirs, output of teenage days and his stay in Georgia, turned out unexpectedly be a gold mine. He first considered the title *Primitives* for these pieces, but Philipp-who always addressed his six-foot- four student as *mon petit*-advised against it. So it was that these *bloshki* were sold, one after another under various other names: *Bagatelles*, *Episodes*, Suites, etc., and the proceeds, augmented by concert engagements and some help from Wyschnegradsky, were enough to live on for approximately three years.

There is an irony, cruel in some aspects, in this tale of emigration. Alexander left Russia and Georgia much against his will. He did not fear new political experiment during the upheavals of either 1918 or 1921; in both cases he was taken from extremely satisfying professional milieux. He had enjoyed the St. Petersburg Conservatory; he had enjoyed even more the musical life in Tiflis, where he was, in effect, a big fish in a small pond, scoring a string of solid successes as a theater composer, a virtuoso pianist and even a music critic. Leaving all this behind troubled him deeply.

Yet Alexander's art and career flourished in the West as it probably never could have in the Soviet Union. Here, he had a chance to test his compositional muscles by pursuing music in the most abstract terms, something that would have been frowned upon in Russia, even in the relatively relaxed climate of the 1920s. More important, here he had the opportunity for world travel-his later work in China and Japan would have been out of the question for a Soviet national. This musical citizen of the world in fact needed virtually the whole world to expand into, if he was to serve his talent to the full. The exile that Alexander endured with such reluctance was in reality a golden passport to international success.

Nicolai Tcherepnin, by contrast, was leaving what in his eyes was a world with no immediate promise for him. Although he had long been a well-loved composer in his native land, and had reached the verge of solid international success a few years before, he could not see the continuation of his career through and beyond the revolutionary disturbances. He was anxious to get to the west where a "normal" musical climate prevailed, and he could get back to the real business of his life.

Yet in Paris he found that Diaghilev had abandoned him, and the western public did not treat a permanent Russian emigre as it treated a "Russian ambassador." Pavlova continued to commission works from him, but these alone could not sustain an important career. The normal business of his life needed, after all, the Russian integument in which it had flourished. Back in Russia, he would certainly have been put in charge of a major ballet orchestra. In the West, he never procured a regular position as a conductor; and while the occasional engagements he received usually had a "prestige" aura about them, they did not succeed in bringing his career as a performer back to life. Gone was the middle-class security he had known in St. Petersburg. In Paris he was sometimes unable to earn enough to support his family, and had to rely on the bounty of his far more successful son in order to make ends meet. The emigration that Nicolas embraced with such alacrity was, in fact, little more than a passport to neglect and obscurity.

❋ ❋ ❋ ❋ ❋ ❋

A sketch for Préludes Nostalgiques (1922) made on notepaper in London

III. ENCOUNTERING THE ENGLISH

English was the last language that Tcherepnin mastered; and this is not the only reason why it seems so appropriate that England became his last love—the site of his last composition. Ultimately, the English took Tcherepnin to their hearts. But his early experiences in the country were an odd mixture of heartening successes and peculiar humiliations, adding up to a Horatio Alger-like story whose turning-points involved the device of *dea ex machina* at least twice (in the persons of one Lady Dean Paul and the immortal Anna Pavlova).

Shortly after Tcherepnin and his family emigrated to Paris, the young composer became a frequent guest in the home of Madame Ernesta Stern, a wealthy patroness of the arts who fancied herself a poetess. During one visit there, he met two young touring violinists, the d'Aranyi sisters, great-nieces of the great violinist Josef Joachim. Hungarian by birth and longtime friends of Bartók[1], they now lived in England, where the elder, Adila, was married to an English political functionary, Alexander Fachiri, the secretary of the Liberal Party leader Lloyd George.

Adila was impressed with Tcherepnin's Violin Sonata and invited him to come to London to play in a concert with her and her sister Jelly d'Aranyi in November 1922. Unfortunately, she blithely forgot such practical matters as visas and money. For Tcherepnin, a stateless Russian, obtaining a passport was no easy matter, and procuring a re-entry visa to France from the Paris *préfecture de Police* proved just as difficult. Having obtained these documents after endless formalities, Tcherepnin arrived at the British Consulate only to be denied admittance to England. But he returned there again and again, and finally obtained a visa that enabled him to leave on November 14—only one day before the concert, and only a few hours before he was scheduled to play at a private reception at the Fachiri household.

Tcherepnin boarded the noon train at the Gare St. Lazare with no more than a hundred francs in his pocket. Yet he was not unduly worried because he had been offered the hospitality of the Fachiris. In the dining car he was seated with three Englishmen who were engaged in animated conversation. Listening to a language totally foreign to him, Tcherepnin was seized by giggles—finding it unbelievably funny that these bizarre sounds could constitute articulate speech. At the time, he hardly knew more than a few phrases in English, such as "a match" (*i. e.*, "how much") and "thank you." His tablemates, Tcherepnin later wrote, undoubtedly took him for some kind of idiot, but pretended, with typical English politeness, to take no notice of his behavior.

As he expected, he "gave back" his lunch at the Channel crossing—seasickness was to remain his usual reaction to travel by boat-but tea on the train to London calmed his innards, and he arrived at the Fachiris' just in time to change into the one man's dress-shirt that the impoverished Tcherepnin family owned—a garment that made him look like a scarecrow, as it fitted Nicolai, who was much shorter.

Although the guests at the reception showed little enthusiasm for Tcherepnin's playing, the concert the next day was a success. Yet even before the composer had a chance to read the (unanimously favorable) reviews, he met a curious reversal in fortunes. On arriving back at the Fachiris' after the concert, he was unceremoniously put out of the house! Adila told him that his presence was "not good for her reputation"; Fachiri ordered him to pack his things, and then took him to a hotel near Victoria Station.

Fachiri made no accusations, and Tcherepnin stated that he did not find Adila particularly attractive. Yet, as he wrote, "evidently, poor [Fachiri] became jealous [for] no reason whatsoever—or perhaps Adila felt tender towards me without my noticing it, because at that time truly I was like *der reine Tor* [*i. e.*, 'the pure fool'— a reference to *Parsifal*], absolutely unaware of any sexual appeal that I [had]…" and, perhaps more important, unable to recognize a "pass" for what it was.

Stranded in a foreign capital, Tcherepnin "had less than one pound in my pocket. Of course, I had my return ticket to Paris. But somehow, I [had expected] to earn some money in England, and to return to Paris penniless would be—in my mind—the sign of complete failure."

Realizing that his funds were insufficient to keep him in a tourist hotel for even three nights, he promptly withdrew to squalid digs in Pimlico, a room at 33 Berwick Street near Victoria Station. It was a room straight out of a Dickens nove—a coffin for half a crown a week, lit by a coin-fed gas lamp. The landlady was a pale, thin, sickly mother of an indeterminately large number of equally pallid and ill-fed small children. After paying his rent for a week in advance, Tcherepnin survived on a shilling a day, of which tuppence was for the stamp on his daily letters to his parents in Paris and the rest for a diet of three teas a day (one with cake).

His new neighbors were kind to the tall, gaunt penniless Russian, the waitresses in the tea shops occasionally slipping him an extra cake with his brew. Soon, however, a surreal note was added to their impression of him, as Rolls Royces and other luxurious cars with uniformed chauffeurs began coming to the grimy neighborhood to pick him up.

---

1   Bartók dedicated both of his Violin-Piano Sonatas to Jelly D'Aranyi, and Ravel would soon compose his Tzigane for her. Adila D'Aranyi Faschiri later recorded Beethoven's last violin-piano sonata with Sir Donald Francis Tovey at the piano.

For the wealthy had begun to take an interest in Tcherepnin, thanks to the efforts of a certain Lady Dean Paul, an influential socialite of Polish descent who herself composed music (published under the *nom de plume* of Poldowsky), and counted the violinist-composer Henri Wieniawski among her ancestors. Within ten days, he was invited to stay as a guest of one of the branches of the Guinness family on a huge property at Sunnyhill in Ascot. These Guinnesses had two girls and a young boy—Alec, the future celebrated actor. Mrs. Guinness offered Tcherepnin 2,000 francs for a month's stay of composing in peace and quiet. Although quite homesick for Paris, he found the offer too good to refuse. He received half his fee in advance and promptly remitted it to his parents. Earning ten pounds at a benefit concert at the Guinnesses, he returned to Berwick Street bringing presents for his landlady and her children—oranges, bananas, useful things for the house—and some flowers for the kind tearoom waitresses.

At Sunnyhill, he worked on his Second Piano Concerto, in which he hoped to achieve a breakthrough, composing a purely musical concerto, in distinction to the crowd-pleasing virtuoso effort he had produced in his First Concerto. He also wrote his *Préludes nostalgiques*.

Thoroughly pleased with his day-to-day progress on the concerto, he was dismayed to find himself suddenly put out of his second British home, at least temporarily! The Guinnesses asked him to leave the countryside for a few days, during which he would be accommodated at their London establishment. Tcherepnin was sure the change of scene and disruption of the routine he had established would spoil his work on the Concerto. It was later explained to him that the Guinnesses were hosting a hunting party and needed Tcherepnin's bed for some guests, but the composer became even more distressed that the family hadn't bothered to explain this to him. He confronted Lady Guinness, demanding the rest of his 2,000 francs, furiously protested against the damage she had done to his work, and eventually burst into tears.

Fortunately, Lady Dean Paul found him a patron with a sumptuous Belgrave Square home at which there were two Bechstein grand pianos at his disposal. Tcherepnin's troubles in London were past, and he was later able to return to Paris with a feeling of significant accomplishment.

Tcherepnin next visited England the following year. In July 1923, Anna Pavlova returned from India determined to do a ballet centering around various *objets d'art* she had acquired there. Normally, she would have turned to Nicolai Tcherepnin, her favorite ballet composer, but she had previously commissioned another ballet from Nicolai, which had to be concluded by August. Nicolai thought Alexander might be able to provide suitable music, and persuaded Pavlova to engage him.

Pavlova's husband brought the young composer a phonograph and several records of Indian folk music, which Tcherepnin would play every morning, to get "into the mood." In the end, however, he made little use of folk material, for he was convinced that his nine-step materials sounded suitably exotic.

The ballet that resulted, *Ajanta's Frescoes*, Op. 32, drew warm applause at the premiere on September 10, 1923, but Pavlova could not persuade the 24-year-old composer—still preternaturally shy—to take a bow. After a radio broadcast of *Ajanta* the next day, Tcherepnin was surprised by the number of people who told him they had heard it. Pavlova proceeded to take his ballet on tour, and it remained in her repertory ever after. As for Tcherepnin, his name was now well-known enough in England to interest several publishers.

Ultimately, of course, it would be on the continent and America—rather than in England—that Tcherepnin built his musical reputation; the British lost interest in him after his initial successes, and it was only in his sixties that they began welcoming him back as a Grand Old Man. But the highly favorable reception that young Tcherepnin enjoyed in London for two years running proved a permanent encouragement to a naïve, stateless and penniless composer whose name was still virtually unknown in the other major musical capitals of the world.

❈ ❈ ❈ ❈ ❈ ❈

IV. A TASTE OF NEW YORK

When Anna Pavlova arrived in America for coast-to-coast appearances in late 1923, she brought her latest London success with her: *Ajanta's Frescoes*, which now became the first Tcherepnin score to be heard in the United States. Soon, some of Tcherepnin's other music began to attract American performers and the composer's name gained a vague familiarity with big city concertgoers.

Yet it was primarily for personal rather than professional reasons that the twenty-seven-year-old Tcherepnin undertook his first visit to America in 1926. He had recently married the extremely wealthy American socialite Louisine Weekes (nee Peters), a woman of forty-one, and she now wished to introduce her new husband to her family and friends on Long Island.

Although Alexander had been comfortable in his two-year love affair with Louisine, he was terrified by her announcement early in 1926 that she could now marry him because she was divorcing Mr. Weekes. As he candidly admitted in his English autobiography, he went through the wedding with secret reluctance. He did not, however, entirely conceal his resentment of his "50-50" agreement with Louisine: half the time he would devote to the travel and concertizing necessary for his career, the other half he would reserve for her, sharing her Islip home and accompanying her to the fashionable and expensive vacation resorts frequented by those of her social set. This visit to America belonged to Louisine's half.

So it was well before the beginning of the New York concert season, on August 25, 1926, that Tcherepnin embarked from Cherbourg by slow steamer (the S. S. Homeric) with his new wife, his step-daughter Hathaway ("Happy"), the latter's governess, Miss Roger, and two dogs, Maud and Touchkan. He arrived in New York after eight days of almost constant seasickness. "As it did with so many people before me," he wrote, "and as it still fascinates practically every ocean traveller, the panorama of New York, as seen from the boat, impressed me greatly. New York with its skyscrapers slightly hidden by foggy atmosphere seemed like Mont St. Michel, or like the Bayan Island of Russian fairy tales (so splendidly pictured in Rimsky-Korsakov's opera, *Tsar Sultan*)."

Tcherepnin's family had not accepted his marriage with especially good grace. The composer later revealed that his affair with Louisine had been the only youthful love relationship with which his fiercely possessive mother had not had any opportunity to interfere. Prokofiev had often teased the adolescent Alexander by calling him-quite justly-a "mamma's boy," and the circumstances of emigration, with its financial hardships for the family, had kept Tcherepnin closer to home than might otherwise have been the case. In taking up with Louisine, Tcherepnin was taking a step toward independence, and only later did he begin to understand that he had, in effect, exchanged his mother's apron strings for those of a wife fourteen years his senior. In any event, Tcherepnin's parents were absent from his wedding, and their coolness was matched by Louisine's: she resented their opposition to the marriage, and she felt that they had shamelessly exploited their son, accepting a share of his by no means opulent earnings when they should have been shifting for themselves.

When the couple arrived at Louisine's home in Islip, described by Tcherepnin as "a copy of some French chateau, with towers, garden surrounded by walls, and forests all around," the composer was touched to find that Louisine had not only arranged to have a Steinway grand piano rented for him, but had also had the servants procure a copy of his *Bagatelles* and put it on the music rack.

Thoughtful as this gesture was, the piano was useless to him for work, since it was in one of the "public" rooms of the house; fortunately, Tcherepnin found a sufficiently isolated dressing-room alcove where he could put a small upright piano for composing in private.

Finding his *Bagatelles* was an unexpected pleasure, however, and, moreover, when Tcherepnin later went into New York City he was surprised to learn that many of his compositions were available at Schirmer's Music Store. The copies of his works that he had brought with him from Europe were thus quite unnecessary.

The meeting of family and friends was a qualified success. On the one hand, it is doubtful whether these aristocrats—mostly of the card—playing set-knew what to make of Louisine's exotic new acquisition. When watching Tcherepnin play the piano, his mother-in-law leaned over to her daughter and whispered that he "looked like a congenital idiot." Other family members and friends could not understand why Tcherepnin had to take money for his music and performances: people in their circle sometimes pursued music as a hobby, but no working professional in the arts could be regarded as a true gentleman—Tcherepnin was thus putting his new family in an embarrassing position.

On the other hand, everybody behaved with impeccable kindness and politeness. "Practically each day," Tcherepnin wrote, " there was a party in [our] honor [given] by Louisine's friends, who also had their summer homes in Islip or in the neighborhood. All of them were friendly, hospitable, openhearted. At that time I could not speak English, hardly was able to understand [a] few words (with Louisine and Happy we always spoke French), yet everyone tried to speak with me [in broken] French or German; asked me about Russia, about music; mostly asked me to play on their pianos, [which] were grands, and [which] they had tuned when I was to come. All of this was very touching…"

Tcherepnin added, "While in Islip I was trying to compose an orchestral piece—a *Radiénie*, a wild dance of [the] Russian 'old believers' sect. Nothing came of it, however. The great impression[s] I received from a new country, from a new people, were diverting me from inner concentration."

With his visit drawing to a close, Tcherepnin thought that it would be "a pity" to miss performing in the USA. Remembering some advice given him by Mary Garden, the famous opera singer, he got in touch with her manager, a Mr. Wagner in New York. Mr. Wagner did not care to handle a composer who played his own compositions, and introduced him to a minor manager of his acquaintance, Miss Catherine Bamman, who arranged Tcherepnin's first concert appearance in New York. The debut was scheduled for Wednesday, October 20, 1926, at the now-long-vanished Chickering Hall on 57th Street, where Tcherepnin was required to play a Chickering piano.

The program included Tcherepnin's Sonata, Op. 22, Romances, Op. 31, Toccata, Op. 1, *Four Slavic Transcriptions*, Op. 27, *Petite Suite*, Op. 6, and *Étude de concert*, along with two Tcherepnin transcriptions: Nocturne in F by Anton Rubinstein and *All' offertorio* by the eighteenth-century Italo-Argentine composer Domenico Zipoli.

As Tcherepnin was preparing for Chickering Hall, he met an old friend: the violinist Emmanuel Zetlin, with whom he had given concerts as a high school student in Petrograd. Zetlin had a New York recital of his own the night after Tcherepnin's debut, and agreed to put the Tcherepnin Violin Sonata on his program—if the composer would come and play it with him. As it turned out, Tcherepnin's music was heard that week in *four* New York concerts on four consecutive days; for the pianist Grace Hofheimer performed his *Pièces sans titres* (Pieces Without Titles) in her Tuesday recital at Aeolian Hall, and another pianist, Herman Reuter played his *Bagatelles* on Friday in Town Hall.

Out of the six reviews in New York papers after his debut, only two were favorable to him as a composer. Most found him praiseworthy as a pianist, while the *New York Herald Tribune* critic concluded his end-of-the-week summary by writing that it was "Tcherepnin week in New York," and gave him a good notice.

As a result, Chickering Pianos offered to pay him $100 each time he used the company's pianos, and its Director, Lionel Tompkins, engaged him to record two Ampico player-piano rolls, for a fee of $100 each: one featuring Rubinstein's Nocturne, the other, three numbers from *Petite Suite*. Tcherepnin was pleased at last to have some American money that had not come through Louisine's largesse.

On October 22nd, he embarked on the S. S. Olympic for Europe, feeling quite happy over "this unexpected and most welcome artistic achievement and also quite warmed up by the kindness and friendliness that I found in all circles—family, social and artistic."

A man of lesser character might have had his artistic ambition sapped by living the luxurious, gracious life of the very rich. Tcherepnin, perhaps aware of the dangers, spurred himself on to even greater challenges. The following April found the composer and his wife back in New York. As it was then impossible to arrange a concert (the season was just about finished) he decided he would instead devote his efforts to composing a major work. And so, over the next months, while those around him glided unthinkingly through the minuet-like rituals of aristocratic life, Tcherepnin wrestled with the fierce intellectual constructs and barbarically energetic rhythms of his most ambitious score to date-the First Symphony.

V. CHINA AND JAPAN

During his extensive travels, Tcherepnin established ties with concert managers in virtually every major musical capital, and in 1933, his representatives in New York, London and Vienna relayed several exotic offers to him, involving concerts in India, the Philippines and Hong Kong. He then received a proposal from the firm of A. Strok[1] for appearances in China and Japan, and a 1934 world tour seemed to be taking shape almost by itself. Although thrilled by this far-ranging prospect, Tcherepnin feared it would never materialize; for Louisine had an inviolable claim on half his time, and would bitterly oppose any extended separation. The composer could thus arrange such an excursion only if his wife were prepared to go with him.

Fortune, however, put Louisine on Tcherepnin's side. "When I spoke to her of my desire to undertake a world tour," Tcherepnin wrote, "to my great surprise she became entranced with the proposition." Louisine, in fact, thought that a long absence from Europe would solve a delicate family crisis. Her daughter Happy had become romantically involved with a Hungarian count, who had followed her from Vienna to Paris to Cherbourg, and Louisine was looking for a way to keep the lovers apart in order to prevent a marriage she regarded as premature at best and unsuitable at worst. Long before Henry James, foreign travel had been a well-worn aristocratic expedient for inducing a young girl to fall out of love with an undesirable suitor, and Louisine, in traditional fashion, was sure that a round the world trip for Happy with her mother and stepfather lasting the better part of a year would be just the thing to cure her of her infatuation.

The tour, ironically, not only met Louisine's therapeutic expectations, but surpassed them in a manner she would come to rue: for Happy was not the only one in the family who underwent a ruptured relationship because of it. Had Louisine been equipped with hindsight, she would have moved heaven and earth to keep Tcherepnin away from the Far East.

Tcherepnin's attitude toward his marriage—now in its seventh year—had long since been one of quiet desperation. Louisine, no less than Tcherepnin, resented the "50-50" arrangement they had made about balancing his professional concerns with her personal life. By Louisine's standards, Tcherepnin's musical income was contemptibly meager, and this made it difficult for her to accept that his composing and concertizing was anything but a hobby, perversely pursued to keep him from her side. To be sure, she never denied him money he needed for professional reasons: when he had to pay for full-orchestra rehearsals of his First Symphony, it was Louisine who footed the bill. However, she made a point of holding aloof from Tcherepnin's musician friends. Begrudging the time he spent with them, she insisted that, in recompense, he participate fully in her own social round.

Since it was Louisine who supported the Tcherepnins, it was usually she who decided when and where they traveled and how they lived. This was fortunate when Louisine's taste for globetrotting coincided with Alexander's own. For their wedding anniversary on August 4, 1931, he composed a droll pastiche for her, studded with "national" themes representing the various places they had been during the previous twelve months: "USA VIII 1930, Paris VIII 1930, Baden Baden VIII 1930, Czechoslovakia IX 1930, Munich X 1930, Warsaw X 1930, Vienna X 1930, Paris XI 1930, London XII 1930, St. Moritz Xmas 1930, Monte Carlo I-II-III 1931, Egypt IV 1931, Jerusalem IV 1931, Greece V 1931, Venice V 1931, Vienna V 1931, Paris V 1931, London VI 1931, Monte Carlo VI-VII 1931, Gstaad VII-VIII 1931." (See page 134 for the first page of this piece.) But Louisine also insisted on long stays at her Islip home, where Tcherepnin, dispirited by his isolation from the music world, was obliged to sit opposite his wife afternoon after afternoon in interminable sessions of bridge, a game that bored him silly.

Financially, Louisine kept Tcherepnin on a very short rein, paying his individual expenses as they arose rather than giving him money to handle on his own. He soon came to feel that she was using her wealth to control him. Support for his parents was another sore point. Sometimes Louisine would send them substantial sums without a murmur (totalling, in all, tens of thousands of pre-inflation dollars); on other occasions, a bitter altercation would erupt when Tcherepnin asked her to help them.

At the same time, Tcherepnin knew that Louisine's personal devotion to him was unquestionable. Showered with gifts of beautiful jewelry and clothed in the height of fashion, he felt that Louisine was pampering him like some kind of rare, exotic, delicate pet. Years later, he told his student Gloria Coates about a typically tense incident in the marriage. Tcherepnin was at his desk composing when all at once Louisine appeared to tell him it was time to dress for a party that evening. Loath to interrupt his creative train of thought, he asked her to go without him, and a furious argument ensued. In such arguments, however, Louisine-who held the purse strings-was invariably the winner. When Tcherepnin arrived at the gathering with his wife, he felt so frustrated that he assumed the character of a pet dog in tow, exclaiming "woof-woof" as a counterpoint to each handshake as he went around the room greeting the other guests.

---

1   The Latvian-American impresario Awsay Strok understandably did not use his first name in his extensive management dealings, which included at times representing Heifetz, Piatigorsky and Arthur Rubinstein. He died in Tokyo in 1956.

In sum, Tcherepnin felt that Louisine's love and financial support placed him under deep obligation, yet resented the professional and personal sacrifices that this obligation entailed. Despising himself for his spineless subservience to Louisine, he despised himself no less for his ingratitude toward her. Their fourteen-year age difference presented another complication: how could he be so heartless as to dream of deserting a woman nearing fifty? Louisine, for her part, recognized Tcherepnin's restiveness, but loved him, and had every reason for believing that his dependence on her-and his very real personal affection for her—would bind them forever. This was the state of the Tcherepnins' marriage as they discussed his offers from the Far East.

At first, the prospect appeared benign. Overjoyed that the tour would not provoke any of the familiar family friction, Tcherepnin told his managers to proceed with plans. "The itinerary," he wrote, "was arranged as follows: I was to start in China, by the end of April, to continue in Japan in early fall, then to appear in Manilla, Hong Kong, Singapore, and in India up to Kashmir; from there to Europe [with] concerts in Palestine… on the way. Leaving [the] USA early in April (at that time there were no trans-sea planes) we would be back in Europe by February or March of the next year—this because of the slowness of transportation and not-too-well-arranged coordination in concert dates, due to the fact that they were [handled] by different managers."

Realizing that the tour would keep him away from his parents for at least a year, Tcherepnin invited them to New York for a farewell visit. Unfortunately, Nicolai had quarreled with Louisine the previous November and would not accept her hospitality. Tcherepnin's mother perforce made the journey alone, arriving with her one-footed canary, Gavroshka. After spending a month as a guest in New York and Islip, she saw Alexander, Louisine, Happy and their dog Maud off on the train west.

The travellers broke their journey in Arizona to see the Grand Canyon, then continued on to Los Angeles, drove to San Francisco for a stay of eleven days, and at last boarded the S. S. President Hoover for the Orient on March 23, 1934. Reaching Yokohama on April 6, they paid the customary visit to the statue of Daibursu and proceeded immediately to Tokyo.

At the Imperial Hotel, Tokyo's famous Frank Lloyd Wright palazzo (now demolished), Tcherepnin was greeted by his impresario for this first leg of the tour, Mr. A. Strok, known as "the Hurok of the Orient." A violinist himself, Strok loved artists and loved even more to talk about music. He told Tcherepnin how much he regretted having refused to handle Prokofiev when the latter came to Yokohama in 1918 intending to play a series of all-Prokofiev recitals (Prokofiev's music was then unknown in Japan, and the impresario had seen the venture as far too risky). Strok said that he did not want to make the same mistake with Tcherepnin and promised to do his best to promote him in the Orient.

Four days later, Tcherepnin arrived in Shanghai, where his vast concert tour was to begin. Much to his surprise and pleasure, he was met at the steamer by a group of reporters prepared to interview him. It was an auspicious beginning; indeed, Tcherepnin was now embarking on what proved to be a lifelong love affair with China, her people, her traditions, her music—an affair that would soon prompt him to cancel most of his eagerly-awaited tour!

Another surprise to Tcherepnin was the large colony of Russians in Shanghai, among whom was an old friend of his father, the pianist Boris Zakharoff. Tcherepnin's official debut in Shanghai, with the Municipal Orchestra under the Italian conductor Mario Paci, was slated for mid-May; but as it turned out, he played three chamber and solo programs prior to the scheduled concert-one at the American Women's Club, one at the Shanghai Conservatory and one at an Association of Russian poets and writers called "Vostok."

By SAPAJOU

SHANGHAI THE MELODIOUS

A tip to a visiting composer, Mr. A. N. Tcherepnine

Tcherepnin's name and general appearance soon became so well-known to local newspaper readers that one journal made him the subject of a friendly caricature. This cartoon showed the tall, lanky Western composer in the street, straining-so the caption explained-to hear traditional Chinese music and instead being bombarded by the sound of American Jazz and French chansonettes from every direction.

In actual fact, however, Tcherepnin's desire to hear genuine Chinese music was soon gratified under unusually propitious circumstances, for when he visited the Shanghai Conservatory, several professors treated him to a carefully planned demonstration of Chinese instruments. Professor Chou Ying, a *pipa* virtuoso, played some pieces that Tcherepnin found spectacular, and a young composer, Tang Xiao-Lin, played a traditional piece on the *er hu* (Chinese violin), an instrument which impressed him nearly as much as the *pipa*. For Tcherepnin, this experience provided "an unexpected revelation for my Eurasian tendencies."

On May 13, 1934, the composer duly appeared with the Municipal Symphony, performing his Piano Concerto No. 2. The hall was filled to overflowing, and Paci's conducting was excellent. But, to Tcherepnin's consternation, the entire orchestra was foreign: not a single player was Chinese; likewise few Chinese were in the audience. After the concert, however, a young student of Zakharoff's, Miss Lee Hsien Ming, came to the green room and invited him to give a recital at Shanghai University. Tcherepnin was immediately attracted to the young lady, and in the aftermath of this encounter his sense of discontent with his domestic life began to become acute. The idea of obtaining a divorce from Louisine ceased to be an idle fantasy and began to assume concrete shape as his love for Ming continued to grow.

Partly as a ploy to get to know Ming better, Tcherepnin proposed to include his Second Concerto in his program at the University and suggested that she play the accompaniment on the second piano. Ming promised to do so, provided her teacher approved. Unfortunately, this scheme backfired, for Zakharoff insisted on doing his duty as a host by accompanying Tcherepnin himself.

Yet the composer could not be so easily thwarted; and as he was on his way to play at Shanghai University, his thoughts of the young lady took musical form as he jotted down the beginning of a piece that later was to become *Hommage à la Chine*-a piece whose "inner content," as he wrote, was the birth of his love for Lee Hsien Ming.

Quite early in Tcherepnin's stay in China he attended a performance of Chinese opera. The Chinese singing style unquestionably influenced him in his fleshing-out of the unfinished

Tcherepnin plays the *pipa*, suitably garbed.

Mussorgsky opera, *The Marriage*, a project that he had brought to China with him. (Mussorgsky had abandoned the work after completing one act in piano score; Tcherepnin had been commissioned to orchestrate the existing music, and to compose some sort of conclusion to the piece.)

Tcherepnin continued take an active interest in Chinese music—one of the first European musicians to do so. He explored tradition by taking *pipa* lessons, and made every effort to examine new scores by young Chinese composers. These, however, he often found disappointing, for when the Chinese wrote for western instruments, they tended to employ European classical cliches, abstaining from Oriental sounds in a manner he found inexplicable. "I firmly believe," he wrote, "that perfect[ed] European instruments can serve to express any national idiom: for instance, the piano can sound Spanish when used by a Spanish composer, French when used by a French one, Russian if used by a Russian, etc. I tried to explain [this] to the young Chinese composers, and to persuade them to use international instruments to write Chinese national music. To encourage them to do so, I sponsored a competition... open to any Chinese composer, for a piano piece written originally for piano, but in [a] Chinese idiom."

Launched in May 1934, the contest was administered with the assistance of Hsiao Yu-mei, President of the Shanghai Conservatory. Tcherepnin donated a cash prize (in Mexican pesos, then the preferred currency, as the previous year's collapse of the international silver market had left China's own money all but worthless). The winners and their works were announced in the November issue of *Musical Magazine* (Shanghai). First prize, by unanimous vote, went to *Buffalo Boy's Flute* by Rodin Ho (in modern transliteration, He Luting). The award proved a godsend to the young composer, for he was then in such financial difficulty that he had been forced to take a leave of absence from the Conservatory. The prize money enabled him to resume his studies at the Conservatory, and eventually, he became its Director.

Originally, only one award was to be conferred; but when the jury decided to give four second prizes, Tcherepnin doubled his contribution, and the additional sum was divided four ways.

Tcherepnin left Shanghai once the contest was organized and arrived on May 21 in Peiping (formerly and subsequently Peking, now Beijing). There he was reunited with the relatives with whom he had spent his boyhood summers at Sudak in the Crimea, his Aunt Camille (his mother's younger sister) and her husband, General Horvath, neither of whom he had seen for seventeen years.

"By this time," Tcherepnin wrote, "Louisine, Happy and I were captivated and fascinated by China, although for various reasons. My reasons were sentimental; I wanted to stay near Lee Hsien Ming. Of course I would… mention [this] to no one. But there were plenty of other pretexts I could produce: interest in Chinese culture and in Chinese music; demands… to contribute to the musical education in China by lecturing and teaching; various proposals for concert appearances."

Indeed, Peiping held him in thrall. With Louisine and Happy he never tired of visiting the temples, palaces, *hutungs* (small lanes), bazaars, lakes, the Forbidden City, the Temple of Heaven, and the theaters. The city's beauty—its art, its ever- azure skies, its air—he declared beyond description. To him, there were "three world towns worthy to live in": it was only in Rome, Jerusalem and Beijing that one truly sensed the infinite human richness of an "eternal" city. "They all have this in common: they were the greatest cultural centers of the past," and, as a result, he found that anything or everything in these cities might be imbued with profound meaning. "To say that we all fell in love with Peiping would be to express inadequately, and in [a] common[place] way the great internal joy that one feels when one has the chance to be in Peiping."

While Tcherepnin was thrilled by the physical and historical actuality of Beijing, he was dismayed that his concerts there and in Tientsin were attended almost entirely by Westerners. In the hope of a broader audience, he asked his Peiping manager to advertise his concerts in the local Chinese-language newspapers, and to make special reduced-price tickets available to Chinese students, because regular admission fees were far beyond their means. It was also on the dogged insistence of Tcherepnin, who prevailed over managerial indifference only by threatening to cancel performances, that programs were finally printed in both Chinese and English—a historical first.

Tcherepnin now began to consider the special problems of Chinese piano students. These young musicians-the first generation of Chinese to be trained on Western instruments-had to deal with a repertory totally alien to the native idiom of their earliest musical experiences. Confronting both an unfamiliar instrument and an unfamiliar musical style, they were, in effect, "operating with two 'X's," as Tcherepnin wrote. In order to "eliminate one of the 'X's," he prepared a set of graded piano studies based on the pentatonic scale, the standard scale of Chinese traditional and popular music. These etudes, he hoped, would provide familiar-sounding material through which students could master the alien instrument.

After a busy season of concertizing and teaching in China, Tcherepnin returned to Japan in a little boat which landed in Kobe on July 8, 1934. Although his concerts in Japan were not to begin until the fall, he had decided to spend the summer there, resting and composing. Peiping was traditionally shunned by all who could afford to leave in the summer months, just as Paris, in the West, is deserted by its residents in August.

From Kobe the Tcherepnins went by car to Myanoshita, where a luxurious resort hotel had been recommended to them. But he, Louisine and Happy all took an immediate dislike to the highly European atmosphere there, and after spending but one night they found a hotel compound where they were able to rent a small Japanese private house, complete with Japanese garden and bath. A piano was brought in for Tcherepnin and put in his room overlooking the garden, where he could work in complete seclusion and quiet. On August 8, less than a month after his arrival, he completed the short-score of his second act for Mussorgsky's *The Marriage*, and it amused him to think that Mussorgsky, sixty-six years before, had completed the first act piano-score in much the same kind of "peasant's" house.

In the meantime, through extensive correspondence, Tcherepnin had managed to withdraw from all of his engagements outside of Japan and China, so that he would be able to stay in China until at least February of 1935. Strok was so angered by these cancellations that he broke off communication, and as a result, the composer was in the embarrassing position of not knowing when and where he was scheduled to appear in Japan that fall.

His repeated inquiries to Strok left unanswered, Tcherepnin decided to act on his own and was ready to sign with a Japanese manager; but at the last moment, he happened to run into Strok at the Imperial Hotel, and the strained relations were repaired. He learned that he had a recital on September 29 and a concert with the radio orchestra on October 4.

Late in September, Tcherepnin went to a party given in his honor by several Japanese composers and a singer, Yeinen Yuasa, who was fluent in English and served as interpreter. Tcherepnin's vivid account of the evening and his hosts' performances of their own music, apparently written for a lecture around 1937, begins as follows:

"A reserved space at a popular cafe. At our arrival, composers are busily helping to place an upright piano kindly sent by a piano store. Picturesque group of men, mostly young… We bow, sit down, and I ask the composers to show me their compositions.

"Evidently confused, one pushes the other. Timidly smiling, a tall thin man whose face is slightly unshaven rises, takes out of an overfilled briefcase a small manuscript and seats himself at the piano.

" 'Two Dances, by Yasuji Kiyose,' announces Yuasa.

"Kiyose plays with a dry touch, rhythmically incorrect; he takes time at the difficult passages as if it were the first reading of his own composition and he himself were surprised to find the piece difficult. Whilst he is playing, his music speaks for itself and one becomes aware of the originality and spontaneity of his musical thoughts. "

That evening, the works of three composers—Kiyose, Tadashi Ota and Yoritsune Matsudaira—particularly impressed him. Tcherepnin asked Yuasa about finding a Japanese firm to publish their music, only to learn that no establishment would do so: the Japanese publishers were too busy reprinting pieces by modern European composers, who were not protected by local copyright laws. (The entire piano *oeuvre* of Ravel, for example, was available for 5 Japanese yen—about 1½ cents.) Tcherepnin then thought he might recommend some Japanese works to one or two western publishers when he arrived back in Europe.

On November 5, Tcherepnin returned to China intending to surprise Ming with the news that he would be in her country for much of the winter. But Ming, bizarrely, had a "Gift of the Magi"-like surprise for *him*: she was shortly to leave for *his* home continent as the winner of a three-year Boxer Fund scholarship for piano study in Brussels. Realizing that this was a magnificent opportunity for her, Tcherepnin swallowed his disappointment at the unexpected separation, and on November 13, he accompanied Ming on the tender to the S. S. Ruhr. He saw her to her cabin and the last moment, as the tender began to carry him away from the ship, he threw her one of his gloves to keep until they saw each other once again.

On November 23, 1934, Tcherepnin presented both acts of *The Marriage* at the Russian society, "Vostok," playing the orchestra part on the piano and singing all the roles himself. Two days later, he performed his Piano Concerto No. 1 with the Municipal Orchestra of Shanghai under the baton of Mario Paci, the program also including Tcherepnin's *Festmusik*. He subsequently appeared in numerous recitals, playing not only his own works but also several of the Chinese competition pieces. Tcherepnin had now completed his pentatonic piano study, and a local publisher, Shanghai Commercial Press, immediately agreed to issue it. However, when he proposed that the firm also print the prize-winning scores of, He Luting (*Buffalo Boy's Flute*) and Lao Chih Chen (*Shepherd's Pastime*), he received a flat refusal—as in Japan, there was no commercial interest in local music. Since he could find no firm to publish Chinese and Japanese composers, Tcherepnin decided to establish one himself. The first scores he acquired were the winning efforts by He Luting and Lao Chih Chen, along with four songs by Liu Shea An. "The contract for publication was concluded on January 29, [1935]," Tcherepnin wrote, "and I intended to publish [the pieces] in Japan. As a trademark for the publication, I chose a little ivory figure of a boy riding a buffalo, playing flute," which, of course, corresponded to the title of He Luting's piece.

Tcherepnin's altruistic gesture was not universally appreciated. One American music columnist branded him a profiteer, since he did not pay royalties. But, in fact, the works he published never came near to making back their costs, and the venture would not have been possible at all had not Tcherepnin and Louisine been willing to bear the costs. No such complaints came from the composers, who were thrilled to have their works in print, and gratified by the knowledge that Tcherepnin himself was playing these works in concert after concert, first locally and then in Europe and America.

As Tcherepnin prepared to leave China in February, he was named "honorary professor" at Ming's alma mater, the Shanghai Conservatory. Learning with avuncular pleasure that Ming's younger sister, Hsien Ping, had just passed the entrance examination to that institution, he persuaded Mario Paci to accept Ming's gifted baby brother, the five-and-a-half year old Lee Sing, as a student.

"We [took] a small Japanese boat in Shanghai to cross the Yellow Sea," wrote Tcherepnin. "The sea was rough and I was seasick all the way to Nagasaki. Strok arranged [rooms] at the Hotel Imperial in Tokyo and wrote me that they [would allow] Maud (my dog) to share the room with me.

"But when we arrived at the desk—[entrance] was forbidden to Maud. I became cross: so cross, as a matter [of] fact, that I broke the hotel reception desk…

"In Tokyo, I founded my publishing house, [which] I [later] named 'Tcherepnin Collection.'" Managed by Yeinen Yuasa, the firm followed up *Buffalo Boy's Flute* and the other Chinese pieces with piano compositions by Kiyose, Koh, Kobune, Ota, and Matsudaira. The collection's first orchestral score was *Etenraku*, a modern-instrument arrangement of ancient Japanese ceremonial court music by the western-trained Viscount Hidemaro Konoye. Covers and contents pages were a tri-lingual delight, with titles and composers' names printed in Chinese (or Japanese), Russian, and a sometimes-quaint variety of English.

On February 28, 1935, Tcherepnin and his family left Tokyo on the S. S. Tatsuta Maru. They docked in San Francisco on March 13, and took the train for New York on the following day, arriving on March 18. Spending two months in New York, Tcherepnin made concert appearances and submitted his article "Music in Modern China" to *The Musical Quarterly*, in which he secretly declared his love for Ming by citing her baby brother as "China's youngest composer" (see pp. 328-332). The composer now longed to see his parents, while Louisine wanted to stay and spend more time with her mother, so the two agreed that Tcherepnin would go ahead to Europe, with his wife joining him later.

After visiting his father and mother, Tcherepnin attended a Baden-Baden music festival which he found shockingly Nazified, and then traveled to Brussels to visit Ming. He spent most of a day with her, discreetly chaperoned by one of her friends, a Chinese violinist, and the next morning she saw him off on the train for France. He soon registered Ming for Alfred Cortot's ten-day series of master classes in Paris; and, as he wrote, "it was not long until the happy day when I met her at the *Gare du Nord* arriving from Brussels. Lipatti was one of the students of the *cours d'interpretation*. I [had] known him from Bucharest, and was glad to introduce him to Hsien Ming. I also introduced her to many musical friends. to Ania Dorfman, to Marguerite Long, to the Louis Fourniers, to Blondel, to my publisher Benno Balan… I felt more than ever how dear [she was] to me, and [that] my life would [be] straighten [out in a manner] corresponding to my goals. if it [ever became] possible for us to become united."

As Ming's train for Brussels left the station, Tcherepnin hurriedly went to pick up his chauffeured car for a drive to Cherbourg, where he arrived barely in time to meet Louisine's boat.

Louisine arrived alone. Happy now had an independent income, thanks to her grandmother's generosity, and had taken an apartment in New York, "which made Louisine upset," Tcherepnin observed, "as she was accustomed to have Happy around and to influence her life.

"This made my problem of leaving Louisine more difficult. She had practically no friends in Paris and only very few in New York. To walk out on her while she was alone in a foreign town would be a hard blow. Yet soon after her arrival, I told of my meeting Hsien Ming, of Hsien Ming's visit to Paris and of my feelings toward Hsien Ming. It was as dreadful to hurt her as it must have been for her to be hurt. Probably it would [have been] better for both of us if I [had had] the courage to leave her at once. "Instead. I accepted her suggestion to wait and see if our relations could be mended." The two went to Prague to see a new staging of Tcherepnin's ballet *Ajanta's Frescoes*. But relations were more strained than ever. Louisine refused to meet any of Tcherepnin's musical friends, and the composer felt more than ever that he needed to be with Ming-that Ming would willingly include herself in his activities, allowing him at last to live a fully professional life. Back in Paris, Tcherepnin announced that he would not accompany Louisine to Monte Carlo. The break seemed a *fait accompli*.

"Before leaving, however, Louisine. left an envelope for me to open after her departure: I found in it a [notice] from Morgan Bank that she [had] deposited. 1,500 dollars for me, and a note from her wishing me the fulfillment of my dreams and promising further help if I should need it." Tcherepnin was surprised and deeply disturbed. Louisine, in her beneficence, now reminded the composer of the elderly, noble-spirited bridegroom in his own opera *The Wedding of Sobeide*, who selflessly opens the door for the bride Sobeide at the end of the first act, leaving her free to go to the young man she truly loves.

"Sobeide was equally surprised, but walked out through the door generously opened to her. I had no [such] courage. Beaten by Louisine's generosity. I felt like a skunk, selfish and guilty." And so, when Louisine came back to Paris, Tcherepnin was there waiting for her. The marriage resumed its rocky course.

Later in the summer, Happy came to Monte Carlo to provide company for Louisine, leaving Tcherepnin free to attend the Salzburg Festival. He wired Ming, asking her to meet him there. But when he reached Austria, the strain began to tell. "I became more and more nervous. I spent time crying, accused myself of treachery towards everyone; towards Louisine for the meeting with Hsien Ming, towards Hsien Ming [for putting] her in a compromising position; towards my parents, who expected me to leave Louisine and to remain with Hsien Ming, of whom they approved; in my mind I was [at] fault with everyone who was dear to me. "

So it was that Tcherepnin came to a decision: "I saw clear[ly] that I [had] no right to expose Hsien Ming to the talk of Salzburg, [had] no right to associate with Hsien Ming until [I became] free. to make [her] my wife, and that my duty [was] to return to Louisine and to stay with her until I [found] the courage to terminate our relationship." He wired Ming, saying that he would have to leave Salzburg before their planned meeting; later, he wrote her a letter explaining the situation.

The Tcherepnins had been discussing a return to the Far East the following winter, and now the idea seemed even more attractive. Louisine was reassured by the prospect of an extended period during which her husband would be half a world away from Ming (who was committed to staying in Brussels for two more years). She was also pleased that Happy wished to accompany them back to the Orient. Tcherepnin, for his part, felt that he could "materialize" his love for Ming "by helping Chinese musicians in China and promoting the cause of music in China."

For more than a year, Tcherepnin had been working in desultory fashion on the orchestration of *The Marriage*. He completed it on October 13, 1935, in Berlin, and then made a concert tour, during which he played Chinese and Japanese compositions along with his own.

The Far East now further claimed his attention, in connection with a competition for Japanese composers that he had sponsored before leaving. Similar to his venture in China, this contest was for orchestral works in the Japanese musical idiom. All Japanese composers were invited to compete: manuscripts were to be sent to Tcherepnin in Paris under pen names, with each composer enclosing his real name in a sealed envelope. When the scores had all arrived, they were submitted to a jury composed of Tcherepnin's composer colleagues and several musicologists: included were Albert Roussel, P. O. Ferroud, Alexandre Tansman, Jacques Ibert, Henri Prunieres, Henri Gil-Marchex, and Arthur Honegger. Thus, in a sense, the *École de Paris* was finally functioning as a "school," conferring honors!

On November 26, the jury convened at Roussel's home and, by unanimous vote, awarded the first prize to *Japanese Rhapsody* by Akira Ifukube, a forest engineer in Hokkaido. Tcherepnin found this score picturesquely Japanese in character, bearing the stamp of definite talent but in need of editing before publication. The second prize work was *Pastorale* by Yoritsune Matsudaira, a Tcherepnin pupil whose piano Prelude was already published in the Japanese Album of "Collection A. Tcherepnine."

Tcherepnin now had a full month free in Paris for composition, and he decided to write some extended piano pieces in the same pentatonic vein as his recently completed *Hommage à la Chine*. During January, he made substantial progress on the Five Concert Etudes, Op. 52, completing the last piece in March 1936. Before leaving on his westward journey back to the Orient, he paid Ming one more visit for a few hours in Brussels. He kept her abreast of his domestic situation, and explained his decision to spend another year in the Far East.

Returning to Japan with Louisine, Happy and Maud in April 1936, Tcherepnin went directly from the dock at Yokohama to the Tokyo Radio Station to rehearse with the orchestra, under Walter Herbert, who, in Vienna, had conducted his opera, *The Wedding of Sobeide*, and who had come to Japan on the same boat. After the rehearsal Herbert and Tcherepnin were made to wait interminably until the former's patience entirely wore thin. It turned out that the directors of the station were discussing the performers' fees, and that the bizarre result of their deliberations was a double fee for Tcherepnin as a composer-pianist, and a single fee for Herbert as a "mere" conductor!

In May, Tcherepnin left Japan for China. His stay began ominously, for he now had the unpleasant duty of helping to put his faithful dog Maud to death. The animal had been in excruciating pain, and cancer was diagnosed. The grim irony was that this may not have been necessary, for after Maud died, two ticks emerged from her urinary tract, which could well have been the source of the trouble.

Tcherepnin was soon cheered, however, by the unexpected arrival of one of his Japanese pupils, Bunyah Koh, who had followed him to Peiping to continue studies with him. Koh was hesitant about a group of experimental songs he had written-their texts contained no coherent words, consisting entirely of exclamations. But Tcherepnin, who believed in the young man's talent, found these "Seiban Songs" excellent-and that exclamations had a positive advantage for performers and listeners abroad, needing, after all, no translation.

Back in Japan for the summer of 1936, Tcherepnin revised the score of *Japanese Rhapsody* with Akira Ifukube, who came to Yokohama expressly for this purpose. In spite of the language barrier, the lessons (which lasted many hours) ran smoothly. Tcherepnin played through the score measure by measure at the piano, pointing out places that would gain by an alteration in the instrumentation or texture, while Ifukube asked questions that he had formulated beforehand with the help of a dictionary. Tcherepnin became very fond of Ifukube, who was, in his eyes, "a type of Japanese Mussorgsky: extremely delicate, charming and kind."

Many years later, on August 6, 1987, Ifukube wrote to the composer's widow, Ming Tcherepnin, "I have kept...some autograph of his lecture notes with much care, these were written when he was giving lessons to me at Yokohama in 1936, for a long period of time without any fee. These are very happy souvenirs and treasures of inestimable value to me." He also informed her that his *Tryptique Aborigène, Trois Tableaux pour Orchestre de Chambre*, dedicated to Tcherepnin half a century before in 1937, and published in his "Collection," had recently been recorded in Japan (this work received its U. S. premiere in Carnegie Hall, New York, in May 1985 with the IMAS Chamber Symphony of Tokyo).

Another young student of Tcherepnin's in Yokohama was Kojiro Kobune, a guitarist by profession. Tcherepnin considered Kobune's set of children's pieces "perfect, varied in melody, in rhythm, in modes." He decided to publish them and asked if Kobune knew any Japanese painter who could illustrate them. A few days later, Kobune brought him a set of watercolor pictures that Tcherepnin found exquisite. The painter turned out to be none other than Kobune himself.

Surprised and delighted, Tcherepnin published the set with the composer's own beautiful illustrations in typically discreet Japanese colors.

Works by all of Tcherepnin's students eventually appeared in the Tcherepnin Collection, and thanks to Tcherepnin's astute arrangements, these scores were distributed from Peiping and Shanghai (Commercial Press, Inc.), New York (Shawnee Press Inc.), Tokyo (Ryuginsha), Vienna (Universal Edition), and Paris (A la Flute de Pan).

Decades later, the well-known Japanese composer Toru Takemitsu characterized himself as a "grand-pupil" of Tcherepnin because he had studied with Kiyose, who was Tcherepnin's pupil. Likewise Toshiro Mayuzumi, whose works in the late 50s and early 60s were played all over Europe, was a pupil of the Tcherepnin student Ifukube.

Tcherepnin's whirlwind concert tour of Japan in the fall of 1936 would have daunted many a seasoned barnstorming virtuoso: it started in Tokyo where he gave successive piano recitals at the Takaruzaka Theater on October 5, 7, and 10, with three different programs of Japanese, Chinese and Russian music (from Bortniansky to Stravinsky), plus some of his own compositions in each program. On October 11, he played in Osaka; on October 12, at the Kobe College in Kobe; on October 14, in Nagoya. From there he went by train and ferry to the northern island of Hokkaido. On October 21, he played on the radio in Sapporo; on October 22, he gave two consecutive piano recitals at two Sapporo high schools, where all the young students sat on the floor, Japanese fashion; on October 24, he played a recital at Otaru, on the eastern coast of the island facing Vladivostok.

Back in Tokyo, on October 28, Tcherepnin played his Piano Concerto No. 2 with the Tokyo Symphony, under Joseph Rosenstock; on October 30, he gave a benefit recital in Yokohama for the Yokohama Hospital. The same evening he left for Kyoto to give a recital there on November 1. The concert tour ended on November 3 in Hiroshima.

Some of Tcherepnin's fees for these concerts were substantial, some modest. He never accepted payment for playing in schools, however, and whatever was left of his earnings went to support the publication of music by Japanese and Chinese composers. Neither in Japan nor in China did he ever receive remuneration for his teaching.

Following this tour in Japan, Tcherepnin took a train passing through Korea and Manchuria en route to Peiping. But no train could carry him away from the hearts and memories of his Japanese disciples. Sometime later, he received the following letter, dated August 15, 1937:

> Dear Mr. Alexandre Tcherepnine,
> Please allow me for my long silence....
> Some time ago, I received my Rhapsody published from Mr. Yeinen Yuasa. What was my joy when I opened the parcel, how fine it is. It was too fine to believe that it is my own composition, and thrill was beyond descriptions.
> After the first revision of Rhapsody by your kindness at Yokohama, just one year was passed, and souvenir the dear memories, Yokohama-days, and all your kindness since the time, besides I cannot express my thanks enough, so generously adopted my design and crest on the score.
> Between China and Japan, as you know, the war has happened after all. I cannot write the details of TAPANA. When will wars become extinct from the human race? Unavoidably, unwilling, we must make war with *Buffalo Boy's Flute* or *Shepherd's Pastime*. We must resign ourselves to our fate.
> By my diary, the before yesterday of last year I started Tokyo for Hokkaido but this year you are in very faraway land....
>
> With my best wishes, I remain
Sincerely yours,
Akira Ifukube

The cold war between China and Japan was, indeed, rapidly heating up again as Tcherepnin journeyed back to China for the last time. He had been scheduled to stop over in Korea, and Manchuria for appearances in Dairen, Port Arthur and elsewhere, but when he saw the tyrannical nature of the Japanese occupation in Korea he was so upset that he canceled the concerts, proceeded to Mukden, and caught a direct train to Peiping. Back in that ancient city, he played a benefit concert for Chinese soldiers resisting the Japanese invasion.

The end of 1936 was trying. A winter freeze made the Tcherepnins' house in Peiping uninhabitable for several weeks. When they finally got back in, it was still uncomfortably cold, and the composer was unable to procure a piano. After an engagement in Shanghai—a city he loved because of its congenial work atmosphere and its associations with Ming-he told Louisine that he would not return to Peiping. Louisine, however, disliked Shanghai, and made her dislike known in no uncertain terms. Happy, who had fallen in love with a Shanghai Eurasian boy, took the composer's side against her mother, and before long Tcherepnin found the domestic climate well-nigh unbearable.

He responded by immersing himself still more deeply in his work in Shanghai where, in fact, there was a great deal to keep him busy: "Toshitsugu Ogihara came to study with me. I gave free lessons to Chinese composers and pianists." Tcherepnin was also a familiar presence as Honorary Professor at Shanghai Conservatory. "I was glad to participate in all possible ways to music education in China…

"Finally, Louisine and Happy returned to Peiping [at] the end of January [1937] and I stayed in Shanghai alone. I was to return to Peiping to rejoin Louisine, but failed to return. Once more, this time with no Hsien Ming around, there was a 'rupture.' Louisine was revolted by my staying over. Sent me an insulting cable. I obstinately refused to return to Peiping. Louisine changed from anger to love…[I] returned by plane to Peiping on February 18. When I entered the plane, I was warned not to lean on the door, because it was not s[ec]urely closed… I would have been relieved [had] I fall[en] out of the door, so fed [up was] I. with all the situation. But it was not my day."

Again, Tcherepnin found solace in his educational work, and in warm friendships with his Chinese colleagues. On March 1, he gave his farewell recital in Peiping; his last performance in the Orient was a recital at the McTyre School in Shanghai on March 11, 1937. A few days later, he embarked for North America on the S. S. Empress of Asia.

"The night before arriving in Vancouver," wrote Tcherepnin, "I had an [episode of] hysteria—could not stop crying: somehow I felt that it [was]—if not definitive—at any rate [a] long-term good-bye to the Orient that I [had] learned to love."

The death throes of Tcherepnin's life with Louisine persisted for five more weary months. "When I finally left my wife in September 1937, in Hagenals, Austria, I had only a ticket to Paris and not a penny in the world. I had to rebuild my whole life. The trouble was that no one believed that I did not have a penny, which made earning money all the more difficult.

"From the luxury on Park Avenue, the apartment in Paris, I found myself in a small furnished room in Brussels, without a bed, without running water, without a telephone (but with a piano), and did not know how I was going to pay the rent.

"My wife thought that this financial need, if nothing else, would bring me back. But she miscalculated. If my wife had only known how happy and well I felt in spite of this penury, she would have given up all hopes of ever getting me back right then."

"Hsien Ming helped me, and gradually I rebuilt my life, this time correctly."

The rupture with Louisine in September 1937 was not, in fact, as definitive as Tcherepnin indicated. He still used the salutations "Lula" and "Cherie petite" in his letters to her; he arranged for her and Happy to attend the premiere of *The Marriage* in Essen, which took place on Louisine's birthday, November 14 ("please come to see our child's first steps") and on that occasion he even presented her with another hand-drawn birthday card. He also continued to accept sums of money from her. While they no longer lived together, Tcherepnin stayed with Louisine at Wereholme between January and March; and once back in Paris without her, he had her permission to work at the piano in her apartment. Not until September 24 did, he ask for a divorce, telling her that Ming and he were expecting a child in January.

The gratifying ending to this was that Tcherepnin and Louisine ultimately emerged from their troubles as good friends, and that Peter, the eldest son of Alexander and Ming Tcherepnin, developed close ties with his "Aunt Happy."

Tcherepnin's visits to the Far East wrought not only a permanent change in his life, but a permanent change in his musical style as well. The results of his Chinese pentatonic research were immediately evident even in a nominally Russian piece like the ballet *Trepak*, composed just after his return to the West, and continued to be apparent even in works as late as the Fourth Symphony (1957).

Indeed, the exchange between Alexander Tcherepnin and China was mutual. His generous support will not soon be forgotten in the annals of Chinese musical history. Many of those whose lives were touched by the composer from abroad in the 1930s later became directors or deputy directors of important conservatories in China, some forging careers as composers and performers in their own right. During 1945 or 1946, the Chinese government invited Tcherepnin to harmonize and orchestrate the national anthem—which he did. The subsequent Communist regimes, of course, generally discouraged the suggestion that *anything* worthwhile was accomplished in China during the regime of the hapless Generalissimo Chang. The educational work of Tcherepnin, however, was a significant exception. The composer has continued to be the subject of praise in government-controlled publications of more recent years, and regular anniversary concerts have been presented, showing that Tcherepnin's contribution to Chinese musical life is still treasured. Typical is a tribute that appeared in 1982 in a Shanghai periodical, *The Art of Music*:

> Mr. Tcherepnin had a great love for China. He recognized the heritage that lies in the treasury of China's music and musical talent. Unfortunately, he bid us farewell too soon. Only the kindness of his face, his noble artistic spirit, and his unique love for China will remain forever in our hearts.

❀ ❀ ❀ ❀ ❀ ❀

EPILOGUE:

ALEXANDER TCHEREPNIN by Phillip Ramey

September 29, 1983, was a pleasant, sunny day in Paris. The morning saw unusual activity in the Rue Furstenberg, that picturesque Left-Bank passage graced by a tiny, tree-shaded *place* containing the Atelier Delacroix, lying almost in the shadow of the medieval belltower of the St. Germain-des-Pres Church. Municipal workers arrived early to sweep and wash the street, and as the morning wore on, police began to cordon the area with barricades. A wooden lectern had been positioned at No. 2 Rue Furstenberg and above and left of the doorway a cloth covering hung from the building. Later in the afternoon a crowd began to gather, consisting of notable figures in Parisian musical life. Speeches were given—by a high government official (Maurice Fleuret), by two eminent musicologists (Jacques Chailley, Vladimir Jankelevitch), by two well-known composers (Marcel Mihalovici, Alexandre Tansman). Then, with a flourish, the cloth came down, unveiling a marble plaque inscribed with gold lettering: "*Le compositeur Alexandre Tchérepnine—1899–1977—habitâ cette maison*" ("The composer Alexander Tcherepnin—1899-1977—lived in this house").

The ceremony, on the sixth anniversary of Tcherepnin's death, demonstrated that gone is not necessarily forgotten. Even better evidence of that fact are the many recent and projected performances of his music around the globe from Chicago to Beijing. Numerous new Tcherepnin recordings have appeared since the composer's death, both here and abroad, and several posthumous works have been published by the firms of Belaieff, Peters and Schott.

In his biography of Alexander Tcherepnin, Willi Reich pronounced him a "musical citizen of the world," and it was no exaggeration. Although Tcherepnin maintained a home in Paris for more than half a century and was resident in the United States for much of his last thirty years, his background and culture were Russian. He was an almost constant traveler during a long career, composing and concertizing as a pianist not only in the major European and American capitals, but in less familiar places like the Soviet Caucasus region, China, Japan and Egypt. The international cosmopolitan aspect of Tcherepnin's life and career rightly informs much of the commentary on him by critics and colleagues. Yehudi Menuhin, for instance, termed Tcherepnin "this distinguished composer, original in concept and expression, whose works reflect a synthesis of many cultures."

Tcherepnin was born into an old and cultured family on January 21, 1899, in St. Petersburg, Russia. The Tcherepnin name was already well known in Russian musical circles because of Nicolas Tcherepnin, Alexander's father, a distinguished composer, conductor and pedagogue. Alexander's mother, Maria, was also musical, gifted with a fine mezzo-soprano voice and given to singing Russian, German and French songs in the parlor.

Alexander's maternal grandfather was the French painter Albert Benois, pioneering watercolorist in Russia and brother of the stage designer Alexander Benois. Nicolas Tcherepnin was conductor of Serge Diaghilev's famed Ballet Russe, and thanks to him young Alexander met most of the great figures of Russian music and dance, among them Rimsky-Korsakov, Liadov, Glazunov, Stravinsky, Chaliapin, Diaghilev, Pavlova and Fokine. Sergei Prokofiev, a conducting student of Nicolas Tcherepnin, frequently played his latest compositions for Alexander when he visited the apartment for a lesson.

"In our home," remembered Tcherepnin, "music was religion," and one of his earliest recollections was that of praying to an icon to become a composer. His mother taught him the fundamentals of music when he was five years old, predating his knowledge of the alphabet. Alexander soon began to improvise at one of the family's two pianos, but, as he said, "I never dared to touch a piano in the presence of my father for fear of disturbing him." His mother, however, encouraged his initial efforts at composition. "At first, my father did not approve of my plans to be a composer, insisting that it would be a hard and nerve-wracking life. He wanted me to become a gentleman-farmer but, when he saw the seriousness of my intent, he gave in and even embraced the idea."

By age 15, Alexander was a prolific composer, with several symphonies, piano concertos and operas, dozens of piano pieces, and at least seven piano sonatas behind him. Some of this music was later published, notably a set of Bagatelles that became as renowned in its way as Rachmaninoff's Prelude in C-sharp Minor and that is to this day part of the experience of most student pianists.

In his 18th year Alexander enrolled at the St. Petersburg Conservatory, where his father taught. His long-standing preoccupation as a composer with the major-minor triad began about this time. That harmonically ambiguous entity was much in his ear, but he heard it as a fundamental and stable chord. "I used it as a final consonance [and] the acceptance of the major-minor triad resulted in further acceptance of many other unorthodox chords." The practical result was that in many of Tcherepnin's earliest compositions the function of dissonance as requiring resolution was lost. In his works until about 1921 is found a hybrid style successfully linking the Romantic impetuosity (but not the Romantic textures) of Rachmaninoff and Scriabin with the grotesquerie of early Prokofiev. The result was fresh, imaginative music, such as the *Bagatelles* and *Sonatine Romantique*, that quickly made a reputation for the young composer. Tcherepnin's fascination with the major-minor triad and its modal possibilities would cause him to devise a nine-tone scale (formed from the superimposition of two such triads), which he would use to greater or lesser degree in much of his mature music. (This, which in fact became known as the "Tcherepnin Scale," reads, from C: C, Db, Eb, E, F, G, Ab, A, B, [C].) He subsequently made the interesting discovery that his instinctively composed music "did not just lean toward this nine-step synthetic scale, it was actually based on it and could be explained by it. From then on, what had previously been done instinctively was done through theory and conscious application." Further, "The devices of melodic, free, chromatic scale formation, of serial writing, of using the early medieval polyphonic devices for the formation of chromatic, linear writing was all found and elaborated while isolated from any contact with Western music [because of] the First World War and Russian Revolution… three years ahead of the serial conception of tropes of [Josef Mathias] Hauer and Schoenberg."

Late in 1918, the Tcherepnin family fled famine and cholera in St. Petersburg (which had recently been renamed Petrograd) for the relative peace of the still-independent republic of Georgia in the Caucasus, where Nicolas had been appointed director of the Tiflis Conservatory. In that city, Alexander came under the spell of Georgian folk music, another lifelong influence, and, continuing to compose, began to practice the piano diligently. In 1921 the Red Army brought the civil war that had been raging elsewhere in Russia to Tiflis, and not long afterward the Tcherepnins were again on the move, this time out of Russia for good, to France, where they settled in Paris.

Alexander finished his studies in Paris (composition with Paul Vidal, piano with Isidore Philipp), saw a sizable number of his early pieces published, and began an international career as a composer-pianist. His Western debut came in London in 1922, and the following year his ballet *Ajanta's Frescoes*, inspired by ancient Indian cave painting and imbued, said Tcherepnin, with "the idea of integrating Eastern and Western musical conceptions," was presented at Covent Garden by the immortal Anna Pavlova.

Tcherepnin came to the United States in 1926, and in 1927 gained notoriety through a *succès de scandale* at age 28 when his First Symphony nearly provoked a riot at its premiere, police being summoned to the Paris Theatre du Chatelet to quell an audience aroused by the work's scherzo for unpitched percussion and stringed instruments tapped with the bow as if they were wooden drums. In his book *Music Since 1900*, Nicolas Slonimsky cited this as "the earliest known example of an integral percussive movement in a symphony," and here, as in portions of the orchestral work *Magna Mater* (1926-27) and the piano piece *Message* (1926), which ends with tappings on the wood of the piano, Tcherepnin indulged in pure rhythm for its own sake.

Perhaps stimulated by the near-volcanic musical climate of the 1920s Paris, where he found himself "mingling with such people as Ravel, Stravinsky, Prokofiev, Honegger, Milhaud and Martinu and hearing their music," the young composer began producing work of more distinctive character than before. Tcherepnin once observed, "Interestingly, the influence of Paris has generally had on foreign composers has been to make them find and to be *themselves*. Chopin didn't develop a French style because he lived in Paris, but became, if anything, more Polish. The same thing happened to composers like Albeniz and Cop-land." Tcherepnin joined a group of composers known as the *École de Paris* (the other members, Arthur Honegger, Bohuslav Martinu, Marcel Mihalovici, Tibor Harsanyi, Conrad Beck).

At first, Tcherepnin followed "the road of simplification" in lyric, mordantly witty works of neo-Classic bent, sometimes based on motor rhythms, often on variation techniques, such as the *Rhapsodie géorgienne* for cello and orchestra (1922) and Piano Concerto No. 2 (1923). This process culminated in what became one of his most often-played chambers works, the tiny Piano Trio, and Tcherepnin then realized that if simplification continued "nothing will be left." As a consequence, he began to move in the opposite direction by introducing complications, especially increasingly complex polyphonic structures. "Interpoint" was the name he gave to a system of often-dissonant polyphony wherein rhythmic units were employed thematically. "Meditating about progress in music," he wrote, "and rejecting traditionalism and the vagueness associated with it from my early youth, I found that, to my mind, progress would be achieved via clear part-writing and, therefore, by polyphony." Tcherepnin's works of the late 1920s and early 1930s tend toward larger forms, clear textures (here, the influence of neo-Classic Stravinsky was significant, as was Tcherepnin's rejection of Impressionism) and highly active part-writing. The Piano Quintet (1927), Piano Concerto No. 3 (1931-32) and Symphony No. 1 (1927) illustrate this trend.

After 1933, coincident with concert tours to the Middle East and the Orient, Tcherepnin began to look for a way to escape what he called "my own self-imposed technical formulas," and he soon found it in folklore. He reinvestigated Russian, Georgian, Armenian, Azerbaijan and Persian music, later becoming especially intrigued by Chinese and Japanese folk melodies. Results were immediate: the 1933 *Russian Dances* for orchestra, a lightweight though effective melange (which, in a graph-like appraisal of his output he himself made in the late 1950s, found only recently in his papers, he classed rather harshly as one of his low points); the Five "Chinese" Concert Etudes for piano of 1934-36, brilliant yet delicate and lyrical; the *Suite géorgienne* for piano and string orchestra of 1938, subtle, refined, emotionally restrained.

Throughout his visits to the Far East between 1934 and 1937, Tcherepnin taught composers in China and Japan and, with the receipts from his concerts, generously established in Tokyo a press, *Collection Tcherepnine*, for the publication of his pupils' works. (The prominent Japanese composer Toru Takemitsu once told the author that many in his country consider Tcherepnin a father-figure of Japanese serious music.) It was in the Orient, in Shanghai, that he met a talented young Chinese pianist Lee Hsien Ming, who later became his second wife. Ming had won a scholarship to study in Brussels, so Tcherepnin was able to continue his courtship back in Europe.

During World War II, Alexander and Ming and the composer's father and mother had no choice but to remain in Nazi-occupied Paris, having tried unsuccessfully to escape. Tcherepnin supported the family on his meager earnings from composition lessons and what he called "utility music." He noted that there was a great decline in the quality of his work during the war. "To live through the Occupation was not easy, and I had to compose lots of trash—for dancers, for music halls, and so on, which had to be signed by another name because I was Russian." Little of Tcherepnin's wartime music has survived, which is perhaps just as well, for on his aforementioned graph the year 1944 ranks as the nadir of his entire career.

"Immediately after the end of the Occupation, even before the end of the war," he wrote, "my fertility returned." Once again, he began to compose worthwhile music and to resume traveling and concertizing. After he toured America in 1948, he and Ming accepted teaching positions at DePaul University in Chicago, and he later wrote that coming to the United States in 1949 was "the great change in my life." In 1950 his children arrived, and the family stayed in Chicago for 15 years, becoming U. S. citizens in 1958. Tcherepnin resigned from DePaul in 1964 and settled in New York, in order to devote himself entirely to composition and to performing in American and Europe. The Tcherepnins had three sons, Peter, Serge and Ivan, the last two of whom became the family's third generation of composers.

Tcherepnin himself quite accurately labeled his music from 1950 on as "synthesis." He was involved in a conscious effort to consolidate and develop all the previous elements of his style, the instinctive, the simplified, the systematic and synthetic, the folkloristic. "I was looking," he said, "for pure creation, broader forms, rhythmic development and free application of everything I had obtained and experienced."

There is no question but that the synthesis process made possible some of Tcherepnin's most imposing works, scores replete with melody so wide-ranging as to suggest atonality, dramatic contrasts between simple and complex part-writing, polytonal chords so complex and dense as to form tone-clusters, and free, invented forms—all constituting an emotionally cool, impressively balanced neo-Romanticism. Among the masterpieces of this last period are the 1959 *Symphonic Prayer* for orchestra, with its powerfully discordant nine-tone opening and its stunning, perhaps unique, *alleluia* climax, and the dramatic, intensely lyrical Symphony No. 4 (1957—premiered by Charles Munch and the Boston Symphony Orchestra), tightly argued yet expansive, full of invention and contrast, culminating in a majestic, dissonant polyphonic finale based on a medieval Russian church chant. Also notable in this regard are the Symphony No. 2 (1947-51), Twelve Preludes for Piano (1952-53), Eight Pieces for Piano (1954-55), *Divertimento* for Orchestra (1955-57—premiered by Fritz Reiner and the Chicago Symphony), Serenade for string orchestra (1964) and Piano Concertos Nos. 5 (1963) and 6 (1965—premiered by Margrit Weber).

In 1967, Tcherepnin became the second White Russian emigre composer officially invited back to the U. S. S. R. for concerts, the first having been Igor Stravinsky five years earlier. In Moscow, Tcherepnin was soloist in his Second Piano Concerto, and many of the Soviet Union's finest musicians, among them Emil Gilels and Sviatoslav Richter, came to honor him; he then went on to play in Leningrad and Tbilisi, the cities of his childhood and youth.

Being on his native soil after nearly half a century and finding his music enthusiastically accepted was a heady experience. In a letter to the author from Moscow dated May 15, 1967, Tcherepnin described the previous two weeks as "an uninterrupted going," with concerts, broadcasts, "meeting old friends, making new ones, extravagant hospitality… wonderful, attentive, warm audiences. Altogether unique experience, seems to me so natural, so familiar, to be here as if I had never left." In another letter: "Most important and stimulating for me is the 'open door' to the country of my origin—for me and my music—which certainly will mark the rest of my life and is a sort of guarantee that after my death I will not be forgotten."

That Tcherepnin will be forgotten, either in Russia or in the West, is unlikely. He left, at his death, too much of genuine worth. He thought of composing as a duty, "I feel that the process of composition is for the professional composer (at least for me) not a pleasure but a heavy responsibility, a continuous effort resulting from the urge to create. Pleasure comes only when the composition is completed." He himself had rigorous standards, and he once gently but firmly admonished an aspiring student, "Remember Stravinsky's advice: the most important utensil of the composer is the *eraser*. More you erase, better will be what stays."

Tcherepnin, of course, heeded Stravinsky's counsel the greater part of the time, but, as with all fecund artists, there were occasional lapses. His art, as he frankly acknowledged in his graph appraisal, had its peaks and plateaus—and canyons. As an example, only one opus number from the towering Fourth Symphony is an orchestral suite called *Georgiana*, a treacly confection gummed together with Georgian folk tunes. (Tcherepnin seemed to me to be less than delighted when Leopold Stokowski programmed *Georgiana* in the 1960s.) But it should be noted that this was a composer who thought it necessary to write not only works that might stand the test of time but also to provide more accessible, useful scores. Tcherepnin was not a believer in another Stravinsky dictum that every piece should be a masterpiece; and, partly as a rest from his more serious efforts, he took pleasure in creating occasional crowd-pleasers-like the brilliant *Symphonic March* of 1951 and the genial Harmonica Concerto of 1953. To sum up, Tcherepnin was a major figure, a fact well known in Europe if not entirely appreciated here in his adopted country. At this writing, more than five years after Tcherepnin's death and not long after the 85th anniversary of his birth, there are increasing indications across the United States that his music is enjoying a revival. One anticipates his major works being performed more often by American orchestras and instrumentalists. After all, as Virgil Thomson put it, Tcherepnin's art "has at all periods been filled with poetry and bravura"-qualities too often at a premium in 20th-century music.

Alexander Tcherepnin was a "compleat" composer, an elegant pianist, a discerning, sympathetic teacher, an extraordinarily civilized man. Those who knew him suspect they will not see his like again.

Teaching Phillip Ramey

Teaching Robert Muczynski

Tcherepnin in class at DePaul University

The first page of Tcherepnin's anniversary pastiche for Louisine commemorating their extensive previous year's travels.

ALEXANDER TCHEREPNIN:
A COMPENDIUM

INTERMEZZI:

TCHEREPNIN AND HIS COLLEAGUES

PART I: TRIBUTES

TCHEREPNIN PRELUDE

Artists [live] in a regime of constant flattery; no one who comes to greet an artist after the concert [in] the green room ever [utters] anything other than compliments… And of course there [is] applause after each performance.

AARON COPLAND

Alexander Tcherepnin was a remarkable and fascinating composer, because his art represents an unusual fusion of differing cultures; his Russian upbringing; his long sojourn in Europe, particularly Paris; his extensive travels in the Orient; his many years in the United States. Because of this last, I came to think of Sasha as a kind of honorary American composer, a valued colleague and friend. His music, expert and individual, was often dashing and affecting, from charming early scores like the *Bagatelles* for piano and the Second Piano Concerto to impressive later efforts such as the Fourth Symphony and Serenade for Strings. As the years pass and his work becomes more widely known, I feel convinced that the prolific Sasha will be seen as a major figure-an important composer of our time who successfully assimilated several artistic worlds.

❈ ❈ ❈

VIRGIL THOMSON

Alexander Tcherepnin was a sweet man and probably a great one. His friends loved him; his wife and his sons adored him. He was a remarkable pianist and a composer both highly skilled and deeply original, personal, not quite like any other. The range of his music was wide, comprehensive, covering all the forms and practically all the occasions... A great family! and I am sure a great man! Mastery and distinction are the qualities of them all.

❈ ❈ ❈

ELLIOTT CARTER

The remarkable and the unusual characterize the musical side of the Tcherepnin family. To have been the son of the outstanding Nicolai and yet not to have been dominated by him but to have a personal, commanding, avant-garde style of his own, puts him in a special category of present-day composers who have been for the most part in reaction against their upbringing. For Sascha was a greatly respected creator of new music of highly developed skill and imagination. He wrote works that gave him his reputation while leading an especially agitated life, moving from Russia to China to France and then to the United States—drastic changes that would have prevented many from completing such a large body of work and distracted them from the single-minded effort to maintain and develop a personal musical style. Along with this he found a way to bring up two sons as composers, who, in turn, have become in their own way original and skillful.

❈ ❈ ❈

HENRI DUTILLEUX

I feel I have always known Alexander Tcherepnin. He is a figure that could never be overlooked; to use the familiar French expression, *il a de la branche* (he has an air about him). The human warmth, the natural curiosity and the appetite for everything new that have animated [his] entire existence are paralleled in his work, and [the passing] years have only heightened his faculty for enthusiasm and intensified the youthfulness of his spirit.

❈ ❈ ❈

DARIUS MILHAUD

You can be proud of the music of your family: your father and now your sons. As to you, you have known how to assimilate orient and occident into your work, as you have into your life.

❈ ❈ ❈

LENNOX BERKELEY

Alexander Tcherepnin, besides being himself a composer and pianist of great distinction, has endeared himself to countless musicians by his capacity for friendship and by his interest in their work. This generous appreciation of the qualities of others is equalled by his sensitive and intelligent understanding.

❊ ❊ ❊

VLADIMIR USSACHEVSKY

Whatever Tcherepnin wrote, the work possessed a wonderful clarity, no matter how complex the language, and an elegant and forceful style. He showed an unfailing surety in determining the proper form for his works. [His scores] included instances of prophetic ventures into some musical fashions of the future. In [his First Symphony] there is evidence of the early use of dodecaphonic principles and medieval polyphonic artifices. In his First Cello Sonata (circa 1924) there was also clearly pre-Messiaen thematic use of bird-calls. He [created] a masterly synthesis of [folk] materials, quite unlike the chinoiserie and fake orientalia we are running across in some fashionable music writing today. With his passing, we have lost one of the last links with that circle of musicians who did not have the opportunity to carry out their revolutionary musical ideas in post-revolutionary Russia. Yet through them and their fellow exiles, artists such as Balanchine, Vladimir Nabokov and Diaghilev, *et. al.*, the vocabulary of the arts gained a Russian accent.

❊ ❊ ❊

WERNER EGK

I first encountered Alexander Tcherepnin's music and the composer himself more than four decades ago during the founding of the Munich Society for Contemporary Music. Through the decades, I have maintained a warm friendship with him and a lively interest in his wholly personal, carefully crafted music. [I] thank him for his unfailing affection, and for his work.

❊ ❊ ❊

NED ROREM

His music colored my Chicago childhood. It never occurred to me then that one day I would actually know him. But years later, when we occasionally chatted during Parisian intermissions or at Manhattan parties, I would always draw a parallel between the cosmopolitan likability and tall elegance of his person, and the expert economy and healthy sensuality of his art. And now today, I continually return to the notion of the man as to the sound of his music, and realize that my life—indeed, the life of our planet—would be much lonelier without the fact of Alexander Tcherepnin.

❊ ❊ ❊

BORIS BLACHER

You belong to a group of composers who for many decades—to be exact, since World War I—have been buffeted back and forth as "citizens of the world," or, in less high-flown terms, as stateless persons, between countries and languages, not always willingly. You were one of the first to build artistically viable bridges between the Far East and the Western World. Warmest greetings from your friend, colleague and compatriot (for 35 years also stateless).

❊ ❊ ❊

MARCEL MIHALOVICI

[Tcherepnin's music] is of a superb originality—I love it for the perfection of its forms, for that of its realization, for the nobility of thought that informs it.

❊ ❊ ❊

HE LUTING

We saw him off at the [Shanghai] train station. As the train was pulling out of the depot, he waved goodbye with a sheaf of manuscript paper rolled up in his hand as a reminder that we should always compose diligently. Little did we know that that was to be our last glimpse of him. As the composer of *Buffalo Boy's Flute*, [which won] the competition Tcherepnin had sponsored for compositions in a Chinese character, how sorely I missed him! But all I could do was silently remember him in my heart. I was not allowed to communicate with him in the ten awful years when the Gang of Four was in power. This I count as one of the great regrets of my life… Mr. Tcherepnin is the only Western composer who so passionately loved Chinese music. He was tireless in his efforts to promote Chinese music around the world. Many of his own compositions reflected a Chinese character. We Chinese musicians will love him and miss him forever. He has our eternal devotion and esteem.

❀　❀　❀

ROBERT MUCZYNSKI

… When I was still a pupil of his during the late '40s and early' 50s I was witness to the fact that some of the greatest orchestras and conductors of the day performed Sasha's music: Kubelik, Reiner, Steinberg, Munch, Malko, Sevitzky, and so on. Invariably, Sasha's music generated a powerful impact upon audiences and I was thrilled to be present at many of these events: in Orchestra Hall, Chicago, when Kubelik and the Chicago Symphony Orchestra presented an all-Tcherepnin concert featuring the premiere of the Second Symphony plus a performance of the Second Piano Concerto with Tcherepnin as soloist; at Carnegie Hall when Sevitzky and the Indianapolis Symphony premiered the Third Symphony; a radiant performance of the Suite, Op. 87, by Reiner and the Chicago Symphony; the marvelous Fourth Symphony presented by Walter Hendl and that orchestra at the Ravinia Summer Festival Concerts; the unique and utterly charming Concerto for Harmonica and Orchestra as performed by soloist John Sebastian with the Grant Park Summer Symphony Lake Front series of concerts under the direction of Nicolai Malko (who later presented Mr. Tcherepnin's dynamic score *Symphonic Prayer*)… For a young, aspiring composer this was not only a vital part of my education but also served as a source of inspiration. I owe the man so much. Without his encouragement and faith in my earliest primitive attempts I am quite certain that I would have pursued a different path. He guided me, assisted me, inspired me. In addition to all these professional kinds of direction he so generously extended to me I must mention that Alexander Tcherepnin was also one of the most remarkable men it was my privilege to encounter, to know and to love. I still miss him. He was devoted to his family, worked harder than anyone I know and yet maintained a sense of joy. Sasha was the most positive-thinking and dedicated artist I have ever known. I am certain that his creative work will emerge and receive its fullest and most deserving recognition in the years to come.

❀　❀　❀

RAFAEL KUBELIK

My dear Sascha!

With us musicians, words are only appropriate where they can be realized in music. I wish that… I wa capable of writing a cantata whose music could fully portray your large warm heart, your noble personality and your love for music, humanity, nature and everything of beauty. So accept these modest words from me, with my most heartfelt wish that you may continue for many years to bring *caritas* to music, to the joy of all who love it.

❀　❀　❀

FERDINAND LEITNER

My strong artistic and personal harmony with Tcherepnin has induced me to recommend the work of this very great composer to my colleagues as something quite special.

❀　❀　❀

IGOR MARKEVITCH

In you I salute a rare, singular, eminently aristocratic artist, whose qualities have the merit of always appearing natural. One does not know whether you should be more admired as a man or as a creator, so thoroughly are the two mixed in the course of your life. But your most attractive trait is undoubtedly the seignoral elegance in which you sheathe your profound musical science.

❊　❊　❊

KURT REDEL

Alexander Tcherepnin is a man with abundant heart, magnificent elan and the sort of indescribable charm that communicates beyond the circle of his friends. These great human qualities are strongly perceptible in his music…

❊　❊　❊

RUDOLF BAUMGARTNER

In recent years, several works by Alexander Tcherepnin have been introduced at the Lucerne International Music Festival… Along with celebrated soloists and conductors, musicians of large symphony orchestras and the Lucerne Festival Strings have gotten to know him, not only as a world-famous composer, but as a lovable, profound, simple man. How fortunate that his spirit, and with it, the soul of true music, has endured in his latest works despite all the changes in stylistic fashions over the years.

❊　❊　❊

ALFREDO ANTONINI

I have known Alexander Tcherepnin for many years and we have been working together on many occasions. He is a great artist, a warm human being and a delightful person. Alexander Tcherepnin is one of the greatest composers of the twentieth century.

❊　❊　❊

JOHANNES SOMARY

As a choral conductor, I have had numerous occasions to program some of Alexander Tcherepnin's liturgical music, which not only blends magnificently into the worship service but also creates an exquisite aura of mysticism, peace and tranquil joy. His music exudes a serene optimism that makes his compositions a pleasure to sing and a pleasure to conduct.

❊　❊　❊

YEHUDI MENUHIN

Alexander Tcherepnin is to music the living and lovely echo of that magic that Serge Diaghilev brought to Western Europe adding a dimension to all the arts: painting, composing, dancing, theater unrivalled before or since his advent. The grace and charm, warmth and color, as well as the boldness of imagination that flowered in this halcyon time is what nurtured the young Tcherepnin and what is inherent still in all his music. Profoundly Russian in conception, it yet bears the stamp of a Paris that was the capital of the Arts—was significantly where Asia, Africa and Europe met and fused, and which served as a catalyst for the ideas and creations of artists from all three Continents. It was through this civilizing filter that the great and natural essences of Russian art passed, producing just such a musician and composer as my dear and valued friend Alexander Tcherepnin.

❊　❊　❊

ALFRED LOEWENGUTH

I have had occasion to play several works of Alexander Tcherepnin and also had the pleasure of making his acquaintance. The man measures up to his work, that is to say, simple, sincere and cogent. One cannot but wish that his work will live in all nations.

❀　❀　❀

TOSSY SPIVAKOVSKY

Although Tcherepnin's Violin Sonata is an early work, the composition is undimmed in its freshness of emotion, its richly-colored and eloquent musical diction and its harmonic interest.

❀　❀　❀

LEONARD SORKIN

As a member of the Chicago Symphony Orchestra and later on as 1st violinist of the Fine Arts Quartet, I developed a great appreciation for his music, particularly in the chamber music form… His music to me has always expressed a great charm and warmth, coupled of course with complete mastery of whatever musical form he was dealing with. I shall always treasure the opportunities I have had to work with Mr. Tcherepnin and to perform his music.

❀　❀　❀

PAUL TORTELIER

I only play the music I love, and one can count many classic works in that category. On the other hand, where modern music is concerned, the repertory for me becomes very limited. That is why I am so grateful to Alexander Tcherepnin, for having brought so valuable a contribution to the literature of my instrument, especially with his Suite for Cello Solo and his remarkable Duo for Violin and Cello. His compositions prove that, in the world of music as in the world in general, variety is endless and that originality in the expression of feelings is not a question of fashion or of novelty. Alexander Tcherepnin does not seek to "amaze the bourgeois." He is original in spite of himself because he has an original talent of composing and the gift of making his public feel a sensitivity which is all his.

❀　❀　❀

PIERRE FOURNIER

I address my warmest good wishes to my friend Alexander Tcherepnin. Once more, I express my admiration for his great talent as composer, whose ceaselessly renewing inspiration constantly enriches the world.

❀　❀　❀

JANOS STARKER

Mr. Tcherepnin has long ago passed the stage where his unquestioned mastery and creative powers need to be deliberated on. He is one of the handful of true giants of twentieth-century music. His music will stay and the esteem will increase.

❀　❀　❀

GRANT JOHANNESEN

Alexander Tcherepnin has remained a rare phenomenon over the turbulent decades of this century: quite simply, he is a "man of music," whose civilized ear follows its own civilized inspirational course. We are the better for his integrity, since he has produced a body of music full of real quality, sensitivity and brio. In spite of his deep Slavic inheritance he never appears slave to a pat nationalism; indeed, his music ever reflects a highly sophisticated international mind…Tcherepnin's great contribution to the piano literature deserves the gratitude of all artists who love the piano and its perpetuation.

❀   ❀   ❀

MARGRIT WEBER

[Tcherepnin's] music opens for us an almost unattainable world in which every sound, whether spoken or played, is true. That is why his music, in its art and virtuosity is beyond cavil. It mirrors his spirit, aglow in all its facets with his richness of ideas and his beautiful inner world.

❀   ❀   ❀

YVONNE LORIOD-MESSIAEN
(Letter of condolence to Ming Tcherepnin)

I should like with all my heart to tell you of the sadness we feel at the loss of our dear master, A. Tcherepnine. You know that I play his music as often as possible, and give it to my pupils to play. He represented for me the discovery of the East through his *Études de Concert* and my first concert with orchestra, more than 30 years ago, was his *Suite Georgienne*. A part of my childhood disappeared with him. So many memories come back: the birth of your little baby in a motorcar, rue Furstenberg, you, so pretty and happy, he, so tall and proud! And now he has left the earth and is in heaven. Think, chere madame, that he is now happy, that he has the answer to all his questions, that he sees the Light and Music in their very essence, in contemplating God. Continue to smile at him as he continues to love you with all his heart.

❀   ❀   ❀

WILHELM KEMPFF

Dear Alexander Tcherepnin,
    Do you know where we first encountered each other?…The setting was Japan…After a concert in Hiroshima, my wife and I boarded the steamer crossing the inland sea to Beppu. It was a clear, starry night. I can still see the bejewelled light of the temple lanterns wreathing the shore like a string of pearls as it slowly faded. Suddenly, the captain appeared, [saying]: "There's a concert, Radio Korea or Hong Kong. Perfectly clear sound tonight. Do you want to hear it?"
    So I listened, and indeed the sounds were no ordinary affair—sounds that seemed like a tonal likeness of the Japanese night. The piano rose clearly above the orchestra, and yet the lines flowed together in a unity. Who was the soloist? Who was the composer? The announcer revealed it: Alexander Tcherepnin was playing his own music. He, mediator between east and west, who has nevertheless preserved his personal musical signature.

❀   ❀   ❀

ROLAND KOHLOFF
(Principal timpanist, New York Philharmonic)

Dear Mrs. Tcherepnin:
    I wanted to tell you just how much I loved your husband's composition *Sonatina* for Three Timpani and Piano. It has long been a favorite of mine since I first studied it and played it at the Juilliard School in the 1950s. And it has given me great pleasure to have played it and taught it to students from coast to coast…

❀   ❀   ❀

H. H. STUCKENSCHMIDT

Alexander Tcherepnin is one of the few genuine world citizens of contemporary music. Earlier than others, he understood the cultural importance of non-European music. Moreover, he is a great musical inventor...and in his oeuvre almost all musical genres are represented by works of great originality.

❋　❋　❋

OLGA KOUSSEVITZKY

Alexander Tcherepnin, as the son of Nicolai Tcherepnin, is an heir of the great Russian musical tradition, and represents today one of the foremost creative talents on our musical scene.

❋　❋　❋　❋　❋　❋

Manusript of Tcherepnin's *Opivochki* No. 1, originally intended for his Fifth Symphony.

TCHEREPNIN PRELUDE

(In response to the question, "Who is your favorite contemporary composer?")
Now I am sixty, and at this very moment, I can accept much more than I ever accepted. I [have] learned that it's not a question of the means the composer used in his composition but of the message that he has. When I was young, I felt that Debussy is one to be fought. I felt that Rachmaninoff or Faure would… not even need to be fought because they were already finished… But now I find… good in Faure, in Debussy, in Rachmaninoff. I think Stravinsky is the greatest Russian composer that ever existed… I find good in Prokofiev. I find good in Copland. I find good in Thomson. I find good in Harris.

TCHEREPNIN ON PROKOFIEV

There was several years' difference between Prokofiev and myself-that is to say, I was 12 and he was 20. When I looked at him, a tall young man, I myself was still a boy. I admired him and his music immensely.

… Both Nicolas Benois and I were ardent *priverjeszy* [partisans] of Prokofiev; we called him "The Great" and counted years from the birthday of Prokofiev—April 11th (old style), which we took as the beginning of our year and [called] January 1st. Once we sent him a birthday card saying, "Happy New Year!" to which he answered: "Congratulations on your commitment to the lunatic asylum."

… I remember once, in 1918, just prior to the Revolution, on a bitterly cold night, when we were all hungry, he played his last recital of his own works in St. Petersburg. There was only a handful or so of people present in the hall—some 15 or 20. Nicolai Benois, my cousin, and I clapped our hands as loudly as possible until they were red at the end of each work and elicited many encores—trying to give the impression of success despite the poor attendance. My father was the only professor at St. Petersburg Conservatory who encouraged Prokofiev. At the Conservatory's graduation concert, Prokofiev played his First Piano Concerto. Although it was not customary for a student to play his own composition at a graduation concert, my father nevertheless proposed and persuaded the other faculty members to permit Prokofiev to do so. Glazunov, who was at that time the Conservatory director, got up and stalked off from his first-row seat in a motion of protest as Prokofiev proceeded to play the first movement. Prokofiev had my father's permission to come to the music library at our home, refer to scores there and study them whenever he liked. During that period, he brought all his compositions to my father for comment and advice, listening very attentively to all my father's counsel. Naturally, I was full of interest and did not miss any of these sessions. I can still recollect him telling me with an emphatic tap on my head, "Remember, what you've just heard should not be known outside of this house!" I remember the first work that he brought to father was "Kudesnec," for voice and piano. When he had left, my father told me, "This man has great talent." Prokofiev dedicated three works to my father: the first, Sinfonietta, Op. 5—he told us that he had been able to compose this without a piano. The second was his Piano Concerto No. 1, and the third, Scherzo for Four Bassoons, which was later published as a piano piece. When I was 16, I composed a piece for orchestra called *Laugh, Laugh and Laugh*. Prokofiev was in my room and looked at this work. Then he said to my father, "It's fascinating how Sashinka has learned the craftsmanship. You should try this piece with your orchestra at the Conservatory." My father asked me to copy the material and said he would play it. But he never did, alas, and I was too timid to broach the subject to him myself.

{Tcherepnin also liked to recount this other anecdote about Prokofiev}

Tcherepnin recalled that during his teens the experience of performing often rubbed his emotions raw. Suffering from something like stage fright, he was often so dissatisfied with himself after playing at concerts that upon returning home he would go to bed and weep. However, when he heard Prokofiev, he saw that the latter had perfect self-control when playing, with no signs of stage fright or other emotional upset, only effortless ease and faultless spontaneity. In this respect, as in others, Tcherepnin decided to take Prokofiev as his model, deciding, "if the great Prokofiev has no stage fright, why should I?" From that moment on, Tcherepnin was able to dispel any sign of stage fright or nervousness. But this story was to have a most unexpected twist: on November 12, 1926, Tcherepnin participated at the *Palais du Trocadéro* in the annual Russian Culture Day concert. Through the years, it had become customary for all noted Russian artists present in Paris to perform at these events. This particular date was especially memorable for Tcherepnin as Prokofiev was also to be one of the performers. So they sat together in the artists' room, each awaiting his turn. Suddenly the manager appeared and said to Prokofiev, "Sergei Sergeievich, you are next." Prokofiev became wild with rage: "Didn't I tell you," he fumed, "that you have to give me 15 minutes notice because I have to take drops to keep calm while playing?" Another artist went out instead. Prokofiev in the meantime took lily-of-the-valley drops (which were supposed to calm the nerves) and, in 15 minutes, walked serenely and calmly onto the stage to perform. So Prokochka had fooled him all these years by seeming so calm, whereas in truth he was as nervous as any other colleague of Tcherepnin's—and his composure was due not to his character but to his drops! Fortunately, this disillusionment came too late to do any harm; it was now impossible for Tcherepnin to find his way back to nervousness. He could only feel happy and self-possessed when on the stage.

{Tcherepnin admiration for Prokofiev works did not blind him to the flaws of some individual works, as his cool assessment of the Fifth Piano Concerto shows.}

I heard Prokofiev's 5th Piano Concerto played by himself in N. Y. in 1938. It was the last time I saw Prokofiev. I do not remember what I thought of it at that time, but lately when I heard it performed by Samson François in Minneapolis and by someone [else] in some other town the piece [disappointed] me. It dates from the time when Prokofiev still felt that he had to be a "bad" boy, while his heart was already elsewhere, dreaming of simplicity and clarity. The contact with his native soil helped him to find his own way without continuing the *épater le bourgeois* style, which is the style of his 5th Concerto. I remember that when I have asked Prokofiev sometime in the early thirties why he preferred Russia to the Western world he answered, "it is because in Russia I can compose large scale works… " The 5th Concerto is precisely the opposite of [that]: small scale forms with "shocking" power which no [longer] shocks!

❀　❀　❀

TCHEREPNIN ON SCRIABIN

Nearly all of my fellow students belonged to the Scriabin cult; they saw him as the musical and philosophic prophet and followed him. In spite of the fact that I had romantic feelings toward Scriabin's daughter, Elena, who was in piano class then, I was not attracted by Scriabin's music. His early works seemed to me conventional, the later ones seemed far-fetched, pretentious. Many of his sonatas (except the 9th and 10th) seemed to mill the wind, caught in the mousetrap set by the composer himself. His orchestral works—especially the *Divine Poem* and the *Poem of Ecstasy*—shocked me by their colorless and heavy instrumentation, the *Prometheus* by its fixedness and affectation. And although in the course of fifty years I have gone through many changes in my estimations, my opinion of Scriabin has remained the same, only perhaps I am now able to see in his music—relieved of the home-made high-flown philosophy—some [motivic] and rhythmic aspirations in harmony with the present day.

　　… Mozart, Tchaikovsky, Reger, Prokofiev were in those days in harmony with my thinking: and against the cult of Scriabin I made my undisputable and enthusiastic cult of Prokofiev.

❀　❀　❀

TCHEREPNIN ON STRAVINSKY

… In October 1952, during my stay in Los Angeles, I had the pleasure of visiting Igor Stravinsky, a master whom I admire profoundly. He invited me to his home for supper. His wife Vera—as beautiful as ever—whom I had known in 1920 in Kodjori near Tbilisi—where she was vacationing with her husband of the time, my friend the painter Sudeikin—prepared the menu that she remembered I had liked in Kodjori, and showed me the autograph of several bars of my First Concerto that I had inscribed in her "golden book" in 1920! Stravinsky, whom I had known when I was little, and of whom I retained many personal memories (and many more artistic memories!) touched me by his graciousness and hospitality. He had me listen to several orchestral excerpts from *The Rake's Progress* recorded in Holland, showing me the score and following important lines with his finger. All in all, I spent an unforgettable evening: as presents, he gave me the French edition of his *Poetics of Music*, which he had autographed, along with a recent photo inscribed to my mother, whose beauty he remembered.

❀　At first, the ballet *Firebird* was commissioned by Diaghilev from Liadov. But time passed and Liadov was delaying—when Diaghilev asked him to play something from the ballet, Liadov would play a few bars and say: "see, here is a little star falling" [or something of the sort]. In desperation, thinking he would not get the score, Diaghilev, on the advice of my father, decided to "try out" the young Stravinsky and commissioned him to compose *The Firebird*, which Stravinsky did brilliantly and in [good] time. In those years, during the creation of *Firebird* up to the [completion] of *Petrushka*, Stravinsky often visited my parents, valued my father's opinion, appreciated his orchestration and played some fragments of his [own] works in our house. After *Petrushka* and especially after the *Rites of Spring*, the relations between Stravinsky and my father [came to an end], an event that coincided with the rupture of relations—not without Stravinsky's [instigation]—between my father and Diaghilev.

❀　[Stravinsky] is not a twelve-tone composer: for me, he is a kind of folklore composer. First of all, he worked on Russian folklore—so came *Firebird*, so came *Petrushka*, so came *Rites of Spring*, so came the *Noces, Le Renard*. Then… he started to folklorize [the] eternal line of great composers. So he used Bach as folklore, and on Bach's themes he wrote up [to the] octet-then, not even on Bach's themes, but [in] Bach's ways. On Tchaikovsky, he wrote *Baiser de la Fée* and on Rossini he wrote *Jeu de Cartes*… Lately, on [Alessandro] Scarlatti he wrote *Rake's Progress*. Now… he is using twelve-tone material, but he is using [it] just as he would use folk material. And in that sense there is something absolutely unifying in all Stravinsky, because whichever material he uses [his] approach is the same… And the material which he chooses is always eternal material… He is probably the greatest composer that exists [at present], and certainly in my mind he is absolutely equal to Beethoven. Well, perhaps not Beethoven…

❀　❀　❀

TCHEREPNIN AND BARTÓK

Tcherepnin's initial meeting with Bartök took place during his first year in Paris (1921-22). Tcherepnin recounts that he was invited to call on the composer Karol Szymanowsky and the violinist Paul Kochanski in order to accompany them to a reception. "After a brief talk, we all went together to the home of Henri Prunieres, the director of *Revue Musicale*, [where], according to Szymanowsky, I was to meet *tout Paris musical*. The reception, incidentally, was given in honor of Béla Bartók-and indeed, just as Szymanowski said, *tout Paris* was present. At the piano, Poulenc and Jacques Février were playing jazz. The few rooms were overcrowded. Prunieres and his wife were busily circulating, yet failing to introduce anyone to anyone—for, of course, *tout Paris* was supposed to be well acquainted. Everyone was chatting; everyone seemed to enjoy the party.

"Shy, as I was, I was pushed by the crowd towards a corner—finding myself near. another wallflower, [like] myself completely abandoned and looking [forlorn], as if he were saying, 'why am I here?' For a long time we stood near each other without saying a word. I do not know who. was the first to break the silence—I guess it was [he], because the language [we spoke] was German, in which I would have hardly approached [anyone] in a French gathering.

"It happened that the man with whom I was speaking was Bartók. Nobody paid attention to the 'guest of honor'— so we had an hour-long talk. The theme was folklore: Bartók spoke of his interest in Hungarian, Rumanian, Bulgarian folk [music]; learning that I was Russian, he inquired about the rhythmic and modal aspects of… Russian folklore, and seemed particularly interested in what I was able to tell him about… Georgian folklore, and about the first inversion of a triad built [of] fourths, which is the basic Georgian chord. We spoke also about [the] relation[ship] of language to music, specifically about rhythmic correlations of language and musical phrases… At that time the music and even the name of Bartók was entirely unknown to me; undoubtedly… Bartók [knew just as little about] me. But this long, friendly conversation, the exchange of names and… addresses, aroused our mutual interest in each other and in each other's music which was to show itself in the future in many a way."

❀ ❀ ❀

TCHEREPNIN AND RACHMANINOFF

Tcherepnin told Phillip Ramey that he always felt some remorse when he recollected an encounter with Rachmaninoff in Paris during the 1920s. At that time, Tcherepnin and his fellow avant-gardists had little respect for Rachmaninoff as a composer. In their view, his brand of full-blown post-Tchaikovskian Romanticism represented everything that was detestable about the past. Some even shrugged him off as a has-been: for after leaving Russia, Rachmaninoff composed no music for eight years, and when he finally returned to his desk, the dismal result was his Fourth Concerto, an unqualified failure at its 1926 premiere.

A concert of music by contemporary composers had been scheduled in Paris, and Rachmaninoff and Tcherepnin, among others, were to be presented to the audience and to perform. Backstage, the younger composers chatted together, leaving Rachmaninoff standing silent in isolation. Finally, Rachmaninoff approached Tcherepnin almost shyly and asked him if he would say a few words to introduce him to the audience.

Unfortunately, at that moment Tcherepnin's youthful modernist pride asserted itself. To be associated in the public mind with a musical dinosaur like Rachmaninoff—to open himself to the accusation that he might approve of this hopeless reactionary—would, he felt, put a significant blot on his reputation. Coldly, he refused Rachmaninoff's request.

In later years, Tcherepnin became uncomfortably aware that he had been guilty of gratuitous rudeness; and he had all the more reason to regret his snub as he grew to realize—once his own battle for modernism was won—that there was much to admire in Rachmaninoff's music.

❀ ❀ ❀

TCHEREPNIN ON DEBUSSY

Contrary to most of my colleagues in the Conservatory, I saw the music of the future in simplification and not in complication, in clearness… I fought the impressionists in those days, and, not having understood the genius of Debussy, called his music "sketchy and formless." I confess [this] now in shame: [for] the [longer] I live, the more I admire the imagination and freedom of Debussy and consider his creative genius a revelation.

❀ ❀ ❀

TCHEREPNIN AND RAVEL

In February 1932, Tcherepnin attended a concert of Ravel compositions in Vienna conducted by the composer himself. While listening to the *Boléro* (which he was hearing for the first time) Tcherepnin developed a dreadful toothache. It increased in intensity during the performance, but disappeared as soon as the piece was over. After the concert, he went to the Green Room to greet Ravel and Marguerite Long, who was the soloist for the Ravel Concerto. Ravel immediately asked him what he thought of the *Boléro*. Tcherepnin told him about the toothache. But instead of being offended, Ravel was all excited. "So my music can have a physical effect!" he exclaimed, "It's wonderful!"—and went and told his friends about the incident.

A few days later, Ravel and Marguerite Long were present at the reception of the Dowager Queen Mary at her castle in the vicinity of Bucharest, where Tcherepnin had been asked to perform. Ravel had a concert in Bucharest a week after Tcherepnin's, and so Tcherepnin had several occasions to be with Ravel and Marguerite Long. One evening Tcherepnin invited them to a local restaurant, where the celebrated violinist Dinicu—admired equally by Ravel and Tcherepnin—was playing. The evening was a great success. When ordering dinner, Ravel said, "By all means spare me another chicken. I am fed chicken on all official occasions—give me a steak!" One of these official functions was a luncheon at the King's palace where Ravel was invited alone. He forgot all about it, or, rather, he remembered being invited, but forgot who invited him and where he was supposed to go. A phone call from the palace finally settled matters for the puzzled Ravel.

❋　One evening, the violinist Jourdan Morange, a close friend of Ravel, invited Tcherepnin to accompany her in the Tcherepnin Sonata for Violin and Piano. After they finished playing, Ravel suddenly came out from behind a curtain and declared that he had liked the sonata very much.

❋　Tcherepnin retained vivid memories of Ravel's tragic deterioration during his last years. Their penultimate meeting was a chance encounter. Sometime in 1935 or even later, Tcherepnin went to visit someone in the Clinique Piccini in Paris, and, to his astonishment, saw Ravel standing alone in the corridor. Tcherepnin knew that Ravel was already suffering from aphasia, that he was often unable to recognize music or remember his friends. Yet Ravel immediately recognized Tcherepnin, and he seemed quite normal and himself. They had a long talk and exchanged news. Ravel was very interested to learn of Tcherepnin's China experience. Their talk was joyful and animated. Wonderfully surprised to see Ravel in such good form, Tcherepnin offered him his wholehearted congratulations. They were already making plans for their next meeting when Ravel's doctor appeared. No sooner did Ravel espy the man than his face changed drastically, as did his whole demeanor. Without saying, "good-bye," he turned blankly away in mid-sentence and followed the doctor like an obedient lamb, as though hypnotized.

"It was not many years after this visit," wrote Tcherepnin, "that I was in the area where [Ravel] lived, and chanced to stop in for a brief visit. This wonderful gentleman was so glad to see me, but not fully aware of just who I was… his mind was leaving him. He went to the piano and played one note over and over and over, and kept asking me what I thought about his newest work. It was very sad."

❋　❋　❋

TCHEREPNIN AND SHOSTAKOVICH

Ming Tcherepnin recalled her husband telling her the following anecdote about Shostakovich, a story that has never before appeared in print and may well come as a surprise to many readers. Sometime in the 1930s, Tcherepnin received a letter from Russia. It came from the young composer Dimitri Shostakovich, who knew of him by reputation. Shostakovich wrote that he was very dissatisfied with life in the Soviet Union, and asked Tcherepnin to help get him out.

At that period, some emigrations were still being arranged, and Tcherepnin consulted many of his fellow exiles, leaving no stone unturned in trying to find some means to help Shostakovich come west. All of his efforts went for naught, however: it was too late, and Shostakovich was too prominent.

As news of worsening dictatorship in the Soviet Union spread, Tcherepnin realized that Shostakovich could be put into serious danger if the Soviets found out about the letter he had written. In the atmosphere of the times, spies seemed to be everywhere; and, in fact, nobody knew who, among the emigre community, might be currying favor with Stalin by feeding his agents information about foreign contacts established by Soviet nationals. Determined to keep the letter from prying eyes at all costs, Tcherepnin removed it from his correspondence files and found a secret hiding place for it, some location where no one would think of looking.

Tcherepnin selected all too well. Several years later, when he tried to locate Shostakovich's letter, he found himself totally unable to remember or imagine where he had secreted it. Search as he might, he never found the incriminating document, and it has remained hidden to this day.

❀　❀　❀

TCHEREPNIN ON MILHAUD

When I was in San Francisco in January [1953], I visited Darius Milhaud at Mills College—and I discovered with shock and admiration that he was already orchestrating his opera *David*—completed in composition—which he had not even begun when I saw him at Aspen in summer 1952!

❀　❀　❀

TCHEREPNIN ON COPLAND

{*Tcherepnin had both admiration and affection for his student Phillip Ramey, calling him the "brother to my sons." When Ramey later developed close ties to Aaron Copland, Tcherepnin by no means resented Ramey's enthusiasm for a "rival" composer, but wholeheartedly encouraged it.*}

Again and again [I am] happy about your association with Copland. First because he is a fine musician, outstanding composer, big shot in every respect, second—precisely because he, more than anyone, can help you. Do not be embarrassed by looking on him also as a person who can be of great use for you and for your music. It is only natural. And as it should be. Compose the orchestra pieces for which he asks. Study his scores. Both his music and he himself are the best influence that you, as [a] young American composer can have; and there is nothing wrong for you to depend on his judgment and on his assistance in your struggle. He knows how to struggle. He was not only born Copland—he became Copland! And he knows it better than anyone—both in music and in life. Cherish your association with him. It is worthy in every respect.

❀　❀　❀

TCHEREPNIN AND ORFF

One evening during the 1970s, Ramey arrived at the Tcherepnins for a late supper, having come straight from a performance of Carl Orff's *Carmina Burana*, a piece that he had disliked on records but never before heard live. Ramey is seldom one to mince words about what irritates him, and barely had he greeted the Tcherepnins when he launched into a vehement denunciation of Orff's relentlessly repetitive score. Ramey fully expected Tcherepnin to join in with criticisms of his own, but there was no comment, and on he raged.

Finally, Tcherepnin said, "I must tell you, Phil, that I love this piece." There was an awkward silence. Ramey then learned from his host and hostess that part of the blame for the irritation Orff had caused him earlier could, in a sense, be placed on Tcherepnin himself. For Orff, as a young and unknown composer, had taken the score of *Carmina Burana* to Tcherepnin, and Tcherepnin was so impressed that persuaded one of his own publishers to issue the piece. Tcherepnin had thus played a role in launching *Carmina Burana* to world-wide fame.

Somewhat bemused, Ramey remarked that he still hated the piece. Tcherepnin just smiled.

❀　❀　❀

TCHEREPNIN ON MUNCH AND REINER

The French conductor Charles Munch was a dear friend of mine. He loved my compositions and was very generous in performing them on various occasions. Incidentally, at his debut concert in Paris, when he conducted the Paris Philharmonic Orchestra in 1936, he gave the Paris premiere of my *Russian Dances*. Among others, he gave, also in Paris, the world premiere of my *Suite Georgienne* for piano and string orchestra with Ina Marika as soloist. Very soon after, he was appointed principal conductor of the Boston Symphony Orchestra. He engaged me as soloist to perform my 2nd Piano Concerto with him in Boston in 1951. In 1953, when I was performing my *Suite Georgienne*, in Boston with the Zimbler Sinfonietta, he came to the concert, had me at his home for dinner, and asked me to compose for him a symphonic work. When I gladly consented, he went to his desk and wrote me a generous check, leaving me free to choose any form I would like and be free from any deadline.

It so happens that at the moment I was still busy completing commissions previously received (*Suite* for the Louisville Orchestra; *The Lost Flute* for Thor Johnson), also I was teaching approximately 40 hours a week, and had many concert engagements in the USA from coast to coast. Some illnesses occurred in my family, so it was only by the summer of 1955 that I was able to put my mind to the composition.

I decided to compose a Symphony during the Autumn of 1955. Although overburdened by my teaching schedule and by concert engagements, I succeeded in sketching the first movement and started on the second—a slow one with a dramatic outburst, that was to bring the agitated middle part of the movement. Strangely enough, I sketched this sudden, dramatic **FFF** in the morning of a long teaching day—on this day I taught classes and private lessons at the University (in Chicago) from 9 A.M. till after 7 P.M. with the only small stop for luncheon at the neighboring cafeteria with my composition student, Robert Muczynski, who came not for a lesson but to ask advice. After classes I had to go to the concert hall to attend a concert by David Oistrakh—at which—to my great surprise, I saw my son Serge at the stage, turning the pages for the accompanist. My wife and I were supposed to attend a party in honor of Oistrakh, after the concert, but I felt tired and by midnight we were at our home.

That night, most unexpectedly, out of the pure sky, I suffered a severe heart attack. Three weeks at the hospital, three other weeks of convalescence in Florida—back to the same schedule and concert engagements after this.

Soon I had another extended concert tour, and the Chicago conductor Fritz Reiner, whom I met in New York, and who previously already conducted my Suite, Opus 87, in Chicago, persuaded me to take the same train with him to return to Chicago so that we could have a good visit together. I usually went by plane, but accepted his suggestion. We had supper together in the restaurant car, and he suggested that I compose especially for him, a symphonic piece in any form except that of a symphony. I had great respect and admiration for him, so I accepted.

So it happened that by the end of 1956, I had to compose two symphonic works—one for Munch, the other for Reiner. Before my heart attack in 1955 I was a chain smoker for thirty years (often as much as three packs as day). Doctors advised me to stop smoking after the heart attack, and I did so. But the habit of smoking while working was so related to composition work, that for an entire year, 1956, due to the abstinence from smoking, I was unable to compose. I spied myself when musical ideas came to my head-rejected them before doing something with them-and lacked the necessary concentration.

[At] Christmas, 1956, I had to do a very quick composition of two Chinese songs for the Basso Yi-Kwei Sze, who already had announced these uncomposed songs in the program of his New York recital, early in January 1957. In order to push myself, I tried to smoke a pipe. After a few days, I returned to cigarettes, and as a miracle, the two songs were composed in two days.

Thus I returned to chain smoking and—with this—to composition.

As said, I had one and a half movements of the Symphony sketched before the interruption by the heart attack. Instead of using them for the Symphony, I decided to use them for the Reiner piece, but before completing the second movement, I composed the third. After this I completed the second, and changed the coda in the first. It became now the Divertimento, Op. 90.

When I sent the score to Reiner (at the beginning of the summer) he immediately replied enthusiastically, and even fixed the date of the first performance by the Chicago Symphony under his conductorship. That was to be in November 1957. I immediately started then with the composition of the Symphony, for Munch, completed the first two movements very quickly, but took my time to compose the third, at the coda of which I used the *requiescat in pace* theme from medieval Russian liturgy. I was still busy orchestrating the Symphony in November when Reiner successfully performed the Divertimento in Chicago. The critics were favorable to me, but attacked Reiner for a cut that he made (by the way, with my full consent) in the last movement (the publisher unfortunately provided the critics with scores—this without my knowledge).

Reiner became furious and for a long while we were not on speaking terms. I erased the dedication to him (that, I now regret) and he never performed either the Divertimento or any other composition of mine after this, although, in a year or so, when he became sick, I visited him and we made peace. He died, by the way, quite soon after our reconciliation.

Shortly before Christmas 1957, I completed the score of my Symphony No. 4, and phoned from Chicago to Boston to tell Munch that the symphony was ready. He told me to take the first plane and to bring him the score. His chauffeur met me at the airport and brought me to Munch's home in a Boston suburb. Munch himself opened the door and with a suspicious, sarcastic smile asked me, "Tell me, how many 'fortes' at the end of the symphony?" "Sorry," I answered, "it ends not forte but with **ppppp**—it is in complete *pianissimo*."

He immediately asked me to play the symphony for him, which I did. After having heard the music and followed on the score, he went to his desk and wrote me again a generous check. I protested, assuring him that he had already paid me in advance. "Do you think it is not worthy of it?" he asked. "Of course not," I answered. Then he said, "One is never generous enough." We had a pleasant supper together. I spent the night at his home, then returned to Chicago with the check, which was quite handy for Christmas-time, and gave me extra fuel to acquire Christmas presents for the family.

In November 1958, when I was with my son Serge in Paris, I received a telegram from Munch that he would perform the symphony early in December. I decided to return to the USA for the premiere, together with my son Serge; we flew to Chicago, and I had the chance to see my ailing—nearly blind—mother for the last time in my life. (She died on December 19th, at which time I was back in Europe, in the midst of a concert tour with my son Serge in Vienna.)

But before returning to Europe, I went to Boston, was joined there by Ming. Serge also came along, and I had the joy, not only to attend the three successive Boston performances of the Symphony, but also the performances of it in New York and in Brooklyn (Munch included the Symphony in the tour of the Boston Symphony Orchestra). Later, he performed it in Tanglewood, and in Chicago, and intended to conduct and to record it in Paris with the Orchestre de Paris, when he became its director, which unfortunately could not take place because of his sudden death during the American tour of the orchestra. Incidentally, this Symphony became the most played of my Symphonies…

❀　❀　❀

TRIBUTE TO ISIDORE PHILIPP

My dear teacher Isidore Philipp, who died two years ago in an accident at the Paris subway at the age of 92, remains for me the most sacred example of what a teacher should be. At the time I was studying with him in Paris in the early twenties he was Professor at the Paris Conservatory, Professor at the Ecole Normale and combined it with teaching private students who came to him from all parts of the world. He also composed in all fields (yet mostly in the teaching material field) and was best with editing compositions of all epochs.

His day started early in the morning teaching private students, and all day long he was busy teaching. Yet during the night hours he read through every new piece published, examined it and-if finding it worthy as teaching material or for performance by his advanced students and ex-students-he included [it] in his teaching repertoire. It went this way all his life. What is more, he understood that the duty of the teacher is not only to teach, but also to promote his young student-artists. Therefore he was equally busy in contacting conductors, managers and associations to help the young artist to become known and to find funds for those in need.

I owe everything to him, and as much as I can I am trying to follow his path, and to show him my everlasting gratitude by trying to be helpful to my students in every way, as he was helpful to his. And not only this; I am trying to be helpful wherever I can in the cause of music and musicians. We are all here in this world on a round trip from the unknown to the unknown. We have to hold together while we are here and try to do our best in every direction, continuing what our predecessors have done and preparing the way for our successors.

❀　❀　❀　❀　❀　❀

ALEXANDER TCHEREPNIN: A COMPENDIUM

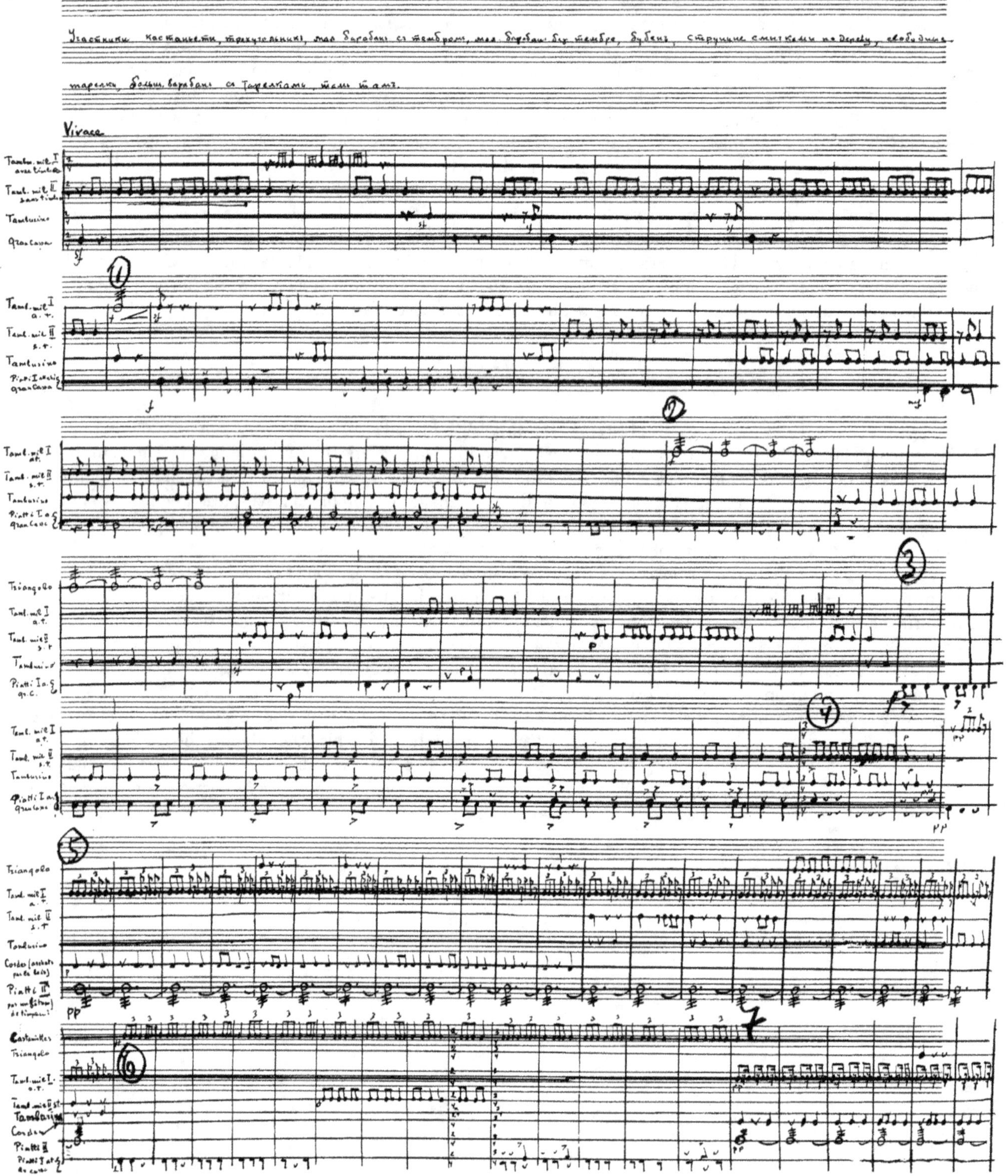

Preliminary version of Symphony No. 1, *Scherzo*.

ALEXANDER TCHEREPNIN:
A COMPENDIUM

BOOK II

SEVENTEEN
TCHEREPNIN
MASTERPIECES

BOOK II: SEVENTEEN TCHEREPNIN MASTERPIECES

INTRODUCTION

Book II of *Alexander Tcherepnin: A Compendium*, entitled *Seventeen Tcherepnin Masterpieces* was conceived as something more than a collection of independent program notes. Although the individual essays on selected Tcherepnin scores may be read separately, they have been embedded in a more- or-less continuous narrative. The works are examined in chronological sequence rather than being grouped together by genre, and passages of general critical commentary have been interspersed between the analyses, where discussion of Tcherepnin's artistic development seemed desirable. Significant cross-references will also be found among the individual annotations. If all this adds up to something less than a unitary survey of Tcherepnin's most important works, it at least constitutes—so the editor hopes—a more coherent aesthetic and technical appraisal than would have emerged from completely separate annotations.

The essays here concatenated often draw on Tcherepnin's own analyses; however, the editorial viewpoint—for better or for worse—differs somewhat from Tcherepnin's own—a viewpoint that has been reflected without scrutiny in many of the standard writings about the composer. In those, much attention has properly been paid to the melodic and harmonic consequences of nine-step material and the workings of Interpoint: less careful analysis has been given to the overall formal designs in which these textural details fulfill their localized destinies; and thus in preparing the present analyses it seemed important to lay particular stress upon the broad dramatic outlines of the musical forms-following Tcherepnin's own dictum that "it is the form that makes a composition long-living." Commentators have also readily adopted Tcherepnin's own classification of his works into sharply defined periods; both Reich and Tcherepnin tend to suggest, in fact, that the composer's stylistic peregrinations were motivated by abstract aesthetic constructs-arbitrary leaps from success to success, having little to do with his satisfaction or dissatisfaction with the music he was producing. While the stylistic divisions are unquestionably valid, it is equally useful to examine Tcherepnin's development as an unbroken continuum, with the composer continually modifying his style in response to day-to-day composing discoveries and in accord with his sense of place within the musical community.

Few would presume to deny that a great composer's truest and most revealing autobiography lies in his musical output, although many would deny that such an autobiography can necessarily be deciphered in non-musical terms, let alone translated into words. Nevertheless the present annotations will suggest that there exists—in a modest number of instances—a closer relationship between the outer circumstances of Tcherepnin's life and the inner content of his music than has heretofore been suspected. True, such speculations risk foundering on the unsavory shoals of so-called "psychohistory"-a pseudo-discipline that in popular biographies of recent decades attempted to prove—among other absurd theories—that Pierre Boulez and Leonard Bernstein were psychologically identical. The truth is, however, that some composers, in their music, do reveal their psychological concerns and exhibit identifiable reactions to their biographical experiences, and Tcherepnin seems to be one of these—in fact, we shall see him pointing out some such connections himself.

THE EARLY YEARS

As a rule, the compositions from Tcherepnin's early years do not need structural analysis: most of them are cast in uncomplicated three-part forms thoroughly consonant with their clearly delimited expressive values. However, the quality and nature of the gift that young Tcherepnin displayed in the *Bagatelles* and elsewhere should not be underrated or misrepresented. Almost from the beginning, Tcherepnin demonstrated an insight that perhaps 99% of the world's composers never succeed in developing: he was able to recognize the crucial distinction between what an idea actually was and what that idea merely resembled. From that idea, he was thus able to extract the portion of its content that made it genuinely unique. With this insight came an understanding of how to compel the listener's interest (rather than merely seizing the listener's attention). Young Tcherepnin's gift was, in fact, only partly musical—or, to put it more precisely, his gift lay partly in the interstices between musical genius and other qualities such as inventive intelligence and the psychological understanding of communication. In any case, it made it possible for the boy-even with a limited musical technique—to produce little works of permanent beauty and value.

The adolescent Tcherepnin, then, was an astute purveyor of musical anecdotes, usually composing for an audience of one and blissfully unaware that that single listener (as a member of the Tcherepnin-Benois clan) was a highly sophisticated one with unusually refined musical tastes. The composer later so broadened his musical scope, of course, that the symphony became a natural means of expression for him: still, a mastery of the miniature was the foundation of his work, and was an important factor in defining the nature of all of his subsequent music. One indication of these origins is his life-long penchant for self-developing themes—*i. e.*, themes that grow from successive permutations of a single brief motif or several brief motifs, such as the first subject of the First Symphony's opening movement or the second subject in the Fourth Symphony's first movement. As with Brahms in his Third Symphony second subject, it is only a master miniaturist who can deploy such cellular building-blocks with so elegant a lyric balance.

When Tcherepnin began to concertize in Tbilisi as he approached adulthood, he found it no less easy to communicate with listeners, discovering that large audiences with questionable taste responded enthusiastically to piano fireworks and other appurtenances of *Sturm und Drang*. Supplying these, however, was a less innocent matter than making *bloshki* jump through their paces for beloved Benois uncles, although the process, at first, must have been no less instinctive.

The truth is that the ability to compose the *Bagatelles* was a veritable gift of nature, akin to uncommon personal beauty or innate sweetness of social manner. Tcherepnin seems to have realized that, had he chosen the path of least resistance, he could have coasted through a pleasant provincial career as a composer-pianist merely on the strength of his flair for charming or exciting people through music. His situation was ironically akin to that of a hackneyed figure of comedy: the woman who, naturally endowed with astonishing beauty and ineluctable sex- appeal, longs to be admired for her brains. For Tcherepnin, it was not enough—indeed, it began to seem somewhat immoral—to bask in general approval of his natural endowments; and this conviction was now strengthened within him as he undertook the intensive study of Beethoven, in whose music beauty, significance and nobility are present in direct proportion to the intellectual power and effort that informs it. Tcherepnin saw his true mission; emulating Beethoven, he was determined to merit admiration for his brains.

If the works of Tcherepnin's earliest period may be likened to anecdotes, those of his earliest adulthood are akin to lyric poems of exceptional imagistic density and technical complexity. Tcherepnin's most characteristic movements at this time still exhibited miniaturistic proportions, but their musical content now extended beyond the aphoristic, and their organization often reveals the composer's growing awareness of problems of large-scale continuity.

No longer trusting entirely in his natural communicative power, Tcherepnin entered an "awkward stage" during the mid-twenties. He was determined to produce music that convinced audiences through its cogency of argument rather than its charismatic charm: but, in fact, there is a certain overlap between those two qualities. After all, an argument, even when based on a bedrock of substance, may need rhetorical enhancement to be fully effective. We shall see that in these years the more fully Tcherepnin attempted to purge his music of rhetoric, the more problematic it became.

THE NINE-STEP SCALE

Exploring the possibilities of the nine-step scale brought Tcherepnin to a major breakthrough in his style, as Reich has already recounted. Here it will be useful to diagram the nine-step scale on bass C, with its intervalic content:

C	half step	Db	whole step	Eb	half step	E	half step	F	whole step	G	half step	Ab	half step	A	whole step	B	half step	C

Because of the half-full-half symmetry, this scale, in its note content, is identical to the nine-step scales on bass E and bass Ab (or G#). (As aforesaid, the other three nine step scales are those on bass Db [F, A], bass D [F#, Bb] and bass Eb [G, B].)

This scale has two additional "modes," but it is best to postpone a discussion of these until its characteristics in its basic form are studied—the form on which Tcherepnin's early nine-step work centered.

Three notes are lacking from this scale: D, the major second; F#, the tritone; and Bb, the minor second. As a result, it cannot produce all three of the common chords of functional tonality: it contains tonic and subdominant triads, but offers the dominant seventh chord only in an exotic "French sixth" version (G-B-Db-F). Further, the flatted seventh is not available for the tonic-seventh chord: as a result, both the V-I and I-IV paths of conventional harmony are short-circuited. Nothing prevented Tcherepnin, of course, from going *outside* the nine-step scale to borrow missing common-note chords, but this procedure required "modulating" to another nine-step scale, and so, destabilized the "tonality." When using this basic form of the scale, Tcherepnin often contented himself by harping on the dominant *note* to prepare a new key, but such preparation inevitably lacks some of the power of dominant-chord emphasis.

The gap left by the absence of dominant and other tonicizing chords is filled, to some extent, by three tonicizing agents that are basic to the nine-step scale and are not present at all in the diatonic scale—the half-step cluster-aggregates (B-C-Db; Eb-E-F; G-G#-A). Indeed, in these aggregates, the homing in on the center note is so salient to the ear that the listener almost always gains the impression that any extended passage utilizing the basic form of nine-step has more than one tonic. Particular stress falls on the aggregate below the tonic—that is to say, a piece in E nine-step will often seem to present C as a secondary tonic (G#, curiously, rarely makes the same tonic impression because it is prominently used for another very audible purpose—along with the G, it is indispensable in defining the major/minor context of the E—and thus seldom gets the chance to assert its own tonal identity).

This aggrandizement of a secondary tonic that does not disappear via modulation can be a source of weakness, depriving some closing passages and strategic cadences of their intended sense of finality and inevitability.

Another limitation of the basic form of nine-step is that the four scales, in their common-tone relationships, are equidistant from one another: there are neither "remote" nine-tone "keys" nor, for that matter, closely neighboring keys. Any two of the scales will have six notes in common. Since the tonal effect of a return from a vast distance is lacking, modulation ceases, to some extent, to be a tool for expressive differentiation.

However, as indicated, the nine-step scale forms "modes" which considerably widen its possible harmonic vocabulary. Just as the white keys of the diatonic C major scale yield different modes when "white-key" scales are begun on notes other than C (D=Dorian, E=Phrygian, F=Lydian, etc.) so the notes of C nine-step produce different interval patterns when the bass is shifted: the tonicizing clusters fall on different degrees of the scale, and the gaps in nine-step also fall in different places. Tcherepnin calls the basic form of the scale "Mode I." Owing to the symmetrical interval patterns of nine-step, there are only two other modes. Here are Modes I, II and III of C nine-step—tonicized notes are in bold face; both tonicized and unavailable notes are intervallically identified at the right:

MODE													Tonicized				Unavailable		
													C	E	Ab	C		D	F#	Bb
I:	C	Db	Eb	E	F	G	Ab	A	B		--------		I	III	#V	I	---	II	#IV	bVII
II:		Db	Eb	E	F	G	Ab	A	B	C	Db	-----	bIII	V	#VII	--		bII	IV	VI
III:			Eb	E	F	G	Ab	A	B	C	Db	Eb	--	bII	IV	VI	---	#VII	bIII	V

The differences are striking. One highly suggestive feature is the congruence of Mode II with traditional tonality. Both the dominant and the major-seventh (a dominant surrogate) are tonicized—and the tonicizing of the dominant is a basic strategy of all functionally tonal music. Moreover the II[7] chord, another gateway to the dominant, is eminently available. Within a few years, Tcherepnin came to rely very heavily on Mode II with its tonal affinities, particularly when working with large-scale structures.

By contrast, Mode III is the harshest and most "modernistic" of the group. Lacking the dominant and major seventh, it demands the invention of new harmonic pathways; lacking the minor third, it is devoid of the modal ambiguity that had inspired Tcherepnin to develop nine-step in the first place; moreover the interval structure—with its two half-steps rising from the bass, tends to be the source of dense chromaticism in Mode III materials.

Further potential of nine-step contrasts, despite the lack of variety in tonal "distances," is provided by "enharmonic" relations, as becomes evident when Mode I of C nine-step is compared to the other two modes that provide C to C scales:

											unavailable		
Mode I of C:	**C**	Db	Eb	**E**	F	G	**Ab**	A	B	**C**	D	F#	Bb
Mode II of B:	C	D	**Eb**	E	F#	**G**	Ab	Bb	**B**	C	Db	F	A
Mode III of A:	C	**Db**	D	E	**F**	F#	Ab	**A**	Bb	C	Eb	C	B

It should be stressed, however, that in steadily modulating passages it becomes difficult to differentiate between a particular nine-step scale and one of its modes. Mode II of B (with its bass on C) uses the same notes as G nine-step, for example, and in a C context there is something arbitrary about distinguishing between what are, in fact, two different forms of the dominant nine-step scale.

All in all, however, it seems that nine-step has somewhat less technical scope than did functional tonality. The latter, with its complex geography and its sense of key-distance offered a limitless range of perspective, which does not exist in nine- step; on the other hand, the flattened perspective of nine-step may be likened to tonal cubism and could be creatively exploited both analytically and synthetically to create beautiful abstract mindscapes that could have come into existence by no other means. The small-boned symmetry of the nine-step scale (a four-note pattern overlapping three times within a single octave) makes it malleable for miniaturists, but this can also be a weakness, for the scale's limited and repetitive interval-structure tends to generate short-breathed thematic materials and to encourage excessive sequencing.

The potentialities of the nine-step scale in its several modes, however, were very real. Its interval-patterning had been validated long since in several exotic folk-musics, including our Western Phrygian mode (indeed, Mode I even shares with the Phrygian—*i. e.*, the white- key mode on E—a predilection for C as a secondary tonic). It is easy to see why Tcherepnin found it fascinating to immerse himself in nine-step, and just as easy to see why, several years later, he saw fit to widen his vocabulary to include other scale-patterns. It should also be pointed out that Tcherepnin exaggerated when he called the nine-step scale "the exclusive basis" of his music during the mid-twenties: pieces such as the *Rhapsodie Georgienne*, the *Transcriptions Slaves* and above all the opera *Ol-Ol* were plainly folk-inspired, yet fit quite naturally into the sequence of his works even in this, his most intellectual period.

TCHEREPNIN AND TONALITY

As we have seen, the most astringent form of nine-step tended to remove music from the traditional tonal orbit altogether: even Mode I tended to behave in a manner alien to functional tonality. Yet, like many composers of his era, Tcherepnin was long disposed to pay lip-service to the conventions of tonality even as he was moving beyond them in his music. As late as his French autobiography he still punctiliously referred to his scores as being "in" one or another key—writing, for example of his "Cello Sonata in G" or his "Concerto in A" even though the music may have had little or nothing to do with the G or A major sounds of previous centuries. (We shall see, in fact, that while some nine-step scores, such as the *Concerto da Camera*, seem quasi-traditional in their tonal orientation, others suggest a single tonic only obliquely.) In his last years, Tcherepnin decided to discard the traditional nomenclature, removing the key designations from his Symphonies, Concertos and other scores. It is nevertheless clear from his own analysis of the Second Concerto, prepared in later years that even at that point, he still had a healthy respect for the local function of a dominant. One thing Tcherepnin never does is totally negate the difference between consonance and dissonance, though he prefers consonances more piquant than would have been countenanced by nineteenth-century experts: he counts on the sense of arrival that comes from the resolution of certain intervals; the Schoenbergian ideal of "equal" semitones related only to each other would not have let him make the musical points he repeatedly aimed at.

THE SEVENTEEN WORKS

The seventeen works analyzed in the subsequent pages were chosen largely for their intrinsic musical value and their significance within Tcherepnin's oeuvre. Another determining factor for inclusion, however, was the availability of interesting analytical and anecdotal commentary by Tcherepnin himself; on the other hand, some important works have been excluded because Reich has discussed them in detail.

The specifically analytical sections were conceived as aids to listening or to intensive study, and may be safely skimmed or skipped by the more casual reader. In these, the Editor has not hesitated to disagree with Tcherepnin, particularly where principles of Classical sonata form are involved. This was a more flexible genre than the Russian teachers of Tchaikovsky, Rachmaninoff, Prokofiev and Tcherepnin knew. As a result, Tcherepnin's perceptions about his relationship to classical orthodoxy are, in the Editor's view, sometimes overblown, but sometimes quite overmodest, his classical instincts, in the latter incidences, proving better than his classical theory. Even if the Editor's comments merely lead the reader to a reinforced conviction of the validity of Tcherepnin's views, they will have fulfilled one of their purposes. It is hoped that some readers will form analytical views that contradict both Tcherepnin *and* the Editor.

❋　❋　❋

TCHEREPNIN PRELUDE

All these explanations might give an impression of [a] "formal" or "technical" approach [to] composition[—] it is not so.

In my mind the form and the technique of musical speech are nothing but ways to organize the musical emotion, and by no way could be considered as goal[s] in [themselves].

SEVENTEEN TCHEREPNIN MASTERPIECES

PART I (1922-1932)

CONCERTO NO. 2 FOR PIANO AND ORCHESTRA, OPUS 26

Tcherepnin began work on his Second Piano Concerto while enjoying the patronage and hospitality of the Guinness family at Sunnyhill in Ascot, England during the last weeks of 1922. This was the first time that supporters of the arts had accorded this kind of recognition to Tcherepnin's work, and the receipt of his initial large monthly stipend from the Guinnesses came as a climax to a series of early professional triumphs that had included the offer of free piano tutelage from Isidor Philipp, the sale of his music to several enthusiastic Paris publishers, and his successful debut in London. For the first time, he had left his parents behind in another country to pursue his own professional engagements, and he had proved fully able to cope with the situation, even when unexpected difficulties cropped up—notably, the sudden withdrawal of Adila Fachiri's hospitality which had temporarily cast him adrift in London with scarcely a penny in his pocket.

The concerto composed in the wake of these experiences turned out to be one of his finest works to date, and one that broke new ground in his art, as he had recently begun breaking new ground in his career. In fact, in tracing Tcherepnin's composing life it will become evident that every crucial experience of his life tends to be "ratified" shortly afterwards by a score of unusual importance, almost as if his compositions were rites of passage commemorating his artistic journey. This is not to imply that the Second Concerto is exactly "about" the joy of being discovered by publishers, foreign audiences and patrons; but it is safe to say that after this exhilarating series of events, Tcherepnin, as a composer, found himself with something special to say.

In the Second Concerto, in fact, Tcherepnin consciously aimed at a new artistic maturity. "The fact was," he wrote, "that I was dissatisfied with my 1st Piano Concerto—a typical *Sturm und Drang* piece, with all the artificery of conventional pianism—octaves, chords, 'pathos' and brilliancy. So I wanted to compose a concerto with an 'honest' piano part, with musical rather than virtuoso content.... I was sick of hearing so much boom-boom-boom."

Although Tcherepnin was not especially fond of living and composing in the countryside, and was homesick for his parents and Paris besides, he found that his "work on the Concerto progressed and became more and more stimulating, especially after I found the material for the second theme..."

The story of Tcherepnin's rupture with the Guinnesses has already been told in Book I "Encountering the English" (pp. 161-164)—how Tcherepnin, asked to vacate his room and move to the city for a few days, reacted with panic, fearful that the change in background would derail his progress on the Concerto. And after breaking with the Guinnesses, he found that he did indeed temporarily lose the thread of the piece. Back in Paris, he busied himself with a concerted work he had begun earlier—the *Rhapsodie Géorgienne*—along with a new set of piano preludes (opus 24) which complemented the *Préludes nostalgiques* written in England.

Tcherepnin stated that when he resumed composing the Concerto in February, "I decided to use the variation-form as a part of the development, reworded the initial theme to serve as theme for variations, giving it to cello solo; each of the variations had to be in different rhythm and, at the end, culminate in the reexposition of the variation theme in retrograde reading, which I designed for a horn solo."

Despite his impending French debut in late March 1923, in Monte Carlo, he continued work on the piece, and in April he was able to play it through from short-score to Philipp. Tcherepnin wrote that his teacher "approved the Piano Concerto, although he told me that [it was] hardly a concerto but a *Konzertstück* (right he was)." In contrast, in fact, to what Tcherepnin scornfully termed "the 'eloquence' and 'grand pathetic art' of the First Concerto," the composer had persevered in his intention "to treat the piano more discreetly, avoiding any recourse to external virtuosity." The solo part of the Second Concerto is by no means lacking in brilliant sounds, but the motivation behind these is wholly musical: solo and orchestra dovetail into a unified narrative rather than competing.

Tcherepnin's accounts of the orchestration of the Concerto seem contradictory: in his later personal autobiography he says that he completed it by the end of the season, which would indicate the end of spring. In the French autobiography, however, he states that the autumn was devoted to the orchestration of both the Concerto and the *Rhapsodie Géorgienne*.

Tcherepnin did not play the piece in public until the beginning of the following year, and then only in a version for two pianos. This performance, in which he was accompanied by Nadia Boulanger, took place on January 26, 1924, at the Societe Nationale in Paris. By now, in fact, the composer's First Concerto had begun to make the rounds, receiving performances by other pianists in France and Holland in late January, so Tcherepnin was well advised to have a second concerto ready for performance.

Apparently, Tcherepnin failed to make a diary notation of the date on which he premiered the Concerto with orchestra. In his writings, he notes vaguely that the performance took place about a year after the Paris performance, in Brest, with a local orchestra (reinforced by Marine Band brass players) under the direction of an "excellent" conductor named Merlin. The one surviving early-1925 review of Tcherepnin in the Brest Municipal Library (in the *Depêche de Brest*) states that Tcherepnin appeared with orchestra at the *Amis de Colonne*'s first gala concert of the year on January 29, playing his own music and also accompanying his violinist friend Dany Braunschwig in works of Pugnani. Although the reviewer merely comments on Tcherepnin's avant-garde "revolutionary" modernism and does not identify which of his own pieces the composer played, it is almost certain that Tcherepnin did, indeed, premiere the Second Concerto at this concert. The *Depêche* gives the conductor's name as "Merle," and this (rather than Tcherepnin's "Merlin") is probably correct.[1]

Although Tcherepnin did not remember the exact date of the premiere, he always enjoyed recalling a moment of hilarity that he experienced at the opening of that performance. This came about because the auditorium was quite small and the stage was only partly elevated, so that a soloist in a piano concerto was actually close enough to listeners seated in the first row center to shake hands. At the concert, these favored seats were occupied by the mayor, a corpulent middle-aged gentleman with the ruddy complexion of a *bon vivant*, and his equally comfortable looking wife, and as they settled into them it was obvious that the mayor was preparing to sleep off a hearty dinner with a pleasant nap. When the Concerto began with its aggressive snare-drum roll and blaring trumpets, the poor man jerked erect and practically jumped to his feet, while, as Tcherepnin tells it, "the expression of the angelic visage of his wife was that of agony and fear. I had to bite my lips to restrain from laughing. Otherwise the performance went well and the concerto nicely baptized." Ultimately, this piece was to become the most-played concerted item in Tcherepnin's repertory, receiving over two hundred performances at his hands. The published score bears a dedication to the French pianist Jeanne-Marie Darr.

Rather inexperienced in instrumentation, Tcherepnin originally scored the work for a very modest, almost classical complement: 2 flutes, 2 oboes, 2 clarinets, 2 bassoons, 2 horns, 2 cornets a piston, timpani, percussion and strings. In 1950, at the prompting of Charles Munch, a far more skilled Tcherepnin replaced the cornets with trumpets, added a piccolo, 2 horns, 3 trombones and tuba to the ensemble and rescored the piece completely. This new orchestration was first performed by the Boston Symphony Orchestra directed by Charles Munch with the composer at the piano in December 1950, and was considered by the composer to supersede the original. In later years Tcherepnin also dropped the key designation of what he had once called his "Concerto No. 2 in A"—a well-advised decision, given the tonally oblique opening of the piece.

Tcherepnin's papers contain no fewer than four analyses of the Second Concerto. The most detailed of these is a handwritten roll of four pages taped together horizontally with the succeeding sections of the piece described in columns of prose accompanied by musical examples. The progress of the music is charted through themes A and B of the exposition, the succeeding development, themes A and B of the recapitulation and the Coda. The English here requires editing, but Tcherepnin's meaning is clear. This analysis serves as the basis of most of what follows.

"The work is in one movement, its form that of the Sonata-*allegro*," Tcherepnin wrote, stating elsewhere that the piece "opposes a theme of military character to a theme of timid romanticism."

It should be said that, as in many French mid-Romantic and Russian late- Romantic concertos, the single sonata movement contains elements of a slow movement and a finale. Although it lasts some sixteen minutes, the single movement does not exhibit the characteristics of a large-scale narrative, for it is distinctly articulated into individual sections: indeed, the variation-episode that constitutes the slow movement may justly be considered a separate structure.

Exposition

The **principal subject** (A), *Vivo* 4/4, in A nine-step, starts with a *fortissimo* snare-drum roll, *pianissimo* string harmonics and trill-like piano figuration, all of which provide a background for the principal theme, a twelve-measure melody proclaimed by the trumpets:

---

1   Enrique Arias, in his bio-bibliography of Tcherepnin, has the conductor's name as "Nevlin," which appears in no other source: presumably Arias misread his own handwriting when transcribing his notes from Tcherepnin's accounts.

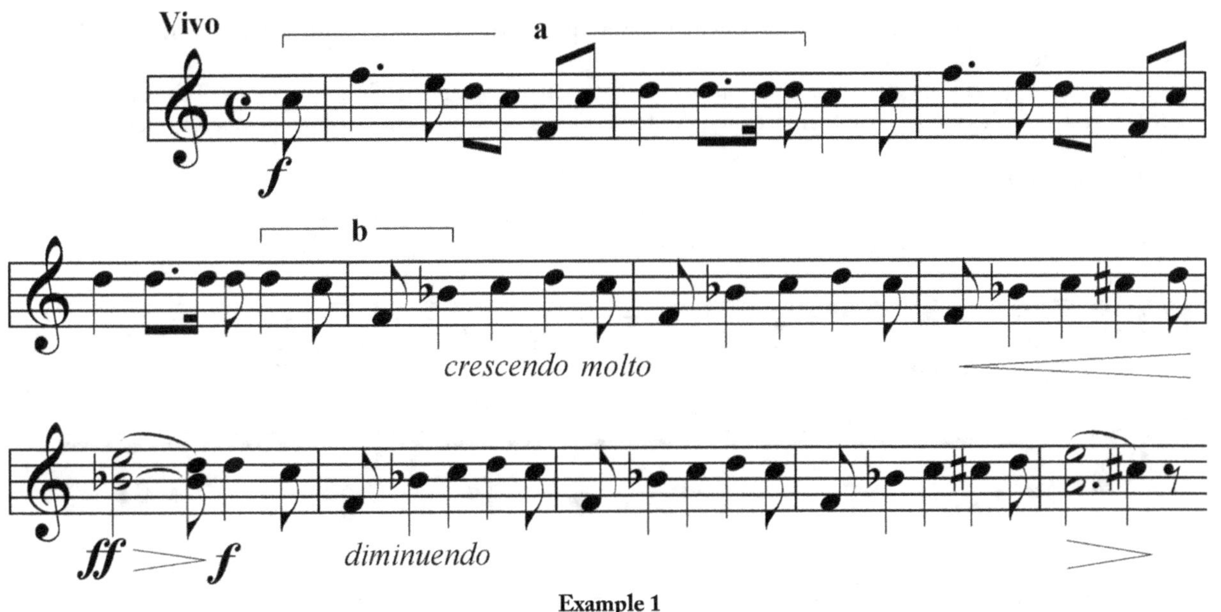

Example 1

The *g#* and *a* held in string harmonics and trilled by the piano constitute at the same time the major-minor third of F (the basic tonic of the first part of the melody) and the root (A) with an *appogiatura* (G#) of A nine-step tonality. (Notice the typical nine-step proclivity for a secondary tonic a major third lower.) The two motifs marked a and b will later have separate importance.

The theme is then developed, alternatively appearing in the piano and in different orchestral groups, also passing through an antiphonal episode.

The meter changes to a 3/2 based on a rhythmic ostinato (piano chords on the beat, orchestra syncopated). The principal theme is heard and echoed in different groups: this entire section takes place on a pedal D, which proves to be the dominant of the subordinate theme's tonality (G).

A general *diminuendo* leads to a pause of cadential character, preparing the tonality of G.

The **subordinate theme** (B), *Moderato*, 3/4 in G nine-step, is of lyric character. Introduced by the piano solo, it is twenty-four measures long:

Motifs c, c¹ and d will generate future developments.

The theme is taken up by the flute in two-part counterpoint with the piano, then continued by the strings with mutes, accompanied by the piano.

In the *codetta*, in G nine-step, an antiphonic display between the piano and different groups of the orchestra, based on motifs a and a^1 of the subordinate theme, concludes the exposition and bridges towards the development

Development

A lengthy passage for orchestra alone begins with the strings obstinately repeating the "a" motif of the subordinate theme (in E, in 3/4), after which the principal theme appears as a counterpoint in 4/4 (Example 3).

Example 3

This procedure is repeated and developed using different orchestral registers and tone colors; the root changes consecutively from E to F#, then to G (all in nine-step scale) and there is a climax on A as a pedal. (This will serve as the dominant of D minor, the key of the next episode.) After the climax, a general *diminuendo* (still on pedal A) leads to a cadential stop similar to that heard at the end of the principal theme in the exposition. The piano now reenters with a brief, meditative passage that leads to a

Theme and variations

This episode is so plainly in D minor that Tcherepnin employs a key signature from this point on until the beginning of the recapitulation. It should also be observed (in connection with the bitonal character of the main theme) that D minor is not only the sub-dominant of A but also the relative minor of F major.

Theme: a modification of the principal theme, lyrical in character, *Andantino*, 4/4, 8 measures long, in D minor, is introduced by unaccompanied solo cello.

Example 4

Variations
First four variations for piano solo (all *Allegretto*, D minor)
    1) theme, figurations in quarter-notes
    2)   "   "   " eighth-notes
    3)   "   "   " eighth-note triplets
    4)   "   "   " eighth-note triplets (with chords)
  5)-6) *Vivace risoluto*: two-part canon, at the interval of a fifth and the
      distance of half a measure in alternation between the piano and strings.
    7) *Alla breve*: Against running piano figurations, the theme is heard
      transposed to D nine-step (and therefore modified), appearing successively in trumpet, piccolo and string *pizzicatos*.
      (There is some canonic imitation between piano and orchestra).
    8) *Presto*, 9/4, starting with a piano solo in D minor, with four measures of 6/4
      added at the end.
    9) *Molto animato*, 8/4 divided 2+2+3, D minor.
  10) *Maestoso*, 4/4, D minor. Theme in a large unison cantilena of all strings
      sustained and embellished by piano passages.
  11) Continuation of previous variation in two-part counterpoint over a pedal A
      (still D minor), the piano at first playing the counterpoint voice in trills and ending on a sustained trill in sixths.
  12) Theme in the piano in 3-part counterpoint over a pedal D held by the violoncelli.
  [13] Postlude. [Example 5] The variation theme *ex-cancerans* [*i. e.*, retrograde form] played by solo French horn
      unaccompanied.

Example 5

Bridge toward the recapitulation (*Allegro moderato*, D minor, 2/4).
    Separated from the French horn solo by a short rest, the piano enters solo with the retrograde theme hammered in repeated notes; then the piano accompanies alternating entrances of the theme and the retrograde in different solo instruments of the orchestra.

Recapitulation
    The principal theme (A) reappears in trumpet as before (F major in A nine- step) with the background of string harmonics, but the snare-drum roll is omitted. The piano's trill-figure is now in octaves and deviates into little drum-roll-like eruptions. The theme is extended as before, but the argument is shortened. At the 3/2 section on pedal E (dominant of A), rhythmic roles are switched, the orchestra now playing on the beat and the piano in syncopation. This episode is also curtailed and leads, as before, to a cadential stop (different in detail) on the dominant of A.
    The subordinate theme (B), *Moderato*, 3/4, in A nine-step, is recapitulated in the tonic key in shortened form; the "a" and "a¹" motifs are divided between violins and piano solo, and the flute solo is replaced by first violins. A climax on pedal E establishes the independent value of the subordinate theme's motif "b."

Coda
    Pedal E of the A nine-step scale is constantly felt till the end of the concerto. Running piano passages (*Presto*, 6/8) are heard, with the orchestra developing motif "b" of the subordinate theme reduced to three notes, thus:

Example 6

alternating with motif "b" of the principal theme also reduced to three notes.

The principal theme reappears in 4/4 and descends ladder-like from flutes to trumpets to trombones and finally to the bass trombone and tuba. The pedal-note has suddenly jumped to D, but this is not insisted on and the E soon returns. This last reentrance of the principal theme is accompanied by a snare-drum roll and trill-figures at the extreme ends of the piano.

A *prestissimo* ensues (2/4), built on a rising two-note figure derived from the subordinate theme's motif "b."

Prestissimo

Example 7

The piano is constantly interrupted by a six-voice dominant chord in woodwind and brass instruments, then by isolated outbursts of inverted bits of example 7, and ends abruptly when the tonic A is reached in the bass.

In his French autobiography, Tcherepnin wrote, "A comparison of this concerto to its predecessor reveals the distance I had traveled in the four years separating their composition. I consider the Second Concerto clearly superior to the First, and I do not know why it is the First that has enjoyed the favor of pianists and the public." In subsequent years, the "favor of pianists and the public" once enjoyed by the First Concerto has evaporated, and Tcherepnin's own recordings of the Second, distributed by two major labels (DG and RCA) helped to establish it as one of his best-known pieces.

II. Veranstaltung

Freitag, den 7. März 20 Uhr   Tonhalle

ORCHESTERKONZERT
des Konzertvereins

Leitung: Adolf Mennerich

Ernst Krenek

Conzerto Grosso II. op. 25
Allegro — Adagio — Allegretto — Andante, allegro

Igor Strawinsky

I. Orchestersuite (1917—1925)
I. Andante II. Napolitana III. Española IV. Balalaika

II. Orchestersuite
Marsch — Walzer — Polka — Galopp

Alexander Tscherepnin

II. Klavierkonzert a moll op. 26
deutsche Urauff.
vivo — allegretto — allegro — presto
Solist: Alexander Tscherepnin

Paul Hindemith

Vorspiel zu „Neues vom Tage"
Konzertfassung

Tcherepnin performed his Concerto
No. 2 at the Zurich Tonhalle on
March 7, 1930.

CONCERTO DA CAMERA, OPUS 33

The *Concerto da Camera* was the score that propelled Tcherepnin to international prominence. Composed for a competition sponsored by the German publisher B. Schott's Sohne, it won a prize and received a featured performance at the 1925 Donaueschingen Festival. Tcherepnin had read of this contest in Monte Carlo the previous autumn. "Among the members of the jury," he wrote, "figured the name of Paul Hindemith, which was a sign that there [would] be a chance for a composition written in a modern idiom. I... composed a *concerto da camera* for flute, violin and chamber orchestra (strings, 2 horns, 2 trumpets and timpani.)" As required by the contest rules, Tcherepnin submitted the score pseudonymously, identifying himself as "Schaffen"-a clever choice for a German competition, since this plausibly name-like word means, "to create" or "to undertake actively" in that language. In March 1925, Schott notified him that he had won one of the five prizes awarded that year and sent him a check for 6,000 Francs, by far the largest sum he had yet received for a score.

That summer, Tcherepnin was invited to attend the Donaueschingen Festival for the first performance of the Concerto, con-ducted by Hermann Scherchen. "I spent there," he wrote, "perhaps one of the happiest weeks of my life. The artistic atmosphere of the Festival was unique and highly stimulating.

"It is there where I first met Hindemith, who was busily writing choruses at a table in the garden of the Schlitzen Hotel in the midst of conversing with colleagues. [Scherchen] also stayed at the Schlitzen...: he advised me that the dynamics of my *Concerto da Camera* were not balanced and spent the night in readjusting them [so that] the comparatively small number of strings [would] balance...with cornets and horns. The performance of the *Concerto da Camera*, wonderfully conducted by Scherchen was a great success and established at once my name and reputation in Germany." The *Concerto da Camera* was premiered as the closing number of the third and final Festival concert on Sunday, July 26, 1925, with Gustave Kaleva, flutist, Licco Amar violinist, and a chamber orchestra conducted by Hermann Scherchen which included Paul Hindemith as one of its two violists. Tcherepnin's piece immediately followed the first public performance of Igor Stravinsky's Piano Sonata, the program also offering world premieres by Paul Dessau, Felix Petyrek, Otto Siegl, and Paul Hindemith. The published score was decorously dedicated to "Mrs. Louisine Weekes," then the composer's mistress, later to be his wife.

Unique among Tcherepnin's works in its biographical significance, the *Concerto da Camera* is also singular in style: indeed, it can scarcely be an accident that in this piece, written for German contest judges, the composer adopted a Baroque Germanic tone notably closer to *echt deutsch* than anything else in his music. Tcherepnin, as we have seen, was well aware that Hindemith was to be on Schott's jury; he surely had some familiarity with Hindemith's initial chamber concertos (*Kleine Kammermusiken*), and knew of the growing German appetite for neo-Baroque evocations of Bach and his Italian contemporaries. Fortunately, the aims of such music were compatible with Tcherepnin's own, and if the antiquarianisms, the tonal balance and the teutonicized motor rhythms of the *Concerto da Camera* are somewhat atypical for Tcherepnin, they nonetheless emerge therein with the most perfect naturalness.

One consequence of Tcherepnin's stylization in the work is a recrudescence of the functions of traditional tonality. For once in a Tcherepnin title (Schott issued the piece as *Concerto da Camera* in D major) the key-designation is appropriate and necessary. Key signatures (which were dispensed with for much of the Second Concerto) are employed here in three of the four movements; and while the nine-step scale is used throughout, the important thematic material exploits it to emphasize its major/minor aspect, with the F# and B natural of the major continually played off against the F natural and Bb of the minor. The tonal orientation here is astonishingly different from that of Tcherepnin's Piano Trio, which was written shortly afterward and also utilized the D nine-step scale: there, at least in the outer movements, the scale is made to seem almost incompatible with a stable tonal center.

Tcherepnin's use of Bach-like elements was, of course, selective, just as he made no effort to avoid a certain eclecticism in his evocation of older music. The three-movement Bach-Vivaldi concerto layout is rejected in favor of a more modern four-movement plan that admits a highly organized waltz-scherzo. The work is decidedly Baroque in its conciseness, however, and in its use of recapitulation as well. Tcherepnin the miniaturist is still plainly evident in the small proportions of these movements, especially the first and second. The recapitulations (in the context of such brevity) are surprisingly extensive, perhaps even disappointing in a young composer whose inventiveness shows unquestionable mastery. Then again, perhaps part of the Baroque ethos is that the composer is expected to play it safe. Tcherepnin, in any case, had no qualms about this piece: on one occasion he described it fondly as "a happy child."

I.   The first movement, *Allegro maestoso* (key signature D major), is framed by a *ritornello* which opens the work and reappears at the end of the movement, where it is followed by a brief coda. The flute and violin play in unison in this recurring *tutti*, joining in the presentation of the following theme in D nine-step:

Example 8

Against climactic slashing chords, the trumpet takes up motif a, and intertwining lines effect a modulation to E nine-step, where the violin, accompanied by flute, begins the solo exposition with a lilting new theme:

Example 9

The rhythm of c is, of course, the rhythm of a in reverse (an important point later). Note the similarity between d here and b above; note also the elegant counterpoint (unquoted) that the flute provides for d. Flute and violin then exchange parts as example 9 ap-pears in F nine-step.

A descending-scale passage brings some development based on motif a, heard both in its normal form and with its rhythm reversed. A *crescendo* on a rising five-measure sequence is continued in rhythmic compression with 5/8 measures of rising nine-step bass scales (over A as pedal) and swelling brass chords.

A reprise begins with the soloists playing a variant of ex. 9 in the home key of D nine-step:

Example 10

Note the new rhythmic form c¹ (actually, a in rhythmic reversal). Taken up in A nine-step by the violin, the theme passes to flute, moving to E-flat and G, whereupon the opening *ritornello* reappears. This time, the closing trumpet-*cum*-slashing chord episode is slightly extended, after which c¹ blares out as a culmination.

II. *Andantino* (key signature Bb major). This brief tri-partite slow movement is in B-flat nine-step-the same scale, of course, as D nine-step. The accompaniment figure played by lower strings at the outset, a tick-tock pattern of grotesque charm proves to be omnipresent, and may well have been a sly reference to the Haydn "Clock " Symphony (Example 11).

Example 11

As the violin continues, the flute enters with its own theme; when the soloists' colloquy reaches the highest register, they take up the tick-tock pattern, which continues through the central portion of the movement against brief brass and string solos. There is a mysterious legato climax, and the opening section is reprised with new *sul ponticello* coloring in the accompaniment. In 1926, Tcherepnin made a transcription of this movement for piano solo, published the following year by Schott as Op. 33a.

Example 12

Example 13

III. *Vivace* (no key signature). The opening "motto (Example 12) will later serve as a cadence to every important episode in the movement. Note that the bass has dropped from the slow movement's Bb to A as dominant preparation for D major. The home key arrives as a theme is presented by flute, then (with a significant variant) violin (Example 13). After a climax on the motto and some descending passagework, the bass-pattern (Example 14, overleaf) appears (later to be heard in single-note variants),

Example 14

which serves to accompany two different themes, one (marked A) associated with the flute introduced in C# nine-step, the other (B) also first delivered by the flute and harmonized in B nine-step:

Example 15

and repeated by flute and violin in octaves in C nine-step, with a *crescendo* that culminates in the motto. In the lengthy following *diminuendo* (all over pedal E) theme A is prominent. The motto cadence brings a central section in foreshortened A-B-A form, the outer portions based on a wistful colloquy between soloists, the center section introducing a Romantic homophonic orchestral waltz.

After a grand pause, the whole opening of the movement is reprised, up to the first climax. Descending scales bring a determined discussion of theme B by the soloists, a climax on the motto (in Bb nine-step), a blaring parody of the orchestral waltz, and an unexpected *pianissimo* dissolution of the motto.

IV.   *Allegro molto* (key signature D major). The solo violin participates in the bold opening theme:

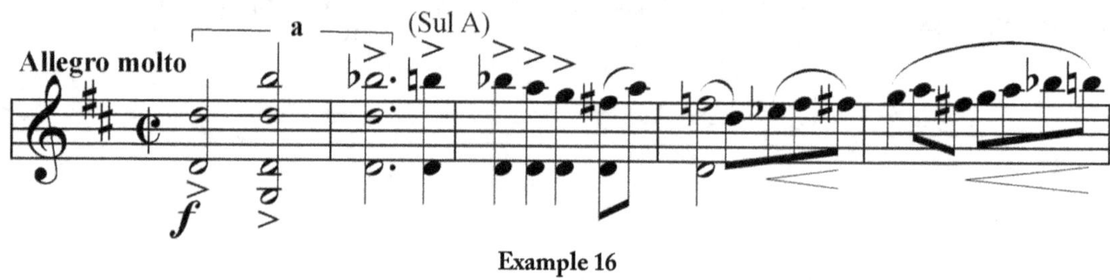

Example 16

The flute enters with its own repeated-note theme, which is presently fragmented and transformed against violin *arpeggios*; later the fragments are played against a heroic octave displacement version of motif a (Example 17). The key signature disappears as the music moves to C nine-step and there is an orchestral discussion of the opening theme and the flute theme. A climax brings a *tutti* on the opening theme (differently harmonized), and an impassioned discussion of motif a ensues in flute-violin antiphony.

The fragments return in the flute, and the violin soon begins to reiterate motif a, now pregnant with Romantic promise, first reaching a climax, then in *diminuendo*. The key signature returns and the main theme reenters, *dolcissimo*, delivered by the soloists in octaves. A sudden slashing climax brings rhythmic cadential gestures, and the *Concerto da Camera* reaches a jubilant conclusion with all the instruments playing reiterated Ds in various registers.

Example 17

Tcherepnin with cast of *Ol-Ol* as performed in New York on February 7 and 9, 1934.

The militant modernism with which Tcherepnin approached music did not dominate his attitude toward the other arts. The subjects he chose for his operas, for example, indicate that he felt no need to rebel against the psychological realism of turn-of-the-century theater. Puccinian *verismo* may well, in his eyes, have suffered from a severe lack of artistic verity; yet the protagonists of Tcherepnin's first two operas, Ol-Ol and Sobeide, would probably have been quite congenial to Puccini as operatic heroines. It will become evident that Tcherepnin himself had good reason to identify with these heroines, both of whom faced predicaments analogous to those in his own life.

On the occasion of the first performance of *Ol-Ol* in its original Russian (New York, 1934—see also Book III, p. 317), Tcherepnin wrote this account of his early attraction to the Andreyev play on which the opera is based:

"It was in 1918 in Tbilisi that I first made the acquaintance of Leonid Andreyev's drama *The Days of our Life*.

"Imagine a company of amateurs on a tiny stage lit by a few inadequate lamps, a pale, sickly Gloukovtzev [the hero], a tall, gray-eyed flaxen-haired Ol-Ol, a gay, animated Onoufry. I myself was a student at the time, and this performance, with its truthful portrayal of student lives by students themselves, without make-up, without theatrical costumes, almost without scenery, before an audience of students, made a profound impression upon me.

"And I immediately seized upon the idea of putting this drama to music.

"A few months later at the Tiflis Opera, I attended a performance of an opera by the composer Glouharev on the same subject. It disappointed me as profoundly as the dramatic production had moved me. The music, so it seemed to me, utterly failed to express the deeply and typically Russian content of the play.

"And once again I began to cherish the idea of composing an opera on this subject myself. But the times were not favorable for so ambitious a project. And the disruptions of the years that followed continued to prevent me from realizing this wish. It was only in 1924, in emigration in Monte Carlo, that I finally had the long-desired opportunity to undertake the project."

It is not surprising that Andreyev's portrayal of Russian big-city student life appealed deeply to Tcherepnin, who had been extremely happy in the Petrograd student milieu and had been forced to desert it much against his will. The young composer had felt guilty about leaving his country in its hour of need, a feeling that was only reinforced upon his later departure for the west. Like Ol-Ol, he had allowed parental authority to dictate the course and surroundings of his life, suppressing his own inclinations and abandoning or betraying many of the people and things he loved most. It is doubtful, of course, whether Tcherepnin ever went so far as to equate his own betrayal (emigration) with Ol-Ol's (prostitution); yet it is certain that he believed he had done a shameful thing in fleeing a nation to which he belonged so completely by birth and education.

It was in March 1924 that definite plans for an opera on *The Days of our Life* began to take shape in Tcherepnin's mind. The composer was then in unusually buoyant spirits. His love affair with Louisine Weekes, begun only a few weeks before, had come into full bloom, and by sheer luck he had received a concert engagement that obliged him to stay in Monte Carlo, where he could be near her. Because his father had recently been conducting at the Monte Carlo Opera, Tcherepnin had free entry to the theater, and had gotten to the habit of attending almost every performance. "In this lyric mood," he wrote, "I felt more than ever the great desire to compose an opera." The Tiflis performance of Andreyev's drama was still vividly in his memory: he even recalled that the role of Ol-Ol had been played by one Miss Krijanovsky. To his great joy, he found a copy of the play in a Russian bookshop in Nice, and he quickly prepared a libretto in three scenes. Remembering that Glouharev's opera had used Andreyev's original title, Tcherepnin decided to call his own setting *Ol-Ol*, after the heroine. On an upright piano that Louisine had rented for his convenience, Tcherepnin finished up the composition of his *Transcriptions slaves* and immediately began to work on *Ol-Ol*.

By the end of April, the first scene was almost complete. Subsequent progress was slower, however, because Tcherepnin became involved with other projects. His father enlisted his aid in orchestrating an enormous old ballet for Pavlova against a dead-line, and he was also asked to help orchestrate his father's new ballet, *The Romance of the Mummy*. After finishing these tasks he felt he had fallen out of the groove for original composition, and decided that the best way to find his way back in was to start on some new pieces. He returned to *Ol-Ol* in the fall, beginning the second scene, but repeatedly put it aside to work on the *Concerto da Camera*, which had to be finished in time for submission in the Schott contest.

The short score of *Ol-Ol* was finally completed in May 1925; Tcherepnin proceeded cautiously with the orchestration, conscious of his inexperience, and finished it in early August, shortly after returning from the premiere of the *Concerto da Camera* at the Donaueschingen Festival.

For the opening of his very next work, the Trio, Tcherepnin used the same theme that begins *Ol-Ol*, rhythmically varied. More than half a century later, he told Ming that he had deliberately resorted to self-quotation in this case (something he almost never did) because he feared that the opera would never appear in print.

Tcherepnin could not, in fact, realistically expect the opera to be engraved until it was staged, and his publisher (Universal Editions) had some trouble placing *Ol-Ol* in a theater, partly because it furnishes only a half an evening's entertainment and must be given as part of a double-bill. A performance was finally arranged, however, for Weimar in early 1928. "When... I arrived in Weimar and entered the opera house from the stage entrance... I heard the sounds of the first scene of *Ol-Ol*," wrote Tcherepnin. "It was a wonderful feeling. And when I entered the hall and saw German singers dressed in the traditional uniform of Russian students, dear and familiar to me, I nearly cried, so moved... was [I] by this artistic materialization of my native country. The conductor, Ernst Praetorius, the singers and the orchestra did an excellent job; the scenery of the Vorbiev mountains, of a boulevard in Moscow, of the room in a Moscow hotel, [was] authentic, and the policem[a]n—in his typical uniform of the pre-Revolutionary years-was as authentic as if he [had] just arrived from early XXth Century Russia."

On January 31, 1928, *Ol-Ol* was introduced in Weimar in a double premiere with another one-act opera, *Don Juans Sohn* by Hermann Wunch. Tcherepnin's score was well received, and he was immediately commissioned to produce an opera for the following year's Baden- Baden Festival (this project, however, never materialized).

Soon after his initial joy at seeing the opera come to life in rehearsal, Tcherepnin found that he was not totally satisfied with it. "I... felt," he wrote, "when listening to *Ol-Ol* in Weimar, that the libretto [was] too episodic, that instead of relying only on what is said, some dramatic situations should be enacted. A plan for two supplementary scene[s] that could be played before the lowered curtain came [in]to my head: the first of these... would... show that Ol-Ol really wanted to quit her call-girl life but could not...because of the domination by her mother and fear of her. The second... would bring together Onoufry and Kolya... with the provincial officer... thus explaining to the public how all of them [come to be] together in the last scene."

The composer decided that he would write these scenes only after finishing another operatic project, *Die Hochzeit der Sobeide*, and it was not until January or early February 1931, that they were completed. The five-scene version was premiered on October 19, 1933, in Yugoslavia, at the Ljubljana Opera House, under a conductor named Polic. Tcherepnin was present (he had played four concerts in Yugoslavia during the previous week), and observed "[The opera] was given in Slovenian, so it was hard for me to understand the words, but the new version seemed to me much better than the old one." The published score of the opera bears a dedication to the composer's wife. It may be noted that Louisine Tcherepnin also prepared an English translation of the libretto from the French, which was apparently issued for the score's New York premiere in 1934.

Ol-Ol could scarcely be called a repertory piece, but it receives performances from time to time, and a tape of it from a French broadcast is in informal circulation among collectors. It might be mentioned that the opera's title ("Ol-Ol" is a nickname for Olga) is singularly prone to misconstruction by English-speaking readers and typesetters: in Tcherepnin's *New York Times* obituary it was transformed, bizarrely, into the tautological, pseudo-arithmetical equation "01 = 01."

Subtitled "Scenes from Student Life," *Ol-Ol* was scored for an orchestra of modest, almost classical size: piccolo, 2 flutes, 2 oboes, 2 clarinets, 2 bassoons, 4 horns, 2 trumpets, 3 trombones, tuba, timpani, other percussion, harp and strings. The major characters are:

Eudoxia Antonovna . . . . mezzo-soprano
Olga Nicolaievna (Ol-Ol), her daughter . . . . soprano
Nicolai Gloukovtzev (Kolya), a student, in love with Ol-Ol . . . . tenor
Onoufry Nicolaievich, an older student . . . . buffo baritone
Mischa, a student . . . . tenor
Grigori Ivanovich, an officer. . . . . bass

A chorus appears in the first and last scenes.

The plot of *Ol-Ol* has few complexities. After a choral drinking song about the shortness of life, the curtain rises, revealing that the singers are university students enjoying a picnic outside Moscow. In a comic aria, Onoufry tells the story of his eviction from his last lodgings. Ol-Ol enters with Kolya, and the two sing of their love for each other as, simultaneously, Mischa leads the students in a song.

However, when Ol-Ol and her mother Eudoxia appear in the following entr'acte, their conversation makes it clear that Eudoxia is a procuress who lives by selling her daughter's sexual favors to male clients. Eudoxia has found a new customer for Ol-Ol, an officer. Ol-Ol longs to give up prostitution, for she truly loves Kolya, but her mother demands that she forgets about the penniless student and concentrate instead on the officer, who has money to offer. Eudoxia threatens that, if necessary, she will chase the boy off by telling him that Ol-Ol is a kept woman.

Ol-Ol finds Kolya in a Moscow street with some of his friends and tells him the sordid the truth about herself. After an initial outburst of anger, his pity is aroused when he learns that Ol-Ol has been refusing to work for her mother and consequently has had nothing to eat for two days. But Eudoxia then arrives with the officer-client in tow and browbeats her daughter into going off with him. Kolya is crushed.

The officer, Grigori, is next seen confronting Eudoxia; he has come to complain that Ol-Ol has run away from him. She promises to find her daughter and bring her back. Left with time to amuse himself, Grigori now joins a group of drunken students, including, coincidentally, Onoufry and Kolya, who are bent on a pub-crawl.

The revelers find their way to Grigori's room in a Moscow hotel. Grigori, very drunk, sings a sentimental friendship duet with Onoufry. When Ol-Ol and Eudoxia enter, the situation, of course, becomes awkward. Eudoxia tries to smooth things over, but Kolya is infuriated at Ol-Ol's presence here and begins to heap insults upon her; Grigori, unaware of what is going on, takes offense. Kolya threatens Grigori with his own sword, Grigori draws a revolver, the broken-hearted Ol-Ol tries to separate them, and Onoufry manages to restore peace, persuading the lachrymose Grigori and the shattered Kolya to embrace. As the opening chorus is again heard in the distance Ol-Ol and Kolya are both miserably aware that, without revolvers or swords, their lives have been destroyed through the destruction of their love.

When a composer becomes deeply involved in abstract musical theory, there is the danger that he may approach the composition of opera as a mere technical puzzle, filling his score with formal ingenuities but failing to give it dramatic shape or to differentiate his characters by musical means. These defects are disconcertingly manifest in Hindemith operas, and might have also been expected from Tcherepnin, who was gaining a reputation as a neo-Classicist with some surprising Teutonic attributes. One reason that this did not happen with *Ol-Ol* was that Tcherepnin was determined that the Russian character of the play should be reflected in the music (his chief objection to Glouharev's setting of the drama was that it failed to do this). Thus, Tcherepnin filled his score with folk material, and the contrast between this and Tcherepnin's "modern" music became one of his basic techniques for differentiating the characters of the drama by musical means. Thus on the simplest level, the care-free students and the hedonistic officer sing music of a distinctly populist cast (here key signatures are very much in evidence), while nine-step themes are employed in connection with the play's darker elements.

Tcherepnin goes beyond these simple distinctions, however, showing a still-rudimentary but unmistakable flair for subtler musical characterization. For example, although Onoufry and the officer inhabit the same populist world, Onoufry's theme has a mirth and wit that clearly sets it apart from the officer's sententious and platitudinous utterances: indeed, in the final scene, the officer's shifting mood in drunkenness, from the euphoric to the lachrymose, is resourcefully mirrored in the music. Eudoxia's shrewish, non-stop nine-step nagging, combined with her unfailing melodic triviality, renders her as a caricature rather than a flesh and blood creature-nevertheless the results are vivid: she emerges, in fact, as one of the most unpleasant characters in the entire operatic literature.

Much of Ol-Ol's music is based on a descending motif (called "motif a" in the analysis that follows) that lends a generic sadness to her utterances; there are also moments, however, of peculiar desolation where her overall lyric appeal gains individualized character. Gloukovtzev's music, predictably, is much bound up with Ol-Ol's. On the whole, however, Tcherepnin's flair for character and concern with dramatic values are obvious throughout.

In the opera's brevity-particularly in the initial version, which did not contain the two interludes-we again see evidence of Tcherepnin the miniaturist, determined to tell his story in a few deftly-executed tableaux. Tcherepnin was well advised to add those episodes, not only for dramatic reasons, but for musical ones as well. While dissonant passages tend to be more prolonged in them than in the original scenes, the result is far from a mismatch—indeed, the contrast proves to be an advantage.

In *Ol-Ol*, brevity is accompanied by straightforwardness and simplicity of manner. The leitmotives given the characters are not developed and redeveloped in the full Wagnerian manner, but are, instead, trotted out more or less unaltered when they come on stage, much in the manner of the motives in Puccini's *La Bohème*. Motif a, to be sure, is designed for versatility and durability, for, like a good deal of nine-step material, it can be harmonized in a number of expressive and highly varied ways.

A brief orchestral prelude introduces three significant themes. The most important of these, labeled "Theme I," owes its poignancy to the special intervallic character of the nine-step scale. Often stated in abbreviated form as motif a, Theme I is associated throughout the opera with Ol-Ol's despair and hopelessness. The prelude rises to a climax on theme II in E minor, then E-flat minor.

THEME I

Example 18

Over a figure of two alternating notes (F and Eb), the opening chorus appears in Ab major, based on the following traditional student theme:

Example 19

Onoufry sings an F major aria, based on the extensive use of the following cheery motif, which will be identified with him in all subsequent scenes:

Example 20

Mischa begins a traditional song in A minor with the chorus, and soon Ol-Ol and Gloukovtzev's often canonic protestations of love are touchingly interwoven with it:

Example 21

The ensemble grows in lushness and complexity with impressive high-note climaxes for the lovers.

A lengthy "bells of Moscow" episode ensues, and the lovers are left alone. Ol-Ol, chromatically accompanied by strings, reveals her anxiety as, for the first time, she sings motif a of theme I; Kolya tries to comfort her with theme III:

Example 22

Kolya expresses his love in an extended cantabile accompanied by string "heartbeats," but Ol-Ol's answer is melancholy, reprising much of the prelude as she alternates theme I with theme II.

Onoufry reenters, his theme heard at first in diminution in the strings, and later delivered in pompous augmentation as he sings of marriage. After a sprightly "fire chorus" in D major, there is an orchestral postlude, in which theme I appears in the cellos.

The orchestral prelude to the first entr'acte limns the coarseness and raucousness of Eudoxia, in three motifs-a shrill, descending nine-step flourish (A), a trivial fragment (B), and a menacing rising figure (C):

Example 23 (A, B)

Example 23 (C)

These themes are hurled about as Eudoxia chatters on. The combination of the rising figure (C) with a variant of its near in-version-motif a-will be of considerable importance later (Example 24):

Ol-Ol answers in recitative over a trudging bass, *Lento*, but Eudoxia flares up again, introducing yet another theme (Example 25).

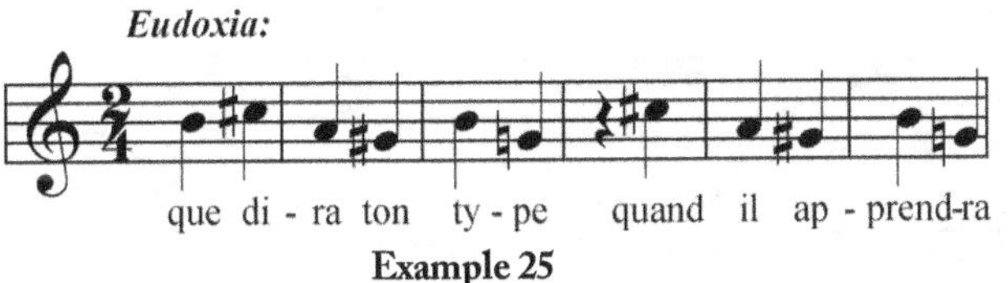

Example 25

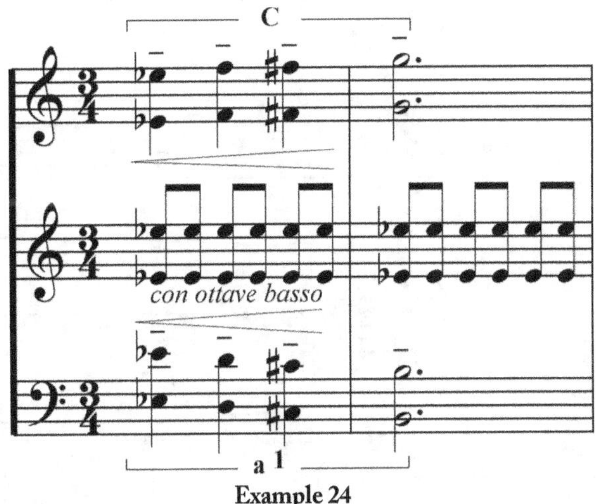

Example 24

At the end of the entr'acte, the beaten Ol-Ol sings two pathetic phrases, both followed by mournful flute musing, the first suggesting motif a, the second quoting and extending it. Eudoxia's shrill flourish concludes the episode.

The second scene opens with a somewhat plaintive melody for oboe, accompanied by close chromatic harmonies in running sixteenth-notes, and continues with a more march-like affair. The students' adventures are characterized by the expected folk-like material. The plaintive melody returns, and its sixteenth notes slow into motif a in lower-register strings as Ol-Ol enters. She sings a poignant F# minor aria, in the second phrase of which Theme II takes her into her highest range. Theme III is played in canon by oboe and bassoon, accompanied by a "fluttering heart" rhythm, and Kolya tries to console his love, but she returns dolefully to motif a. As Kolya becomes more importunate and Ol-Ol begins to confess the truth about her way of life, theme III and motif a are heard in diminution and obsessively developed in a passage of steadily mounting agitation. After a climax, there is a recitative-like passage accompanied only by oboe, playing motif a in vast augmentation; then as the two lovers renew their vows of devotion, motif a blossom into a more extended melody, sung by the two in lushly-harmonized free imitation (Example 26).

Example 26

The return of Onoufry brings another sprightly tune. When he departs, the temporary optimism of the lovers is indicated by a new element- which will here be called motif b-a kind of inversion of motif a, ascending where the latter had descended, and representing hope where motif a had represented despair. Motif b now extends into a melody, sung by Kolya in free canon with the orchestra:

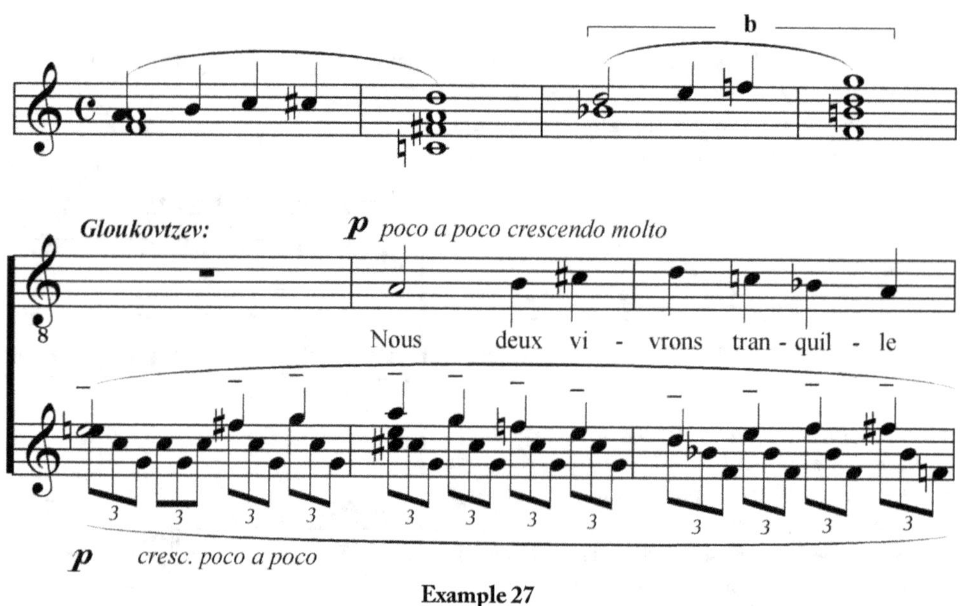

Example 27

In the most richly romantic passage in the whole opera, Kolya builds motif b into a tenorial climax of Puccinian sonorousness, at which point Ol-Ol joins in at the octave. Even as love appears to be triumphing, however, Eudoxia's vulgar tune (B) is heard, and the procuress enters with the officer Grigori, her prospective client for Ol-Ol, in tow. Her themes are developed, and the combination of (C) with motif a[1] snarls out with distinct viciousness as reinforced by the trumpet. Ol-Ol fearfully sings motif a; Kolya, in a rage at Ol-Ol's vacillation, warns her, in a stentorian statement of theme II, that all is over between them if she leaves with the officer. Ol-Ol twice reiterates the moaning strains of motif a, arriving at theme II for a piercing, high-register climax before she departs.

Left alone, Kolya sings an aria of lament, accompanied by a "sobbing" rhythm and mostly based on new material but incorporating references to theme III when sectional cadences approach. Onoufry enters with his usual jollity, but shows unexpected musical gentleness when he undertakes to comfort Kolya. The plaintive music from the opening of the scene returns to provide a conclusion.

The second entr'acte begins with a nasty 5/4 brass variant of example 25, which is extensively developed in the opening pages, often in connection with the following tune:

Example 28

The students enter, their drunkenness suggested quite economically by orchestral hints of staggering and hiccuping. Grigori essays brassy nobility of utterance, somewhat impeded by his own intoxication, and a grand climax dies away as the unsteady tread of the drinkers is again suggested.

The opening of the final scene is again populist in tone. The distinctly military theme of Grigori's fatuous opening aria in praise of Moscow, with its trumpets, dotted rhythms and confident rising scale, later yields to other folk and folk-like material as Grigori professes his love for the society of students and is joined in a racy duet by Onoufry. Suddenly, as Eudoxia's raucous theme (B) is heard, the old harridan comes in with her daughter, the orchestra playing motif a as, with a shock, Ol-Ol recognizes Kolya. The two lovers tensely question each other in a recitative accompanied by simple triads. Grigori, totally unaware of the personal relationships or emotions involved, resumes burbling with musical bonhomie; Ol-Ol can do little more than moan motif a. In a *crescendo*, as theme (B) is worked over, Kolya hurls insults at Ol-Ol. This provokes Grigori, who sings the following melody as he lectures Kolya about the politeness that a gentleman must accord to women:

Kolya yells out in anger, Ol-Ol sings motif a once again; in the confused shouting, as weapons are drawn, brasses blare theme III. Soon slashing chords reach a climax, and a gong stroke is heard. From the ensuing near-silence, a desolate waltz for flute and cello begins. Ol-Ol joins them, singing motif a, which now develops into an extended and poignant melody as the heroine bewails her departed and never to be recaptured happiness. The

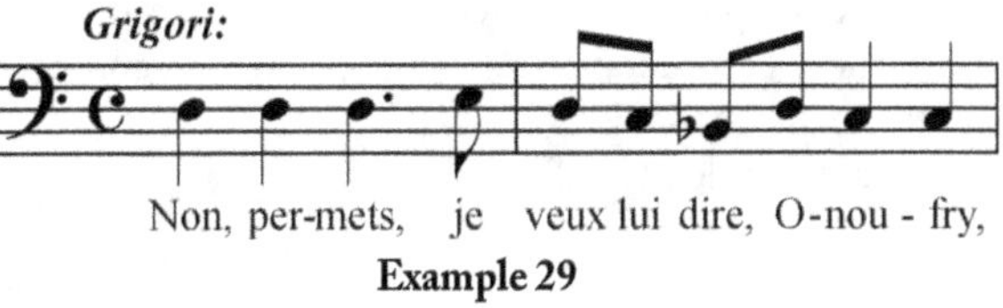

Example 29

tempo speeds and the other characters muse about the situation; then as the piece again becomes a solo aria, motif a is again heard, and continues to repeat in a descending chain:

The waltz resumes and concludes its desolate course. Grigori, feeling sorry for himself as the innocent victim of Kolya's inexplicable abuse, vents his grievance through example 29. Onoufry smooths things over, as his theme makes a humorous

Example 30

appearance in the tuba. In the distance, a chorus sings the song that was heard at the very opening of the opera: this time, Onoufry and Grigori add their comments. Then Ol-Ol has a final plaint that begins with motif a and proceeds to theme II: a brief orchestral return of this theme brings the opera to a conclusion.

A case can be made that up to the completion of *Ol-Ol*, Tcherepnin's work consisted of two strains, a folk-strain and a modernist strain-these strains tending to alternate with and interpenetrate each other. After *Ol-Ol*, however, Tcherepnin's folk impulses went into exile, as it were, as the composer set about producing a group of scores marked by a passion for naked intellection.

❆ ❆ ❆

POETRY AND RHETORIC

Further consideration must now be given to the notion of an "awkward stage" in Tcherepnin's creative journey. He had developed a self-consciousness about manipulating the audience-a conviction that an artist should refrain from doing so. The danger was, of course, that he might become so uncompromising about guiding his audience's attention that his music-like excessively cryptic lyric poetry-could simply fail to project its content to the public.

Tcherepnin was now finding, in fact, that when he produced music that he deemed "honest" in its use of expressive devices, it often failed to communicate directly with an audience. Conversely, his attempts at "audience pieces," particularly those written for his piano recitals, emerged as tawdry (in his own estimation, at least) and quickly dropped from his repertory. The problem he now faced is evident even in a relatively popular work such as the Piano Trio, which represented an attempt to present a musical argument almost without rhetorical trimmings. This tiny, ultra-dense score makes a strong impression on the listener, but it is doubtful that it genuinely communicates the full range of its contents. Its formal framework, in both the first and last movements, is frankly too small to support the panoply of emotional issues implicit in the music's violently contrasted and hyperexpressive episodes. Tcherepnin did not deign to guide the listener toward the high-spots, nor to provide breathing pauses to let anything sink in. Hearing the Trio is like being bombarded by simultaneous questions yelled by a team of interlocutors who never wait for a reply. It was presumably plain to Tcherepnin that in subsequent works he would do well to allow more scope for narrative connectives. What was the use, after all, of "honest" music that flew by too quickly to be communicative?

Tcherepnin also noticed that his piano output in the Paris period had consisted almost entirely of miniatures. From these considerations arose the desire to compose a big piano piece that would be at once brilliantly effective and intellectually challenging.

He decided to call it *Message.*

MESSAGE, OPUS 39

In *Message*, it was Tcherepnin's conscious intention "to compose a major work for piano solo, of the dimensions of [a] Sonata, yet not in conventional form. I wanted to use… all the technical devices that [were] introduced in my chamber music compositions, such as nine-step scale-fundamental and modal-[and] Interpoint, and yet not make it a goal *per se*, but the way to express my inner world, which at that time, I have to admit, was far from being in peace." By now Louisine's first husband had initiated divorce proceedings, and Tcherepnin realized that he would soon have to choose between marrying her and breaking with her altogether. The composer was unable to bring himself to discuss his grave doubts with Louisine or anybody else, and he may have hoped to gain a sense of confessional release by encoding them in his *Message*.

Tcherepnin apparently began work on this score in March 1926, in Monte Carlo, while still putting the finishing touches on the so-called "Well-Tempered Cello," Op. 38. That collection codifies nine-step language, with each of its twelve preludes set in one of the three modes of the four possible nine-step scales. *Message* completed in Paris in April, similarly delimits the boundaries of nine-step, presenting a tonal journey that twice cycles systematically through all four transpositions—C, D#, D, C#- of his scale (measures 1-203; measures 204-254). The score is cast in a single movement which "in one way," according to Tcherepnin, resembles "an enlarged Sonata form." This description, however, is surely suppositious. Here, as the previous Second Cello Sonata and in many subsequent works, Tcherepnin incorporated a development section, but chose to avoid the sort of full-scale recapitulation he had considered acceptable in the *Concerto da Camera*; and this step forward into modernism is unarguably a step away from the historical sonata-prototype. In the purest classical treatment, as many slow movements by Haydn, Mozart and Beethoven illustrate, the recapitulation is an absolute necessity for the form—it is the development section that may be dispensed with as an unnecessary luxury. *Message* begins with a sonata-exposition and continues with a development section, but its feint at genuine recapitulation veers off, almost before it has begun, into a coda. Musical analysis lacks a name for this kind of post-sonata form (which Tcherepnin would use again as late as the Second Symphony) but no confusion with the classical model should be risked.

The first important material heard in *Message* has its origins in a short theme introduced in the tenth measure: (Though ear-catching, the rhythm of this theme is uncomfortably like a nursery-rhyme platitude, and must be accounted a weakness in the score. By changing the rhythm later, Tcherepnin does succeed in making variants of this theme considerably more attractive-which makes one wonder why he was satisfied with the initial form of it. This tendency to use all available variants of a theme, even those that are unappealing, is a feature of *Message* that listeners may find irritating.)

Example 31

The work itself starts with what Tcherepnin called a "rhythmic introduction" (7/8 meter), based on motif a:

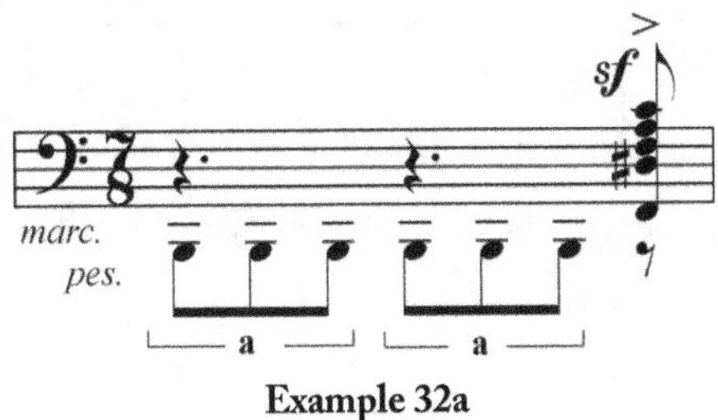

Example 32a

and continues (at the pick-up to the eleventh measure) with what will here be called the main theme, which is based on motif b:

Example 32b

This theme is extensively discussed, first in quiet interpoint, later over insistent repeated note patterns. (The interpuntal treatment of the main theme has already been examined by Willi Reich on pp. 15-16.) Tcherepnin wrote, "The same tonality...(E in the nine-step scale) is used for all the...principal [group] themes, but the tonal center changes...from E to C, then to the second mode of C ([*i. e.*, the mode beginning on D-flat]). " It is at this modal change that scale-like passages begin to swirl upward.

Example 31 appears in this mode, and another first-group theme is introduced:

Example 33

The opening 7/8 returns; then example 31 appears with a new pick-up and, in this form, becomes the basis of a bridge passage that brings the "modulation" (the quotation marks are Tcherepnin's own), and the second of the scale's four transpositions brings a new theme, as the subordinate group, musically related to motif a, appears in G nine-step:

Example 34

The short coda centers on E-flat (same notes as in G but the tonic changed from G to E-flat), as example 34 climbs the "circle of thirds" so characteristic of nine-step music, rising from Eb to G to B to Eb.

"The development section," wrote Tcherepnin, "starts with the appearance of an entirely new theme...in the second mode of [nine-step] D, which has its tonal center on E-flat." Again, a new transposition brings a new theme: a melody that stands as one of Tcherepnin's loftiest lyrical inspirations, imbued with dignity, poignancy and epic inevitability:

Example 35

This theme, "conceived in three-part song form uses, among other [devices], 'added values' such as a [sixteenth note] added to the 4/4 measure":

In the center of the three-part song-form, ex. 34 appears slightly varied to fit the current transposition, and the return of ex.

Example 36

35 is a moment of high passion, the theme now in canon in F# nine-step accompanied by throbbing chords.

The development section continues with an interpuntal discussion of two variants of example 31 (mutually transparent to each other in rhythm), in a passage of steadily mounting tension marked *sempre avvivacendo*. The variants are combined with example 33:

Example 37

a shortened version is combined with the theme from example 32:

Example 38

and soon that theme appears *fortissimo* in augmentation in the highest register over thunderous repeated bass-notes.

An imitative passage on example 31, rising by the characteristic circle of thirds, leads to a combination of example 34 (the second subject) with material from example 31. Example 33 rises to a climax and the fourth and final transposition of the scale appears as example 34 roars out in augmentation in the bass. At the climax of a *crescendo*, the opening 7/8 rhythmic pattern reappears, here heard half a tone higher than in the introduction.

This seeming recapitulation proves abortive, however. Example 34 (the second-subject theme) is heard at an extremely slow tempo as it brings us back to the first scale, and Tcherepnin now cycles again through the four transpositions, but far more rapidly. Next a purely rhythmic chordal passage emphasizing 5/8 patterns broadens (second scale) to a climax (third scale). Now a jittery, syncopated version of the once majestic example 35 combines with the main theme, then descends to the bass, after which example 33 appears in the treble, bringing us back to the initial scale for the remainder of the piece. Soon there is a climax on smashing chords. Example 31 appears a final time; the introductory music returns *piano*, and *Message* concludes with this unusual passage:

Note that the final knocking on the wood of the piano is in no sense a gratuitous sound effect, for it is carefully prepared by what precedes it: low, dissonant chords that have already brought the piano some distance to-ward sounding like a non-pitched percussion instrument. In effect, Tcherepnin has executed a "timbral modulation," with the music evolving from piano sound to percussion sound.

Example 39

One may question, however, whether that knocking-written in rapid note- values—provides a truly satisfying conclusion. Tcherepnin may have fallen into the trap here that would later ensnare many composers of the 1970s, who experimented with piano-percussion and sustaining-pedal effects: that of creating a timbral effect that sounds magnificent to the player himself but fails to project into the auditorium.

Also problematic is Tcherepnin's reluctance to return to the wonderful melody of example 35 for *cantabile* restatement. Every listener hopes to hear this noble theme again; and indeed, in bypassing the expository themes in his vestigial reprise, Tcherepnin gives the listener good reason to think that example 35 will again sing out, even after it is thrown into the contrapuntal mixmaster in a rhythmicized version. To accord such short shrift to an element as attractive as this, especially in a piece with such overall difficulties for the listener, is veritably suicidal.

Tcherepnin let more than five years pass before he performed *Message*, finally giving the premiere on June 10, 1931, at Grotrian Hall in London. "This concert was a flat failure," the composer wrote. The reviews were uniformly negative, as they tended to be for Tcherepnin's very infrequent performances of the score in later years. In fact, *Message* yields its message resentfully, shooting its quills at the listener, disdaining to ingratiate itself by any lush doubling in the piano writing. As noted, Tcherepnin shows a perverse pride in artificial thematic derivations while treating his lyric inspirations with something approaching contempt. It is, however, the combination of this sullenness with the white-hot emotion that obviously underlies so many of the musical manipulations, that gives this piece its unique cachet. Performances of *Message* will probably always be few; but they will seldom fail to be special events.

❀   ❀   ❀

SYMPHONY NO. 1, OPUS 42

It is surely significant that a few months after he crossed an important threshold in his journey to maturity by marrying Louisine Peters Weekes, Tcherepnin crossed a no less important threshold on his path to musical maturity by writing his first work for orchestra (juvenilia excepted)—*Magna Mater*. One aspect of that score that stamps it as a nuptial utterance is its epigraph, which glorifies the eternal feminine from the point of view of a pagan phallic cult; and if the epigraph is murky and confused, Tcherepnin's state of mind at this point—in his hesitancy and pessimism about his marriage together with his realization of his dependence on "apron strings"—was no less so. We have already encountered the notion of Tcherepnin's major works as autobiographical landmarks or "rites of passage" in the analysis of the Second Concerto: now, as with that piece, Tcherepnin's reaction to drastically altered circumstances in his life was to make a conscious effort to rise to a new aesthetic plateau-this time by devoting himself to the symphonic milieu.

Tcherepnin's embrace of this new medium was quite gingerly. In his view, the sensual blandishments of the orchestra were no less suspect than those of late romantic and impressionistic piano writing, and thus he approached symphonic composition almost as if Wagner and Rimsky-Korsakov had never existed. For *Magna Mater* and the work to which it was a prelude, the Symphony No. 1, Tcherepnin chose an ensemble of astonishingly modest size—the standard classical double- wind orchestra with the important addition of a few percussion instruments. Percussion apart, the instrumental was of veritably *skoptsi*-like asceticism, as if Tcherepnin were consciously renouncing seventy-five years of modern orchestral mores, comforts and conveniences. This went further than merely disdaining Strauss-Stravinsky-Dukas-Ravel resources such as basset horns, saxophones, Wagner tubas, alto flute, heckelphone and sarrusophone; Tcherepnin even refrained from using instruments that most of his contemporaries would have considered absolutely essential for orchestral music, such as English horn, E-flat clarinet, bass clarinet and contrabassoon, limiting himself, moreover, to two trumpets.

His tendency at this time, as he himself remarked, was to treat the orchestra merely as an enlarged chamber ensemble—one containing extra instruments that enabled a composer to achieve denser polyphonic textures and climaxes. In fact, the Symphony contains numerous passages where strings are divided in order to accommodate unusually profuse polyphonic elaboration. In these episodes, there is a certain nobility in the coloristic neutrality of the instrumentation. Other climaxes tend to sound somewhat gray. For Tcherepnin rejected the type of doubling found in traditional orchestration, obstinately ignoring, by his own testimony, the possibility that such procedures might be founded in acoustical laws. It was chiefly in chamber-like passages involving solo instruments that his coloristic imagination truly came alive, and fortunately these are numerous.

Tcherepnin began work on his First Symphony in April 1927, almost immediately after his arrival in New York for his second extended stay at his wife's estate. Facing months of artistic isolation among the aristocracy of Islip, with no activities more exciting than interminable sessions of bridge-playing, which Louisine loved and he loathed, he was determined to break new ground in his art.

Another spur to the production of an intellectually dense symphony may have been the recent appearance of such a work by his old idol, Prokofiev, the Symphony No. 2—modeled on no less profound a work than Beethoven's last piano sonata and bristling with complex developmental polyphony.

"Analyzing what I [had] done before," Tcherepnin wrote, "and especially my first orchestra piece, the *Magna Mater*, I found that… while I was navigating freely in the medium of [the] chamber orchestra, I was not… expert enough in orchestral writing as such; and *Magna Mater*, with its duration of hardly over eight minutes, seemed over condensed and stiff. My ambition became now to compose a regular symphony in large form, more relaxed than *Magna Mater*, Apollonic, not Dionysiac"—a work "marked by more fully-developed, purer forms and more flexible ideas."

"The first night after arrival in New York I heard in my ears the character of a theme that was to become the subordinate theme of the First Symphony. And immediately started to work, promising myself not to hurry, but to try to develop the ideas [on] as large [a scale] as I could.

"On beginning the Symphony, I saw it as a strictly formal edifice of sound. My nine-step scale furnished the tonal basis for both this piece and *Magna Mater*; my polyphonic, rhythmic and interpuntal procedures attained their full amplitude in the symphony.

"At first, I thought of a symphony in three movements—of the first being strictly polyphonic, of the second of dreamy character and of the Finale as a rondo…

"For the second movement, I wanted to use 'birds Folklore'; Islip was rich in all kind of birds. We slept in the tower at the porch and… in the early morning hours… used to listen [to] and admire… fascinating bird calls, [which] I notated as far as possible…

"Yet… having composed the 'bird' movement I discarded it as not fitting into the picture of an 'Apollonic' symphony[1] and started composing [the slow movement] anew. This time I started [with a piece of] six-part polyphony: three themes with their vertical interpoints… The movement seemed rather scholastic and dry, but I needed something of this kind to precede the lively Rondo finale.

"Yet I felt that an extra movement [was] needed between the polyphonic first movement and the scholastic second; so the idea came to me to reduce the thematic material of the first movement to its purely rhythmic value and to free the rhythm from pitch by conceiving the entire movement for non-pitch[ed] percussion instruments only… [T]his movement fulfilled the function of the classical scherzo.

"The composition and the writing down of a clear sketch of the Symphony were completed by the end of June. Like a race horse after a long race I was unable to stop the creative imagination, and to smooth it down, composed an Elegy for Violin and Piano. Thus calmed down, I started to orchestrate the Symphony and completed [it] by the end of July. I dedicated the Symphony to the memory of Louisine's father, S. T. Peters, 'founder' of the Islip estate."

Tcherepnin's first efforts to launch his new score confirmed his fears that his marriage to an extremely rich woman had placed him in an equivocal position as a composer. When he offered the symphony to the publisher Jacques Durand, Durand said he would have to hear it played before making a decision. Tcherepnin accordingly asked Gabriel Pierne to read through the piece with the Colonne Concerts Orchestra, and was told that this could not be done during the Orchestra's normal rehearsal time, but that a special rehearsal could be arranged if Tcherepnin would pay for it. With Louisine footing the bill, the composer arrived for the rehearsal on October 7, only to find that Durand had been detained in Fontainebleau. Another paid rehearsal had to be scheduled a week later especially for the publisher. Tcherepnin, at these readings, was "thrilled by the sonority" of his piece, but Durand's attitude was distinctly condescending. He said that he would publish the Symphony only if Tcherepnin made cuts in the middle movements and changed the ending of the third movement. Tcherepnin was not disposed to agree to these alterations, and the two postponed further discussion until November.

Now, however, the musical merits of the Symphony began to work in its favor. Pierne, having gone through the piece twice with his orchestra, was convinced that it was worth playing in public, and persuaded the Colonne Concerts committee to program it on a regular subscription program on October 29, where it was tucked in between Wagner's *Meistersinger* Overture and Rimsky-Korsakov's *Scheherezade*.

The full story of the concert, with the riot provoked by Tcherepnin's revolutionary scherzo for unpitched percussion, has already been told in the present volume by Willi Reich. After riot police removed a few of the most obstreperous demonstrators, Pierne was able to resume the performance with the third movement. There were some derisive whistles at the end of the Symphony, but the applause went on long enough to allow Pierne to return to the stage for a bow.

Tcherepnin soon received a letter from the head of Universal Editions in Vienna offering to publish the Symphony. With this in his pocket, the composer went to Durand and advised him that if he wanted the piece, he would have to print it exactly as written. Durand not only issued the Symphony with the full score and instrumental parts beautifully engraved, but also bought Tcherepnin's other piece from the summer of 1927, the Elegy for Violin and Piano.

The First Symphony is a work of extraordinary intellectual density. As the composer himself observed, it achieves fullness and richness of sound not through any felicities of orchestration, but through its complex polyphony. The materials, in fact, are exceptionally well-suited to manipulation, the manipulations free from the odor of artifice. Indeed, the mood of the first movement is as far removed as one could imagine from detached intellection; the atmosphere is one of relentless tension and obsessive activity.

I. Maestoso; Allegro risoluto. "The first movement," wrote Tcherepnin, "use[s] two themes: [one] of fanfare-like character and… only three measures [long], the [other] of a sort of *perpetuum mobile* type, long and non-stop [in] movement; although based on two themes, the first movement was not in sonata form…" In fact, the movement is closer to the sonata-style than Tcherepnin admits—something that becomes clearer when it is recognized that the fanfare-like motto is not (as Tcherepnin calls it) the principal theme, but actually a slow introductory theme which reappears at the beginning of the *second* subject. Few experienced listeners will fail to sense a short introduction, a sonata exposition with first and second groups, and a highly polyphonic development. What follows, however, is a kind of re-exposition; for while the same first and second themes are used, they are presented in retrograde statements! This procedure does not sound like recapitulation, but lends a certain recapitulatory coherence nonetheless. Tcherepnin, also stated, rather apologetically, "in the first movement (sonata-allegro) I proceeded more by the variation and juxtaposition of the themes

---

1   It would become the prelude to Act III of *The Wedding of Sobeide*

than by their organic elaboration," observing, wryly, that "development' ('*Durch-führung*') was never a strong point of the Russians." Here, too, his estimation errs on the side of timidity. The self-developing nature of the main (*perpetuum mobile*) theme precludes many obvious methods of development (which, in the context, would sim-ply sound redundant), but the polyphonic elaborations fulfill the symphonic requirements of development handsomely. The fact is, of course, that Tcherepnin's success in building an extended theme by manipulating small motivic kernels is as surely a mark of his miniaturistic origins as of his growth beyond them.

The first movement opens with a three-measure *Maestoso* introduction, in E nine-step, which is reproduced in Example 40 along with its later incarnation as a second subject:

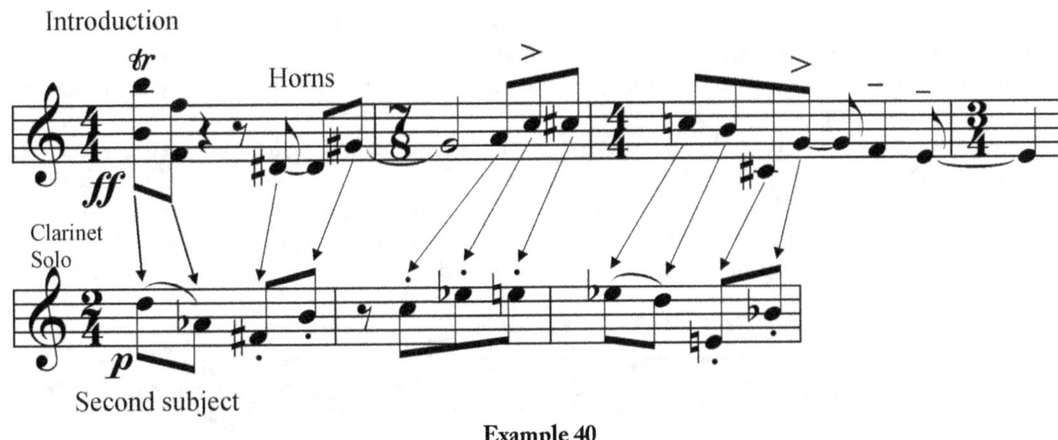

Example 40

The main theme, interestingly in B nine-step, begins with the following four measures:

Example 41

Each of these measures is a module, with an extended paragraph built up by the juxtaposition and re-juxtaposition of the rhythms of these measures. If the opening section is represented as A B C, the theme continues as follows (rising sequences are designated by ^{r}, falling sequences by $_f$):

$$\text{A B B}^r\text{--A d}^1\text{--A B B B}^r\text{ B}^r\text{ C C}^r\text{ C C}_f\text{--A B B B}^r\text{ Bv Bv Bv Bv}$$

culminating in a rising sequence (statement plus three restatements) on a variant of B called Bv (with a third beat of two eighth notes instead of a quarter). Note the powerful juxtaposition of short and long phrases. At the climax, A is tossed back and forth antiphonally by basses and horns; at the same time, a slow-rise-fast-fall figure and its inversion are discussed in complex interpoint (displacement by a single measure and by two measures):

After a *decrescendo*, the second subject arrives in the clarinet (see example 40) in E nine-step. This theme (II) alternates with a

Example 42

first theme pattern (A B C in lower instruments: simultaneously with C, higher instruments enter and play A d^1) which can be called K. The sentence is built:

$$\text{(II) K (II) K K C C}^r\text{ C}^r\text{ A B C A A Bv A A Bv A A B (A B)}$$
basses   rising sequence

(The bass sequence on C is overlaid with swirling string figures: ABC is a piccolo statement.) At the end of the sentence "lettered" above, trombones play B; (A B) begins in lower instruments and passes to the bass drum, clearly indicating that a section has been completed-in fact, these drum notes mark the end of the exposition (and, in their prominence here, provide a foretaste of the extensive use of unpitched percussion in the movement that follows).

It should be stated that there is nothing un-sonata like about the appearance of first-theme motives in the second subject: it is only in oversimplified definitions of sonata form that each subject is confined to its own material. In the hands of sonata masters such as Beethoven, Mozart, Brahms and even Dvorak, first-theme material will be used in masterly fashion throughout the exposition.

Up to this point, the themes have alternated. Now, in the development, they are combined. As the winds pursue a polyphonic discussion of the main theme, the violas introduce (II) in broad augmentation (Example 43), a form in which it will be imitatively discussed by the other strings. These simultaneous contrapuntal procedures continue in steady *crescendo*. As theme (II) reaches the trumpet, the three trombones begin a canon on an augmented version of A Bv. At the climax, there are two simultaneous versions of (II), one in equal eighth-notes (strings) and one in equal quarters (brass).

Example 43

There is a sudden *pianissimo*, and then flute and clarinet enter with a retrograde version of A B C-in Bb nine-step, un-classically enough-beginning the retrograde exposition that does duty for a recapitulation-note that the eighth-notes of A have been compressed into triplets, and that the music has been re-barred:

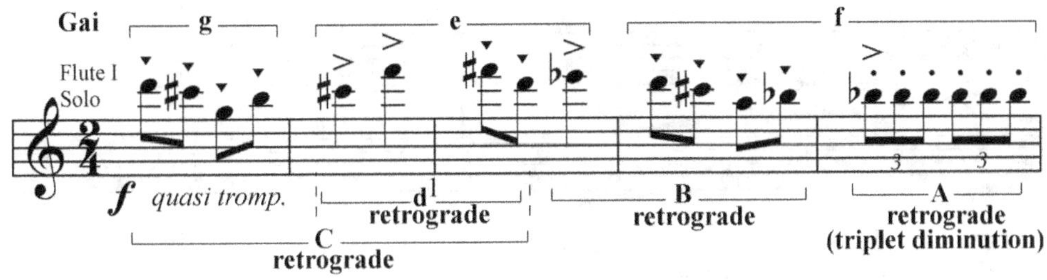

Example 44

The triplets are, in fact, a master-stroke. They call the listener's attention to the repeated notes at the *end* of the theme—in contrast to the exposition where repeated notes had been at the *beginning* of the theme: in short, they are a red flag signalling the presence of a retrograde statement! At the same time, the triplet rhythms established here take on increasing prominence as the movement proceeds, their evolution becoming an important structural element.

This retrograde theme, henceforth designated (III), acquires mysterious violin echoes upon its flute repetition; and these persist as the oboe presents (III) in augmentation against flute statements of f and, later, bassoon statements of e. The discussion (example 46, overleaf) becomes quite complex at a climax where, simultaneously,

1. upper strings interpuntally sequence on g.
2. g, augmented and rhythmically reconfigured in the syncopated shape of theme II, is heard in trombone.
3. violas present the trombone material inverted.
4. horns present the trombone material in further augmentation.
5. cellos play an augmentation of the f rhythm.

Procedure 2 constitutes a kind of "thematic modulation" to the second subject—another indication of how thoroughly this movement is pervaded by sonata strategies.

Now the retrograde of theme II appears (again in Bb nine-step): Note that the reverse quotation begins with the penultimate note of example 40 Introduction, and that these intervals are rhythmically adapted to the theme as it was in the exposition; the accompanying chords are also retrograde, falling where they had been rising. As in the exposition, discussions of this theme (II^r) is interrupted by the appearance of first-theme material—the flute-clarinet statement leads to a variant of g+e in trombone, clarinet and flute; a cello-bass dialogue on the inversion of II^r results in another return of g+e.

Example 45

At a climax, g assumes the second-theme syncopated rhythm in strings (g^2), its first measure at the same time continually reiterated in augmentation by trombone. As a fortissimo culmination, a condensed version of the main theme is tossed from flutes to trumpets (A in triplets+d^1 in eighths). Now against insistent repetitions of g^2 in the strings (rising sequence on a non-syncopated variant) winds play g in augmentation in off-beat staccatos. Eventually brasses add a further rhythmic *frisson* by joining in with g, twice as slow as the winds and an eighth note behind, the *crescendo* ever continuing. Sustained notes for bassoons and brass pile up in chords, with the trombones thundering out g in half-notes.

As catastrophe nears, the meter returns to 3/4 and the rhythm simplifies, with g^2 reiterated in upper strings, trudging bass and snare-drum figures. Finally, the opening tritone returns, bringing back the introductory fanfare. Divided doublebasses provide a low pulse while making a start on the main theme again (A B B B), but as it rises, B is transformed into a sinuous wind figure that passes from bassoon to clarinet to flute to piccolo as it dies to silence. Two quiet unison notes in the strings, B-E, provide a conclusion. These, of course, were justified by Tcherepnin's original designation of the piece as a "Symphony in E," but today this hint at a tonal cadence seems dated; indeed, Tcherepnin's effect in "framing" the movement between the opening tritone and the concluding cadence seems a trifle overcalculated. This cadence, one should hasten to add, is not blatantly ineffective: but it is not the best imaginable end to this wonderful movement, and one feels Tcherepnin would not have used it had he realized, in 1927, just how far he had come in emancipation from the superstitious context of traditional tonality.

Example 46

II. Vivace. Tcherepnin wrote, "I conceived the second movement for unaccompanied percussion neither as a gesture of bravado nor as a pretext for experiments in timbre, but solely in an intent to create a purely rhythmic musical construction."

This statement needs to be taken with a grain of salt. Tcherepnin was surely aware that this movement was quite unlike anything his audience had heard before, or indeed, anything he himself had heard before. One obvious feature of this Symphony, in fact, is Tcherepnin's manifest desire to stretch himself to his limits—to extend his interpuntal grasp to its ultimate, to find sound combinations he had never employed before (see the passage in the slow movement for solo violin and solo doublebass). What is perfectly true is that Tcherepnin's intention here was to challenge himself, not his audience. The result was the first known example in Western classical music of a movement for unpitched percussion alone. The percussion complement includes castanets, triangle, snare drum, side drum, tambourine, the full orchestral string section (tapped like drums), crash cymbals, suspended cymbal, bass drum and tam-tam.

"In a way," Tcherepnin continued, "this movement (in the form of a scherzo with a central trio) complements the first movement—in that it reduces several first movement 'themes' to their intrinsic rhythmic value." This is quite exactly stated. The thematic connections are not stressed, nor are they especially apparent to the ear—indeed, at the faster tempo of this movement, the first-movement rhythms have a different character.

The opening of the movement fits a repeated eighth-note pattern against slower materials. Later, there is a passage exploring the short- short-long pattern against its reverse and its augmentation and a syncopated bass- drum pattern taken up by tambourine.

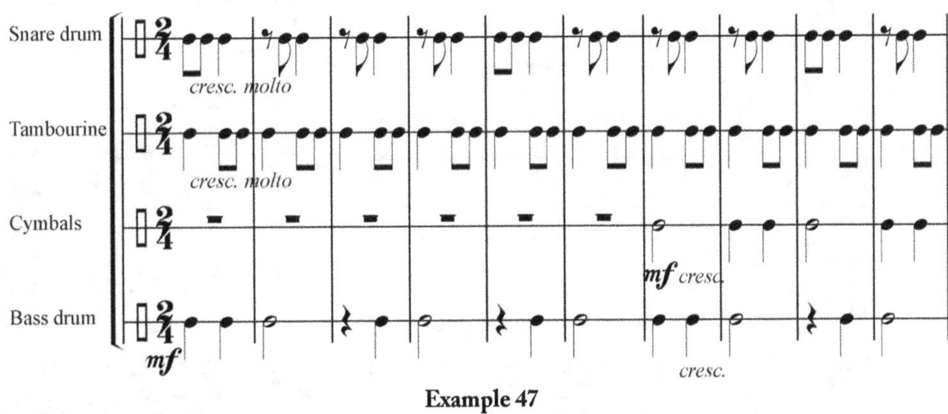

Example 47

The opening theme returns, leading this time to a superimposition of three different versions of rhythm d^1 (bass drum, tambourine and side drum).

With the entrance of a triplet rhythm, the trio section begins. This itself is in A-B-A form. Here, over an extended quiet cymbal roll, the string players tap the wood of their instruments with their bows in an interesting rhythm that is almost "non-retrogradable" (the rhythm is twelve measures in length, and its last four measures are a retrograde version of the first four measures. In the center, two displaced quarter-rests keep the music from being completely palindromic). After a passage begun by snare drum and continued by triangle, the cymbal roll stops and there is a central episode, for castanets and bass drum. The string taps duly return with a more animated accompaniment.

The return of the scherzo is identical with the opening for about fifty measures; this time, however, the d^1 episode is not heard, but replaced by a final build-up on triplet and sextuplet rhythms (as in the first movement "retrograde exposition," such rhythms achieve a new prominence in the present reprise).

III. Andante. "In my opinion," wrote Tcherepnin, "the third movement is still the most problematic. This movement employs three pairs of interpuntal themes which unite at the close in a six-voice coda, which I called 'Formula.' Presented as a culmination, this was, in fact, my starting point for the movement." The Formula (Example 49) is twelve measures in length. Each of the interpuntal pairs is introduced in a complete statement and developed in later pages. The movement commences with pair I; a counterstatement, with the two instruments exchanging parts and Ib lowered an octave, has a new continuation. Pair II appears, mysteriously accompanied by *sul ponticello tremolando* strings. In its counterstatement— perhaps better called a development—IIa takes on a nostalgic, faintly jazzy air, its first two measures being passed from trumpet to oboe to strings to woodwinds as IIb is transformed into a rocking lower-string figure and rich brass chords provide a background. Soon, beneath later figures of IIa, horns begin an imitative discussion of Ib-first-system as lower strings play Ib-second-system.

A quiet antiphony for violins upon IIa dies away and pair III, with its lone violin and doublebass soloists in ghostly extremes of register, receives its exposition. IIIb material provides the basis for the strange, post-Sibelian climax in example 48 (overleaf). Then IIIa is passed from trombone to bassoon to horns over quiet string *tremolos*; these instruments then present IIIa polyphonically as, meanwhile, IIa appears in violins and a *crescendo* on its triplet rhythms ensues. Later, the trombones switch themes, discussing Ib. At a climax, the opening tune of IIa is stated twice. A *tutti* outburst in dry chords and low trills suggests pair III; then the formula brings the movement to a quiet end.

2 Fl.
2 Ob., 2 Cl.
2 Bsns., Hns. 3,4
Vn. 1, Vn 2
Vla.
Vc. & Cb.
2 Fl.
2 Ob., 2 Cl.
2 Bsns., Hns. 3,4
Vn. 1, Vn 2
Vla.
Vc. & Cb.

Example 48

Example 49

Reich calls this conclusion "the thematic and dynamic climax" of the movement. With all due respect to him, it is nothing of the sort. The point is, of course, that it should be: the reunion of all the themes ought to be an episode that, like the five-theme combination in the coda of Mozart's *Jupiter* Symphony last movement, makes the listener gasp at the astonishing inevitability of the music. Here, however, the passage merely has a certain strangeness; the transparency of the counterpoint attracts notice, yet this "formula" coda has no appreciable unifying effect on the movement, partly because the various themes do not enhance each other. Moreover, although Tcherepnin refers to the formula as a "culmination," his actual musical treatment of the materials here shows that he knew better. Realizing that the formula did not, in fact, provide a climax, Tcherepnin took care to precede it with a relatively conventional build-up that, by itself, gives a satisfactory impression of resolution. The formula's subsequent appearance seems like an almost casual afterword.

The abrupt ending of the movement—the music trails off as if in mid-sentence, indeed, in mid-word—also seems to be a miscalculation. Durand, be it remembered, wanted Tcherepnin to change this conclusion. In fact, it is doubtful that a different coda would impoverish the *Andante*. In the last analysis, in other words, the complex polyphonic calculation that went into the planning of this movement's materials proves quite irrelevant. Pleasant though the music may be, Tcherepnin's overall scheme simply did not come off. The liability of Tcherepnin's intellectual style to such failures was a problem that it became more and more difficult for the composer to ignore with the passing years: indeed, in this movement, it was already apparent that Tcherepnin might soon be due for a little stylistic stock-taking.

IV. Allegretto con anima; Tumultuoso; Presto. "As to the finale (in rondo-form)," wrote Tcherepnin, "I truly do not understand how anything in it could have been shocking to the ears of Colonne Concerts listeners in the year 1927." Again we see the composer's miniaturist origins, for the main theme of this movement (comfortably in E nine-step) is scarcely more than an elaboration of an opening three-note motif, which will be designated motif (h):

Example 50

(h) continues to be heard in the bass beneath a repeated-note violin tune, then emerges in a *tutti* trumpet statement after an ominous series of descending brass chords, and subsequently thunders out in a syncopated full orchestra statement:

Example 51

The first episode then presents two new themes simultaneously, one (m) in trombone and the other (n) in tuba:

Example 52

Counterstatements of the example 51 complex alternate
with tense assertions of the simultaneous 5/4 *vs.* 5/8
rhythm in example 53. At a climax, timpani thunder out
the rhythm of m.

There is a sudden *pianissimo*, and the main theme
appears again in an eerie, high-register 5/8 version for
divided violins:

The repeated-note tune is restated and when the music
becomes *forte* the menacing brass chords are counterstated.
In the next episode, (example 54) theme n and its augmentation are elaborated upon.

As the discussion continues, a 4/4 version of the main theme is blared out staccato by antiphonal trumpets. A
grandiose retrograde version of m is stated (with a measure added) and sequentially restated four times (Example 55).

Two brass statements of m (back in normal form) are answered by chordal syncopations and dramatic silences,
and in a *decrescendo* m passes from piccolo to oboe to bassoon to timpani. Cellos and basses make a feint at another main
theme statement. But it is the winds who continue to reiterate and counterstate this theme's motif (h) at *presto* tempo, a
discussion that naturally leads to example 52. There is now a steady build up of (h) in strings against its augmentation in
brasses, and a grand peroration ensues, intensely syncopated, sprinting toward a wrenching final cadence.

Tcherepnin was quite aware that he had produced a problematic piece. The third movement conclusion has already
been discussed, and the use of retrograde material proved another source of trouble, for many critics singled it out either for
ridicule or for condemnation. The program notes for the first performance, surely at Tcherepnin's instigation, had plainly
discussed the "crab-wise" restatements and their place in the sonata-like structure of the first movement. In his subsequent
program notes and other writings about the Symphony, however, Tcherepnin almost always avoided mentioning this device,
presumably to avoid being accused of arid intellectuality. Even with the "triplet expedient" in the first-movement reprise

(or, reexposition) many listeners would fail to hear the retrogrades for what they were; and with a composer so concerned with always making himself clear, this must have been somewhat worrisome. Never again, in fact, would Tcherepnin exploit retrogrades to this extent.

Yet there is little question that Tcherepnin had produced, in this Symphony, his greatest work so far. Unfortunately, the piece did not succeed in catching on: after a few performances the score, as Tcherepnin liked to put it, "went to sleep," and remained in that somnolent state for decades. In the 1960s and 70s, however, there was a flurry of interest in the piece, particularly in England, where Colin Davis took it up after Tcherepnin himself had conducted it successfully. In 1999, conductor Lan Shui and the Singapore Symphony at last provided the score with its badly-needed first commercial recording (on the BIS label), as part of a series encompassing the complete Tcherepnin symphonies and concertos.

❀ ❀ ❀

Jolanthe Garde (Sobeide) pleads with Kurt Preger (Ganem)
in the first production of *Die Hochzeit der Sobeide*,
premiered at the Vienna Volksoper on March 17, 1933.

THE WEDDING OF SOBEIDE, OPUS 45

Even before beginning his First Symphony, Tcherepnin had begun thinking about his first full-length opera. His previous stage-work, *Ol-Ol*, had been a cautious first step, as we have seen; the challenges it presented to his powers of musical and dramatic construction were distinctly limited, not only because of its brevity, but also because its scheme had enabled him to veer off from his own original materials into traditional songs. Now, however, after his marriage and his initiation into orchestral writing through *Magna Mater*, Tcherepnin was determined to succeed in the largest musical forms.

It was in early March 1926 that Tcherepnin broached the matter of an opera to the director of Universal Editions, Emil Hertzka, who was then in Monte Carlo negotiating with Tcherepnin for new scores (the publisher acquired *Magna Mater* and the composer's Third Cello Sonata).

"I spoke to Hertzka," Tcherepnin wrote, "about my old desire to compose an opera on [Hugo von] Hofmannsthal's early play *Die Hochzeit der Sobeide* and together with him I wrote to Egon Wellesz to approach Hofmannsthal for the permission to do so…"

[That summer], while I was still in Islip, Hertzka cabled me that Hofmannsthal agreed to let me compose *Die Hochzeit der Sobeide* as an opera, gave me the right to make cuts and agreed to collaborate with me for possible changes and addenda."

Securing the consent and cooperation of Hofmannsthal unquestionably enhanced Tcherepnin's prestige. Rightfully considered one of the great lyric poets in the German language, Hofmannsthal was also admired for his highly successful series of librettos for Richard Strauss, who, since Puccini's death, had reigned unchallenged as the preeminent operatic composer of the era. Securing admission to this milieu was indeed a coup for Tcherepnin.

"As the libretto still was to be worked out, I postponed the beginning of composition until the time I would meet Hofmannsthal and started to work on a Piano Quintet [which] I intended to send to a competition in Philadelphia."

The meeting with the poet did not take place until January of 1928. "Soon after the New Year," wrote Tcherepnin, I received a letter from Weimar [saying] that the premiere [of *Ol-Ol* was] scheduled to take place on January 31. Before going to Weimar I went to Vienna. to make final arrangements with Hofmannsthal concerning *Die Hochzeit der Sobeide*. He received me most cordially—I told him that when I was in my teens I [had] read *Die Hochzeit der Sobeide* in Russian, loved it and already then wanted to compose it as an opera.

"He was amused to hear it and told me, that he was very young when he wrote *Die Hochzeit der Sobeide* and that if he would write it now, he would have written it differently. He himself warned me [against] taking the text in its integrity and advised substantial cuts.

"He also expressed his readiness to cooperate with me should I wish some alterations in text, or should I feel that I need some extra words. We agreed that we [would] keep in touch while the composition progress[ed]. We both signed the contract with the Universal Edition and I expected to have the opera ready by fall."

In setting Hofmannsthal's "dramatic poem" Tcherepnin was choosing another heroine who reflected his own self-sacrificing devotion to his parents. The young Sobeide, against her deepest inclinations, has married an older man, a wealthy merchant, in order to rescue her father from the poverty into which he has descended. Tcherepnin's father, too, had declined so severely from a position of affluence that he frequently needed financial help from his son, and the latter had been quite conscious that marriage to a rich woman would make it easier for him to extend that help; at the same time, these thoughts gave the younger Tcherepnin a guilty conscience, since he never wavered from his conviction—either before or after his wedding—that union with Louisine was a mistake, and that he was sinking ever more deeply into a financial dependence from which he would never free himself.

Sobeide's saintly husband throws open the door for her, allowing her her liberty; and while Tcherepnin surely realized that such idealism is rarely found in everyday life, he realized just as surely that his only hope of freedom lay in just such a gesture on Louisine's part. (Indeed, when Tcherepnin told her, in the late 1930s, of his determination to separate, her altruistic response reminded him vividly of his operatic merchant.) Sobeide's dream of blissful poverty with Ganem had been based on cruel deceptions-real life did not offer such happiness: the best the fictional heroine or the genuine Tcherepnin could practically hope for-barring the operatic suicide—was a cordial marriage to an older spouse of genuine decency with whom he had once been deeply in love, amid luxurious physical surroundings.

Tcherepnin's enthusiasm for this Hofmannsthal project was boosted substantially by the success of *Ol-Ol* at the end of January 1928. "We arrived in Monte Carlo by the middle of February," he wrote, "and I immediately started the. composition of *Sobeide*."

Work on the opera went so slowly, however, that a fall completion soon seemed out of the question. Part of the composer's problem, as Reich has pointed out, was in dealing with the Hofmannsthal text in its original language. Wrote

Tcherepnin, "although German… is very familiar to me—I was educated by German *Fräuleins* and for the three first years of the high school learned everything in German at the Schule der Reformierten Gemeinde in St. Petersburg—I found that to compose an opera in German is much more difficult for *me* than to compose in Russian.

"Russian… which is my own language, the language in which I am thinking, gives me direct 'hint[s]'. When I composed *Ol-Ol*… the language often. helped me to find the right accent, to find the musical materialization of the word, of the phrase or the sense of the phrase… In *Sobeide*, I had two problems: the one of the German languages and the one of poetic language (*Ol-Ol* is composed on [a] text in prose). In poetry the formation of a phrase, the position of words in it, is often 'unnatural,' unrealistic expressed in poetic rhythm instead of colloquial language…

"Also in the time between the composition of *Ol-Ol* (1924-25) and the composition of *Sobeide* (1928) I composed chiefly chamber music and orchestral compositions—I mean to say 'pure music'—and my musical language became more complex.

"Although [from] the very moment when [the] contract with Hofmannsthal and UE was signed I [had been] reading and rereading the text preparing myself for the composition, when I actually put myself to work in Monte Carlo, I had to start from a scratch."

Tcherepnin decided that, while he would use individual themes to characterize the personages, these themes would also play a part in defining large-scale musical sections from which the opera would be built. The themes, in other words, would not only establish the mood, but also be altered "according to the moods of respective scenes."

"I started the composition by the first aria of the Merchant in the first scene. The First Act was not composed from A to Z but according to the scenes for which I had material and found the form. [It took] me 2 and half months-from February 20 till May 5, with only one short trip to Paris, where I played with Paul Grlimmer at the concert of SMI on March 28 my 3rd cello sonata.

"After our return to Monte Carlo early in June I resumed the work on *Sobeide*, but the way of life we were leading—with picnics, short [excursions in the car] etc.—did not [help me] to concentrate, so that by the end of July I had progressed in the second act very little—only up to the moment where I decided to introduce a dance scene…

"I had no concert engagements in [the] U. S. A. this autumn, [which] proved however to be a blessing for my composition work. We spent our time between Islip and New York, and from the beginning of September up to the second half of November I completed the second act. The dances [still] had to be composed, but this I postponed until later, and when by the end of November we returned to Paris and inaugurated our flat at 5 rue Colonel Combes, I started with the third act."

Tcherepnin devoted the first two months of 1929 to an intensive concert tour. "During the trip," he wrote, "I worked on the third act of *Sobeide*, then, after we returned to Monte Carlo on March 18, [made one] last effort and completed the composition of the opera (with the exception of dances) on April 7th….

"As soon as I arrived in Islip [in May] I started the orchestration of [*Sobeide*] and the composition of [the] dances. The dances were composed but the orchestration progressed slowly and I did not even. complete the first act.

"At the beginning of August [while attending] the Musikfest… in Baden Baden I learned the news of the sudden and tragic death of Hofmannsthal.

"I developed fever on our way from Baden Baden-in an open car-to Vienna and when, after the crisis was over, a Viennese doctor—a Frau Doktor Domes—examined me, she found some irregularity in my left lung, prescribed some mountain air and forbade [me to] work. Yet it is Louisine and Happy who went to the mountains… while I obstinately decided to stay in Vienna… I was still not well, having fever every afternoon, but felt… well [in morale for I enjoyed] being on my own and working without stop on [the] orchestration of *Sobeide*… But then again, when we returned to Monte Carlo [my] spells of fever [and] various colds handicapped the orchestration, while the way of our life—social and professional—was even a greater handicap… I earnestly wished all this time that the illness would liberate me from the life that seemed. more and more [to have come to] an impasse.

"On January 7, 1930, I completed the orchestration of *Sobeide*—and strangely enough—the health became, like by miracle, restored. "

Like *Ol-Ol*, *The Wedding of Sobeide* did not immediately attract theaters. Tcherepnin observed that, "with only one handwritten orchestra score and only one also handwritten vocal score of *Sobeide* one hardly could expect an active promotion."

After a long discussion with the publisher in the fall of 1930, Tcherepnin, "obtained [Hertzka's] promise to publish *Sobeide* and a Suite from *Sobeide* consisting of the Overture and Dances not later than by the January 1st of the next year, and [I] was sure that [through] this the promotion might bring some results." The opera was, in fact, published in 1931 with a dedication to Louisine P. Tcherepnin.

Ultimately, the suite from *Sobeide*, entitled *Festmusik* and published as Opus 45a (with a dedication, for some reason, to Serge Koussevitzky) was of no particular help in promotion. The opera was already scheduled for production by the time the suite received its first performance, which according to Tcherepnin, took place sometime in January 1933 (not, as Arias states, in June of that year).

As the premiere of the opera approached, ill omens proliferated. First, Tcherepnin's beloved dog Touchkan, a companion of some fifteen years, died in the composer's arms. Then Tcherepnin fell ill with a "grippe" in January, which was to persist until the early spring. Suffering from high fever, he had given the first performance of his Third Concerto in February, in Paris, and the piece proved a complete failure. The Tcherepnins arrived in Vienna around the beginning of March for the rehearsals of *Sobeide* at the Volksoper to find all in chaos: the scenery and costumes were not ready, the singers were complaining about the difficulty of their parts, the orchestra was also complaining, and making life miserable for the conductor, Walter Herbert. One day, the Tcherepnins found that a large sum of money and pieces of valuable jewelry had disappeared from their lodgings; and, as a last straw, the thief turned out to be their own butler, whom they had liked and trusted. "The time in Vienna," Tcherepnin observed, "was not a joyous one."

The Wedding of Sobeide was premiered on March 17, 1933, at the Volksoper in Vienna. "It had success with [the] audience," wrote Tcherepnin, "and with the press. I was thrilled to hear it, and liked it." But the composer's hopes were quickly dashed. "Although...the reviews [were] most enthusiastic," he wrote," the second performance had a hall only half filled; we left after the second performance for Monte Carlo, and soon I heard that the third performance was the last one, and was given for a nearly empty hall. If I am not wrong, *Sobeide* was given only once more, in the spring at the Wiener Festwochen. Yet I feel that this opera, if given another fair chance and performed adequately, would be able to survive."

Indeed, Hofmannsthal's prestige may now have worked to Tcherepnin's disadvantage, for audiences, reading reports that the composer had preserved the poet's seriousness, dignity and intellectual elevation, may have concluded that the opera was bound to be a crashing bore.

Die Hochzeit der Sobeide reflects virtually the full range of Tcherepnin's style as it was in the period 1928-30. On the one hand, nine-step materials and interpuntal elaborations abound; on the other hand, folk-like material, which had essentially been absent from Tcherepnin's work during 1926-27, is used again in the opera, blended with nine-step, but discernible nonetheless—notably when dances are performed or sung about, and when the plot involves the courtesan Glilistane. Again it is possible to see Tcherepnin's intellectual and folk styles as pursuing parallel and simultaneous courses, with the two-year abstention from ethnic material constituting a mere inter-ruption. What should be noted, of course, is that the use of folk material is nowhere near so extensive in *Sobeide* as in *Ol-Ol*, and this factor in itself explains much about the difference in what Verdi called "*tinta*" between these two operas.

While the dissonance quotient in *Ol-Ol* (particularly the first version) is lower than that in *Sobeide*, the operatic technique in the two works is more similar than Tcherepnin and other commentators would have us believe. In both works, the various characters have their *Leitmotifs*, but the scenes tend to be fairly self-contained. Again in *Sobeide*, characterization is especially strong in the minor roles. It is unquestionably true, however, that here, Tcherepnin's treatment of leitmotives is freer and more developmental than in the previous work.

Tcherepnin's care in setting the German is also quite evident-indeed, he is almost too scrupulous about rhythmic adjustments, sometimes sacrificing the melodic curve to achieve prose-like declamation: one sometimes has a *Die Meistersinger*-like impression that text has been added to a purely instrumental piece. Fortunately, there are moments where the vocal lines are allowed to soar. Despite his asceticism, the composer shares the normal opera lover's taste for climactic high notes.

Tcherepnin scored *Die Hochzeit der Sobeide* for his standard orchestra—a rather modest complement, as has been previously observed—of 2 flutes (2nd doubling piccolo), 2 oboes, 2 clarinets, 2 bassoons, 4 horns, 2 trumpets, 3 trombones, tuba, timpani, percussion, harp and strings. The major characters are:

A rich merchant . . . . baritone
Sobeide, his young wife . . . . soprano
Bachtiar, a jeweler, Sobeide's father . . . . baritone
Sobeide's mother . . . . mezzo-soprano
Schalnassar, a rug dealer . . . . bass
Ganem, his son . . . . tenor
Glilistane, a courtesan, widow of a ship's captain . . . . .contralto
A Gardener on the merchant's estate . . . . tenor
His wife . . . . soprano

Bahram, house-servant to the merchant . . . . bass
A young man in debt to Schalnassar . . . . tenor

(The merchant is not designated by name in the dramatis personae of either the play or the opera. In a single passing reference at the end of the second scene, he is identified as "Chorab.")

Cast in three divisions (which, for no obvious reason are designated as "scenes" rather than acts) and containing about an hour and forty minutes of music, the opera makes greater demands upon singers than had *Ol-Ol*. The part of the merchant, with its lengthy soliloquies, high-lying climaxes and frequent lyrical *pianissimo* and *piano* passages above the staff (ranging up to high G and demanding full voice without falsetto admixture) requires a veritable Verdi baritone. Sobeide is a considerably heavier role than Ol-Ol; a real *spinto* soprano is required, with rich, well-projecting low notes, yet there is one murderous climax where the singer must vehemently deliver a series of high As and then proceed rapidly up to a high C#! The role of Ganem is not long, but needs a seductively attractive voice with a ringing high B if the part is to make its full dramatic effect.

In an interview given in Vienna before the opera's premiere, Tcherepnin said that he had been able to show Hofmannsthal the first two acts of the score, but did not discuss the poet's reaction. A conference of that sort—which could have taken place only in the last months of 1928—would, of course, have given the composer and the poet an opportunity to discuss changes in the last scene of the libretto. The fact is, however, that neither of the composer's autobiographies mentions playing the opera for Hofmannsthal and it is possible that Tcherepnin's interview account was a necessary fabrication-after all, to tell the public that Hofmannsthal had never heard any of the music (if that was indeed the case) could only have sown prejudice against the opera, damaging its chances without serving any good purpose beyond the purely documentary.

Indeed, it is difficult, if not impossible to determine exactly how much input Hofmannsthal had into Tcherepnin's opera. The original work, a product of Hofmannsthal's twenty-third year, was designated as a "dramatic poem," and shows its author concerned more with lyric and imagistic beauty than with stagecraft. (Walter Koons, whose synopsis of the opera appears in Arias' bio-bibliography of Tcherepnin, mistakenly ascribed the drama to Hofmannsthal's eighteenth year.) Still, whatever the theatrical failings of the piece, its poetry is in no sense immature—nor would any immaturity be likely, since the amazingly precocious Hofmannsthal had sprung to the first rank of German-language poets at age 15.

In fashioning the libretto, Tcherepnin jettisoned a good half of the play, but such radical surgery is scarcely rare when a verse-drama is used for opera-after all, in preparing the libretto for Verdi's *Otello*, Boito discarded about three-quarters of Shakespeare's tragedy. No incidents from Hofmannsthal's rather static play are cut; moreover, Tcherepnin makes an effort to preserve the integrity of key speeches, cutting these only minimally, and sometimes salvaging particularly attractive lines from excised passages by finding new places for them.

In between these "set pieces," the dialogue is considerably trimmed and tightened in order to speed the unfolding of the plot. As indicated, some lines have been shuffled and, in the process, tailored for continuity, but virtually every word in the libretto appeared in the original drama (with the small but significant exception of the "earring" episode discussed below). Koons' statement that Hofmannsthal provided Tcherepnin with "an important new soliloquy" is quite erroneous. As it happens, Tcherepnin combined speeches from two separate episodes in the third scene into a single soliloquy; perhaps Koons failed to recognize this conflation for what it was.

One suggestive feature of the libretto, however, is that in its third scene—which, of course, was set after Hofmannsthal's death-the departures from the original play are far more extensive than elsewhere. The merchant's entrances are shifted around, and a brief but crucial re-entrance is added for Schalnassar's Old Servant, who now presents Sobeide's earring to the merchant, hoping for gold. This episode, by alerting the merchant to Sobeide's presence, prepares the final catastrophe in a much more dramatic fashion than had the original scene. Was Hofmannsthal himself responsible for this and other changes in this last scene? Their high quality would suggest he was. On the other hand, the new dialogue is built almost entirely from fragments of the original lines, and while Hofmannsthal would have no reason to construct dialogue in this fashion, a reviser determined to be faithful to the deceased poet's verbal style would be likely to choose a synthetic method of this sort.

Perhaps the most provocative detail of all involves a line which is cut from one of Sobeide's closing speeches and reassigned (by Tcherepnin or Hofmannsthal, we do not know) to the merchant as the last line of the opera.

The Wedding of Sobeide takes place in an old city of the Persian kingdom. After a vigorous overture representing marriage festivities, the curtain rises upon a bedroom. As a servant brings in a mirror, the bridegroom, a rich, middle-aged merchant, expresses his concern that his young bride, Sobeide by name, seems unhappy. The more lights he brought to the wedding supper table, the more darkly veiled she appeared. She ate nothing but a single pomegranate seed, and could only gulp down half a cup of wine by forcing herself. Left alone, the merchant addresses the mirror, which had belonged to his mother, wondering if he looks old in his bride's eyes. His musings develop into a rapturous apostrophe to the stars. A servant announces that the guests are departing.

The scene changes to a spacious room overlooking a garden. Sobeide enters, led by her father and mother, who take their leave of the merchant and bid their daughter a tender farewell. The merchant tells Sobeide how much he loves her, how he has longed to marry her ever since seeing her dance for her father's guests—her smile, while dancing, had had a sadness he had last seen in his mother's smile. Sobeide asks, through clenched teeth, if he wants her to dance now. Shocked by the wildness of her tone, he asks what is wrong. She tells him that if he should ever hear her crying in her sleep, he must wake her—because these will be tears of erotic yearning for another man, and she thinks it wrong to bring them to his bed. For three years she has been in love with Ganem, son of Schalnassar the rug dealer; for the past year, however, she has seen nothing of him, and is now determined to be totally honest about it.

As the merchant gasps, inarticulate with distress, she continues with unpleasant truths. Her father was poor—not born poor, but even worse, had slid into poverty; it is to help him that she has married the merchant, her father's chief creditor. Ganem could not marry her because he and his father Schalnassar, too, were poor. This confuses the merchant, for, as far as he knows, the evil old Schalnassar is anything but poor. But Sobeide insists. Now that she has wedded the merchant, she will content herself and try to be a good wife to him. Their marriage is like a newborn bird, weak and blind; she begs him not to kill it. Looking out the door into the garden, she says, with an anxiety that steadily mounts to a near frenzy, that the day must never come when she goes out through that door; the day must never come when she goes into the world which has made no place for her.

The merchant, deeply moved by her plight, offers to open the door for her. She chides him for mocking her. But he is serious. He cancels her father's debt to him and tells Sobeide she may leave whenever she wishes. He feels no more her husband than if he had brought her home to shelter her from a storm or a highwayman. Sobeide is thrilled by his generosity, but feels impelled to go immediately; belonging to Ganem, she cannot spend the night in a stranger's house. She rushes out, still dressed in her bridal array. Left alone, the merchant meditates upon the way of the world; in humans down here he seeks to divine the same truth he finds in the stars above.

The second scene takes place in a sumptuous hall in Schalnassar's house. To a young debtor's vain entreaties for leniency, Schalnassar sneers that the man must pay up or take his wife and children into the streets begging. The debtor pleads that his wife is too delicate for penury, that if Schalnassar only saw her, he would take pity on her. "Very well, send your wife to me," the old reprobate demands. After the debtor departs, Schalnassar chuckles over the man's foolishness. If the wife comes and satisfies his desires, he will be more than generous; if not, she can learn to sleep on straw.

Tonight Schalnassar, who has recently been enfeebled by illness, will break his convalescent's regime. He will shower gifts on the widow Glilistane and move her into his own room. He leaves the hall, and a woman's voice in the distance sings a wordless, oriental-sounding melody. This is Glilistane, who now enters as Ganem emerges from an alcove. Ganem lusts after her, curses his father's physicians, and tells her of his plan to procure an undetectable poison and kill the old man, so he may have her all to himself. The two exchange endearments, then Glilistane warns Ganem away, just in time to avoid his father.

The old man returns, presents her with an onyx box, promises her other treasures, and brags of his skill in choosing gifts. He claps his hands and the two are regaled by a dance spectacle: antic capers by a malicious dwarf are followed by a dance for male gymnasts, a dance for women and a final bacchanale.

A servant tells Schalnassar that a young woman is at the door; she has been fleeing a highwayman and had been attacked by dogs. The old man assumes this is his debtor's wife. Pleased by the thought of having two women, he gets rid of Glilistane by asking her to dance for him—this will require her to go upstairs and have her hair arranged, which she does. The young woman enters. It is Sobeide, her bridal veil torn off, the pearls in her hair askew. Schalnassar makes lewd advances to her, only to find that she is not his debtor's wife; and after she repeatedly calls for Ganem, he petulantly has his son called and leaves.

Sobeide now first has a chance to notice that the house is one of riches. And "poor" had been the second word out of Ganem's mouth: he has lied to her, not once but a hundred times. Glilistane enters, divines Sobeide's feelings toward Ganem and ridicules her as she stalks out again, determined "to protect what is mine." At last Ganem comes. Sobeide, by now almost at her wits' end, greets him ecstatically, telling him that she is his alone, now that her husband has freed her. Ganem tries to quiet her, lest they be overheard, and says that she must go home immediately. He asks her when he may come to her and strokes her hair.

As he tries to persuade her to leave, he hears music in the distance. Schalnassar and Glilistane enter on their way to bed, accompanied by drummers, a dwarf playing a *zurna*, several torch bearers and a eunuch with a whip. When Ganem realizes where they are going, he explodes in rage. Seizing the whip, he lashes the musicians and torchbearers, decries the foulness of his father's bloated body and putrid mouth and angrily orders Glilistane not to go with Schalnassar. Glilistane mockingly suggests that he go to bed (with the pointed observation that "tomorrow is another day") and sarcastically gives Sobeide permission to go with Ganem.

The entourage heads up the stairs, with one old servant lagging behind. "You are dying to lie with her," Sobeide exclaims to Ganem, torn apart by fury, despair and shame. She loved him so much, and he betrayed her so totally. Ganem, still sulking at his humiliation by Glilistane, claps his hands and orders that Sobeide be removed. She longs to leave, and at her request, Ganem instructs the old servant to take "the wife of the rich Chorab" home.

After a lengthy orchestral prelude, the curtain rises on the final scene of the opera, set in the rich merchant's garden. It is just before dawn, and the gardener and his wife are surprised to see the merchant awake and alone so early on the very morning after his wedding; truly he is not like other men. The merchant delivers an extended soliloquy. He sees the world as a grim soulless reflection in a mirror, and muses on how very much he had loved Sobeide.

After he leaves, the gardener and his wife see Sobeide at the gate. She enters, still accompanied by the old servant, and asks if the pond in the meadow is nearby. Learning that the merchant has gone in that direction, she starts off the other way and catches sight of a tower-a tower which, she ascertains, is always open. The old servant begs leave to depart, and Sobeide gives him an earring, as she has no money, telling him that her husband will give him a gold-piece for it.

Left alone, she resolves to rush up to the tower. The old servant encounters the merchant and presents him with the earring. As the merchant hears that she has headed for the tower, the gardener's wife shouts that Sobeide has climbed it and is leaning out. With a scream, Sobeide jumps down. Horrified, the others rush off to aid her. The gardener returns, holding Sobeide in his arms. The merchant kneels before her. "You must live," he says. "I must die," she answers. "I see your face as never before.... Do not weep; I can't bear to see that, because I love you so much now." Sobeide dies, "noiselessly as a falling star," the merchant says: "Our soul lives within us like an imprisoned bird. When the cage is smashed, it is free."

Scene I:
The Overture unfolds in a single stream of manic energy. As with *Ol-Ol*, Tcherepnin introduces the opera's most important motif at the very outset:

Example 56

The figure marked a is, of course, Tcherepnin's favorite major/minor *arpeggio*; here it will reappear again and again in varied forms, giving birth to a significant "family" of themes and motifs personally associated with the merchant and Sobeide. There is a curious similarity between this opening and the third act prelude of Wagner's *Lohengrin*, with its jubilant *arpeggio* commencement evoking-as does *Lohengrin*-euphoria during the celebration of a foredoomed wedding. Tcherepnin may have been conscious of this kinship, because he carefully attempts to avoid a notorious flaw in the Wagner score-a serious loss of energy that causes the music to "fizzle out." As the swirling string triplets continue, a broad countertheme appears in the brass, followed by a busy horn-trombone colloquy:

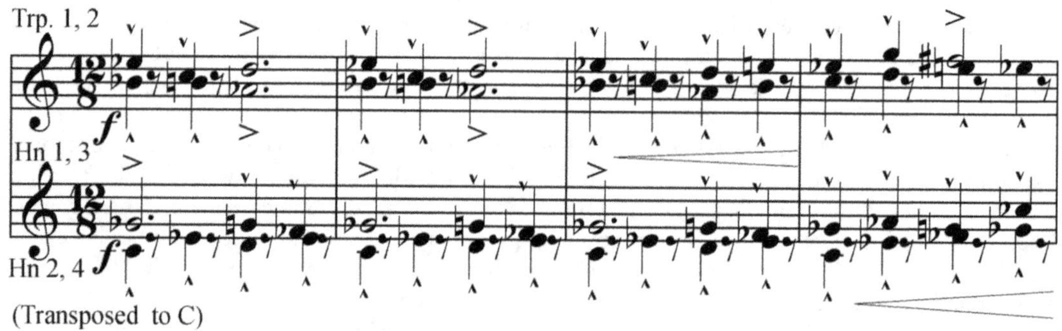

Example 57

After motif a reappears in the brasses, another theme is introduced:

Example 58

Eventually, the entire opening flourish returns. The curtain rises on the final chord of the overture. A reiterated rhythm:

Example 59

continues in the overture's wake, and the following type of melodizing is heard:

Example 60

These elements continue as the merchant and his servant begin discussing Sobeide, example 60 developing into major-minor triad outlines and branching into diads:

Example 61

Also of considerable importance is the cadence of this type which continually recurs: usually in lower registers, always in connection with the merchant.

The music from the overture returns quietly, representing the sound of merry-making from a distance. Soon the merchant embarks on a lengthy monologue: the first part is recitative-like, accompanied by animated rhythmic fragments, the second more lyrical, becoming centered on major-minor triad outlines as it builds toward the climax in example 63.

Example 62

Example 63

The music of the overture returns again as the scene changes. As it continues, the merchant's cadence is heard several times, superimposed in syncopation. Sobeide's first entrance provides an impressive climax indeed as the music rises to *forte* with a significant theme derived entirely from the major-minor triad (example 64):

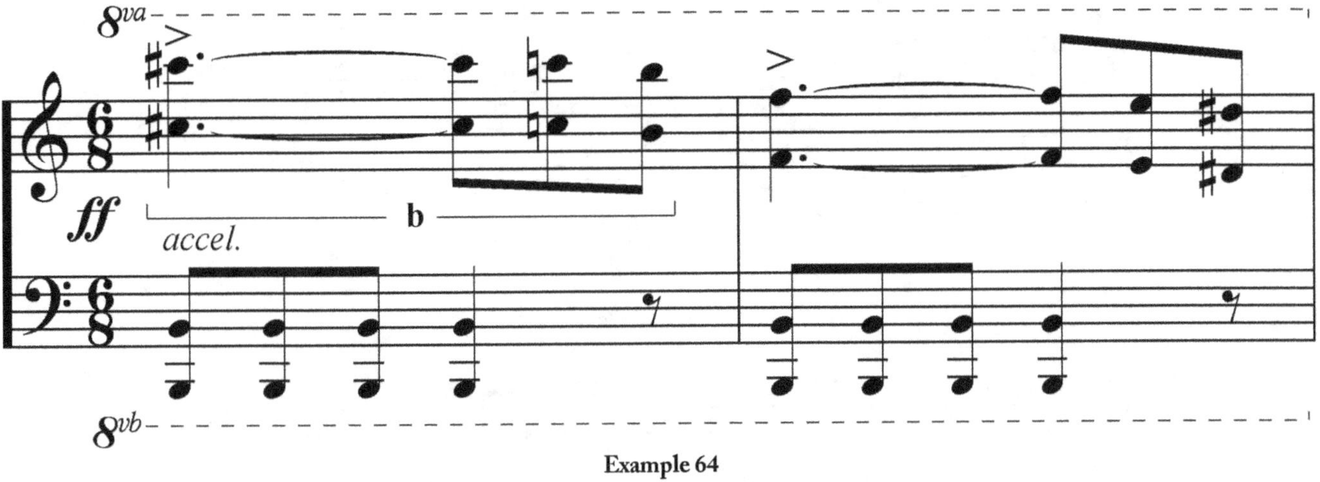

Example 64

The culmination is another important motif here labeled motif b.

Sobeide's parents take their leave of her in a scene of notable beauty, based on a dotted-note theme that seems to be descended from the first movement second subject of Schumann's Piano Quintet (seen here in the accompaniment as Sobeide sings the music of example 64):

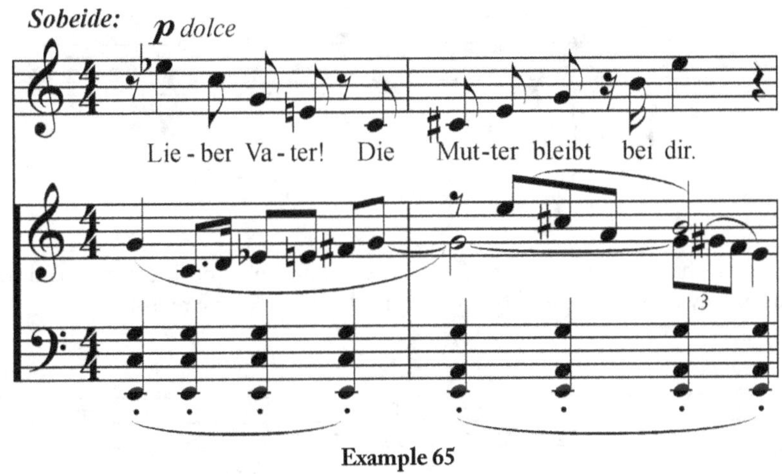

Example 65

The merchant tells Sobeide of his love, accompanied by a dense, dissonant polyphonic discussion of example 63, which is later combined with example 57. His reminiscence of Sobeide's dance is evoked:

Example 66

Sobeide finally begins to voice her misery, and motif b takes the forms heard in examples 67a and b.

Example 67a

Example 67b

She sings of dreaming of another man in variants of examples 62 and 63, and the accompaniment builds in whirling sixteenth-notes. The words "my father was poor" bring an episode of bleak lyric repose:

Example 68

The merchant's agitation is expressed by example 58. A short, imperious theme (c) introduces a lengthy, sparse-textured passage based on continual reiterations of a syncopated rhythm (d), over which Sobeide expresses her hope that the marriage can work. Presently (c) and (d) are combined.

Example 69

Sobeide's passionate monologue alternates build-ups on short, fretful motifs seemingly bent on breaking out of step-wise bondage:

Example 70

with mysterious, wide-spaced *tremolo*s. Eventually (d) reappears *fortissimo*, and there is a *crescendo* culminating in a climactic, thunderous combination of Sobeide's example 64 themes with (c).

Over a trudging bass, the merchant offers to open the door for Sobeide. This is soon revealed to be an inversion and augmentation of the fretful motif, which now appears in its original form. Fragments of example 63 are intermixed, and the tension mounts as the merchant declares Sobeide free (as he tells her she may leave at any time, his cadence is heard again). Sobeide's resolve to go to Ganem mounts, and the fretful motif is mixed with the opening of example 63.

The tempo slows; Sobeide drinks a farewell to the merchant, accompanied by this notably attractive combination of example 63, the inversion of motif a, theme c and the fretful motif:

Example 71

The merchant is left alone, and several features from the opening scene return: the nervous reiterated e, the sparse chords, and the chromatic wind figures. The stars upon which the merchant muses are glitteringly evoked in the orchestra, and a meditative colloquy on motif a brings the quiet curtain and a parting evocation of the merchant's cadence.

Scene II

The first section of scene two is a mordant triple-time scherzo, relieved by some lyricism as the debtor sings of his love for his wife. A theme in the bass, representing Schalnassar's lechery and cunning, coalesces from rhythmic patterns when Schalnassar tells the young man what to say to his wife in order to get her to visit (example 72). After the debtor leaves, another Schalnassar

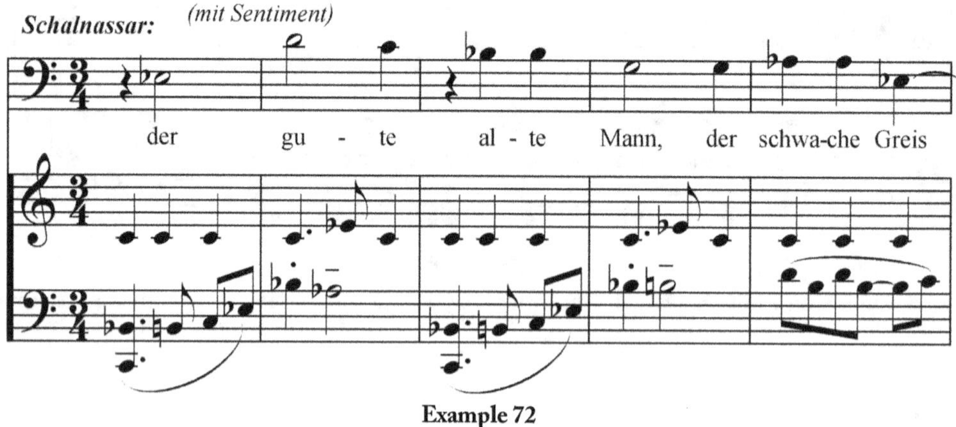

Example 72

theme appears:

Example 73

evoking the lurching gestures of an enfeebled man attempting to strike an imperious pose. During his aria here, the sixteenths are slowed to flowing pentuplet eighth-note *arpeggio*s. Schalnassar exits to example 72, and Glilistane, offstage, sings an oriental-sounding vocalise:

Example 74

to which she presently enters. The figures of this theme, always lushly harmonized, will be prominent throughout the coming scene.

Ganem greets Glilistane with tender-sounding melody, but his conniving character is revealed by this sinuous motif: which he later sings while deploring the medical art that cured his father. As he speaks of his plot to poison Schalnassar, the theme is heard both in scurrying sixteenths (treble), and in octave-displacement augmentation (bass):

Example 75

Example 76

There are sensuous climaxes on Glilistane's vocalise. When she senses the return of Schalnassar, motif e from example 74 takes on a life of its own, repeatedly strumming on a single note (often e natural again) or sounding in simplified harmonies throughout Schalnassar's subsequent presentation of gifts to

Glilistane, the rhythm combined with examples 72 and 73 and lyrical fragments from the vocalise.

Here the *corps de ballet* enters for a three-movement dance (the last three sections of the *Festmusik*-Example 77). The opening episode, the dance of a malicious dwarf, is a brilliant essay in the grotesque with its timpani solos and eccentric wind figurations. The subsequent sections do not rise to the same level of invention, becoming somewhat monotonous in their 5/8 and 12/8 kicking and twitching.

A reiterated 3/4 variant of e emerges from the end of the ballet, and continues during a complex episode that also features continuous development of the materials in example 77.

Glilistane exits to a somewhat sinister version of her vocalise theme (strangeness is lent by its combination with the inversion of a, which is, of course, the beginning of Sobeide's big theme). As Schalnassar boasts of what he will do with two women, example 19 sounds forth, now provided with a pompous dotted-rhythmed continuation.

After Sobeide's climactic entrance, there is a *subito piano*, and over a breathless repeated rhythm (three sixteenth-notes and a sixteenth rest), she begins her conversation with Schalnassar accompanied by a low and mid-register concatenation of motifs c, a and b. Schalnassar answers, supported by his pentuplets and dotted rhythms. Sobeide's desperation mounts in *crescendo*; and when she says "today was my wedding day," her big theme, example 64, is heard in the orchestra, followed by a combination of motifs c and b. At a sudden quiet moment, she says she is Bachtiar's daughter, and a brief remembrance of the Schumannesque example 65 is heard. Schalnassar stalks out with a flash of furious pentuplets, and rhythm e resumes.

After Sobeide's climactic entrance, there is a *subito piano*, and over a breathless repeated rhythm (three sixteenth-notes and a sixteenth rest), she begins her conversation with Schalnassar accompanied by a low and mid-register concatenation of motifs c, a and b. Schalnassar answers, supported by his pentuplets and dotted rhythms. Sobeide's desperation mounts in *crescendo*; and when she says "today was my wedding day," her big theme, example 64, is heard in the orchestra, followed by a combination of motifs c and b. At a sudden quiet moment, she says she is Bachtiar's daughter, and a brief remembrance of the Schumannesque example 65 is heard. Schalnassar stalks out with a flash of furious pentuplets, and rhythm e resumes.

Sobeide is left alone and an eerie new theme rises into mysterious treble harmonizations accompanied by spectral tremolos as she muses over the mystery of Ganem's riches, her vocal line now containing fragments of motifs a and c:

Example 78

When Glilistane enters, her vocalise is transformed into staccato mockery. Sobeide pleads against an inversion of c; later she is accompanied by down-up statements of a + a-inverted. The once-flowing second measure eighth-notes of the vocalise are heard in shrill diminution as sixteenth notes, these interrupted by vulgar oom-pah passages. Glilistane exits in a triumph of ridicule.

After a gloomy recitative, Sobeide nerves herself (a is heard again, and rhythm d returns *fortissimo*). Her big theme appears in inversion, answered by developments of c, b and a, the latter building to a chordal climax that signals Ganem's entrance.

The confrontation scene is a breathless *allegro*, accompanied by repeated-note triplets. Sobeide's pleadings reflect ma-jor-minor mixtures, and introduce a new, romanticized motif (g).

Example 79

Ganem's answers are accompanied by the sinuous intervals of example 75. There is a fragment of Sobeide's big theme, and then example 79 is heard in canon. As she continues, motif a is extensively discussed, appearing also in augmentation; Ganem fends her off with example 75-this alternation continues, with Ganem offering to stroke Sobeide's hair and then send her home. Sobeide tells Ganem that her husband has freed her, and the fretful motif from example 70 is developed.

Rhythm e now appears with material from example 77, for Ganem hears music in the distance. Against a reiterated rhythm, theme c makes its ominous appearance when Sobeide tries to get Ganem's attention. At a faster tempo, the opening of Sobeide's big theme is proclaimed in rising sequence, and appears in broad *fortissimo* augmentation as she rises to a high c.

Glilistane and Schalnassar are heard just offstage and the patter of example 77 sounds in a sudden *piano*. After an enormous climax, pitched instruments fall silent, rhythm e continuing on percussion alone. A dwarf enters playing a *zurna* (a kind of middle eastern shawm) accompanied by a drummer and followed by a group of torchbearers, who are leading Glilistane and Schalnassar to his bedchamber in state. Glilistane's vocalise accompanies her complaint that she has lost the onyx box. Ganem's theme is heard as he demands that she explain her dalliance with his father; Schalnassar chides her for delaying (to the music of example 73, with example 72 now mixed in as accompaniment). Glilistane tries to smooth things over with her vocalise music, but Ganem bursts out in a fury reflected by the two transformations of his theme in example 80.

Example 80

"His father, both after the woman," exclaims Sobeide against a brief polyphonic passage based on motif b, heard in normal form and in augmentation. Glilistane's vocalise theme resumes, and becomes lushly colored when she makes to exit, punctuated between each of its figures by the first four notes of Ganem's theme as he urges her not to go.

Sobeide vents her despair to a *presto* passage based on motif a and its inversion, with a reiterated syncopated e in the bass. The climax, based on a descending three-note figure derived from theme c, is cruelly demanding-pitched unrelievedly in the highest register of the singer's voice and taking her up to high c#.

After some bare recitative, the three-note theme is lengthened into a very slow descending *arpeggio*. When this reaches bottom, a trudging pattern of two alternating notes (a minor third), representing the old servant, appears in the bass. It shifts to treble, where it accompanies the three-note theme and a fragment of example 70, then returns to the bass beneath Sobeide's big theme and example 67. There is a final climax on an accelerating version of Ganem's theme 2 from Example 80.

Scene III

A slow, lengthy prelude establishes the scene of antelucan dawn in the merchant's garden. It begins with a new bass motif and some rhythmic interplay evoking nature sounds (exmple 81). Presently, the motif speeds to eighth triplets and acquires a last note another half step down. Merchant's-cadence material *à la* example 62 leads to the opening of ex. 63, heard over a throbbing figure; it is restated in sequence and then treated imitatively, building in *crescendo*.

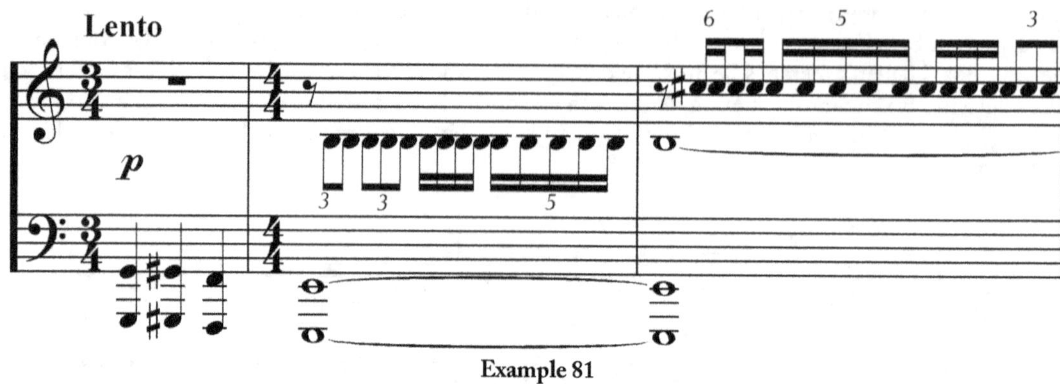

Example 81

A climax on the opening rhythms subsides, and a reference to motif a introduces a new motif (h) and a new theme (j):

Example 82

These are developed at length, leading to two climaxes on the nature rhythms; they are ultimately stated in a peaceful major-mode version with luminous high accompaniment. A final cadence one (major-like, if not quite major) is punctuated by a bird-song figuration.

The garden scene proper is set by a lilting 6/8 *moto perpetuo*. This rhythm of motif x, heard beneath flowing sixteenth-notes is omnipresent, and in the quoted form will prove to be of importance. As the gardener and his wife espy the merchant, there are breaks in the steadily murmured sixteenth notes. The opening of example 63 introduces a sparsely accompanied recitative. Merchant-cadence chords presently lead to an agitated reiterated rhythm. Theme j is now given a lengthy, lyric statement, almost unaccompanied, and this proves to be the introduction to a doleful aria for the merchant, "I loved her so!" Motif h is prominent in the accompaniment, and the merchant-cadence motif also makes frequent appearances. With unusual formal strictness for this opera, most of the aria's introductory theme is reprised in the singer's closing measures, with the merchant cadence and motif j luxuriantly worked over to provide a coda.

motif x

Example 83

The *moto perpetuo* returns as the gardener's wife espies Sobeide at the garden gate. It builds in leisurely fashion through the conversation. When Sobeide enters, her theme is transformed into the following tense and mysterious *tremolo*-accompanied version:

Example 84

In the subsequent scene, during which tension continually mounts, this theme is heard in a number of var-ants, of which four are identified here as k, l, m and n:

Variant k is heard as Sobeide asks where the pond is; l bursts out when she fears that she will meet the merchant. As she resolves to go to the tower, k is heard again in the bass against syncopated sixteenth notes. When the old servant speaks, his trudging bass is heard; m breaks in, followed by k and n. Motif b puts in an appearance, then the first four notes of Sobeide's theme are superimposed in syncopated fashion against the bass. Sobeide's theme resumes its original form, heard in rapidly rising sequence and building to a climax on motif c as she runs off to the tower.

An orchestral triplet passage descends from the high register to the deep bass; then a tense polyphonic passage ensues based on motif x in both normal and rhythmically augmented forms. Example 63 makes a plaintive appearance as the merchant reenters; the trudging rhythm accompanies the old servant, who offers Sobeide's earring. As Sobeide is seen at the top of the tower, there is another agitated build-up on motif x, which is heard at four speeds (in sixteenths, eighths, quarters and halves), and becomes chordal. Sobeide shrieks and a *presto*

Example 85

on repeated notes (e-flat) breaks out, the rhythm (periodically combined with a pentuplet cross-rhythm) continuing as a rising major-minor triad theme is stated and restated. The merchant-cadence chords provide a climax, and there is a long *diminuendo* as the throbbing rhythm persists.

Sobeide is carried in as the tempo slows. Example 63 receives a tender statement, and the merchant sings "you must live." Sobeide expresses her regret accompanied by rhythm (d). There is a tender cantabile on example 63, a luminous chordal theme derived from example 70, a hint of theme c, and-as Sobeide dies-a new radiant version of example 78. A final hint of her big theme is heard. Then, the merchant's slow bass version of example 70 provides a dirge, persisting as the luminous chord version returns. The four opening notes of the dawn prelude accompany the merchant's last words ("then it is free") with motif a ultimately taking him up to a soft, sustained high g. The merchant-cadence chords are evoked, and over the four-string basses' lowest e, there is a final ultra-high register statement of motif a.

Tcherepnin himself observed, "I found that the virtue of *Sobeide* is its good music; the *défaut* of it [being] that the music is too important and dominates the situation." Whether the score adds up to a viable opera is an open question. Certainly there is much beautiful music; there appears to be a sense of theatrical pace as well. The dramaturgy of the play, however, courts monotony in its long first-scene discussion between Sobeide and the merchant and in its string of two-character episodes during second scene. Tcherepnin differentiates his characters effectively, but it might be that there are too many scenes based on repeated-note rhythms. The opera must be seen and heard before a definitive assessment is possible.

What is undeniable is that in *Die Hochzeit der Sobeide* Tcherepnin showed that the largest musical genres were now comfortably within his grasp. He no longer had to prove himself-to himself, or to anyone else. His artistic challenge was now in finding what to do now that his major technical challenges had been surmounted.

❀   ❀   ❀

TRIPLE CONCERTINO, OPUS 47

No work of Tcherepnin's was recast so many times as the Triple Concertino. The composer's changes even extended to the title, which was originally merely "Concertino" and assumed its present form only in the final revision (1965). And yet the many alterations—there were six different versions of the piece—were equivalent to little more than changes of clothes: the musical substance remained unchanged despite the many remodelings in instrumentation.

"On January 7, 1930, I completed the orchestration of *Sobeide*," wrote Tcherepnin. "Immediately after[ward], I started to work on a concertino for two viole da gamba, piano and string orchestra [which] I [had] promised to compose [for] my friend Paul Grlimmer." Interestingly-and, as will become clear, inevitably—various source materials seem to disagree about the complement of this original version of the piece. Arias, following Tcherepnin's commentary, lists it as a two-gamba concertino. In the Paris Tcherepnin Archives, however, it is catalogued as a concertino for violin, viola da gamba, piano and strings, and the original reviews of the first performance gave a similar description.

Neither designation, as it happens, is wholly accurate; for the score, in this first version, was not the solo-*vs.*-orchestra piece it later became. It was a chamber concertino for 4 violins, 2 violas, 2 gambas, 2 cellos, bass and piano. Considerable solo exposure was given to the first violin and the first gamba, although other instruments also had solo opportunities. Only at a few times in the first movement were the two gambas presented as the soloistic pair suggested by Tcherepnin's description. The real problem is that there is no commonly accepted designation for such a piece. A Baroque composer might have called it "Concertino a 12"; perhaps it would be best listed as "Concertino for String Ensemble (with Gambas) and Piano."

The Concertino owes its existence to the intense proselytizing efforts on behalf of the viola da gamba by Tcherepnin's close friend Paul Grlimmer. Grlimmer, a distinguished cellist who frequently appeared in recital with Tcherepnin (he was the composer's favorite partner for *The Well-Tempered Cello*), was also an enthusiastic gamba player in a Baroque-style string ensemble which he himself had founded. His fascination with ancient instruments was an attitude shared by many other German musicians of the time, including, of course, the viola-playing Hindemith, who composed himself some works for viola d'amore. (The novelist Thomas Mann reflected this aspect of the *Zeitgeist* when he made the ostensible narrator of his *Doktor Faustus* an amateur viola d'amore player.) Tcherepnin had dedicated his Third Cello Sonata to Grlimmer; nothing was more natural than that the cellist should discuss the potential of the gamba with Tcherepnin and ask him to compose for it.

One thing that apparently excited Tcherepnin about the gamba was the fretted fingerboard, for this assured fixed pitch, eliminating the constant pitch-adjustments of the "expressive intonation" automatically used by players of modern stringed instruments. For several years Tcherepnin had been pleading for fixed (equal-tempered) pitch as a *sine-qua-non* for nine-step music, and with the gambas he at last had it (at least for two-twelfths of the ensemble of the Concertino). The irony here is that now, with the experience of *Sobeide* behind him, he had arrived at a more flexible approach to nine-step, using it in adulterated forms, as will be later shown in examining the opening of the Concertino. The idea of mixing gambas with instruments of the more modern violin family was not new (Bach had done it), but the gamba's featured solo role in such a context is unusual. Even more so is the combination of gambas with the modern piano: a seeming anachronism which is apt to elicit automatic feelings of distaste from devotees of period instruments, but surely cannot be faulted *a priori*. When composing this score, Tcherepnin apparently paid close heed to the special characteristics of the gamba. Passages like the chromatic motif that answers the first movement's opening theme (called motif c in the upcoming analysis) and the last movement's rustic main theme seem to have been designed especially for the gamba's thin, reedy, somewhat whining tone. The low chords at the beginning of the slow movement were also apparently conceived with the hollowness of gambas in mind.

After completing the first movement, Tcherepnin put the Concertino aside to work on a group of piano pieces that he owed to the Durand firm. Concert engagements cut into his composing time during the next few months, and it was not until June, when he and Louisine arrived in New York for their annual stay, that he resumed intensive work on the score.

That summer, Tcherepnin came upon a book by a Russian named Vernatzky in which the "Eurasian" theory of Russian culture was propounded. The Mongols, according to this theory, had unified the feudalistic entities of Russia into one state, provided this state with its system of communications and built its infrastructure. The modern (pre-Revolutionary) Russian nation developed directly from the Mongol state as the Mongols themselves assimilated into local life. As a result, Russian culture had some of its basic roots in the east and could only wither if these were ignored in an attempt to become wholly European; the Oriental heritage had to be recognized if a true Russian tradition was to thrive.

Even before reading this book, Tcherepnin had already been using Oriental (*i. e.*, "Eurasian") materials—in *Sobeide* and the recent set of piano pieces (*Entretiens*, Op. 46)—and now the third and fourth movements of the Concertino became "consciously Eurasian." Work was sporadic, "interrupted by many visits to friends of Louisine in East Orange, Boston [and] in and out of New York, [also] by parties for Happy, who [was] now 15, preparing for [her] not-too-far-away 'coming out.'...We left America [at] the beginning of August and, after a few days in Paris, arrived in Baden Baden on the 22nd [where I completed] the score of the Concertino... on September 7th."

Tcherepnin recounted that the premiere took place on December 17, 1930, in Cologne, "with Grlimmer playing the first gamba and with me at the piano. But without conductor! This was [a] most trying experience; I certainly would never believe that such [a] thing would have been possible-but thanks to the great musicianship of the members of Grlimmer's chamber orchestra all went well. Yet never since [have I] performed this Concertino without conductor, and do not believe it is recommendable, nor feasible in spite of this example of the conductorless first performance."

Although it contained some of Tcherepnin's most attractive music, this first version of the piece could be nothing but a white elephant to a publisher: gambists being decidedly few in number, the exiguous sales and rental income from a score that required two of them, one a virtuoso, would not begin to earn back printing costs. And so, when Tcherepnin offered the Concertino to Emil Hertzka at Universal, the latter agreed to publish it only if the gambas were eliminated. Tcherepnin saw the point of Hertzka's proposal, and decided to make a new version of the piece, recasting it as a concertino for violin, cello, piano and string orchestra. "The work to transform the Concertino into a form of a triple concertino proved to be quite exciting, but not as easy as I thought," wrote the composer. "The fact was that the old version was written for an orchestra of twelve including the soloists and that all the twelve were supposed to be quasi-soloists, with numerous soli for each instrument. Now I had to decide what really is solo and what orchestra. And doing so I perhaps isolated too much the soloists, especially the piano, giving them less to play than I could [have], in order to reserve them for the purely solo parts."

The premiere of this revision took place on November 18, 1931, with Fabien Sevitzky conducting the Philadelphia Chamber String Simfonietta (sic) at one of its regular concerts in the Bellevue-Stratford Hotel ballroom. The composer played the piano part with Alexander Zenker, violinist and Benjamin Gusikoff, cellist. It was in this string-orchestra recasting that the work was first published-the original chamber-version remains unpublished to this day.

"In 1944," wrote Tcherepnin, "I made a version for clarinet, bassoon, piano and string orchestra... as well as a version for trio (violin, cello, piano—or—clarinet, bassoon, piano) which was premiered over French National Radio in 1945 with me at the piano." The clarinet-bassoon-piano-orchestra treatment had been premiered on December 3, 1944, in a Paris Conservatoire concert by the Wind Instrument Society, with Pierre Lefebvre, clarinetist, Paul Hongne, bassoonist, and the composer as pianist; the orchestra was directed by the distinguished French conductor-bassoonist Fernand Oubradous.

Tcherepnin returned to the score yet again in 1960. "During the autumn," he wrote, "I made a new version of the Concertino, Op. 47, for piano, violin and cello, bringing [the whole orchestra part] in[to] the parts of the soloists... and called it Trio Concertante. Such [a] version could be used by the soloist[s] to study the Concertino among them, and also as a regular Piano Trio.[1]

"I always found that the parts of the soloists are not [interesting] enough in the Concertino... that the soloist plays his part and then waits until the next occasion instead of participating in... orchestra *tutti*s. The new version... could serve as sketch for a further new version giving to soloists more to play and reducing sometimes what the orchestra is playing. And also in such [a] case I would do a new orchestration for full orchestra, not only for strings. Just as I promised to the Universal Editions in 1958."

Tcherepnin fulfilled this promise several years later, completing the final version in Bach, Switzerland, in October 1965. Here, the solo parts were extended, but Tcherepnin decided not to use a full orchestra, adding only timpani and one each of flute, oboe, clarinet, bassoon, horn, trumpet and trombone to the original strings. The premiere of what was now called the Triple Concertino took place with the composer at the piano in February 1967, in Paris; Fernand Quatrocchi conducted the Paris Chamber Orchestra. The added winds, it may be noted, sound like an integral part of Tcherepnin's original conception, and there is no doubt that the final version represents an improvement over the 1931 string-orchestra scoring.

Still dedicated to Paul Grlimmer in its final incarnation, the Triple Concertino marks a notable relaxation in Tcherepnin's style. The "Eurasian" approach, very much present in the first two movements (which Tcherepnin does not mention), gives a newly songful air to several of the themes and melodic fragments. Interpuntal passages are far less frequent and somewhat less complex here than in the First Symphony or the Piano Quintet. While there are still no key signatures, the feeling of traditional tonality is patently stronger here than in those ultra-intellectual scores. There is also considerably more exact recapitulation: in the original gamba version, repeat signs appeared at the ends of both halves of

---

1   How, or if, this version is related to the trio-transcription premiered on the French radio is not known, because the latter seems not to have survived.

the first movement. For the subsequent rescorings, however, Tcherepnin wrote out the repeated music in full so that he could vary the instrumentation.

There is also more freedom in the use of nine-step. The opening major-minor chords indicate a tonality of D; but the main theme actually begins in A nine-step,[2] and modulates when reaching its first climax, rising to a G which is not in the A nine-step scale. (The First Symphony had also created an impression of its tonality [E] through a main theme built on the dominant's nine-step scale [B].)

I. Allegro marciale. Tcherepnin wrote: "the first movement (march-like in atmosphere) of the Concertino is constructed in two parts, of which the first is in equal measures of 4/4 and the second is anything but that, [being cast] in unequal measures-7/4, 5/4, 3/4, 1/4, 3/4." A notable feature here, in fact, is Tcherepnin's success in unifying a movement that is ostensibly disjunct in structure. (It is obligatory to point out that the unequal-measure part of the movement was re-barred by Tcherepnin in the versions postdating the description quoted here, divided entirely into measures of 2/4 and 3/4, as will be seen in the musical examples.)

The opening theme, heard over striding reiterated chords, is a lengthy cantilena of Slavic grandeur played by the strings and soloists, and deserves to be quoted in full:

Example 86

After a wind-piano cadence based on b, there is a new episode which will be called II. Chromatically shifting where the opening had been tonally solid, this section begins with the a solo-cello variant of c and continues with a[1]-*cum*-a and the b cadence. II is counterstated, and a climax on descending chords brings back the opening theme, now played by the soloists in its entirety. The b cadence is delivered by strings, and II and its counterstatement also return, now confined almost entirely to soloists until the descending-chord climax.

A contrasting section ensues, based on the alternation of a fanfare with sinuous chromatic chords (Example 87, overleaf: note the way the intervals burst the bonds of nine-step). The fanfare triplets are passed from soloist to soloist, rising inexorably step-wise with every statement. Suddenly they subside into a lower-string murmur, whereupon b[1] is tensely introduced by the solo cello and builds in a dramatic Interpuntal *crescendo* that culminates in restatements of a[1] and a. This entire section is now reprised from the beginning of the fanfare (which is introduced by the orchestra this time) and its climax leads to a brief coda. What holds this movement together is the strategic use of b[1]. A factor that ensures that "balance is attained," according to Tcherepnin, is that "each of the [movement's] two parts contains an equal number of quarter-notes."

---

2   Tcherepnin would probably label the tonality C# nine-step, mode II. But the editor believes that A as dominant best explains the theme's tonal geography.

Example 87

II. Lento. The second movement, which, as Tcherepnin says, "features concertante solos," is quite freely organized, in the manner of one of Bartök's bucolic nocturnes. A somber-sounding series of two-note chords, originally conceived for gambas: accompanies a rhapsodic, free-ranging violin outburst. After low repeated-note jagged-rhythmed piano mutterings, the chords pass to violins, and the cello rhapsodizes. The piano then breaks into fantastical figuration, with jagged rhythmed repeated note

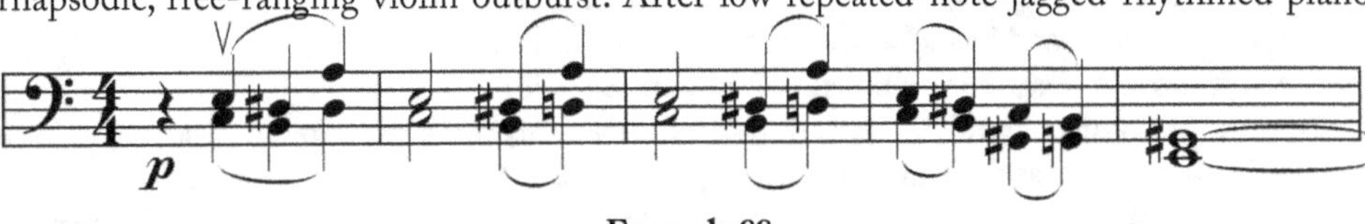

Example 88

effects again prominent. Indeed, as the soloists continue their quasi-improvisational way, the syncopated repeated-note rhythms proliferate in the accompaniment and rise to an enraged climax. The discussion breaks off suddenly, and ex. 88 returns as the opening of a brief, highly atmospheric coda.

III. Allegro. This movement, "a type of scherzo," according to Tcherepnin, seems to begin in a kind of B-minor/major and is largely in fast 7/4 time. At the opening, this rhythm tends to be strictly divided into 5+2-with five grinding string chords supporting a pervasive motif that we will call figure c:

Two beats of solo interjection follow. Extra beats are occasionally thrown in, but it is only considerably later, after several episodes of piano figuration, that these last two beats become integrated into the rhythm, in a series of equal piano chords.

Soon, there is some delicate sparkling high-register interplay, and a full-throated, folk-like theme, virtually on one note, appears in piano and solo cello. Its continuation proves to be figure c in augmentation,

Example 89

and this element is sprinkled into the fragmented thematic mix-more often, of course, figure c is heard unaltered, rapidly jumping from key to key as it is bandied about. Eventually, the music achieves a kind of harmonic stasis in its elaborations of c, and in what sounds like a D major context, a high-spirited melody appears in violin:

Example 90

The cello takes this into B-flat, a *tutti* builds it to a climax in G; then quiet piano figures in B major/minor provoke a sudden loud close.

IV. Presto. This decidedly ethnic Rondo begins with a puckish oboe theme in D nine-step over bassoon accompaniment (in the original version this theme was for gamba accompanied by cello):

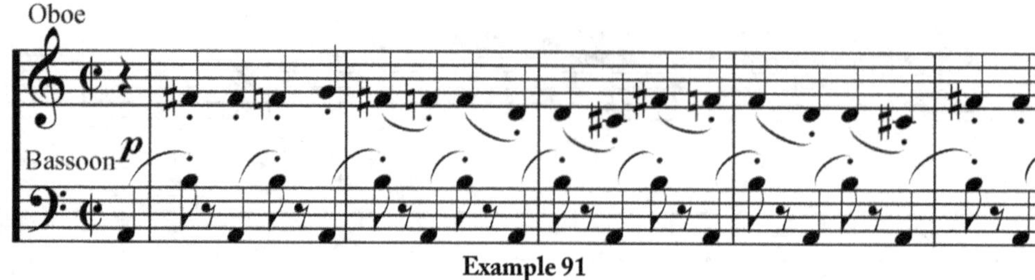

Example 91

Example 91, according to Tcherepnin, "uses the rhythm (but not the actual notes) of a Georgian 'dialogue' folk-song, and the movement, in rondo form, alternates this theme with another in faster values":

This second theme often leads to whirling triplets. At a climax, example 91 is heard in augmentation in sonorous piano chords. When quiet is restored, this tune is restated in its original rhythm, and continues as the bass rises step-by-step. Soon strings tenderly play the opening measure of 91 in augmentation; and just after the cello enters w ith the theme in its normal form, the violin chimes in with a version

Example 92

in diminution. Syncopated augmentation (orchestra) and insistent triplets (soloists) rise to a climax. There is a sudden

tremolo in the strings, and we are back in the world of the slow movement with what Tcherepnin calls "a third-middle-theme, of a recitative type," and repeated-note figures of nocturnal mystery. In a resumption of the original tempo, whirling triplets build over a throbbing pedal, and continue to churn even after the main theme reappears in oboe and solo cello. The theme blows away when heard in diminution in the violins, and more triplets bring example 92, now in D-flat major, rather than the original D-a key that persists notably. A return of ex. 91 in augmentation initiates a furious argument in which the theme

Example 93

in all three versions—augmented, normal and in diminution— "divides itself and goes to buffets" (ex.93).

As the bass returns to A, a syncopated version of 91 appears in agitated dialogue with a descending woodwind figure. But when the tumultuous storm suddenly clears, the loping original theme is heard on solo violin and solo cello, and soon trails off in fragments. There is a slow, nostalgic coda, and, as Tcherepnin wrote, "the movement ends with a 'fishtail,' as the initial phrase of the first movement is evoked," (along with the opening D major/minor triad).

❈   ❈   ❈

DUO, OPUS 49

Some time in mid-1932, Tcherepnin began a correspondence with a young, enthusiastic publisher named Benno Balan, who had recently established a firm in Vienna, and was in the process of acquiring works by many composers who had left Universal Editions. "He asked me for compositions," wrote Tcherepnin, "and especially wanted to have an orchestral composition on Russian themes-Russian dances. The idea… appealed to me. On the other hand, the New York League of Composers approached me to compose a chamber music composition for their Tenth Anniversary Season. At first, I expected to compose for them a Trio (later on it [turned out] to be a Duo) and I signed [a contract] with Benno Balan… for the Russian Dances and the Trio. " It was in July that the composer began work on the Duo.

Tcherepnin was evidently in a state of considerable dissatisfaction with both his life and his work at this point. "Early in September," he wrote, "we arrived in New York. This year was Happy's coming out party and we were to remain in [the] USA until January 16… which meant 132 days of nearly total artistic isolation.

"To cheer myself, I wrote in my diary on the date of October 3, 1932: 'Be happy that you can compose, be happy that by accepting the life you are leading you can attend to the needs of your dear ones in Paris (my parents, grandfather and Alik {*NB* a Benois uncle}) and give joy to your dear ones here (Happy, Louisine, Madame Peters); do not ask yourself how it could be different, but accept… life as it comes.'

"But immediately [following] I wrote, 'Eat less, smoke more, by all means try to endanger your health and harm your physical being, harm your body: exercise your will of power in your soul.'

"And concerning the composition of the Duo I wrote: 'I am facing an evolution in my approach to. music (in my creativity): instead of searching for [the] right geometric proportions, I search for 'beauty,' [which may be] geometrically proportionally constructed, but [is also] imaginative and unregular. It looks [as if] precisely in the form of [a] Duo it is possible for me to find a new 'primitive,' [beginning a] search for 'unmaterial' forms, away from any abstract formula. And out of this primitive… it will be possible to find the way towards becoming 'human.'"

Tcherepnin completed his Duo for Violin and Cello on November 7, 1932. Remarkably, two other compositions produced for the League of Composers Anniversary also turned out to be duos: Aaron Copland's *Elegies* for violin and viola (later withdrawn by the composer) and Serge Prokofiev's Duo for Two Violins. Perhaps this use of the most modest means was a subliminal response by all three composers to the desperate financial condition of a world rapidly headed for the rock bottom of the Great Depression.

Tcherepnin's Duo was premiered on a League concert on April 10, 1933. The performers, Ivor Karman, violin, and Sheridan Russell, cello, reportedly devoted sixty hours of rehearsal to the piece. Prokofiev's Duo was premiered on the same program.

Originally, Tcherepnin's Duo was planned to be the first work in a series of "Eurasian Notebooks, Op. 49"; it was accordingly published as Op. 49, No. 1. This numeration later proved unnecessary, however, for the only other piece in the projected series to appear was the Russian Dances, and this was assigned its own opus number.

"The idealistic background [*i. e.*, the artistic ideology] of [the Duo] is 'Eurasian,'" wrote Tcherepnin, "but due to the inspiration of Egypt, Israel and Greece, the 'Eurasia' became enlarged and outgrew the geographical site of the Russian Fatherland. The nine-step scale and Interpoint are still present, but no longer to the point of exclusivity: elements of folklore (Asiatic) have been incorporated, though not in their pure form-they have been digested and transposed into a tonal language derived from the six-step hexachords, the nine-step scale and a system of 'hard' intervals (chord combinations eliminating the thirds)."

Tcherepnin's new primitivism becomes evident in the texture of the Duo's very opening gesture. Gone is the classical chamber ideal of pristine linear interplay between equal voices. Each of the players here must be like the folk performer at dances and other public festivities who is obliged to make his instrument sound like a whole orchestra. Double-stops and drones abound throughout; indeed, there are passages that might well be transcribed as music for a string quintet with two cellos.

Nine-step influence is still sometimes evident in a preference for half-step/ whole-step/half-step melodic gestures. More fully manifest, however, is a free chromaticism: this, too, is evident in the first two measures, which present every chromatic semitone from g up to e-flat (and, in the process, fill in several intervallic gaps that would be present in strict nine-step use). The use of dissonance is still modernistic, but simplified, often centered around minor ninths used as drones.

Compared to the Triple Concertino, the Duo seems to have a higher dissonance quotient and a less relaxed organization, making recourse to exact recapitulation considerably more seldom. Perhaps these "elitist" aspects represent a residue of resistance to the siren song of Eurasia.

I. Allegro. According to Tcherepnin, the opening movement is based on two themes, the first introduced by the cello at the beginning:

Example 94

the second played by the violin against a cello Interpoint:

Example 95

The thematic material and its development are interrupted by purely rhythmic passages. The central portion of the movement is dominated by example 95, which is imitatively passed back and forth between violin and cello and, at a climax, is reduced to assertions of its first three notes. After the opening theme is reprised, example 95 is again discussed, and the movement ends in a meditative *Lento.*

Example 96

While the movement is not exactly tonal, G is insisted on as a "home bass" throughout, and D is stressed as a "dominant-key bass."

II. Maestoso; Allegretto. The second movement begins by establishing a Db tonic and its Ab dominant. It is in two parts: the first part is like a cadenza, "improvised" by the violin, with rhythmical responses by the cello. "The second part (*Allegretto*)," wrote the composer, "is another story. The idea of it came to me while in Egypt on a *dahobeah* on the

Nile sailing from Luxor to Aswan. In the evenings the sailors used to give a 'concert'-the chorus would sing some short phrase, self-repeated [in continual] *accelerando*, while a solo singer would sing over it [with] the most fantastic *fioraturas* [which had] no relation to it. I tried to take this form as my basis: the cello plays a self-repeated ostinato phrase:

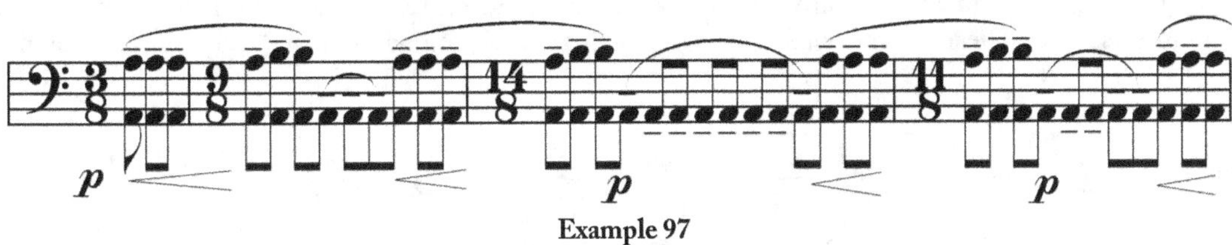

Example 97

over which the violin interprets free melodic figures in Interpoint to the cello. The tempo, [initially] *allegretto*, becomes faster and faster; [and] at a certain moment [measure 23] the violin takes over the self-repeating phrase while the cello [indulges in] melodic *fioraturas*; then both cello and violin participate in [a] simultaneous [reduced version] of the self-repeating phrase [measure 25], alternating [this] with [fragments from] the melodic parts.

Example 98

The highly agitated movement ends unexpectedly [with] a short *Maestoso* conclusion."

III. Moderato. The third movement is a "home bass" of D. "To the activity of the West, [the] East imposes its passive meditation.... The melody is sung by the violin, accompanied by the cello.

IV. Allegro. The fourth movement, on a C bass, was "inspired by insect folklore." Here Tcherepnin evokes the sounds of the various insects he often heard on the porch on autumn nights at Islip, among these the "Katy-did, Katy-didn't" pattern.

Example 99

The closing section, marked *Maestoso* is "a sort of Chorale to the Glory of God..."

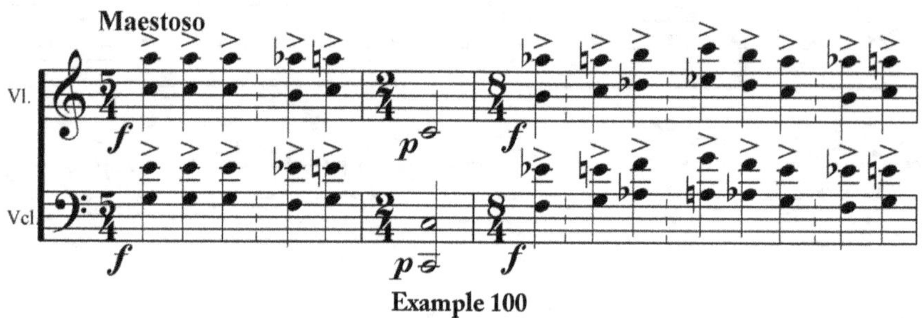

Example 100

V. Allegro moderato. Returning to G, the finale "is in free form, using two themes alternately, rich in rhythmical passages and building up to a long, elaborate climax."

Example 101

Alexander Tcherepnin in 1933

SEVENTEEN TCHEREPNIN MASTERPIECES
PART II (1942-1965)

ROMANTIC OVERTURE, OPUS 67

A great deal of water passed under the bridge in the nine years that separated Tcherepnin's Duo from his *Nevsky Prospect* Overture, written in Paris in 1942; an equal amount surely flowed in the nine-year period that subsequently elapsed before that orchestral score was published in its definitive form (1951) under the title Romantic Overture.

Had Tcherepnin not broken out of ivory tower isolation of his own accord during the mid-1930s, with his embrace of the pentatonic scale and other Eurasian materials, he would in any case have been forced out later in the decade by the external circumstances of his life. During the time that he was married to Louisine, he literally had not needed to worry if his music was salable or not. For, even in his most successful years his earnings as a composer constituted no more than a negligible portion of the enormous family income. After his separation from Louisine and his later marriage to Ming, however, he was obliged to support himself entirely on the income from his music and his concerts. Fortunately, Tcherepnin was now well-established enough to receive a steady stream of commissions; but he was in no position to pick and choose among proposals—he had to accept the assignments that came, and to make the best of them artistically. It might almost be said that in between 1937 and 1947 Tcherepnin was primarily a ballet composer, and secondarily concerned with music as an adjunct to words and with educational scores. In fact, between the Russian Dances (1933) and the turning point of World War II ten years later, Tcherepnin composed only one full-orchestra concert piece—the *Nevsky Prospect* Overture.

This score, although rather lightweight in absolute terms, is of considerable interest as an indication of Tcherepnin's approach to the delicate question of program music—a question that cannot be avoided by a composer who, as Tcherepnin did during the 1940s, regularly produces music for the stage. Varying programmatic material was attached to this Overture over the years; yet there is implicit, unchangeable extramusical content at the core of its sounds as well, and Tcherepnin evidently felt that neither he nor the listener should ignore it.

The overture stands out strikingly as one of the very few pieces that Tcherepnin ever subjected to extensive revision—a revision that went beyond mere changes in scoring and extended to alterations in the basic form of the piece. It is impossible to overstress how exceptional such second thoughts were in Tcherepnin's body of work: certain pieces, to be sure, underwent extensive instrumental refurbishing, such as the Second Piano Concerto, the Triple Concertino and the *Bagatelles*, but in that process the original musical content was almost always preserved as sacrosanct. Yet, the *Nevsky Prospect* Overture, a thirteen-minute piece, was revised into the Romantic Overture, an eight-and-a-half-minute piece; the one-time miniaturist now found it necessary to curb his carefully developed powers of expansion. Several episodes, both brief and extended, were omitted, and the original exposition was tightened somewhat. The largest change was an eighty-four-measure cut, which considerably shortened the lyrical central episode, the music jumping directly from this to the original coda. A clue to Tcherepnin's motivations for such changes can be found toward the end of his letter to Slonimsky (see p. 122): evidently the initial version of the score struck him as excessively eclectic.

In the overture's first context, however, eclecticism may have seemed a desirable trait. The piece was intended to serve as a temporary overture to an unabashedly eclectic work, the Mussorgsky-Tcherepnin opera *The Marriage*, at a performance scheduled by an emigre Russian opera company in Paris during the German occupation. Ordinarily, *The Marriage* fills only half an evening, but the for this production, director decided to flesh out the spectacle by including, as spoken interludes, scenes from the original Gogol play that had been cut from the opera; some additional music was also deemed necessary, and an overture appeared *de rigueur*. Because Tcherepnin had carefully avoided making any musical connection between the opera's two acts, however—Act One is Mussorgsky orchestrated by Tcherepnin, Act Two is pure "Eurasian" Tcherepnin—the Overture could not very well make specific musical references to either act. The most that could be done was to provide a certain romantic nostalgia. As it happens, there were other stimuli to bring Gogol and his period to Tcherepnin's mind at this time (whether before or after the opera project was broached we do not know). Tcherepnin wrote: "At the time of World War II...private cars and taxis were not allowed to circulate on the streets of Paris. Some few old-fashioned horse driven coaches made their reappearance. One night the usual silence of the Rue Furstenberg, where I was living, was interrupted by the sounds of a passing cab. The sound of horse-steps on the pavement awakened in me the [memory] of the epoch to which these sounds belong."

Tcherepnin was reminded of the Gogol novella *Nevsky Prospect*, with its coach rides along that major thoroughfare of St. Petersburg. Indeed, the Nevsky Prospect at the time of Tcherepnin's youth, so he said, "differed only a little from the Nevsky Prospect of Gogol's time and the Gogol description of it is quite similar to the one my memory recollects."

Tcherepnin continued, "the Gogol novella [recounts] a story of two young men's romantic adventure with two young girls. The romance, the conflict, the 'drama' [are] all framed by the animated 'neutrality' of the Nevsky Prospect."

If *The Marriage* had to have an overture at all, a "period piece" evoking Gogol's world was just the thing. So it was that ideas took shape in Tcherepnin's mind for a musical scenario where the opening and closing hustle-bustle of horse-drawn traffic on the Nevsky Prospect frames a central episode redolent of Tchaikovskian Romanticism and nineteenth-century comic intrigue.

There appears to be no printed record of the date or conductor of the first performance: the occupying Nazi authorities permitted neither newspaper accounts nor public advertising of the Russian Opera venture. For this reason and various others, the production of the Mussorgsky-Tcherepnin opera was a failure (See "The Marriage," pp. 458-459). But Tcherepnin thought the overture worth saving and reorchestrated it some time before completing his French autobiography in 1947, listing it in his catalog as *Nevsky Prospect* Overture, with the subtitle "Return of the Coach Driver." When the final revision was completed in 1951, however, all references to the Gogol novella were dropped. The piece, as said, was retitled Romantic Overture, and an epigraph—containing an embarrassing grammatical error which some editor at G. Schirmer should have caught-was placed at the top of the page where the instrumentation was listed. It read: "The sound of horses' hooves on the pavement evoke [sic] the romantic era to which it belongs."

It is relevant here to recall that Mussorgsky's *Marriage* was intended to work a revolution in Russian musical prosody. The composer took great care to preserve the rhythms and accents of normal speech, so much so that melody seemed to be virtually abandoned in favor of continual recitative. Presumably it was this circumstance that prompted Tcherepnin to use "orchestral recitative" in two episodes of the Overture's initial version, matching the music to the words of unspoken conversations between the passenger and the driver. Thus, this jolly C major Overture had originally begun with a seven-measure orchestral "dialogue":

Passenger:	Ei! Izvostchik!	P:	Hey! Taxi!
Driver:	Pojalouite barin.	D:	At your service, sir.
Passenger:	Na Gorokhovouiou ougol Voznessenskogo!	P:	Gorohovaya street at the corner of Voznessenski!
Driver:	Poltinnik pojalouite.	D:	Fifty kopeks, if you please.
Passenger:	Podavai!	P:	Fine!

This musical conversation was expunged in the 1951 version, which begins with the cab-ride itself.

Tcherepnin summarized the remainder of the original version as follows:

Measures 7-165)	ride. A panorama of St. Petersburg's streets. Accents indicate (sic) how the izvostchik beats the horse with a knout. There are some rhythms of street vendors, a church carillon, different street scenes.
165-169)	arrival at Nevsky Prospect
170-259)	romantic adventure (music in this part is in "style" of Russian romanticism)
260-294)	scandal scenes
295-308)	escape
309-312)	istvostchik
312 to the end [378])	a ride on the iztvostchik through the animated Nevsky Prospect.

The revised version of the overture is only 270 measures long. The romantic adventure begins at measure 145, for Tcherepnin not only eliminated the opening recitative, as we have seen, and made a twelve-measure cut in the allegro, but also excised *another* orchestral recitative in which the cabby had announced the arrival at the designated corner (as the piece was no longer connected with *The Marriage*, prosody had ceased to be an issue). This second recitative, the original bridge to the romantic central *Andante*, was replaced by a brief chordal transition. The lyrical middle section, in F major, retained its first portion, 60 measures in length, but the original half-cadence, coming to rest in C major and thus promising more to come, was rewritten so that the music ends in F, rounding off the episode. A slightly faster section, with this attractive theme:

Example 102

is omitted, as is the busy and eventful "scandal and escape" episode, which had contained some hints of thematic development. The final section is retained at full length.

The overture was definitely rendered less episodic by the revision-indeed, it lost all of its connection with Gogol's story and most of its own musical plot. Tcherepnin was musically justified, so it seems, in removing the instrumental recitatives, particularly the one before the central section-as a transition, it is far weaker than the passage that is now in the score. As for the drastic cut from the *andante* to the coda, the composer might have gone too far. The absence of any thematic recurrences in the last portion is a trifle worrisome, and while the music moves smartly along to its conclusion with no hint of lagging, its progress may strike some listeners as too efficient. The surviving orchestral material shows, however, that Tcherepnin experimented with shorter cuts: it is possible that none of these worked out as well as the published version.

In the instrumentation, Tcherepnin has notably progressed from the abstract chastity of his previous concert works for orchestra. The wind complement is still classically small (after all, the piece was originally conceived for an opera orchestra), but Tcherepnin has unbent to the extent of employing an English horn doubling second oboe. With this group, however, the scoring is quite coloristic; moreover, the percussion group, given a good deal of splashy, high-spirited display is quite large, consisting of triangle, castanets, wood block, side drum, cymbals, bass drum, glockenspiel, chimes, xylophone and sleigh bells; these are often used in conjunction with the harp and the piano.

Premiered in its final form on October 23, 1951, in Kansas City, Missouri, under the direction of Hans Schwieger (to whom the piece was later dedicated), the Romantic Overture is a feather-light score of zest and charm. Its contemporary *scherzo à la Russe* quality inevitably brings Prokofiev and Shostakovich to mind, but the scathing satirical edge of their work is quite lacking, with the result that their depth of expression is not achieved. However, the cleverness of the imitative writing and the *panache* of the whole make the score well worth hearing; it would undoubtedly be received with delight on a Pops concert program.

"The composition, generally speaking, is in three sections," wrote Tcherepnin, in an analysis of the final version. "The first section, *Allegro*, describes a ride on a horse-driven carriage through the streets of St. Petersburg. The [viola] figure [in example 103, doubled by harp and xylophone] gives the horse-steps sound; the C major chords are to depict the driver's knocks on the horse's back by the stick. The phrase of the violins in measures 7-10 names the different streets:

Example 103

Example 104

All kinds of street scenes follow."

Soon, the figures of ex. 104 are delivered by the lower strings, and amid a kaleidoscope of brief, evanescent motifs there is a wholesale replacement of the expected Fs with F-sharps, as if the Lydian mode were in use. This sharping seems to explain itself as a way of creeping up on G major, but in fact, the appearance of that dominant proves a false alarm. The music moves back to C and now the horse-motif-*cum*-F-sharp emerges as a real theme the orthodox concept of a "first subject" being reduced, as it were, to a belated afterthought:

The music exuberantly overshoots the dominant, careening through E major to F (as dominant of B-flat), and here a second theme is introduced by bassoons and violas:

Example 105

Example 106

which repeats its motifs with Stravinskian rhythmic variations and soon displays this characteristic modulation:

At a climax, the hoofbeats become a low bass-timpani rumble, and a kind of cantus firmus appears in the trombones. Later, the trumpets break in with ex. 106 in augmentation, and a chordal *allargando* leaves the music poised on the brink of F major.

"The second section, *Andante*," wrote Tcherepnin, "begins the romantic adventure;

Example 107

the music is here in the style of the romantic *epoque*." Here there are climaxes of unabashed lushness leavened with some interesting harmonic leaps. "At the end, in measures 195, 197 and 198 the oboe, piccolo and flute imitate the street vendor's phrase that I often heard in my youth in St. Petersburg:

Example 108

"The third section, *Allegro*, brings us back to our own time."

Here, neither first theme nor second theme is recapitulated. The hoofbeat motif, however, is again omnipresent, and its interval-the third-is filled in to produce a new trumpet theme which displays the same characteristic modulation as ex. 107. A salient rhythm from the opening allegro (3+3+2) is also recalled.

Example 109

Example 109 builds, sequencing in a self-repeating *crescendo*, to a jubilant climax on final cracks of the cabby's whip.

SHOWCASE, OPUS 75

<table>
<tr><td>Les levriers en verre et</td><td>The glass greyhounds and</td></tr>
<tr><td>la vache en porcelain</td><td>the porcelain cow</td></tr>
<tr><td>Les écrevisses</td><td>The crayfish</td></tr>
<tr><td>La grenouille</td><td>The frog</td></tr>
<tr><td>Le furet</td><td>The weasel</td></tr>
<tr><td>Le cerf</td><td>The deer</td></tr>
</table>

Almost all of Tcherepnin's piano works are, among other things, artifacts of his concert touring. We have seen that even so abstract a work as *Message* was intended specifically for performance; and throughout the twenties and thirties Tcherepnin continually supplied himself with new material, which he promptly performed in public. A relatively small number of his works remained in his permanent repertory, but those that did represented almost every creative period. (This pattern was to continue in his later years with the cycles Opp. 81, 82, 85 and 88, and the Second Piano Sonata, Op. 94.)

No piano collections were composed during the years of enforced idleness in wartime Paris; the appearance of *Le Monde en Vitrine*, Op. 75, (at first called *The World Under Glass* by Tcherepnin in English but later published under the title *Showcase*) marked his return to concertizing as a pianist on tour. The overt musical portraiture in these pieces, unprecedented in Tcherepnin's piano works, reflects his orientation at this time as a composer of ballets and other stage-works: a theatrical or otherwise extra-musical program had become a welcome, perhaps even necessary stimulus to creativity.

The sparkling zest and *affetuoso* charm that characterizes these little virtuoso pieces is echoed in the delightfully arch program notes that Tcherepnin had included in both French and English in the printed score. These are reproduced here, amplified to include analytical commentary, and with some of the French comments rendered more accurately into English than they were in the original edition.

Example 110

"All artistic Paris knows Madame Amos, a great patron of contemporary painting, of art in general and music in particular. Her collection of paintings and *objets d'art* is world famous. Numerous masterpieces of painting, sculpture, poetry and music owe their existence to her initiative. Tcherepnin wanted to express in music his impressions of the figurines in Madame Amos's show-case. *Showcase* was composed in 1946 and consists of five movements." Tcherepnin himself gave the work its first performance on February 28, 1946, at the home of Mathilde Amos, to whom the published score was later dedicated.

"The first movement is inspired by a group of miniature greyhounds in glass, which in the showcase stands next to a porcelain cow of imposing dimensions. The greyhounds are all motion. The cow is torpid. This contrast fascinated the composer as an image of life, where our enthusiasm is so often thwarted by bovine placidity!"

Cast in a loose A-B-A form with coda, the music indicates the friskiness of the greyhounds not only through the cheerful themes and sizzling scale passages, but also by restless modulations that take the music from C major through C minor, B-flat major, D-flat major, B major and back to C where, after a few rhythmic chords, the opening theme is heard again. The immobile cow appears in the coda in the form of a sustained B-flat that steadily seems to sap the vitality of the melody, which loses direction and fragments.

"The second movement presents the crayfish. We can picture two crayfish, male and female, noticing each other from afar and approaching each other backwards." For some reason, the publisher decided to call this piece "Crabs" in English, which is a blatant mistranslation. Tcherepnin, who knew a crab when he saw one, always insisted that Mme. Amos's figurines were creatures of another kind. This piece, an absorbing and slyly humorous study in dissonant intervals, grows entirely out of a simple constructive paradox. At the opening, a harmonically stubborn three-voiced chord (I, #4, #7, softly sounds at the extreme ends of the piano (Example 111) and individual treble and bass notes begin creeping toward one another, mostly by scuttling step-wise and half-step-wise motions, with the conflicts between drifting parts in opposition generating weird-sounding ornamentation identifiable with writhing claws (Example 112).

Example 111

The process continues in a steady *crescendo* until the two chords coalesce into a single *fortississimo* middle register chord—which itself, in a sudden turn to *pianissimo*, at last undergoes rapid shrinkage into a single unison.

(Note that, as in the previous piece, the introduction of a stubborn, static element-there, the b-flat, here the chord, signals the impending close of the piece).

Example 112

Example 113

Of this depiction of two massing into one, the program note reads:

"There are two versions: one for the children, wherein the crayfish devour each other (which is true to zoological law), the other for adults, which we leave to their imagination, and which is equally faithful to the laws of nature.

"Assuming that the second version takes place, the frog, a turquoise figure next to the porcelain crayfish, begins to gossip, thus scandalizing all the creatures in the showcase." The frog's croaks and leaps are evoked by this opening motif in major/minor thirds (Example 114).

Presently an insinuating chromatic motif is heard, and the two reappear in alternation.

Example 114

Example 115

The opening motif is extended into a theme in an agitated *crescendo* featuring extremely wide spacing; then a distinctly Ravel-like waltz figure emerges.

The chromatic motif combines with this and builds to a ferocious climax that yields to quiet croaks and trills. Then the opening motif theme (3/4 + 3/4 + 2/4) is humorously interpointed with a reiterated 5/8 bass pattern. There is a lyric climax, and again an end-signaling sustained note is sounded (C-sharp, baldly alien to the prevailing G major). As the frog hops away in a final scherzo

Example 116

gesture, Tcherepnin writes a G below the bottom A on the piano.

"The uproarious noise of the poultry, followed by the scurrying of the weasel, provides the rhythm of the fourth movement." An opening "signal" (a cock-crow?):

Example 117

is twice answered by flutterings, then sounds twice again. A low-register *sempre piano* toccata of great virtuosity, in a Russian vein also mined by Prokofiev, represents the scurrying weasel. After a brilliant triplet episode, the opening signal is incorporated into the continuing *moto perpetuo*, becoming a dominant force:

The music dies away into repeated low Bs, and the signal is heard a final time, its last note sustained, before a closing low-register flourish.

"The big porcelain deer, Tcherepnin declares, is one of the most beautiful pieces, if not the most beautiful, in Madame Amos's collection. Contemplation of the deer reminded Tcherepnin of an incident which he relates. It was in Austria in the forest of Hagen-gut, near Mariazell, where, before the war, he spent a few days' holiday on the estate of his friend Alfred von Porada. Walking peacefully in the forest, Tcherepnin suddenly found himself confronted by a deer advancing in his direction. Both stopped and stared, but only for a few seconds."

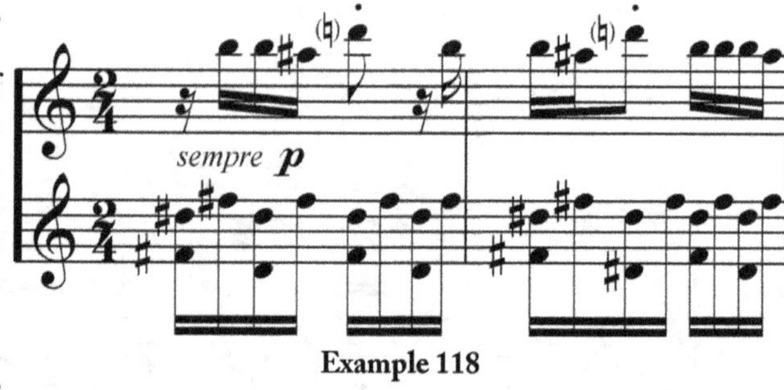

Example 118

Tcherepnin evokes the image of the deer with a serene, tender richly chordal cantabile (the piano writing here utilizes stretches so wide that only performers with exceptionally large hands can manage it). A second theme, a kind of woodland *arpeggio* answered by *Rosenkavalier*-like chords, provides an almost sentimental touch. The opening cantabile returns, more densely accompanied, extended in its counterstatement and rising to a climax; then the second theme duly reappears.

"Thanks to the music we shall know the thoughts of Tcherepnin, but we shall never know those of the deer, which swiftly fled." In an *animato*, the woodland figure prances up the piano:

Example 119

The music then evaporates in a fleeting downward scale and a final contrary-motion *glissando* from a unison middle D to Gs six octaves apart.

"It is with this confrontation of the human and animal worlds that this portrait of the world of the Showcase concludes."

SYMPHONY NO. 2, OPUS 77

At the beginning of 1946 I received a telegram from my friend Hugo Winter, one of the directors of Associated Music Publishers in New York, proposing that I write a symphonic work of 15-20 minutes duration to be issued by this firm and premiered over NBC, and offering me a substantial sum in the event that I consented to undertake this task.

Naturally, I accepted and, wishing to use this opportunity to write a work in which I could spread myself, proposed to Winter that I produce a symphony.

The contract was signed, and while making sketches, I waited for a propitious moment to begin fully intensive work.

Almost twenty years had passed since my First Symphony. My mentality, my language, my artistic perspectives had evolved.

As the First Symphony was the culmination of a period devoted to pure forms in the chamber music or chamber-orchestra works that preceded it, there was a solid equilibrium between its "what" and its "how." I do not recall having had any doubts at that time, neither about its form-which I accepted as being classic-nor about its language, tonally and harmonically based on the nine-interval scale and polyphonically developed through the procedures of interpoint.

Of all the times in my life, the year 1927 was the most suitable, the best chosen for the composition of a symphony. The rapidity and the surety with which the First Symphony was composed are proof of this.

It was only after undertaking the composition of the Second Symphony, after having thrown myself into the water, so to speak, that I perceived the difficulty of the task that I had voluntary imposed upon myself.

With a few exceptions, the works that I had composed during the previous decade had been commissioned pieces of "applied" music, mostly ballets and dances.

The "purgative cure" by folklore, begun in 1933 with the *Russian Dances*, had liberated me from technical artifice, from the *deus ex machina* of abstract language, but in its turn needed to be cured in order to liberate my thoughts and my language from localized geographical and stylistic formulas.

That is probably why none of my works cost me so much difficulty, reflection and effort; never did I have so many doubts about my powers as when I worked on the symphony, rejecting one idea after another, cringing at the mediocrity of everything that came into my head, spending days and weeks in unprecedented confusion.

It was only in January 1947 that, after multiple attempts, I finally felt myself back on the rails: the third movement, preceding the others, was composed in January-February, the second in March, the first in March-April and the last in May.

At the moment I write these lines (August 1947) the orchestration remains to be done.

What I attempted to achieve in composing the Symphony was that its form be "realized" through material entirely "composed," or, in other words "discovered" and not "worked out" or "written." A piece of music doesn't exist on paper, its existence begins only at the moment of interpretation; to be worth interpreting it must encompass elements of dynamism, must be the result of the "felt" and the "experienced"-and must make it possible for the interpreter to recapture the feelings, the thought processes and the temperament of the author....

The Second Symphony, like the First, is unrelated to any program but, in contradistinction to the schematic, almost algebraic construction of the First, its construction is dynamic and emotional; the problem of language is eliminated: the "how" and the "what" are one.

Without being descriptive, and entirely without a "program," the music of this symphony somehow reflects the agony of the war years, the rising hopes of a better world, the desolation which I felt at the death of my beloved father, the mystery of death itself, the controversial feeling of a post-war period. The great task was to construct without any innovating technicalities, and to find an adequate form The work is dedicated to Hugo Winter.

❊   ❊   ❊

Most of the preceding account by Tcherepnin appears in his French autobiography; the last two paragraphs and the quoted analytical comments on the pages that follow are taken from a program note by the composer.

Tcherepnin's frank confessions indicate the degree to which he had become used to hanging his music on some kind of representational, if not exactly programmatic peg, and to framing it for a utilitarian design. Unable to apply an extra-musical rationale to the "absolute" music he was now again composing, he apparently had some difficulty in identifying *any* intrinsic rationale in the ideas that came to him. This may have been all the more problematic, given Tcherepnin's apparent conviction that a symphony, composed at this time of his life and this stage in history, could be no ordinary musical utterance, but had to make the most significant statement of which he was capable. In the First Symphony he had sought profundity through materials that were susceptible to complex technical manipulation. Now neither these, nor other overtly "invented" themes, satisfied him as having natural musical substance. Indeed, when he finally began work on the Symphony, it was with the *scherzo*, a "character" movement informed by deliberate thematic grotesquerie, and hence the least "abstract" section of the piece.

Ultimately Tcherepnin's attempt to forge a score that depended entirely on its purely musical content was successful. It should be noted, however, that in his next concert piece, the Fourth Piano Concerto, he again resorted to programmatic references.

In another respect, the compositional crisis that preceded the Second Symphony seems more ominous, prefiguring longer dry spells that would increasingly overtake Tcherepnin in his later years. In one of his stranger English locutions, Tcherepnin several times used the phrase "I spied myself" to describe the state of uncertainty that periodically reduced him to creative sterility. What he meant was that he would unleash his critical faculties prematurely, impatiently discarding ideas long before they could reasonably be expected to reveal their full potential. In the Second Symphony, he worked his way out of this impasse with the partial aid of a jester's mask donned for a Scherzo. Later crises would not yield so easily to such a ploy; but through the 1950s these remained limited in extent, still allowing him to produce a series of extremely impressive works.

Although the composer completed the Symphony in short score in 1947, he did not finish the orchestration, as Reich has already recounted, until four years later. Why he waited so long is something of a mystery. To be sure, he had other commissioned works to worry about, some of them stage works with specific deadlines; moreover, Tcherepnin began carrying a full college teaching load in 1949. (It was Mary Garden who had finally persuaded a hesitant Tcherepnin to accept his DePaul Professorship, saying, "Chicago brought me luck; it will bring you luck too.") Finding it difficult at first to combine his academic duties with his creative work, he did no composing at all during the fourteen months between late 1949 and early 1951, as he wrote to Slonimsky. It was only in the latter year that he tackled the orchestration of the Second Symphony in earnest.

The press of time aside, however, the fact that the Symphony was not the only project that Tcherepnin left on the back burner is suggestive. The composer similarly procrastinated about bringing out his Fourth Piano Concerto. Although it was announced, in the late 40s, that he would premiere the concerto soon, no performance materialized; there were also reports in the press that the premiere would be entrusted to the composer's wife, Ming, but she did not present the piece either. In her last months, Ming recollected that there had been a two-piano reading, one in which, it seems, she accompanied her husband, but Tcherepnin never played the Fourth Concerto with orchestra at all, either in any of his post-war European concerts or at any other time; indeed, the premiere, which took place in the unlikely locale of Oakland California, did not occur until 1958.

It could be that Tcherepnin found the Concerto uncomfortable to play, or that it demanded more practice time than he could give it-the piece was, after all, a real virtuoso concerto, quite unlike his Concertos Nos. 2 and 3. But it is also possible that Tcherepnin had other good reasons to avoid presenting his most recent concert works in Europe during these years-reasons related to the politics of musical modernism. Much time had now passed since Tcherepnin had made his reputation as an ultra-modernist, and in that interim his music had changed significantly; more to the point, so had the avant-garde climate in Europe. In Paris, the Age of Serialism, fostered by the proselytizing efforts of Rene Leibowitz, had dawned under particularly acrimonious circumstances. Stravinsky himself had been booed as an outmoded neo-Classicist: Boulez had proclaimed the utter "irrelevance" of any music that did not reflect the serial principal, and many of the most prestigious critics had jumped on the bandwagon. While Tcherepnin's First Symphony had been categorized by the critics and audiences of 1927 as a work of the far left, his Second Symphony and Fourth Piano Concerto would surely impress even the friendliest European judges in 1947 as works just to the right of center. Tcherepnin may have thought it prudent to withhold his new concert scores until the fashion for militant serialism waned.

Another possible element must be considered within what was probably a congeries of motivations. Almost all of Tcherepnin's previous major pieces had been sent into the world accompanied by information about their distinctive technical or artistic rationales. In calling attention to the nine-step scale, to interpoint, to Renaissance-like polyphonic manipulation, to the Eurasian ideology, to the pentatonic scale, to the Georgian chord, Tcherepnin had been able, to some degree, to control what would be written about a new piece. In the Second Symphony, however, Tcherepnin had deliberately held aloof from all such premeditated stylistic and technical features, creating a piece that had to be sent out naked, as it were- just at a time when the absence of polemical propaganda actually placed a new piece at a disadvantage in Europe. He may well have believed that for the Symphony to succeed, the climate had to be such that his abstinence would be viewed as a positive advance rather than as a mark of artistic exhaustion.

After coming to DePaul in 1949, of course, Tcherepnin had totally different concerns. It became necessary for him to procure commissions that would get his name before the American public under circumstances as prestigious as possible. In the United States, post-Webernite fever was still years in the future. A Chicago Symphony premiere of a sizable score under Rafael Kubelik was a feather in any composer's cap, and it was in those circumstances that Tcherepnin introduced his Second Symphony on March 20, 1952. As to the Fourth Concerto, Tcherepnin now did not have to spend valuable time practicing it because audiences in major American concert centers, unlike those in Europe, had never heard the composer play his Second Concerto, a work of proven success that fitted him like a glove.

Tcherepnin's Symphony No. 2 was cordially received by the critics but did not immediately catch on as the composer had hoped, apparently remaining unperformed for the rest of the decade. It was only in later years that it was revived and recorded. Tcherepnin good-humoredly noted this neglect when inscribing a copy of the score to his student Phillip Ramey (referring also, in his inscription, to an occasion when Ramey had unexpectedly met him at the airport during a heavy snowstorm). Tcherepnin wrote: "To the redoubtable snowman with gratitude but *never do it again* (alike [*sic*] this symphony that was never done again). Wholeheartedly, A. Tcherepnin 16 IV 61."

The orchestration of the Second Symphony indicates how thoroughly Tcherepnin's orientation had changed in the years since he had last cultivated the form. For, at sometime during the wartime era (exactly when cannot be determined, because several manuscripts from that period are missing) Tcherepnin at last embraced the concept of the full modern symphony orchestra. As previously noted, his earlier works, up to the dismal experience that had prompted him to revise the *Russian Dances* (1933), had utilized woodwinds in pairs, 4 horns, 2 trumpets, 3 trombones and tuba along with strings. In subsequent years, Tcherepnin took tentative steps to expand the wind complement. *Trepak* (1938) had required a third trumpet, the *Nevsky Prospect* Overture (1942) utilized an English horn, although more for its Romantic local color than because of its potential for expanded orchestral expression. A more substantial change, however, became evident in Tcherepnin's *Evocation: Childhood of Saint Nino*, Op. 69, begun in late 1943 and finished the following January, for here the composer called for woodwinds in threes.

This concept of the large orchestra now became a permanent feature of Tcherepnin's style. To be sure, for works where a modest scale of tone was desirable-some of the ballet scores, the Harmonica Concerto, the Fourth and Sixth Piano Concer-tos-Tcherepnin would return to double wind. But the Second Symphony, conceived as a work of normal orchestral scale, called for 3 flutes (3rd doubling piccolo), 2 oboes, English horn, 2 clarinets, bass clarinet, 2 bassoons, contrabassoon, 4 horns, 3 trumpets, 3 trombones, tuba, timpani, xylophone, small bells, tubular bells, castanets, woodblock, triangle, snare drum, tambou-rine, cymbals, bass drum, gong, celesta, harp, piano and strings. Triple wind would also be used in both of Tcherepnin's subsequent symphonies, as well as the Divertimento and the Fifth Piano Concerto.

Tcherepnin used to say that it was only after the death of his father, in 1945, that he finally became comfortable in dealing with the orchestra. He was inclined to take a mystical view of this artistic advance-as if his father's unquestioned instrumental mastery had been a heritage posthumously transmitted to him. Freudians are apt to take a different view of the matter, seeing the orchestra in this context as a potential battleground for Oedipal confrontation that the younger Tcherepnin, consciously or unconsciously, avoided so long as his father was alive.

In any case, the instrumentation of the Second Symphony is assured and sonorous. Stylistically, the work is coherent and distinguished, firmly tonal in its outlines (here, one wishes that Tcherepnin had kept the original designation, Symphony No. 2 in E-flat major), yet easily and confidently passing back and forth between diatonic passages and episodes of dense chromaticism in which any sense of a tonal center vanishes.

As might be expected from Tcherepnin's previous practice, sonata-form recapitulation occurs only in fragmentary fashion, and while rondo recurrences remain normal in his style, the narrative method here has, at least ostensibly, more freedom than in the First Symphony: the new material that appears in the first- and last-movement codas and the second movement's picturesque central portion is seldom thematically deducible. Increasingly, the elemental compositional question "what next" is answered by neither formula nor logic, but, rather, by cultivated instinct; Tcherepnin has, in other words, come some distance toward the novelistic method of construction that would inform some of his later works.

That he has by no means discarded all of his fastidiousness is evident, however, in his refusal to recapitulate the attractive second subject in his first movement. Indeed such a return, although artistically justified and of great potential popular appeal, is crowded out by the composer's "message," and by the ending dictated by symphonic momentum-a coda whose rhythmic imperatives seem veritably biological in origin. This description is also germane to the *Scherzo*, which some judges might be tempted to underrate on the basis of the spoof-banality of its tune: here, the motion never degenerates into mere vibration, but derives continually renewed urgency from the exercise of sheer compositional stamina.

It should not be thought, however, that the proto-novelistic approach here was without its artistic risks. Thematic loose ends were unquestionably left in the first movement, and although this was surely a conscious decision, the result may disturb some listeners-creating the impression that Tcherepnin has changed his agenda in mid-course, or has created an unbalanced structure. The second movement, too, opens itself to criticism for, in its continual introduction of new material, it inevitably seems somewhat diffuse. This, however, is surely a venial flaw in so relatively brief a movement, and does not prevent the strangely sweet poignancy of Tcherepnin's elegiac coloration from making a deep expressive effect.

"In the work as a whole," wrote Tcherepnin in his analysis, "there is a pause after the first movement, but the following movements are intended to be played without break."

"The first movement begins with an Introduction (*Sostenuto*)." In an atmosphere blending serene dignity with dispassionate mystery, thematic materials are discovered, or revealed through the step-by-step introductions-both chordal and melodic-of the basic pentatonic elements. The sequences of fifths:

Eb Bb F C G / Eb Ab etc.

are additively unfolded in a spacious series of hushed, sporadic single staccato chords; the pentatonic scale is introduced in string *pizzicato*s (these lines at times quasi-canonic). The motif Eb-F-G emerges as a significant factor (this was pointed out by Arias in his analysis). It is often, however, the extension of this motif *beyond* the pentatonic, *i. e.*, to four-note and five-note diatonic scale patterns, that generates action in this symphony.

The opening materials first display a decided subdominant bias. When the dominant appears, it is immediately obscured as chattering woodwinds enter at double tempo and extend the vocabulary to the chromatic in a passage of densely harmonized mockery. A return of the hushed chords signals a transition to the main body of the movement via the dominant and, curiously, the low-register pattern B, G, D (simultaneously sounded, of course, these notes form the triad of G major, which will prove of considerable importance).

"The *Allegro*, which follows," writes Tcherepnin, "offers a short exposition of the thematic material [beginning with] a principal theme of agitated character":

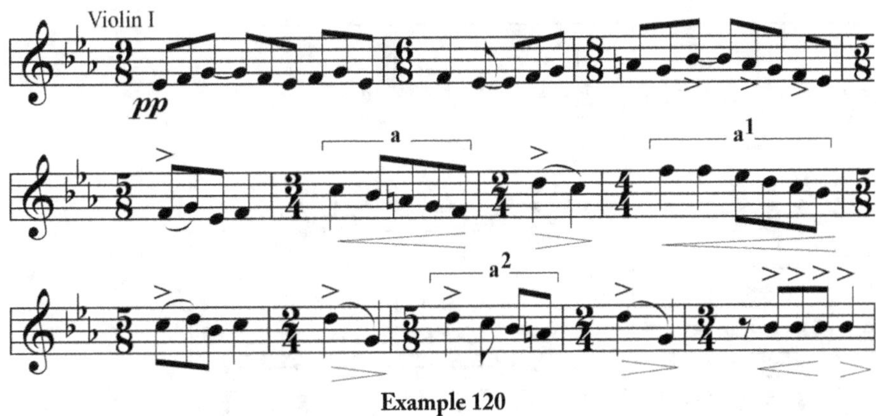

Example 120

The rhythms, of superb ambiguity, were presumably "discovered" through elimination of other possibilities that proved less open-ended. Note the hints of Lydian mode in mm. 40, 42 and 48, a predilection previously seen in the Romantic Overture; here, too, as in that work, the first theme will generate a modulation to #III. Even before the counterstatement at measure 56, motifs a and a[1] take on a life of their own, and at measure 60, they provide the first hint of the G major#III tonality prefigured at the end of the introduction.

A bridge motif (unquoted) moves from A to G to D major, and here, with motif a and related scale motifs subjected to a great deal of working over, there is a leisurely and climactic transition to G major.

Here, we have, according to Tcherepnin, "a subordinate subject, more lyrical, [example 121] but with a rhythmic conclusion" [example 122]. This theme too begins with pentatonic elements, but soon moves beyond them.

Example 121

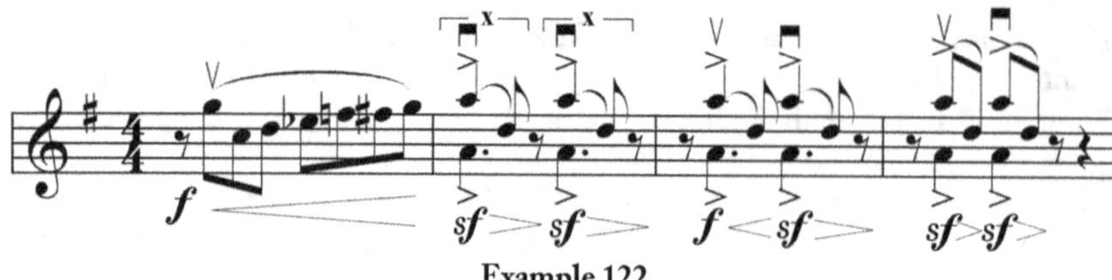

Example 122

"The development combines some new material with that already presented…" A new theme, similar in character to the main theme but with no actual connection to it appears "on" rather than "in" the dominant and displays new rhythmic variants (3+2+2+2; 3+3+2+2):

Heard again against material in contrary motion and vibrantly contradictory interpuntal rhythms (note the bassoon part), it modulates rapidly, passing through D, Db and A on its way to indeterminate chromaticism. By the time the dynamic reaches **p** it has virtually shed definite pitch (the chords now pit the notes A B and C against a snare-drum).

Example 123

Example 125

After a sudden flare-up, a new theme appears:

Example 124

and moves to the bass following a brief intervention by ex. 123. There is an enormous build up on the ex. 123 rhythm, beginning over a pedal G, but then taking on dominant implications as swirling accompaniment figures are heard.

Following an unexpected pause at the climax, the hushed rhythmic chords of the opening are reinvoked, now accompanying a lugubrious horn-theme (Example 125). The *pizzicatos* of the opening are also reinvoked, but the colors here are even more atmospheric. The new theme continues its dirge-like course, building in steady *crescendo* till the dominant is reached. Then the tempo quickens, and the opening motif of the principal subject and example 123 are discussed. With culminating reference to the principal subject promising a return of E-flat, it seems as if the beginning of a full reprise is on the tip of the orchestra's tongue. "But," as Tcherepnin says, "instead of an orthodox recapitulation there is given only a light reminiscence of the formal material…" for what is heard is only a few references to the main theme, followed by the passage that had announced the impending second subject (see example 121), "and this passes directly into a largely developed and rhythmic coda." This brilliantly energetic episode is almost themeless, but there is a reference to the motif marked x in example 122. "Like a question mark, the movement ends with a repetition of the first three measures of the Introduction."

"**II.** The second movement in my mind is dedicated to the memory of my father." The movement, surely a nocturne, begins with a dissonant pentatonic- related high-register chorale for violins divided into five parts. The rhythmically shifting patterns on a single pitch introduced by the viola, later taken up by horns, recall similar passages in the introduction to Act III of *Die Hoch-zeit der Sobeide*. As a throbbing repeated-note accompaniment figure appears, nature-like sounds reminiscent of the slow movements of the Triple Concertino and the Duo are heard and, as Tcherepnin says: "There is even in it a realistic touch in the form of a 'family whistle' that I reproduced at measure 350, which is given out by the clarinet and later is developed in the coda."

Example 126

Picturesque piccolo and violin comments contribute to the nocturnal aura as tension mounts. The reappearance of the chorale-sounds brings an end to the throbbing rhythm, and a pause, after which a new section commences with an oboe melody, darkly accompanied in a plaintive pungency of Stravinskian dimension. Final references to the single-pitch horn-pattern and the chorale complete the movement.

III. The third movement, *Allegro*, begins without a break. Tcherepnin describes it as "an energetic rush in a constantly mounting *crescendo*." It opens with a grotesque timpani pattern in fourths: related, of course, to the pentatonic. Much of the movement, a brilliant exercise in the comedy of mania, is centered on fragments of this derisive theme:

Example 127

Example 128

which is constantly adumbrated, but not actually heard in full until the piece is well under way, and so reprised only a few times. In later restatements, it is combined with the timpani pattern.

As the movement progresses, the originally square rhythms are enlivened by superimposed 5/8 interpoints. There is a last statement of the main theme, and an orchestral buildup over the timpani pattern brings the opening of the finale.

IV. "The fourth movement [begins] with a short introduction [and] evolves into a rondo (*Allegretto*)." The opening, a rather harsh brass chorale is answered by doleful woodwind sounds; four-note scale patterns (rising and falling superimposed) serve as transition to the main body of the Rondo, based on the following theme:

Freely nine-step but suggesting E-flat major, it is accompanied by hints of G major (notably, the first clarinet *arpeggio*). The characteristic "rhythm c" suggesting first-movement introductory chords appears (Example 130), and a one-note melody (repeated Ds in G major) is presently restated by woodwinds in more fully-pitched form (example 131) with notably Stravinskyesque effect passing then to horns and back to violins. A half-step figure heard between its phrases (Example 132) will also bear watching.

Example 129

Example 131

Example 130

The Rondo theme reappears, now expanded into a *moto perpetuo* underpinned by brass chords. There is a brilliant codetta for piano and woodwinds which promises an E-flat cadence, but instead, a new theme erupts in trumpets, again exemplifying the characteristic scale-pattern of motif a:

Example 132

A developmental passage on the rondo-theme soon dies away into rhythm c in timpani. A new piccolo theme, taken up by brass, provides a route to an extensive development of the one-note melody and its variants (ex. 131) in alternation with example 133, example 132 also being heard in a continually reiterating version. Fragments of the main theme are now mixed into the discussion. There is a jubilant climax on the melody; then *pizzicato*-accompanied woodwind fragments of the main theme lead to a full thematic restatement in the strings.

Example 133

Rhythm c returns; repetitions of motif b (flute-piccolo) then alternate with the opening of ex. 133. The theme begins one last time, now leading to a new rhythmic triplet figure; then massive chords, suggesting the opening of the symphony in a context of accrued grandeur, bring the work to a close with a controlled yet shattering sonic explosion.

❄ ❄ ❄

SYMPHONIST ON COMMISSION

Perhaps no work of Tcherepnin's has elicited judgments so wildly contradictory as the Symphony No. 3. Reich thought most highly of it, as a repository of "urgent personal confession," others adjudge it a surprisingly weak effort, given the high level of achievement that marks Tcherepnin's other works in the form. The composer himself tended toward the latter opinion, and would certainly not be pleased to know that, of all his symphonies, it was this one that first became available on compact disc.

Some Tcherepnin scholars, however, made a point of telling the composer's widow, Ming, that they were pleasantly surprised by the music that emerged from this disc. In the habit of dismissing the piece as warmed-over slumgullion, they discovered it was considerably better than they thought.

It may be argued, in fact, that the Third Symphony was a necessary and beneficial step in Tcherepnin's development into a composer whose natural and normal means of expression was-at last-the symphony. Producing this piece proved to him at least that he did not need the stimulus of dreading the marriage-trauma or suffering the privations of a world war in order to unlock his capacity to think on the largest musical scale.

Tcherepnin's experience with the Third Symphony also gave him valuable, if unpleasant, experience in accommodating to, or exercising control over, the patrons who would commission some of his works in his newly adopted home of America.

To be sure, Tcherepnin did not need to come to America to experience unpleasantness in connection with patronage. An enigmatic passage near the end of his French autobiography describes a deep shadow that was suddenly cast over the creation of his Fourth Concerto (originally called Fantasy for Piano and Orchestra).

"In the basement of Mme. Amos's Rue de Rivoli apartment," wrote the composer, "there is a Chinese room decorated entirely by furnishings, paintings, rugs and Chinese objects that Mme. Amos had herself brought back from China on one of the many voyages that took her to all corners of the world. In this room, its draped windows lit by a little lamp adroitly hidden in a censer before a golden statue of Buddha, I completely recaptured the feeling of being in China.

"The idea came to me to compose a work for which my point of departure would be this room, whose evocative charms set my imagination in motion. In August 1946, I spoke to Madame Amos about this project, which she greeted with her habitual benevolence, and I set about composing the work which would become a Fantasy for Piano and Orchestra.

"I only had the time to sketch the opening of the first movement-'The Enchantment of the Eastern Chamber'-when, in this same room, an unhappy event took place that transformed the place into a 'haunted room' for me.

"Time, the unique healer of all wounds, permitted me to come to the moment that I could pass beyond this event, [and] in June, 1947, I resumed composition of the Fantasy."

Tcherepnin never revealed what the traumatic experience was that had interrupted the composition of the Fourth Concerto for almost a year. The composer's son Serge explored the question, however, and now believes that the nature of the event may be inferred from the following piteous plea, which Tcherepnin reportedly made to an artist who was then also working at Mme. Amos's: "Don't leave me in that apartment alone with that woman!"

The composer's experience with the American patroness Patricia Gordon had ups and downs of a different kind. It began with her commissioning his Third Symphony—on terms of such absurdity that one is inclined to wonder whether Tcherepnin was ever able to take the work quite seriously.

Briefly, the Third was to be Tcherepnin's "Dog" Symphony, a piece inspired by Ms. Gordon's written musings on the basic relationship of man and dog. Presumably Tcherepnin had told her of his affection for his old dogs Touchkan and Maud, and this casual remark had prompted the patroness to type up at least two versions of a "Dog" Symphony program for the composer's guidance. The more detailed of them-presumably, the lady's definitive synthesis of her pantheistic insights-read as follows:

DESIGN FOR PROGRAM MUSIC BASED
ON THE FRIENDSHIP OF MAN AND DOG

Commissioned to Alexander Tcherepnin by Patricia Gordon for Symphonic Composition, August 15, 1951

1. The opening mood suggests the bleak, precarious life of primitive man and wild dog; each making a separate struggle against cold, hunger and wilderness enemies. The deep yearning of both man and dog for friend and ally form the prelude to their first encounter. Man and dog meet and there is a conflict. Man wins and the dog accepts man's mastery

as the price of his friendship and protection. They hunt together happily in a sylvan setting. The movement ends in a sympathetic expression of the bond between the dog and mankind's children.

2.   Casually skipping a few thousand years to the present, this movement playfully views the fashionable dog show. The music bounds along through a rising, deafening jumble of dog voices in every key. Humor flashes bold and gently ironical—sketching the "Vanity Fair" side of the man-dog picture. Reaching its hilarious culmination, the movement stops abruptly. A measure of rest bridges over into the third movement.

3.   The faithful soul of the dog, as exemplified by those animals which spend a lifetime watching for the return of their lost masters, the incredible devotion of the "seeing eye" dogs, provides the substance of the movement. The primitive themes of loneliness and yearning reappear transmuted and refined.

4.   The introduction depicts preparation for a modern hunt. An atmosphere of tension and nervous expectancy pervades these preliminary passages. With a burst of trumpets the hunt begins; and races to its peak of excitement as galloping horses, hunting horns, join with voices of the pack in full cry. The composition ends with a paean to man's steadfast friend, the dog.

Tcherepnin apparently made a show of considering this preposterous scenario for just long enough to flatter his patroness, then explained that at this point he felt artistically impelled to write a symphony in pure form, and would present this to her instead of the "Dog" Symphony. By now, he had Ms. Gordon "hooked," and she accepted this proposal.

However, Tcherepnin had a great many other projects on hand at the same time, some with specific deadlines. It will be remembered that he had found little or no time to compose from the fall of 1949 through most of 1950. By 1951, he was at last learning to combine a full University teaching load with outside work, but the Symphony could not be an immediate priority: for, during that year and the next, he had to orchestrate his Second Symphony, to work out a final version of the Romantic Overture, and to set about reorchestrating *Pan Kéou*-retitled *The Farmer and the Fairy*-for performance at Aspen; moreover, Charles Munch had asked him to reorchestrate his Second Piano Concerto; as if all this were not enough, he also felt that he needed to compose new piano pieces for his increasingly frequent recitals-indeed, as Reich has demonstrated, the piano works from the 1950s were of vital importance in the further development of Tcherepnin's artistic language.

With all this activity, the composer's work on the Symphony, not surprisingly, was sporadic. After four months, Tcherepnin had done little more than begin the first movement. What he had composed, however, pleased him a great deal. At Christmas, he played Ms. Gordon the opening of the Symphony and presented her with a musical autograph, which she had framed and hung in her salon. Having grown impatient, however, she soon confronted Tcherepnin with a work schedule, specifying deadlines for each of the four movements tied to incremental payments of his fees. The composer was thoroughly disgusted at being treated like a tailor stitching a ball-gown, and decided to finish with his patroness as quickly as possible. Putting aside the music he had composed, he reached into three old Paris ballets-*Dionys* (1940) *Atlantide* (1943) and *Vendeur des Papillons* (ca. 1945)-for material he could plausibly recycle for a symphony. By spring 1952, he was able to play a completed four-movement short-score for Ms. Gordon, and the orchestration was finished in the fall.

Partly because of the nature of the material, ballet music that was not motivically suited to conventional formal exposition or development, Tcherepnin hit on a method of interspersing continual thematic evolution with episodic interludes, resulting in a form that he called "novelistic." (Ironically, the "abstract" music discarded from his initial work on the Third Symphony found its way into a ballet, *La Colline des Fantômes*.)

Tcherepnin's transformation of ballet music in the Third Symphony was emblematic, in more ways than one, of his reorientation as a composer for America. Here there was no way he could continue the ballet-centered career that had flourished in Paris, a career in which he constantly collaborated with the most admired French choreographers and set designers. The significant Dance culture in America was centered in the east. Composing for dance in Chicago could not give Tcherepnin the prominence he had enjoyed in Europe. Here, the most significant commissions were for Symphonic, operatic and concerted works, and, indeed, once Tcherepnin was immersed in the American swim, he quickly procured commissions for two symphonies (Patricia Gordon; the Louisville Orchestra), two lengthy symphonic works (Chicago Symphony; Boston Symphony), two operas (Aspen Festival; Koussevitzky Foundation) and a Harmonica Concerto (John Sebastian). With the Chicago and Boston commissions, his career would reach its peak.

❈   ❈   ❈

DIVERTIMENTO, OPUS 90

In order to give Marjorie Glock the information she needed for her translation and revision of Reich's erroneous statements about the Divertimento and the Fourth Symphony, Tcherepnin wrote his own account of the geneses of these works. The composer's very informal piece of writing is somewhat too discursive to quote in full in an analytical essay. To chop it up, however, would have been a pity; and accordingly the Editor has elected to reproduce it in its entirety on pp. 149-151, as "Tcherepnin on Munch and Reiner." The basic facts of the story are included in the present narrative.

Many composers would be thrilled by the opportunity to produce a score for a single major American orchestra. Yet Tcherepnin, in the mid-1950s, had reached a point where, enjoying a veritable embarrassment of riches, he could begin composing a score for one leading ensemble-the Boston Symphony-and, part way through, decide to give the piece instead to another top-notch group-the Chicago Symphony. What made this situation all the more remarkable was that Tcherepnin had never received a commission for a concert work from a major European orchestra (to be sure, he had lived much of his life in Paris where no major orchestras existed).

This symphonic odyssey began in 1953, when Charles Munch, Music Director of the Boston Symphony, gave Tcherepnin a check for \$1,000 as prepayment for any orchestral work he chose to write, to be delivered whenever the composer wished (ironically, now that Tcherepnin had cleared the way for producing new symphonies, he was being offered other opportunities). In fact, Tcherepnin had two other orchestral projects to finish first: the copying of the Suite, Op. 87, together with the orchestration of its last movement from the two-piano original, and the composition of *The Lost Flute*, Op. 89. As a result, almost two years passed before he was able to begin the piece for Munch, planned as a three-movement symphony.

The score shaped up impressively as a truculent utterance of unflagging intensity and rhythmic energy-a piece in which, Beethoven-like, hard work and fierce concentration were being transmuted into expressive power.

One morning in September 1955, Tcherepnin rose well before dawn to work on this symphony, conceived a shattering climactic passage in the second (slow) movement, which he notated in sketch form, and then left the house for a full day's teaching. That evening, he was obliged to attend a concert and a reception. Having finished this killing day, Tcherepnin went to bed, only to be awakened around midnight by severe chest pains. He had had a heart attack.

More than a year passed before Tcherepnin returned to the piece. Indeed, he composed almost nothing during 1956: having given up smoking after his illness, he found that, without cigarettes, he was inclined to "spy" himself-*i. e.*, to pounce on and sabotage inchoate ideas, preventing them from developing into anything worthwhile.

Meanwhile, Fritz Reiner, conductor of the Chicago Symphony had asked Tcherepnin for a composition while the two were on a train returning from New York to Chicago. As with Munch, a symphony was not necessarily required, indeed Reiner made it clear that he did *not* want a symphony; evidently he thought that the term scared audiences away, at least, where new music was concerned. According to Arias, Reiner suggested that Tcherepnin write, instead, a divertimento.

By the beginning of 1957 Tcherepnin had resumed smoking, and was again in a frame of mind for composing. For some reason, he decided that the symphony he had been writing for Munch would now be retitled Divertimento, finished in short order and handed to Reiner; he would then produce *another* symphony for Munch.

Why the change was made we do not know. Unfortunately, the pages that might tell us in Tcherepnin's first autobiography are missing (there is a gap between the completion of the Twelve Piano Preludes, Op. 85 in April 1953, and the premiere of the Fourth Symphony, in December 1958). Tcherepnin's decision may have had something to do with the vastly different personalities of Munch and Reiner. Munch, an easygoing, generous, warm Alsatian, was an old and dear friend of Tcherepnin's. He had emphasized that Tcherepnin should feel no pressure about finishing the commissioned work, and was evidently prepared to wait patiently. Reiner, by contrast, was widely regarded as a terror-a merciless, sharp-tongued Hungarian with a Toscaninian capacity for anger, which, however, he vented with an icy, sadistic intensity. In 1956, Tcherepnin was in Reiner's best graces: the conductor had programmed the Suite, Op. 87, and was obviously anxious for a new piece from a composer who was being increasingly feted as a leading citizen of Chicago. But a friendship with Reiner could not be guaranteed to last; and Tcherepnin might have felt that with this most difficult man, it was best to strike while the iron was hot, giving Reiner a finished symphonic work quickly as possible, before that maestro found reason to lose interest. The fact that "Divertimento" was, as Arias has observed, a grossly inappropriate designation for the spiky, grimly bellicose score studded with flashes of desperate Romantic frustration did not seem to bother Tcherepnin unduly.

There is, however, another possible reason that Tcherepnin decided to reassign the two pieces as musical ideas returned to him. During the hiatus in his work Tcherepnin had had, for the first time, a serious brush with death; and this experience surely left its mark on him. He had subsequently resumed smoking in the face of sober warnings that cigarettes might kill him. He was also acutely aware that his aged mother's health was now steadily failing. Thoughts of mortality are, in fact, impossible to dissociate from the last movement of the Fourth Symphony, with its piece of Requiem chant; and it may be that Tcherepnin had begun to form plans for this symphony even before he returned to the interrupted piece-plans for a score with a slow, elegiac finale that clearly could not have been handed to Reiner under the title "Divertimento."

The unfinished piece-so Tcherepnin may have reasoned-would be much less implausible as a Divertimento: at least it was designed to have a vigorous and instrumentally brilliant finale. That work, then, would go to Reiner; Munch had said he would wait and, unlike, Reiner, he would surely have no objections to a genuine symphony. The foregoing scenario, of course, is purely speculative, and could conceivably prove unfounded. However, the remarkable promptness with which Tcherepnin finished the Fourth Symphony-it was ready shortly before Christmas 1957, a mere six months after the completion of the Diverti-mento-lends support to this theory, indicating that the two pieces were, to some extent, simultaneously conceived, and thus may have been switched to satisfy Reiner's requirements.

When Tcherepnin began composing again in early 1957, he did not resume the unfinished work where illness had halted it, but skipped ahead to write the finale. He then returned to the first two movements, and in June or early July, he was able to present Reiner with a completed work.

Reiner wrote Tcherepnin the following enthusiastic letter on July 6:

> Thanks for sending me the score so promptly. I sat down at once to study it and hasten to salute you with an enthusiastic Bravo, Bravissimo! I do not have to reiterate at this point my sincere admiration for your craftsmanship. Your inspiration seems to have grown new wings, the thematic material has sharp individuality, the climaxes develop logically and without undue verbosity-theme C in the 3rd movement with the explosive "A"-and many other fascinating details, like the farcical tuba at the close of the 2nd movement!
>
> The thing that puzzled me at first reading is the return of theme C in the 3rd movement before the B lyrical climax. Maybe I am wrong but it seems a bit "Zuviel des Guten" [*i. e.*, "too much of a good thing"]. Wouldn't [sic] B recapitulated and extended to a lyrical climax (omitting measure 625 to about 667) be sufficient?"

Tcherepnin never stated an opinion about this proposed cut. When he himself conducted the Divertimento in a BBC broadcast years later, he gave the score complete, as he had written it; clearly he thought a cut unnecessary then, and it is probable that he had also thought it unnecessary in 1957. At the same time, however, he could not have believed that the cut would do much damage, for he gave Reiner his unqualified permission to jump directly from measure 623 to measure 666.

Reiner was quite enthusiastic about the piece during rehearsals and talked of making a commercial recording. Tcherepnin furnished one of his most detailed program notes for the concert, announcing therein that the score was dedicated to Reiner. The Divertimento was premiered on Thursday, November 14, and repeated the following afternoon (Arias' date of December 14 is an error, surely inadvertent). The performance, of which a broadcast tape exists, was nothing short of magnificent-Reiner not only proved a rhythmic dynamo, but also reveled in an expansive lyric flexibility fully in accord with Tcherepnin's episodes of superheated Romanticism; the difficult woodwind and brass parts emerged with scintillating, devil-may-care virtuosity; the lyrical string lines soared with passion, the whole bristled with urgent communicative energy.

Within two weeks of their joint triumph, however, Tcherepnin and Reiner were no longer on speaking terms. It seems that Tcherepnin's publisher had given the score to all of the major critics, and one of them, Robert Charles Marsh of the *Sun-Times*, took Reiner to task for making the cut in the finale. He expressed a hope that the conductor would soon play the Divertimento again, this time restoring the missing measures as a suitable act of contrition.

Reiner was furious. He concluded that the composer was the secret ringleader in a nefarious plot to make him look bad and hotly denounced Tcherepnin for duplicity, evidently determined never to play another note of his music. Tcherepnin, annoyed at the groundless accusation, and presumably mortified at being cast into outer darkness by the home town conductor (a potential catastrophe for a symphonic composer) withdrew the dedication to Reiner from the Divertimento's first page.

It was only about a month after this contretemps that Tcherepnin went to Boston and played through his Fourth Symphony for Munch. One hopes that Munch's warm enthusiasm for the piece, coupled, as it was, with a most unexpected financial generosity, helped to dissipate the bad taste left in the composer's mouth from the Chicago affair.

The three symphonic scores that Tcherepnin completed in the late 1950s, the Divertimento, the Symphony No. 4 and the *Symphonic Prayer*, constitute a peak in his mastery, each illustrating a different aspect of his aesthetic range. The Divertimento and the Symphony are highly contrasted and could justly be said to represent, respectively, the Dionysiac and Apollonic; the *Symphonic Prayer* contains elements of both approaches, reflecting something of the agitation of the Divertimento and the spirituality of the Symphony.

The Divertimento, in particular, is the work of a rejuvenated artist in two respects: it not only displays the vigor, imagination and urgency of youth but also shows Tcherepnin returning to some of his compositional concerns and moods of the twenties (for one thing, an important episode in *Message* is evoked several times). It is Tcherepnin's renewed immersion in nine-step here that is largely responsible for his reanimation; but his approach has evolved considerably. Just as conflicts in the Second Symphony evolved from the juxtaposition of the pentatonic with the diatonic and chromatic, so in the Divertimento, nine-step material is constantly played off against chromatic motifs. Here, some influence of serialism, with its ultrachromaticism, is plainly evident. Tcherepnin does not exactly work with rows, but repeatedly fills in virtually the entire chromatic space, as is evident in the principal first movement theme quoted further on. There is even a proto-serial element in Tcherepnin's manner here of using nine-step as a kind of theme-generator within a wider harmonic context, rather than as a hermetic system.

Notable also in the Divertimento is a true thematic power in its Interpoint, going beyond the mere rhythmic emphases that often mark Tcherepnin's use of this device. The expositional subjects now unfold as complexes of pregnant motives. University teaching seems to have renewed his interest in "intellectual" manipulations. The "modular" themati.c construction of the First Symphony is also evoked, as are the asymmetries of rhythm and phrasing arising therefrom, particularly in the Divertimento's first movement development section.

Unlike the many Tcherepnin works in which the question of recapitulation is skirted or rendered moot, the Divertimento has a genuine reprise in the first movement, albeit an unorthodox one. Where the First Symphony's recapitulation had been a reexposition, reprising the themes in order, but in retrograde versions, the Divertimento's reprise recalls the themes in retrograde *order*, drawing new expressive qualities from them through this change of sequence.

An aspect of Tcherepnin's expositional approach that may be called the thematic red-herring has been noted earlier: in *Message* the "basic" form of the principal subject did not emerge until its motifs had been introduced in a different form; in the Romantic Overture there was a good deal of motivic throat-clearing before identifiable themes appeared. This method is taken further in the Divertimento's first movement and, indeed, becomes a point of structural integration, for several themes are "foreshadowed" by motivic second-cousins before they themselves appear. When the material returns in reverse order, the resultant "aftershadowing" produces an unique narrative effect.

Considerably higher in its dissonance quotient than the Second Symphony, the Divertimento was never given a key designation, although it does start and end in G and observes some of the formal gestures of tonal sonata music. Even more than in the Second Symphony, coloristic innovation and brilliance is exploited to expressive ends. The E-flat clarinet is now added to the complement, with special concentration on its piercing top tones and its potency in instrumental doubling. (In the list of instruments opposite page 1 of the printed score, four trumpets are specified. This is a publisher's error, however, for the music never calls for more than three trumpets.)

On the other hand, the piano and celesta, "luxury" instruments that Tcherepnin relied on in the Romantic Overture and Second Symphony, are dispensed with. The composer also refrains from using percussion instruments (timpani excepted) in the first two movements, and is subsequently satisfied with a percussion group much smaller than those he used in the first two symphonies. This modesty, however, presents no bar to substantial and effective percussion exposure in the finale.

Even had Reiner continued to promote the Divertimento, the piece would probably not have found a great many sympathetic listeners in the 1950s. Chicago's anti-serialist critics thought highly of it, but the score's tough-mindedness would undoubtedly have alienated listeners outside of big cities; this was not a piece like *Georgiana* that could have been entrusted to a second-line orchestra. In subsequent years it has been overshadowed by the Fourth Symphony, the benign philosophical resignation of which is a doctrine considerably more comfortable than the nervous strivings of its symphonic predecessor. But in fact Tcherepnin's music has now become specific rather than generalized in expression. He has come a long way: back in the 1920s, his first two Cello Sonatas sounded as if cut from the same cloth even though he took some pains to differentiate them. Nothing of the sort could have happened with the Divertimento and the Fourth Symphony. It is as if, in order to attain the spiritual equilibrium of the latter, Tcherepnin had to suffer the spiritual unrest of the former.

Tcherepnin's program note, penned in a delicate and eminently legible hand, begins: "Composed in 1957 on suggestion by Mr. Reiner and dedicated to him." But on the photocopy made available to the editor Ming had pencilled the comment, "later not dedicate [sic] to Reiner-a long story!" Tcherepnin himself then noted that the piece was "scored for piccolo, 2 flutes, 2 oboes, English horn, E-flat clarinet, 2 B-flat clarinets, bass clarinet, 2 bassoons, contrabassoon, 4 horns, 3 trumpets, 3 trombones, tuba, timpani, percussion (side drum, bass drum, cymbals, chimes)-of which the use occurs only in the last movement, harp and strings.

"The performance of November 14th will be the world premiere.

"The tonal basis of [the piece] is the nine-step scale [with] the major/minor triad c e-flat e natural g [as] the fundamental triad..." We have seen, and will continue to see, that this statement is an oversimplification. "Among other proced[ure]s, it u-ses...Interpoint (punctus-inter-punctum)-a polyphonic device which together with the nine-step scale, I have introduced and which both are characteristic for my musical speech.

I. "The first movement-*Allegro*-in G, starts by a **sf** *tutti* of a minor second (with G on its basis and on its top) in all the octaves. It is a sort of a haunting sound which all along the Divertimento serves as a 'teaser' stimulating the chain of musical events. Only in the last measure of the last movement of the Divertimento [is it] 'resolved' into a unison of G.
"At the beginning it is used in Interpoint with the principal theme of the first movement announced by strings":

Example 135

Commencing with an array of nine of the chromatic tones (ten, including the opening chord) the theme proceeds-beginning with the major-minor triad (motif b)-to nine-step patterns. Note here and later the painstaking sequential asymmetry.

"[Now] follows the development of the principal theme," in which more motivic elements are introduced over a steady pulse of staccato eighth notes. Motif x will prove to be a red herring. There is then a culmination as the lower strings turn from motif z to the principal theme's opening.

Example 136a

Example 136b

"[This extension] is succeeded by a bridge passage with… new thematic material in slower tempo. The roles are now reversed: the new theme," having been foreshadowed by motif x, "is proclaimed in four octaves by the wind instruments while the [chordal] Interpoint to it is played by the strings." At this point, there is another red-herring: a lyrical passage for violins that serves as a kind of "false second subject." Hyper-expressive solo-cello fragments are heard, and then "[t]he bridge leads to the appearance of the subordinate theme in slow tempo" [Example 138] "introduced by the violins in high register, resting on a rhythmic basis of contrabasses in the lowest register and opposed by the Interpoint of trombones starting in low register and moving

Example 137

upwards in contrary motion to the theme." This theme, as mentioned above, suggestively resembles the lyrical theme introduced in the development of *Message* (was there a "message" here, too, as in that secretly confessional work?-note also the appearance of motif b in the viola continuation).

In passionate counterstatements (one in lush imitation) this theme acquires a rising-octave upbeat: these restatements alternate with repetitions of this seemingly neutral but significant horn theme in anapestic rhythm: "The 'exposition' part of the first movement finds its conclusion in a cod[etta], … **pp** [throughout], in which the thematic material" *i. e.*, a rhythmic abstraction of the second-subject melody," is indicated by violins and violas playing *saltando* [in] the background of a moving woodwind web and of *pizzicato*…violoncello and contrabass" (Example 140).

Example 139

Example 138

Example 140

The Interpuntal intricacy here is particularly felicitous. Bass clarinet and contrabassoon outline a 5/4 pattern against a 5/8 pattern in flute and oboe and a 4/8 pattern in clarinet and bassoon. In the example as printed, the editor has taken the liberty of re-beaming Tcherepnin's flute and oboe parts to clarify the rhythmic structure (the published score presents these lines in conventional four-note groupings).

"At the end of the coda 2 solo violins are moving upwards in contrary motion with 2 solo violas, then 2 solo violoncellos, finally 2 solo contrabasses [all] moving downwards" and all outlining motif b's major-minor triad.

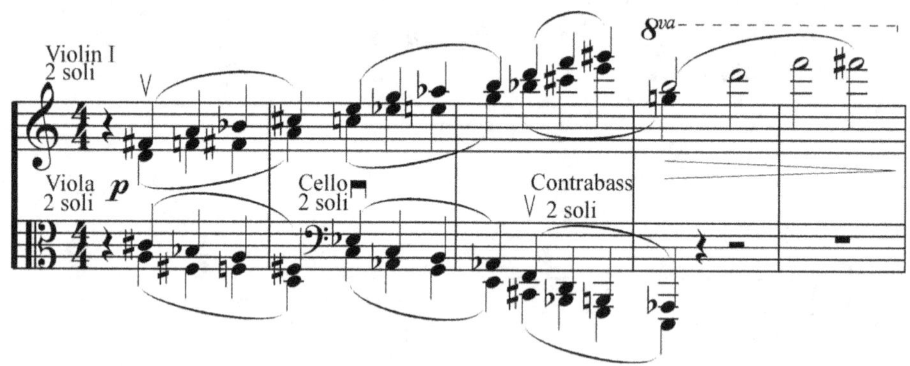

Example 141

Mention should be made of the singular orchestral coloration that so chillingly enhances the profoundly disquieting atmosphere of these passages.

This is an appropriate point to think of Sir Donald Francis Tovey's instructive game: if this were all we knew of the music, what would we expect to happen next? There are a great many possibilities, and the one Tcherepnin chooses may be the most improbable of them, and certainly one of the riskiest. To introduce new material is surely to diffuse the tension, and so Tcherepnin does. But when he begins to gather earlier thematic threads, the risk begins to pay off.

"The development (Presto 2/4 *in una battuta* [*i. e.,* one beat to the bar-ed.] starts abruptly with a new [theme] like a sudden interruption of the previous musical thought."

Example 142

Nominally a piece of na"ve Russian barbarism with the characteristic three-bar phrasing thereof, this actually emerges as 3+3+3+4, thanks to a "modular replication" in the last phrase. The gain in suppleness is surprising; and at the counterstatement, as the first violins re-enter, the stamping rhythm quickly expands to a five-beat pattern, the steadily pulsating rhythm continuing all the while. This pattern immediately contracts to 4+4, and in the subsequent 3+4+3+3 (against an accompaniment of 3+2+3+2) familiar material-motif a-appears in the second horn:

Example 143

The opening theme now bursts out in augmentation in the lower strings. This seven-beat pattern is shortened on reiteration to five beats, then three beats (quarter-notes, against a 4/8 Interpoint). Example 142 returns, but now the pattern is 3+3+4, and the up-and-down-eighth- note-scale measures take on a life of their own. The second subject (example 138) brays out in the horns, accompanied by spiky contrary motion quarter-note major-seventh leaps, along with swirling scales for strings alternating with winds. More development pits variants of example 142 against the "moving web" in a sudden piano; then 142 is replaced by a kind of "changeling"-a visitor from *Le Sacre du Printemps*, perhaps-similar to 142 in mood and drive, but beginning with repeated notes, the first tied over and syncopated.

Repeated-note and repeated-chord patterns of various lengths (some in eighth-notes, some in quarters) build the rhythmic tension, and there is a pounding climax over thundering timpani and a gentle flute-cello interlude in plaintive nine-step harmony, utilizing motif b. Then the main theme opening (motif a) asserts itself with powerful syncopations, the development, as Tcherepnin says, "reach[ing] its climax at the moment of recapitulation, which proceeds in the inverse sense of the exposition, first featuring a new version of the subordinate theme" with example 139 heard in trumpets.

Interpuntally intertwined with a reiterated pattern of a thrice played sustained chord derived from 139 (three quarter notes followed by two quarter rests) example 137 reappears, now in deep bass instruments. The "false second subject" is then invoked by strings in a violent *crescendo* up from piano, winds joining in with example 137. Suddenly, a hushed figure of two alternating chords appears, a spectral derivation from the once-rambunctious example 142. As these chords continue to undulate, motif x from example 135 is heard in flutes and E-flat clarinet, then trumpets, and there is a *crescendo* for doublebasses in octave *tremolos*. This dies away into what Tcherepnin calls "a[n extensively] developed new version of the cod[etta]," which begins with a sudden radiant warming of the atmosphere as cellos and harp evoke the 5/4 bass-pattern of Example 140. Violins contribute a 5/8 element of the "moving web." But the music that is woven becomes motif a in divided violas (inverted and normal 3/8 versions) and cellos (normal, 3/4), and the oboe begins to ring rhythmic changes on motif y from example 136. Motif z answers in horns and trombones (the 5/4-5/8 web returns).

From here on, moods vary kaleidoscopically. The changeling passes from staccato woodwinds to confident brass; then through the web, an anapestic figure from the codetta appears in violins, develops in trumpets into a jaunty fairy-tale fanfare against skirling upper winds, and then, as if waking with a start from a reverie, expands into a version of motif w from example 136, duly answered by violins with example 135. A *crescendo* culminates in a restatement of the opening theme, transposed up half a step and continuing in free imitation between upper and lower strings, and this, as Tcherepnin wrote, is "followed by a gradual *crescendo* of a scale passage in contrary motion in progressively slowed-down metrical values-which reaches its climax in the last chord of the movement."

For one who hopes to see steady artistic progress in Tcherepnin's works, a first glance at the slow movement of the Divertimento is not particularly reassuring. Its appearance on paper is very similar to that of many previous Tcherepnin slow movements, including several analyzed here (*i. e.*, in the Concertino and the Second Symphony)-similar, in other words to the standard Tcherepnin nocturne complete with string-chorale, interrupted "unpredictably" by virtuoso bird or insect sallies in the woodwinds, the whole freely organized, inevitably taking on an improvisatory air. What saves Tcherepnin from repeating him-self here is the expressive content, which deals with neither the pleasurably exotic nor the objectively mysterious, but resonates with a bitter grotesquerie: this is not an Arabian nights adventure but a real-life experience, and a rather unpleasant one.

II. Marked *Lento*, the slow movement, as Tcherepnin notes, "is in a five-part form. The first section is confined to the strings in a 6-part harmony writing":
The movement begins, in effect, with a resumption of the contrary motion that had ended the first movement.

Example 144

"The second section starts by a sudden interruption by a trumpet solo **ff** with a quarreling motif and progresses by a series of short and long solos: horn solo, tuba solo, bassoon solo, dialogue between clarinet and bassoon, bass clarinet solo, oboe solo, flute and piccolo solo, E-flat clarinet solo, harp solo-which are accompanied Interpun[tally] or harmonically by the orchestra.

Example 145

"The third section starts suddenly, like an explosion, with an entirely new theme," [Example 146] which [is extensively] developed. "

A passionate motif [Example 147] is introduced by violins, and a climax

Example 146

provoked by its return leads to the-

Example 147

"Fourth section-somehow similar [to] the first section as to the thematic material, yet in different time values: over the strings moving in eighths woodwinds are duplicating it in triplets (Example 148)

-bringing, [through] a gradual *diminuendo*, the- "Fifth sec-tion-which recapitulates by a new version and under new aspect some-what the thematic material of the second section." It should be pointed out that the bridge passage to this section is weird indeed, as the gurgling low woodwinds thin out to a single contrabassoon

Example 148

which now has a "new version of the [previous] bassoon solo...while the quarreling intervention of the trumpet is now proclaimed by tuba solo. The movement ends in **pp** by a rhythmic solo of timpani over the contra C held by contrabassoon and by the contra-bass."

III. The final "*Allegro* is in Rondo Form. The principal theme:

Example 149

is announced by the first violins" in a passage for strings alone, "and after reaching its climax is immediately followed by the first subordinate theme: entrusted to the trumpets"

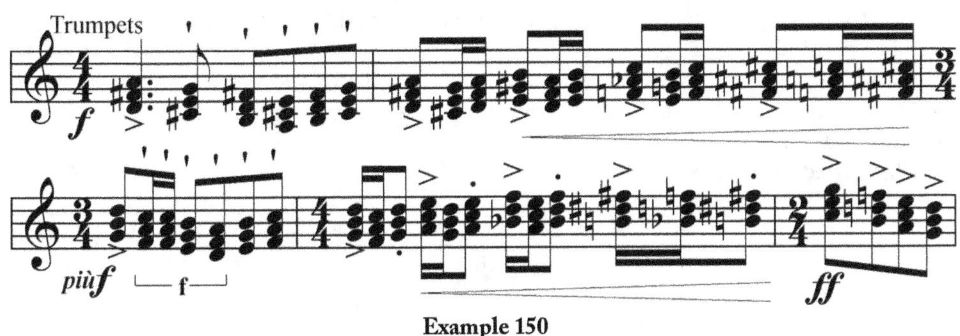

Example 150

and accompanied by delightful contrary-motion trombone figures and descending major-seventh leaps for horns and bassoon. This theme's similarity to example 139 in the Second Symphony is suggestive-both clearly reflect a buoyant "finale archetype" in the composer's symphonic gestural language. A climactic string-wind antiphony shortens the last measure of example 150 from four notes to three, then two. "It is followed by a bridge," a quintessential Tcherepnin passage for basses and violins spaced five octaves apart creating a bizarre color indeed as they play an out-of-phase sixteenth-note trill on the notes B and C, against which horns and bassoon are heard in rising major-seventh leaps.

These leaps, when they reach the woodwind and harp, become descending, and are filled in via fourths, "after which the same subordinate theme reappears presented in a rather lyrical way and widely developed in association with the thematic material of the principal theme. The same bridge which separated the two versions of the subordinate theme reappears now in a new version with added [elements] of the principal theme, reduced to their purely percussive value and entrusted first to timpani, then to the side and bass drum.

"This time the bridge leads to the second subordinate theme":

"—in tripartite form: it is of ascetic, religious, psalmodic character and is announced by the trombones and bassoons, interrupted here and there by the sounds of chimes on the note A. After a contrasting middle part" curiously reminiscent of the opening of Mahler's fourth symphony! "the religious theme returns, this time entrusted to the strings. [As] before it is obstinately interrupted here and there

Example 151

by the sound of A which [turns] out to be an *idée fixe* and finally brings all the orchestra to the unison A in all the octaves.

"Then the principal theme—this time 'transposed' in[to] ternary rhythm—returns and receives a new development [among its new features is a quirky sextuplet figure for woodwinds]—[as] before, it is directly followed by its 'satellite,' the first subordinate theme, [also] transposed into ternary rhythm…" The subordinate theme's climactic string-wind antiphony is reprised, and leads to a sonorous *tutti* where strings recall the earlier trilling figuration and winds reiterate the rhythm of motif f from example 150.

The second subordinate theme returns, decorated by harp and wind flourishes, and is developed in a syncopated chordal passage (the accent displaced by an eighth-note for many measures on end). After a climactic broadening of the rhythm culminating in a *rallentando*, the first subordinate theme receives an apotheosis "in a majestic, slowed-down version" of exalted fervor, "leading to a climax.

"The coda, which follows directly, is in two sections. The first section [is **pp**] all through… the woodwinds and strings are engaged in an antiphonal run in fast triplet-semiquaver values. It is interrupted by a sudden **ff** [roll] of the side drum which brings in the second, final, section of the [coda], based on [new] fanfare-like material announced by the trumpets, answered by horns, continued and built up to a climax by all the winds of the orchestra. The measure before last brings a sudden **pp** with the identification of the sound of the haunting minor second heard in harmonics of strings, while the last measure resolves it to a unison *on* G which directly follows the reminder of the first three notes of the principal theme in semiquaver values.

"All these explanations might give an impression of 'formal' and 'technical' approach to the composition. "It is not so.

"In my mind, the form and the technique of musical speech are nothing but ways to organize the musical emotion and by no way could be considered as [a] goal in itself.

"The ultimate goal of the Divertimento is to 'make music' ([the] German word would be *um zu musieren*), to bring to the listener the product of musical imagination free from any extra-musical program, free from any abstract speculations or manipulations of musical material.

"It is what I have tried to achieve."

❃ ❃ ❃

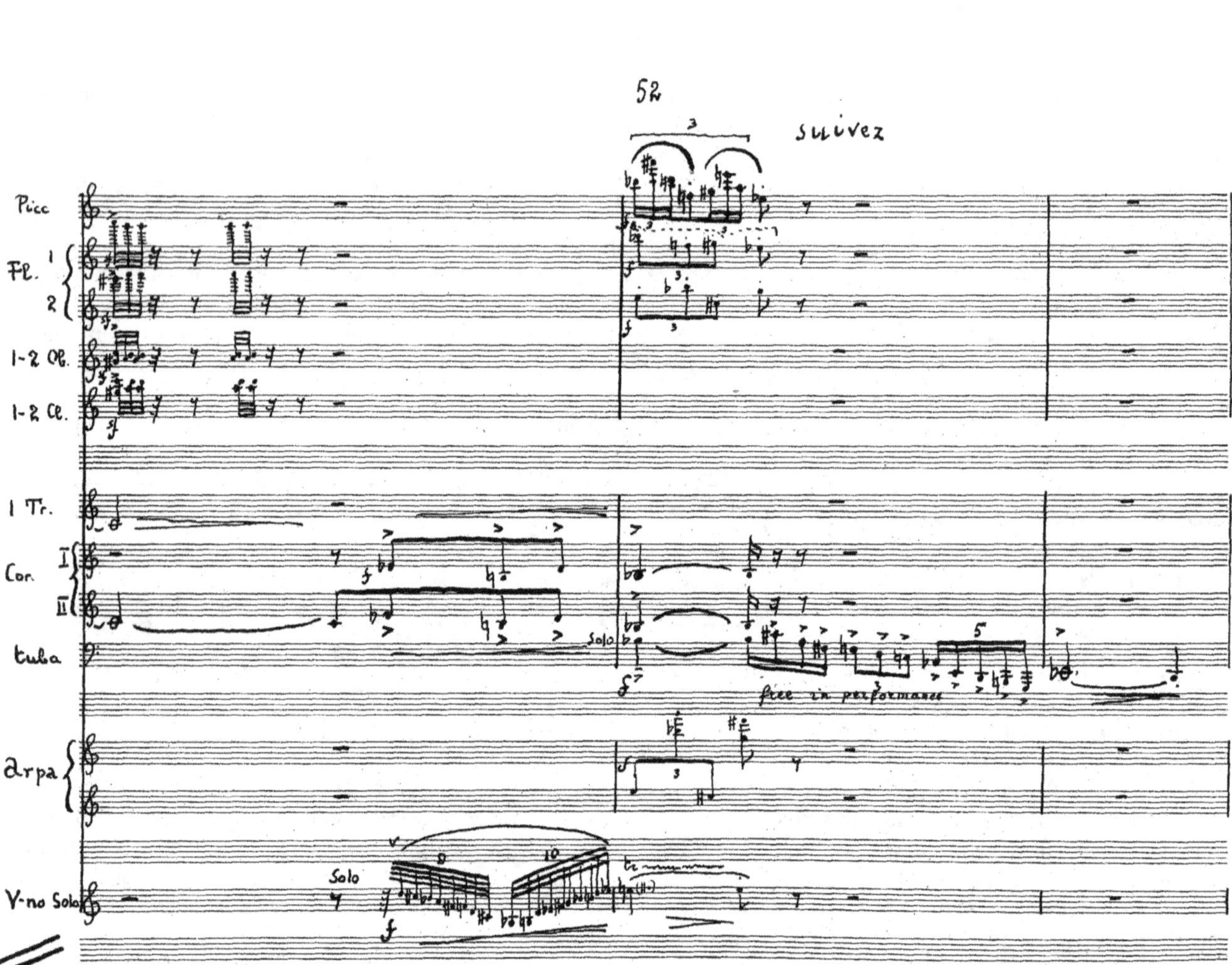

Violin and tuba solos in movement two of Tcherepnin's *Divertimento*

SYMPHONY NO. 4, OPUS 91

The complete story of the Fourth Symphony's origins is told by Tcherepnin himself in memoir called "Tcherepnin on Munch and Reiner," found on pp. 149-151. Much of the information given there has also appeared in the preceding account of the Symphony's companion score, the Divertimento.

Commissioned by Charles Munch for the Boston Symphony in 1953, the Symphony was not ready until four years later. As has been noted, however, it was actually written very quickly. When Tcherepnin returned to composing in early 1957, his Divertimento was less than half finished: yet by late December he had not only long since completed that work and seen it through performance, but had also produced the entire Fourth Symphony, having written the equivalent of one and a half symphonies in seven or eight months.

Tcherepnin conceivably felt a certain time pressure; for while Munch had assured him that he could deliver the piece as belatedly as he wished, that assurance was surely not an invitation to Tcherepnin to ignore the commission indefinitely while he went about producing scores for other conductors. And so, once Tcherepnin had given the Divertimento to Reiner, he presumably thought it wise to present Munch with a work as soon as possible—before the Boston maestro had much time to wonder whether he was being bypassed or taken advantage of.

The composer may also have been motivated by a sense of *tempus fugit*; for, as has been and will be discussed, he had new reasons to be conscious of the progress of "time's winged chariot."

When Tcherepnin telephoned Munch after finishing the Symphony, on December 18, the conductor immediately proposed that Tcherepnin bring it to Boston and stay as his house guest in Milford while they examined it together. Tcherepnin arrived two days later.

Whatever Munch thought about waiting for four years, he was delighted with the Symphony when he at last received it. According to Tcherepnin's autobiography, somewhat different in small details from the account in the memoir cited above, Munch looked over the score at his desk, then turned to the composer and asked: "How do you spell your name in English?" Tcherepnin answered, somewhat mystified, then realized that Munch was writing him a check. This proved to be for $1,000, even though Munch had already paid Tcherepnin a $1,000 fee (When the composer pointed this out, Munch observed, "one is never generous enough.") The conductor was quite prompt in programming the Symphony (although he did not match Reiner's lightning speed with the Divertimento), scheduling the premiere for February 1959. In November, however, Tcherepnin learned that the date had been advanced, and the Fourth Symphony was in fact introduced by Munch at a Boston Symphony concert on December 5, 1958.

The premiere was an intensely satisfying experience for Tcherepnin. "The music of the Symphony," he wrote, "seemed to me relaxed—balanced as to form and musical substance; I had tears in my eyes when listening to the last movement. [It was] encouraging… that Charles liked the Symphony, that the orchestra members expressed [to] me their approval, that both Charles's conducting and the orchestra's playing showed that the music of the Symphony was not indifferent to them, that they [gave] their love to the work. It was that that projected the music of the Symphony and reached the hearts of the audience."

Munch performed the piece again the following week in his two New York concert series (at the Brooklyn Academy and Carnegie Hall), and later included it in a summer program at Tanglewood, a clear indication of his high regard for it.

Like the Divertimento, the Fourth Symphony was subjected to some conductorial abbreviation. In the last movement, Munch removed the four spasmodic staccato wind chords that follow the **fff** climax before the reprise, inserting a grand pause instead. Fortunately, no critic made an issue of the cut, but Tcherepnin reinstated this anti-sentimental passage when he conducted the piece himself. The minor excision apparently did not diminish the composer's deep admiration for Munch's interpretation of the piece, and it was to Munch that Tcherepnin dedicated the published score, issued in 1959.

Ironically, Tcherepnin ultimately paid a price for Munch's generosity *vis-à-vis* the Fourth Symphony. Offered the opportunity, shortly after the premiere, to have the piece recorded in state-of-the-art stereo by Igor Markevich in London, for the new, then-prestigious Everest label, Tcherepnin squelched the project through inaction, feeling that Munch had earned the right to make the first recording. The Symphony's fortunes would have benefitted immensely from a first-class disc by the celebrated Markevich, and the composer later had reason to regret that it was never made; for Munch died just before his projected taping sessions of the score.

And yet all in all, there is an ultimate justice in Tcherepnin's decision to reserve the score for Munch, since the conductor's style unquestionably influenced its musical language. The composer's son Ivan reports that Tcherepnin consciously gave the Fourth Symphony an expressive character congruent with Munch's musical personality: it was accordingly planned as an "emotional" rather than "cerebral" work. Tcherepnin was conscious that this approach would enable him to do something he had never risked before—namely, to compose a real Russian Symphony in the Tchaikovsky tradition.

Indeed, from the stylistic point of view, the Fourth Symphony is preeminently a work of reconciliation. Modernistic narrative is reconciled with traditional forms such as the classical sonata-allegro and the romantic waltz, and with the nineteenth-century notion of the "cyclical" recurrence of first movement material in later movements-something Tcherepnin had usually avoided in previous works; nine-step writing, hints of the pentatonic, and complete twelve-note series are reconciled with functional tonality; even the rhythms and phrase structures bow to tradition: for, while they have Tcherepnin's customary suppleness, they are much closer to Romantic symmetry than was the case in the Divertimento. The obsessive pentuple cross-rhythms and willfully irregular counterstatements of that work take second place here to a more nominally "square" metrical treatment, more fully approximating the broad periods of Romantic narration.

The first movement form is particularly exceptional for Tcherepnin. As far back as *Message*, in 1926, he had virtually eliminated the reprise from a sonata-allegro, and this modernist distaste for exact or parallel repetition became a fairly predictable feature of his extended works. The first-movement recapitulations of Tcherepnin's first three symphonies were all heterodox as a matter of principle: in the First Symphony a reexposition with the themes in retrograde replaced the standard reprise; the recapitulation was almost nonexistent in the Second Symphony and became completely so in the Third Symphony; in the symphony that Tcherepnin styled "Divertimento," the recapitulation presented the themes in reverse order and was overtly developmental in cast. In the Fourth Symphony, however, the first-movement reprise is normal (albeit too compressed to be completely Classical), rounding off the movement so convincingly that only the briefest and most allusive of codas is subsequently needed.

In a yet more elegant abstention from frills, Tcherepnin dispenses with the opening introduction, even eschewing preparatory rhetorical gestures. The musical argument instead commences *in medias res* with the most unpretentious simplicity. Tcherepnin had similarly begun the Divertimento with its main musical argument, but in his previous three symphonies he had required slow introductions, and had resorted to such prefatory passages in smaller-scaled works as well-even such tightly-woven efforts as *Message* and the first movement of the Piano Trio. The Editor does not mean to imply that a slow introduction is a fault; merely that in some cases, a composer demonstrates a special grace and finesse of movement by avoiding one, as Tcherepnin has done in this Symphony. Another dividend of such reticence is that an impression of exceptionally clean formal lines emerges, reflecting the genuine classical spirit.

The key scheme here also follows the traditional classical outline. Tcherepnin originally called the piece Symphony No. 4 in E, and it seems a pity that he later withdrew the key designation, because here it is eminently suited to the distinctly selective musical language from which the work's basic character stems. The first movement begins in an unambiguous E minor and soon makes a feint toward the dominant (B major), but then introduces a second group in the normal G major (the relative major); in the reprise, both groups appear in E. The second movement is firmly in C major despite highly chromatic episodes; the finale, like the first movement, begins in E minor and has a second subject in G major, and its closing episode affirms E minor/major in elemental, almost abstract fashion.

Tcherepnin told Phillip Ramey that he adopted an orthodox symphonic plan here because he thought that at least one of the symphonies in his output should reflect the classical tradition. The composer's impulse, in other words, was to put his life-work in order-an attitude quite germane to the valedictory character of the Fourth Symphony as a whole. Mention has been made in the previous section of Tcherepnin's heart attack, with its intimations of mortality, and of his growing realization that his mother, now institutionalized because she needed full-time supervision, would not live much longer. If it was not yet time for him to compose his own Requiem, he had by now experienced, at least, the penultimate rite of passage: the acceptance of death as a distinct present possibility-no longer to be shrugged off as something confined to the vague, distant future.

Such a realization was bound to leave a mark on Tcherepnin's art; and death is, indeed, unmistakably a subject in the Fourth Symphony, evident in the brooding lament of the finale long before the reprise, where the Russian Requiem chant is combined with the movement's opening music. The contrast with the Divertimento's last movement is suggestive. There, Tcherepnin had used a lugubrious, chant- like theme as third subject, but had done so almost in a spirit of mockery, adorning it with comically overenthusiastic punctuation in the chimes. The effect was unmistakably that of macabre laughter in the face of tragedy. This derisive gesture was clearly appropriate for the Divertimento; but it was emphatically not Tcherepnin's last word on the subject-or so the Fourth Symphony, with its rapid genesis, would seem to indicate.

Although penning a slow, mournful finale was not without precedent for Tcherepnin (see his Piano Sonata No. 1)-the Fourth Symphony example suggests very special subject matter. The direct ancestor here was the closing *Adagio* of Tchaikovsky's *Pathétique* Symphony, although Tcherepnin may have also been influenced by the bleak finale of Vaughan Williams' Sixth Symphony (also in E minor). While Tcherepnin's effort has some of Vaughan Williams' exhausted otherworldly estrangement, the Russian's piece is differently conceived as a whole, for it seems to retain a connection-and a painful one-to the life instinct, keeping, as it were, one foot in this world even as it sets one foot into the next.

Indeed, Tcherepnin, like Tchaikovsky, heightens the pathos of his lament by preceding it with a movement of bubbling *joie de vivre*; but the two composers' overall narrative methods are not otherwise similar. Tcherepnin's finale, when it comes, seems inevitable, yet it is not prepared by any Tchaikovskian foreshadowings of gloom and doom in previous movements: there are no fate-fanfares, no sepulchral bass colorations, no self-pitying string sighs. Indeed, there is an oddly child-like innocence-a mood not usually associated with mortality-about many of the themes in the Fourth Symphony, much of which stems from the instrumental coloration, and even more particularly from high-register instrumental spacings that are direct consequences of the work's basic harmonic premises.

The special unity of the Fourth Symphony's three movements is in fact abstract rather than programmatic, stemming from an inextricable linkage between thematic and harmonic factors. The simplest basic element is Tcherepnin's beloved major/minor triad; next simplest is what might be called a six-step scale derived from two chromatically adjacent minor triads, beginning on E and reading E F# G A# B D# E. The consequent "privileging" of chromatic neighbor tones, particularly lower neighbors, is reflected in the Symphony's thematic materials to a surprising degree. Most of the themes and motifs are generated by juxtapositions of major and minor thirds in a triadic context-juxtapositions that involve not only the "supersaturated" major/minor triad (actually a tetrad) with its privileged minor third, but also tetrads in which the supersaturation provides the altered tonic or altered fifth degree. In the *pizzicato* chord reiterated at the opening (G-B-D#-E), the supersaturating D# sharp is privileged in this manner, and as the principal theme unfolds, this privileging is broadened, first harmonically, then melodically, to include an entire D-sharp minor chord against an E minor chord. The opening melodic figure itself (G-B-A#) provides another, related, major-minor third context.

By outlining triads with contradictory thirds, chromatic "chains" are also generated, as in the transition to the second subject (D F Db Bb A C Ab F, or, G# E B G F# D Bb F C#). The initial second subject passage, in similar fashion, is based on a G minor triad, with privileged F#s and Ebs; the closing theme, analogous to the first, intermixes G major triads with F# major triads.

The main point of the second-movement opening theme is its alternation of major and minor thirds-the theme that immediately answers it is also based on high-register triads and chromatic neighbors thereof. Minor thirds predominate in the last-movement themes (notably, E-F#-G, F#-E-D# in the principal subject), and the peroration over the chant consists largely of superimposed minor-third patterns exploiting chromatic neighbor conflicts.

Born of so elemental a principle, the themes of the Fourth Symphony have, to a remarkable degree, the air of being "discovered," rather than "invented." In the editor's view, they have the inevitability of natural phenomena to such a degree that it is difficult to imagine that there was ever a time when they did not exist.

Unfortunately, this is a virtue that cuts two ways in a century when originality is prized as a *sine qua non*. To Hermann Scherchen, in 1959, these "elemental" themes merely seemed like cliches, and the piece so irritated him that he handed the score back to Tcherepnin after hearing the first movement on tape, refusing to listen any further. Tcherepnin maintained his good humor in his account of this affair, professing sympathy for Scherchen as a poor harried soul ambushed by a Symphony during the midst of a much-needed vacation. Nevertheless, the criticism must have rankled, and may have been in Tcherepnin's mind when he set about composing the *Symphonic Prayer*, a decidedly less conservative achievement. Other conductors and composer colleagues reacted more favorably: in 1958, the Fourth Symphony was awarded the Glinka prize, and it soon became the most frequently-played of all Tcherepnin's orchestral works.

The orchestra utilized by Tcherepnin in the Fourth Symphony is identical to that in the first two movements of the Divertimento, consisting of piccolo, 2 flutes, 2 oboes, English horn, E-flat clarinet, 2 clarinets, bass clarinet, 2 bassoons, contrabassoon, 4 horns, 3 trumpets, 3 trombones, tuba, timpani, harp and strings. With classical chastity, Tcherepnin banishes unpitched percussion instruments, according, however, a prominent role to timpani.

The instrumental treatment shows a brilliance comparable to that of the Divertimento, but Tcherepnin explores new subtleties as well. Right at the opening, the use of the E-flat clarinet as a bass to the two flutes, replacing a third flute, is resourceful and astute. These three instruments are later briefly answered by doublebasses divided in three, another indication of Tcherepnin's delight in discovering the obvious. A related "elemental" treble-*vs.*-bass contrast, one in which Tcherepnin reportedly took pride, occurs in the second movement, where the theme is superbly suited both to piccolo and to tuba.

At the first performance, the Symphony was accompanied by a brief program note purporting to be by the composer's son Serge. Actually, Tcherepnin had written this himself (following a tradition of using a family member as a mouthpiece that dated at least as far back as the beginning of the seventeenth century, when Claudio Monteverdi used his brother's name in what was obviously his own preface to a book of madrigals). The note calls attention to the nine-step scale, the procedure of Interpoint (*punctus inter punctum*) and "the rhythmic intensity characteristic of [Tcherepnin's] works."

    I. Moderato. "The first movement of the symphony…is concise in form, based on three groups of thematic material." Subtleties abound in the nominally simple opening. The music begins "on the run," for the tonic chord is not presented in root position. The reiterated first-inversion E-minor seventh *pizzicato* chords give the illusion of metrical squareness; at the same time, a sophisticated 11/8 rhythm is suggested, since eleven chords precede the opening wind "signal," and that signal itself-which will be called motif a or rhythm a-is eleven eighth-notes in length in this statement. Its repetition continues the theme in syncopated fashion, largely as an outline of the six-step scale.

Example 152

Root position is reached only at the end of the bassoon passage, where the aforementioned divided doublebasses play an E minor triad. The *pizzicato* chords then blithely step to the exceedingly remote key of B-flat (the bass G moving to F with root position again avoided) and a follow-up theme introduces elements of nine-step and an important triplet upper-lower neighbor motif:

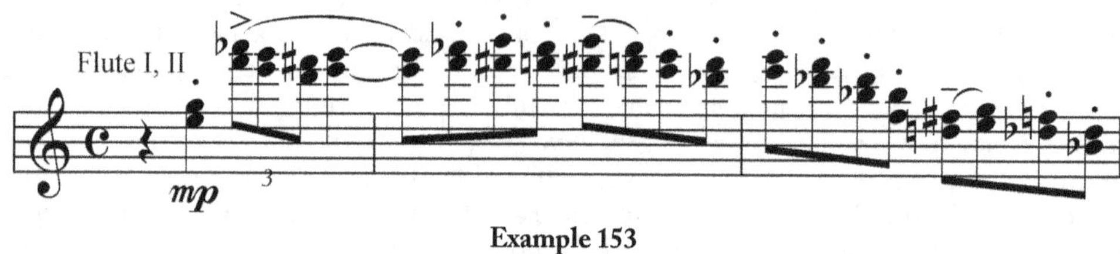

Example 153

Rising-scale woodwind swirls and horn interjections on rhythm a are accompanied by 5/8 + 5/8 + 5/4 string oom-pahs. Melodic thirds in the trumpet line, played off the doublebass intervals, lead to D-minor[7] and this important figure:

Example 154

Rapid falling sequences on motif a alternate first with example 154, and then with elaborations of half-step-*cum*-perfect-fourth patterns (both in eighth-notes- brass-and sixteenth-notes-strings):

Example 155

After a violin figure, motif c^1 (later to be of great importance): a rising bass of six-step and nine-step intervals leads to a *tutti* climax (example 157), where motif a is progressively shortened in its repetitions.

Example 156

The orchestra falls silent except for cellos and basses, which provide a bridge built on modulating triad-chains:

Example 157

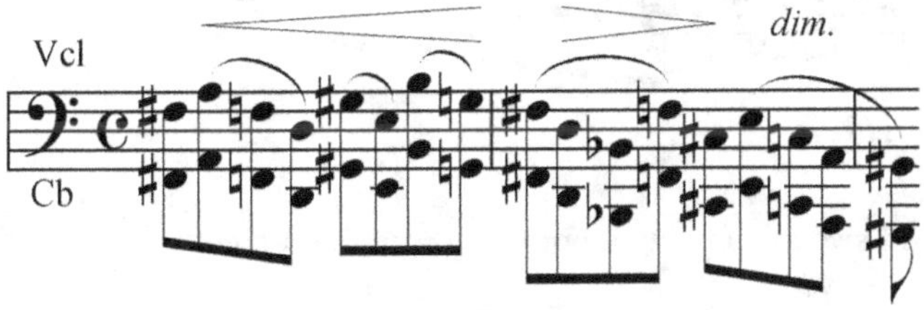

Example 158

The oboe begins the second subject (Example 159) with plaintive, self-developing G minor melody over a constant half-step viola buzzing of what will here be called motif c^2, the bass-line in bassoons showing the Symphony's characteristic obsession with half-steps and major-minor triad outlines:

Example 159

The theme is extended by the flute, with an exquisite hint of E-flat minor. As the clarinet delivers a further continuation, a descending quarter-note scale in horns and cellos passes through every chromatic note except E, which then appears to begin melodic figure b, and this, in turn leads to a triumphant pentatonic-flavored theme.

Example 160

After a climax on superimposed alternating major-minor thirds:

Example 161

another climax begins building from *subito piano*, as the following important accompanimental motif in the c family is introduced in two variants, c^3 and c^4-an interesting echo of *Die Hochzeit der Sobeide* (where a similar figure served as a flight motif for the desperate heroine) and of the opening of *Mystère*. These variants support major-minor-third melodizing in oboe (unquoted).

Example 162

The closing group introduces a six-step toy march. Like the opening theme, this is dominated by the sound of chromatically adjacent high-register triads. It is diatonically accompanied by an A-G-A-G pattern in the bass:

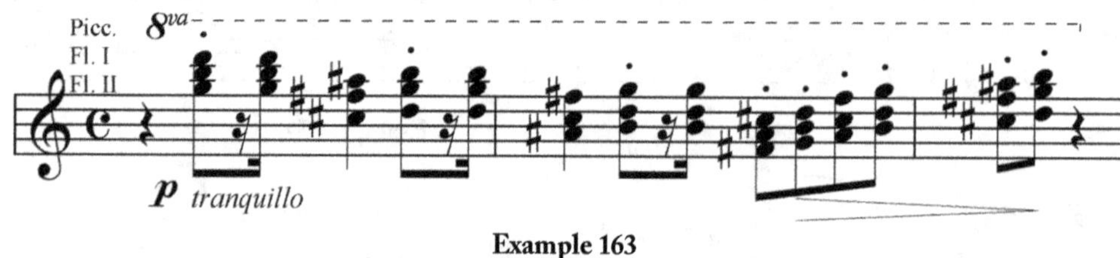

Example 163

A piquant trumpet comment and quasi-*glissando* woodwind swoops provide a note of comedy, and a coda follows of quintessential major-minor third and chromatic neighbor make-up .

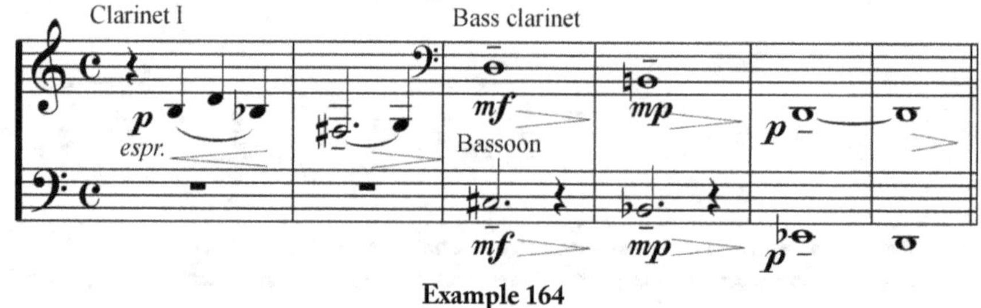

Example 164

Trumpets begin the development with *tremolo*-accompanied variant-statements of motif c^2, which are answered by flurries of sixteenths and falling motif a cascade in the manner of example 155. These materials are now extensively developed along with new material, which is usually based on half-steps alternated with larger intervals than had been heard in previous themes, and often accompanied by nine-step bass patterns. A repeated-note theme eventually blares forth:

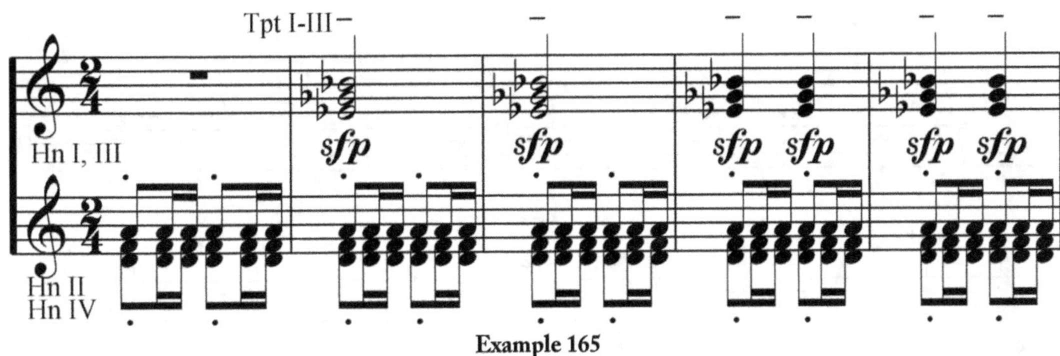

Example 165

accompanied by rhythm a obsessively hammered in repeated brass chords. Now example 154 reappears (violins), provoking this variant in diminution of the example 158 bridge:

and a fragment of the second subject in oboe over an agitated string rhythm (related to rhythm a) precedes nine-step melodizing. Woodwinds and violins reiterate motif a in falling sequence over ominously rising six-step

Example 166

trombone-tuba cello-bass chording, trumpets and horns briefly discuss motif c as six-step chords rise, with motif a then becoming obsessive in strings. Patterns in the manner of example 165 (trumpet) introduce an extended discussion: after a new bassoon theme alternating descending major seconds and descending fourths (unquoted), the pentatonic-like theme is begun by clarinet and answered by cello as flutes provide motif-a fragments; the oboe now picks up the theme, which later passes to cello and then appears in grandiose augmentation in the brasses. There is a climax with marching scales superimposed upon major-minor patterns *à la* example 158 (the contrary motion here recalls the Divertimento's first-movement close).

The return to the opening key is achieved by scalic and neighbor tonicizing rather than through the workings of functional tonality. A preliminary dotted-quarter note is added to motif a (two sixteenths and a quarter), and repeated chords are drummed out in this extended rhythm—first B major, then C# minor open fifths, then D-sharp minor, then a doubled bare fourth C-F. The D# and F indicate a close on E, and here the opening music of the symphony reappears.

The recapitulation veers off from exactness almost immediately. Timpani strokes replace the double-bass triads; the rising wind scales are heard only once; the antiphonal discussions of motif a are elided as are the 5/8 rhythms and example 154. Instead, the bass of the plucked chords steadily descends from G to F to E-flat to D, and Examples 155-158 are restated a minor third below original pitch, the rhythmic *stretto* on motif a now reproduced with lighter texture and orchestration, *pizzicato* eighth notes replacing the original agitated string figurations (here, it is the harp that provides the sixteenth-note vibration). The cello-bass bridge is presently restated on higher instruments, which raise it to the tenor and mezzo-soprano ranges.

The second subject duly appears, but in a weird recoloration, for the melody, in viola in the tonic (E minor), is doubled several octaves and a minor third above—*i. e.*, at the original pitch of G minor—by piccolo. In effect, the subsidiary key of the exposition reappears as a ghost that must be exorcised. This organ- register-evocation—famously used by Ravel in *Boléro*—gains a new dimension here, transcending the world of sound effects in a manner Ravel did not attempt.

As the melody continues and the eleven-note descending scale begins, the pentatonic-flavored melody, example 160, enters prematurely—superimposed over the continuing theme—in the cellos in E major, with basses joining in the repetition of the phrase (D-flat major). The upshot is that vastly different harmonies are produced as the original climax on example 160 is approached: motif b is chromatically deprived of its harmonic stability: A-flat major seems pentatonically inevitable, but through contrary motion resolution, the motif c episode is bypassed completely and the closing group appears in E major with the little march in flutes and E-flat clarinet. The movement ends with a last high-register evocation of motif a.

II. Allegro, tempo di Valse. Described as "sectional" in the composer's account, the second movement opens with a puckish piccolo melody, quintessentially Tcherepninesque in its major-minor vacillation (example 167, overleaf).

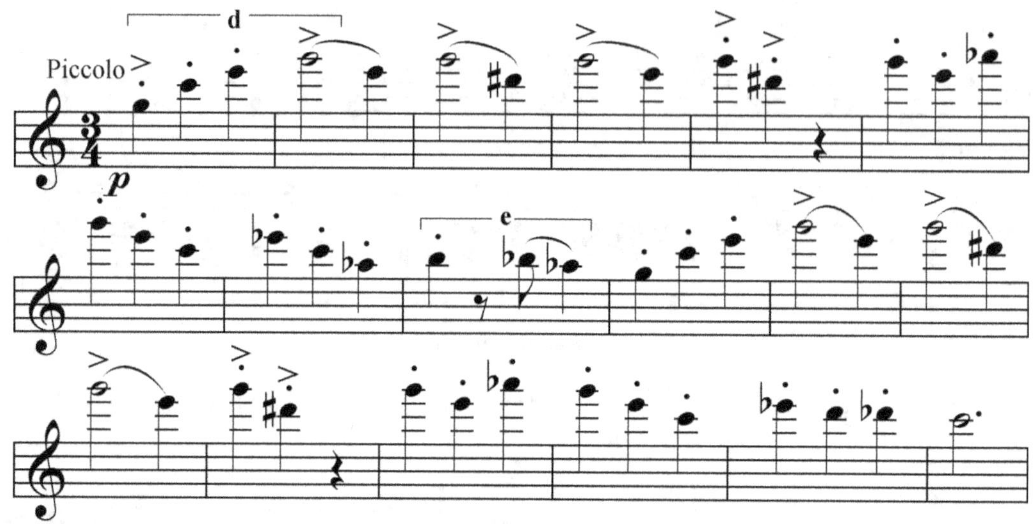

Example 167

A satellite theme, at once mischievous and elegant, and strongly reflecting the characteristic high-register chromatically adjacent triads of Fourth Symphony themes, is delivered by flutes and e-flat clarinet:

Example 168

and motif e appears in oboes-with-English horn, then French horns in a self-developing cadence-theme:

Note that here, in a manner so characteristic of this Symphony, tonicizing is achieved through scalic bass motion (Eb-Db-C) rather than chordal function—in fact, the Georgian chord (CFG) replaces the expected tonic triad.

Example 169

"In the second movement, serial chromatic patterns are used as bridges between the movement's sections." In an even quarter note waltz rhythm, the lower strings play a deadpan twelve-note theme which is echoed aggressively by lower woodwinds in augmentation; and after an oboe reference to example 167, the twelve-note theme and its augmentation return in inversion, then in retrograde inversion. Now, back in C major, example 167 is played by the tuba, the satellite theme is delivered by trombones, and the cadence-material passes from trumpets to oboes to piccolo-flute and then piccolo alone.

In an independent section, an aggressive, highly syncopated theme appears *subito* **ff**, its rhythm suggesting a barring of 3/2 + 4/4 + 3/4 + 2/2 + 1/4:

The changes are rung on these rhythms in brusque counterstatements, and in alternation with a rakish major-minor third tune:

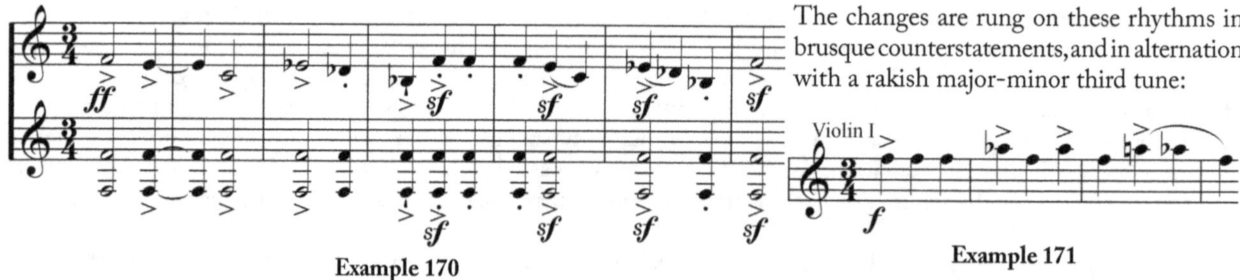

Example 170

Example 171

This discussion is interrupted by a mercurial violin solo, very lightly accompanied, somewhat evocative, in its exotic intervals, of the slow movement nocturne-flourishes heard in many previous Tcherepnin works. A trill- like continuation of this for the full violin complement continues as the discussion of example 170 resumes.

A singular type of reprise now occurs, the opening music in a sense recomposed in a romanticized dream. With long, euphonious low-string chords sustained throughout, Example 167 becomes a plaintive affair for horn and the solo second violin, adorned with a brief flute-piccolo bird-call; example 168 is irradiated by accompanying *divisi* violin harmonics; motif e is stated and varied in ghostly *saltando* chords for divided second violins and violas.

In the next independent episode, the timpani let loose with a lengthy solo. After a brief quiet interlude featuring high string chords, E-flat clarinet and a derisive piccolo:

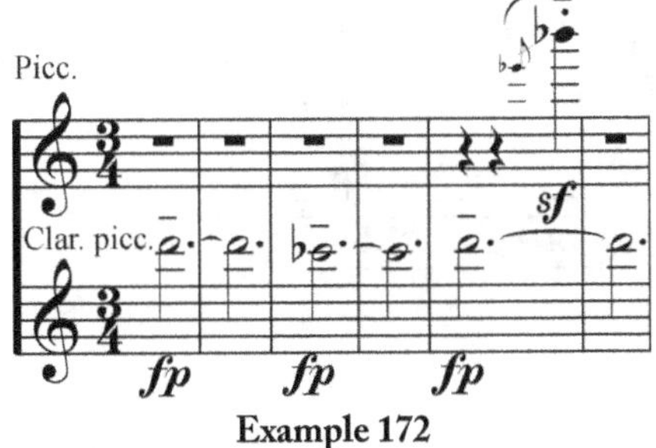

Example 172

the timpani solo returns and is taken up by the upper strings. Motif e is then tempestuously reiterated against an ominous series of three long chromatically descending notes. In a sudden hush, a mysterious twelve-note theme (beginning with three chromatically ascending notes) is stated by cellos and basses in tenths (!), answered by its retrogrades (a third apart) double tempo in upper strings:

Example 173

Horns and trumpets immediately erupt in motif e, with the three long descending notes in contrabasses and tuba. Violins, piccolo and flute then play example 173 in inversion, which is accompanied by its augmentation a third lower in viola and trombones—this, in fact, is a continuation of the contrabass-*cum*-tuba line. There is a huge climax on the motif e rhythm, repeated in a *tutti* against slowly descending chords.

When the subsequent *diminuendo* reaches **pp**, lower strings embark on a breathless discussion of examples 170 and 171. The example 170 opening is answered by the beginning of the principal theme, motif d, in horns accompanied by woodwind swirls. Motif d is now bandied about imitatively against brilliant wind or string scale passages, and a *stretto* brings a joyous full-orchestra reprise of the entire thematic complex. In a vast coda, Example 169, with its repetitions of motif e, undergoes festive antiphonal expansion (the hemiola rhythms of example 170 are intermixed), and the climax of the contrary-motion chromatic harmonies is a *fortissimo tutti* C major 6/4 chord. The horns are left to bray motif e alone as if they were visitors from Beethoven's Seventh Symphony. Then, with sly, serpentine rising-scale wind passages, the movement evaporates into an ambiguous near-tonic high-violin haze. Soft, lengthy Georgian-like horn chords tonicize *via* descending bass (Eb-D-Db), and a *tutti* unison outburst of motif e closes the movement.

III. Andante con moto. "The third and last movement," according to the original program note, "is of liturgical character." Some interest thus attaches to the fact that, up to this point, Tcherepnin had never written a note of music for liturgical use-nor would he until, as an obvious gesture in support of the ecumenical spirit (and against the exclusivistic promises of salvation offered by various sects claiming to be the "one true church") he produced his English language Mass, Op. 102, in 1966.

The opening cello-bass scale-figures trudge inexorably downward:

Example 174

providing a processional and funereal back-ground, and the violas deliver a lament as the principal theme:

Example 175

Oboes are soon joined by clarinets in a bittersweet codetta (here, the Symphony's characteristic thematic sound of chromatically adjacent triads is much in evidence). Then, through a luminous web of triadic ambiguities woven by piccolo, flutes and six solo violins, spectral muted horns deliver a triplet theme reminiscent of example 153 near the opening of the first movement.

Cellos and basses enter with the main theme and its trudging bass, respectively, now in A minor. Violas and, later, higher strings provide freely imitative counterpoints of great expressivity. As the music reaches G major, a second theme appears in first violins, violas and horns:

Example 176

After a *tutti diminuendo* on sequence f, the oboe plays the main theme in a B^7 context, and some development ensues, leading to a ferocious brass outburst. Then the second theme makes a quiet, tense reappearance over interwoven fragments of the first subject. The repeated notes of 176 are insistently restated with mounting passion in rising sequence, and there is a titanic climax on coruscating 32nd-note string-figurations, which culminates with two **fff** *tutti* chords. A pause is followed by four dry clucks from the winds. Then basses and cellos introduce the motif in Example 177, which is related to the opening of example 176, and much more saliently connected to the motif c family that had been so important in the first movement—and will continue to be so here.

Example 177

This theme persists against a varicolored series of slow, ominous chords, and tonal orientation vertiginously disappears in an astonishingly unsettling *agitato crescendo* on dense cluster-like string figures, which later die away, however, as ex. 177 reasserts itself and restores a tonal footing. Suddenly, there is a moment of radiant consolation as flutes and clarinets deliver the beginning of a serene quasi-mixolydian G major chorale, corporating the repeated-note opening of the second subject and example 177. But this mood is immediately contradicted by a stark, implacable F mino r chord, made harshly bell-like by harp doubling, and reinforced by the timpani's reiterated descending minor third (Ab-F), a clear intimation of mortality.

The G of last rites and the F of death provide tonicizing preparation for the free reprise in E, which now begins with fragments of the opening descending scale at double tempo:

Example 178

The trumpet enters, intoning the *Requiescat in pace* theme from the Russian orthodox liturgy: (This, with its repeated-note opening and rising minor third melodic outline is a kind of loose inversion of the second subject, which had begun with repeated notes and a falling-third outline.) The trudging bass then reappears at its original half-tempo, and the principal theme is restated (ex. 179 being superimposed upon it like a *cantus firmus*) with its original woodwind codetta (abbreviated).

Example 179

Now the strings intone a haunting major-minor third array (note the 3/8 + 3/8 + 2/8 + 2/8 bass rhythm). Trombones play the chant in C minor and, as the violin line shifts to the notes C-Eb, horns deliver the chant in A-flat minor and trumpets again intone it in E minor, completing the circle of thirds:

Example 180

Supported by ghostly string *tremolo*s, a series of steadily descending melodic thirds, outlining the E-bass (second) mode of D# nine-step appears in upper winds against a chromatically rising bass-a passage of elevated valedictory:

Example 181

When only the figure G E is left, the opening bass line returns, and the rising notes of the E-bass second mode scale are played, added one by one until the entire nine-note chord is assembled. Against this, basses and cellos deliver the chant theme one final time.

Example 181a

But the melody does not resolve to the anticipated low E; and nothing could be more unexpected than the brief violin solo which follows instead, outlining four supersaturated triads with romantic dolor. Winds enter with a shrill G minor chord (C# added), and, again, it is the bass that tonicizes, moving G E F# E, the music concluding on a richly ambiguous E chord.

SYMPHONIC PRAYER, OPUS 93

If Tcherepnin indeed felt, as Reich reports, that to compose a symphony was "to live life to the full," he must have felt a certain emptiness when fulfilling the obligations that piled up on him in the year following the completion of the Divertimento and the Fourth Symphony—obligations that involved musical activity on a distinctly more mundane level. In early 1958 his leave of absence from DePaul ended, requiring him to resume teaching. On April 1, Alexander and Ming Tcherepnin became naturalized United States citizens, and about a month later the composer received another of his pedagogical commissions. This was for a series of "chopsticks-like" four-hand pieces, with an easy, repetitive part for the student and what Tcherepnin called a "more glamorous part" for the teacher.

But, ironically, it was largely thanks to his reestablishment of ties with long- time publisher- and musician-friends during his visit to Europe beginning in June 1958 (ending an eight-year absence from the continent) that Tcherepnin found himself saddled with projects that impeded new creative work. First, Dr. Eulenberg asked to publish the Symphony No. 4, and since that piece had already been given to Boosey and Hawkes, Tcherepnin decided to provide Eulenberg with something else by reworking his *Chota Rostaveli* (a "lost" ballet that had just resurfaced) into a five-movement suite called *Georgiana*. This revision gave Tcherepnin more trouble than he had originally envisioned, for his approach to orchestration had so changed in the thirteen years since he had written the piece that "the original score for large orchestra… done hastily… proved to be rather a hindrance than a help." Moreover Tcherepnin realized that this old ballet music was on a lower artistic plane than the one he now occupied.

On the same trip, Tcherepnin was commissioned by Simrock to produce a performing edition of Tchaikovsky's Piano Sonata. The task, although not exactly creative, fascinated him, and he begrudged none of the effort he lavished upon it. Discarding the previous (textually corrupt) Simrock edition, he worked from the perfectly accurate text published in the Soviet Union, and was thus free to concentrate on fingerings, pedalings and dynamics, over which he took much care, spending "much more time than I expected."

It was also on this European visit that he met Margrit Weber and heard her play his *Bagatelles* at her home. Later the same evening, she mentioned that she had been wracking her brains trying to think of a ten-minute piano-and-orchestra work that she could put on a record along with Weber's *Konzertstück* and a new concerto she had commissioned from Martinu. At that moment, Tcherepnin had no suggestions for her, but the following morning, it occurred to him that he could devise a piano and orchestra version of the *Bagatelles* which would fill the gap very nicely. Mme. Weber greeted this idea with enthusiasm, and the result was yet another "recycling" commission.

It was April 1959 before Tcherepnin managed to complete these projects (he had not yet decided to do the second, piano-and-string version of the *Bagatelles*). Just about then, he received a proposal from Mrs. Geraldine Freund, a member of the Women's Committee for the "Festival of the Americas," which was to be held in Chicago in conjunction with the Third Pan-American Games in August 1959. A three-concert Pan American Music Festival had already been scheduled for the event, and Mrs. Freund asked Tcherepnin to write an orchestral piece for the opening concert. Tcherepnin accepted the assignment "in principle," but no specific details were discussed, and when the composer left for Paris on May 30, he doubted that the commission would materialize.

The time, in any event, was not a propitious one for composing. Tcherepnin arrived in Paris to find his apartment turned upside-down by painters, who dawdled on day after day, making the house almost uninhabitable. In order to escape, he arranged a few brief trips, including the visit to Scherchen described in the previous section, at which the latter was so censorious about the Fourth Symphony. On each return to Paris, the composer busied himself at his typewriter, bringing his autobiographical materials up to date, as Willi Reich needed them for his biography. Tcherepnin had also agreed to serve for a week in June as a piano judge in the Marguerite Long-Jacques Thibaud Competition, and he was to spend July in Nice teaching at the Academie Internationale de Musique d'ete. It was thus a not altogether welcome surprise when, at the end of June, Tcherepnin received a cable from Mrs. Freund confirming the commission for the orchestral work and specifying an August 1 deadline. And it was still more disquieting to Tcherepnin that, when he left for Nice on July 7, he still had "no ideas concerning the piece." By the ninth, however, the composer was comfortably installed in an apartment with Ming, Serge and Ivan, and—as a stimulus to work—a piano had been procured.

"Having thought of the character of the piece to compose for the opening of the Pan American Festival I decided finally to compose a solemn piece, a sort of Russian *Moleben*—by which in old Russia one would inaugurate any enterprise.

"I gave to it the title 'Symphonic Prayer.'

"And with this idea started the composition of July 10. I conceived a sectional form " Tcherepnin described the five parts of the score as "Processional, Emotional, Prayer Proper, Recapitulation [and] Coda."

"The establishment of the clear form was a help. Each day the composition was progressing further, and [well] before ending [the piece], I started. writing [out] the clean orchestral score on transparencies. Each day counted in this race against the deadline.

Yet we found time to go to Aix-en-Provence...to attend. a splendid performance of Haydn's charming opera *Il Mondo [della] Luna*....At that time I was behind the schedule with my [clean copy], and even with the composition. [but I eventually] completed the score at. night on August 2."

The Tcherepnins were by then staying at an apartment in Rovello, near Lugano, and the extraction of instrumental parts for the eight- and-a-half minute long *Symphonic Prayer* became a family industry. "With the help of the children and of Hsien Ming the orchestra material of the *Symphonic Prayer* was copied and partly photostated in Milan. The last part I sent to Zurich to be photostated there and picked it [up] in Zurich on August 11 on my way to Cologne. I mailed the orchestra material to Chicago from Zurich and another copy of same next day from Cologne."

Tcherepnin received no confirmation that the parts had arrived, and was thus in some suspense until Mrs. Freund informed him, by cable on August 21, that the *Symphonic Prayer* had been successfully premiered at the festival's opening concert in Grant Park on August 19, with Eleazar de Carvalho conducting the Chicago Symphony, and would be repeated at the closing concert on August 23.

Apparently, the Women's Committee decided that, as they "owned" Tcherepnin's score, they could call it what they chose, for it appeared on the program under the title *Symphonic Prayer for Peace*. Phillip Ramey, who was in Nice when Tcherepnin was composing the piece and had come back to Chicago in time for the first performance, reported that after the orchestra had finished, a man ran up on to the stage to harangue the audience about peace, demanding a "hands off Cuba" policy, and was carried out in mid-tirade by the police.

The score enjoyed a notably favorable critical reception. Tcherepnin dryly observed, "Miracle! All the four Chicago papers have reviewed the piece favorably." Because the work was supposed to be "for peace," someone came up with the idea of sending the music to the White House. Eventually, Tcherepnin received a letter expressing the President Eisenhower's thanks and good wishes for the success of the *Symphonic Prayer*. Tcherepnin later remarked that these wishes may have brought him luck, as the *Symphonic Prayer* soon became one of his most frequently played pieces.

The composer did not hear the work himself until the autumn, when Mrs. Freund brought him a tape. In listening, he "found some shortcomings in orchestration and decided to revise certain parts." This done, he persuaded Walter Hendl to read through the altered portions with the Chicago Symphony at the end of a rehearsal, and then sent the score off for publication. It appeared in print in 1960 with a dedication to Geraldine Freund. (By then, Tcherepnin had decided to make a second accompanied version of the *Bagatelles*, one for piano and strings, and he completed this in short order early in the year.)

Tcherepnin scored the *Symphonic Prayer* for what had now become his standard string, wind and brass complements, restoring, however, much of the percussion battery that had been absent from the Fourth Symphony: the instrumentation is for 3 flutes (third doubling piccolo), 2 oboes, English horn, E-flat clarinet, 2 clarinets, bass clarinet, 2 bassoons, contrabassoon, 4 horns, 3 trumpets, 2 trombones, bass trombone, tuba, timpani, wood block, xylophone, snare drum, field drum, cymbals, bass drum, tam-tam, harp and strings.

With its air of forbidding grandeur, the *Symphonic Prayer* was consciously designed to present a striking contrast to the Symphony No. 4: indeed, Tcherepnin told Ramey, while working on the score, that it would be quite different from the Symphony. Where the numerous woodwind solos and small instrumental "family" groupings of the Symphony and the Divertimento had suggested episodes of intimacy, the *Symphonic Prayer* is massive almost throughout and thus decidedly "public" in expression, its dense harmonies fraught with rebarbative dissonances, its gestures displaying a broadly oratorical, quasi-Teutonic character rarely heard elsewhere in the composer's work; this is music eminently determined to "make a statement."

As the Fourth Symphony represents Tcherepnin's reconciliation with traditional symphonic ideals, the *Symphonic Prayer* shows the composer coming to terms with the serial principle. To be sure he had made desultory use of tone-rows in the Scherzo of the symphony, but in a playful, almost mischievous fashion; in the *Symphonic Prayer* serial organization not only has considerable structural significance, but also plays an important role in determining the overall expressive character of the piece.

During his years in America, Tcherepnin had unquestionably been aware of the post-Webernites' dominant position in the European avant- garde; but their work (even Stravinsky's twelve-tone music) was then still dismissed by many American musicians as dry and formulaic. Thus Tcherepnin might well have been rather surprised to see, on his return to the Old World in 1958, how thoroughly serialism had gained the allegiance of European modernists. It is likely, in fact, that he regarded these European attitudes, so humiliatingly exemplified by Scherchen's cold dismissal of the Fourth Symphony, as a challenge-all the more so because avant-garde techniques were by no means beyond his grasp: indeed, the proto-serial aspects of nine-step (which demands that a composer deal with what George Perle calls "tropes") had prepared him to handle full serialism as if it were child's play. Tcherepnin may even have been struck by Stockhausen's remark that the early serialists' preoccupation with the number twelve was a mere superstition-that the mere existence of twelve chromatic tones did not preclude the manipulations of tonal, timbral, rhythmic and other series of any length.

In any case, the *Symphonic Prayer* happens to provide a perfect illustration of Stockhausen's post-dodecaphonic dictum, for here Tcherepnin approached serialism in a characteristically personal way, choosing a nine-step series as the first basic tone row, and working with additional series, one of them metrical.

In another provocative respect, to be sure, the avant-garde *Symphonic Prayer* begins where the conservative Fourth Symphony left off: for one of the most striking events in the coda of the symphony's last movement is the gradual accumulation of a nine-note chord from the sustained tones of a rising nine-step scale, and the *Symphonic Prayer* opens with a similar building of a nine-note chord-this, however, arising from the statement of an actual theme based on the notes of the nine-step scale. It is a measure of Tcherepnin's inventiveness that these two passages utilizing the same basic technique are so totally different in expressive effect.

Without going into great analytical detail at this point, it should be said that the "tone-rows" in this piece are quite unusual, in that they are not totally fixed in pitch content, but undergo systematic alteration to conform to the different nine-step scales. Here, for example, are the pitches of the principal row, first, as originally stated in G nine-step, then as restated in A nine-step:

D E G F# Bb B Ab Eb C--original (G nine-step)

D E F# F A Bb G# D C--restatement (A nine-step)

The metrical content of the *Symphonic Prayer* is almost ceaselessly concerned with the cross-rhythmic aspect of Interpoint. Against unchanging 4/4 bar-lines, melodic or accompanimental rhythmic patterns of 5/4, 3/4, 2/4, 1/4 and 9/4 are repeatedly superimposed. Rather than conveying dance-like vigor, as these generally do in Tcherepnin's works, the present cross-rhythms, in the *Maestoso* context of the opening and recapitulation, produce an impression of grand melodic expansiveness and freedom, along with psalmodic eloquence.

Tcherepnin's desire to evoke liturgical music in the *Symphonic Prayer*, to an even greater extent than in the Divertimento and the Fourth Symphony, is almost too obvious to require comment. The composer himself wrote that the motto of the piece is "Glory to God on high, and on earth peace to men of good will"-the opening phrase of the Gloria of the Catholic Mass. The grandiose "Processional" beginning the work is congruent with the fearful exultation that may be found in this phrase. Moreover, it is reasonable to see the percussion outburst in the "Emotional" second section as an evocation of war and unrest, with the following chant- like "Prayer Proper" as a pious reaction to the violence. The "Recapitulation" brings a new expressive note of hushed awe to the opening music (and hence to the motto) and the triumphant "Coda" is described by Tcherepnin himself as an Alleluia.

Tcherepnin provided several analyses of the *Symphonic Prayer*. Some of these are short generalized program notes, some are more detailed structural descriptions. The most illuminating is a precis of the piece, which deals with its harmonic and motivic aspects in almost bar-by-bar fashion-except, oddly and yet inevitably, with the percussion episode, which receives only cursory comment. Even though this analysis can be fully understood only when studied with the score in hand, it is not completely impenetrable to casual perusal, and, in any case, is of such importance that the Editor has decided to reproduce it here, adding some remarks about the textural and expressive character of the music, inserting some discussion of the percussion episode, and providing musical examples (in the original, Tcherepnin quoted only the principal theme).

[First Section (Processional)]

Measures 1-9 [Theme, overleaf]
Mode G III³ Nine-step tone row (principal tone row)
The tone row, [as each note is sounded and sustained], becomes a chord of 9 sounds.

Example 182

[At the 1/4 values-*i. e.*, the three repeated Ds-the chord is] "transposed" [into] modes of the other three fundamental nine-step scales:

Mode A II2   Mode D I1   Mode E III3 [this last
against a sustained D],
which is absent in mode
E, bringing the chord
to 10 sounds

thus closing the circle
of modulation

[There is also a] metrical row of [rhythmic] values, [diminishing] in length and number (number zero [bringing] the end):

4 in 5/4; 3 in 3/4; 2 in 2/4; 3 in 1/4

Measures 10-18 [First variation: theme (brass) accompanied by imperiously striding, wide-leaping quarter-notes]

Trumpet: principal row I transposed to A Mode II^2
2nd and 3rd trumpet, 1st and 2nd trombones-starting from unison building harmony

Bass trombone, tuba, vlc, cb: principal row I transposed to A mode (in octaves) II^2 and inverted
Vn I, Vn II, Vla:

a) 2nd row in mode   A II^2 straight - -   in   equal   quarter   values
b) 2nd row in mode   A II^2 retrograde (crab)   "   "   "   "
c) "   "   "   "   A III^1 inverted   "   "   "   "
d) "   "   "   "   A III^3 straight   "   "   "   "

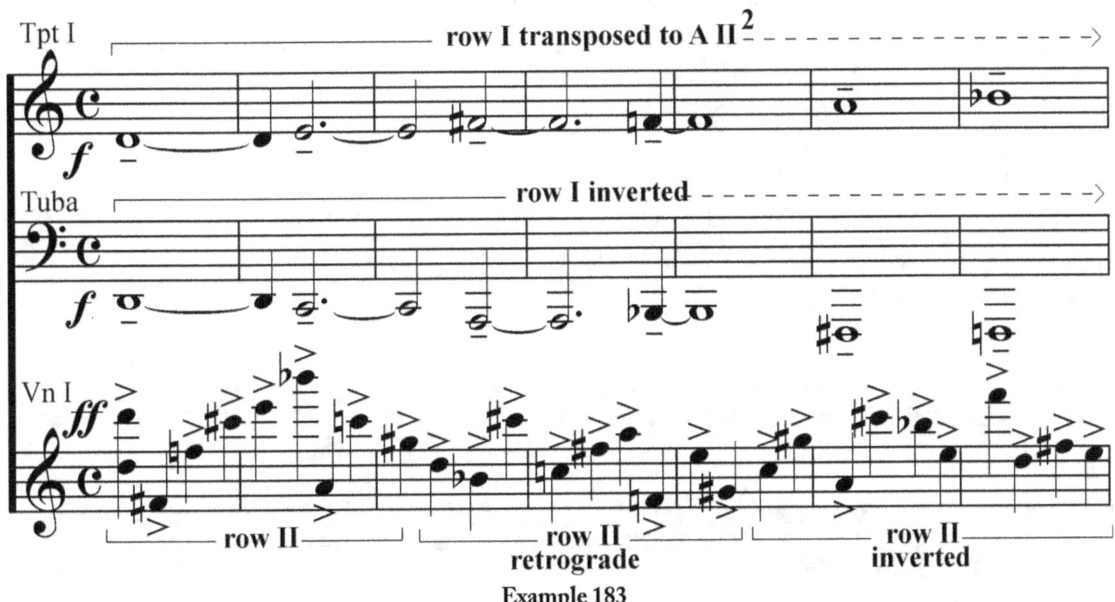

Example 183

Measures 19-29 [Second variation: Theme in chords, (chords presented by woodwinds and brass in regular alternation-striding rhythm simultaneously alternating as upper strings accompany brass and lower strings-*cum*-bsn., cfg. accompany winds).]

5/4 D I^2	5/4 G III^3	5/4 A II^2	5/4 E II^3
3/4 G II^1	3/4 D I^3	3/4 E III^2	3/4 A I^1
2/4 A I^1	2/4 A III^2	2/4 A III^3	[2/4 patterns overlap
2/4 D I^3	2/4 A III^2	2/4 D III^1	by one beat]

The free rows using the notes of the corresponding 9-step scales that are not present in the chords.

Measures 30-43   [striding rhythm continues against four sustained brass chords:

1st chord   2nd chord   3rd chord   4th chord]

9/4 A II^1 9/4 D I^1 9/4 G III^3 28/4 E (bringing (E II^2 [5th] chord)

Vn I-II,   2nd row mode   2nd row mode   2nd row   scale passage going upward E II^2
Vla,   A II^1 direct   D III^2 inverted   G III^3

2nd row   scale passage going down E II^2

Bass Cl.	2nd row	2nd row	G II^1	
Fg. Cfg.	A III^2	D II^1	direct	gradually changing from stepwise
Vlc. Cb.	inversion	retrograde		holding of E scale
Brass	holding the A II^1 nine-step scale	holding D I^1 scale	holding G III3 scale	

disposed stepwise in the limits of one single octave during the 9/4 to a buildup of the same scale by thirds, thus filling the distance between the melodic voice and the bass part.

Second Section (Emotional)

Allegro risoluto-regime of hard intervals and chords of hard intervals

[measures 44-50:   *moto perpetuo* sixteenth-note timpani outburst-repeated notes (Bb) and outlining hard intervals with low F and high Eb.

measures 51-57:   soft snare-drum triplets, bass drum punctuation]

measures 53, 54, 55, 56:   horizontal interpoint: the measures in strings are displaced by 1/8.

measure 57:   horns, bass tbn. and tuba in horizontal interpoint with the [other brass]

measures 58-64:   xylophone restates timpani solo

measure 64:   violins take up xylophone solo.

Example 184

This is presently discussed in rising sequences, repeated-note salvos alternating with the hard-interval horizontal interpoint patterns in rhythmic diminution. These materials tempestuously developed in original and diminution forms.

measure 76:   descending nine-step scale (Bb, mode II) in bass instruments, rising triplets (from snare drum) in vls. vla, cls.

measure 79:   trumpets and horns join in with repeated-note triplet salvos.]

measures 81-92:   hard triadic chords in mutual appoggiaturas with each other and in vertical, gradually diminishing in values, interpoint-

[measures] 94-95:   vertical interpoint

Meno mosso after stop announced by the gong, the soft third, in all octaves, resolved in major seconds (hard) in all octaves.

measures 98-100½: bridge passage in hard-interval chords in equal, then augmented values.

Third Section: The Prayer Proper

Here the regime is in Major and Minor pentatonic and the theme of the Prayer is treated in [an] antiphonal way- with announcements and responses (like a Russian liturgical *Ektemia: Mirom Gospodi Pomolimsia, etc.*)

Background: "hard" chord A Bb Eb E [held] in high register by harmonics of Vn I and II.

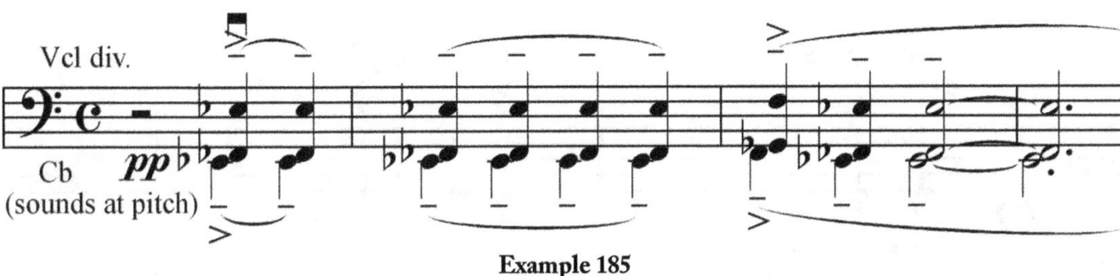

Example 185

Theme of the prayer "recited" by Horns opening in octaves same theme doubled by vle, vlc, Cb. **pp** with semitone added. Responses in pentatonic "regime" by woodwinds

NB at measure 112 first appearance of diatonic tetrad: Ab C Db Eb
Harp in metrical interpoint

Poco meno mosso **measures 113, 114, 115:**
        climax of the prayer, returning to hard chords.

116, 117, 118:   Bridge passage in hard chords first in equal, then in augmented values.

Fourth Section

[The atmosphere of hushed reverence here, so different from that created by the same themes at the opening, deserves comment. The throbbing reiterated D in the timpani has been tonicized by the E-flat bass of the prayer, in the stepwise approach we have seen so often in Tcherepnin's music of this period.]

measures 119-127:   recapitulation of the beginning in new orchestration (**pp** strings) Pedal D is [held] by fg. cfg. cb. important is the repetition of the Ped. note (D) in equal 1/4 values by the timpani

measures 128-132:   recapitulated as before in new orchestration.

measure 133:   modulation in E followed by extension and bringing new development [**pp** till now, the music embarks on a steady *crescendo* here, becoming increasingly triumphant as it reaches **ff** in measure 139 (where trombones deliver the opening of the prayer again) and **fff** at measure 151.]

measures 138-140:   chord and figuration in E theme in G III[2]
      bitonality

measures 141-142:   chord and figuration in A theme in F III[1]
      bitonality

measures 143-144:   figuration in hard intervals,
      theme in diatonic G minor
      bitonality

measures 145-149:   melodic "pattern" of five successive notes is repeated three times in isotheric way

measure 150:   *Sostenuto*-melodic unison in chords (although marked **f** will sound **p** in comparison [to] what was bef-ore and will come after)

measures 151-155:   preceded by uplift of *glissando* on harp and **sf** on bass drum, the diatonic tetrade D F# G A gives the basic harmony to a sort of...antiphonal "Hallelujah"

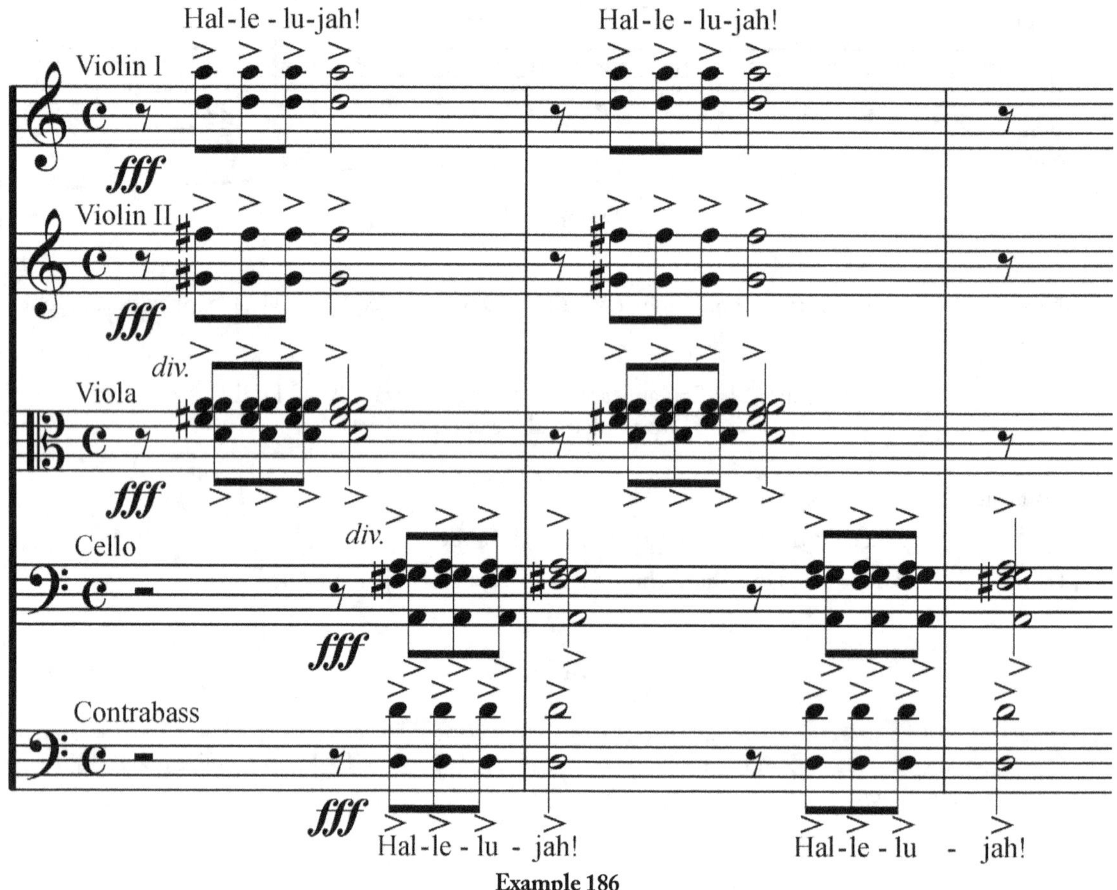

Example 186

measures 156-157:   strings [breaking into whirling sixteenth-notes provide]:
two nine-step tone rows
one eight-step tone row and   G, A, D, C
one six-step tone row: 9 9 8 6
while the woodwinds are doing the same in values of eighths and in abbreviations.

measures 158-159:   the brass brings three inversions of the diatonic tetrade, after which the composition is closed on diatonic pentade D F# G A C# taken up by orchestra *tutti* in all octaves.

While the diatonic pentade is [held] during the 2 last measures of *allargando*, the timpani, playing [with] wood sticks *marcatissimo*, are continuing the movement in equal eighths, *sempre crescendo molto*, the last three of these being helped by [bass drum], ending the composition on the last 1/8 of the last measure.

❅ ❅ ❅

CONCERTO NO. 5 FOR PIANO AND

ORCHESTRA, OPUS 96

None of Tcherepnin's more detailed autobiographical writings cover the period between May 27, 1962 and his death a decade and a half later. Thus apart from sketchy program notes, there are no accounts by Tcherepnin of the origins of the last three pieces analyzed here in Book II. Fortunately, the anecdotal material that Reich supplied is usually sufficient, and some of the gaps are filled by information found in Tcherepnin's correspondence and in tapes of his lectures and radio interviews. It is also fortunate that one Tcherepnin memoir contains an explication of the tetrachord system that he was to use in several important scores of the 1960s.

Since the *Symphonic Prayer*, with its reconciliation of serialism and nine-step, was a notable artistic and public success (the composer said in a 1965 radio interview that he regarded the piece as a kind of good luck charm), Tcherepnin might have been expected to follow it up with other works utilizing the same technique. But in fact the ever inventive composer soon began to pursue wholly different theoretical concerns, which he discussed as follows:

"[It was] probably via Japan [that] I became attracted by a sort of triad buil[t of] intervals of [a] minor third and [a] major second-which first appeared in my music early in 1940, in the little ballet [called] *Dionysus* (later I used the music of this ballet in the first and last movements of my Third Symphony).

"The chord E G A appeared in some other of my compositions as [the] fundamental chord...particularly in the ballet *La Femme et son Ombre*, and if I am not [mistaken], in some passages of the second movement of my Second Symphony.

"...In the middle part of the last movement of my Fourth Symphony...without any knowledge of it, subconsciously, I have used... the same chord, both [in its original form and] with the addition of a semitone between the whole-tone step, thus [changing] the triad to a tetrad-the chord reading now E G G# A.

"...Somehow always in my life, practice precedes the theory (so it was with the nine-step scale...) [and] I found out only later-to be precise, in March 1960-that this [tetrad] was not just...a tone cluster agreeable to my ear, but [was] a chromatic Greek tetrachord taken as [a] chord.

"So after having found [this], I understood that [the chord] was 'logical' and highly 'justifiable,' and started to [determine] if a PERFECT SYSTEM-similar to the Greek Perfect System [which] was buil[t] on diatonic tetrachords and on their modes-could not be built on chromatic tetrachords."

It is appropriate to note here that in the Ionian mode of the Greek Perfect System, an ancestor of the major scale of functional tonality, the tetrachord C B A G is joined to the intervallically identical tetrachord F E D C; the interval between the two tetrachords (G-F) being a whole step. Tcherepnin felt, however, that since a chromatic tetrachord such as A G# G E was built only on intervals of a half-step and a step-and- a-half, *excluding*, whole-steps, it was not "justified" to place a whole-step between two such tetrachords (as, for example, A G# G E; D C# C A, joined by the whole-step E-D). He observed also that "a construction of the SYSTEM by joint tetrachords" (*i. e.*, by overlapping tetrachords, such as A G# G E; E D# D B) "would bring the return of the same [*i. e.*, first] tetrachord only at the fifth octave.

"So I decided to build the PERFECT CHROMATIC SYSTEM [on] two chromatic tetrachords [separated] by a half-tone. This immediately gave a scale of 8 intervals and [afforded] the possibility [of] four fundamental modes of the Chromatic tetrachords, which I would call:

Chromatic Dorian E	D# D B, Bb A G# F, then E D# etc.
Chromatic Phrygian	D# D B Bb A G# F E, then D# D etc.
Chromatic Lydian	D B Bb A G# F E D#, then D B etc.
Chromatic Mixolydian	B Bb A G# F E D# D, then B Bb etc."

Tcherepnin pointed out that displacements of the tonic produce the following "four chromatic tetrachords:

E D# D B	Chromatic Dorian
E D# C B	Chromatic Phrygian
E C# C B	Chromatic Lydian
E D# D C#	Chromatic Mixolydian

"Of course, there are infinite possibilities of [combining] two different tetrachords.

"And the interesting feature of [the] so-constructed CHROMATIC PERFECT SYSTEM [is] that in all four modes...the missing notes [form] a chord with hard intervals only (this, however, I found only later, in Summer 1961, and certainly was delighted at that [discovery, which] brought the hard intervals into the System).

"The theor[etical formulation] of this CHROMATIC PERFECT SYSTEM was about the only semi-'creative' occupation during the second semester of the season, and proved to be of importance only more than a year later."

In fact, this system provided the basis for Tcherepnin's Second Piano Sonata, composed during the summer of 1962, and would also be a significant factor in the Fifth Piano Concerto. (A somewhat shorter discussion of this tetrachord system, containing, however, a useful diagram, appears in "Basic Elements of My Musical Language," Book I, p. 100.)

For much of his life, Tcherepnin's concerto output, as we have seen, mirrored his practical expectations as a touring composer-virtuoso. The First Concerto was apparently written with an eye to performance in Tiflis (although there is no evidence he ever played it there); the Second was produced to demonstrate the greater maturity of his artistic ideals once he had come west, but in fact both works figured prominently in his repertory throughout the 1920s and early 30s. Tcherepnin wrote his Third Concerto because he felt that he badly needed a concerto to perform in places where his first two were both well known; the reason he dropped it from his repertory after two performances was that audiences thoroughly disliked it.

Had Tcherepnin not gone to the Far East in 1934, it is conceivable that he would have then composed a fourth concerto to take on his well-worn European rounds. In China and Japan, however, he could play his first two concertos without any fear that audiences or critics would find them overfamiliar; and on his return, his need to earn a living by his pen kept him at his desk, curtailing his activity on the old concert circuit (touring had never provided him with substantial profits, for many of his fees in smaller cities were dismayingly modest). During the war, of course, no international concertizing was possible.

The Fourth Concerto seems to have been planned for post-war touring, but before Tcherepnin got around to presenting the piece with orchestra, circumstances had brought him to the American Midwest—another milieu where his Second Concerto (by now splendidly rescored for larger orchestra at Munch's behest) was unknown and could thus serve as a warhorse; nor was there any objection to the Second Concerto in Europe when Tcherepnin resumed performing there in 1958, for audiences in the old world had not heard it for at least ten years (in some cities, in fact, Tcherepnin had last played it some quarter of a century earlier). However, after the Second Concerto had been reintroduced in its large-orchestra version, it seemed desirable to Tcherepnin to have another modernistic Concerto in his repertory.

The Third Concerto might have filled the bill, but the frigid reception it had received apparently made him hesitant about presenting it now. The Fourth Concerto represented the Oriental period, and Tcherepnin, in the Europe of the early 1960s, preferred to emphasize his more modernistic output; moreover, the Fourth Concerto was an extremely difficult piece, requiring long hours of practice that Tcherepnin did not have to spare, and it was by no means guaranteed to appeal to audiences (the reviews of the San Francisco premiere had been discouragingly unfavorable).

In short, Tcherepnin needed a new concerto, and in 1963, a commission from the directors of the Berliner Festwochen provided him with a pretext to write one (Tcherepnin's Second Piano Sonata, a major work, had been commissioned for the same festival several years before, and its premiere had enjoyed notable success despite the serious last-movement memory lapse suffered by the composer during his performance). Thus Tcherepnin took his own present keyboard capabilities into account when designing the music, intending to produce another "ensemble work" in the manner of the Second Concerto, with a solo part of no exceptional brilliance, prominence, or, indeed, mechanical difficulty (and thus relatively easy to prepare for performance), but one that presented more subtle problems of rhythmic projection, solo-orchestra integration and cantabile expression.

The Fifth Concerto turned out, however, to be more difficult than Tcherepnin expected. During a radio interview, the composer told Robert Sherman that, while he had written the score to suit the style of his pianism, "I also gave myself some headaches." And in a letter to Phillip Ramey dated March 13, 1964, Tcherepnin said that, in order to make an adequate recording of the work, "I would have to practice, practice and practice—and have played it at least a dozen of times." It was apparently only around 1967 that he began to feel that he had gotten the piece comfortably into his fingers.

Actually, Tcherepnin's original plans for the 1963 Berliner Festwochen had not involved a piano concerto at all. For a long time he had been looking for a big project, and during the last months of 1961 he made preparations for composing another symphony. By the end of the year, however, he was beginning to think better of that idea: "I felt [a] stronger and stronger [conviction]," he wrote, "that the right thing for me actually would be *not* [to] undermine the success of the Symphony No. 4 [and the] *Symphonic Prayer* by composing a new symphonic work." It would better benefit his career, he thought, "to push the Divertimento and Second Symphony to follow the Fourth and the *Symphonic Prayer*—and by all means to try to find a suitable opera libretto and to compose the long overdue opera": that is, the opera that had been commissioned by the Koussevitzky Foundation (it was only later that Tcherepnin renegotiated this as a symphonic commission).

Tcherepnin first considered Tolstoy's *Ivan the Fool*, but regretfully concluded that it did not lend itself to operatic treatment (later, of course, he would provide some fifty minutes of music to a British radio play on the subject). He then looked over a libretto dealing with Stenka Razin that had been submitted to him—Tcherepnin had already written a ballet about the exploits of this legendary figure-but decided that the proffered treatment did not do justice to the hero. Tolstoy's writings were still very much on his mind, however, and soon another project began to take shape.

"I thought more and more of Tolstoy's novella *What Men Live By*, of which the moral was so dear to me," he wrote. "One day the idea came to me to reverse the development of the action and to start the opera [with] the scene in paradise: the angel coming to God to [plead] *mea culpa* for not taking the woman's soul, and God giving him the order to take it, and not to return to Heaven until he has learned the three truths. From then on, the libretto would develop according to the development of the Tolstoy story-starting with Simon returning to the village, meeting the naked man (the Angel), clothing him, bringing him home. The gradual conversion of Matriona. Teaching Michael (the Angel) to work. Then the scene with [the] General (excellent scene) and finally the scene with the woman and the two girls, culminating [in] the ascension of the Angel to heaven.

"When I understood how to do it, I 'smiled' for the first time; then, after writing down the libretto (using exclusively Tolstoy's dialogues) I 'smiled' for the second time. The next time to 'smile'—for [the] third and final time—will be when I have completed the composition—if I have the imagination and the strength to do it.

"Because Martinu… used the title of this novel for an opera based on another novel, I decided to name the opera *The Three Truths*—which will fit and seems to be a good title."

Tcherepnin began by composing the paradise scene, but immediately ran into the problem of "How to make Paradise exciting and attractive?" Other tasks intervened, but when writing the close of his first autobiography on May 27, 1962, with the prospect of a year's leave of absence from DePaul before him, Tcherepnin had confidence that he would finish *The Three Truths* promptly: "On June 2," he wrote, "we will leave for Paris, will teach in Nice in July, in Salzburg in August; then fly over the North Pole to Honolulu to stay there six weeks—to lecture, concertize; to attend the wedding of my nephew Tan Tak, for which I promised to compose a wedding march, but chiefly to compose opera. [I] probably will have my opera performed at the Berlin Festival [at the] end of September 1963…. *L'homme propose, Dieu dispose* "

Things were, indeed, disposed of differently. Tcherepnin produced the desired wedding march-two of them, in fact (one for the entrance one for the exit)-but did not go to Hawaii himself, for, as he wrote to Ramey, the summer was so "exhausting" that he elected to stay in Europe until October. Nor, ultimately, did he compose the opera, having decided instead, by spring, to write a concerto that he could perform at the Berlin Festival. In a March 29 letter to Ramey, Tcherepnin discussed his recent activities and his future plans with characteristically self-deprecating humor:

"Here are some of your old teacher's marks:

2nd Symphony Bielefeld	C
Divertimento Munich	B
2nd Concerto Munich	B-
Opera Lubeck	d
Ballet Kiel	A
2nd Concerto Vienna	B
Basel 2nd Sonata	B

"No comments about the rest, [which] included Berlin, Bonn, Mainz, London, Paris etc., but souvenirs of airports, limousines, packing and unpacking, rehearsing, dressing, performing, and lately the long overdue haircut.

"Now will look for a place where to compose the Concerto. Have canceled teaching in Nice and in Salzburg, so will have time for the next few months to round the egg. Will let you know where I. find the hermitage."

Tcherepnin's composition of the Fifth Concerto was destined, unfortunately, to take place against the background of a cruel family ordeal, as Reich partially related. In late 1961 and early 1962, the Tcherepnins had lived through the death of Ming's sister Lucy from cancer. Recognizing cancer as a family threat (it had previously killed their mother) Ming underwent a precautionary operation during the same year. Now, in April 1963, she received word that another sister, Louise, was dangerously ill in Honolulu. Ming went off to Hawaii, and Tcherepnin was alone in Switzerland as a guest in the home of his friend Paul Grlimmer, who was also seriously ill.

It was there, in a state of unusual emotional vulnerability, that Tcherepnin began work on the concerto, which, according to Reich, occupied him between April and September 1963. On the aforementioned Sherman interview, Tcherepnin said that the piece was completed in August, but the data he gave Reich was probably correct. In any case, he confessed to Sherman that with less than two months to practice the piece, he had to labor mightily to get it into presentable shape for the premiere, which took place during the Berliner Festwochen on October 13, 1963, in Berlin, with the composer as soloist and Miltiades Caridis conducting the Philharmonia Hungarica. The story has an unhappy post script: for Louise Lee Lum did not recover, and the Fifth Concerto was eventually dedicated to her memory.

Tcherepnin had already dealt with the personal tragedy of death in the last movement of his Fourth Symphony, and there are musical and emotional echoes of that work in the slow movement of the Fifth Concerto. Such thoughts of mortality as might be present in the concerto's first movement, however, take a more pantheistic, even Buddhistic form, for here we have a direct descendent of Tcherepnin's beloved nocturne-like evocations of the glories and the terrors of nature. Like the Second Concerto, the Fifth begins with measured trills—consciously or unconsciously, the composer here embarked on a road that had previously led to great success-but the trills here outline a middle-register "hum of nature" cluster that is quite different in mood from the low menacing rumble heard in the earlier work. (The notes of this cluster in fact comprise a mixolydian tetrachord in Tcherepnin's chromatic system.) What was new here for the composer was the use of nature-nocturne effects in a first movement—and, for that matter, in a movement cast in a sonata-like form.

Indeed, these effects produce an overtly "contemporary" sound-one that reflects, to be sure, the central European character of the old Bartök-Tcherepnin axis, but that evokes at the same time the pointillistic details, luminous coloration and complex, viscous rhythms of the post-Webernites. The attempt to assimilate these into a movement governed by a more typically Tcherepninesque narrative approach results in a more expansive and discursive argument than is usual for the composer. At structural turning points, full use is made of what has previously been referred to in this series of analyses as Tcherepnin's "red herring" technique, although such passages tend more often to resemble the motivic throat-clearing observed in the Romantic Overture, for they do not always have the long-term structural significance here that they do in the Divertimento. The remaining two movements are decidedly less modernistic in flavor-so much so that Phillip Ramey told Tcherepnin that they seemed to belong to a different piece. Tcherepnin conceded that Ramey's objection might have some validity.

The method of recapitulation in the Fifth Concerto's first movement stands somewhere between the allusive abbreviation found in *Message* or the Second Symphony and the extended restatement featured in the Divertimento, Fourth Symphony and *Symphonic Prayer*. Toward the close of the Concerto movement, there is indeed a section where two themes are reprised, and the subsequent coda recalls the work's opening music; but this "reprise," in context, is far more a simplification or distillation of the exposition than a true recapitulation (for here the red herrings are ignored), and the coda is as much a transformation as a restatement. Overt cyclical thematic treatment, on the other hand, takes on a new importance for Tcherepnin in the Concerto.

Tcherepnin's arrival at a symphonic orientation in America is evident in the Fifth Concerto's orchestral complement, which is significantly larger than any the composer had used in a previous concerto. The scoring is for 3 flutes (3rd doubling piccolo), 2 oboes, English horn, 2 clarinets, bass clarinet, 2 bassoons, contrabassoon, 4 horns, 3 trumpets, 3 trombones, tuba, timpani, a percussion battery conceived for 4 players and consisting of snare drum, xylophone, castanets, triangle, tenor drum, wood block, chimes, bass drum, gong and cymbals, harp, and strings. Tcherepnin is thoroughly alive to the timbres of instruments he once would have considered "extra," such as the English horn, the bass clarinet and the lower brasses; indeed his restrained and magically atmospheric use of harp to enhance the piano's timbre deserves special mention.

There seems to be a consensus that the concerto's opening orchestral introduction and its slow movement raise profound emotional issues; and indeed Reich does not successfully conceal his regret that the rest of the Concerto, particularly the last movement does not concern itself with the same subject matter. This veiled censure is perhaps unfair. Not so far into the concerto, Tcherepnin begins to introduce new material in a slyly comic manner, pairing each lyrical element with a grotesque element—a use of contrast that Reich labeled "dialectic." The warning to expect contrasts is evident, and the tenor of the finale, a quite new element for the concerto, presents just such a contrast: here, at the opening, the intended atmosphere is of a childlike awakening, with all the subsequent playfulness that such a tableau might imply. Tcherepnin would not be Tcherepnin without his entertaining moments of childlike glee; and it might be more just to regard the Fifth Concerto as a picaresque entertainment that periodically raises some deep artistic issues rather than as a sermon *manqué*.

I. Allegro moderato. As if in "dialectical" equipoise between mystery and paradox, the first movement begins with material that at first seems improvisatory and metrically shapeless, but later reveals a strong underlying pulse. Tcherepnin treats the 12/8 rhythm with subtlety, now privileging weak beats, now superimposing cross-rhythmic patterns such as 4 against 3, 4/4 against 12/8 (producing 2 against 3), and the equivalent of 3/2 against 12/8.

Out of an opening harp-*cum*-string *pizzicato* chord (a chromatic affair with E major-minor 6/4 in its ancestry), a measured cluster-trill emerges in the piano. Fragmentary answering wind comments lead to mysterious rising chords for three solo violins (unquoted).

Example 187

These fragments actually constitute a theme, which is subjected immediately to free restatements over continued piano trilling:

Example 188

Meanwhile, right after example 188A, against a rising-scale line for solo violins (a sort of red herring) the piano unobtrusively introduces this figure above its trills:

Example 189

(oboes and bassoons, then flutes and clarinets.)

which is immediately restated a minor third lower by the xylophone (with example 188B following).

At an explosive *tutti* chord, *forte* strings and winds take up the trilling, which continues in **pp** strings as the piano imperiously delivers a new theme in hard intervals:

A counterstatement against sonorous piano trills, in which winds snarl out motif e and variants thereof, leads to a stepwise red-herring theme of surging lilt

Following a display of flashing downward piano scales, the strings play syncopated chord figures which alternate with sparkling, quasi-imitative piano-comments involving motif b. The piano then breaks into wide-ranging scales as winds deliver a version of the main theme (Example 187, motifs a, b and c) in diminution, whereupon the piano

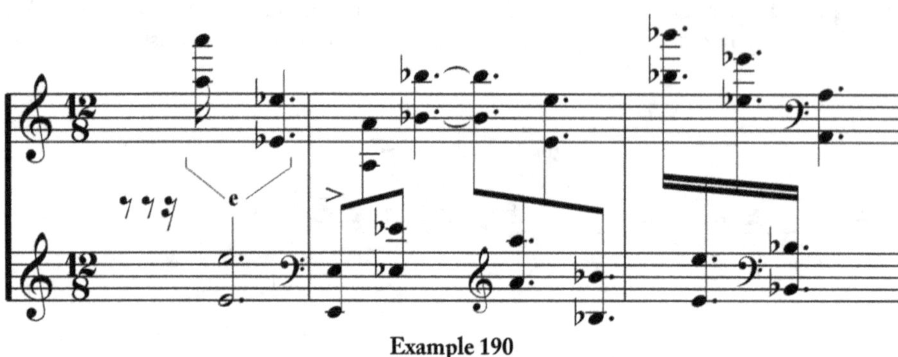

Example 190

propounds a new version of its own main theme (example 190). A bridge passage evokes the stepwise red-herring theme, and there is a climax on example 189 (strings) against flailing repeated piano chords.

An improvisatory passage with piano cadenzas follows. Then a staccato low-register theme is offered by strings, harp and percussion, but the piano interrupts with a contrary motion scale. The ensemble now gets to the real thematic business, as two new melodic subjects are introduced almost simultaneously:

Of these, the piano theme (g), which disappears after a fragmentary counter-statement, seems at first to be another red herring; but later pages will tell another tale. For now, the discussion develops as a *scherzando* elaboration of the "mountain-king" string figure f. Tcherepnin's recording of the Concerto reveals that teasing speed-ups and slow-downs such as those marked in measures 75-77 should be applied to the entire passage between here and measure 103. Meanwhile, during the course of puckish piano-orchestra interplay, the piano finds following theme:

Example 191

Example 192

There is a joyous climax on a new tune, which is heard in two variants:

Example 193

then the mood suddenly mellows as the theme of example 192 appears in English horn, revealing poignant, unsuspected lyric qualities:

Example 194

Soon, figure f creeps in in the lower strings, beginning the development section. A new variant of example 193, all the intervals changed into thirds, precedes a triumphant restatement of that theme in its original form. In the ensuing discussion, example 194 is dissected into its basic intervals, which are bandied about by the orchestra against sparkling piano figuration that sometimes suggests the rhythm of motif b. The percussion eventually joins in, and the material is distilled to an interplay in thirds (example 195).

Subsequently, in an almost Tchaikovskian outburst, piano chords adorned by a snap-rhythm march up and down through five octaves against sustained string chords (Tcherepnin is careful, however to provide metrical variety here). The piano then resumes its graceful b-motif figurations, but a climax (still on the thirds principle) presently ushers in the reprise, as the strings break into a *tremolo* and the piano delivers its principal theme (example 190), which is accompanied with new ferocity. This theme-elaborating statement (in which a syncopated dotted rhythm from the beginning of the exposition becomes prominent) leads to a lush piano version of example 194. An ardent full orchestral expansion of example 194 follows, accompanied by piano chords that range widely through the registers.

At the close of the preceding episode, a coda begins punctually: cluster trills are played by high-register violins and low-register cellos and basses, the spacing narrowing as violin trills descend and cello-bass trills rise. Against the strings, the piano delivers the opening orchestral theme in fragmentary form, concentrating largely on motifs a and b. After the trills have

Example 195

amassed into a *pianissimo* middle-register violin array, the piano gives a last statement of example 187, and concludes with mysterious wide-spaced trills, outlining the notes B C and C# (cf. the last movement of the Divertimento) as horns sound sustained spectral Ds.

II. Andantino. In its rapt, chorale-like spirituality, this brief, remarkable movement is philosophically akin to several *religioso* slow movements of Bartök's (*e. g.*, the Third Concerto). The mental atmospheres created by the two composers are curiously dissimilar, however. One might say that while Bartök is serene beyond emotion and corporeality, Tcherepnin, no less serene, conveys a gentle air of plaintive regret, condolence for which is provided through fastidious sensuality, perhaps out of the conviction that music, however spiritual, is a physical experience.

There are two themes, the first a string-chorale punctuated by piano meditations:

Example 196

Note the similarity, even in tonality between this piano answer and the main theme of the finale to Symphony No. 4, example 175. The piano, at its third answer, provides a new theme:

Example 197

which, however, seems to refer to the original theme via the repeated eighth-note melody begun in the penultimate quoted measure.

Trumpets and flutes continue the chorale, with bassoons providing a countermelody in the bass. Then example 197 appears in solo cello, with a piano accompaniment that luminously outlines thirds in a manner technically similar to the third-treatment in the first movement. This accompaniment continues as the theme passes to solo violin. After a short, meditative interlude (violins, contrabasses, piano figuration), double counterpoint is employed with atmospheric strangeness, for the chorale reappears in the tuba as a bass-line, with the countermelody heard above it in the flute. The piano's answer now becomes a reiteration of a single figure; then questions and answers are reduced to short fragments, and a rising half-note motif in cellos (C-D-E) leads directly to the finale.

III. Animato, ma poco rubato; Molto animato. As the first movement had been redolent of ambiguous chromaticism and the second of modal harmony, the third movement conveys a strongly diatonic atmosphere (although there are harmonic complexities at times, including bitonality). The movement itself is a rondo with very clear outlines. Its main theme is introduced hesitantly by the piano:

and then launched jubilantly in sustained momentum by the orchestra.

Example 198

This theme, (which, more than incidentally, exhibits the same kind of stepwise rise and fall as is found in the sec-ond-movement chorale) is especially susceptible to rhythmic manipulation, and Tcherepnin makes full use of his opportunities to vary the syncopation. Note also that while the melody of example 198B is unambiguously in D major, the accompaniment figure (Bb-Ab) seems to suggest D-flat major; this superimposition of adjacent tonalities will appear in later pages as well.

A brief episode featuring heightened syncopation:

Example 199

leads the soloist into main-theme figures, and the orchestra then returns with that theme, now accompanied by a falling-fourth figure:

Example 200

During the next episode, which begins with brilliant descending nine-tone piano scales, the falling-fourths continue to sound:

Example 201

Rapid solo passagework soon leads to a new melody:

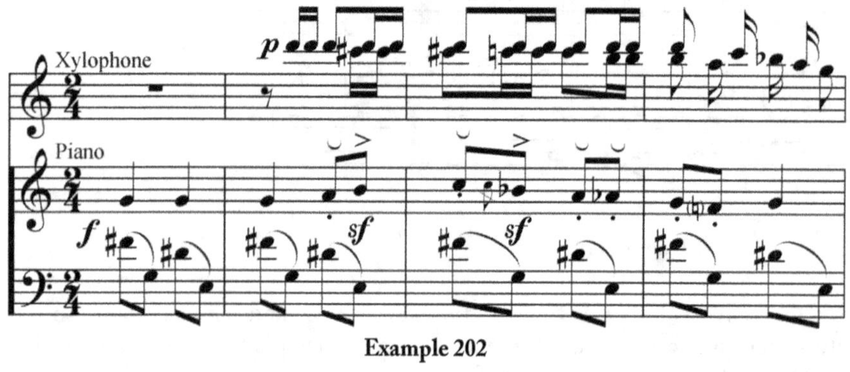

Example 202

which, like the second movement chorale, begins with three repeated tones. While this tune itself seems to be poised on C as the dominant of F, most of the accompanimental notes in the piano left hand and xylophone suggest B major-minor. The tune is restated by the piano against rapid woodwind figuration outlining thirds (as in the first movement); it is then taken up by orchestra. When it loses its opening three notes, it proves to be first cousin to the main theme, and there is a lengthy sequential build-up, culminating in a return to the original key, where that principal theme appears in an exuberant piano statement.

After an unexpected pause, the music grinds to a halt with harmonies built on a series of reiterated low-register C-sharps, and an extended lyrical episode now commences with the following theme:

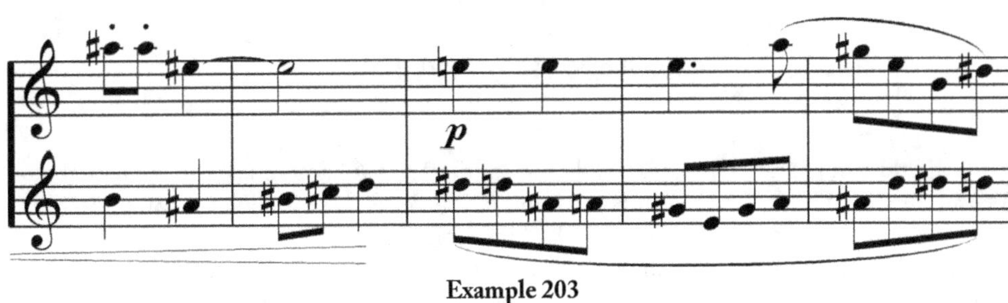

Example 203

The accompaniment figure, motif h, will bear watching. In a free restatement, example 203 is imitatively treated by piano and cellos and passes upward through the strings. Suddenly it dovetails into the interval-configuration of the main theme, and the following passage:

Example 204

becomes the subject of a rhythmically free quasi-sequential build-up.

A massive *rallentando* chordal climax subsides, whereupon gro-tesque low-register croaks introduce a comically florid trombone mini-oration. Shivering *sul ponticello* string *tremolo*s and mysterious timpani strokes follow. These gestures, however, turn out to be tantalizing red herrings; for now, the long absent theme g from example 191 in the first movement (where it was a kind of false second subject) reappears in a limpid, leisurely piano statement.

It is always risky to introduce relatively slow music into a short fast movement-the momentum may be irretrievably compromised—and experts are divided as to the efficacy of that procedure here. On the other hand, the cyclical reappearance of this slow theme serves to tie the movements together—and serves, moreover, to unify the finale, because figure h is now revealed to be the melody's opening motif. This melody is presently counterstated by violins against sonorous, undulating piano chords, and then passes to bass clarinet.

After an ultra-romantic *crescendo*, the original fast tempo resumes, and the main theme reappears in woodwinds and xylophone in a simplified staccato 6/8 version. The piano takes this up bitonally:

Example 205

with the right hand in F major and the left hand G-flat major, while the strings suggest a third tonal context (E major/C# minor). A substantial rhythmic peroration ensues, motivically based on the main theme, replete with relentless timpani urgings, descending-fourth motifs in the bass and piano figurations that alternately glitter and thunder. Two brief chordal outbreaks for the piano (the second in augmentation) precede the heroic conclusion.

Tcherepnin related, with amused satisfaction, that the final notes of the piano part were chosen partly for their visual effect. Leaping from bass through the middle register to the treble, they would swing his body around to the right so that he was directly facing the audience when the piece came to a stop.

❀ ❀ ❀

SERENADE, OPUS 97

Tcherepnin retired from DePaul University at the end of the 1963-64 academic year. He had no doubts that it was time to leave. As usual, he had a backlog of commissions, and felt he needed more time for composing than academic life had afforded him; moreover, at 65 years old he had reached retirement age.

In many respects, Tcherepnin had not been happy at DePaul, for while the eminence of his established reputation was of value to the school, his continued achievements as a composer and performer were of no interest to the administration. His leaves of absence for concert tours were openly resented in the Music Department, and his Dean treated him with genuine rudeness.

The consolations of his position were two: first, the financial security offered by the Tcherepnins' salaries was an enormous relief to him after the gnawing uncertainty and actual penury he had endured during the war years; second, he truly adored teaching, and he was truly adored by his students. Tcherepnin always maintained, in fact, that he would not have left DePaul in 1964 had he then had any outstanding composition students who needed his guidance—his sense of responsibility toward his star pupils was proudly and protectively parental. However, Robert Muczynski was no longer serving as his occasional assistant at DePaul, having moved on to Tucson after receiving a Ford Foundation grant; Phillip Ramey, with his Bachelor's degree completed, had also left; and none of Tcherepnin's current students was on a comparable level—another indication that the time was ripe for a change.

The Tcherepnins' decision to pull up stakes in Chicago and move to New York made sense for several reasons. New York was a somewhat more convenient starting point for their extensive international travel, and was frequently visited by many of their European friends and associates who only rarely ventured further west. Tcherepnin was already familiar with the city because his professional dealings had required him to make frequent trips there; in fact, he and Ming had lived in New York when on unpaid leave from DePaul during the fall semester of 1961-62, subletting Mr. and Mrs. Elliott Carter's apartment in Greenwich Village for six weeks beginning in November and then moving to the Westover Hotel on West 72nd Street, where they remained until early February.

An unpleasant truth that Tcherepnin discovered during these months—that in New York, the musical capital of America and perhaps even the world, his work was but little recognized by the general public—may also have convinced him that his residence in the city was important for his career. In the "second city," after all, Tcherepnin enjoyed a genuine local celebrity, not only as a composer respected as a leading light by the musical community but as an "eminent Chicagoan" accorded steady newspaper and broadcast coverage and exposure; the President of the United States himself had acknowledged that Tcherepnin, with the *Symphonic Prayer*, produced for the Pan-American Festival, served as a kind of national spokesman.

It was thus with some irritation that Tcherepnin wrote, "there was not one performance of my major works in New York during my stay." He went on to recount that during those months the Chicago Symphony had played *Georgiana* at home and on tour in Milwaukee under Stokowski (although he and Ming scarcely dared read the reviews, for, as she wrote, "we presume they will be terrible"). In addition, his Second Quartet and Concertino had been performed in Chicago at that time, the *Symphonic Prayer* was heard in Bonn, Bamberg and Cologne, and John Sebastian presented the Harmonica Concerto in Tokyo, Denver and Fort Wayne. "All this was very encouraging," he observed, "but New York is certainly a difficult town."

Moreover, Tcherepnin was convinced that Chicago was an artistic backwater. While boasting a superb orchestra, it did not then offer the cultural variety found in New York and the major European capitals. Little new music was played there; little of the new music that *was* played there represented the most progressive trends (fortunately, the situation has changed considerably during the intervening years). When Phillip Ramey was about to graduate, Tcherepnin repeatedly told him that Chicago was no place for a young composer and urged him to get out of the city at all costs. "I feel that New York would be the best place for you," he wrote on June 3, 1962. "Every establishment there can be OK provided you decide to learn: Columbia, N. Y. University, Mannes School, Manhattan School, 'New School' (on the 13th St)—Juilliard—wherever you enroll you will be able to work; the essential however is the artistic climate in New York, all the acquaintances that you will make, all the opportunities for you to [promote] yourself, to make friends with young composers of your age—to be in the right, dynamic artistic 'milieu.'

"So it is less important in which establishment you will study—the most important [thing] will be to be in New York-which is by now the world's center of music and art."

Tcherepnin's advice to Ramey presumably reflects his growing conviction that it was time he himself move to the center of his adopted nation's musical activities. Tcherepnin, after all was on cordial social terms with just about every important composer and performer of his generation, and it seemed likely that his constant presence among them as they passed in and out of New York was bound to result in increased attention to his work. Indeed, the Tcherepnins eventually arranged things so that when they retired from DePaul they were able to move into a permanent New York home a few days later.

During his final semester at DePaul, Tcherepnin had three commissions on his agenda, all involving Switzerland: a piano concerto (No. 6) for Margrit Weber, a string orchestra piece for the Zurich Chamber Orchestra and Edmond de Stoutz, and a cantata for the Lucerne Festival Strings. The two latter works were scheduled for performances in the late summer, so it is not surprising that he informed Ramey, in a letter dated March 13, 1964:

"The No. 6 had to be postponed." He continued, "Am now working on the piece for string orchestra and [am] hav[ing] fun with it." (According to Arias, Tcherepnin had actually begun this score in January.) On April 3, he wrote to Ramey:

"The title of the piece for strings is Serenade
"   "   "   "   "   "   "   and voice is Cantata
"The composition of the Serenade is progressing, but I still was unable to find suitable text[s] for the Cantata."

The Serenade was Opus 97; the cantata, *Of Things Light and Earnest*, in which Tcherepnin had clearly changed earlier plans to use harpsichord, became Op. 98.

On June 10, the Tcherepnins moved from Chicago to New York, where they had rented an eighth-floor apartment on Amsterdam Avenue and 73rd Street, only a short walk from the Westover, in an aged building once erected for luxury and now occupied by middle-class tenants. The Tcherepnins' residence was the front half of what had originally been an enormous apartment, and offered amenities such as art-deco moldings, huge hall and bedroom closets, high ceilings and parquet floors. To the right of a central entrance hallway were two smallish northern-lit bedrooms, the first of which the Tcherepnins sometimes used as a formal dining room. The end of the hall formed a right angle with a narrow corridor that gave access to two adjacent bathrooms. Opposite the bedrooms, to the left of the hall, a pair of double glass doors opened on to a nearly square living room (facing south into the courtyard) which abutted on a moderate-sized dining alcove, creating a comfortably open space that easily accommodated a Hamburg Model L Steinway along with various tables, comfortable chairs and a couch. Icons graced the mantle-piece of the false fireplace, and the walls were covered with pastel, ink and watercolor representations of the settings of various Tcherepnin stage works, made by the distinguished artists who had collaborated on them.

On the far side of the alcove was the kitchen, which faced west into the courtyard, and beyond the back door of the kitchen was a square of hallway with yet another bathroom to the right—this with an ancient pull-chain toilet—and an unusually commodious westward-facing maid's room straight ahead—probably intended for a domestic couple, since it was fully eight feet wide and twelve feet long in comparison to the ordinary five by ten servants' quarters of vintage Manhattan apartment buildings.

This maid's room was Tcherepnin's studio. Here, to serve him for composing, he installed an upright piano with a silencer that muted the sound to bare audibility, which still left enough space for several bookcases to accommodate his printed scores and manuscripts. It may well have been this room that led Tcherepnin to take the apartment, for it offered the kind of atmosphere he needed for creative work: being isolated from the rest of the house, it allowed him to compose without being overheard.

And yet, among the various composing nests that Tcherepnin occupied over the years (beginning with the Monte Carlo *pied-à-terre* discussed by Reich) the New York room was least ideal; for even with both the kitchen back door and the maid's room door closed, the isolation from the rest of the apartment was sometimes imperfect—traffic in and out of the kitchen could be bothersome. Tcherepnin had had more privacy in his attic studio in his Chicago house, reached by a kind of catwalk and totally removed from the circulation of normal household business. In Paris, Tcherepnin was equally fortunate, for in his Rue Furstenberg building he was able to rent one of the top floor studios originally constructed as servants' quarters, in which wealthy lower-floor tenants had generally housed their domestic help in the years before elevators. The dimensions of that room were small, but the sloping roof and dormer window lent an air of charm, and there was enough space for a piano and a desk, which was all Tcherepnin needed. At the Marlow cottage, Tcherepnin's nest was another sufficiently cloistered upstairs room.

If the New York studio was somewhat disappointing to Tcherepnin, the progress of his New York career was even more so, for his presence did not give the substantial promotional boost to his music that he had hoped. Ming assumed the generalship of a campaign to launch Tcherepnin's work in New York, cultivating professional associates and giving elegant parties at which no expense was spared, but the gains were largely social. The Tcherepnins were soon welcome and familiar figures among New York's musical luminaries, a milieu the composer thoroughly enjoyed. But performances of Tcherepnin scores out of town continued to be notably more frequent than those in New York; indeed, it remained a sore point with the composer until his dying day that the New York Philharmonic had never played a single one of his scores (a neglect that persists even at this writing [February 1992]).

Tcherepnin was full of optimism during his first days as a New Yorker, however. The slight flaws of his studio were not immediately apparent, and the disruptions of the move had proved brief. On June 24, he wrote to Ramey that he found the apartment "comfortable, cool and large," and that he was quickly settling in:

"By now, thanks to the wonderful gift of organization, energy and wisdom of Hsien Ming, the flat is already in fine shape. With the exception... of paintings that are decorating the mantlepiece or leaning towards the wall, waiting for 'hanging'-all is [in] its place and quite comfortable.

"My 'hiding place' behind the kitchen—with desk, piano and temporarily empty bookshelves, is quiet and stimulating.

"I think I wrote you that I have completed in Chicago the composition of the Serenade, but that I learned since, that the first performance in Venice had to be postponed until next year due to change in program.

"Still in Chicago I finally compiled a text for the Cantata and composed a good part of it. But the settlement in new surroundings and the interruption cooled me down about the text. So I have started here all [over] from scratch. 'Composed' myself a text and then the music and completed the composition in 5 days. The title—in German—is 'Vom Spass und Ernst,' it is for contralto and strings, is in five movements with a duration of performance of 15 minutes. The first performance will be in Lucerne on September 3rd."

The premiere of Tcherepnin's cantata *Of Things Light and Earnest*, Op. 98, took place as scheduled (Arias' date of September 5 agrees with the Marjorie Glock version of Tcherepnin's biography; Tcherepnin's date of the 3rd, also found in the Reich's German text, is apparently incorrect).

As the performance of the Serenade had been put back a year, the composer postponed the task of preparing a full score from his detailed score-sketch. Now facing a heavy European concert schedule, the Tcherepnins had sublet their New York apartment only shortly after moving into it; and the autumn found them based in one of the two large villas on the Webers' estate in Bach. Although the Sixth Piano Concerto still remained to be written, Tcherepnin had by now taken on two additional tasks. For his 1938 ballet *The Wandering Scholar who Exorcised the Devil*, which was being performed in Kiel in January, he agreed to supply a new orchestration, since the original full score had disappeared during the Second World War. He was also planning to write a concerto for two viole da gamba: indeed, in a schedule he circulated of events during the upcoming season, the premiere of the two-gamba concerto was listed for May in Switzerland. No score materialized, however, and the project later evolved into a work on a more modest scale, the *Sonata da Chiesa* for viola da gamba and organ, Opus 101.

In a letter to Ramey, dated November 2, 1964, Ming wrote: "My husband [has] decide[d] to stay here until Jan. 31st. He wants to compose the new concerto and to attend the world premiere of his ballet in Germany. But between time, he will be concertizing quite a lot (too bad, he said)....

"The concerto for Gamba[s] has not yet beg[u]n, first he has to finish the Serenade for chamber orchestra, and the piano concerto." By the close of the year, Tcherepnin had completed the ballet orchestration and the final score of the Serenade, again postponing work on the Piano Concerto.

The Serenade for String Orchestra, Op. 97, was premiered on September 11, 1965, at the Venice Biennial Festival by the Zurich Chamber Orchestra conducted by Edmond de Stoutz. A dedication to this ensemble and conductor appeared at the head of the printed score, published the following year.

Highly acclaimed at its first performance, Tcherepnin's Serenade may justly be considered the next logical step in the composer's continuing process of stylistic self-renewal. For it seemingly represents an attempt to sustain, through a full-length work (sixteen minutes), the kind of avant-garde atmosphere that pervaded the materials introduced in the first few minutes of the Fifth Piano Concerto. The very opening of the Serenade, with its mysterious, wide-spaced, contrary-motion trills behind rhythmically ambiguous melodic fragments recalls episodes in the concerto (with ancestry, in fact, in the Divertimento). Indeed, in the Serenade, Tcherepnin exploits such motifs in a new, expanded context, working with two double trills, and the striking dynamic element of *crescendo-decrescendo*s and *sforzando*s. Bitonality and polytonality, explored with a new overtness in the Fifth Concerto, are also put to more fully extended and systematic use in the Serenade, particularly in the second movement.

Curiously, Tcherepnin had never before conceived a piece for string orchestra (the Concertino, Op. 47, was written as a chamber piece for twelve soloists before being recast for string orchestra with soloists; *Suite Georgienne*, Op. 57, for piano and strings had originally been a two-piano piece; *The Twelve*, Op. 73, used harp, piano and percussion along with the string-ensemble to accompany the narration—the composer had heard a string-orchestra version of his First Quartet by Fabien Sevitzky, but would not make his own version in collaboration with Kurt Redel, called *Musica Sacra*, until 1973). Yet Tcherepnin had always shown a keen ear for the sound of massed strings, particularly in *divisi* passages and solo-*vs.*-*tutti* interplays, even in relatively "gray" scores such as the First Symphony.

Moreover, the "nocturnal" solo string excursions in works ranging from the Duo and Concertino to the Second Symphony were always notably effective—perhaps even too facile, sometimes, for the composer's own good. Tcherepnin's ready invention in this vein served him well in the Serenade; for while such episodes in earlier works had usually been improvisatory and discursive they are subsumed here in an economical and unfailingly urgent narrative. This superb score, replete with provocative coloration and compelling drama from first note to last, belongs near the top of any short list of Tcherepnin masterpieces.

Tcherepnin's papers contain a short program note on the Serenade which was evidently prepared either by the composer or with his approval; moreover, Marjorie Glock's final version of her Reich translation contains analytical remarks that are not in the original German text—these were almost certainly added at the behest of Tcherepnin himself. The analysis that follows draws on both of these sources.

The size of ensemble required by this score is defined on the second page, where the violas are divided in five. In addition, cellos are divided in four at the end of the movement and doublebasses are not infrequently divided in two. Lily Chou, in her catalogue of Tcherepnin's works, lists a string complement of 8 first violins, 6 second violins, 6 violas, 4 cellos and 2 doublebasses.

"The Serenade is composed of five movements closely linked together and played without interruption. As the title implies, this is 'nocturnal' music in its various moods and aspects. The writing is chromatic but not serial. The musical thought is expressed in different patterns which progress in parallel passages-at one time completing [each] other mutually, at another time in opposition."

Reich oversimplifies somewhat when he says that all movements reflect a single formal archetype, proceeding from unstructured beginnings to more fully organized passages; such a design undoubtedly underlies the first movement, and perhaps the fourth, but looking for it elsewhere can only cause misunderstandings. On the other hand, Reich is eminently correct in finding that the movements spill over into one another. Throughout, in fact, Tcherepnin innovatively plies what might be called a technique of cyclical allusion, recalling characteristic textures and gestures rather than themes *per se*.

I. Mesto. In what Tcherepnin describes as "a sort of dialogue," violins, cellos and basses provide a menacing background of measured trills:

Example 206

for thematic fragments, now dolorous, now agitated, introduced by solo viola (Example 207).

The trills die away into a middle-register *tremolo* chord for divided violas, and four solo violins provide brief glinting comments. As the *tremolo* chord begins to rise, spasmodic and varied interjections are heard from two solo cellos, two solo violins and the contrabasses. The first solo violin gains dominance as the shuddering chord reaches the upper register and breaks off, whereupon a vehement downward solo *arpeggio* passes through two violins to cello, then bass.

A desolate chorale-like *tutti* [Example 208] now begins with motif a:

Example 207

Example 208

In its continuation the stepwise element of the trills reappears, transmuted into scale-like motion (the two passages quoted in Example 209 are separated by a climax). The interval-patterns of the coda (where rising violins- playing half-steps in alternation with minor thirds-combine with falling cellos and basses) have a decidedly Tcherepninesque ring (*cf.* Divertimento, example 141). At the end of this prefatory movement, wide-spaced reiterated half-step motions subtly evoke the opening trills, and with their undulations, a sense of closure is avoided.

Example 209

II. Allegretto. This madcap scherzo, cast in free arch-form (A-B-C-B-A) begins with the whimsical interpuntal deployment of three different accompanimental *pizzicato* patterns, all fixed in notes, but all continually shifting in rhythms: the two opening four-note patterns (E, C#, B, e; g#, B, f#, G#) are joined by a three-note pattern (F#, E, C#). ("Layered" passages such as this are unquestionably ancestors of a good deal of the so-called "process" music of the 1980s.) The key-signature (and sound) indicates E major.

Example 210

Suddenly, against these, the violins deliver a jaunty tune in Bb major, of all possible keys the most remote from E. After a short *crescendo*, a rather violent theme (Example 212) appears in lower strings (of great importance later), reminiscent

Example 211

of the Duo. Violins join in as this passage is echoed, then example 211 makes a cheerful reappearance, with the tune now in E major (violins) and the *pizzicato* accompaniment (lower strings) in Bb. Other important motifs that appear at this juncture are: vigorous *moto perpetuo* sixteenth-note *tutti*-out-bursts in tetrachordal patterns, and a group of three repeated notes, which evolves into this determined theme:

Example 213

Example 212

Minor-third-emphasizing vibration of this sort is, of course, by now a veritable calling card for Tcherepnin (*cf. Mystère, Sobeide,* Fourth Symphony, etc.; we shall also meet it in the Sixth Concerto).

Soon the main theme (example 211) appears briefly in F major in the violins (accompanied in F#), and, after an angry interruption, resumes in G major as it passes almost pointillistically from doublebasses to cellos to violas (accompanied in Ab).

Beginning a kind of reverse reprise, Example 212 erupts, and is extended in this restatement, as it is tossed from lower to upper strings and back. Then the violins alone, in robust two-part writing, present the main theme in Eb major, and the accompaniment patterns soon reappear in A major. After the *pizzicato*s gently die out, the violins suddenly play a *fortissimo* fragment of the tune, back in Bb, and, after a grinding dissonant chord, the movement ends with a harmonically ambiguous sustained high note in the violins.

The movement is marked by kaleidoscopic juxtapositions throughout, and according to the Glock(-Tcherepnin?) commentary the interpoint principle, beginning as note between note, is quickly "generalized to include passage against passage, loud versus soft, high versus low, solo passages versus *tutti*s," and is also manifest in the polytonal clashes.

III. Vivace. This exercise in "perpetual movement" (Tcherepnin) begins with an obsessive theme for the violins harmonized in grating major sevenths:

Example 214

which contains an allusion to motif a and continues largely in hard intervals. Soft intervals are introduced by violas and cellos, which then begin a counterstatement harmonized in major sixths:

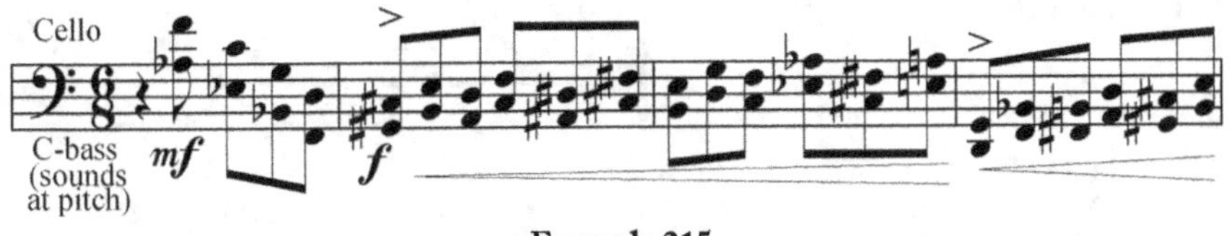

Example 215

The minor third (prominent in example 213) assumes importance and example 212 is also furiously evoked (Example 216, overleaf). The opening theme is then mischievously elaborated (the violins still in major sevenths, the lower strings in major sixths). Contrabasses stress the minor thirds in long notes (E-G-E-G) and the insistent patterns of example 216 return. As the irresistible motion continues, a scintillating discussion that begins with high, closely-harmonized violins gradually descends, passing to cellos and basses—here, a descending chromatic-scale passage is salient—and ending with basses alone in spooky *diminuendo*. There is a sudden calm, characterized by Tcherepnin as "a bridge," as the hard intervals are evoked in augmentation by *pizzicato*s which rise from the lowest bass note to the veritable top of the violin range as the music disappears in nocturnal mist.

It now becomes clear, according to Glock-(Tcherepnin?), "that the entire Serenade is built upon the *Principle of Contrasts*, the fast third movement being followed by a dramatically tense and slow fourth movement...."

IV. Lento. "Visionary and mystic, with a dramatic explosion in the middle" (Tcherepnin), this modified A-B-A movement commences with a spacious, rather bleak theme for divided first violins, mostly harmonized in astringent parallel minor seconds (related, of course, to the violin major-sevenths of the previous movement).

The minor-second is emphasized by the accompanying figure here (Example 217)-an ominous descending chromatic-scale fragment (motif b) for *pizzicato* second violins with *sul ponticello tremolando* violas-and further highlighted by quizzical major seventh leaps in *pizzicato* cellos.

Soon, the violins embark on a lyrically musing passage (Example 218), elevated in sentiment and eloquent in effect (its close intervallic spacings may conceivably have been inspired by some of the high-string writing in late Stravinsky). The lower strings gradually join in, increasing the richness of texture and chromatic pungency of the harmony.

Suddenly there is a ferocious *forte tremolo* eruption for virtually the full complement, in which the chromatically descending violin-viola figure of example 217 is extended; the music here, after a swirling *tutti* uprush, is then abstracted from *tremolo*s into chords in an imperious evocation of example 212. Another swirl provides a climax; then, in a sudden hush, the fragmentary comments of the Serenade's opening pages are evoked as mysterious and mercurial solos appear. Doublebass trills soon begin to mutter, and the opening violin theme, with its sustained minor-second now an octave higher, begins again. Motif b also returns, interrupting the doublebass trilling, which, however, resumes. After a last mournful violin solo die away, three choked second violin *pizzicato*s (a broken memory of motif b) provide a close.

Example 216

Example 219

V. Allegro moderato. Characterized by Tcherepnin as "a drawn-out Rondo [of] gaiety and vigor," this finale begins with a humorous, bustling fanfare-like theme on the edge of

Bb major-minor (Example 219). There is a short build-up on bouncy repeated-note melodic patterns (which have been heard in the Serenade with increasing frequency); the note repeated here is E, again setting up the Bb *vs*. E confrontation of the scherzo. After a rising-scale flourish, the main theme puckishly appears in viola in a kind of D

Example 218

Example 217

Example 220

major-minor. Now a slashing theme of the example 212 type (Example 220) exuberantly breaks out.

The descending figure is a variant of motif b. Climactic chords now punctuate a viola statement of the main theme, successive phrases of which are heard in E, F, C# and G. The first movement trills are then transformed: and there is a fierce, decidedly triadic descending sixteenth-note *tutti* flourish (example 222).

Example 222

Then solo violin and cello begin an elegantly inquisitive theme of three phrases (separated by punctuations), based on widening interval patterns-half-steps, then half- steps alternating with minor thirds, then triadic rises (Example 223), and an energetic elaboration of example 220 figures is followed by quasi-lyrical developments of b. These, in turn, culminate in a scale-*cum*-repeated- interval *moto perpetuo* descent, in which strands of falling minor thirds and rising major seconds are juxtaposed with conjunct chromatic motion. After a heroic antiphonal chordal climax, example 223 suavely resumes,

Example 221

Example 223

its continuation culminating in sixteenth-note scrubbing and a *tutti* flourish on a rising chromatic scale.

Suddenly, the music quiets, and the bass becomes a series of thuds on a single inexorably reiterated minor-ninth bass-cello dyad. Repeated-sixteenth-note figures appear in the viola, and the higher voices soon chime in with fragments of exam-ple 223; then the opening theme buoyantly reappears in the cellos in Ab. Soon (with the swirls from the first statement returning) the theme appears in the violas in C major-minor and is shouted down by the music of example 223. An irate repeated chord passage ensues. Then, in an idyllic lull, trill-like figures appear in first violins and basses while the middle strings play a piquant F major version of the main theme in augmentation:

Example 224

A striding 5/8 rhythm appears in the cellos and basses as other instruments briefly drop out, cellos soon providing a contrasted 4/8 pattern with violas playing a 6/16 = 3/8 figure. Five sonorous repeated chords climactically broaden the rhythm to 5/4; then the main theme appears in the violas against example 223 in the basses and cellos, passing to the upper strings, which repeat it with mounting excitement in higher and higher keys. This passage leads to a brilliant restatement of the triadic descending flourish (example 222). After two sizzling chromatically rising swoops (upper strings, then lower strings) and a last abrasive reference to example 212 (*i. e.*, 220), the work ends in jubilation with a decisive D-majorish chord (reading upward, D-A-D-F#-G-A-D).

CONCERTO NO. 6 FOR PIANO AND

ORCHESTRA, OPUS 99

The story of Tcherepnin's Sixth Piano Concerto is a story of delays. Many months passed between the time the score was commissioned and the time it was finished; seven years passed between its completion date and its premiere.

The chain of circumstances that kept Tcherepnin from this concerto through much of 1964 has been described in the essay on the Serenade. On the last day of that year, the composer wrote to Phillip Ramey with yet another non-progress report: "Because of too much concertizing the work on the new Piano Concerto is still handicapped, and not much hope to have it ready before leaving Europe. On top of it, have accepted other commissions:—will have to stand on my head for the rest of my life!" According to Reich, Tcherepnin finally got a start on the score in January 1965, before arriving back in New York at the end of that month.

On March 30, Tcherepnin was at Columbia University participating in a marathon recording session for a series of radio programs devoted to his works, produced and hosted by Ramey for WKCR-FM, the college radio station. Tcherepnin was interviewed, provided brief oral program notes on pieces ranging from the *Bagatelles* to the *Symphonic Prayer* and taped both of his piano sonatas, the *Préludes nostalgiques* and the Prelude Op. 85, No. 9 on the concert grand Steinway in MacMillin Theater at the edge of the campus, using the facilities of the Columbia-Princeton Electronic Music Center (the engineer and tape-editor was a then-unknown electronics expert, then named Walter Carlos).

When asked by Ramey about his future plans during one of the programs, Tcherepnin responded: "My plans for the summer are such that I am very delighted to think of them, because from June 1st I will close my piano for practicing, and will be in a little village in Switzerland, to be able to stay there for three months, without concert[s], without any other doings than to compose… I will compose a new piano concerto, a commission that is long overdue, and that I feel that I have absolutely to finish before I go to do any other thing."

To Ramey's observation that this would be Concerto number six, Tcherepnin answered, with a chuckle, "It is very dangerous for a composer to have five piano concertos; and I am rather at a crucial moment of five piano concertos and four symphonies." Tcherepnin, meant, of course, that some of the better-known composers only lived to produce five piano concertos, including Beethoven, Saint-Saens, Prokofiev, Anton Rubinstein, Martinu and (if the Rhapsody on a Theme of Paganini be counted as a concerto) Rachmaninoff; moreover Schumann, Brahms, Taneyev, Roussel and Ives completed only four symphonies.

Tcherepnin's stay in Bach that summer was not quite the uninterrupted idyll he had hoped for, but in a July 15 letter he could report to Ramey: "The concerto progresses slowly, have now [the] 1st and 2nd movements ready in sketch, working on the Finale.

"It is as beautiful as ever here. No concerts until October. So I do hope that before I will have to start practice, the No. 6 will take final shape." Reich states that Tcherepnin finished the work in September. It might have merely been the short score that was ready that month, however, for Tcherepnin did not announce to Ramey that he had "completed No. 6" until December 8. In the last movement, as Reich observed, Tcherepnin used the name of the village where the concerto was composed, spelled in English B-A-E-C-H, as a *soggetto cavato*; in fact, the sprightly motif derived from these letters is given considerable prominence as a bass-line.

Having been kept waiting for the score by Tcherepnin, it was now Margrit Weber's turn to keep the composer waiting. Somewhat weary after her busy concert schedule of the previous few years, she decided at this juncture to curtail her professional activities for an extended period so that she could devote time to her husband and children. There was little point in her learning Tcherepnin's concerto if she was only to give it a few sporadic performances over the next three or four years, thus she postponed working on the piece until such time as she was prepared to resume extensive touring and take it to a series of major European cities.

The interim, as indicated above, lasted seven years. The first performance of Tcherepnin's Sixth Piano Concerto was finally scheduled for September 5, 1972, at the Lucerne International Music Festival, with Margrit Weber as pianist and Rafael Kubelik conducting the Amsterdam Concertgebouw Orchestra. By that time the printed score, with a dedication to Margrit Weber, had already been in print for four years.

Shortly before Tcherepnin left New York to attend the premiere, he was interviewed for the September-October, 1972 issue of *Music & Artists* magazine, where he made the following comments about the concerto:

"About 1958 in Zurich I heard a Swiss pianist, Margrit Weber, play my *Bagatelles* for piano solo, composed when I was a teenager. Strongly impressed with her playing, I wrote an orchestral accompaniment to the *Bagatelles* for her. She recorded this version on Deutsche Grammophon with Ferenc Fricsay and the Radio Symphony Orchestra of Berlin and played it throughout Europe and in New York.

"Hearing Margrit Weber perform this version of the *Bagatelles* I became eager to compose for her a full-size Concerto for Piano and Orchestra that would reveal my admiration for her talent and artistry.

"I was not the first to do so; Stravinsky composed for her his Movements for Piano and Orchestra and Martinu a concerto, and so did many others.

"The 6th Piano Concerto, a virtuoso work in three movements, has a brilliant, fervent first movement. The middle, central movement I think is the most important of the three with its many contrasting sections, moods and tempi. The final movement starts in a rhythmic, percussive style, followed by a lyrical Russian folk song alternated and combined with the rhythmical material. In all three movements, there are sections when the piano plays alone but they are not regular cadenzas as such.

"At the premiere Rafael Kubelik, my dear friend, will conduct."

Some weeks after the performance, Tcherepnin informed Ramey: "The No. 6 was successful in Lucerne-Margrit Weber played brilliantly, Kubelik and Concertgebouw Orchestra did their best. It was also projected on TV and obtained excellent reviews." Ms. Weber went on to perform the Concerto in numerous Swiss, German and Austrian cities, sometimes with Tcherepn in conducting.

The virtuoso character of the Sixth Concerto—especially at this late stage of Tcherepnin's career, requires a word. It will be remembered that the composer's original designation for his earlier Piano Concerto No. 4 was "Fantasy for Piano and Orchestra." Tcherepnin later told Phillip Ramey that he had decided to change the title because the score was a "real concerto," containing the expected elements of brilliant solo display. In this respect, it resembled the First Concerto, Tcherepnin said, and differed from the Second and Third, which were basically ensemble pieces.

Similarly, while the composer produced the Fifth Concerto as an ensemble piece, he designed the Sixth as a "real concerto," a brilliant and demanding showpiece requiring a player of extraordinary ability. Tcherepnin confessed that he himself was unable to perform the Sixth Concerto (the only one of his concertos of which this was true). This was a piece for one of those titans of the keyboard who maintain the ability to toss off Rachmaninoff and Prokofiev Concertos with nonchalance by ceaselessly maintaining a four to six hour daily regimen of practice.

Discussing this score in a radio interview with Robert Sherman, Tcherepnin remarked: "I think the happiest compositions are those that are written for a special performer that you know… You know his abilities, his technique, his ways of approach and then you make [the piece] just like a tailor-made suit. [The] Sixth Concerto for Margrit Weber. was written after I have heard her many many times, so I know what she can do—and not her limitations but her special attributes."

Despite Tcherepnin's praise for Margrit Weber, it seems that she was not the ideal pianist for this concerto, at least, by 1972. Her interpretation, as preserved on tape, sounds cautious and reticent—far inferior to the work's first commercial recording, taped by Murray McLachlan in February 1994 (with Ivan Tcherepnin attending the sessions). In the interim, the piece attracted other virtuosos. A live performance in Ming Tcherepnin's cassette collection by the German pianist Christof Amtmann, had consider-able panache and excitement, although the ensemble tended to be helter-skelter. The late British pianist John Ogden also once performed the piece, and his rendering was probably superb, given his demonstrated ability to strike the proper balance between brilliance and solidity in works of great difficulty.

Tcherepnin's Sixth Concerto, in contradistinction to his recent *Symphonic Prayer* and Serenade, was influenced little if at all by the new music culture of the late 1950s and early 1960s. Not unlike the weightier and even more ostensibly conservative Fourth Symphony before it, this score took shape as a work of consolidation, providing a musical journey with periodic diatonic signposts, as Tcherepnin here was not primarily concerned with orienting the aural traveler amid the hitherto uncharted highways and byways of a self-sufficient chromaticism. Indeed, the tonal aspect of this last of the composer's concertos is not its only overtly retrospective feature: reminders of themes and techniques from previous works such as *Mystère*, the First and Fourth Symphonies, the Divertimento, the Fifth Concerto, the *Symphonic Prayer* and the Serenade abound within the score.

What is almost disconcerting about these reminders is how thoroughly they are divested in this piece of their original expressive trappings. The emotional tensions, the demonic shadows, the bereavement, the anger, the bewilderment, the awed reverence implicit in those earlier works are infrequently discernable in the Sixth Concerto, for it is essentially a carefree piece. Such tensions as are present usually resemble those of the determined athlete: more often the music is apt to display wit, rakish adventure or a sensuous, almost lupine lyric elegance; and a good-humored eye for the ridiculous underlies the episodes of grotesquerie. All in all, the work has a zest that makes it a first cousin (once removed) to some of Prokofiev's earlier "white-note" music.

It is tempting to find a connection between the youthful ebullience of this work and the composer's quotidian milieu at the time he wrote it. If the Serenade reflected, to some degree, a harried and overworked composer-teacher's parting contemplation of the accrued resentments and conflicts of his experience at DePaul (where he was loved by the students but periodically sniped at by nit-picking colleagues and administrators), and of the uncertainty of his prospects as he faced, for the first time in many years, a freelance existence without a safety net, then the Sixth Concerto surely manifested itself as the work of a rejuvenated man, overjoyed at being relieved of burdensome worries. No longer hampered by the daily grind of teaching, Tcherepnin was able to schedule things so that he had time to breathe—indeed, as noted, he could now set aside months at a time for composing without distraction, and this new freedom filled him with elation. The actual act of at last composing the Concerto—and thus clearing his agenda of a major obligation that had long weighed upon him—must have also been a source of cheer.

The eupeptic kinetic panache of the piece is surely informed as well by Tcherepnin's relish at the legitimate opportunities that composing such a concerto gave him to be "bad"—to indulge in a measure of rip-roaring virtuosity for its own sake, with the devil-may-care bravado of a schoolboy on a lark, rather than ceaselessly concerning himself with the subtle solo-orchestra integration of an essentially symphonic concerto.

Largely because of its air of uncomplicated athleticism, the Sixth Concerto has inevitably been undervalued; both Reich and Wuellner treated it with faint (though probably unconscious) patronage. True, this score has no passages that plumb the emotional and spiritual depths found in a few episodes of the Fifth Concerto; but there is nevertheless no good reason to regard it as shallow or facile. The formal design shows all of Tcherepnin's wonted sophistication, the serene lyric nostalgia of the slow movement is freshly inspired, as are the episodes of unabashed Romantic ardor—in short, there is no falling-off here of the composer's technical or imaginative powers. Tcherepnin chose to devote himself to an optimistic piece that would keep the listener alert, and succeeded brilliantly in this Haydnesque aim.

The notable prominence of the piano in this concerto, cited by several commentators, results not so much from any suppression of the orchestra as from the voluminous and unusually continuous nature of the solo part. The piano's long uninterrupted stretches of toccata-like music in the first movement, in fact, put considerable strain on the performer. On the other hand, more prominence is given to the percussion here than in any other Tcherepnin concerto. There are also effects of a Romantic luminosity unusual for Tcherepnin that involve complex *divisi* deployment of the strings.

While the orchestra is not scanted in this work, Tcherepnin decided to forgo the large instrumental apparatus he had used in the Fifth Concerto. The Sixth merely requires what is essentially a double-wind orchestra: piccolo, 2 flutes, 2 oboes, 2 clarinets, 2 bassoons, 4 horns, 2 trumpets, 3 trombones, tuba, timpani, castanets, wood block, triangle, crotales in G, side drum, tambourine, snare-drum, cymbals, bass drum, glockenspiel, xylophone, chimes (G in two octaves), harp, and strings.

Appropriately, this last of Tcherepnin's major works is very much concerned with the major-minor triad and its corollary, the six-step scale discussed in the essay of the Fourth Symphony (here, G-A#-B-C#-D-F#-G). The score's first movement sonata form is an adroit compromise between the Classical model, with its full-scale recapitulation, and the type found in the Fifth Concerto, where the narrative function of the curtailed reprise is almost that of an epilogue: the sonata form is undeniably foreshortened, but there is no reversion to the Second Symphony or *Message* type of structure in which recapitulation is crowded out.

One surprising feature is Tcherepnin's indisposition to begin the reprise with a restatement of the principal theme in its original key—all the more remarkable because the tonal scheme of the exposition is solidly within classical parameters. This formal quirk, however, is a necessary consequence of the movement's thematic economy; for the development concerns itself so completely with first-subject material that a reprise that began classically would be ineffective. Indeed, Tcherepnin decided instead to make the development dovetail almost unnoticeably into the recapitulation (to the ear, the beginning of the reprise at first seems to be an episode of dominant preparation). To draw an analogy with prose, the progress from the opening of the development section to the start of the second-subject reprise is covered in one paragraph; and that paragraph, moreover, ends with a colon rather than a period.

In his article on Tcherepnin's works for piano and orchestra, Guy Wuellner places the beginning of the "Subtheme Group" (second subject) at measure 98. In the editor's opinion, it is at measure 83 that the subsidiary group actually begins, marked by a tempo change that draws a narrative line and by the establishment of E minor as the first subsidiary key (this related to G major; another subsidiary key-area related to G minor appears later). True, some first-group motivic material is used in measures 83-98, but the necessity for a new theme at the opening of the second subject is, as we have seen, a post-classical superstition.

I. Allegro. Delivered by the piano with spiky orchestral punctuation, the determined G minor-major *moto perpetuo* opening theme of the concerto:

Example 225

recalls similar repeated-note-*cum*-major-minor-third materials in works such as the Serenade, the Fourth Symphony, *Sobeide*, *Mystère*, etc. Following brilliant thirty-second-note solo scale-figuration (which will periodically reappear throughout the movement), the main theme continues in Eb, and the ubiquitous major-minor triad (motif a) is introduced via treacherous cross-hands leaps.

With considerable subtlety, Tcherepnin avoids any suggestion of the dominant key in the opening 19 measures (the note D itself is virtually absent). Other important thematic cells (Example 226) are introduced here against the continually hammered sixteenth-note rhythm. The momentum is broken by sonorous cadence-preparing eighth-note chordal piano leaps. These bridge from the neighborhood of Bb to the dominant, which, having been withheld, appears with great effect as a brief orchestral *tutti* begins (example 227).

The piano immediately reenters, continuing its toccata-like thrumming, while the opening motif of example 227 continues to be restated—first by lower strings, then bassoon, then horns, then in wind polyphony.

More materials are added to the ongoing discussion (Example 228) and assume a predominant role. Eventually, dense piano eighth-note chords are pitted against string sixteenth-note scales and brass half-notes in a massive step-by-step contrary motion climax (treble instruments up, bass instruments down–*cf.* Divertimento first movement close). The piano then returns to the opening theme, beginning on E-flat, against which winds deliver a passage based on motif a:

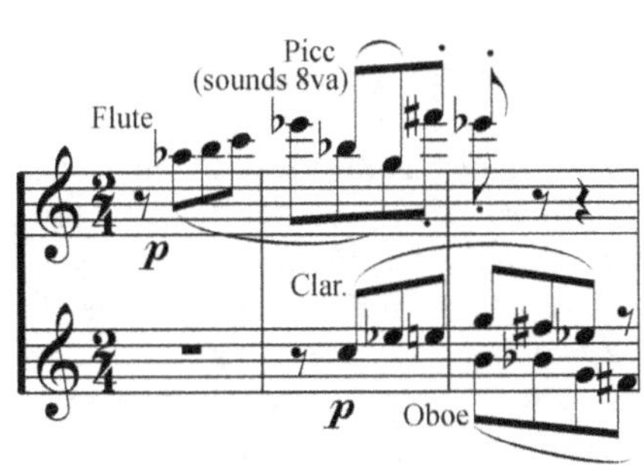

Example 229

Example 226

Soon, the repeated-note figure is heard in minor seconds and climbs steadily upward against a shrill rising trumpet solo. The orchestra then falls silent for a sixteenth-note piano passage in

Example 227

low-register fourths which ushers in the second subject, beginning in E minor (subsidiary to G major). Here, the music slows into a grotesque march, in an episode reminiscent of the third movement of Prokofiev's Second Concerto (Example 230, overleaf). Note the piano fourths outlining the six-step-*cum*-major-minor triad harmonies, the mock-military brass and wind comments and, oddly, the staggered lower-string minor thirds , redolent of something far more serious in the Fourth Symphony. Chuckling repeated sixteenth-notes soon appear Again, dissonantly harmonized chords (brass quarter-notes) pursue a scale-ascent to a climax.

In a sudden calm, the piano is left alone for a lyrical solo of notably seductive elegance, beginning in E-flat major, subsidiary to G minor (example 231)

Example 228

which eventually leads to a piquant *pianissimo* array of dissonant high-register triplet chords as the march-rhythm returns in the orchestra in bizarre divisi-string scoring that colorfully mixes *pizzicato* and *saltando* (example 232).

With a final nostalgic reminiscence of example 231, the piano ends the exposition in the orthodox key of B-flat (relative major of G minor). of B-flat (relative major of G minor).

Surprisingly, yet inevitably, given the character of the principal theme, the development begins with a zestful 22-measure episode for percussion alone. The theme is played (or shall we say abstracted) by timpani with cymbal and bass drum, then by xylophone with wood- block, and passed back to timpani. The general procedure resembles the First Symphony scherzo, where originally-pitched materials were rhythmically restated. (The xylophone recalls the *Symphonic Prayer*-however, it here conveys none of the

Example 230

Example 231

war-fever atmosphere it had in that piece. This is because this sort of repeated-note drumming has already been established as "normal" discourse in the concerto, while in the *Symphonic Prayer* this effect disrupted the majestic orbital cycle of a set of slow variations.) Sixteenth-note spasms of four notes, then three notes, then two notes are tossed about between xylophone, side drum, snare drum, wood-block and xylophone; the xylophone,

timpani and snare drum then return to the theme in a kind of semi-pitched canon.

The piano reenters with first theme material in A major-minor (repeated-notes, thirty-second-note scales, cross-hand leaps), proceeding to a counterstatement in Bb, accompanied all the while by percussion. Then the orchestra breaks in, ferociously stating the theme in a D major-minor version, and this, in retrospect, proves to be the beginning of the recapitulation.

When the music reaches G, the piano reenters, continuing the abbreviated yet normal reprise. After piano and orchestra rapidly bandy example 226 back and forth, a climactic leaping chord-*cum*-hammered octave transition drawn from the exposition leads to the second subject march, with the derisive wind materials from example 230 now roared out by the piano as well. Soon the piano adds a barbaric new melody:

N.B. The divided strings are further divided as to mode of execution: half play *pizzicato* with the other half playing *col legno saltando*.

Example 232

Example 233

and an immense contrary-motion chord climax prepares the return of example 231, now heard in a torridly romantic piano and orchestra restatement that begins in C major (Example 234-subdominant emphasis, it should be noted, is a normal feature of

Example 234

the classical recapitulation). Eventually, as the piano thunders out fourth-outlining octaves as in Example 234, another contrary-motion array in slow chords fans out. This concludes in titanic unaccompanied chordal piano leaps requiring four staves for notation, which at last coalesce on a final G in octaves, the note being reinforced by crotales, chimes, cymbals and gong.

    II. Andantino. This slow movement is in modified A-B-A form (foreshortened, as is the composer's wont) with a brief final coda. An aura of innocent nostalgia tinged with unabashedly romantic coloristic radiance pervades the A portions, and it would not have been inappropriate had Tcherepnin called the movement *Romanza.* The wistful opening theme for oboe:

Example 235

suggesting B minor and containing motif a is rounded off by flutes and clarinets. Rarefied, wide-ranging piano figuration and sustained string chords (example 236) then create a halo in glowing D major- the piano part even has a key signature-as a background for a sweetly naive motto (Example 237). Augmentation of the motto will later be of particular importance.

The piano then begins a counterstatement of example 235 in limpid soprano-range two-voice writing. As the keyboard writing thickens, the motto (b) is heard in treble, and answered by c (with the dotted rhythm evened out) in the bass. Soon, the example 236 halo reappears in F major, and horn and flute deliver the motto. Another piano interlude culminates in delicate rising scale filigrees accompanying a codetta where the motto, in overlap-ping statements by horn, oboe, horn, flute, trumpet, flute and piccolo, is progressively augmented and simplified (Example 238).

The piano falls silent, and the B-section of the movement begins (itself in three parts) with an oboe melody, accompanied by a rhythm in the horns (Example 239) that will prove persistent. The melody, however, is but another Tcherepnin red herring, for it is not until the violins join the oboe that the real thematic agenda is revealed and counterstated, a new tune also derived from motif a (Example 240), which is presently given out in a lush

Example 236

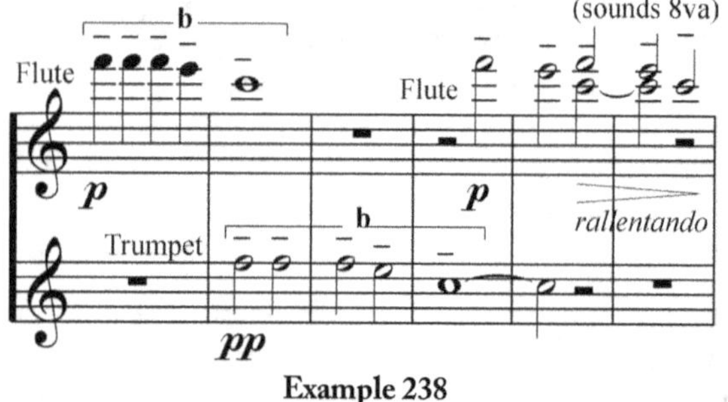

Example 237

version by piano, followed by an even lusher piano-string version that rises to a climax. In a suddenly quicker tempo, the piano impishly plays a chromatic prank and sails off into a gossamer, dazzling cadenza-like excursion-the middle part of the B-section (example 241-perhaps the central presto in the Tchaikovsky Concerto slow movement was on Tcherepnin's mind here; the effect of the two episodes is strikingly similar). Soon, however, as Example 241-like figurations continue, the previous discussion is resumed as the oboe returns to Example 241 and is answered by the violins. (The horn-rhythm from example 239 does not reappear, however). After a *crescendo*, a delicate *subito pianissimo tutti* rounds off the B-section.

Left alone, the piano plays the first three notes of the opening theme-and, as if wondering "what next?," repeats this melodic figure after delivering a quiet *arpeggio*. Then a bridge passage, based on quiet, pedalled octaves in contrasted registers that set the whole piano aglow, brings back the opening theme. The scoring here is of exquisite delicacy: the piano delivers the melody in single notes two octaves apart (in a variant that encompasses motif c) and *divisi* strings provide a sustained chord

Example 238

and quiet *pizzicatos*. The strings now have an Eb major key signature: the piano begins in an enharmonically related B minor and swings around to Eb major in the counterstatement, where the flute continues the melody with motif a and cellos and basses take up motif b.

A sonorous piano continuation prepares the return of D major and motif b, which passes tenderly through the winds (horn, oboe, horn, clarinet, flute). Serenity again yields to elfin mischief as the piano reverts to the pranks of

Example 239

Example 240

example 241, beginning a brief coda; but the solo comments soon take on the air of whispered valedictory flourishes, and the movement ends peacefully with an enchanting Ab (string) to D (piano) cadence.

Example 241

III. Animato. Two bustling orchestral themes are proclaimed at the outset, the first tuneful in the Russian folk manner, the second quite rhythmic (Examples 242 and 243).

As a climax approaches, the B-A-E-C-H theme appears in lower strings doubled first by trumpets, then trombones, then bass trombone (Example 244).

The piano enters in Cossack-like exuberance with a clashing, dissonant extension of example 243-the sixteenth-note figure (second measure) soon appears in snare drum, and later

Example 242

passes to the piano as the orchestra takes up the syncopated eighth-note figure, and at the same time, a "misspelled" version of the BAECH motif appears in the piano left hand.

There is an orchestral *crescendo* where the violins play repeated G eighth notes, and the piano, finally taking the

hint, joyously proceeds to hammer out a variant of the opening theme which is continued by winds. After more discussion of other themes, a similar piano climax on the first theme ensues.

A slackening of tempo brings a noble three-note figure, motif d, imitatively treated by winds, strings and piano in a rich texture (Example 245). Lower strings try to reestablish the first theme's rhythm, but the piano again embraces motif d, extending it into a broad, soulful melody, which is continued by clarinet (Example 246,

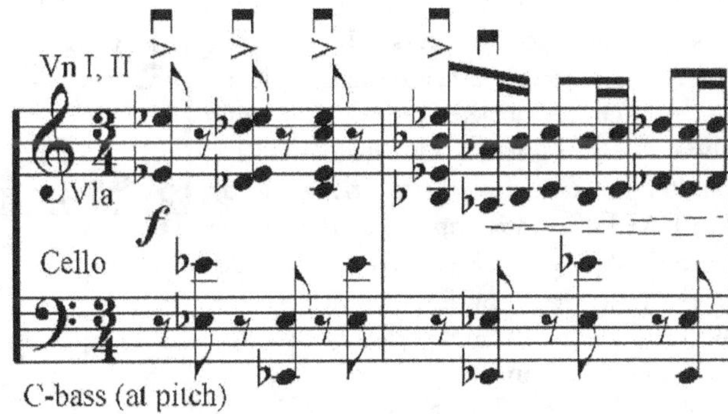

Example 243

motif e). Motif d is then restated imitatively, and soon motif e and its aftermath are ardently delivered in a *tutti* supported by sonorous piano chording. The tempo then quickens, and after a snare drum-*cum*-trombone interlude, motif e appears in a luminous wind-harp statement.

Example 244

A heroic question-and-answer horn tune, its "answer" piquantly harmonized in parallel tritones by piccolo (Example 247) and a descending string sequence on motif e lead to a dark-colored piano build-up that culminates in the luxuriantly romantic reappearance of example 246, now aglow in Elgaresque grandeur, with example 247 appearing in the bass at the pick-up to the sixth measure. The counterstatement is even more emotionally intense,

Example 247

presenting rising sequences on the melody's first two measures.

Abruptly, the piano returns to its crashing-staccato-chord version of example 243, interjectively accompanied by timpani, snare drum, cymbals, bass drum and side drum. The opening theme now breaks out in strings, its fragments tossed back and forth by strings and piano; both this and example 243 are referred to in rapid alternation, and there is a final grandiose restatement of example 246, climaxing in majestic canonic pyramiding of motif d.

Suddenly the tempo quickens. The BAECH motif appears, beginning on G rather than the original Bb—the "wrong" key for spelling purposes, but the right key for the concerto, which has now come around to the opening key of G major. Vigorously rhythmic at this tempo, the motif

Example 245

is heard first in strings, then in winds, each of these statements followed by short bursts of piano octaves. Motif and alternating piano answers both grow progressively shorter as the tension mounts, and are finally reduced to single chords hurled alternately by piano and orchestra. Then, against brilliant rising piano figuration and pulsing string chords, the BAECH motif appears at the proper "letter" pitches in long stately tones, each of its five notes played by different instruments: Bb (*B*) by 2nd trumpet and 1st trombone, A by 2nd trombone, E by 1st trumpet, C by bass trombone and B (*H*) by tuba, just before the ebullient G major chordal conclusion.

The music of the Sixth Concerto pulsates with youthful expectation. It is the work of a man who lives in the present and in the future, a man whose superabundant ideation would indicate that many major projects lie before him. Indeed, it is tempting to say that, having produced his ripely philosophical "late" works-the Fourth Symphony and the *Symphonic Prayer*-between

Example 246

his fifty-fifth and sixtieth year, Tcherepnin could now again, in his mid-sixties, go about composition with the endurance and abandon of a young man.

It is thus doubly ironic that the Sixth Concerto should have turned out to be Tcherepnin's last major score.

Yet, ultimately, Tcherepnin was not a man much concerned with composing epitaphs for himself. One cannot imagine him consciously planning his "last musical testament": the idea of writing a piece that would leave him with no more to say would have unutterably depressed him. How could one make such a summation when the potential of music, always limitless, was continuing to grow with each passing day? To live, in Tcherepnin's mind, was to have new worlds to explore.

The stylistic range of the composer's last masterpieces offers proof that his continual attraction to delimited "systems" in his search for new modes of technical mastery, far from ever permanently inculcating a more definitive ethos of composing, ultimately multiplied the possibilities that he saw before him. Perhaps it was the continual proliferation of these new possibilities, these unrealized potentialities, leaving more and more of his life still before him, that allowed him to grow young enough to produce a work with so fresh an animal and intellectual vigor as the Sixth Concerto in his sixty-sixth year.

❋   ❋   ❋

Chamber Music of Alexander Tcherepnin
The American String Quartet
with the Composer at the Piano
Tuesday Evening, October 24, 1967 at 8:30 P. M.
CARNEGIE RECITAL HALL

China

Russia

Г. Александар Н. Черепњин
Цртеж г. Вл. И. Жедринског

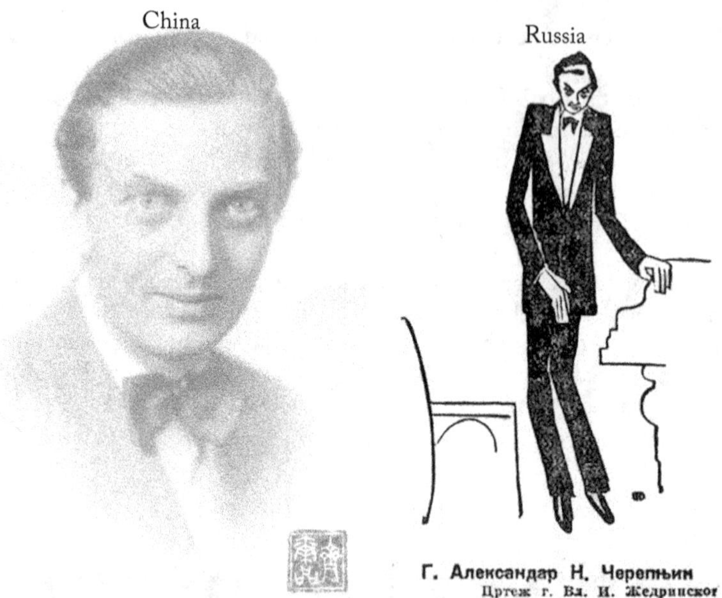

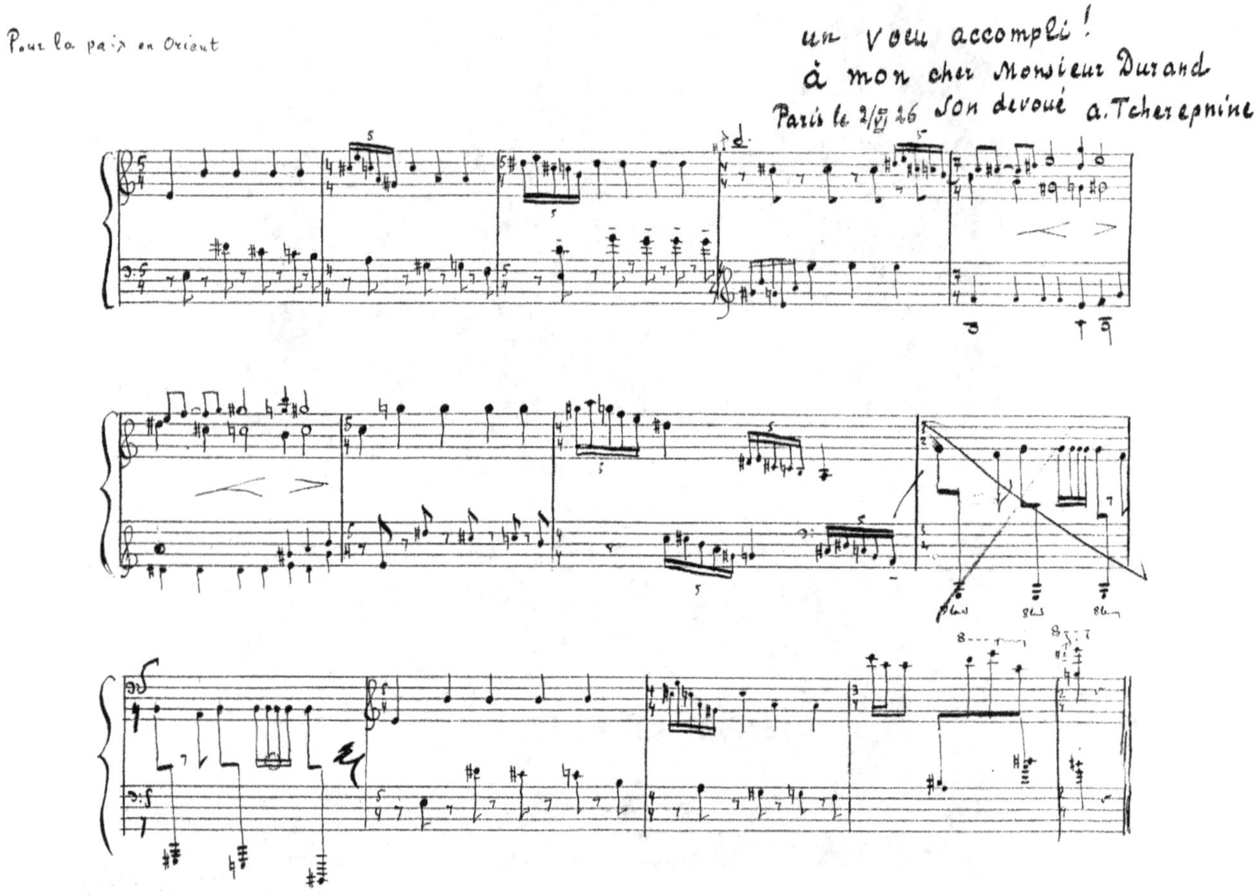

Tcherepnin's *Voeux* ("Wishes"), Op. 39b (1926) originally included this piece: a "wish" *For Peace in the Orient*. When the Abdul Krim uprising was put down, however, Tcherepnin removed the movement from the set and gave the manuscript to his publisher Jacques Durand as a memento, inscribing it as "a wish fulfilled!"

Alexander Tcherepnin in his early twenties

Alexander

Louisine

Tcherepnin records his Piano Concerto No. 5 with Rafael Kubelik conducting the Bavarian Radio Symphony Orchestra (1968).

ALEXANDER TCHEREPNIN:
A COMPENDIUM

BOOK III:

TCHEREPNIN SPEAKS

INTRODUCTION

Part one of Book III contains comments by Tcherepnin on a wide range of subjects, drawn from a wide range of sources. Most of them are taken from his autobiographical accounts, the rest coming from letters and from published, taped or scripted interviews and lectures. The remarks as arranged here proceed from what might be called analects to more extended and detailed discussions.

In connection with Tcherepnin's observations, political matters demand a word, as they so often do. Tcherepnin was frequently accused of political na"vete. Many of his fellow Russian emigres found it infuriating that, despite his fierce instinctive loathing for any kind of personal compulsion, he refused to utter condemnations of the tyrannical Soviet system that they had fled. They thought him unduly influenced by his friend Boris Schwarz, a distinguished Russian-American musicologist who discounted reports of Soviet artistic censorship as propagandistic exaggerations.

The reasons behind the composer's reticence, however, were more complex. To begin with, Tcherepnin was always conscious that he had not "fled" communism, but had departed unwillingly: he left Russia and Georgia only to avoid a separation from his parents, who were determined to go. He himself was unreservedly pleased to see the czarists toppled and he believed in the egalitarianism the communists professed; indeed, his growing career in Georgia put him in a position to make a cultural contribution to the formation of a new order.

Yet, to his secret shame, when his country needed him most, he had abandoned it. Having thus shirked his obligation to help shape Soviet society, he presumably felt that he had forfeited any right to condemn it. And so, during thirty-seven years (1921-1958) of exclusion from the political process as a citizen of any nation, he conformed to an etiquette of statelessness, maintaining a guest's tactful silence and putting down roots chiefly in the supranational realm of art.

TCHEREPNIN PRELUDE

My papa didn't want me to go through all the things he thought were so troublesome. But I did not feel it was troublesome. I loved everything about music. I love to compose, I love to teach, I love to play the piano, I love to conduct, I love to listen, I even love to copy music.

ON COMPOSITION

❀ There are Sunday painters; but there could not be Sunday composers. Borodin was probably the only exception. But, as said—the exception confirms the rule....

❀ In a pattern (or theme) there is an embryo of its growth, just as in a human seed there is an embryo of the future human organism—blood, bones, arteries, etc.

❀ I know nothing; I feel.

❀ Creative ideas are in the air and we composers are antennas. We pick up these ideas and somehow prove their validity.

❀ A composer or performer never has to stay where he does not want to stay; his field of action is unlimited and his "home" travels along with him Homesickness is unknown to one who loves people, is in peace with himself and feels that he has a mission to fulfill.

❀ People are more united by music than by any other art. You go to an exhibition and look at pictures and it's an individual experience; at a concert we are sharing a common interest and feeling.

❀ Nobody really understands music. Technique? Yes, maybe. But music? Never. It can only be heard and felt. Without that it is nothing. It is completely meaningless unless it is played.

❀ People like to say they can tell about a composer's moods or his state of health and such things from his music. I am always suspicious of such claims. I have devoted my life to music and, personally, I do not believe that such a direct relationship exists. If there are exceptions, they are probably intentional.

❀ A composer composes whether he is commissioned or not. It helps, of course, if he can count on some remuneration. He must live, after all. But his real reward is in the performance of his work.

❀ The masterpieces of the pre-war music are still with us: "modern" yesterday, "classified" today. But the general tendency has been revised. The ideal of the 19th century was to be strong and profound. The ideal of the first half of the 20th century—to be new. We have inherited the aim of the first and the language of the second.

❀ The music which fixes the present is the music that will live in the future.

❀ Art must reflect its epoch, as Van Gogh reflects his time and Picasso reflects his. Yet art must stand apart from the movement of the epoch or suffer the stigmata of localism instead of universality. The very crux of the problem is that the artist remains stable through it all, and how then can he reflect an unstable epoch?

❀ At each epoch of musical history there were limitations in musical speech due to the standard of the cultural environment of the composer. But there were and are no limitations to the deepness of a composer's thought.

❀ I always preferred city to countryside. It is the city and human beings that inspire me to work and not the chickens, cows and trees.

❀ I can only compose when I "have the itch." My work is much more intuitive than calculated.

❀ I wish the day [were] twice as long and my gray matter twice as alert.

❀ Good music is good, no matter what the means, and bad music is boring.

❀ [Serialism] is a means to an end, and to that extent is valid. Unfortunately, [it] can act as a cover for mediocre talents that have little natural inspiration but can construct a perfectly logical, and therefore defensible, serial composition.

❋ Personally, I [accept] every medium of musical expression—it is not the medium that "makes" the composer, but the composer that makes any medium acceptable by writing good music.

❋ I [never] had a continuous perfect pitch—at some moments, especially when composing, I… enjoyed perfect pitch, while at certain other moments the color of the tonality often escaped my attention and I heard everything in a relative pitch.

❋ A composition method is useful: everyone can become a composer: [the] only important [thing] is the right approach. What is usually considered as "gift" is the right approach plus work.

❋ Anyone who understands English should be able to write a letter in that language; anyone who can read music should be able to compose it.

❋ Greater is the talent, greater must be the work to materialize the potential that it has.

❋ Once a piece is composed, it can't really be changed—I don't play them up and I don't play them down. Some of a composer's creations turn out to be good children, some are problem children, but they are all still his children.

❋ A composer is to a certain degree a computer. You see, if you put a [program][1] in a computer [it] will produce music according to that [program]. And in order to produce a new composition, the composer has always [a] kind of [technical program] in mind that he will use. Now the difference between the mechanical computer and the composer computer is perhaps that what the composer computer does [is] a compromise between this [program] and his ear and way of thinking.… Now to tell you honestly and truly, [in some pieces] I forget what [the] program was [after I] become accustomed to the music.… and when I am playing these I am not thinking of the [program] that produced them, but mostly of a kind of sentiment or inner content of these pieces that I am trying to project while playing.

❋ I believe in the "reality" of music, in its "existence," in the world of music that is just as realistic a world as the visual one. The visual we can "touch" by seeing it; the musical one we can "touch" by hearing it. Sometimes, when in my attic I am deeply sunk in composing, the reappearance of the visual world in form of an opening of the door and a dear person entering seems to me like a "ghost"—so different are the dimensions. Scares me and gives me a shock. So I am sure that the world of music "exists" and that a composer has to "listen" and to take the "existing" material to construct with it, just [as] an architect constructs houses, churches, orchestra halls and bars out of "existing" stones or wood or whatever else.

❋ [When] guiding my imagination towards composition of a new symphony, it came to my mind that all my compositions starting from the middle thirties became more and more homophonic, and that it [was] time for me to look for [a] new polyphonic approach—via independent "plans," further development of interpoint, "non-imitative" thematic work. [On] days when my imagination was not working, I wrote "polyphonic exercises"—sketches.

❋ Pedagogy is a sort of exodus for creativeness: teaching to compose or to orchestrate exhaust[s], to a certain degree, the [compositional] imagination… teaching piano fills one's head with compositions of others; there are [a] thousand pretexts to escape the effort of composing.

❋ You can only teach the technique of composing, not the composing itself. That depends entirely on talent, instinct and temperament.

❋ For more than a hundred years, I think, the conservatories all over the world have taught the musical language as an historical language, not even as a [living] language, mostly as a summar[y of] what was already acquired… in Classical and Romantic times—not even so much Romantic… The composer… was aware that nothing of what he was taught could be used as such in his compositions. It was not the same in Classical times; [for] instance, whatever Mozart was taught he immediately used. Beethoven also studied with Haydn [and] Albrechtsberger in order to acquire a technique that he [could immediately] use.

---

1   Tcherepnin's original word was "device." The Editor has substituted the word "program," which conforms more closely to today's computer idiom.

❋ Analyze all the Beethoven sonatas, for they will teach you all you need to know about composition.

❋ The student's work should begin [with] monodies, melodic and rhythmic. Next step: to find [their] Interpoint.

❋ Avoid the *ostinato*; it is the Achilles [heel] of modern music.

❋ The university is too late to begin specialized and concentrated work on music. Much talent is lost or dissipated for having been discovered or attended to too late.

❋ Learn to think in silence and learn the beauty of the music of silence. In our modern times we are surrounded by too much noise. We stand the chance of losing all the inner beauty by the intrusion of too many extraneous sounds. Choose quiet living quarters, patronize silent eating places and, occasionally, dynamite the music machines.

❋ One should not flatter the bad taste of people, but also should not indulge in bolstering one's own ego by producing puzzles.

❋ [The] older I am, [the] more difficult it is for me to concentrate, to respond by the work to the inner urge for creation. And the most difficult [thing] is to "start," and to arrange my schedule drastically in order [to] keep the desire to compose alive.

❋ [My father and I] had an arrangement: It was his ambition to compose an opera, and we agreed that when I had written a thousand *bloshki*, he would compose an opera. I never did reach a thousand—just two hundred....

❋ When Cui asked my father to complete and orchestrate [Mussorgsky's] *The Fair of Sorochinski*... and my father... found no time... I did the orchestration of the whole opera... in secret... and was proud to present my father with the completed score. The good intention was handicapped by [my] lack of skill in orchestration. I do not know what became of the score—probably it was left in Petrograd... It had, of course, nothing to do with the version of *The Fair of Sorochinski* that my father did in 1922... {*Editor's note:* nor did it have anything to do with the ballet version of *Sorochinski Fair* that Alexander himself did in Paris in 1940.}

❋ When a composition is completed I cannot imagine that it could be different from what it became. And never have the urge to change the music, that somehow becomes as definitive as a[n] incarnated child. The only thing that I have often the urge to change—and am changing—is the orchestration. Here I am often dissatisfied with the balance and am urged to revise it (and often do so). Another thing that is subject to change [is] the dynamics and the tempi. Here I feel that I. should carefully edit practically all my compositions of [the] early period. Wonder if I ever will accomplish it.

❋ I feel that every good piece, old or new, has one thing in common—a "vertical" spontaneous impression on the listener. It has something that catches our ear, sticks in it, gives us the desire to hear it again without our realizing at first why and how this is so. Provided we have felt this vertical action on us, we [be]come intrigued to find out how it [was] produce[d]. We start to analyze it. Sometimes, as a result of such analysis, we find out that we have been fooled. At other times the close analysis shows us the presence of great "order" and as we go deeper into the piece, we discover that it is a masterpiece. The virtue of a piece is a combination of vertical projection plus internal order. Vertical projection without internal order is of no value and fades away after close analysis and after repeated hearings. Order alone without vertical projection is a [still]born piece of music.

❋ There are two special things about music. First, we cannot actually go back in time but the composer fixes a given moment in time for us. For example, the first movement of Schubert's "Unfinished" Symphony and Bach's Passacaglia each take 13-1/2 minutes, and those particular 13-1/2 minutes are fixed forever.

  Second, the composer also evokes the climate of that period in his life when he was writing the music. So music should reflect the best moment of the time in which it was written.

❋ Never has the composer had the opportunities that he has today; at the same time, never has he had so many responsibilities. A bad composer in Mozart's time would just be a bad composer and nobody would ever know his name. But a bad composer today—especially one who is also a bad teacher-might spoil the taste of a generation.

❀ The folklore[s] of all countries have this in common-they represent an objective musical truth.

❀ While the diatonic scale can normally be "natural" or "well-tempered," the nine-step scale can be only "well-tempered." The accidentals… are simplified, and related mostly to the major-minor accidentals if taken from the same tonal center: therefore, they have rather practical than theoretical value, and there is no difference between, let us say, A-flat and G-sharp (and so on)—[even after] displacing the tonic [and] naming [the note] differently according to accidentals.

❀ Gradually I think [our] chromatic language is becom[ing] as well organized as the Classical language—diatonic language- was [after] we passed from modes to major and minor scales. Now I think we [are] proceed[ing] in a kind of synthesis of many chromatic approaches… the formation of a new language that will be [the] same for a composer [in] New York [as] for the composer in Tokyo [or] the composer in Paris; and it will be rather a question [of] what they will say and not how they will speak, because how they will speak will be already established as [well] as it was established in Classical times.

❀ [When I first got to Paris], Boris Schloezer, whose sister was the second wife of Scriabin… became interested in my compositions, particularly in the theoretical basis of them. For his [information] I [wrote] down the system of hexachords, the nine-step scale and, as illustration, copied for him some of my two-voice inventions. [He] told me of his intention to write an article about my musical "speech" and my musical ideas… He did nothing of the kind. However, the writing down of a sort of small treatise about the hexachords, the nine-step scale and the rhythmic approach to… polyphony consolidated the results of my personal approach… made it even more conscious and pushed my mind toward further research.

❀ I do not believe in living in an ivory tower. I do not seek a hermitage. My place is with human beings. I put my faith in them—I love them-they inspire me. And I try to serve them by way of music.

❀ I feel that the process of composition is, for [a] professional composer… not a pleasure, but a heavy responsibility, a continuous effort resulting from the urge to create. The "pleasure" comes only when the composition is completed and I am writing down the completed version, or see the completed score. Therefore I compare the process of composition to the state of a pregnant woman. There is no pleasure for a woman in pregnancy—on the contrary, lots of unpleasant and uncomfortable moments. The joy comes only when—after the delivery—the mother has the child brought to her, lying near her in a *berceau* [i. e., cradle]—alive and born.

Who does not like to make love? But how many women would prefer not to have the act result in pregnancy.

So the "amateur" composer [to] me seems like a lovemaker [who has none of the] troubles of pregnancy as a result. The amateur composer takes pleasure in composition; but… composition [produced in this way] fails to give pleasure to the listener; while the professional composer does not take pleasure in composing, but the composition that comes as a result of his urge and of his effort projects his message to his fellow human beings and might become a source of their pleasure.

So difficult to have the will (at least for me) to become pregnant!

❀　❀　❀

CHAMBER MUSIC PIANO

In my chamber music with piano, I have never let the piano vie against its partner. My aim has been to treat the piano and the strings as equals, never overloading the piano writing, but reducing its weight to a necessary minimum. The writing of Beethoven's sonatas has been my ideal. The writing of Rachmaninoff's Piano and Cello Sonata, or that of Cesar Franck's Sonata for Violin and Piano has been my "public enemy no. 1." That is why I was quite satisfied with my success in conceiving and realizing my Sonata in G for Cello and Piano [i. e., No. 2] in three-voiced texture [throughout].

SOLO PIANO MUSIC

❀ While I was still in Russia, I used to include in my concert programs a group of short piano pieces, using [different] selections [on different occasions]. However, whichever… short pieces [I chose], I always used the piece that was to become *Bagatelle* No. 1 as a framing piece[:] not only did I play the *Bagatelle* No. 1 at the beginning of the [group], but [I] also repeated at the end.

There was one difference in dynamics: when playing the *Bagatelle* No. 1 at the beginning of the group I would keep playing **p** till the end… When played at the end of the group, I started [a] *crescendo*… in [the] third measure from the end, and finished the piece **ff**.

In the versions for piano and orchestra and piano and string orchestra, [No. 1] is repeated at the end, and should follow No. 10 without interruption.

❀ Some time in April [1923], I played [Isidore] Philipp the *Préludes nostalgiques* and the new Piano Concerto [No. 2]. He… disapproved of the *Préludes nostalgiques*. "Ne vous compliquez pas trop—vous avez assez de talent pour se passer des telles betises que font les musiciens modernes," was his advice. ["Don't get too complicated—you have enough talent to dispense with the stupidities that modern musicians perpetrate."] On April 22… Ania Dorfman played [the *Bagatelles*] at her Salle Érard concert… the first performance of this group of pieces under the title *Bagatelles*… I was present at the performance, and was quite ashamed of being the author of such childish pieces, [which] seemed to me naïve, stiff and "home made." Philipp was right when he observed the change in my style of writing, so just as he disliked the *Préludes nostalgiques*, I disliked and belittled the *Bagatelles*.

Now I am accustomed to listen to the *Bagatelles* with more indulgent ears, and to perform them myself— and am ready to grant them the virtue of spontaneity, which my piano compositions of the twenties—such as the *Novelettes*, Preludes, *Voeux*, etc. do not have. I can even understand now people preferring the *Bagatelles* to the *Voeux*, or 4 Preludes; but I still cannot understand the success of the *Bagatelles* over other pieces of my youth written in [the] same circumstances by [the] same composer at the same time. After all, the *Bagatelles* were only a choice among hundreds of small piano compositions… and *Petite Suite*, *Pièces sans titres*, Episodes, 10 Etudes and others belong to the same stock. [Why are] the *Bagatelles* still going strong and not the others? It is a mystery to me.

❀ After the virtuoso *Sturm und Drang* pieces, such as the Nocturnes, Dances, Toccatas, *Novelettes*—which somehow served their goal as concert piano pieces—I started (still in Tiflis, with the Inventions) a process of "purifying" my piano writing: the Inventions were the most primitive pieces—the *Préludes nostalgiques*, the Four Preludes and finally the *Romances* followed the trend, but became more and more complex. Still there was a gap between the "concert pieces," which were useful for performance, and those piano pieces written for the sake of music. In my recital programs, I stuck to the old "warhorses"… Of the "honest" piano pieces (without *Schmalz*) only the 2nd Piano Concerto stayed in my repertoire.

To combine "honesty" with virtuosity, as I tried in the *Novelettes* and the Second Toccata, did not succeed: the *Novelettes*, especially (which I played for one season and then stopped) were seated royally between two chairs.

So… I wanted to produce a strictly unconventional and yet virtuoso piece that I could use in my concerts. To avoid any allusion to a conventional form, to underline its psychological inner sense, I called the piece *Message*… It was not easy to play, nor easy to memorize. I never succeeded in keeping it in my "standard" piano repertoire[;] after first performing it in London [I] returned to it only in the forties for my Paris piano recital, and then—again after more than a decade—played it at my recital in Chicago in 1960.[1]

This composition, which never met with favorable reviews, is still somehow puzzling to me: in one way I feel that I have achieved my goal, in another way I feel that it is still problematic as a piano piece.

❀ In the summer of 1926, I composed… a series of piano pieces entitled *Voeux* [*Wishes*] (of which *Voeux pour le bonheur bourgeois* ["Wishes for bourgeois happiness"] acquired a certain notoriety and was reproduced in a Swiss music box).

[*Voeux*] had some relation to my psychological state… to the problems of family, life, faith and even to political problems (*La paix en Orient*—which [related] to the liquidation of the Abdel Krim uprising). When giving the composition to Durand… I changed the title of *Voeux pour le Prolétariat* ["Wishes for the Proletariat"] to *Voeux pour la vie* ["Wishes for Life"] and left out the *Voeux pour la paix en Orient* ["Wishes for Peace in the Orient"]—presenting Jacques Durand with a separate manuscript of this *Voeux*, with a little dedication mentioning that this wish is not to be printed because it was already fulfilled.

Truly I was in despair and greatest indecision at that time:… should I take the courage [to] get away from [a] way of life absolutely contrary to my education, to my career, to my ambitions, could I enjoy the little *bonheur bourgeois*… by accepting [a] bourgeois type of companion, should I follow my original revolutionary inclination of accepting the ideology of [the] Russian revolution and… be bold enough to leave my parents and return to my country, in [whose] ideals and struggle I believed… [having] spent by now five years outside my country? While in the *Message* all the same feelings gave birth to a pure, non-programmatic composition, in the *Voeux* the problems became hidden behind the

---

1   A performance in San Francisco in the late 1940s evidently slipped Tcherepnin's mind.

titles: I asked my Saint, Alexander Nevsky, for guidance; I expressed my devotion and love to my Parents, I analyzed my Sentiment, which was that of longing for tenderness; I thought of a simple, unpretentious *bonheur bourgeois* with a girl who would endorse my life and not put me in a climate of "high life"; and finally, I expressed my admiration for the struggle of my country—*Voeux pour le prolétariat*, which it was easy for me to change into *Voeux pour la vie*, because I strongly believed in its ideals-those of healthy work for building a new human society.

THE ORGAN

[I] decided to take some organ lessons from the organist of Baden Baden's most prominent cathedral. This was the most trying experience, because between lessons I had to practice at the cathedral, and felt conscious that some people prayed silently or visited the church while I was practicing, and [I was] ashamed to disturb them by the wrong notes of the footwork, [experiments] in instrumentation (registration) and advanced harmonies. So it [was] not long before I gave up...

CELLO WRITING

Piatigorsky asked that I compose four pieces for him—of the kind he could put at the end of a program, which is to say, in a popular and virtuoso genre (he insisted above all that I employ the penetrating high register—contrary to my own conception of the cello, which was, rather, to treat the cello as the equivalent of the human baritone voice). I happily accepted this proposition along with an advance of three hundred dollars (half the total price—the other half to be turned over at the moment I "deliver the goods").

{*Editor's note:* Tcherepnin's high register writing turned out to be all the cellist desired-and more: playing through the score, Piatigorsky pointed to a particularly stratospheric passage and exclaimed: "Did you suppose I am a violinist?"}

❀ I became dissatisfied with [my boyhood cello teacher] when he described Prokofiev's Ballade for cello as "degenerate." It so happened that I loved this piece, and was so outraged that I... sold my cello and bought a bicycle.

DRUMS

While composing the Prelude No. 2 of the Twelve Preludes... which I rather pretentiously entitled *The Well-Tempered Cello*... I wanted the melodic line of the cello to be accompanied by purely rhythmical Interpoint: first, in the bass; [then], in the middle [of the piece]—where it becomes associated with horizontal Interpoint—in the treble. The pitch value of the interpuntal part was indifferent to me: only the register (low or high) seemed to be important. The first version of this prelude was for cello accompanied by bass drum and side drum.

To unify the twelve preludes, I "transposed" the rhythms to appropriate pitches, and in this form [the piece] was published. Yet when performing it... with my friend the cellist Paul Grlimmer, I [often] accompanied this prelude on drums instead of piano, and adopted the same procedure for the Prelude No. 4, although No. 4, like all the other [remaining] preludes of the set, was originally composed for cello and piano.

❀ ... One of the drums (the small one) that I used [for a performance] in Cologne had a big negro face painted on its skin. This, together with an unexpected (due to [clumsy] footwork) and unplanned huge *sforzato* on the bass drum [produced] hilarity in the audience.

❀ ... In London, on December 15, [1927], I gave a sonata evening with Paul Grlimmer at the Aeolian Hall at which we played my 1st Sonata, the Ballade by Prokofiev, the *Well-Tempered Cello* and the Reger A major Sonata... For this concert I went, as usual, to rent the drums. Found a splendid bass drum and side drum—with English military insigniae—at the instrument shop of Hawkes. The director of the shop... persuaded me to buy these drums instead of renting them. I did so. And from [then] on, I had the perfect instruments to play when performing the *Well-Tempered Cello*.

The funny thing was that all during the Second World War, during the occupation, these drums were in my flat [in Paris]. Had some German by any chance searched my apartment, I certainly would have been under suspicion for keeping English military drums. But, thank God, no one searched my flat; the drums survived the occupation and I sold them to a Canadian *antiquaire*, who made the bass drum into a low table for his den, to [hold] glasses, bottles or ashtrays. I do not know what he did with the side drum.

PROFESSIONAL DISCOUNT

During my stay in London [in March 1946], having received an urgent telegram requesting delivery of the orchestration of *Chota Rostaveli*, I spent my days and nights working on the instrumentation.

Not having counted on doing this work in London, I hadn't taken the precaution of bringing music paper with me. After many fruitless inquiries, I found excellent paper at my publisher's, the Chester firm. At my request, the director of the company sent me an impressive quantity of beautiful paper, but included a no less substantial invoice in the package!

Annoyed at being required to pay "in cash," I composed two melodies for voice and piano on words of Marguerite Tuck, a young poetess who had been kind enough to put her studio with a marvelous Bechstein at my disposal-thanks to which hospitality I had been able to do the orchestration.

… The director of the Chester firm was nice enough to accept the two melodies-which I put on 2 pages of his beautiful paper-in total payment.

PERFORMANCE FEES

[In Constantinople], sounds of a street organ, playing a tune from a Greek operetta were heard at intervals; the funny part was that the organ grinder wandering from hut to hut would stop playing while collecting the money, sometimes… on a half of a beat of a measure, or so, and then, after the "collecting" intermission, start again from the same place-[the same] middle of a beat.

PIANO TEACHING

The beginning of piano teaching should be done by ear, not by eyes. First, make the student sing and then make him find on the piano the familiar melody. Next step: incite him to search for the melody in another voice, and eventually a harmony, still by ear. As a further step, play for him a simple piece and make him memorize it by ear. Give him the name of notes. Make him transpose the same melody from one tonality to another, thus showing him the sense of accidentals, giving him the idea of tonality. Only after a long period should you show him how the notes are written.

SUFFERING FOOLS GLADLY
(overheard at a music convention)

Piano teacher: (to Alexander Tcherepnin) I have a student who can play all of Mozart and Beethoven and who has gone through all the Schaum books. What should I do with him now?
Tcherepnin: Send him to me.
Teacher: But we live in Detroit. How could I get him to Chicago?
Tcherepnin: Put him in a box and mail him.

✸   *(An explanation of nine-tone, given in response to a somewhat impertinent question at a college lecture)*

Quite near to DePaul University was a little kind of a joint. It was called "Enriched Hamburgers." So I would say my music, my tonality is "enriched tonality."

ELECTRONIC MUSIC

Looking on… electronic music [as] an all-prepared, finished product of music in [the] form of a carefully recorded and prepared [tape], I feel [that] this is a medium for the future, quite logical and quite suitable. Here a piece of music will become as finished and preestablished as a painting. And it brings the composer back to the time when [he] was also the interpreter. It will also guarantee a piece of music [freedom] from misinterpretation by a mediocre interpreter and give to composition its complete finality.

THE POWER OF A TITLE

Having heard nothing from Chicago… I was wondering if the *Symphonic Prayer* ha[d] reached its destination.… Finally, on August 21st [, 1959,] came a wire… that the *Symphonic Prayer* was first performed at the opening of the Festival on the 19th and due to the success w[ould] be repeated [at] the closing of the Festival on the 23rd.

… The amusing part was that the piece was put on the program under the title *Symphonic Prayer for Peace*, and that at the second performance it was marked by [demonstrations] for peace and [the] oratory of a propagandist.

PERCUSSION AND THE "FOUR GROUP" ORCHESTRA

[From] my earliest youth—and especially in the 20s—I have felt the need [to depart] from conventional pitch and to enrich the musical palette by sounds outside of the chromatic tempered staircase.

To enlarge the number of sounds that we call "music."

People who objected to [this], who object to electronic music [and unpitched] sounds of percussion—why do they not object to a cymbal crash, or a drum display, [as] so often used in Romantic music without anyone doubting the composer's sincerity? [Indeed] without realizing it [they receive] great emotional uplift [from] this non-pitched addendum.

The fact is that the future of music—of orchestral music in particular—seems to me [to lie] in the growth of the percussion group in the composition of the orchestra.

We already have, of course, a multitude of percussion instruments, yet hardly any orchestra has more than three percussion players.

Our symphony orchestra is the same apparatus, [the] same instrument, [that] served Romantic music—and later on, Impressionistic music—so well.

[As long as] the apparatus (*i. e.*, the composition of our symphony orchestra) stay[s the] same, it will play essentially the compositions produced for [it], such as the masterpieces of Romantic music and also of suitable Classical music from Haydn on. Indeed, the programs of our symphony orchestra are chiefly devoted to the compositions of the past, for [which] the present orchestra is an appropriate medium.

On the other side, Bach, Handel, etc. are played less-and [then] mostly in a version for larger orchestra.

If we start from Haydn, as the Father of our Symphony Orchestra, we have in his scores the embryo of the four groups. Yet only the string group and the woodwind group are equal, and for general use. [The] brass was handicapped [during] his time, and for a long time to come, by the "natural" instruments and their limitations, while percussion [was limited]—with a few exceptions—to only one player.

The Romantic school… added the brass group, thanks to the progress in instrument[-making], as a full-sized, powerful group for general use. The Modern [era] brought more and more emphasis to percussion… [Eventually], the percussion group will grow to an independent, full-sized group and the orchestra will become [a] four-group orchestra.

First step—to augment the number of [percussion] players and introduce some new instruments, among them electronic instruments. Next step—by general use of microphones—[to] liberate the strings from slavery [to] the concertmaster, individualize them and reduce their number. [The] result will [be] a new symphony orchestra… able to serve the cause of modern music in the same way [that] Haydn's orchestra served the music of his time, and the Romantic orchestra served Romantic music.

When, as the consequence of the changed balance and enrichment of orchestral colors and possibilities, we will have to "reorchestrate" the scores of Beethoven, Tchaikovsky, etc. for the new orchestra, the cause of modern music will be won and programs will change radically in favor of the new [music] for which the four-group orchestra [is] the appropriate medium.

In this fourth group, electronic-instruments-to-come will have an important part.

RUSSIAN MUSIC

❋ Western art music is a product of the Catholic Church, and of its progressiveness—in allowing polyphony to develop, providing music with the system of notation, organiz[ing the] church modes [and] allowing instruments to be used in church service[s]. The backwardness of the Greek Orthodox Church, [while] having its religious virtues, retarded the development of art music in Russia for many a century; Russian art music owes its origin still to the influence of the Catholic Church's western music product, which reached Russia first via Poland, then, [at] the end of the 18th century, via Italy.

❋ I must say that the Greek Orthodox church is not very receptive to the new productions [of composers]. They [insist on] keeping to the mutilation of the old chant that was [perpetrated] in the 18th century by Bortniansky, Beresovsky and Fomin, who were appointed by Catherine the Great to go to learn harmony and counterpoint in Italy. [Later] they [were] busy spoiling all our medieval chants [with] Italian harmonization, and that's what our church is [still] singing.

❋ Tchaikovsky never pretended to be clever; he wrote what he felt and consequently revealed both the greatness and the weakness of sincerity.

❋ The development of the Russian school grew from creative genius *plus* a close comradeship of work and a guiding influence of expert criticism *while* the work was being done. It would be interesting to see how such a close, strong combination would work in other lands.

❋ For a Russian, there's no exoticism in Oriental music.

CRITICISM AND CRITICS

❋ Artists [live] in a regime of constant flattery; no one who comes to greet an artist after the concert [in] the green room ever [utters] anything other than compliments. So it is quite… a shock for an artist to find that someone does not like his way of playing, of composing, and dares to express it publically. And of course there [is] applause after each performance. For my part, I am always interested to read the reviews… In that way I [learn] what is said behind my back. Of course, I am happy if the reviews are good, but I am never angered by bad reviews, whether I find them justified or unjustified….

❋ Early in the morning of the concert [in Tsin Tsin], a group of Chinese newspapermen came to my hotel and interviewed me. After the interview was over they [made no effort to] leave and seemed [to be] waiting for some[thing]. When I asked the interpreter… he explained [to] me that they were waiting for me to play the Recital program for them. When I expressed my astonishment [I was told] that in order to have a review of the concert in the next day's Chinese paper, they [had] to hear the concert in the morning to meet the deadline. I had an upright piano in my hotel room and was glad to play the entire program for the newspapermen.

❋ After [my Monte Carlo debut concert], a very enthusiastic critique appeared. and before long the author of it, a Mr. Joly, asked me for a rendezvous. I was highly flattered when he came and expressed his full admiration for me both as a composer and as a pianist. Then he told me that, as a correspondent of the Paris magazine *Courier Musicale*, he would like to write a long article about me. I was even more impressed. But then he produced various sizes of articles in that magazine and asked me which size [seemed] good for the article, and did I wish to have my photo reproduced, etc. Still unsus[picious] of anything, I produced a photo… Then, finally, he explained to me that I would have to pay for the reproduction of the picture, and [for] the article according to its size—and produced [a list of prices]. I felt like an honest girl, a virgin, who was mistaken for a prostitute and approached with a lewd proposal. I explained to Mr. Joly that even if I [had] the funds, I would never… pay for a favorable article, but [in fact] I [had] no funds… It amused me a month or so later to read his article… it was as enthusiastic as if I [had] paid for it, but at the end he [observed], "Mr. Tcherepnin will not fail to become a perfect and widely celebrated pianist as soon as he ceases to put his left foot under his stool while playing."… Evidently, my left leg was covered by the side of the pants with the pocket in it.

❋ My sons are very generous about my music—they sit in different parts of the hall and applaud very loudly!

PROFESSIONAL MUSICIANS

❋ This is a difficult time for musicians, because they seem to feel that there is little future for them. Fortunately, I feel just the opposite. There is a *very* secure future for musicians. Maybe there are no easy "staff" jobs available, but certainly, the future of music has not come to a standstill just because of a scarcity of staff jobs. If a true musician wants to become a professional, he can very easily. But he must not be lazy. Stravinskys were not born; they were made. Work, work and more work is necessary. In Paris, during the occupation, I was allotted only three cigarettes a day. For me, this was not enough. I wanted more. Because I wanted them badly enough, I got them. In fact, I could get quite a supply for myself by merely looking for them. This taught me a great lesson. If a man is resourceful enough, he can get anything he wants. There is nothing a man can't do, if he has all of his health. So it is with musicians. Many have bastardized themselves artistically, so that they must work hard to rise up to their former standards. This is hard to do, but once it is done, then he can have a very creative and secure future. Unlike the man in business, who must depend on others for his work, the musician always has his "business" right with him. He can bring it wherever he goes. It never leaves him. This is his security.

❋ As a musician I have many activities: I am composing, I am teaching, I am playing piano, I am conducting.

Assume that I am composing on commission, and I receive the highest price I have [ever] been offered: [even then], one hour spent composing will bring me one cent. [But] when I start to teach the same [music] to some kind of private student, for an hour I can already think [I will earn] not one cent but about fifty dollars. And when I start to play this on a concert—this same piece that was paid *one cent an hour*—for one hour [of] a concert [I receive] a little over a thousand dollars. And if I take a baton and start to conduct it, [the fee would be] *much* larger.

Now I ask you, what would a conductor do—the greatest, Toscanini of Toscaninis, super-Toscanini—what would he do with his baton if there were no composer?

THE PERFORMER'S LOT

❋ The concert stage is like a church for me, the place where I can serve my religion-which is music-and thus accomplish my mission towards human beings.

❋ Someone has estimated that I have spent, in all, about two complete years on ships (mostly being seasick), trains and planes.

❋ I was shy, but as children were supposed to sing for guests, I would hide under the piano and sing from there.

❋ One of my fondest childhood memories is of playing the piano with my father. He would designate some notes or short patterns for me to perform in the treble while he improvised an accompaniment. In playing my indicated notes and adjusting my dynamics to those of his accompaniment I felt as though I was contributing to a real musical performance.

❋ I used to practice piano wildly with a hard touch which, as I was told, would strengthen my fingers. Before presenting myself [at] the [Paris Conservatory] entrance examination, for weeks I did practically nothing other than to practice. After having heard me, [Isidore] Philipp, with his great kindness, told me: "Your hand is very tired, *mon petit* (he always called me "my little one"). Do not practice too much and do not practice hard—learn to practice *piano*: it will relax you and bring progress."

❋ The audience [provides an] invisible but feelable radiation of assistance which I always feel when performing and which helps me to give my best.

❋ The day will come when we will no longer have a Romantic cemetery on our concert stage.

❋ [In Paris], Adila [Fachiri] stayed at Mrs. Stern's home… and one evening we were asked to play. Mrs. Stern had a huge music room, which had very high ceilings and was surrounded at the mezzanine level by a narrow balcony with comfortable chairs for listeners. At that evening, the aged but still passionate Mrs. Stern had a guest—a boxer whose name I forgot, but who, strong and young, was supposed to be her lover (not disinterested, however). Lots of stories were going around about this affair. The room was plunged in dark[ness]—with the only lights near the piano… While Mrs. Stern and her boxer friend were able to see us from the balcony, we were, of course, not able to see them…

We were asked to play some soft music: among the selections were the first movement of the Cesar Franck Violin Sonata followed by Bach's Chaconne for solo violin. No sound from upstairs after our playing. So we were to continue. It was my turn to play solo, so I chose to play the Nocturne, Op. 2. When I finished I heard Mrs. Stern's exclamation, "*C'est merveilleux!*" This gave me the idea to continue in no soft way—I played the Danse, Op. 2, and then finished with the Toccata No. 1. The result was that Mrs. Stern and her boxer friend (. buttoning his pants) came down, the hall [was lighted] and both paid me heartiest compliments…

❋ [When] I appeared with my 1st Piano Concerto under Aime Kunc in Toulouse… the pedal… stopped function[ing] in the middle of the concerto. I continued and played the second half without pedal. The funny part [was] that no one noticed it: listening to the compliments… in the green room I learned once more not to take [them] seriously.

❋ Early in February [1927], I went alone to Arnheim in Holland to perform… my 2nd Piano Concerto. The fee that I received hardly paid for the trip and hotel, and it proved once more to Louisine that what I do professionally is chiefly for my own amusement.

❋ {*London, November 1972*} Hectic time, overburdened schedule, working under pressure, traveling and all this at an age at which any composer of self-respect should enjoy eternal rest or gossiping with his ancestors at the Elysian Fields.

❋ {*Written on Air France stationery*} It is 1:50 AM in Chicago, but it is already full sunshine over the ocea—the stewardess announced that in 1 hour 15 minutes we shall land in Paris-When I think of all the dreadful weeks that before the war I spent on steamships on the ocean— I am especially blessing this wonderful way of getting over the ocean like in a bus drive. Mrs. T. is still sleeping-not [many] people on the plane, and thus was able to stretch herself along the three empty seats.

❋ What a privilege it was to the performer who first performed, let us say, the Beethoven *Moonlight* Sonata, or to Gieseking, who first had the nerve to put Debussy's Preludes on the musical geographic map of pieces to be performed. The performer today can find pieces worthy of his attention at all stages of difficulty.

❋ It was very warm [in Nanking]. The piano on which I played had a non-adjusted closing cover over the keyboard. A young Chinese girl had to stand during the entire-nearly one hour long-performance to hold the cover, which otherwise would [have] fall[en] on my fingers. There were many mosquitos circling around—observing their maneuvers while playing I was scared that if the mosquitos… attack[ed] the girl she might take her hand from the cover-board, [letting it] fall on my fingers. But she was a brave girl. Mosquitos or no mosquitos she [did] her job perfectly and never lost her vigilancy keeping my fingers under her protection.

❋ The Sgambati Hall at the Academia Santa Cecilia was filled to capacity and [the onstage] audience [for our Rome trio concert] practically surrounded us. While playing solo, I observed that two ladies seated near the piano were chatting without interruption. When the conversation would stop, it was evident that one of the ladies [was looking] for a new subject to continue the animated conversation. And they were not [the only ones] to chat during the performance. It did not disturb me, but I [feared] this behavior was the result of our boring playing. On the next day, however, I attended the same hall… and observed that the audience was [just] as chatty. Later on I observed [the same thing] at La Scala [during] Italian operas and Russian ballets. Evidently, the Italian temperament accepts it as necessity.

❋ I was due to take the train in Athens for Salonika to appear there at a chamber music concert performing my Trio and some other selections. But I was tired, out of practice, so I wired to my friend, the Greek conductor Loris Margaritis, that I [would] be unable to come. As he told me afterwards, in order not to [disappoint] the audience, he replaced me performing the piano part of my Trio and attached a beard to his face to pretend [he was] me…

❋ Champagne never brought me luck! A 97-cent Spanish Rose will do!

❋ After [a] concert [in St. Brieuc, the violinist Dany Brunschwig and I] were invited by the president of the [concert] society and expected to have something to eat… It was a large gathering of St. Brieuc musicians—but alas, no food in sight. What's more, the President, an amateur organist, started to play….Far after midnight. I persuaded Dany to leave [and] hunt for an eating place. He bet that such could not be found… Still I insisted—so we walked along the pitch-dark streets.

    Finally, I saw a light—a red light—and an entrance door. I entered and pushed the shy Dany in with me. The room was brightly [lit]; many ladies in low-necked dresses were seated around, and a huge red-haired lady greeted us and wished us welcome.

    Dany whispered, "Let's go, let's go." I was more courageous and asked the lady if we could have something to eat. She answered, "Nous ne vendons ici que de la chair humaine. "[1]

---

1   "Here we sell only human flesh."

THE EARLY YAMAHA

❋ [In 1936], Japanese Victor Recordings asked me to record the [first] Japanese pieces [in the Tcherepnin Collection] for them. I found that the Japanese Yamaha concert grand piano that I played at the Radio [was] an excellent instrument and suggested to use it for the recording, in order to patronize Japanese instrument making. It was an event in Japanese musical life that a foreign artist would care to play on a Japanese piano.

The piano was so big that it was impossible to place it in the elevator (the Victor Studio was on the top floor of a tall building)—so it had to be lifted through the window. The lifting of the piano was photographed by the press. Before the beginning of the recording session I was interviewed and photographed at the piano. Then the press photographers and interviewers left, leaving us free to record.

Recording done… I found that the sound was uncolorful, dry and spinet-like. Suspecting my touch, I recorded again, trying to play softer with more pedal. The result was [no] better. Then I suspected the engineers, and asked [them] to play for me some other piano recordings done by them. The other recordings sounded normal. So gradually the engineers and I started to suspect the piano. There was a baby grand Steinway in the room that was used for recordings. On advice of the engineers, I recorded the pieces on that Steinway. The result was unbelievable: the little Steinway sounded colorful, beautiful and powerful! So after all the press boom the pieces appeared [as] recorded on the baby grand Steinway piano.

THE OPERATIC GAUNTLET

{*Editor's note:* Tcherepnin enjoyed several notable operatic successes; however, like almost everyone involved with the singular world of opera, he had his horror stories as well-which he wrote about with characteristic gusto-beginning in 1922 with his "pocket opera" *Idylle Astrale*.}

IDYLLE ASTRALE

❋ *Idylle Astrale*… gave me much… trouble because of the text, [which], with all due respect to Maria Star, I felt [was] extremely corny. In order to push myself to produce it, I had to imagine another plot or program which would fit… the form of the *Idylle Astrale*, yet give me more desire to compose it. So I imagined a cathedral with the religious service going on, and then a celestial vision of the Eternal Truth. [This] approach helped me to fulfill the assignment: I conceived it for tenor solo, speaking voices, flute, string quintet and an organ. [Later,] the music of the *Idylle Astrale* became my String Quartet, Op. 36.

OL-OL

❋ … The [world premiere] performance of my opera *Ol-Ol* in Cologne… was scheduled for the middle of March 1927. Receiving no news from Cologne, I sent a wire with a prepaid answer to the Intendant of the Cologne Opera asking about the date. No answer came… [In] March [I] went to Paris… and from there to Cologne.

Here I learned the reason for the silence of the Intendant (although I did not understand why I could not have been advised of it). *Ol-Ol* was not to be given, and the reason… was that some months before, the production of Bartók's ballet *The Miraculous Mandarin* [provoked] a huge scandal due to [its setting]—a Chinese brothel… The Intendant [and] the Opera [personnel were mocked] as brothel-keepers. Ol-Ol being a prostitute would only throw new oil on the still-burning fire of mockery… so, as the Intendant said, he had to ask Universal Editions to release him from his obligation to produce [the opera].

It was a great shock to me, yet, when the Intendant phoned me to explain and to apologize, it was I who tried to comfort him, saying that I understood and could not blame him for it.

❋ [In late 1933], my old friend, the young composer Alec Steinert insisted on introducing me to a Mrs. Irion, a lady who was about to sponsor a season of Russian operas at the Casino Theater in New York with a troupe consisting mostly of Russian singers. When I told her that I had a half-evening opera, *Ol-Ol*, she jumped [at] it because she was looking for [something to fill] a double-bill with Tchaikovsky's *Yolantha*. She asked me if I would be willing to work with the singers, and… I had… to write the original Russian text [into the] vocal scores, which [contained] only German and French translations.

It was a hard ordeal to coach Russian singers [owing to] their lack of knowledge of *solfège*; I had to chew into them practically every note. It was equally hard to teach American singers to sing in Russian—the Americans knew their *solfège*, singing intervals was no problem for them, but pronouncing Russian was their ordeal (and mine, as their teacher). The premiere took place on February 7th…

The performance was pitiful: the tenor… had hardly learned his part and constantly missed [entrances], singing out of tune…; [even] the best [singers] had not learned their parts thoroughly. The orchestra, under the [leadership] of Steinert, then absolutely inexperienced, was catastrophic.

[Before] the second performance, the baritone…became sick, and I ventured to replace him. It was great fun to rehearse, to move on stage and to sing the part with full expression. Yet it was fun only for me; my voice must have sounded dreadful, [for] after the rehearsal, the direction resurrected the [ailing] baritone, who sang in the evening, while I missed my only chance to make my stage debut as a baritone…

THE WEDDING OF SOBEIDE

❋ [The year 1930] found Universal Editions in panic: Nazism was in progress in Germany and as a result, fifteen contracts for opera or ballet performances of works of leading UE composers were canceled. *Sobeide* lost its chance to be performed in Berlin, where she had been tentatively accepted by the *Unter den Linden* Opera, and there was great pessimism at UE about what would come. And [this] was still [only] 1930—three years before Hitler came to power.

❋ While I was in Vienna, [a publisher] told me that the Deutsche Oper in Prag [was] interested in *Sobeide* and advised me to make a short trip to Prag and to play *Sobeide* for Szell. I did so… Hitting… a black key [at the wrong angle], my thumb started to bleed, and at the end of the first act the keyboard was covered by blood. Szell became aware of it. But I became aware of Szell's disapproval. I never played further than this first "bloody" act and returned to Vienna with a negative result, which Szell did not tell me at the time but which was easy to guess.

ST. VEIT'S ORGAN

❋ … at the premiere of *The Wedding of Sobeide* [in March 1933], I met an Austrian author whom I had long admired, Hermann Heinz Ortner. He submitted a libretto to me, *St. Veit's Organ*, in which mysticism was joined to realism, and which pleased me so much that I decided to compose it.

… I met Ortner in July at Salzburg and played him the half of the first act. It seemed to me that Ortner was shocked by my music. Whether because of his stunned reaction, whether because of lack of encouragement on his part, whether because I had realized that the clearly Teutonic libretto was basically quite contrary to my Eurasian mentality, the fact remains that I suddenly "cooled off" and abandoned the composition—("momentarily," as I then thought)…

THE MARRIAGE
(as the subject of an unhappy experiment)

{*Editor's note:* The phrase "unhappy experiment" is Tcherepnin's own. A reminder: *The Marriage* consists of two tableaux, the first composed by Mussorgsky, the second by Tcherepnin: both were orchestrated by Tcherepnin.}

The Musical Society of Russia Abroad, under whose auspices the 1939 Paris performance of *The Marriage* had taken place, proposed organizing a series of performances of Russian operas [during the occupation], and wanted to include *The Marriage* in this series.

The scenery and direction were entrusted to the painter Annenkov.

Annenkov's conception involved using the entire text of the Gogol comedy—all passages not included in the libretto of the opera would be presented as spoken dialogue. He asked me, however, to fill out my score with several new scenes, and I decided that I would compose a substantial overture as well.

Everything was ready by the beginning of 1943, and the "Season of Russian Opera" took place at the Salle Pleyel that May and June. Since the occupying authorities, at the last minute, prohibited any account or mention of these performances either in advertisements or reviews, nobody knew anything about this "season" except the Russians, who came to weep through *Pique Dame* and *Eugene Onegin*—and did not seem to enjoy sitting through *The Marriage*.

Nor was I enthusiastic. In *The Marriage*, Mussorgsky wanted "once and for all to fix the intonation, the expression and the dynamism of the Russian language in music."… My design was similar… [a] "recitative" embedded in a music that pursues its own development in accord with the dramatic thrust of the text.

In short, we wanted to create an "operatic realism": and unfortunately this realism, juxtaposed with the genuine realism of "speech without music" and alternating with it, was killed by it. Every time the music resumed, the action appeared to be slowed down, and the "operatic realism" seemed like a pretentious stylization without a *raison d'être*.

From this failed and disappointing effort, I retained nothing positive except the overture, which I had composed in complete thematic independence from the opera, under the influence of a Gogol novella, *Nevsky Prospect*; I completely reorchestrated this piece after hearing it, and it acquired an independent place in my catalogue under the title *Nevsky Prospect*, Overture for symphony orchestra. Acceding to the demands of my editor, I used *The Return of the Coachman* as the subtitle of this work.

THE FARMER AND THE FAIRY

❋ [In the spring of 1962], DePaul University Opera Workshop programmed *The Farmer and the Fairy* [on a] double bill with *Trouble in Tahiti* by Bernstein at the DePaul Center Theater.

Of course, no orchestra was available, and it had to be done with piano, to which viola was added for the viola solo places, and 3… percussion [players]. The director… put all [her] zeal in[to] the production, but zeal is not enough when one has not the slightest knowledge of stage direction. And the "staticness" of the opera makes the stage direction even [more] important and indispensable.

[I] did all I could to [get] the singers to give expression instead of just vocalizing, to move around purpose[fully] and not [aimlessly], to act…; by far the worst was the narrator—a pin-up type girl of Yugoslavian origin. Tried to teach her how to [speak] the text expressively.

But all was in vain.

On Friday, May 1st, Hsien Ming and I attended the first performance. It was probably the most painful experience of all my life—everything was wrong… The (vocally fair) singers did not know what to do with themselves, walked like zombies or did not walk at all; the piano, hidden backstage, was shot and hardly audible… And the words pronounced by the Yugoslav… were [incomprehensible]. And with [all] this, I had to bow from the stage and listen to compliments…

A JOHN BROWN PROJECT

❋ I visited the American poet Steven [Vincent] Benet, who suggested that I compose an oratorio on the subject of John Brown and declared himself ready to write the text for it. The figure of John Brown interested me very much. We undertook… a trip to the battlefields of the Civil War… to Harpers Ferry, where John Brown was caught… to Charleston, where John Brown was hanged… At the Library of Congress I looked for Civil War battle music. Outside of the epic poem of Benet, I read quite a deal about John Brown… It was enlightening to learn that he preferred to be executed, instead of accepting the insanity plea suggested by his lawyers, [which] would certainly have saved him from the gallows. He was fully aware that his execution [would serve] his cause better than his survival and consciously preferred the execution. His self-sacrifice was Christlike. As much as I admired it and his ideas, I was not enthusiastic about its relation to the Old Testament, [which] I always felt like rejecting for its bloodiness and cruelty. For me religion starts with the New Testament and has no relation to the Old Testament. When Jesus comes, all becomes Love, Charity, Pity, and [this] is in what I believe. But when I suggested to Steven Benet to separate John Brown from the Old Testament, he felt it would be historically untrue. My idea to make of John Brown a purely political humanitarian figure outside of any religious background was dear to me… and [I] spoke one time with Bert Brecht about it, [who] suggested. a libretto in two parts: the one how it really happened and the one how it should have happened. Nothing came of this [either] and in spite of accumulating… two other [John Brown] scripts, I never composed any.

JAZZ

❋ I am not much qualified to speak of jazz as such, because perhaps I was one of the rare composers of the 20th century who personally escaped any influence from this music… Still, I know about jazz and I feel that here we have. a popular art [that] is an art in itself. Just like in the olden times, when there was [music for] the church and there were minstrels, [who] were not regarded as particularly honorable people… Where did the minstrels get their training? They learned… how to write music from the church [and] out of this music, [which] they composed at first for the sake of entertainment… our great music later [developed]. So who knows if today's jazz, which is composed for the sake of entertainment of people, is not the seed from which the future great music might grow?

❋ Whether it's "pop" or "serious music," whoever has talent is right.

❋ Already with jazz and Gershwin—United States music of that field made a world conquest… because it was something that was true, something that came [at] the right moment, [and] was produced with talent. A monopoly of entertainment music is [still] in the hands of American music all over the world with no exception. Now at the same time [there] is also [an] avant-garde American music where [the] American composer is unbeatable, because they bring something that European composer[s] cannot do. I would say that just [as] Russian music [in] the 20th century [influenced] the [fate] of music in all the world… the 21st century… will be the century of American Music.

MUZAK

❋ This is the *most* terrible thing that has happened to the world! It was bad enough when people moved out of the active role of *playing* music into the passive role of listening, but now they are not even listening—they are eating to it, reading to it, and thinking *to* it but not *of* it. The origins of music required active participation, but now, with the advances in technical skills, we have only to turn on a hi-fi and there is muzak. Eventually, people will not even know *how* to listen to music. It will truly be a lost art. I say that we must get back to active participation in music. More group playing, either in trios, quartets or other. This way, a person need not rely on the abilities of other[s] when he wants music. It will be available to him through his own resources.

COMPOSING FOR FILM AND TELEVISION

❋ In Paris [in 1933] I was asked to compose music for two documentary films [about] India—about one hour duration. As always in the film business, the budget was scanty for music and the time even scantier. I went to the studio of *Éclair-Journal* where the film was shown to me. Of course it would be impossible to compose and to write one hour of music for even small orchestra in a few days—so I suggested that I… do it by an improvisation on an *orgue Mustel*.[1] This was accepted. A beautiful Mustel organ was brought to the studio—the little practice in Baden Baden proved to be a help, and during the single day of November 23, improvising from morning till late in the afternoon while the film was projected… I succeeded to provide the films with practically uninterrupted music.

❋ In [late 1961] came an assignment to do the orchestral version (without chorus) of the final Gloria from the *Nativity Play* to serve as a frame for Margaret Truman's Christmas show on. CBS television, and [no] sooner [did I do] it, copying the parts myself, than came the long awaited commission to compose music for [a] CBS Twentieth Century production-documentary film—*The Crisis at Suez* Isaac Kleinerman projected for me some films that they did before—among them *The Battle of Stalingrad* (music by Auric) and *Okinawa* (music by Creston). I found both [scores] too noisy and too aggressive.

   Then Isaac projected *The Crisis at Suez*, and [a] few days later we went through it at the Moviola, Isaac giving me stimulating indications as to the moods of the music at each particular moment. I was given the script, in which all the shots were expressed in feet—so I had to transform the feet into seconds, according to the chart that was given to me. Hsien Ming [bought] a stopwatch; Virgil Thomson kindly loaned me his, and Hsien Ming also bought for me a pocket metronome that was easier to handle than the huge standing one.

   So on December 19th I embarked [on] compos[ing] the music [against] the deadline of January 3rd, [on] which the music was to be recorded (so the deadline was actually on January 1st, giving me but 13 days to compose and to orchestrate about twenty minutes [of] music).

   The most nerve-wracking [part] was the conversion of feet into seconds. I certainly spent more time doing it than in composition and orchestration. Thank God I had the help of Ivouchka,[2] who came to spend Christmas vacation with me, and who always was ready to help me with mathematics with his usual skill and wonderful good nature….

   [I] finished the…123-page-long score late at night on the 1st of January.…On January 3rd. the recording was done in 3 hours and everyone was pleased. It was amusing to hear a score that I completed only 36 hours [before], and I was satisfied with the results.

---

1   a kind of harmonium.

2   Tcherepnin's three sons, Peter, Serge and Ivan, rejoiced in the Russified nicknames Petinka, Serioginka and Ivouchka.

❊ For [the next documentary], *Catch the Graf Spee*, I insisted that the feet [be] transformed into minutes by an engineer for each of the sections…I had only six days to write down the whole 150 pages [of the orchestration]…[When] we went through the score with Alfredo Antonini, all was OK [except] that all my metronome [markings] were wrong, evidently due to the different atmospheric pressure, which influenced the sensitive pocket metronome that I used. Poor Alfredo probably spent [a] few trying hours before establishing the rate of difference. *Catch the Graf Spee* was on the dramatic side, with [cues] up to four minutes and… complex, sometimes polyphonic texture… I used much percussion, and this proved to be of help, by leaving the percussion parts to the end of the recording session, thus guaranteeing against overtime [that might otherwise] be needed for the whole orchestra.

RELIGION

❊ Religion is wonderful, but Churches are terrible! It seems the more organized religion gets, the worse it is. Wherever I am living at the time… that is the religion I practice.

Buddhism is a beautiful religion. If you compare the teachings of Christianity with those of Buddha, you would find them almost identical… only Buddhism is much more profound.

I never go to church… I give up my seat to those who want to go much more than I do.

❊ The tales of Tolstoy, [especially] "What Men Live By," "Two Old Men," "Where Love is God is" [and] "The Godson" [show] that God is in us, helping us to do good in life. I love these tales dearly—also "The Story of Ivan the Fool" which in spite of being slightly Utopic is congenial with my belief in the way to achieve peace.

THE AYA SOPHIA

I must admit that although I am not a fanatic of my own Greek-orthodox Russian religion, it… shocked me to see this great historic church transformed into a Mohametan mosque; to see Mohametan rites [and] praying in it, on large carpets, seemed unnatural and somehow blasphemous. Yet it seemed great when I visited the Mohametan mosques, heard the psalmodies of [the] Mullah; when I saw Mohametan praying in the parks at the sunset—there it was [in] its place and had all my admiration.

THE LANGUAGE PROBLEM

❊ Here [in Salzburg, August 1962] I have quite interesting students of many nationalities (French, German, Austrian, Japanese, American). The problem is that the French [do] not understand German or English, the Austrians do not understand French and English, and the Japanese and Americans do not understand German and French: so I have to repeat my remarks in three languages, and [the] same when I am discussing various [individual students'] problems.

THE GERMAN PROBLEM

❊ … A row of Baltic governesses took care of my preschool education. They were changed after the end of [each] year: Bertha Koch, Leontine Traks, Akina something and again Bertha Koch. All of them were Baltic Germans and trained me according to the system of Pestalozzi—making me do useful house[hold] duties and certain work; because of them I mastered the German language completely. Evidently [this] was [intended], because when I was 9 years old I was placed in the Reformat School in which all the teaching was done in German, and which at the time was one of the best schools in Petersburg. [It is] probable that scholastically the school was very good and was worth its reputation. But the custom there was rather strange: it was [believed] that fighting among the boys was [normal] and developed their bravery/?/. During the recesses, real battles took place between the classes and the teachers did not pay any attention. It [seemed] that fighting was even encouraged, [for] the fighters were never punished. I was tall but very weak. I did not know how to, and did not want to fight. Thus I was often beaten, and would return home with bruises. Considering it a shame to have been licked, I concealed my mishaps from my parents. [One day] I returned from school beaten up so [badly] by my [schoolmates], with so many bruises on my body that I collapsed into bed…. [When] I confessed…to my parents about the beating[s]…they decided to take me out [of] the Reformat School.[1]

---

1 Tcherepnin told his wife Ming that about the only time he got into a school fight willingly was when he rushed to the defense of a Jewish boy who was being pummeled by a gang of schoolmates as they shouted ethnic slurs. Unfortunately, young Tcherepnin's attempts to break up the fight were hopelessly ineffectual, and he merely suffered a beating for his pains.

❁ …The [1929 Baden Baden] Musikfest with Hindemith's *Lehrstück* as [its] central piece disgusted me. This pessimistic look on life, [which] I felt in *Lehrstück* and later in Weill's *Mahagonny*—just to name a few pieces—[and which] became fashionable and typical in Germany of the early thirties, this propaganda of hatred [spread] via artistic works… was unworthy of art, just what art should not serve.

❁ It [had] long [been] my desire to study algebra, [which] I hated in high school, but [which] seemed to me now to be related to music. I found a young German student, Otto Graf, who [gave] me algebra lessons. But very soon the lessons [evolved into] discussion about religion. I did not believe in church; in my belief, religion should be purely spiritual and should not mix with moral[ity]. Ethics is a social problem, so is human behavior, while religion is purely spiritual and therefore unrelated to the social code. I also believed that the religion of the future will come through science, and all [during the preceding] years [had been] passionately reading books about geology, astronomy, botany, natural science, etc. Otto Graf, [by contrast], was a devoted Roman Catholic. My idea of God independent from morals and morals independent from God shocked him Our discussion covered also the field of German problems. On one side, there was the great pessimism of German artistic production,. already mentioned, [which] seemed to me unworthy of art; on the other side was the rise of National Socialism, [which] replaced this sincere pessimism by a bureaucratic and aggressive optimism. I was interested to know if there [was yet] another way to think in Germany, if there [was] German youth who [was] neither pessimistic nor National Socialistic. Otto Graf assured me that [there was], and that [this] healthy way of thinking and living is professed by the German youth of the Roman Catholic religion…

❁ [In 1935] I went to the *Allgemeiner Deutsche Tonkünstler Musikfest*… in Hamburg. I do not remember what was performed… but I laconically wrote in my diary that I. had a most depressing impression of Germany. It was a great difference from the last *Musikfest* that I attended, in Dortmund two years [before], and even greater with the previous ones…

    Most of the musicians looked scared: there was the jokingly—called *Neue Deutsche Bewegung* {*i. e.*, "new German movement"—when two people were conversing, each would keep turning his head before speaking to make sure no one could overhear him-*Editor*}.

    Some musicians—strangely, foreigners, not Germans, were aggressive and behaved like Nazis: I remember a violent discussion that I had with the Finnish composer Kilpinen, who in my presence attacked Russians. I riposted and [we] finally [had to be] separated by well-meaning friends who [wished] to [prevent] a first class scandal. I remember also how shocked I was by the behavior of some Italians, among them the composer Pizzetti and the conductor Lualdi, who, before starting the concert, greeted the audience with a Hitler salute.

    Strangely enough, I cannot remember a single German musician who would wear a Nazi insignia or who would hold a Nazi talk. German musicians were confused and afraid. So were German publishers: my friend Schlee, who represented Universal Edition, told me, when we were alone, of the difficulties [involved] in [supporting] modern composers [in] Germany: in [the] absence of clear definitions of what could be [and could not be] allowed for performance. all the music directors, intendants and conductors were scared to consider any modern composition, [for] fear of making *faux pas* and losing their jobs.

WESTERN PREJUDICE

❁ On October 22, [1935], I gave a lecture-recital of Chinese and Japanese music in Munich… Munich critics were rather skeptical, and protested against the idea of Chinese and Japanese composing music for our instruments instead of using their own. I do not usually argue with the critics… yet this time I wrote back in favor of international instruments [for] all the nations, and… riposted by saying that if all the nations [used] only their national instruments, the Germans would probably have to use the Luren and similar old German instruments instead of imported Italian violins, French keyboards, etc.

❁ In Seattle at the Pro Musica Chapter on March 18, [1936], I played Chinese and Japanese music and my own compositions. It was amazing that due to the political situation, Japanese music was unwelcome in San Francisco, where I could play only Chinese and my own music; both Japanese and Chinese music were unwelcome in Los Angeles, where my program was reduced to my own compositions; while in Seattle I was allowed to present both Chinese and Japanese music and to complete the program with my own compositions.

THE JAPANESE PROBLEM

❋ Following the concert tour in Japan I had some appearances scheduled on my way from Japan to Peiping-in Korea and Manchuria, among others, in Dairen and in Port Arthur, [which] was dear to me [because of] its long heroic resistance to [the] Japanese during the Russo-Japanese War from my early youth.

But while in the railway train in Korea, I was shocked [in] the dining car of the train by [the] provocative aggressive behavior of the Japanese military "junta." Realizing that I would have to play [in an] "occupied" country, I gave up [any] idea [of] appear[ing] under such circumstances…

THE AMERICAN PROBLEM

❋ {*May 1968*} The other day, while walking in the lovely district of my New York "residence," an illuminating idea came to me, that will be the most practical for LBJ, RFK or similar [figures] among oncle [*sic*] Sam's employees to follow: instead of help for the underprivileged nations, help the underprivileged *race* at home. Give to the 20 million blacks free education up to *super* doctor's degree: make *all* of them the best educated class of [the] USA community, provide all of them (young and old) with a regular income (a la Social Security but with [a] higher stake, starting from the day of birth) and show the world what money and good will can do! Isn't it a bright idea? And why not?

THE RUSSIAN PROBLEM

❋ I was born three times—on January 8, January 20 and January 21, 1899 in St. Petersburg.[1]

❋ On the way from Miami to Louisville the plane stopped in St. Petersburg. It was the first time that I was in a town by the name of St. Petersburg since Petersburg was rebaptized Petrograd at the outbreak of the World War I. I [sent] postcards to my Russian friends and bought little gilded paper tags with [the] "Made in St. Petersburg" *etiquette*.

❋ [After the Red Army conquered Tiflis], the artists and musicians organized themselves in a union. At one of the rehearsals of the Opera, my father corrected the playing of the trombone player. The passage… had to be repeated—same mistake occurred. My father addressed the orchestra, and said, "Gentlemen, I will have to repeat the passage until it goes as it should." [At] this, someone in the orchestra screamed out, "The 'gentlemen' have all run away to Batum; [there] are only 'comrades' here." My father threw away the baton and left.

❋ Not that my father was bossy, nor that he had any political hatred toward the union. It was the usual way to address the orchestra, "Gentlemen"—no conservative mind was attached to this word. But my father had [a] quick temper. He was upset in his artistic feeling: it was not the question of "regime" but the question of orchestra discipline—my father could not tolerate interference with his responsibilities as a conductor and [took] the riposte… as a personal offense. He never returned to the [Tiflis] Opera…

❋ In Batum… we had just enough money to buy our passage as far as Constantinople… The customs officer opened our bags. All was OK with my mother's… which contained [a] few pieces of wearing apparel, [the] same with mine, which contained music manuscripts, but when the bag of my father was opened, the customs officer discovered a program of the Coronation [Gala] of the Ballet Russe in London in 1912—my father [had] conducted… his ballet *Pavillon d'Armide*, and treasured this program, printed on silk. [The officer] became red in [the] face and confiscated the entire bag, which contained letters to my father of Rimsky, Prokofiev and his numerous musical friends… I wonder [what] became of my father's bag? I hope it [fell] into the right hands, and that all the epistolary material… found its place in some library or artistic archives of the Soviet Union.

❋ [We left Georgia on the Mongibello], a small steamer—I guess somewhere around 3,000 tons. Late in the afternoon it started to move slowly. I [noted] how gradually the port and the chain of mountains vanished in the fog: once again it was a departure from my homeland. Why?, I asked myself. Will I ever see it again? Is there any excuse for

---

1   January 8 in the Russian old-style calendar corresponded to the Western January 20 in 1899, and became equivalent to January 21 after 1900 (a leap-year in Russia but not in the West).

one to leave his country, especially when his country is in distress? To leave the community to which one belongs by his birth and by his education?

❀ In October 1945 I composed music to the Blok's poem *The Twelve* for Annie Maurel in the form of "melodeclamation" for speaker and piano. The well-known Blok poem had been translated into French several times. I used a recent unpublished version by Arout, which seemed to me not only faithful to the original text, but also to preserve the rhythm of the Russian prosody. Because Blok in this poem was depicting the ambience of the Russian Revolution, he often used the rhythms of popular songs, even, at the end, the rhythm of [Schubert's] *Erlking*. Through the rhythms, I determined the original lyrics of the songs in question, and attempted through these to "decipher" Blok's thoughts in order to give them the "accompaniment" that matched his intentions.

This text, of supposedly revolutionary character-because it employs slogans current in that era—is only so outwardly: the great individualist Blok never for a moment shared the idea of a dictatorship of the proletariat, of ideological oppression of the individual.

However, my interpreter, Annie Maurel, lent an ear to "friendly advisors" who thought they saw elements of political propaganda in the text and counseled her not to compromise herself by continuing to perform it....

❀ I was invited back to Russia recently. I noticed two things right away. For one thing the basic Russian character has not changed at all; they are as warm as ever. In the old days they had to learn to live with a difficult regime of the Czars, now they have adjusted a bit to live with another difficult regime. They are suspicious of foreigners, but they were always so. It is just the way they are. Politics too are as conservative and difficult as ever—but I don't speak of politics, please. Still, one should not think that the Soviets were completely bad. They have done some really marvelous things for the country. People can read now, whereas less than five per cent could in my boyhood. Anyone who wants to enjoy cultural things has [them] available.

❀ Dear friend [*i. e.*, Willi Reich], please keep this absolutely confidential between us until my death. The fact that even today I regret having left my country and that I am not there, where I belong, must be known only to you until I die.

... But this is what happened. It can no longer be changed—forty-one years of emigration have shaped my life quite differently from anything I could have imagined as a young man; and I will faithfully serve the U. S. A., the land of which I became a citizen in 1958, for I value my place in the American community....

Something else should be said here: in 1925 I could have become a French citizen—my petition for naturalization was accepted, but at the last moment I avoided becoming a Frenchman, for I felt myself too much a Russian. I freely chose to remain "stateless." In 1938, when my petition for naturalization as an American citizen was accepted I passed the "examination" but again refused, of my own free will, to become an American, this time for two reasons: first, because this naturalization would have been granted on the basis of my marriage to an American wife at the exact moment I was seeking to divorce her, and second, because I felt too much a Russian.

Then, after the war, in 1948, I could have chosen to be French or Russian: the French were ready to naturalize me, the Russians to give me back Russian citizenship automatically.

I refused both; I did not feel French and I was no longer Russian...

Only after I finally assimilated into the American community, where I felt that my children belonged because of their upbringing in and acceptance of American principles did I decide to become a U. S. citizen, together with my wife.

❀ There was a Swiss girl-composer who attended my lectures [in Weesen in 1960], did not enroll in composition class but expressed the desire to show me her compositions. My everyday schedule was very busy, and I had to postpone [meetings] with her from day to day. The girl sometimes participated in the discussions following the lectures...

When speaking about the object of music and of the situation of music in the Soviet Union, I usually try to make people understand that the attitude of the government is not as oppressi[ve] to the musician and to the creator as it is believed to be by the Western reporters of the situation. The fact is that both the USSR government and the Soviet composers are animated by the same desire to 'serve' the community of people and to convey the message in a language that [will] be understood. To quote an example, I often refer to. Mozart's letter to the direction of [the] Paris Opera in which he says that he could compose music in every style-French, German, Italian... He composed *Les Petits Riens* and it was just as good [as] anything he... composed. A talented composer should be able to express himself in every style, stay talented under every restriction... be [it] self-imposed or dictated by the [music's] ultimate [purpose].

So in my opinion, the composer who goes "with his folks" and serves the cause of music in his country according to the cultural standard of people is right, while the composer who manifests only his own "ego" or puts on a mask trying to outsmart his fellows is not necessarily a genius.

And one can be talented or deprived of talent in any medium. And that's what counts.

It so happened that the girl disappeared after the last lecture and never showed up again, not even [to say] good-bye or [to ask about] the meeting that I had promised her to arrange.

Later, I… learned from Paul Grlimmer that this girl denounced me to the Swiss police as a Soviet agent… For a while, it created some difficulties for poor Grlimmer, but the good thing [was] that my lectures were taken on tape.

THE UPROOTED LIFE

> Russian composer
> Georgian composer
> Composer of the School of Paris
> Chinese composer
> American composer.

Is this a handicap or an advantage

… and there is more… my name is not associated with another name. Stravinsky met his Diaghilev, Prokofiev his Koussevitzky, then his own Russian milieu; Honegger-Charles Munch. Milhaud's life was bound to his friends of *Les Six* through his association with Claudel, Cocteau, Satie.

But I stand alone.

Befriended by many, but with very few real friends.

Known by many, but with no exclusive patron.

The list of 27 publishers speaks for itself.

Many publishers, no exclusive publisher.

Many artists, conductors who played or play my works—among them Koussevitzky, Pierne, Munch, Mitropoulos, Monteux, etc. etc.— none of whom I was truly a *protégé*.

Many publishers-none who really launched me.

How I succeeded through all this is a riddle to me.

Yet I did succeed, and particularly in the last few years—with the Suite, Op. 87, Concerto for Harmonica, Op. 86, and most particularly through the Divertimento, Op. 90, 4th Symphony, Op. 91, and now in the *Symphonic Prayer*, Op. 93.

… the problem of my "lack of homeland"… can be regarded as a handicap or a *cas special* and thus an advantage.

I love people. Based on my own experience, I understand that all people— whatever the race from which they may stem, whatever color their skin may be, whatever religion or atheism they espouse—serve humanity in the same way.

Not one people, not one race, not one nation; I serve mankind…

Lopatnikoff in his article at the end of the twenties called me an "independent in Central Europe."

I believe that I am following a special road, a road different from that of many of my colleagues and one that is perhaps without precedent in music, at least to this extent.

This could signify either weakness or strength. It all depends on the objective artistic value of my work.

TCHEREPNIN PRELUDE

My papa was avant-garde for his generation; in Russia he defended the newest experiments of Debussy and Ravel. When I was young, I was also avant-garde, that is, for my generation. My First Symphony was hissed by the audience and panned by the critics but both it and I survived. Today my two avant-garde composer-sons are continuing the tradition. It was to my great delight that they wished to study with Stockhausen and Boulez. They are striking out in their own directions, and what they are doing is fascinating to me.

RADIO (1930)

{This brief piece, one of Tcherepnin's earliest journalistic efforts, originally appeared in French. Highly evident, even at this early date, was Tcherepnin's conviction that the world abounded in utopian possibilities}

We know that the origin of chamber music was directly linked with the existence of intellectual enclaves (whether in monarchical courts, aristocratic salons or common society).

The exploration of an intimate, refined and pure art fostered the creation of a body of works whose intellectualism accrued over the years until it attained absolute abstract perfection in the late works of a Beethoven.

The progressive democratization of the social organism deprived aristocratic enclaves of their intellectual primacy. Concerts replaced the gatherings of connoisseurs. Chamber music was imperiled by external virtuosity, or by the dilettantism of salons in decay.

Today we are present at the creation of new intellectual enclaves all over the surface of the globe; these enclaves-radio broadcast stations-are formulating anew the demand for a pure art, stripped of all external virtuosity, impressive in its essential subject matter, not merely in its brilliance of means.

Supply and demand always go together. I am persuaded that music specifically written to be transmitted by radio (and thus, to be heard at home) will be the spiritual child of Classical chamber music, eventually becoming the purest branch of musical art.

MUSIC IN MODERN CHINA (1935)

{This article originally appeared in the October 1935 issue of *The Musical Quarterly*. The version initially submitted by Tcherepnin was obviously subjected to extremely heavy—and rather flowery—editing. While the piece no longer has contemporary relevance, it retains a good deal of interest as a cross-cultural document.}

After a fortnight's voyage from San Francisco, aboard a trans-Pacific liner, you approach the coast of Asia. The Yellow Sea, colored by the mud of one of the world's largest rivers, has really turned yellow: picturesque fishing boats with typical Eastern sails begin to surround you; in the distance there is a faint line of land—your first glimpse of China. The coast grows more distinct. The steamer at last enters the broad estuary of the Yangtze. Soon, on both banks of the river, which are absolutely flat, you see houses built in English fashion, factories, hangars, and *godowns* (or warehouses). The sight so resembles that of a Western city, you hardly believe this is Shanghai.

The steamer stops. Passport examination, a short trip on a tender—and you land in the middle of the famous Bund. Coolies take charge of your luggage, and you hear them sing, or rather intone rhythmically, while a couple of them carry your heavy "Innovation" trunk: one of the pair mutters the beginning of a phrase, the other one brings it to an end. They always repeat it in time to their slow movements. Here the "immaterial" musical rhythm seems to become a help for carrying the hard, "material" burden.

The Shanghai Bund, like the Thames embankment, is known to seafaring men the world over. An international crowd of sailors, tourists, businessmen of all nations, mingles with a preponderant mass of Chinese, dressed in the national blue coat and wide trousers; hurrying in all directions, people are pushing one another, paying little or no attention to constant collisions. In the middle of the wide street, a long-bearded *cheik*-policeman, representative of the English way of governing colonies or concessions, regulates the traffic, consisting of automobiles, rickshas, vehicles of all kinds—from an old-fashioned cab to the newest streamlined motor-car, from a tired looking tramway to the latest model of electric trolley running without rails. Bewildered, you eventually sink into an overstuffed armchair in a luxurious room of one of the large American-built skyscraper hotels.

To see some of the real China, go out and take a walk.

As soon as you leave the main street, or Nanking Road, you find yourself in one of the animated business streets, decorated with all sorts of flags. Here is a popular eating place. In the interior, you see a nimble cook preparing chops from a peculiar grayish stuff. Even from afar you hear the penetrating rhythm of his handiwork, as he beats the chops with his wooden utensils. The rhythm is a definite one. It constitutes his individual "trade mark."

Then you will notice that, wherever work is going on, it is done in a distinct rhythm: the shoemaker will hammer nails into a shoe-sole at a regular beat; the carpenter will work according to a certain "pulse"; likewise the mason, the dishwasher and everyone else. When a job offers no opportunity to produce rhythmic sound, the worker will mutter a sort of song, or rather [a sort] of rhythmic recitation, reminding you of your first acquaintances, the coolies who carried your trunk.

In attracting your attention by sound, the ingenuity of the Chinese knows no limit: each motorman of the street cars proudly clings to his own rhythm for the sounding of his gong, to warn you of coming danger; there are hardly two Chinese chauffeurs who would use the same rhythmic phrase for the blowing of their horns; the street vendors tax your imagination by the variety of their rhythms and by the percussion instruments they use in order to produce those rhythms. You soon discover that rhythm is fundamentally related to the life and work of the Chinese people.

You may, perchance, like to find sound applied in a more imposing form. Go on and look about you. Guided by sounds of a strange music, you elbow your way through a dense crowd. You come to a dry-goods shop, and you are surprised to find a native orchestra in the center of it, playing loud and strident native tunes. The orchestra is there to attract the attention of the passers-by to the opening of a new shop. The celebration goes on for a day or two, without interruption during the night; the better (or louder) the orchestra, the greater the public that is attracted, and therefore the larger the future clientele. This music may fulfill a utilitarian end; but the fact remains that it would never serve its purpose were it not for the inborn musical sense of the Chinese race.

On your return to the hotel you are stopped by a procession. A band of Chinese soldiers, walking at the head of it, is playing a gay western military march. You will probably be shocked at first when you realize that the procession is a funeral. If the practical Chinese discard the dirge for livelier strains, it is ostensibly not for the benefit of the mourners, but to cheer the departed soul on its way to the beyond.

*　　*

*

There is hardly a book on the history of music that does not offer more or less detailed information about the Chinese musical theories of the past. Volumes have been written on the subject. A very interesting article, "The Music and Musical Instruments of Ancient China," by Robert W. Marks, appeared in the October 1932 issue of this magazine [*Musical Quarterly*]. A small pamphlet, by Mr. Chao Mei Pa, lately published in this country, gives a brief and clear account of the development of musical thought in his native land.

China's classical musical theories are well known. China's classical music is still an enigma. The tradition of it, in China, is lost. To hear some of it, you have to travel to Japan, where the orchestra of the Imperial Household, at its annual public concert at Hibya Hall, in Tokyo, performs on ancient Chinese musical instruments a rather complicated, heavy-sounding orchestral music that is supposed to be ancient Chinese—more than a thousand years old. It is preserved by tradition and played by heart. We have no reason to doubt the origin of the compositions or the authenticity of the performance. I must admit that, for my ears, this music sounded too abstract and problematic for me to be able to judge by it what the classical Chinese music might have been. With the music of present-day China it has nothing in common.

Chinese native music is based on the natural pentatonic scale, is melodious, lyric and highly varied.

The melody is never symmetrical, the musical phrase never ends in a cadence. The pentatonic scale is used in its five positions, the fundamental tone changing its place and being C, D, E, G or A according to the development of the melody. The scale is often filled out by insertion of the tones F and B, additions that produce a correspondence with our major scale. When they are used, the half-tone[s are] introduced in descending passages: B follows C and leads to A; E, following F, lands on D.

Chinese popular songs are monodies. When they are accompanied by an instrument, the accompaniment is built up horizontally—the instruments playing the melody from start to finish, and the voice joining in unison with it at the most important spots. Even in the more complicated instrumental music, no deliberate attempt is made at harmonizing the melody or at building up a contrapuntal combination of any kind. In native Chinese music, there is no harmony or counterpoint, as we understand it. But in an orchestra each musician has to play the same melody according to the capacities and register of his instrument. This results in a "false doubling,"[1] which, together with the variety of the often syncopated rhythms played by the percussion instruments, creates a sort of native polyphony, peculiar to Chinese music.

The form of a native tune consists in perpetual variation of the same melody; a musical phrase is never repeated exactly, the melody always progresses, a change in the fundamental tone replaces modulation. Ingenuity in melodic invention seems never to cease, and when, towards the end of a piece, the movement grows faster and faster, the melody adapts itself to the new rhythm. There is a fascination to this type of "everlasting" melody. It is a device that should prove useful, on occasion, to our composers.

Similarly, our opera producers might learn from the Chinese theater. Chinese drama, or, as it is often called, Chinese Opera, is a synthetic production. It comprises elements of the opera, the ballet, the drama and the circus. It is the music that holds these elements together, and the orchestra accompanies the action all through the performance.

The realistic acting and traditional gestures make up to the public for the lack of scenery, which is unknown on the Chinese stage. All the parts are played by men—high falsetto singing is cultivated as an essential. A heavy-weight Lohengrin, a Salome that has to have a substitute for the "Dance of the Seven Veils," would be useless for the Chinese stage, since all its artists must be at one and the same time good singers, good dancers, acrobats and actors. The repertory consists of classical and modern Chinese plays, and in the theater the best native orchestral music, both old and new, may be heard.

Another kind of native music is found in the temples where the holy texts are rhythmically intoned by Buddhist monks to beautiful old monodies. These are sung by the monks in chorus and are accompanied by temple-bells, gongs and wooden percussion instruments of high register. Religious processions are never without an orchestra, composed of all kinds of flutes (even flutes made of human bones), gongs, drums and instruments of percussion.

Equipped with a system of notation of its own, native music was the only kind known to the large Chinese populace before the outbreak of the Boxer Rebellion. Thereafter the country became subject to the influence of western civilization. Progressive Chinese went abroad to seek their education in foreign countries. After the Revolution, Western culture was introduced into China without reserve. Western education created an interest among the educated people in the achievements of Western culture. Native music lost its monopoly.

*　*
*

Shanghai is the representative city of modern China. It consists of an International concession, a French concession and two Chinese towns, and it counts about three million inhabitants, one hundred thousand of them being foreigners. The municipality of the International concession pays a subvention to a symphony orchestra consisting of artists of all nations, well trained under the direction of an enlightened musician and conductor Mario Paci. He came to China eighteen years ago, and it is through his efforts that the Municipal Orchestra has become an important factor in the musical life of Shanghai. Paci looked upon his job as missionary work. In this independent mind he conceived a plan to educate his

---

1   *Editor's note:* this type of texture is now called "heterophonic."

public by introducing it not only to the usual symphonic repertory, but also to the latest compositions of the moderns. He played, sometimes in advance of his Western colleagues, works of Respighi, Rieti, Malipiero, de Falla, Ravel, Kodaly, Bartök, Graener, Hindemith. Although his choice did not always meet with the approval of the Municipal Council, the high standard of his performances, together with his great authority, left no valid grounds for an effective attack on his venturesome programs.

Shanghai is the only city in China that possesses a symphony orchestra; it is also the only one to have a conservatory of music. The National Conservatory of Music was started eight years ago by Dr. **Hsiao**[2] Yiu-Mei, who at present is still the director of the institution. Born at Canton in 1884, Doctor Hsiao from his youth showed an inclination for music. He started studying in Japan at an early age, and finished his musical education in Leipzig as a pupil of Emil Pauer, Riemann and Reger, being graduated from the Leipzig University as a doctor of philosophy. Composer of a ballet, chamber music, songs, choruses and piano pieces, Doctor Hsiao, after his return to China in 1920, started a movement to refashion Chinese music education along Western lines. Assisted by C. T. **Yan** (pianist, graduate of the Geneva Conservatory), he founded, in 1921, the musical department at the Academy of Fine Arts in Peiping, and in 1927 he went to Shanghai to found the National Conservatory of Music. Assisted in his task by Chinese and foreign musicians, he succeeded in winning from the Chinese Government material support for the institution. The Conservatory became the center of musical education in China, and talented pupils from all parts of the country are receiving musical training there.

So far only four students have been graduated, the first of them being the gifted pianist and pupil of Mr. Zaharoff, Miss **Lee** Hsien Ming.

Musical education according to Western style is now being sponsored not only by the National Conservatory but by the musical faculties of the Chinese or mission high schools and universities.

An American musician, Miss Ruth Bugbee, is in charge of the music department of the Shanghai University. This department, of which the distinguished singer **Chao** Mei Pa, well known in Europe and the U. S. A., is a graduate, counts about fifty talented students majoring in music.

Perhaps the most impressive achievements are those of the music department of Yenching University in Peiping, also headed by an American, Mr. Bliss Wiant. Performances of Handel's *Messiah* and Brahms's *Deutsches Requiem* by a chorus of several hundred students are to his credit, also the harmonization of Chinese melodies for the use of church, a fundamental piece of work for the Chinese Christian associations.

The penetration of Western music into China is not yet twenty years old; the first conservatory—as you have seen—is but a seven-year-old institution. Yet, the Chinese Government has lately decided to introduce our Western musical education into all the governmental middle schools. This adaptability is due to the innate musicality of the Chinese race.

*   *
*

I had a chance to come in contact with a Chinese audience even before my first public appearance in Shanghai. In preparing for a chamber music concert, I went to the small concert hall of the Conservatory, where the rehearsal was to take place. On my arrival, I was surprised to find the hall full of students who evidently wanted to attend our rehearsal. As it was a first reading, I objected to the presence of any public, but the dean of the Conservatory assured me that we would not be disturbed, and a curtain that separates the hall from the stage was pulled down. We struggled through our program for about two hours, and I completely forgot about the people in the hall, and there had never been a sound or a movement betraying their presence. When, at the end of the rehearsal, the curtain was pulled back, I found to my amazement that the "full house" was still with us, some of the students having stood all the time.

Later on, in Shanghai, in Tientsin, in Peiping, wherever I played for a Chinese public, I learned that my first impression held good generally: this desire to listen, this capacity to concentrate, are characteristic of Chinese audiences.

The Chinese student who decides to take up music as his profession does so, on the whole, not because his parents or relatives know anything about Western art or Western musical instruments, but perhaps because he found pleasure in playing one of the native instruments, or because he somehow had a chance to hear pieces of Western or native music that impressed him, or because he tried to play a harmonium or half-broken piano during his free hours at a missionary school or church. Whatever the external reasons, it is an inner love for music and respect for art that [motivates] him, often against the will of his family, to devote himself to the study of music. Everything is foreign to him: the notation, the musical idiom, the instruments. An enormous will power is required to overcome all these obstacles.

---

2   *{original footnote}*: The Chinese, if Christians, place their given names before the family names; otherwise the order is reversed. Where, in the printing of this article, names are letter-spaced, they are family names. [*N. B.* In the present reprinting, **bold-face** type is used instead of wider letter-spacing.]

*　　*

*

The political state of China is a kind of democratic feudalism; medieval institutions exist side by side with modern. At the airport of a distant inland city, a traveller by a Chinese mail plane may be met by a sedan chair, and both forms of conveyance will prove their usefulness for travelling purposes. A Chinese Hans Sachs, going to the reunion of his guild, may travel in a Pullman car of a well equipped express train, having made reservation by wireless for his room in a skyscraper hotel. But the wireless operator, who transmitted his message, will be careful to eat the proper and traditional pastry on the day of the Dragon Festival. A Buddhist monk, passing years of seclusion in a corner of a lonely temple, will wear glasses manufactured by Zeiss in Jena, enabling him to read the holy scripts; a high official will take his meals at home with his illiterate servants seated at the same table; a peasant will carry his wheat to an electric mill; a rich banker, proprietor of a racing stable, before the great event will be at the temple burning paper effigies of horses in order to assure the victory of his favorite.

The medieval forms of life, the medieval traditions and beliefs are co-existing with the modern achievements of Western culture. The nineteenth-century experiences of Europe and America have not been passed through by China. In its quick development, that country has practically jumped from the middle ages into the twentieth century.

A Chinese music student of today is able to take our modern music for granted without regard to its past development, by evolution or revolution, from its early beginnings to its present state. Modern music seems to him as natural as any music could be, and is nearer to his psychology than the classical music, for he is acquainted with the culture that produced today's music, but is almost ignorant of our cultural past. His way would be made easier if his practical training, instead of insisting on his learning to know classical works, could be started with the music of the twentieth century.

I had the opportunity of giving some young students pieces of modern music to study, and I was amazed how quickly and easily they caught on to our modern idioms; the same students found it rather difficult to feel at home with Chopin or Franck. The Chinese musical student should be treated in a special way: for a beginner, both the instrument and the music to be played on this instrument are unknown quantities. At least one of these can be eliminated by the use of familiar music, adaptations of Chinese folksongs in a modern manner. These should be followed by modern compositions, beginning with Debussy (especially congenial to the Chinese ear through the Javanese affinity in his art) and Stravinsky, and leading to the best works of the post-war musical literature.

The Chinese composer must discover the way for China's creative musical evolution. A beginning has been made. I have already mentioned Dr. **Hsiao** Yiu-Mei, whose administrative vision is as extraordinary as his musical talent. Then there is Mr. Tzu **Huang**, Harvard graduate, composer of orchestral music, of striking choral compositions, or songs and piano pieces. Dr. K. **Chen**, who unfortunately for more than a year has had to fight a serious illness, has been forced to interrupt his admirable work of arranging Chinese popular melodies for voice and piano, as well as his activity in connection with original compositions, which have included piano and chamber music. Rodin **Ho**[3] is the winner of a prize competition that I sponsored last year in Shanghai for a piano composition of Chinese national character. He does not speak any language except Chinese: his prize-winning composition, *Buffalo Boy's Flute,*[4] shows originality, clarity and a sure hand in counterpoint and form. The second prize, at the same contest, was won by **Lao** Chih-Chin. Born in Canton in 1911, now living in Peiping, he never had any teacher; he taught himself to play the piano, and performs with nice expression his own compositions, works full of life and real artistic temperament. **Liu** She-An, a very young man, shows great promise in his piano compositions and short songs, pieces of a decidedly Chinese flavor.

To anyone interested in modern works for native instruments, I recommend the compositions of the late **Liu** Tien Hwa, who sponsored the modern movement in native music; his favorite pupil, Miss **Tsao** An Ho, plays these compositions of her master admirably on the *pi'bha* (a native string instrument). A gifted composer, and a great virtuoso on the *pi'bha* is Professor **Chou**. Some of his works are inspired by actual occurrences: the titles of his best known compositions are *Flood in Hangchow* and *Sino-Japanese War in Shanghai*. His young pupil Mr. **Tang** Shiao Liang has written an important work for native orchestra called *Notturno*, which has lately been recorded by Pathé.

3　In more modern transliteration, "Rodin" becomes "Luting," and "Ho" becomes "He." Both renderings, of course, are only vague approximations of the Chinese pronunciation.

4　{Original footnote}: Published by Mr. Tcherepnin (price .60), who has also issued the following Chinese compositions:
Lao Chih-Chen, *Shepherd's Pastime* (for Piano) .60
Liu Shea-An, Three Melodies: *Brotherhood; Farmer's Fate; Advice for Saving* (for Medium or Low Voice and Piano) .75

The youngest Chinese composer is but five and a half years old. His name is **Lee** Sing. He began to study the piano six months ago, being taught by his sister.[5] The rapidity of his progress was surprising. I had the pleasure of writing down his first composition for him. He is actually[6] studying with Paci, and his young talent promises well for the future of Chinese music.

That there is such a future, no one can doubt. Great musical activity is going on in China. The Chinese composer has under his hands one of the richest sources of native music. He has the world's most populous country to support him. The more national his product, the greater will be its international value.

{*Editor's note:* The last page of *Buffalo Boy's Flute* was reproduced at the close of the article when it appeared in *Musical Quarterly*.}

❋　❋　❋

MODERN MUSIC

from the

FAR EAST

Published by
ALEXANDER TCHEREPNINE
Peiping and Tokyo

———

Exclusive Selling Agents for U. S. A. and Canada

G. SCHIRMER, Inc.

3 East 43rd Street　　　　　　　　New York, N. Y.

5　Tcherepnin, with his subtle sense of humor, was here perhaps indulging in a private joke at the *Musical Quarterly*'s expense. China's "youngest composer," whose picture was included along with the article, was none other than the baby brother of the woman with whom Tcherepnin had fallen deeply in love-Lee Hsien Ming. Tcherepnin, who was then not in a position to make his love for Ming public, nevertheless found this outlet to tell the world about her, demonstrating his secret affection in the full view of unsuspecting readers. Incidentally, Lee Sing developed into an excellent pianist, and eventually took up residence in San Francisco.

6　A Gallicism. *Actuellement* means "at present."

PERCUSSION: IS IT MUSICAL? (1955)

{The May 1955 edition of *L'Age Nouveau*, an artistic and literary review, was devoted to "Music and the Sound Universe." Tcherepnin submitted the article reproduced here, which appeared alongside contributions by other distinguished and/ or famous musicians such as Henri Dutilleux, Pierre Henry, Maurice Jarré, André Jolivet, René Leibowitz, Frank Martin, Alexandre Tansman and Edgar Varèse.}

One cannot deny that contemporary composers, in their works, reserve a particularly important place for percussion. This fact has attracted the attention of critics, and some have seen percussion as a means of liberating music through a procedure whose emotional value is foreign to that of music itself.

As for me, I would not know how to separate the emotional value of percussion from that of music in general. Percussion is only one of the means that a composer uses to express his musical intentions. On a purely emotional level, a melody sung *pianissimo* by a flute in its low register can communicate more emotion to a listener than an obsessive rhythm assigned to timpani playing *fortissimo*. The emotional value of music is implicit not in the means it employs but in the message it contains.

*

*   *

Why does contemporary music accord so considerable a place to percussion? I see numerous explanations for this phenomenon.

To begin on the most simplistic level, a comprehensive exploration of color leads to the use of all suitable means of obtaining colors. Percussion is one of those means at a composer's disposal.

Note must also be taken of the ever more extensive relations between the dance and the great part of contemporary music.

Has ballet not tended to become a new form of musical expression?

Finally, there is the eminently justified desire of the composer to transcend the limited extent of sounds considered "listenable"—the development of the piano, which is a percussion instrument by its very construction, has represented this attitude.

In my case, the use of percussion represents my attempt to liberate rhythm from tempered sound.

The seven-and-a-half octaves of organized pitches that we consider the sole standard musical sounds constitute only a minimal part of a sound world which is, I am sure, as real as the visual world.

This sound world, which we can sense thanks to our hearing, extends beyond the seven-and-a-half octaves, but remains infinitely restricted in comparison to the world of sound waves that traverse the universe. Like a painter who reduces what he sees in placing it on a canvas infinitely smaller than the real extent that his eye perceives, a composer reduces what comes to him from the world of sound in the form of sound waves as he integrates it into the range of audible (listenable) sounds.

The impulse to compose, instinctive in origin, generally comes to me as a sensation of the presence of sound waves. I feel the existence of these, which, however, are not audible. Little by little, I succeed in expressing them in the course of transposing them into the domain of audible sounds. At least, it seems that I have succeeded in doing so in certain cases. Sometimes, however, I feel betrayed by the means that are considered musical: in any case they do not offer me any of the equivalents I am looking for. It is then that percussion helps me escape from the cage of the seven-and-a-half octaves. Yet I am only looking for an extension of sonic means. I would not dream of executing a musical structure confined to noise. I do not believe that noise *per se* is capable of being music. If it becomes music, it ceases to be noise.

*

*   *

I should like to stress that percussion belongs to the realm of music and not of noise, and to discuss extra-musical explications that have been applied to the use of percussion. These are not lacking. I would answer by saying, however, that I do not know whether percussion engages the spirit or the senses. I would not presume to establish a distinction between the one and the other. Why not ask if percussion addresses the right ear or the left ear of the auditor? The senses cannot be felt without the spirit's consciousness of sensation. Conversely, how could the spirit perceive sounds, how could it speculate upon their meaning if the senses did not communicate their vibrations to it?

Interpretation, extra-musical again, sees in the use of percussion the demonstration of a need to astonish. Has a composer ever wished to astonish indiscriminately? True, I was personally accused of wishing to shock the listener when I entrusted the scherzo of my First Symphony to percussion alone. The first performance of that Symphony provoked numerous commentaries. To tell the truth, my only objective was to liberate rhythm from the conventional sound of our standard notes. No one, at the time, noticed that the rhythms that I used in the scherzo were merely reductions, to their purely rhythmic value, of themes of the Symphony's first movement, which precedes the scherzo.

Continuing to parry extra-musical judgments about percussion, I will say that its use corresponds neither to a composer's desire or need for excess, nor to any bellicose plan of his to suffuse the listener with self-destructive impulses. It is not a means of gratification for the masochist.

*

*   *

It is a fact that the composers of my generation show a tendency to accentuate the percussive character of instruments. I mentioned, above, the case of the piano, which, by its construction, is a percussion instrument. I myself have a tendency to make different instruments of the orchestra alter from "melodic" to "percussive"; in my Suite for orchestra, the rhythm introduced by the percussion instruments at the beginning of the second movement is immediately reprised by the strings, and by the winds; in the final analysis, the orchestral instruments are used like percussion, with rhythm dominating the construction of the work.

This observation takes away nothing from what I affirmed at the beginning of this article: to achieve his ends, the composer has a certain number of means whose use is always legitimate if that end requires their use. Percussion is only one of those means. It is but one of the colors on a palette. It could not conceivably be made an end in itself. There are not music and percussion. There is only music.

❀   ❀   ❀

From "LET UNDERPRIVILEGED INSTRUMENTS PLAY" (1962)

{Tcherepnin's interest in composing for neglected or, as he charmingly styled them, "underprivileged" instruments dated at least as far back as 1930, when he entrusted some of his most inspired musical ideas to an ensemble including two violas da gamba in the original version of his Triple Concertino. His editor, fearing the use of these odd instruments would render sales negligible, insisted on a gamba-less revision. Late in the 1930s, however, an American publisher actually requested a series of teaching pieces for unexplored instrumental combinations, and Tcherepnin responded with such works as his Sonatina for three timpani and piano, Op. 58, his Trio for three flutes, Op. 59, his Quartet for four flutes, Op. 60, the March for three trumpets, Op. 62, and other works, most notably including the *Sonatine Sportive*, Op. 63, originally written for bassoon and piano, but published, instead, as a work for alto saxophone and piano. Later, of course, he produced works for other underprivileged instruments such as the harmonica and the accordion.

The present Tcherepnin article appeared in the January 1962 issue of *Music Journal*. At this time, there was a great deal of talk about suitable educational and recreational opportunities for "underprivileged children." The first half of the essay has been omitted because it merely deals with Tcherepnin's early life, a subject already exhaustively covered here in previous pages. In the remainder, the composer addresses the subject suggested by the title.}

In 1949, DePaul University in Chicago engaged my wife, the Chinese pianist Lee Hsien Ming, and me as members of the faculty. Since then, of course, my home has been in Chicago, and I have had the privilege to participate in the musical life of the country, not only as a composer and pianist, but also as a pedagogue, lecturer and orchestral conductor. I am fascinated by the intensity of the musical life in the States, by the eagerness of young people to study in order to become accomplished musicians. In teaching young composers, I am trying to help them to discover themselves, to find their own individualistic approach to composition.

I am trying also to draw the attention of young composers to the various musical media in which a new work will be welcome. While piano, violin, cello, string quartet and symphony orchestra have been well served by the great composers of the past, and continuously provided with new compositions of high merit by composers of the present, so many other instruments and various other ensembles are *in need of adequate literature.*

There is a tremendous field for a young talented composer if he chooses to compose for the "underprivileged" instruments. Certainly compositions, let us say, for tuba, for accordion, for harp, for band, for brass ensemble, for saxophone quartet, for marimba, for percussion—are *needed*, and it is the young generation's job to fill up the lack of compositions which would give to the new virtuosos the chance to project themselves via good music. And there is the great coming musical medium-the electronics!

When I hear music in myself, I am not always able to find the equivalent of the sounds imagined in the well-tempered pitch. There is always a kind of "transposition" that I have to make when writing down the composition. In electronic music such compromise becomes unnecessary: every sound in every color at any volume on any pitch can be obtained. Here what we call "musical sound" becomes enriched and practically unlimited!

No doubt that the future of music will be associated with all the new ways of sound producing. The door is open to a new world of musical expression. We are living at the most exciting and revolutionary time of musical history.

{It might be observed here that, despite his enthusiasm for unusual instruments, Tcherepnin was, indeed, capable of drawing the line somewhere. Asked during the early 1960s to compose a piece for Hammond Organ, he had one sent to his home and experimented with it for some months, but found it so detestable that he could not bring himself to write for it.}

❇   ❇   ❇

ELECTRONIC MUSIC AND OTHER MATTERS

{In this undated piece, which appears to be the script of a lecture, Tcherepnin summarizes several basic ideas that recur repeatedly in his speculations about the music of the future.}

The artist is not someone living in an ivory tower. He must absorb everything around him and give it back in the form of his art. It is his duty to serve people, to say something to humanity.

Then, some of you may ask, what about electronic music? Are some ivory towers charged with electricity? And has the wiring gone bad?

It is very difficult, even for an experienced musician, to find out the construction of electronic or serial music, until he realizes that it asks nothing more of us than to open our ears. Most of us [need to] have our ears and minds "shocked" open; only in this way are we able to concentrate on the sounds of the present, musical and otherwise, instead of the sounds of yesterday.

Why should we limit ourselves to the sounds of a piano, for example, when cymbals and drums offer overtones that a piano cannot? So many more varieties of sound are made possible with the addition of new instruments. Since Beethoven's time the piano keyboard has grown in both directions—a fifth above and a sixth below. Since the time of Liszt, nothing has been added.

In the field of sound experimentation, I have a great respect for the work of Henk Badings, the noted Dutch composer. He has written in every genre with a style of romantic modernism, but is also experimenting with four-track tape, his use of which is truly great by today's conception of the sounds. But this musical speech can go only as [far] forward as the musical standard of the audience, which wants to be given a language that it understands. A few new words can be added gradually, but a totally new language such as electronic music is initially disturbing and unacceptable at first to the majority.

The musical scientist searches for new worlds of sound and time. The message, his spaceship, is self-expression in terms of his time and culture. New sounds, fed to the audience in the proper amounts, constitute new fuel for the journey.

In 2700 B. C. the Chinese emperor established certain pitch restrictions. They still exist. True, we are experimenting in an epoch where there is a tremendous need for research in every direction. A musician cannot be a ghost of Canterville and refuse to fit into his own epoch. The composer must go as far in research as is necessary to project his ultimate message, which he may sense but not realize fully himself. The research in electronic music—foreign to our ears and perhaps mystic in message—is the means: the act of composing is mystic in itself.

When I listen to music and compose, I am not hearing the music *actually as it is*. First, I feel music and hear nothing. There is a tremendous world of vibration, only *a part of which can be heard*. Our powers of perception need to be developed. Perhaps there are inaudible vibrations that are sensed or felt. It is common knowledge that a dog can hear higher vibrations than the human ear.

The higher pitches of electronic music are fantastically clear, while the lower seem to have less sound value. There is too much *tremolo* in the low pitches, which one day must be stabilized. But the point should be made that all sound-producing instruments should have a literature, whether the medium be human or mechanical.

There is a strange situation in which we are *lionizing* pianists, violinists and cellists. The eternal "lion" is the singer, also the most conservative lion. The underprivileged instruments, however, must also be given a chance to roar—the percussion family, the harmonica, the accordion (there are 3,000,000 players in the United States alone), recreational instruments—*i. e.*, those lacking a broad *serious* repertoire. Composers have written largely for the established lions. More music is needed—*good* music—for the neglected cubs, instead of an overabundance of the same for string quartets and other accepted forms. Serious composers must permit all the lions to roar!

Now there will always be the "high brow" serious composer who looks down on the lighter mediums, the cubs. I know who will be on the mantlepiece tomorrow, but whose music will be heard tomorrow? Quarter-tone music was written by Abbe Vogler in the time of Mozart! It is not the great complication that survives, but the simplification. Bach gave us wonderful polyphony and Schoenberg simplified it. Will oversimplification survive?

The composer always serves a certain milieu surrounding him. Snobbism cannot control the outflow of the artist. Although the creator must give the community the music it needs, it is also his kharmic debt to contribute to the progressive experimentalism so necessary for the perpetuation of the art form.

There is, incidentally, a terrific parallel between the human body and the simple folklore that has survived. The folklore in music is similar to [human] anatomy. The great artists of all time have elaborated upon the simple and beautiful basics that are everlasting. Michelangelo used the lines of the body, magnifying their complexity. He represented deepness of spirit. Da Vinci displayed passion, Raphael expressed celestial proportion; Delacroix, battle scenes; Picasso, eternal lines, and the like. Anatomical music survives; there are superficial changes only.

I cannot say that electronic music, as we know it just now, is anatomical; but a time is coming when revolutionary simplifica-tion will [shape] its life-cycle. And our ears will have to remain open. Electronic music involves new tone color not necessarily related to known timbres. Who knows how the futuristic electronic lion of tomorrow will roar?

❁　❁　❁

ANTHOLOGY OF RUSSIAN MUSIC

{Tcherepnin discussed the origins of this anthology in his 1947 French autobiography. Almost three decades later, he provided a somewhat different account in English for Marjorie Glock. The Editor here has taken the liberty of inserting some information from the French text into the later version. This additional information is enclosed within 'single quotation marks.'}

Since my teens, I [have been] interested in early Russian music, [which has remained almost unknown both] in Russia and abroad. Usually [scholars have been] informed in Russian music from Glinka on, but not before. What really led to Glinka and to the formation of [a] specific[ally] Russian approach to music was… known, if [at all], only through writ[ten descriptions], not [through] actual [musical] examples… 'The music itself [was, in fact,] for the most part unpublished, and often not transcribed into our notation.'

While in Russia in my youth I succeeded [in] collect[ing] here and there—in libraries, [in] old publication—some [examples] of the actual music, and [some] information about the progress of Russian musical development before Glinka. I brought the material along with me when emigrating to Paris in 1921 and continued researches, among other [places] in [the] Bologna Library (some Russian composers of the time of Catherine the Great were sent to Italy, mostly to Bologna, to study music), and in many antique book shops and libraries. At Brentano's in New York… I succeeded [in] buy[ing] the full orchestral score of the opera *First Government of Oleg*, of which the libretto was by the Empress Catherine [herself] and [the] music by Sarti, Paskevitch and Canobbio. In 1923 or so, Chester published my transcriptions for piano of compositions by Russian church composers of the time of Catherine the Great.

'[Eventually], I procured almost all the published scores of this period and almost everything written about them. Guided by the admirable books of Razoumovsky and Mettaloff, and Mesenetz's *Alphabet*, I made a thorough study of Russian neumes (*kriuki*)—the key to reading the *Znamennei Raspev* (plainsong) of the Russian Orthodox church.'

I admired Riemann's *History of Music* in examples, with his comments, so I wanted to do similar work for Russian music—'to edit a work that would deal with the origins of Russian music and its progress up to Glinka, not in a narrative, but in a series of musical examples.'

This I [undertook], finally, in 1938. 'Editing the [music] and preparing notes on the eighty examples that I had assembled required painstaking work. It was only in April 1940, that I completed the book' and furnished the manuscripts to [the] M. P. Belaieff music firm in Leipzig… The war came before anything was done about its publication. When, after the war, by some miracle, a manuscript was found, the difficulty [of] translat[ing] it into German and English [was compounded by the unfamiliarity of] so many technical terms of Russian church music, etc. Of course [my annotations for] the 80 examples, [in which I] explained and commented, [were] also in need of translation. Finally, the Anthology was translated into German by Guido Waldmann and into English by Alfred Swan.

{Although the annotations that Tcherepnin supplied for this anthology were intended primarily as commentary on the musical examples, some are exceptionally interesting and illuminating even out of context, and are accordingly reproduced here.}

CHURCH MUSIC

The liturgical singing of the Russian Orthodox Church has always been and is to this day strictly choral (*a capella*). At the outset it was based on the liturgical singing of the Byzantine Church, but was gradually enriched by the musical genius of the Russian people and developed over the centuries into an independent national art.

Likewise was the notation of this singing based, at first, on the Byzantine notation of the 10th century (paleobyzantine), but, developing alongside the singing itself, departed from Byzantine models. It passed through a number of stages and reached its final shape and form about the time of the Nikon reforms (middle of the 17th century). The Russian staveless neumes were called *znamiona* and all that has been affixed by means of these *znamiona* constitutes the mainstream of the Russian chant, the *znameny*, as well as its tributaries—the *demestvenny*, *Put's* and *Kazan* chants.

Exclusively on the basis of the notation, the history of the *znameny* chant could be divided into **three** periods:
1. 12th to 15th cc., when for each syllable of the text there was a corresponding neumatic sign, the duration and mode of performance of which depended entirely on the phonetics of the language and the meaning of the words.
2. 15th to 17th cc., when the evolution of the Church-Slavonic language necessitated the replacement of the semivowels by mute signs. Since the melody of the chant continued to intone the mute signs they were restored to their semivowel nature (usually by the letter O).
3. 17th century, when the above distorted texts were corrected to conform to actual speech.

Judging by the vast majority of the extant manuscripts, liturgical singing remained purely melodic during all of the three periods. The few manuscripts that have come down to us with several lines of neumes have never been properly read or transcribed. Melody and rhythm minutely reproduced the words of the sacred text. Whenever the latter was poetic, the musical realization was fully subordinated to the poetic form. When it was prose, the melody came nearer to a recitative and in its free unsymmetrical rhythm faithfully reproduced the intonations of human speech.

Similar to the 8 *modi* of Gregorian chant, the Byzantine and *znameny* chants are built on the foundation of 8 echoi (*glassi* in Russian). In the *znameny* chant the Octoechos (*Osmoglassiye*) is the sum total of eight distinct realms of sound each of which is composed of its proper melodic patterns.

THE KIEV CHANT

The Kiev Chant was one of the later (17th century) chants that became popular in Moscow at the time of the abrupt disappearance of the customs and traditions of old Russia and with them, of the *znameny* chant and notation. It grew up in Kiev, in southwestern Russia, as a result of western (Polish) influences on the old *znameny* chant. It was brought to Moscow already written on the five line stave which was at that time referred to as the Kiev *znamia* (notation). While the *znameny* chant recoils from harmonization and may be even meant to remain pure melody, the Kiev chant is saturated with harmonic feeling and became the ideal vehicle for part-singing. Instead of patterns we have here recurrent phrases or periods, of which there are only very few in each of the 8 echoi of the Kiev chant. These phrases have a much more definite rhythm than the lines of a *znameny chant*.

THE DEMESTVENNY CHANT

While the Kiev, Greek and Bulgarian chants were late importations introduced to Moscow at the time of a great upheaval of the whole Russian state, under the impact of the West, (reign of Czar Alexis) the *Demestvenny* chant was a much older rival of the *znamenny* and belongs… to the period of purely melodic singing.

KOLYADA-MALEDA

The songs sung on Christmas Eve and the week following are called *koliadki* (carols). They are of pagan origin: Koliada was the Slavic god of festivities and peace whose holiday was observed on December 24th. Under Christian influence, they have become Christian canticles. Even to this day they are sung in villages outside the windows of people whose names and the names of whose kinsmen are inserted in the words of the song. Just as Christmas superseded the feast of Koliada, Whitsun took the place of the pagan holiday of Semik.

WEDDING SONGS

In old Russia marriage in the life of a girl meant the loss of freedom and was frequently an unhappy event. Most of the wedding songs sung on the eve of the girl's wedding day have a sad, elegiac character.

THE BUFFOONS

The buffoons participated in feasts, weddings and all sorts of popular gatherings, where they entertained the people by singing, playing on instruments, dancing, giving primitive dramatic performances, and presenting puppet shows. The first mention of them appears in Nestor's chronicle under the year 1068. In spite of being banned by the Church and the powers that were, the guild of the buffoons survived through the Russian Middle Ages, while some of its aspects, such as the puppets, "Petrushka," and performances with trained bears can be seen even in our times (early 20th century).

In contrast to the abundance of historical information about the buffoons, not a single contemporary document of their art has come down to us; and only such of their songs and dances as have been merged with folklore enable us to judge, and very approximately at that, the character of their performances. In ascertaining the "buffoon" origin of [some] songs we are [often] aided by the texts.

RUSSIAN HORN MUSIC

The peculiar thing about Russian horn music was that it was played on horns that could emit only one sound. The Czech Johann Marech (1719-94) developed the orchestra of horns into a big instrumental ensemble. Remarkable discipline [was demanded] of the musicians, who were required, above all, to observe and count all the rests. Horn music was very popular in Russia in the 18th and even in the 19th century. In the last years of the 18th c. there were nine horn orchestras in St. Petersburg.

❅　❅　❅

NOTES TOWARD A CURRICULUM FOR COMPOSERS

{This piece shows Tcherepnin's enthusiasm for folklore and folkways at its height, an attitude which was in harmony not only with the spirit of the 1930s in Europe, but also with the mandated populism of Russian art in that decade and later. Most of the present text, as we shall see, was translated by Tcherepnin himself from jottings made in Russian, and his translation has here been subjected to minor copy-editing.}

Pedagogical problems started to interest me even earlier [than my work on pentatonic teaching pieces], and I find in my diary an outline of [an] approach for teaching composition that I sketched during the sea passage between Honolulu and Yokohama in March 1934, previous to my arrival in China... Here it is:

I. Material.

a) The teacher takes the student to the country people.
They listen to how people sing and play; examine the role that music plays in the life of the people. They notate folk materials.

b) At home the student analyzes the characteristics of the folk art:
Examines the material from the point of view of melody, rhythm, harmony and modulation.
Considers each song or piece of instrumental music according to these functions:
Melody separately
Rhythm separately
Harmony separately
After this he learns how to search for a different rhythm for the same melody, how to find another melody to the given rhythm, etc.

c) Studies the bird calls (and bird species of the country) and applies to them the same procedures, considering them as material.

d) Studies the sounds of insects, of wind, of the sea; but also, in cities, the sounds of cars, of factories, of planes etc.: all of it is analyzed as sound material.

II. Form.	The teacher takes the student to the country people. They listen to how people sing and play instruments. They continue to collect folk material. At home the student analyzes the characteristics of folk music forms. He examines the relation of the material to the form, determining what kind of form is needed to project the material and to which kind of form the people are predisposed.
	The student practices adjusting folk material to such forms.
	The teacher also takes the student to town for a similar study of town folk material.
III. Composition.	The teacher visits museums of folk art with the student, visits temples, reads folk literature and acquaints himself with folk philosophy.
	The student learns to understand the people more profoundly by studying the folk art, religious beliefs (including superstitions) social relations, political organization, history and philosophy of the people.
	And learns how to express his musical thoughts: having learned to find musical content correctly, he gains the maturity to find the form that is needed by the material.
	At this moment the student becomes a creator.

Scholarship for a student: a year in the village with country people. Observation of poetic rhythms, but also the rhythms of prose and of free speech.

The rhythm of the language; learning phrasing by rhythmical analysis of the prose.

Horizontal theory in study of lines.

In some way what happened to me in China was similar to what I anticipated for a student in the above outline: I heard people sing (the first were the coolies on the dock who, in order to synchronize their effort in carrying [a] heavy load were humming short semi-antiphonal patterns), I heard popular singing, music played on folk instruments, heard birds, sounds of towns and of villages, became acquainted with forms of folk music, etc. etc.; and as the first result—practical result, I would say— [produced a] piano method on the pentatonic scale that I felt [was] **needed**....

Later on I had the chance to lecture and to speak of this approach to music to my Chinese and Japanese students, and much later to my students in general.

This short outline, written on [the] S. S. President Coolidge, was the embryo: a seed that produced a much more complex growth. That is why I judged it interesting… to include [in] the present life story.

❊   ❊   ❊

HISTORICAL SURVEY I: FIRST SESSION LESSON PLAN (195?)

{These notes, only one page in the copious sheaf of papers connected to Tcherepnin's classwork at DePaul, give some idea of the flavor of a Tcherepnin class.}

What is music?   ask every student in class to give his idea and engage in a general discussion

Make comparison between the "visual world" and "audible world."

We consider what we can touch "real" (what we can see—sight is nothing other than extension of touch).

We consider unreal what we cannot touch

Yet the world of musical waves (of which the audible part is only a very small part) is as **real** as the world of visual waves. (Latest discoveries in astronomy were done by detecting the *sound* of a celestial [body]—it is detect[able] by sensitive sound machines but invisible by the strongest telescope.)

It is through sound that we communicate with each other. Our language is derived from the world of sound and is based on conventional—symbolic—sound combinations.

Yet our language is limited to the objective expression of things, state of mind, etc.

When we laugh, we do not say: "We are laughing!" We just laugh by producing the sound that is the direct expression of our hilarity.

When we are crying we are not saying: "I am crying." We cry in [a non-symbolic] way—producing the sound of distress by crying.

When we are hurt, we scream rather than describing the extension of our hurt by words. ETC. ETC.

So it leads to the conclusion that when we are overwhelmed by some strong emotion—we need something more than our language is able to express—and it is the world of sound that gives us the way to express the emotion. The World of sound is therefore directly related to our emotions-expresses them, and is able to produce them.

How did music start?   ask the students to give their ideas and discuss their ideas.

The science of Comparative Musicology deals with that problem. By studying the music of primitive tribes in some remote Pacific Islands, the scientist of Comparative Musicology aims to pierce the mystery of the origin of music of our ancestors when they lived the same [primitive] living conditions.

❅ ❅ ❅

MY FAITHFUL COMPANION—THE CIGARETTE (1957)

{Tcherepnin intended this piece of whimsy for the *Reader's Digest*. Many who read it were not amused—including, perhaps, the doctors who had advised him to quit smoking after his heart attack less than two years before. The little essay is wholly characteristic, however, of his sense of humor.}

For some time the cigarette has been treated as public enemy no. 1. It is accused of all possible evils. The enlightened medics are tracing the origins of many dreaded diseases to the use of tobacco. The cigarette is subjected to a third degree treatment by the white clothed detectives, by way of costly laboratory researches. Numerous articles, even books, are published to show to the smokers the way out of their "vice." Medical remedies are put on the market as a device to spoil the taste of the cigarette—thus helping the "feeble" to quit smoking… while the will power of the "strong" is praised to tickle his ego and to make him feel like a hero for having been able to give up the cigarette.

Still people are puffing tobacco—some of them with the innocence of an infant, fully unaware of the "dangers" to which they are exposing themselves; some of them with the guilt complex of a dope addict; some of them with the resolution of Faust, expecting the bill to be presented by Mephistopheles at any moment.

None of them have the nerve to hit back—to discard the head-shakers as a package of cards—to say something in defense of the poor cigarette.

For my part, I consider the cigarette to be my faithful companion. I am 58 years old. I am a composer and a pianist. For 33 years of my life I have smoked an average of three packs a day. I doubt that chewing gum, cracking peanuts or eating pickles would help me to keep my balance in life and to be creative—as the cigarette does.

Strangely enough, I did not start to smoke early in my life. My father was a heavy smoker—so were my schoolmates. That is perhaps why, out of pure desire to be different, I obstinately refused even to try a cigarette, leaving my colleagues free to call me a sissy. I met the cigarette in Monte Carlo at the age of 25. The girl whom I dated at that time used to smoke. At first I stayed independent, yet courteous, lighting her cigarette with a match. All was well, except that I was somehow disturbed by the odor of tobacco emanating from her breath. So I decided to smoke myself—in order to become insensitive to that odor. I remember the moment when, in a car riding on the so-called "Grande Corniche," the mountain highway overlooking the Mediterranean, I lit my *first* cigarette. It was an "Abdullah." It tasted neutrally. Not too good—not too bad. The immediate goal was attained; I had stopped being sensitive to the tobacco odor of my date.

But soon I realized that I had gained something more, something infinitely precious, something truly everlasting—a non-stop feeling of life, a bridging between dream and reality, a constant addendum to anything I might be doing, a stimulation to do the best I could, a faithful companion in joy and in distress: the *c i g a r e t t e .*

At that time my father and I shared a room in a hotel in Monte Carlo. My father was conducting the opera season. I had come along with him to appear as a soloist with the orchestra and to give piano recitals.

In the meantime, my romance went on—and one night I was so late to return to my home that my father became worried and went out to look around for me. It was at dawn when I gaily descended the little path that led from the hills to the hotel.

My dear father, when he saw me with a burning cigarette in my mouth, forgot his worries and burst into cheers. "You! You! You ascetic, you are smoking! Show me quickly how you do it! Do you know how to inhale, how to enjoy the cigarette? Tell me how, why and since when have you given up your abstention from the pleasures of life?"

❀ ❀ ❀

There are two different stages in the process of musical composition. The initial one—contemplative—is purely instinctive. The one that follows is a will-powered stage, during which the instinctively produced musical "material" is shaped consciously into an adequate musical form. Nothing is more detrimental than a simultaneous mixing of these two different attitudes. A cerebral approach that comes too early destroys the capacity of intuitive meditation, while the instinct interfering with form-construction endangers the balance of the final achievement.

The cigarette helps me to listen to what is going on in my subconscious, without analyzing it prematurely. It helps me during the next stage to concentrate on construction of the entire musical form-to balance the material, to eliminate the hazards of improvisation.

❀ ❀ ❀

A pianist who studies a piece of music does not learn it by playing it X times from the beginning till the end at full speed, with all the dynamics and with full expression. As a matter of fact, the process of performing a piece is the exact reverse of the process of composing it. In performance, the cerebral approach comes first, and the creative succeeds it only after the technical problems have been vindicated and resolved. During the preliminary stage, while the pianist is dealing with purely technical problems, he has to study various details according to the degree of their difficulties. In my case, the lengthy hours of practicing each hand separately are eased by holding the cigarette in the free hand, and by puffing it occasionally.

Once more, the cigarette proves to be of assistance to remain patient, to be insistent, to feel at ease while accomplishing a work that has, in itself, nothing especially exciting.

And what a pleasure it is to light a cigarette during the intermission, or at the end of a piano recital. How it helps to concentrate before a public appearance, and to relax after it!

❀ ❀ ❀

The cigarette is a faithful companion in loneliness. One never feels really lonely if one has a package of cigarettes in one's pocket. When one congregates in the company of friends, how much nearer one feel to the group with a cigarette in his mouth. It is certainly a help when discussing complicated business matters, or when looking for proper wording of a contract or an agreement. I was told that at the peace conference in Portsmouth—which ended the Russo-Japanese War at the beginning of this century—the breaking of negotiations was avoided by the timely lighting of a cigarette by the Russian delegate, Count Witte. If what was told is true, thousands of human lives were spared by a single cigarette.

❀ ❀ ❀

During the years of World War II, I was still living in Paris. The daily ration of cigarettes was 3 per capita. And even this reduced ration was not always honored. Yet—whether it was through friends, or my concierge, or through a student—I was never without tobacco. Sometimes I walked miles to get it, sometimes I accepted it as a fee for a lesson or a composition. It has taught me a very important lesson. I have learned that if one *really* wants something, and is willing to put everything at stake to get it-he'll get it! And this is equally valid for anything that one goes after in life.

❀ ❀ ❀

After the liberation of Paris, while the war was still going on, many good acquaintances (that sometimes resulted in life-long friendships) were made by GIs and WACs in Europe, via the cigarette. I believe that if the calamity of a new war should ever occur (God spare us this), the best manner to liquidate it rapidly, without bloodshed, would be by way of guns loaded with American cigarettes. It would quickly make friends out of enemies.

❀ ❀ ❀

Soon after the end of World War II, my wife, who is a concert pianist, was engaged to appear at the International Music Festival in Prague, and to give concerts in Czechoslovakia and Austria. In Vienna, her manager missed meeting her at the railway station. There she was alone, in a foreign country, having no knowledge of the German language and no Austrian money in her pocket. Bravely, she hired a cab and asked to be driven to a hotel. At the hotel, the manger coldly advised her that no room was available. Tired and hungry, she asked for a meal. But no meal could be served except to hotel guests provided with ration cards. In distress, my wife opened her pocket book to reach for a cigarette. As soon as the hotel manager saw the package of American cigarettes in her hand, his attitude changed entirely. A comfortable room became available, a royal meal was served, and the manager paid the cab. All of it—for a pack of cigarettes.

❋ ❋ ❋

What is wrong with the cigarette? Why should this true friend of the human being be treated as a snake in the grass, ready to blast mortal poison at the innocent victim? Why should it be suspected of all kinds of "subversive activities?" Why all these warnings against the use of it?

Of course there is some danger—as in everything that we do. But should we not swim for fear of drowning? Should we not walk for fear of spraining an ankle? Should we not ride in a car for fear of accidents? Should we not eat for fear of indigestion? Should we stop dating for fear of falling in love?

I am persuaded that the weaklings are not we, who are smoking, but those who, by fear, persuasion or ego-flattering self-discipline, are quitting. We all will have to die one day or another. I do not know what I will need then. But I do know that to live, to work, to feel the pulsation of life, I have to smoke.

So, from the bottom of my heart, I most enthusiastically proclaim, "Vive la Cigarette!"

❋ ❋ ❋

A HEART ATTACK (1959)

{The following is a later piece of Tcherepnin's devil's advocate humor, this one rather wry.}

One of the most wonderful things that ever happened to me was when I had my heart attack four years ago. The attack itself was not good, but it had very happy results for me. First, it occurred when I was 56 years old. This was wonderful, because this is the average age for getting heart attacks, and I fit into the "average" category. Never before had anything I had done been average, but now, I fit statistically into an average category. This was grand.

Then, for many years, I had been forced to eat many foods I detest. Milk. No one should have to [drink] milk or [eat] any of its by-products. Also, fats and fatty foods. I detest them. The doctor handed me a list of foods which I had to eat. Everything on the list was wonderful. I just carried my little list with me wherever I went and when I was served some food I didn't like, I just handed over my list and was automatically pardoned from eating. So you see, these two nice things happened—and all because of my heart attack.

❋ ❋ ❋

MY FAVORITE WORK OF ART (1959)

{During the late 1950s, the *Chicago American*'s "Pictorial Living" section presented a series of short articles commissioned from notable Chicago residents on the subject "My Favorite Work of Art." Tcherepnin's essay, in which he had been asked to discuss some art other than music, appeared on May 10, 1959, presented as follows.}

COMPOSER, CONCERT PIANIST NAMES HIS
FAVORITE
WORK OF ART

Masterpieces in the arts—painting, music, sculpture and literature—make lasting impressions on men and women and become inspirations in their lives. The Chicago American is asking leading Chicagoans to share inspirations with our readers.

BY ALEXANDER TCHEREPNIN

A fairly small, one-storey white monastery on the island of Crete. A modest reception room ornamented with frescoes in Italo-Byzantine style. The little chapel with icons, candles, lampads [*sic*]. The odor of incense.

An hospitable monk takes me through a long dark corridor to his room. He seats me on a tabouret facing the entrance door. At this very moment, by mere coincidence, a ray of sun creates a spotlight on a little icon placed over the door. The upper part of the icon represents the bearded visage of St. Nicholas. The rest is covered by silver brocade over which lines of tiny mother-of-pearl [beads] are sewn.

The expression of St. Nicholas—is love to mankind.

The covering dress of the icon, decorated by the monk, expresses his love of his saint. The icon, like most, is anonymous. No personal ambition of the artist who painted it could be detected. However the product of his art, better than any recognized masterpiece, reflects the loving soul of the artist, and the ability to project it through a work of art.

Love inspires love. It already inspired the love of that monk, expressed by the care which he gave to the icon by dressing it up so touchingly. It inspires love to mankind for anyone who contemplates it with his mind and his eyes open.

It teaches us to serve, to project the idea with no strings of one's ego attached, to put the ideal above the means, the product above the producer, to follow the way of love in humbleness.

This anonymous icon, together with its homemade dress, is the work of art I shall never forget.

❀　❀　❀

MUSIQUE CONCRÈTE (1960)

{The following letter by Tcherepnin was published in the letter columns of *France Observateur* on October 13, 1960}

I became aware only today of the article published in your August 17 issue under the byline of F.-Christian Toussaint, an article that imputes to me the statement that "musique concrete is excluded from my class as something antihumanitarian."

Now I have not at any time uttered such a judgment, precisely because I believe that the enriched musical vocabulary provided by musique concrete and electronic music promises to be an important means of artistic expression for both contemporary composers and those of the future. And I might add that my personal researches in the domain of music follow a course leading to musique concrete and electronic music.

I would thus be most appreciative if you were to kindly publish this letter in your columns by way of rectification, and in order to dispel this misunderstanding for which I am not responsible.

❀　❀　❀

A LESSON ON TWO BAGATELLES (1963)

{This Tcherepnin article was published as one of the regular "Master Class" features in *The Piano Teacher* magazine.}

Bagatelle No. 4 was originally the final aria from an opera, *Edda*, that I composed when I was quite young. The opera was about a Finnish girl deserted by her lover. In this aria she expressed her longing for him and her despair when she realized that she would never see her beloved again. This feeling and the vocal concept of the piece should be kept in mind to guide the interpretation.

To obtain a good expressive sound in the melodic line in measures 3-14 and 20-24, I recommend that the weight of the right arm rest on the third, fourth, and fifth fingers, and that the thumb and second finger be kept as light as possible to hold the harmony discreetly in the background. Next in importance to this right hand melody is the contrapuntal line of the ostinato left hand, like an *idée fixe*, which should be played with expression; the low bass must be clearly heard too. To obtain this effect, the weight of the left arm should be distributed equally over all the fingers, not only to make the melodic figure expressive, but also to give a good sound to the bass notes. For a large hand it will be advisable to start the bass with the fingering indicated [*i. e.*, fingers 2 and 5 on the first chord with the top line played by fingers 1 and 2 in alternation]; however, for a small hand, the reverse (starting with 1-5, 2, etc.) will bring the same result.

The importance of the melodic line of the left hand becomes evident win the middle section (measures 15-18) when it leads to the melody in unison in both hands, like a dramatic outburst of despair. This middle section should be played freely, "syllabically," as though each note corresponded to a syllable of a word, giving expressive sense to the phrase as a whole. The two successive chords in measure 19 should be played [with a finger] legato; the first, **mf**, the second **p** In measures 25, 26, and 27, the first chord should be played staccato and the second chord (each time louder) held with the fingers; but starting with the middle of measure 27, the three repeated *fortissimo* chords should be played *portamento* and should be held by the fingers rather than by the pedal. Let the last chord continue sounding very long until it has practically faded away; then only, play the remaining chords of measure 28, very slowly, very *pianissimo*, as an echo. Continue holding the pedal from the middle of measure 27 until the instant of playing the first *pianissimo* chord, then use no pedal at all until the beginning of the final measure. Play the last two measures very slowly, chords legato, without expression-cold and neutral as a verdict of Fate.

Bagatelle No. 6

The Russian winter is long and cold. In my home town (now called Leningrad) the snow appears sometimes as early as October, and the Neva River freezes over and stays frozen for six long months. It is not until April or May that the ice melts away and spring timidly makes its long awaited blessed appearance.

Yet occasionally in the middle of winter, just for one morning, rarely for more than a day, the skies become blue, the sun shines, and one has the feeling that spring is in the air. On one such day Bagatelle No. 6 was composed. It expresses the hope for the coming of spring, a longing for it in the midst of winter.

The melody should be played legato, interrupted by the descents to a lower register when right hand crosses over left, which should be played with a different touch. Observe that when these lower right hand figures continue to the first beat of the next measure, the last note has the function of bass.

Give a slight accent to the first of each six-note group in the left hand of measures 1-8, but in measures 9, 10, and 11, accent only the first note of each measure. In measure 11 (still in the left hand), stress the ascending *f*, *g*, *g*-sharp leading to the a-natural in measure 12. In the final measure, make the theme *a*-flat, *b*-flat, *d*-flat, *g*-flat, which now appears in the left hand, clearly heard in spite of the changing octave. Play this measure *rallentando*.

THE WORLD OF SOUND (1964)

{In this article, published in the March 1964 issue of *Music Journal*, Tcherepnin presented ideas about new music that he had discussed elsewhere in a manner at once pithy and evocative.}

Invisible rays. Inaudible sounds.

Rays that we can see. Sounds that we can hear.

The colors that the painter uses are only a little fraction of the infinite variety of colors of the light spectrum.

The sounds that our ear is able to perceive and to differentiate are only a little part of the infinite variety of sounds that are vibrating around us.

And of these sounds only a minimal part is accepted as "musical."

Western music came finally to the arbitrary division of an octave into 12 equal semitones.

Chinese, Hindu and Arabian music use an equally arbitrary although different organization of the so-called "musical" sounds.

The poetic meters, the pulsation of dance rhythms, as organized in music, are only a *few* relative to the infinite number of possible time subdivisions.

In our epoch the Eastern and Western musical languages finally became acquainted, mutually influencing each other more and more and enriching the conventions of one by the conventions of the other.

Stimulated by science, the music of today is trying to liberate itself from the conventions of East and West-thus penetrating deeper into the world of pure sound, becoming nearer to nature, richer in means of expression, freer from the limitations of "musical conventions."

The incubation period of composition is a mysterious one.

From where and by which way does the initial idea, which is to become the seed of a composition, come to the mind of the composer?

In my case, when I start to work on a new composition, I do not hear it. I feel it. I experience the urge to "tune in," to become a "converter" of inaudible vibrations into audible sounds.

What follows is but a partial materialization in forms of sound that even in this stage stay free from conventions of pitch and of meter.

Another effort is needed to bring the idea into what we call "music" and to start the actual work on a "musical" composition.

Since my early youth I dreamed of the liberation from conventions. It is for this reason that I conceived the second movement of my First Symphony (1927) for percussion instruments *a capella*, thus achieving the liberation from pitch. For a similar reason, even earlier, I ended the piano piece *Message* by knocking on the wood of the piano the meter of the principal theme, thus reducing it to its purely rhythmic value.

It was also in the twenties that I used in my compositions what I called then the *bird folklore* and introduced the rhythms of insects, [and] the irregular meter and intonation of spoken language in[to my] music.

The other way to escape conventions was by color: a sound color of the Harp, of the Harmonica, of Accordion, of Tuba or of so many other instruments that are still winning their place under the sun and are *in need of being served by the composer.*

The musical coexistence that soon will result in a happy marriage of East and West, the rise of percussion group as such and as a fourth group in our orchestra, the appearance of electronic devices of sound production, and the introduction of scientifically conceived new musical instruments are of primary importance to the development of music and open an entirely new way for a composer of today.

I am fascinated to live in our epoch and to see the art of music becoming the true art of sound.

❀　❀　❀

THREE HUMOROUS PIECES

{Along with his whimsy, Tcherepnin had a genuine flair for parody, born of a keen eye for pretension of every sort. His deflationary wit was gentle when aimed at himself and his friends, but could, on very rare occasions, take on a cutting edge, when he felt he was ill-treated. The three short pieces here show some of his satirical range.}

1.　Tcherepnin Violin Sonata
{Tcherepnin here spoofed the sort of publicity materials produced for him by his publishers and managers.}

"Since Beethoven's 'Spring' Sonata there could hardly be found a sonata of equal beauty of expression, equal optimism, and equal stature" writes the celebrated critic of *Music Parnassus* in Vienna, Friedrich Meisterwunkel.

At the end of his report of the first Viennese performance of the Sonata, by Jan Kubelik and Leopold Godowsky, he exclaims: "the audience was galvanized by the performance of the great masters of the masterpiece of the young composer. After [a] 15-minute-long standing ovation, the artists had to bow to the will of the audience, and repeated the whole sonata. The same ovations followed. And the screams—bravo, bravissimo—continued long after the electrician put out the lights in the large hall of the Konzerthaus."

The first New York performance of the Sonata, by Jascha Heifetz and Arthur Rubinstein, brought a triumph for the performers and for the composer. Olin Downes gives of it the following account: "Carnegie Hall, overfilled with an enthusiastic audience, was a scene of the strongest ovations in [the] history of the Hall after the performance of Tcherepnin's by now celebrated Violin Sonata. The light comes from Russia. The 23-year-old Russian composer, now resident [in] Paris, can be proud of his work. It is a masterpiece of modern music literature. Not only modern: it bypasses by far Mozart, Beethoven, Brahms, Mendelssohn: truly a new genius is born—if he... composed [no] other piece than this Sonata—he is already eternal." (New York Times, 22 February, 1922)

The best recordings of the Sonata are by Jascha Heifetz and Vladimir Horowitz (Columbia), by Isaac Stern and Van Cliburn (Victor), by Jacques Thibaud and Marguerite Long (Pathe Marconi), by Yehudi and Hepzibah Menuhin (His Master's Voice). Also of special interest is the recording of Pablo Casals of the same sonata with Eugene Istomin. It is amazing that Pablo Casals succeeded to perform the Violin Sonata on cello without changing a note, keeping the violin register. Also worthy of mention is the recording of William Primrose, who performs the sonata on viola, accompanied by Victor Babin.

The orchestral version of the sonata by Toscanini (recorded on Victor Masterpieces label), although disapproved by the composer, was and still is the best seller of Victor records.

And it must be added that the Sonata, since its initial publication by Durand in Paris in 1923, has had 43 editions; and the total number of records of the Sonata sold alone in this country by leading companies [long ago] bypassed the billion marks.

2. A Letter to his Dean

{Tcherepnin's experience at DePaul was not a totally happy one, for, although he enjoyed teaching, he had to endure an undercurrent of jealousy and intramural sniping in his dealings with music department colleagues whom he privately regarded as mediocrities. In 1963, when European commitments prevented him from attending a DePaul music symposium, Tcherepnin sent a collegial telegram of good wishes for the event's success to the Dean of the DePaul Music School (the late Arthur C. Becker) and received, for his pains, a snide reply. Maintaining public silence about this rebuff from a mere "Sunday composer," Tcherepnin vented his annoyance by preparing—for the amusement of his fellow DePaul sufferers Ming and Phillip Ramey—the letter that Becker *deserved* to receive. Tcherepnin saves his heaviest ammunition for the composer Leon Stein. Competent but uninspired, Stein was forever being held up to Tcherepnin as the ideal DePaul composer-because his career never took him from campus, but was virtually confined to Chicago, where he presented a series of works for saxophone, and a violin concerto that Tcherepnin found dismayingly dull and violinistically graceless.}

Hohestrasse 55
Zollikon/Zurich April 17, 1963
Dear Arthur,

You can hardly imagine how happy I was to receive your letter. I read it and reread it. You can be sure that your dear lines have reached Ming's and my hearts and have moved us profoundly. Especially we were happy to hear about the overwhelming success of the symposium. Of course we are not astonished: DePaul's music school, headed by [so] great an artist as you… and having on its faculty such internationally acclaimed members as Magdalen Massman, Herman Shapiro, Miss Mendelssohn, Miss Kenny, and headed by the incomparable, unique virtuoso… our dear Ted [Kozuch]—the Paderewsky of our time, certainly is the greatest music institution of our time-with no equal in [the] USA, and of course, no equal in Europe. The success was a priori there.

You were surprised to receive my telegram: you certainly are too modest, my dear man. You should realize how far reaching is your reputation, how all the musical world is following the great task that is done on Jackson Street. For weeks all the Paris papers were full of news from DePaul: thousands of young music students stormed the American Embassy with the hope of finding [a] way to attend the Symposium, [which] was the talk of the town for months. Students deserted the Paris Conservatory and went through the streets of Paris with big [posters]: "We want Massman!" "Give us Kozuch!" "Enough of the old moisty French teaching." "Chicago, DePaul we want!" Somehow it was learned that I am in town. Messiaen, Dupre, Cochereau were hanging on [the] phone to ask if the[y] could hope to have your instruction if they came to Chicago, while all the young (and not even young, but even such established figures as Boulez, Stockhausen of this world and Roussel, Ravel, Florent Schmitt of the other, with hundreds of their students) asked me to introduce them to our dear Leon Stein.

On the other hand, the celebrated French pianist Yvonne Loriod came crying to tell me that she was unable to obtain [a] visa to come to [the] Symposium, and to [be] trained by our great masters.

In order to escape this universal demand, realizing that I could not help the French artists to fulfill their great ambition to study at DePaul, I fled to Germany.

And there it started all over again. There was not a place where I [was] not [asked] to give the detailed account of our work at DePaul and of the latest developments on the faculty. Please tell Leon that his compositions are appearing on programs of all the major European orchestras, and of course practically every day on programs of recitalists. His brilliant way of treating the violin [has] bec[o]me a proverb: the best compliment you can make to a composer here is to tell him that he certainly is influenced by Leon Stein.

Bravo to you, bravo to DePaul. Be sure to convey Ming's and my profound homage to our great colleagues. I realize now how much I learned from them while at DePaul, and Hsien Ming particularly is indebted to her pianist colleagues on the faculty (and also to Miss Leafeld) for all that she [has] bec[o]me since she came to DePaul.

We are counting the days until we will be back. Hsien Ming is, however, unable to wait until October, so she just made her reservation to fly to Chicago at her earliest possible moment, early next month, with the sole purpose [of being] stimulated by the wonderful artistic and human climate of our Music School. I do hope you will find time to receive her and that she will have the chance to see her celebrated colleagues. Even if for no more than a minute, it will be worth…her trip.

Please be good to her. She is longing to see you and will also bring you my heartiest greetings.
As ever your profoundly grateful

Sasha

3.   A Letter to Phillip Ramey
{By contrast, this letter is a thoroughly genial example of Tcherepnin's droll and self-deprecating humor. To appreciate all the references the reader should know that Ramey was in the habit of writing letters on stationery from various hotels he had visited, that he liked to tease Tcherepnin about wearing a dark blue shirt with a tie and thus looking "like a Russian gangster," and that he had recently written an article about the MacDowell Colony, an artists' retreat.}

153 Highlever Road
    London W 10
25 iii 73
Cher Monsieur Ramey de l'Hotel Montalambert, Paris
  Caro Maestro Phillipo di Hotel Monaco and Grand Canal, Venezia
    Dear Mr. MacDowell Monster of Peterborough, New Hampshire 03458
      Dear Phil with no stationery of your own [:]
Thank you for your most interesting letters, for the exciting continuation of [your] MacDowell [Colony] journal, for mentioning the name of the old Prof. Dr. T and his overseas activities-and [for] the most welcome proposal to meet at Kennedy the citizens of the world: if you really mean it and intend to do so here are the useful indications: March 31, TWA flight 701, scheduled to land at 7:30 PM at the abovementioned airport: F 5 feet 2½, M 6 feet 2. But please keep the press an[d] reporters away, no photographs, our arrival is of strict incognito: no band, no flowers, no speeches. Immediately upon arrival we intend to drive with you to our Manhattan residence and will be looking forward to learn from you the latest news…

For our part we will be willing to inform you about the miracle town piece, London performance of the 46 year old Long Island Symphony, gas strike, railway strike, white paper, situation in Ulster and Tippett's 3rd.

So until quite soon, dear stationery collector, Ming's and my love to you…

as ever yours[1]

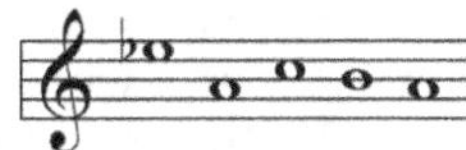

Guess what shirt I will wear!

✻ ✻ ✻

A TRIP TO THE SOVIET UNION (1967)

{This article, discussed by Reich on page 94, appeared in 1967 in No. 4 of *The World of Music*, a quarterly published by UNESCO. The presence of a number of phrases familiar in 1960s Soviet publicity handouts indicates that editing decisions were dictated both by stylistic considerations and by the press policy guidelines of one or more member nations. Some passages are marked by the standard Soviet method of printing names—*i. e.*, the first initial only along with the surname—and these may involve editorial additions, since elsewhere Tcherepnin uses first and last names. It is notable that Tikhon Khrennikov, the notorious hatchet-man for Stalin in the 1948 denunciation and suppression of such "bourgeois formalists" as Prokofiev and Shostakovich, is always referred to here either as "T. Khrennikov" or by surname alone.}

Only now, after forty-nine years, did I have the good fortune to see my native land again. In May of this year I travelled, together with my wife, to the U. S. S. R. upon the invitation of the Soviet Union of Composers which had arranged a concert tour for me.

We were given a most friendly welcome at Sheremetyevo airport by the President of the Composers' Union, T. Khrennikov, and a group of musicians. We were spared customs and passport formalities, and were driven straight into the city where a comfortable apartment in the thirty-storey Ukraina Hotel had been reserved for us.

As I had to practice a lot for my concerts, Khrennikov gave me the use of his office in the building of the Composers' Union. It is equipped with two magnificent grand pianos, a writing desk, comfortable arm chairs, a sofa and a telephone. I felt completely at home and was able to practice several hours a day and receive visitors. The building, the property of the Composers' Union, belongs to a block of houses in which musicians and musicologists live. Shostakovich, Khachaturian,

---

1   Tcherepnin presumably thought that this odd musical spelling of his name, S-A-C-H-A, sounded more interesting than "SASHA" (Note: S=E-flat; H=B).

Kabalevsky, Shneerson, Bernendt, Kisselev, Richter, Sumbatyan, Kogan and Rostropovich live here; the editorial offices of the musical periodical *Sovietskaya Muzika* and the flat of the chief editor, E. Grosheva, are also situated in this complex which includes a club with a concert hall and a friendly restaurant. The whole block is a center for artists that facilitates contacts between the residents and encourages collaboration.

In the vicinity lies the Moscow Conservatoire that celebrated its hundredth anniversary this year: an old, well-preserved building with two concert halls for solo recitals and orchestral concerts. Here I made my first appearance—a piano recital with my own compositions. The Russian public accorded me a most moving and enthusiastic welcome that I shall never forget. A week later, when I played my Second Piano Concerto under the baton of I. Gusman, I received the same friendly and spontaneous welcome, as I did at all my subsequent appearances in other cities of the Soviet Union.

In Moscow I had the opportunity of attending a splendid performance of Prokofiev's *Romeo and Juliet.* I also heard the Second Piano Concerto of the young composer Rodion Schedrin, the humorous operetta *The Hundred Devils and the Young Girl* by T. Khrennikov, Sviatoslav Richter's interpretation of Prokofiev's Fifth Piano Concerto, and also many tape recordings of works by Russian composers.

It appears to me that all these composers of the Soviet Union, independently of personal styles of writing and tendencies, are endeavoring to serve the people with the greatest awareness of their responsibilities. The Russian composer does not live in isolation. His works are performed and his contact with the public, in the widest sense of the word, gives him the necessary corrective for his work. What he receives from the people, he gives back to them in the form of his work of art. Progress in music runs parallel to progress in the general level of culture. To music which is appropriate to the present, belongs also the future. As Bach recorded his "present" in music, as Beethoven reflected the tendencies of his time, as Debussy gave expression in sound to his age, so do the composers of the Soviet Union wish to create a music that arises from the relations between the cultural situation of the people and the creative capacity of the artist.

This attitude on the part of the composer in no way excludes an individual approach; the creative artist has the freedom to determine for himself what means he will employ for the realization of this aim. In the Soviet Union we thus find composers of various tendencies and with very different artistic persuasions; each one senses the present in his own way and tries to record it in sound.

In Moscow I met many musicians: Aram Khachaturian and his wife Nina Makarova who is a gifted pianist and composer, also Rodion Shchedrin and the young pianist Khaimovsky who is making Messiaen known in Moscow and plays the works of the young Russian composers. At the home of T. Khrennikov I met his daughter Natasha, a talented painter who has designed stage settings for Stravinsky's ballets and corresponds regularly with him. I also met my good friend Emil Gilels, the violinist Kogan, Sviatoslav Richter and his wife, and many friends of my youth.

Very valuable and important work is being carried out by the musicologists of the Soviet Union. Nestyev, Bernandt, Kisselev, Pekelis, Dobrokhotov and Martinov, whom I met, have published extremely interesting documents from the eighteenth and nineteenth centuries. My teacher, the distinguished musicologist Victor Belaieff, the author of numerous books on Russian music, gave me his handwritten transcription of polyphonic liturgical chants of the Russian church notated in neumes. Belaieff discovered these chants and is the first to have deciphered them.

From Moscow I flew to Tbilisi, a city that I knew very well in my youth. At that time it had a population of about 100,000; now this has grown to over a million. Tbilisi has become a modern city; however the center is preserved in its original form. Here is situated the old conservatoire in which I studied. By the side of this old building a large new concert hall has been built, and it was here that I gave a piano recital and played my Second Piano Concerto under the baton of the young conductor Djaparidze. It was a most moving experience for me to see this city again—the familiar streets, the house in which I lived with my parents, the old Sion Cathedral and the Maidan Bazaar. I visited Mzhet with its famous old churches, Mziri whose fortified monastery was so effectively described by the Russian poet Lermontov, and Kidjori, where in my youth I was often a guest at the house of the painter Sudeikin whose wife Vera later became Igor Stravinsky's life companion. I also had the opportunity to hear tape recordings of works of Georgian composers, among these a monumental symphony by Machavariani, pieces by Balantchivadze and Taktakisvili. My final visit was to Leningrad. I saw again the house where my parents had lived[1], the Nikolaus Cathedral, and the Conservatoire where my wife and I were received by the director, the distinguished pianist Pavel Serebryakov, and indeed in the very same office where half a century ago I passed my entrance examination under Glazunov. An unforgettable moment! Nothing had changed: the same broad staircase, on the steps of which the witty Prokofiev used to sit and tease his fellow students; the same concert hall in which the student orchestra, conducted by my father, used to rehearse. In those days at the violin desks sat Heifetz, Piastro, the

---

1   In a letter to Frances Clark, Tcherepnin wrote, "[I] visited my own room where I had my piano, my desk, and the icon in the corner, to which I used to pray to become a composer, finding it not changed since the time I left, and amazed that the new inhabitant, a young girl, also has an icon in the same right corner of the room."

Fischberg brothers, and among the 'cellists the most talented Serkin who died young. The orchestra was conducted by my father's pupils: Prokofiev, Steinman, Malko, Gauk and Dranishnikov won their first spurs here.

Back in Moscow again, on the day before my departure I attended a concert of my own chamber music works in the Gnessin Institute. After the concert I was asked to tell the public about my life and give an account of my impressions during my visit to the Soviet Union. In the evening I was invited to Mrs. Grosheva's home. Here I bade farewell to my friends, which was all the more difficult for me since the sojourn in my native land and the heartfelt welcome I was accorded are among the happiest experiences of my life.

❋   ❋   ❋

COMPOSERS HAVE A DUTY

{In this article, written for the 25th anniversary edition of *Music Journal* (1942–67), Tcherepnin strikes the appropriate celebratory tone, at the same time touching on his familiar concerns about the modern music scene.}

There is no doubt in my mind that our time will be remembered as another "golden era of music."

Never before has music had such a prominent place in the cultural life of humanity as it has now. Never before has music reached the large masses of people all around the world as it does now. Never before were the sounds of music projected all over the globe as they are now, whether it be by "live performances" by orchestras, by the virtuosos, by various ensembles, or via radio or records, or (in the case of operas and ballets) by film and by television.

The perfection achieved presently by performers and by the performing ensembles of every kind is unique. Millions of people are exposed to music by listening, millions of people are initiated in music by widespread musical education. Never before has the composer had such a variety of sound-producing means and sound colors at his disposal. Never before was he better served by the performers. Never before was his mission as important, his responsibility as great as it is now, when his production, universally projected, might influence the taste and the "musical morals" of the people for good or bad.

Similar to the progress in our ways of life, the progress in the ways of music making goes on and on. I anticipate the day when our three-and-a-quarter group symphony orchestra will become a fully equipped four-group "instrument" with a percussion section in balance quantitatively and qualitatively with the three other sections. I can also imagine that the piano, as it becomes used in a wider range of sound production, will receive an octave-doubling pedal, when it will be provided with another pedal to move the pitch up and down.

Experiments have already been made to attach a microphone to the violin and to have the engineer plug the microphone in and out, according to the design of the composer, during the performance, thus providing the violin with a set of colors and with a wide range of dynamics that it never had before. When all of this will become of common use, the great "lionized instruments"—such as piano, violin, human voice and the symphony orchestra-will welcome new compositions that will give them the chance to use all of their accrued means.

In the meantime, quite similar to the "foreign aid program" of help to the underprivileged countries, a program to provide the underprivileged instruments with adequate musical literature should be launched, and the task to do it assigned to the present-day composers.

Actually[2] performers of every musical instrument old or new have reached a high virtuoso standard. We have Paganinis of practically every musical instrument who are eagerly looking for pieces to perform.

The flutists, the clarinetists, the cellists, the violinists, with a rich musical heritage from the past, have not enough contemporary musical material corresponding to the present-day possibilities of their instruments.

The harpsichordists and the harpists are in search of contemporary music literature that would give them the chance to display their skill, their musicianship and the accrued possibilities of their sound- producing technique. The long-neglected viola da gamba could be the most appropriate instrument for the chromatic texture, due to its tuning and fingering, for the modern composer to make use of. Oboe, English horn, bassoon, saxophone, horn, trumpet, trombone, tuba and contrabass are waiting to be served by the composers!

Harmonica and accordion, the most "popular" instruments, played by millions, are lacking adequate musical "vehicles" that would use all the sound possibilities these instruments possess. The percussion group, so rich, so varied, so potential, is surely in need of performing pieces.

---

2   *i. e.*, "today" or "at present" (= *actuellement*-a Gallicism previously cited in "Music in Modern China").

And the new instruments—those invented by Harry Partch, those of the Bachet brothers, Ondes Martenot—all the electronic devices that offer the complete freedom from the conventional pitch—could stimulate the imagination of the composer of today and provide him with new means for the materialization of his creative aims. Not only are we living in the golden era of music, but there seems to be (more than ever) things to do; great progress is still ahead of us.

To provide all instrumentalists and ensembles with performing pieces is a duty of the contemporary composer. By accomplishing it he will serve the cause of music and of the musicians, will contribute to progress, and will have the joy of feeling that his production is needed. What could be better than this?

❈　❈　❈

TCHEREPNIN POSTLUDE

We are all here in this world on a round trip from the unknown to the unknown. We have to hold together while we are here and try to do our best in every direction, continuing what our predecessors have done and preparing the way for our successors.

❀ ❀ ❀

ALEXANDER TCHEREPNIN: A COMPENDIUM

CATALOGUES

AND

BIBLIOGRAPHY

THE MUSIC OF ALEXANDER TCHEREPNIN:

A CHRONOLOGICAL CATALOGUE

compiled by Lily Chou

OPUS	TITLE	DATE COMPOSED	DURATION	PUBLICATION
Op. 1	Toccata No. 1 for piano Revised ed. by composer	1921 1957	6'	Belaieff 1922 Belaieff 1957
Op. 2/1	Nocturne No. 1 for piano Revised ed. by composer	1919 1957	3' 30"	Belaieff 1922 Belaieff 1957
Op. 2/2	Dance No. 1 for piano Revised ed. by composer	1919 1957	3' 30"	Belaieff 1922 Belaieff 1957
Op. 3	Scherzo for piano	1917	2' 30"	Durand 1927
Op. 4	*Sonatine Romantique* for piano	1918	13'	Durand 1925
Op. 5	*Bagatelles* for Piano Revised ed. by composer Version for piano and orchestra Version for piano and string orchestra	1912–18 1958 1958 1960	12' 12' 12'	Heugel-Leduc 1923 Heugel-Leduc 1964 Heugel-Leduc 1964 Heugel-Leduc 1965
Op. Posth.	*Sunny Day* (Forgotten Bagatelle) for piano	1915	1'	Presser 1977
WoO	*Old St. Petersburg* (Waltz) For piano	c. 1917	3' 15"	MS
WoO	Ballade for piano	1917	ca. 9'	MS
WoO	Episodes (*Priskaski*) (Fleas) 12 Simple Pieces for Piano	1912–19 or 1920	10' 30"	Heugel-Leduc 1923
WoO	"A Contented Man" for bass and piano	1918	2'	Chester 1938 Belaieff (in preparation)
Op. 6	*Petite Suite* for piano	1918–19	10'	Durand 1923
Op. 7	*Pièces sans titres* (Pieces without titles) for piano	1915–17	9'	Durand 1925
Op. 8/1	Nocturne No. 2 for piano	1919	4'	Durand 1925
Op. 8/2	Dance No. 2 for piano	1919	3' 30	Durand 1925
Op. 9	8 Preludes for piano	1919–20	9'	Heugel-Leduc 1926
Op. 10	*Feuilles libres* (Loose Pages) for piano	1920–24	8'	Durand 1924
Op. 11	5 Arabesques Andantino (piano) Allegro vivo (piano) Allegretto (piano) Presto (piano) Allegretto (violin and piano)	1920–21	7'	Heugel-Leduc 1925
Op. 12	Concerto No. 1 for piano and orchestra	1919–20	16'	Belaieff 1981
Op. 13	9 Inventions for piano	1920–21	6'	Eschig 1925 (Durand)
WoO	Ode for cello and piano	1919	2'	Durand 1925

WoO	*Étude de concert* for piano	1920	3'	Hamelle-Leduc 1924
Op. 14	Sonata for violin and piano	1921–22	13'	Durand 1923
Op. 15	6 Mélodies for soprano or tenor and piano	1921	10'	Heugel-Leduc 1925
Op. 16	8 Mélodies for soprano or tenor and piano	1918–22	13'	Heugel-Leduc 1925
Op. 17	*Haltes* (Stops) for soprano, tenor and piano	1918–22	13'	Heugel-Leduc 1926
WoO	*My Flowering Staff,* a cycle of 36 songs based on a collection of poems by Serge Gorodetsky, for soprano (or tenor), bass, male chorus and piano (Incorporating Opp. 15, 16 and 17 along with twelve unpublished songs)	1918–22	58'	Heugel-Leduc 1925, and MS
Op. 18	10 Études for piano	1915–19	20'	Heugel-Leduc 1925
Op. 19	2 Novelettes for piano	1921–22	9'	Heugel-Leduc 1923
Op. 20	Toccata No. 2 for piano Revised by the composer	1922 1974	7'	Simrock 1925 Simrock
WoO	Romance for violin and piano Version for violin and small orchestra	1922 1922	3'	Simrock 1925 Simrock 1925
Op. 21	6 *Études de travail* for piano	1922–23	12'	Heugel-Leduc 1923
Op. 22	Sonata No. 1 for piano	1918–19	16'	Heugel-Leduc 1924
Op. 23	4 *Préludes nostalgiques* for piano	1922	7'	Heugel-Leduc 1924
Op. 24 Op. 24/3 (posth.)	4 Preludes for piano Prelude for 2 flutes, Arr. by composer	1922–23 1971	5' 15"	Durand 1924 Belaieff 1980
Op. 25	*Rhapsodie Georgienne* for cello and orchestra	1922	16'	Durand 1924
Op. 26	Concerto No. 2 for piano and orchestra (reorchestrated 1950) Original version for small orch.	1923	18'	Heugel-Leduc 1924
Op. 27	*Transcriptions Slaves* (Slavic Transcriptions) for piano 1. *Les bateliers du Volga* (Song of the Volga Boatmen) 2. *Chanson pour la chérie* (Song for the beloved) 3. *Chanson granderussienne* (Song: The Great Russian People) 4. *Le long du Volga* (The Banks of the Volga) 5. *Chanson Tcheque* (Czech Song)w 2. Russian Song (new title) rev. ed. by the composer 5. Czech Song rev. ed. by the composer	1924 1956 1956	16'	Heugel-Leduc 1924 Heugel-Leduc 1956 Heugel-Leduc 1956
Op. 28	Canzona for piano rev., ed. by the composer	1924 1974	3' 30"	Simrock 1925 Simrock 1974
Op. 29	Sonata No. 1 for Cello and Piano	1924	11'	Durand 1925
Op. posth.	Canon for String Trio Canon (transcribed for piano by the composer)	1923–24	3'	Bardic 1987 Bardic 1987
Op. 30/1	Sonata No. 2 for Cello and Piano (second movt. based on Canon for String Trio)	1924	10'	Universal 1925
Op. 30/2	Sonata No. 3 for Cello and Piano	1919–26	9'	Universal 1928
Op. 31	4 Romances for piano	1924	8'	Universal 1925

Op. 32	**Ajanta's Frescoes**, Ballet	1923	30'	Universal 1933
Op. 33	*Concerto da Camera* for flute, violin and chamber orchestra	1924	13'	Schott 1925 Schott Prize, 1925
Op. 33a	Intermezzo (2nd movement of *Concerto da Camera*, arr. for piano by the composer	1926	2'	Schott 1927 (The New Piano Book Coll/2, 1953)
Op. 34	Trio for violin, cello and piano	1925	7'–8'	Durand 1925
Op. 35	OI-OI, Opera, first version in three scenes Final version in five scenes	1924–25 1930	58' 65'	Universal 1926 Universal 1931
Op. 36	String Quartet No. 1 (Love Offering by St. Therese of the Infant Jesus)	1922	10'	Schott 1925
Op. 36a	*Musica Sacra* for string orchestra, arranged from String Quartet No. 1 by the composer and Kurt Redel	1973	10'	Schott
Op. 36b	Histoire de la Petite Thérèse de l'enfant-Jésus (13 Short Piano Pieces)	1926	10'	Durand 1926
Op. 37 /1 /2 /3 /3b	3 Pieces for chamber orchestras Overture *Mystère* for cello and chamber orchestra Version for cello and piano *Pour un entrainement de Boxe* (For a Boxer's Training Bout) Prelude for chamber orch. New version *Training* (unrealized ballet)	1921–25 1921 1925 1925 1922 1964 1922	28' 8' 11' 10' 10'	Universal 1927 Universal 1927 Universal 1927 Universal 1927 Universal 1927 Universal 1927
Op. 38	12 Preludes (The Well-tempered Violoncello) for cello and piano 5 Preludes from 12 Preludes Op. 38, arr. by composer: Nos. 2 & 4 for cello and percussion Nos. 3, 9, 10 for cello and strings	1925–26 1925–26	25'	Durand 1927 Durand
Op. 39	*Message* for piano	1926	10'	Universal 1926
Op. 39b WoO	*Voeux* (Wishes), 6 Pieces for piano *Pour la Paix en Orient* (For Peace in the Orient) Originally one of the *Voeux*	1926 1926	9' 30 1'	Durand 1926
Op. 40	String Quartet No. 2	1926	12'	Durand 1927
Op. 41	*Magna Mater* for orchestra	1926–27	8'–9'	Universal 1931
Op. 42	Symphony No. 1 Scherzo for Percussion Ensemble, from Symphony No. 1	1927 (1927)	24' 3'	Durand 1929 Presser 1974
Op. 43	*Elégie* for violin and piano	1927	6'	Durand 1928
Op. 44 Op. 44a	Quintet for piano and strings Tanz (Dance) for piano, arr. by composer from 2nd movement of Quintet	1927 1928	15' 2'	Universal 1930 Bardic 1987
WoO Op. posth.	Vocalise-Étude for high voice and piano Retitled as Study for high voice (or flute) and piano	1927	1'	Leduc 1928 (No. 60 of Repertoire moderne de Vocalises-Études) Belaieff 1980

Op. 45	**Die Hochzeit der Sobeide** (The Wedding of Sobeide), Opera in 3 scenes after Hugo von Hofmannsthal	1929–30	1 hr 40′	Universal 1931
Op. 45a	*Festmusik* (Celebration Music) for orchestra (Suite from The Wedding of Sobeide)	1930	10′	Universal 1932
Op. 46	*Entretiens* (Conversations) for piano	1930	13′	Durand 1931
Op. 47 WoO	Concertino for violin, cello, piano and string orchestra Original version for 4 violins, 2 violas, 2 violas da gamba, 2 cellos, bass and piano Version for clarinet, bassoon, piano and strings Triple Concertino for violin, cello, piano and orchestra Version for violin, cello and piano: Trio Concertante	1930–31 1930 1944 1965 1960	16′	Universal 1931 MS MS Universal 1973 Universal 1974
Op. 48	Concerto No. 3 for piano and orchestra	1931–32	17′	Schott 1932
Op. 49	Duo for violin and cello	1932	12′	Benno Balan 1933 Bote & Bock 1965
Op. 50	Russian Dances for orchestra	1933	10′	Benno Balan 1935 Universal
WoO	Piano Method on the Pentatonic Scale	1934–35		Shanghai Commercial Press 1935
Op. 51 No. 1 No. 2 No. 3	*Étude du Piano sur la gamme pentatonique* (Piano Study on the Pentatonic Scale) 1st Suite (7 pieces) 2nd Suite (7 pieces) *Bagatelles chinoises* (Chinese Bagatelles) (12 pieces)	1934–35 1934 1934 1935	17′ 30″ 2′ 30″ 4′ 11′	Heugel 1935
Op. 52 No. 1 No. 2 No. 3 No. 4 No. 5	5 Concert Études Shadow Play The Lute Homage to China Punch and Judy Chant	1934–36	16′	Schott 1936
Op. 53	Technical Exercises for Piano on the 5-note Scale	1934–36		Peters 1936
WoO	**Die Heirat** (The Marriage), Opera in 2 scenes by Mussorgsky-Tcherepnin	1934–36	1 hr. 5′	Universal 1938
Op. 54	**Der Fahrend Schüler mit dem Teufelbannen** (The Wandering Scholar who Exorcised the Devil), Ballet—piano version New orchestral version (replacing lost original orchestration)	1937 1964	26′	Universal 1938
Op. 55	**Trepak**, Ballet	1937	40′	Universal 1938
WoO	*Autour des montagnes russes* (Riding the Roller Coaster) for piano	1937	3′ 30″	Eschig 1938 in the "Exposition 1937" Album
Op. 56	7 Études for piano	1938	9′ 30″	Belaieff 1938

Op. 57	*Suite Georgienne* (Georgian Suite) for piano and string orchestra	1938	20′	Eschig 1939
	Version for 1 piano 4 hands by the composer	1938	20′	Eschig (Durand)
	Version for 2 pianos by the composer	1952	20′	
	Dialogue, piano solo, arr. by the composer			Eschig
	from *Suite Georgienne*, 2nd movement	1952	4′	
Op. 58	Sonatine for timpani & piano	1939	7′	Boosey & Hawkes 1940
	Revised edition for 2 or 3 timpani and piano Version	1951		Boosey & Hawkes 1951
	for timpani & orchestra			Boosey & Hawkes 1951
	Version for timpani & band	1966		Boosey & Hawkes 1966
Op. posth.	Sonata in One Movement for Bb Clarinet and piano	1939	6′	Schott 1980
Op. 59	Trio for 3 fluets	1939	6′	Belaieff 1950
Op. 60	Quartet for 4 flutes	1939	6′	Belaieff 1950
Op. 61	Trio for 3 trumpets or 3 clarinets in Bb	1939	6′	Marks 1952
Op. 62	March for 3 trumpets or 3 clarinets in B-flat	1939	2′	Marks 1958
Op. 63	*Sonatine Sportive* for saxophone and piano	1939	6′	Leduc 1943
	Original version for bassoon and piano	1939		Leduc 1975
	Version for piano	1939		MS
Op. 64	Andante for tuba or bass trombone and piano	1939	6′	Belaieff 1950
Op. 65	*Pour Petits et Grands: Douze pièces de moyenne difficulté* (For Young and Old: 12 Pieces of Medium Difficulty) for piano	1940	13′ 30″	Durand 1940 (two volumes)
Op. 66	*Chant et Refrain* for piano	1940	4′ 30″	Durand 1940
WoO	**La legende de Razin** (The Legend of Razin), Ballet, Original Title: **Stenka Razine**	1940–41	50′	Belaieff
	Version for orchestra	1940–41		MS reduced MS solo
	Version for piano	1940–41		
WoO	**The Fair at Sorochinski** Music by Mussorgsky, finished and orchestrated by Nicolai Tcherepnin, pub. Bessel 1941, Ballet version by Alexander Tcherepnin	1940	ca. 1 hr 40′	MS
WoO	**Dionys**, ballet mythologique	1940	ca. 17′	MS
WoO	*Suite Populaire Russe* (Popular Russian Suite) for small orchestra	1941	6′	Bessel 1949
WoO	*Badinage* for piano	1941	3′	Harold Lyche 1947
WoO	*Le Retour du Coche* (The Return of the Carriage) Original title: *Nevsky Prospect.* This is the original, longer version of *Romantic Overture*	1942–43	13′ 30″	MS
Op. 67	*Romantic Overture* for orchestra	1942–51	9′	Schirmer 1955
WoO	*Vivre d'Amour* (Hymn of Love), Cantata for soloists, chorus, organ and orchestra	1942	ca. 6′	Belaieff
Op. 68	Deux Mélodies (Two Songs) for soprano or tenor and piano	1943	5′	Durand 1946
WoO	**Atlantide**, Ballet with French text	1943		MS missing
WoO	*Valse Orientale* for piano, flute, xylophone and strings	c. 1943	6′	MS

WoO	Polka for piano Version for orchestra	1944 1955	2′	Belaieff MS available Belaieff rental
Op. 69	*Evocation, Enfance de St. Nino* (Childhood of St. Nino) for orchestra	1943–44	10′	MS available Belaieff rental
Op. 70	*Mouvement perpetuel* for violin and piano	1944	9′	Durand 1946
Op. 71	7 Songs on Chinese Poems for soprano or tenor and piano (Chinese, Russian, English)	1945	12′	Belaieff 1956
Op. 72	**The Nymph and the Farmer**, Opera in 2 scenes (reorchestration of cantata **Pan Kéou** [Clam Shell], 1945)	1952	40′	Boosey & Hawkes 1972
Op. 73	*Les Douze* (The Twelve) for narrator and small orchestra Version for narrator and piano	1945	16′	Belaieff 1946 Belaieff
Op. 74	*Nativity Play*, Cantata for 2 sopranos, tenor, bass, string quintet and percussion Version for soloists, chorus, string orchestra and percussion Version for voice and piano	1945	30′	Belaieff 1947, 1952 English translation 1962
Op. 75	*Le Monde en Vitrine* (Showcase) for piano	1946	15′	Boosey & Hawkes 1948
WoO	2 Songs for high voice and piano	1945	2′	Chester 1952
WoO	**Vendeur des Papillons** (The Butterfly Salesman), Ballet	ca. 1945		MS
WoO Op. posth.	**Chota Rostaveli**, Ballet (2nd Act) Suite de Ballet (Ballet Suite) arr. by the composer for 2 pianos and percussion, after the ballet **Chota Rostaveli**	1945–46 1946	60′ ca. 20′	MS Belaieff 1982
WoO	*Rondo à la Russe* for piano	1946	3′	Gerig 1976
Op. 76	Suite for solo cello	1946	6′	Durand 1948
Op. 77	Symphony No. 2	1946–51	27′	AMP 1957
WoO	*L'écolier parasseux* (The Lazy Scholar), folksong for voice and piano	ca. 1947	2′	MS French & English
WoO	*J'avais mal* (I was sick), French folksong for voice and piano	ca. 1947	2′	MS
Op. 78	Concerto No. 4 (Fantasy) for piano and orchestra	1947	27′	Hinreichsen 1949 Belaieff
Op. 79 Op. 79a	**La Femme et son Ombre** (The Woman and her Shadow), Ballet Japanese Suite for orchestra, from the ballet **La Femme et son Ombre**	1948 1948	30′ ca. 15′	AMP 1948 MS available AMP rental
WoO	*La Quatrième* (The Fourth Republic) for piano	1948–49	3′	Heugel-Leduc 1954
Op. 80	Symphonic March for orchestra Version for band	1951 1954	6′	MCA 1956 MS (available MCA rental)
Op. 81	*Expressions* for piano	1951	12′ 30	MCA 1951 Belaieff
Op. 82	Songs without Words for piano	1949–51	11′	Peters 1953
Op. 83	Symphony No. 3, incorporating ballet materials from **Dionys** (1940), **Atlantide** (1943) and **Vendeur des Papillons** (1945?)	1951	28′	Belaieff
Op. 84	Songs and Dances for cello and piano	1953	17′	Belaieff 1950
Op. 85	12 Preludes for piano Revised ed. by the composer	1952–53 1972	25′	Marks 1956 Belaieff 1972

Op. 86	Concerto for Harmonica and Orchestra Arranged for harmonica and pianoby the composer	1953	28′	AMP 1956
Op. 87b Op. 87a Op. 87	**Le Gouffre** (The Abyss), Ballet Rondo for 2 pianos Suite for orchestra (excerpts from Op. 87b, with Op. 87a [orchestral version])	1949 1952 1953	30′ 3′ 30″ 18′	Peters 1954 Peters 1957 Peters 1954
WoO	La Colline des Fantômes (The Hill of Phantoms), Ballet	1953	26′	MS
Op. 88	8 Pieces for piano	1954–55	13′	Presser 1957
Op. 89 WoO	*The Lost Flute* for narrator and orchestra Abridged versions for narrator, piano and percussion Abridged versions for narrator and orchestra Pastoral for piano, arranged from *The Lost Flute* (Introduction)	1954 1955 1955 1955	42′ 22′ and 18′ 22′ and 18′ 2′	Belaieff rental available Belaieff 1956 Belaieff Belaieff
WoO	17 Piano Pieces for Beginners	1954–57	9′	Summy-Birchard 1955, 1957, included in "Contemporary Literature" selected & corrected by Frances Clark
Op. 90	Divertimento for orchestra	1955–57	25′	Boosey & Hawkes 1966
Op. 91	Symphony No. 4	1957	25′	Boosey & Hawkes 1959
WoO	Exploring the Piano, 12 duets for beginners and teacher-pianists	1958	6′	Peters 1959
Op. 92	*Georgiana*, Suite for orchestra (from **Chota Rostaveli**)	1946/1958–59	18′	Eulenberg 1959
Op. 93	*Symphonic Prayer* for orchestra	1959	9′	Belaieff 1960
WoO	Trio for flute, violin and cello	1960	10′	Amadeus 1977
WoO	Fanfare for brass ensemble and percussion	1961	6′	Boosey & Hawkes 1964
WoO	Partita for accordion solo	1961	6′	Pagani 1962
Op. 94	Sonata No. 2 for piano	1961	12′	Boosey & Hawkes 1962
WoO	*Processional and Recessional* for organ	1962	9′	Peters 1965
Op. 95	Cycle of 7 Chinese Folk Songs for bass or soprano and piano	1962	15′	Belaieff
Op. 96	Concerto No. 5 for piano and orchestra Version for reduced orchestra	1963	21′	Belaieff 1964 Belaieff
Op. 97	Serenade for Strings	1964	16′	Kunzelmann 1966
Op. 98	*Vom Spass und Ernst* (Of Things Light and Earnest), Cantata for contralto or bass and string orchestra	1964	21′	Gerig-Breitkopf & Härtel
Op. 99	Concerto No. 6 for piano and orchestra	1965	24′	Belaieff 1967
Op. 100	Suite for harpsichord	1966	8′	Peters 1966
Op. 101	*Sonata da chiesa* for viola da gamba and organ Version for viola da gamba, string quintet, flute and cembalo	1966 1967	15′	Simrock 1969 Simrock 1970

Op. 102	Mass (in English) for 3 voices (2 sopranos and alto) *a capella*	1966	5' 30"	C. F. Peters 1969
WoO	*Tzigane* for accordion solo	1966	2' 30"	Pietro Deiro 1968

Op. 103
/1
/2
/3
/4
/5
/6
	6 Liturgical chants for mixed chorus *a cappella*
	   Cherubim Song
	   O my God, I cry to Thee
	   Light so Tender
	   Prayer to the Holy Spirit
	   Transfiguration
	   Alleluia
		1967	
			4' 20"
			4' 15"
			3' 05"
			1' 15"
			2' 45"
			3' 15"
				C. F. Peters 1969

Op. 104
/1
/2
/3
/4
	4 Russian Folksongs for mixed chorus *a capella*
	   Hills
	   Shali-Vali
	   Complaint
	   Nonsense Song
		1967	
			3' 20"
			1' 30"
			4' 10"
			1' 05"
				Peters 1969

WoO	*Ein kleines Lied* (A Little Song) for high voice and piano	c. 1967	1'	MS
WoO	Invention for accordion solo	1967	3' 30"	Pagani 1969
WoO	**The Story of Ivan the Fool** (Music for a Radio Play) for narrator, chorus, solo voices, orchestra and electronic sound	1968	45'	MS
WoO	*Ascension* for piano	1969	1'	Choudens 1970 in album Noveaux Musiciens Vol. 3
WoO	Eleven short pieces for piano	1969	6'	MS
Op. 105	Brass Quintet	1970	10' 30"	Peters 1972
Op. 106	Russian Sketches for youth orchestra Version for band	1971 1977		MCA MCA
WoO	Baptism Cantata for soloists, children's choir, recorders, flutes, strings, organ and congregation participation	1972	3'	MS
WoO	4 *Caprices diatoniques* for harp or celtic harp	1973	4'	Belaieff
Op. 107 (posth.)	Woodwind Quintet	1976	5'	Peters 1984

WoO	2 Pieces for Children
	   1. Indian Trail
	   2. Celebrations
		1976	1'	Willis 1977 in album
				Piano Compositions
				U. S. A.

Op. 108 (posth.)	Duo for 2 flutes	1977	12'	Belaieff 1978
WoO excerpts recorded as Op. 109	"Opivochki" 39 short piano pieces	1975–77	^34'	MS

PIANO TRANSCRIPTIONS

Les Compositeurs Russes du XVIIIème Siècle (Russian Composers of the 18th Century) religious *a cappella* choral music by Bortniansky, Degtiareff and Berezovsky	1920	16'	formerly Chester 1924, now returned to composer
Domenico Zipoli *All' Offertorio, Verso 29,* originally for organ	1920		Ricordi 1925
Anton Rubinstein, Nocturne in F major, Op. 44, No. 5, free adaptation	1920		Durand 1927
Rimsky-Korsakov, *Chant Hindou* (Hindu Song) from the opera **Sadko**	1922		Belaieff 1922
"Pour les enfants," morceaux favorie transcrits et arrangés pour piano (For Children, favorite pieces transcribed and arranged for piano) 12 pieces from the works of Glinka, Borodin, Rimsky-Korsakov, Liadov, Glazunov and N. Tcherepnine	1937		Belaieff 1937

PIANO WORKS EDITED

J. C. Beckel, *The Battle of Gettysburg*: March of the Grand Army of the Potomac under Major General George Gordon Meade into Pennsylvania, July 1, 1863	1939	9'	Hinrichsen 1939—C. F. Peters (in collection *American Civil War Battle Pieces*)
M. Glinka, Pieces de Piano (Three Piano Pieces)	1941		Durand 1941
A. Borodin, Scherzo	1954		Hinrichsen 1954 (Peters)
Borodin, Cui, Liadov, Rimsky-Korsakov, Stcherbachev, Liszt, Paraphrases on the Theme of *Chopsticks* (24 variations and 17 pieces using *Chopsticks* theme as obbligato)	1955		Belaieff A. 1959
P. Tchaikovsky, Sonata in G major, Op. 37	1959		Rahter 1959

CHORAL WORKS EDITED

M. Glinka, Cherubim Song	1954	Summy-Birchard 1954
D. Bortniansky, Cherubim Song No. 7	1954	Summy-Birchard 1954

P. Tchaikovsky, Cherubim Song	1954	Summy-Birchard 1954
G. Handel, Halleluja & Amen from Judas Maccabeus	1954	Summy-Birchard 1954
W. A. Mozart, *Adoremus te, Christe*	1954	Summy-Birchard 1954

MUSIC FOR MOTION PICTURES AND THEATER

L'Inde Inconnue (Unknown India)	1936	Éclair Journal
Le Lac des Cygnes (Swan Lake)	1948	Éclair Journal
Le Bal des Cadets (The Cadets' Ball)	1948	Éclair Journal
King Lear (Shakespeare)	1949	DePaul University, Chicago
Blood Wedding (Garcia Lorca)	1951	Frances Parker School, Chicago
Fenelon	1951	Frances Parker School, Chicago

MUSIC FOR TV FILMS

Crisis in Suez	1961	CBS 20th Century
Catch the Graf Spee	1962	CBS 20th Century
Retreat from Arnheim	1962	CBS 20th Century
Attack on Singapore	1963	CBS 20th Century

ALEXANDER TCHEREPNIN:
A GENERIC CATALOGUE OF WORKS

prepared by Lily Chou

OPERA

Op. 35 **OL-OL**, in 3 scenes after Leonid Andreyev (1924-25)
Final version in 5 scenes (1930) (65')
Original text (manuscript) in Russian (prepared by the composer) Published Version in German by R. Hoffmann; in French by Andre G. Block (manuscript version in English)
Cast: Eudoxia Antonovna, mezzo-soprano/Olga Nikolaievna (Ol-Ol), soprano/Anna Ivanovna, mezzo-soprano/ Nicholas Gloukovsev, tenor/ Onoufry Nikolaievitch, bass-baritone/ Mischa, tenor/Grigori Ivanovitch, basso/ A Student, baritone/A Policeman, baritone/ Chorus
3222/4231/per/hp/strings
Universal

Op. 45 **DIE HOCHZEIT DER SOBEIDE** (The Wedding of
Sobeide), in 3 scenes after Hugo von Hofmannsthal (1928-30) (100') Text in German (prepared by the composer)
Cast: A Rich Merchant (Chorab), baritone/Sobeide, soprano/ Bachtiar, baritone/ Sobeide's Mother, mezzo-soprano/ Schalnassar, bass/ Ganem, tenor/Glilistane, alto/ Slave, tenor/ A Camel Driver, bass/A Gardener, tenor/Gardener's Wife, soprano/Bahram, bass/ A Debtor of Schalnassar, tenor/Ballet
2222/4231/perc/hp/strings
Universal

WoO **DIE HEIRAT** (The Marriage), in 2 scenes after a comedy by Gogol (65')
Music: First scene by Modest Mussorgsky (1863) (30')
Second scene by Alexander Tcherepnin (1934-35) (35') The entire work was orchestrated by A. Tcherepnin
Text in Russian and German. (German translation by Heinrich Burkard)
Cast: Agafja Tichonovna, soprano/Arina Panteleimononva, mezzo-soprano/Fjokla Ivanovna, alto/Dunjaschka, soprano/ Pod-kolessin, baritone/Kotschkarev, tenor/Stefan, bass.
2222/4221/perc/hp/strings
Universal

Op. 72 **THE NYMPH AND THE FARMER**, in 2 scenes (1952) (45')
Based on an ancient Chinese legend. Reorchestration of cantata *Pan Kéou* (1945) Original text in French by Siao Yu; German version by Ernst Roth; English version by Joseph Machlis
Cast: The Nymph, soprano/The Farmer, tenor/Narrator
2121/2200/per/hp pf/strings
Boosey & Hawkes

BALLET

Op. 32 **AJANTA'S FRESCOES** (1923) (30')
Ballet from the story of Buddha by A. Tcherepnin, after an idea of Anna Pavlova and danced by her; choreography by Ivan Cliustin
4 scenes
2232/4231/perc/hp pf/strings
Universal

Op. 37/3b **TRAINING** (1922) (10') (included as No. 3 in THREE PIECES FOR CHAMBER ORCHESTRA, Op. 37—see ORCHESTRA)
Scenario by Georges Isarlov; choreography by Hedy Pfundmayr
1 scene

1010/2200/perc/strings
Universal

Op. 37/3c **TRAINING** (see PIANO) Piano reduction of above by
composer (1930) (10')
Universal

Op. 54 **DER FAHREND SCHULER MIT DEM TEUFELBANNEN** (The Wandering Student Who Exorcised the
Devil) (1937) (30')
Ballet after Hans Sachs
1 scene
original orchestration lost; present orchestration completed 1964 3343/4331/perc/hp/strings
Universal (piano version)

Op. 55 **TREPAK** (1937) (40')
Ballet by Serge Sudeikin and A. Tcherepnin;
choreography by Mikhail Mordkin
3 scenes
2222/4231/perc/hp pf/strings, soprano solo, SATB chorus
Universal

WoO **LA LEGENDE DE RAZINE** (The Legend of Razin)
(1940-41) (50') Original title **STENKA RAZINE**
Ballet based on the legend of Stenka Razine by A. Tcherepnin;
choreography by A. Eltzov
3 scenes
2222/4231/perc/hp pf/strings
Also available in reduced orchestra and piano solo version
Belaieff

WoO **LA FOIRE DE SOROTCHINSKI** (Sorochinski Fair) (1940)
(ca. 100') Music originally by Modest Moussorgsky; finished and orchestrated by Nicolai Tcherepnin; Ballet version
by Alexander Tcherepnin
Manuscript (for information, ask Belaieff)

WoO **DIONYS** ballet mythologique (1940) (ca. 17')
Incorporated into Symphony No. 3, mvts. 1 & 4
Manuscript

WoO **ATLANTIDE** ballet with French text (1943)
Incorporated into Symphony No. 3, mvt. 2
Manuscript missing

WoO **LE VENDEUR DES PAPILLONS** (The Butterfly Salesman) (ca. 1945) Ballet for Boris Knieaseff, Paris.
Incorporated into Symphony No. 3, mvt. 3
Manuscript (for information, ask Belaieff)

WoO **LE DEJEUNER SUR L'HERBE** (Picnic on the Grass)
(1945-46) (30') Ballet based on the music of Joseph Lanner,
orchestrated and freely adapted by A Tcherepnin;
choreography by Roland Petit
Manuscript (for information, ask Belaieff)

WoO **CHOTA ROSTAVELI** (1945-46) (3 hours)
   Ballet in 4 acts;
   choreography by Serge Lifar. Music by three composers:
   Acts 1 & 4: Arthur Honegger (1 hour)
           2: Alexander Tcherepnin (1 hour)
           3: Tibor Harsanyi (1 hour) Manuscript (for information, ask Belaieff)
   For composer's suite for 2 pianos and percussion see
   PIANO 4 HANDS
   For composer's orchestral suite (GEORGIANA, Op. 92) see
   ORCHESTRA

Op. 79 **LA FEMME ET SON OMBRE** (The Woman and her
   Shadow) (1948) (30') Ballet after a NOH drama by Paul Claudel; choreography by Janine Charrat
   2121/2110/timp/hp/strings
   AMP
   For composer's orchestral suite (Op. 79a) see ORCHESTRA

Op. 87b **LE GOUFFRE** (The Abyss) (1949) (35')
   Ballet by Vladimir Dokudovsky after a story by Leonid Andreyev Cast: 4 male dancers/ 3 female dancers
   2222/4231/perc/hp pf/strings
   C. F. Peters
   Three scenes included in composer's Suite, Op. 87
   —see ORCHESTRA

WoO **LA COLLINE DES FANTOMES** (The Hill of Phantoms) (1953) (26')
   Ballet after a story by Tran Van Tung
   3333/4331/perc/hp pf/strings
   Manuscript (for information, ask Belaieff)

ORCHESTRA
Op. 36a MUSICA SACRA for string orchestra (1973) (10')
   Arranged by the composer and Kurt Redel from
   String Quartet No. 1 (1922)
   Schott
   For string quartet original see DUO, TRIO, QUARTET etc.

Op. 37 3 STUCKE FUR KAMMERORCHESTER (Three Pieces
   for Chamber Orchestra) (1921-25) (29')
   1) Overture (8')
       0010/22 cornets 00/strings
           New Version: 2222/2210/perc/strings(86442)
   2) Mystère (11')
       Violoncello Solo/1010/22 cornets 00/perc/strings
           For composer's cello-piano version see CELLO SOLO, CELLO AND PIANO etc.
   3) Pour un entrainment de boxe (Training) (10')
       1010/22 cornets 00/perc/strings
           New Version: 2222/2210/perc/strings (86442) (1964)
           for composer's piano version see PIANO
   Universal

Op. 41 MAGNA MATER (1926-27) (10')
   2222/4231/perc/timp/strings
   Universal

Op. 42 SYMPHONY NO. 1 (1927) (25')
2222/4231/perc/hp/strings
Durand
For edition of Scherzo alone see PERCUSSION

Op. 45a FESTMUSIK (Celebration Music) (1930) (10') Suite
(Overture and Ballet) from the Opera
DIE HOCHZEIT DER SOBEIDE
2222/4231/perc/hp/strings
Universal

Op. 50 DANCES RUSSES (Russian Dances) (1933) (10')
2222/4231/perc/hp/strings
Universal

WoO   SUITE POPULAIRE RUSSE for Small Orchestra (1941) (6')
1111/1110/ perc (4 players)/strings
Bessel

Op. 67 ROMANTIC OVERTURE (1942) (9')
3222/4231/perc/hp pf/strings
Schirmer

WoO   POLKA (1944) (2')
Version for Orchestra (1956)
2222/4231/perc timp/strings
Belaieff
For original version see PIANO

Op. 69 EVOCATION (*Enfance de Saint Nino*) (The Childhood of Saint Nino) (1944) (10')
3333/4330/perc/hp/strings
Belaieff

Op. 77 SYMPHONY NO. 2 (1946-51) (27')
3333/4331/perc/pf cel hp/strings
AMP

Op. 79a JAPANESE SUITE (1948) (15')
(From the Ballet **LA FEMME ET SON OMBRE**-see BALLET)
2121/2110/perc/hp/strings
AMP

Op. 80 SYMPHONIC MARCH (1951) (6')
3222/4331/perc/pf cel hp/strings
MCA—For Band version see BAND

Op. 83 SYMPHONY NO. 3 (1951) (28')
Incorporating ballets **DIONYS** (1940, mvts. 1-4); **ATLANTIDE** (1943, mvt. 2); **VENDEUR DES PAPILLONS**
(ca. 1945, mvt. 3)
3333/4331/perc/hp pf/strings Belaieff

Op. 87 SUITE FOR ORCHESTRA (1953) (18')
2222/4231/perc (3-5 players)/hp pf/strings
C. F. Peters

First three movements from Ballet **LE GOUFFRE**, Op. 87b
—see BALLET
For original 2-piano version of finale (Op. 87a) see
PIANO 4 HANDS

Op. 90 DIVERTIMENTO (1955-57) (25')
3343/4331/perc/hp/strings Boosey & Hawkes

Op. 91 SYMPHONY NO. 4 (1957) (25') (Received Glinka Prize)
3343/4331/timp/hp/strings
Boosey & Hawkes

Op. 92 GEORGIANA, Suite for Orchestra (1946/1958-59) (18')
(From ballet **CHOTA ROSTAVELI**)
2222/4231/perc/strings
Eulenburg

Op. 93 SYMPHONISCHES GEBET (Symphonic Prayer) (1959) (9')
3343/4331/perc/hp/strings
Belaieff

Op. 97 SERENADE FOR STRINGS (1964) (16')
(86642)
Eulenburg-Kunzelmann

Op. 106 RUSSIAN SKETCHES, for youth orchestra (1971)
3222/4231/timp/hp/perc/strings
MCA
For band version see BAND

PIANO & ORCHESTRA
Op. 5 BAGATELLES (1958) (12')
2222/2200/perc/strings Heugel-Leduc
Version for PIANO AND STRINGS (1960)
Heugel-Leduc
For original version see PIANO

Op. 12 CONCERTO NO. 1 (1919-20) (16')
2222/4231/timp/strings
Belaieff

Op. 26 CONCERTO NO. 2 (1922-23, reorchestrated 1950) (18')
2222/4231/perc/strings
Heugel-Leduc
Version for smaller orchestra (original)
2222/22 cornets 00/perc./strings

Op. 48 CONCERTO NO. 3 (1931-32) (18')
2222/4231/perc/strings
Schott

Op. 57 SUITE GEORGIENNE (GEORGIAN SUITE)
for Piano and Strings (1938) (20')

Eschig
For composer's piano transcription of 2nd movement see PIANO

Op. 78 CONCERTO NO. 4 (FANTASY) (1947) (27')
2222/4231/perc/hp/strings
Belaieff

Op. 96 CONCERTO NO. 5 (1963) (21')
3333/4331/perc/hp/strings
Belaieff
Version for Piano and Small Orchestra (21')
3232/3200/perc/hp/strings
Belaieff

Op. 99 CONCERTO NO. 6 (1965) (24')
3222/4231/perc/hp/strings
Belaieff

SOLO INSTRUMENTS AND ORCHESTRA
Op. 25 GEORGIAN RHAPSODY
    for Cello and Orchestra (1922) (16')
    3222/2200/perc/strings
    Durand
    For composer's cello-piano arrangement see
    SOLO CELLO, CELLO AND PIANO etc.

WoO ROMANCE for Violin and Small Orchestra (1922) (3')
    Simrock

Op. 33 CONCERTO DA CAMERA for Flute, Violin, and
    Chamber Orchestra (1924) (13') (Schott Prize, 1925)
    0000/202 cornets 00/timp/strings (86442)
    Schott
    For composer's flute-violin-piano version see WOODWINDS etc. For composer's piano transcription of 2nd
    movement see PIANO

Op. 37/2 MYSTERE for Cello and Chamber Orchestra (1925) (11')
    (included in Three Pieces for Chamber Orchestra
    —see ORCHESTRA)
    1010/202 cornets 00/perc/strings
    Universal
    For composer's cello-piano arrangement see
    SOLO CELLO, CELLO AND PIANO etc.

Op. 37/3 TRAINING version for Oboe and Bassoon with Chamber
    Orchestra, by the composer (included in Three Pieces for Chamber Orchestra—see ORCHESTRA; see also BALLET.
    For composer's piano transcription, see BALLET and PIANO)

Op. 47 CONCERTINO for Violin, Cello, Piano and String
    Orchestra (1930-31) (16')
    Universal
    Original Version by the composer for 12 solo strings and piano
    (4 violins, 2 violas, 2 violas da gamba, 2 cellos, bass) (1930)

Version by the composer for clarinet, bassoon, piano and strings
(1944)
Version as TRIPLE CONCERTINO for Violin, Cello, Piano and Orchestra (1965) (16')
1111/1110/perc/strings Universal
For Version as Piano trio, see DUO, TRIO, QUARTET, etc.

Op. 58 SONATINA for Timpani and Orchestra (1954) (7')
Arranged from Sonatina for Timpani and Piano
(1939) 2222/4231/perc/strings
Boosey & Hawkes
For composer's Timpani and Band version see BAND;
for original version with piano see PERCUSSION

Op. 86 CONCERTO for Harmonica and Orchestra (1953) (28')
2222/4231/perc/hp/strings
AMP
For version with piano see FOR DIVERS INSTRUMENTS

VOICE (OR NARRATOR) & ORCHESTRA
Op. 73 LES DOUZE (The Twelve), for narrator and small orchestra (1945) (16')
Original text in Russian by Alexander Blok; French by G. Arnout; German by J. V. Guenther; English by Peter Ustinov
0000/0000/perc/hp pf/strings (or string quintet)
Version for narrator and piano
Belaieff

Op. 74 NATIVITY PLAY, Cantata for 2 Sopranos, Tenor, Bass,
Chorus (optional), String Orchestra and Percussion (1945) (30')
Text in English, French, German and Russian
Version for soloists, chorus, string orchestra and percussion
Version for voice and piano
Belaieff

Op. 89 THE LOST FLUTE, for narrator and orchestra (1954) (42')
2121/2210/perc/strings
Abridged versions for narrator and orchestra (1955) (22'); (18')
Abridged versions for narrator, piano, percussion (1955) (22'); (18')
Belaieff
For composer's piano arrangement of introduction as PASTORAL see PIANO

Op. 98 VOM SPASS UND ERNST (Of Things Light and Earnest),
Folksong Cantata for Contralto or Bass and String Orchestra (1964) (21')
Russian text version by the composer; German by Robert Marscher; English by Joseph Machlis
Gerig-Breitkopf & Hartel

WoO VIVRE D'AMOUR (Hymn of Love)
Lyric Cantata for Soloists, Chorus and Orchestra,
based on the sayings of St. Therese de l'Infant Jesus (1942) (6')
Text in English and French
Belaieff

WoO **THE STORY OF IVAN THE FOOL**, Music for the Radio-
Play by Douglas Claverdon after a Fable by Tolstoy,
for narrator, vocal soloists, chorus, orchestra and electronic sound

(1968) (45') (Received Italia Prize)
Manuscript

WoO   BAPTISM CANTATA for Children's Chorus, Solo Voice,
Recorders, Flutes, Strings, Organ, and Optional Participation of the Congregation (1972) (3') (for all baptismal religions) Text by Irene Vogel Sulzer
Manuscript

BAND
WoO   FANFARE for Brass Ensemble and Percussion (1961) (6')
3 trpt/4 hn/3 trb/1 tuba/ percussion
Boosey & Hawkes

Op. 58 SONATINA for Timpani and Band (1963) (7')
Arranged from Sonatina for Timpani and Piano (1939)
Boosey & Hawkes

Op. 80 SYMPHONIC MARCH
Version for band (1954) (6')
MCA

Op. 106 RUSSIAN SKETCHES
Version for band (1977)
2142 4 sax 4 cornets/4231/hp
MCA

PIANO
Op. posth. SUNNY DAY (Forgotten Bagatelle) (1915) (1')
Presser

Op. 1 TOCCATA NO. 1 (1921) (6')
Belaieff

Op. 2/1 NOCTURNE NO. 1 (1919) (3' 30")
Belaieff

Op. 2/2 DANCE NO. 1 (1919) (3' 30")
Belaieff

Op. 3 SCHERZO (1917) (2' 30")
Durand

Op. 4 SONATINE ROMANTIQUE (1918) (13')
Durand

Op. 5 BAGATELLES (10 pieces) (1912-18) (12')
Revised and edited by composer (1958) Heugel-Leduc
For composer's piano-orchestra and piano-string versions see
PIANO AND ORCHESTRA

WoO OLD ST. PETERSBURG (Waltz) (ca. 1917) (3' 15")
Manuscript

WoO BALLADE (1917) (ca. 12'40")
Manuscript

WoO EPISODES (Priskaski) (Fleas) (1912-20) (10'30")
12 Simple Pieces for Piano Heugel-Leduc

Op. 6 PETITE SUITE (1918-19) (10')
Durand

Op. 7 PIECES SANS TITRES (8 Pieces Without Title) (1915-17) (9')
Durand

Op. 8/1 NOCTURNE NO. 2 (1919) (4')
Durand

Op. 8/2 DANCE NO. 2 (1919) (3'30")
Durand

Op. 9 8 PRELUDES (1919-20) (9')
Heugel-Leduc

Op. 10 FEUILLES LIBRES (Loose Pages) (1920) (8')
Durand

Op. 11 ARABESQUES (1920-21) (6')
Heugel-Leduc

Op. 13 9 INVENTIONS (1920-21) (6')
Eschig

WoO   ÉTUDE DE CONCERT (Concert Etude) (1920) (3')
Hamelle-Leduc

Op. 18 10 ÉTUDES (1915-20) (20')
Heugel-Leduc

Op. 19 2 NOVELETTES (1921-22) (9')
Heugel-Leduc

Op. 20 TOCCATA NO. 2 (1922) (7')
Simrock

Op. 21 6 ÉTUDES DE TRAVAIL (6 Practice Studies) (1922-23) (12')
Heugel-Leduc

Op. 22 SONATA NO. 1 (1918-19) (16')
Heugel-Leduc

Op. 23 4 NOSTALGIC PRELUDES (1922) (7')
Heugel-Leduc

Op. 24 4 PRELUDES (1922-23) (5'15")
Durand
For composer's two-flute arrangement of Op. 24/3 see WOODWIND etc.

Op. posth. CANON (1923-24) (3')
    Transcription for piano by the composer of CANON for String Trio, on which mvt. 2 of Cello Sonata No. 2, Op. 30/1 is based)
    Bardic
    For cello version see CELLO SOLO etc.; for trio version see DUO, TRIO etc.

Op. 27 SLAVIC TRANSCRIPTIONS (1924) (16')
    No. 1 Les Batelier du Volga (The Volga Boatmen)
    No. 2 Chanson pour la Cherie (Song for the Beloved)
    No. 3 Chanson: Granderussienne (The Great Russian People)
        (Later title: Russian Song)
    No. 4 Le long du Volga (The Banks of Volga)
    No. 5 Chanson Tchèque (Czech Song) Heugel-Leduc

Op. 28 CANZONA (1924) (3' 30")
    Simrock

Op. 31 4 ROMANCES (1924) (8')
    Universal

Op. 33a INTERMEZZO (arranged from 2nd mvt. of CONCERTO DA CAMERA)
    (1926) (2')
    Schott (in THE NEW PIANO BOOK Coll/2, 1953)
    For original version see SOLO INSTRUMENTS AND ORCHESTRA
    For composer's flute-violin-piano version see WOODWIND etc.

Op. 36b HISTOIRE DE LA PETITE THÈRESE DE L'ENFANT JESUS
    (The Story of Little Therese of Infant Jesus)
    (13 short pieces) (10')
    Durand

Op. 37/3c POUR UN ENTRAINEMENT DE BOXE (For a Boxer's Training)
arr. by the composer from his ballet
    TRAINING, Op. 37/3) (1930) (10')
    Bardic
    For original and revised orchestral versions see BALLET; ORCHESTRA; SOLO INSTRUMENTS AND ORCHESTRA

Op. 39 MESSAGE (1926) (10')
    Universal

Op. 39b VOEUX (Wishes) (1926) (9' 30)
    Durand

WoO POUR LA PAIX EN ORIENT (For Peace in the Orient) (1926) (1')
    Originally intended as one of the VOEUX
    Manuscript

Op. posth. TANZ (Dance) (1928) (2')
    Arranged by composer from 2nd mvt. of QUINTET, Op. 44
    Bardic

Op. 46 ENTRETIENS (Conversation) (1930) (ca. 13')
    Durand

WoO PIANO METHOD ON PENTATONIC SCALE (1934-35) (17' 30")
    (Chinese Translation by Dr. Hsiao Yu Mei)
    Shanghai Commercial Press

Op. 51 ÉTUDE DU PIANO SUR LA GAMME
    PENTATONIQUE (Piano Study on the Pentatonic Scale) (1934-35)
    No. 1 Premiere Suite (1st Suite) (1934) (2' 30")
    No. 2 Deuxieme Suite (2nd Suite) (1934)   (4')
    No. 3 Bagatelles chinoises (Chinese Bagatelles) (1935)   (11')
    Heugel-Leduc

Op. 52 FIVE CONCERT ÉTUDES (1934-36) (16')
    No. 1 Shadow Play
    No. 2 The Lute
    No. 3 Homage to China
    No. 4 Punch and Judy
    No. 5 Chant
    Schott

Op. 53 TECHNICAL EXERCISES ON THE 5 NOTE SCALE
    (1934-36)
    C. F. Peters

WoO AUTOUR DES MONTAGNES RUSSES (Riding the Roller Coaster)
    (1937) (3' 30")
    Eschig (in the EXPOSITION 1937 Album)

Op. 56 7 ÉTUDES (1938) (9' 30")
    Belaieff

WoO DIALOGUE (1952) (4') arranged by the composer from
    SUITE GEORGIENNE, Op. 57, 2nd mvt. For original piano-string version see PIANO AND ORCHESTRA

Op. 65 POUR PETITS ET GRANDS (For Young and Old) (1940)
    (13' 15") 12 pieces of medium difficulty
    Durand

Op. 66 CHANT ET REFRAIN (Song and Refrain) (1940) (4' 30")
    Durand

WoO BADINAGE (1941) (3')
    Lyche

WoO POLKA (1944) (2')
    Belaieff
    For composer's orchestral version see ORCHESTRA

WoO RONDO À LA RUSSE (1946) (3')
    Gerig-Breitkopf & Hartel

Op. 75 LE MONDE EN VITRINE (Showcase) (1946) (15')
    Boosey and Hawkes

WoO LA QUATRIÈME (The Fourth Republic) (1948-49) (3')
   Heugel-Leduc

Op. 81 EXPRESSIONS (1951) (12' 30")
   Belaieff

Op. 82 SONGS WITHOUT WORDS (1949-53) (11')
   No. 1 Elegy
   No. 2 Rondel
   No. 3 Enigma
   No. 4 The Juggler
   No. 5 Hymn to Our Lady
   C. F. Peters

Op. 85 12 PRELUDES (1952-53) (25')
   Belaieff

Op. 88 8 PIECES FOR PIANO (1954-55) (13')
   No. 1 Meditation
   No. 2 Intermezzo
   No. 3 Reverie
   No. 4 Impromptu
   No. 5 Invocation No. 6 The Chase No. 7 Etude
   No. 8 Burlesque
   Theo. Presser

WoO   PASTORAL (1955) (2') Arranged by composer from THE
   LOST FLUTE (INTRODUCTION)
   Belaieff
   For original version and composer's arrangement for piano and percussion see VOICE (NARRATOR)
   AND ORCHESTRA

WoO 17 PIANO PIECES FOR BEGINNERS (1954-57) (9') (in
   CONTEMPORARY PIANO LITERATURE selected by Frances Clark)
   Summy-Birchard, Warner Bros.

Op. 94 PIANO SONATA NO. 2 (1951) (12')
   Boosey & Hawkes

WoO   ASCENSION (1969) (1')
   (in album NOUVEAUX MUSICIENS, Vol. 3)
   Choudens

WoO   Eleven short pieces for piano (6')
   Manuscript

WoO TWO PIECES FOR CHILDREN (1976) (1')
   No. 1 Indian Trail
   No. 2 Celebration
   (in album PIANO COMPOSITIONS, U.S.A.)
   Willis

Op. 109 OPIVOCHKI (*i. e.*, "Little Dregs") (1975- 77) (34') A miscellany of 39 short piano pieces in various styles, some based on sketches for works in other media (*e. g.*, a "Merry 'Pickwick' Symphony," the projected Symphony No. 5 and the Flute Duo, Op. 108).
Manuscript

PIANO 4 HANDS FOR 1 PIANO OR 2 PIANOS

Op. 87b RONDO (1952) (3' 30") for 2 pianos
C. F. Peters
For orchestral version as Finale of Suite, Op. 87 see ORCHESTRA

WoO EXPLORING THE PIANO (1958) (6')
12 Duets for Beginner and Teacher-Pianist
C. F. Peters

Op. posth. SUITE DE BALLET (BALLET SUITE) (1946) (ca. 20')
Arranged for 2 pianos and percussion by the composer after the second act of the ballet CHOTA ROSTAVELI (1945-46-)—see also BALLET
Belaieff

Op. 12 CONCERTO NO. 1 (1919-20) (16') Arranged for 2 pianos
by the composer
Belaieff

Op. 26 CONCERTO NO. 2 (1923) (18')
Arranged for 2 pianos by the composer
Heugel-Leduc

Op. 48 CONCERTO NO. 3 (1931-32) (17')
Arranged for 2 pianos by the composer
Schott

Op. 57 SUITE GEORGIENNE (GEORGIAN SUITE) (1938) (20')
Arranged for 2 pianos by the composer
Version for 1 piano, 4 hands, arranged by the composer
Eschig
For solo-piano version of 2nd movement see PIANO

Op. 78 CONCERTO NO. 4 (FANTASY) (1947) (27')
Arranged for 2 pianos by the composer
Belaieff

Op. 96 CONCERTO NO. 5 (1963) (21')
Arranged for 2 pianos by the composer
Belaieff

Op. 99 CONCERTO NO. 6 (1965) (24')
Arranged for 2 pianos by the composer
Belaieff

VIOLIN AND PIANO
Op. 11/5 ARABESQUE for Violin and Piano (1920-21) (2')
Heugel-Leduc

Op. 14 SONATA for Violin and Piano (1921-22) (13')
Durand

WoO ROMANCE for Violin and Piano (1922) (3')
Simrock

Op. 43 ELEGY for Violin and Piano (1929) (3')
Durand

Op. 70 MOUVEMENT PERPETUEL for Violin and Piano (1944) (9')
Durand

CELLO SOLO, CELLO & PIANO, CELLO & PERCUSSION OR STRINGS
Op. 76 SUITE for Cello Solo (1946) (6')
Durand

WoO ODE for Cello and Piano (1919) (2')
Durand

Op. 29 SONATA No. 1 for Cello and Piano (1924) (11')
Durand

Op. 30/1 SONATA No. 2 for Cello and Piano (1924) (10')
Universal
(Incorporating Canon for String Trio-see DUET, TRIO etc.;
for composer's piano transcription of Canon see PIANO)

Op. 30/2 SONATA No. 3 for Cello and Piano (1919-26) (9')
Universal

Op. 38 12 PRELUDES (VIOLONCELLE BIEN TEMPÉRÉ)
(12 Preludes, The Well-Tempered Cello) for Cello and Piano (1925-26) (25')
Durand
Nos. 2 & 4 arranged by composer for cello and percussion;
Nos. 3, 9, 10 arranged by composer for cello and strings Durand

Op. 84 SONGS AND DANCES for Cello and Piano (1953) (17')
Belaieff

Op. 63 SONATINE SPORTIVE (1939) (6')
Version for Cello & Piano by the composer Leduc
For original alto saxophone or bassoon version see WOODWINDS OR BRASS INSTRUMENTS etc.

Op. 25 RHAPSODIE GEORGIENNE for Cello and Piano (1922)
(16') Arranged by the composer from the same work for Cello & Orchestra—see SOLO INSTRUMENTS
AND ORCHESTRA
Durand

Op. 37/2 MYSTÈRE for Cello and Piano (1925) (11')
Arranged by the composer from the same work for Cello & Chamber Orchestra—see ORCHESTRA; SOLO
INSTRUMENTS AND ORCHESTRA
Universal

VIOLA DA GAMBA

Op. 101 SONATA DA CHIESA for Viola da Gamba and Organ (1966) (15')
Version for Viola da Gamba, String Quintet, Flute & Cembalo
Simrock

DUO, TRIO, QUARTET, AND QUINTET WITH STRINGS
Op. 49 DUO for Violin and Cello (1932) (12')
Bote and Bock

Op. posth. CANON for String Trio (1923-24) (2')
Bardic
Incorporated into Cello Sonata No. 2, Op. 30/1
—see CELLO SOLO, CELLO AND PIANO etc.;
for composer's piano transcription see PIANO

Op. 34 TRIO for Violin, Cello and Piano (1925) (8')
Durand

Op. 47 TRIO CONCERTANTE (1960) (16')
Composer's arrangement of Concertino for Violin, Cello, Piano and Strings (1930)-see SOLO INSTRUMENTS
AND ORCHESTRA
Universal

WoO TRIO for Flute, Violin and Cello (1960) (10')
Amadeus

Op. 36 STRING QUARTET NO. 1 (LOVE OFFERING OF ST. THERESA) (1922) (10')
Schott
For string orchestra arrangement by the composer and Kurt Redel (MUSICA SACRA, Op. 36a)
see ORCHESTRA

Op. 40 STRING QUARTET NO. 2 (1926) (12')
Durand

Op. 44 QUINTET for Piano & Strings (1927) (15') Universal
For piano arrangement of 2nd movement as TANZ see PIANO

WOODWIND OR BRASS INSTRUMENTS WITH OR WITHOUT PIANO
Op. posth. STUDY for Flute and Piano (Former title:
"VOCALISE-ÉTUDE" for voice) (1927) (1')
Belaieff
For original see VOICE AND PIANO

Op. posth. SONATA IN ONE MOVEMENT for clarinet and piano
(1939) (6')
Schott

Op. 63 SONATINE SPORTIVE for alto saxophone or bassoon and
piano (1939) (6') Leduc
For composer's cello-piano arrangement see
CELLO SOLO, CELLO AND PIANO etc.

Op. 64 ANDANTE for tuba or bass trombone and piano (1939) (6')
Belaieff

Op. 108 (posth.) DUO for 2 flutes (1977) (12')
   Belaieff

WoO   MOVEMENT for 2 flutes (1977) (2') (*Opivochki*, No. 39)
   MS

Op. 24/3 (posth.) PRELUDE for 2 flutes (1971) (1')
   Arranged from 4 PRELUDES for piano by the composer
   Belaieff

Op. 59 TRIO for 3 flutes (1939) (6')
   Belaieff

Op. 60 QUARTET for 4 flutes (1939) (6')
   Belaieff

Op. 61 TRIO for 3 trumpets or clarinets (1939) (6')
   Marks

Op. 62 MARCH for 3 trumpets in Bb (1939) (2')
   Marks

Op. 105 BRASS QUINTET (1970) (9')
   C. F. Peters

Op. 107 (posth.) WOODWIND QUINTET (1976) (15')
   C. F. Peters

Op. 33 CONCERTO DA CAMERA (1924) (12')
   Arranged for Flute, Violin and Piano by the composer
   Schott
   For original see SOLO INSTRUMENTS AND ORCHESTRA
   For composer's piano arrangement of 2nd movement see PIANO

FOR DIVERS INSTRUMENTS
WoO PROCESSIONAL AND RECESSIONAL for Organ (1962)
   (9') C. F. Peters

Op. 100 SUITE for Harpsichord (1966) (8')
   C. F. Peters

WoO PARTITA for Accordion (1961) (6')
   Pagani

WoO   TZIGANE for Accordion (1966) (2' 30")
   Pietro Deiro

WoO   INVENTION for Accordion (1967) (3' 30")
   Pagani

WoO 4 CAPRICES DIATONIQUES for Harp or Celtic Harp (1973) (4')
    Belaieff

WoO   VALSE ORIENTALE for Piano, Flute, Xylophone, and
    Strings (ca. 1943) (ca. 6')
    Manuscript

Op. 86 CONCERTO for Harmonica and Orchestra (1953) (28')
    Arranged for harmonica and piano by the composer
    AMP
    For original see SOLO INSTRUMENTS AND ORCHESTRA

PERCUSSION

Op. 58 SONATINA for Timpani and Piano (1939) (6') Boosey & Hawkes
    For composer's timpani and Orchestra version see SOLO INSTRUMENTS AND ORCHESTRA;
    for composer's timpani and band version see BAND

Op. 38 PRELUDES (1925-26) From THE WELL-TEMPERED CELLO, Op. 38.
    Arranged by the composer: Nos. 2 & 4 for cello and percussion Durand
    For original version see CELLO SOLO, CELLO AND PIANO etc.

(Op. 42) SCHERZO for Percussion Ensemble from SYMPHONY
    NO. 1, Op. 42 (1927) (3')-see also ORCHESTRA
    Theo. Presser

CHORAL WORKS

Op. 102 MASS for 3 equal voices (*a cappella*) (2 Sopranos & Alto) (1966) (5' 30") (English)
    C. F. Peters

Op. 103 6 LITURGICAL CHANTS for Mixed Chorus (*a cappella*) (1967)
    1) Cherubim Song   (4' 20")
    2) O My God   (4' 15")
    3) Light So Tender   (3' 15")
    4) Prayer To The Holy Spirit   (1' 15")
    5) Transfiguration   (2' 45")
    6) Alleluia   (3' 15")
    C. F. Peters

Op. 104 4 RUSSIAN FOLKSONGS for Mixed Chorus (*a cappella*)
    (1967)
    1) Hills   (3' 20")
    2) Shali-Vali   (1' 30")
    3) Complaint   (4' 10")
    4) Nonsense Song   (1' 05")
    C. F. Peters

VOICE AND PIANO

WoO   A CONTENTED MAN (Turgenev) for Bass and Piano
(1918) (2') (Russian, German, English)
    Belaieff

Op. 15 6 MÉLODIES (Gorodezki) for Soprano or Tenor and Piano (1921) (10')
(French by Andre G. Block)
    Durand

Op. 16 8 MELODIES (Gorodezki) for Soprano or Tenor and Piano (1918-22) (13')
(French by Andre G. Block)
    Heugel-Leduc

Op. 17 HALTES (Stops) (Gorodezki) for Soprano or Tenor and piano (1918-22) (13')
(French by Guillot de Saix)
    Heugel-Leduc

WoO   ЦВЕТУЩИЙ ПОСОХ (My Flowering Staff) (Gorodezki) for Soprano or Tenor, Bass, Male Chorus and Piano
    a cycle of 36 songs (incorporating Opp. 15, 16 and 17, along with twelve unpublished songs.) Russian. (1918-
    22) (57') MS

Op. posth. STUDIE (Study) for Soprano or Tenor and Piano (1927) (1') (Former title: VOCALISE-ETUDE)
    Belaieff
    For flute-piano version see WOODWINDS etc.

Op. 68 2 MELODIES (Tran Van Tung) for Soprano or Tenor and
    Piano (1946) (5')
    Durand

WoO   2 SONGS for Soprano or Tenor and Piano (Margaret Tuck)
    (1945) (2')
    Belaieff

Op. 71 7 SONGS ON CHINESE POEMS for Soprano or Tenor
    and Piano (1945) (12') (Chinese, Russian, English)
    Belaieff

Op. 95 CYCLE OF 7 CHINESE FOLKSONGS for Bass or Other
    Voices and Piano (Chinese) (English by Robert Mok) (1962) (15')
    Belaieff

WoO L'ÉCOLIER PARESSEUX (The Lazy Scholar) Folksong for
    Voice and Piano (ca. 1947) (2') (French and English by C.K. Sie)
    Manuscript

WoO   J'AVAIS MAL... (I was sick...) Folksong for Voice and Piano
    (ca. 1947) (2') (French by C.K. Sie)
    Manuscript

WoO   EIN KLEINES LIED (A Little Song) for Soprano or Tenor
    and Piano (Marie von Ebner-Eschenbach) (German) (ca. 1970) (1')
    Manuscript

MUSIC FOR THEATRE	**MUSIC FOR FILMS**	**MUSIC FOR TELEVISION FILMS**
KING LEAR (Shakespeare) (1950) Manuscript	THE UNKNOWN INDIA (1936) Éclair Journal	CRISIS IN SUEZ (1961) CBS 20th Century TV
BLOOD WEDDING (Garcia-Lorca) (1951) Manuscript	SWAN LAKE (1948) Éclair Journal	CATCH THE GRAF SPEE (1962) CBS 20th Century TV
FENELON (1951) Manuscript	THE CADETS' BALL (1948) Éclair Journal	RETREAT FROM ARNHEIM (1962) CBS 20th Century TV
		ATTACK ON SINGAPORE (1963) CBS 20th Century TV

❅　❅　❅

TRANSCRIPTIONS FOR PIANO
18th CENTURY RUSSIAN COMPOSERS (Bortniansky, Degtiaraff, Berezovsky) Music originally written for church choir.
Arranged for piano solo by A. Tcherepnin (1920)
Belaieff

DOMENICO ZIPOLI: ALL'OFFERTORIO
Originally for organ. Arranged for piano by A. Tcherepnin (1920)
Ricordi

RIMSKY-KORSAKOV: CHANT HINDOU (Hindu Song) from the Opera SADKO. Arranged for piano by A.
Tcherepnin (1922)
Belaieff

12 FAVORITE PIECES FOR CHILDREN FROM THE RUSSIAN MASTERS Selected and arranged for piano by A.
Tcherepnin (1937)
Belaieff

ANTON RUBINSTEIN: NOCTURNE IN F MAJOR,
Op. 44, No. 5 (Free adaptation, 1920)
Durand

REVISIONS/EDITIONS OF PIANO WORKS
J. BECKEL: THE BATTLE OF GETTYSBURG (Revised 1939) (9') Hinrichsen-C.F. Peters

GLINKA: PIECES FOR PIANO (Revised 1941)　　Durand

BORODIN: SCHERZO (Revised 1954)　　Hinrichsen-C. F. Peters

BORODIN, CUI, LIADOV, RIMSKY-KORSAKOV, LISZT, STCHERBACHEV,
"PARAPHRASEN ÜBER EIN KINDERTHEMA"
(Paraphrases on a Children's Theme [*i. e., "Chopsticks"*]) For Piano duet, 4 hands (revised 1955)
Belaieff
TCHAIKOVSKY: SONATA IN G MAJOR, Op. 37 (New edition, revised and corrected, 1959)
Rahter

REVISIONS/EDITING OF CHORAL WORKS
GLINKA: CHERUMBIM SONG (revised 1954)
Summy-Birchard, Warner Bros.

BORTNIANSKY: CHERUBIM SONG NO. 7 in D Major (Revised 1954)
Summy-Birchard, Warner Bros.

TCHAIKOVSKY: CHERUBIM SONG (Revised 1954)
Summy-Birchard, Warner Bros.

HANDEL: ALLELUIA from JUDAS MACCABAEUS (Revised 1954)
Summy-Birchard, Warner Bros.

MOZART: ADORAMUS TE, CHRISTE (Revised 1954)
Summy-Birchard, Warner Bros.

PUBLICATIONS BY A. TCHEREPNIN

"Collection A. Tcherepnin":
Modern Japanese Music, Modern Chinese Music Distributors: Shawnee Press
Universal

BOOKS BY A. TCHEREPNIN

RUSSISCHE MUSIK-ANTHOLOGIE. 80 Beispiele vom Ursprung bis zum Beginn des 19. Jahrhunderts (Anthology of
Russian Music. 80 Examples from the Origins to Beginning of the 19th Century) (Written in 1937) Published in 1965
Belaieff.

TCHEREPNIN'S MUSIC: A DISCOGRAPHY

COMPACT DISCS

ORCHESTRAL MUSIC:

Complete Symphonies (4) and Piano Concertos (6), Symphonic Prayer, Op. 93, Magna Mater, Op. 41, Festmusic, Op. 45a, Symphonic March, Op. 80 (2008)
Singapore Symphony Orchestra
Lan Shui, conductor
Noriko Ogawa, pianist (2008)   BIS-CD-1717/18

Symphony No. 1 in E, Op. 42; Symphony No. 2 in E-flat major, Op. 77
Singapore Symphony Orchestra
Lan Shui, conductor (1999)
(w/ Piano Concerto No. 5)   BIS CD-1017

Symphony No. 2 in E-flat major, Op. 77
Louisville Orchestra
Robert Whitney
(w/ Piano Concerto No. 2; Suite Op. 87)   First Edition FECD 0024

Symphony No. 3, Op. 83; Symphony No. 4 in E minor, Op. 91
Singapore Symphony Orchestra
Lan Shui, conductor (1999)
(w/Piano Concerto No. 6)   BIS CD-1018

Symphony No. 3, Op. 83
Staatsphilharmonie Rheinland-Pfalz
Peter Gülke, conductor (1988)
(w/ Triple Concertino, Rhap. Géorgienne)   THOROPHON Capella CTH 2021

Symphony No. 4, Op. 91, Suite for Orchestra, Op. 87
Russian Dances, Op. 50
Czecho-Slovak State Philharmonic Orchestra
Wing-Sie Yip, conductor (1991)   MARCO POLO 8.223380

Divertimento, Op. 90
Musica Viva Orchestra
Alexander Rudin, conductor (1997)
(w/ Nikolai Tcherepnin Le Destin;
Ivan Tcherepnin Double Concerto)   OLYMPIA OCD 640

Suite for Orchestra, Op. 87
Louisville Orchestra
Robert Whitney
(w/ Piano Concerto No. 2; Suite Op. 87)   First Edition FECD 0024

Magna mater, Op. 41
Symphonic Prayer, Op. 93

Singapore Symphony Orchestra
Lan Shui, conductor (2003)
(w/ Piano Concertos Nos. 2, 4)   BIS CD-1247

Festmusik, Op. 45A
Symphonic March, Op. 80
Singapore Symphony Orchestra
Lan Shui, conductor (2008)
(w/ Piano Concertos Nos. 1, 3)   BIS CD1317

Three Pieces for Chamber Orchestra, Op. 37
Serenade for String Orchestra, Op. 97
Musica Viva Chamber Orchestra
Alexander Rudin, conductor (1995)
(w/ Chamber Concerto, Rhapsodie Géorgienne)   OLYMPIA OCD 584

CONCERTED MUSIC

Complete Piano Concertos (6)
Noriko Ogawa, piano
Singapore Symphony Orchestra
Lan Shui, conductor (2011:reissue)   BRILLIANT CLASSICS 9232 (2 discs)

Piano Concertos No. 1, Op. 12; No. 4 ("Fantaisie"), Op. 78; No. 5, Op. 96
Murray McLachlan, piano
Chetham's Symphony Orchestra,
Julian Clayton, conductor (1995)   OLYMPIA OCD 440

Piano Concertos No. 1, Op. 12; No. 3, Op. 48
Noriko Ogawa, piano
Singapore Symphony Orchestra
Lan Shui, conductor (2008)
(w/ Festmusik; Symphonic March)   BIS CD1317

Piano Concertos No. 2, Op. 26; No. 3, Op. 48; No. 6, Op. 99
Murray McLachlan, piano
Chetham's Symphony Orchestra,
Julian Clayton, conductor (1994)   OLYMPIA OCD 439

Piano Concertos No. 2, Op. 26; No. 4 ("Fantaisie"), Op. 78; No. 6, Op. 99
Murray McLachlan, piano
Chetham's Symphony Orchestra,
Julian Clayton, conductor (1994-reissues 2006, 2007)   FORUM FRC 9110;Regis Records 9110

Piano Concerto No. 2, Op. 26
Alexander Tcherepnin, piano
Louisville Orchestra
Robert Whitney
(w/Symphony No. 2; Suite Op. 87)   First Edition FECD 0024

Piano Concertos No. 2, Op. 26; No. 5, Op. 96
Alexander Tcherepnin, piano
Bavarian State Radio Orchestra,
Rafael Kubelik, conductor (1968)   DG 453 157-2

Piano Concertos No. 2, Op. 26; No. 4, Op. 78
Noriko Ogawa, piano
Singapore Symphony Orchestra
Lan Shui, conductor (2003)
(w/ Symphonic Prayer and Magna Mater)   BIS CD-1247

Fantasy for 2 Pianos, Op. 78
(2-piano version of Concerto No. 4)
in Russian & Armenian Music For Two Pianos
w/Khachaturian, Arutiunian
Reine Elizabeth Duo:
Rolf Plagge, Wolfgang Manz pianos (2011)   TELOS TLS 14

Piano Concerto No. 5, Op. 96
Noriko Ogawa, piano
Singapore Symphony Orchestra
Lan Shui, conductor (1999)
(w/ Symphonies Nos. 1 and 2)   BIS CD-1017

Piano Concerto No. 6, Op. 99
Noriko Ogawa, piano
Singapore Symphony Orchestra
Lan Shui, conductor (1999)
(w/ Symphonies Nos. 1 and 2)   BIS CD-1017

Ten Bagatelles for Piano and Orchestra, Op. 5
Margrit Weber, piano
Berlin Radio Symphonie Orchestra
Ferenc Fricsay, conductor (1961)
(w/ Falla Nights, Martin Concerto No. 5,
Weber Konzertstück)   DG GALLERIA 463 085-2

Triple Concertino for Violin, Cello, Piano and Orchestra, Op. 47
Göbel-Trio, Berlin
Nürnberger Symphoniker
Uwe Mund, conductor (1978)   THOROPHON Capella CTH 2021

Rhapsodie géorgienne for Cello and Orchestra, Op. 25
Reiner Hochmuth, cello
Polnische Kammerphilharmonie
Wojciech Rajki, conductor (1985)
(w/ Symphony No. 3, Triple Concertino)   THOROPHON Capella CTH 2021

Rhapsodie georgienne for Cello and Orchestra, Op. 25
Concerto da Camera for Flute, Violin and Chamber Orchestra, Op. 33
Mystere for Cello and Chamber Orchestra, Op. 37b (in Three Pieces for Chamber Orchestra, Op. 37)
Alexander Rudin, cello/conductor

Nikolai Alexeyev, conductor (in Rhap. & Op. 37b)
Olga Ivusheikova, flute; Nazar Kozhukar, violin
Musica Viva Chamber Orchestra (1995)
(w/ Serenade, Op. 97)   OLYMPIA OCD 584

Mystère for Cello and Chamber Orchestra, Op. 37b
Hai Zheng, cello
Amatius Orchestra of New York
Paul Olefsky, conductor (1991)
(w/ Tchaikovsky Rococo Vars., etc.)   AMATIUS CLASSICS ACCD 1002

Concerto for Harmonica and Orchestra, Op. 86
John Sebastian, Harmonica
Stuttgart Radio Orchestra
Hans Schwieger, conductor (1959)
(w/ concertos by Villa Lobos and Ibert)   URANIA US 5146 CD

PIANO MUSIC

Piano Sonata No. 1, Op. 22
Preludes Nostalgiques, Op. 23
Bagatelles, Op. 5
Expression, Op. 81, No. 9
Impromptu, Op. 88, No. 4
Etude, Op. 56, No. 7
Burlesque, Op. 88, No. 8
(w/ Piano Quintet, String Quartet No. 2, Piano Trio, Duo for violin and cello, Suite for solo cello, /Nikolai Tcherepnin
Songs (2011)
Alexander Tcherepnin, piano
(Groupe Instrumental de Paris, Nicolai Gedda) (2011)   EMI 9 07256 2 (two discs)

Toccata No. 1, Op. 1
Eight Preludes, Op. 9
Sonata No. 1, Op. 23
Canzona, Op. 28
Message, Op. 39
Seven Études, Op. 56
Le Monde en Vitrine (Showcase), Op. 75
Murray McLachlan, piano (2000)   OLYMPIA OCD 681

Toccata No. 2, Op. 20
Five (Chinese) Concert Études, Op. 52
Twelve Preludes, Op. 85
Sonata No. 2, Op. 94
Sunny Day (Bagatelle oubliée), Op. Posth.
Murray McLachlan, piano (2000)   OLYMPIA OCD 682

Sonatine romantique, Op. 4
Four Arabesques, Op. 11
Five (Chinese) Concert Études, Op. 52
Chant et Refrain, Op. 66

Eight Pieces, Op. 88
Opivochki, [Op. 109] (Nos. 3, 11, 9, 4, 17, 37)
Bennett Lerner, piano (1985)   ETCETERA KTC 1033

Bagatelles, Op. 5
Message, Op. 39
Voeux, Op. 39b (with "...pour la Paix en Orient")
Five (Chinese) Concert Etudes, Op. 52
Songs Without Words, Op. 82 Sonata No. 2, Op. 94
Martha Braden, piano (1991)   CRI 896

Bagatelles, Op. 5
(In *Three Centuries of Bagatelles*, w/ Couperin, Beethoven, Liszt, Saint-Saëns, Liadov, Bartók and Denisov)
Julia Zilberquit, piano (2007)   NAXOS 8.570237

Autour des Montagnes Russes
Daniel Blumenthal, piano (1986)
(w/ Auric, Honegger, Martinu, etc.:
Souvenirs de l'exposition-Paris 1937)   NOBLESSE CD 87008

Autour des Montagnes Russes
Bennett Lerner, piano (1988)
(w/ Auric, Honegger, Martinu, etc.:
Souvenirs de l'exposition-Paris 1937)   ETCETERA KTC 1061

Five Concert Etudes, Op. 52
Jenny Lin, piano (2000)
(w/ "Chinese" pieces by Arensky, Busoni, Adams, Chasins, Gould, Orenstein, Ketelby, Grainger, Scott, Rossini, Martinu,
Waeber-Diaz)   BIS 1110

Five Concert Etudes, Op. 52
Tianshu Wang, piano (2011)
(w/ Buffalo Boy's Flute by Heh Liu-Ting,
other Chinese pieces)   ALBANY 1289

Five Concert Etudes, Op. 52, Nos 3, 4
Tsai Chai-Hsio, piano (1996)
(w/ Buffalo Boy's Flute by He Luting,
other Chinese pieces)   THOROPHON CTH 2034

Petite Suite, Op. 6: No. 3, Berceuse
Christian Spring, piano
   (In *Lullabies*, w/Schumann, Liszt, Chopin, Henselt, Grieg, Tchaikovsky, Brahms, Balakirev, Rebikov, Busoni, Casella,
Suk, Tansman, Vladigerov, Villa-Lobos, Wendel, Ringger)   GALL CD 564

ORGAN

Cherubim Song, Op. 103, No. 1 (arr. organ)
(In "Organ History: The Russian Schools")
Arturo Sacchetti, organ (1997)   ARTS MUSIC 47273

HARPSICHORD

Suite for Harpsichord, Op. 100
(*In Revolution for Cembalo*, w/ Ravel, Massenet, Donizetti, Delius, Thomé, Busoni, Strauss, Tansman, Nobutoki, Shostakovich,
Weinberg, Rodrigo, Ifukube, Kingsley)
Sumina Arihashi, harpsichord   Hanssler Classic HAN 98503

CHAMBER MUSIC

Piano Quintet, Op. 44
String Quartet No. 2, Op. 40
Piano Trio, Op. 34
Duo for violin and cello, Op. 49
Suite for solo cello, Op. 76
(w/Piano Sonata No. 1, Preludes Nostalgiques, etc. and Nikolai Tcherepnin Songs)
Alexander Tcherepnin, piano
Groupe Instrumental de Paris,
Yon Pascal Tortelier, violin
Paul Tortelier, cello (2011)   EMI 9 07256 2 (two discs)

Violin Sonata, Op. 14
Duo for violin and cello, Op. 49
Piano Trio, Op. 34
Rhapsodie géorgienne, Op. 25 (cello-piano version)
Rondo for two pianos, Op. 87a
(w/Nikolai Tcherepnin chamber works) (2007)
Sophia Fridman, violin, Dmitri German, violin,
Alexei Tolstov, cello, Nino Barkalaya, piano
Olga Makarova, piano,
Yulia Getallo and Alexander Andreyev, duo-pianists   Vista Vera VVCD-00123

Piano Trio, Op. 34
Cello Sonata No. 1, Op. 30, No. 1
Violin Sonata, Op. 14
Suite for Solo Cello, Op. 76
Duo for Violin and Cello, Op. 49
Alaria Chamber Players (2006)   Alaria: www.alaria.org or CD Baby

Suite for Solo Cello, Op. 76
Yo-Yo Ma, cello (1999)
(w/ Kodaly Sonata, Wilde, Sheng, O'Connor)   SONY SK64114

Complete Music for Cello and Piano
Three Cello Sonatas (Op. 29; Op. 30, No. 1; Op. 30, No. 2)
The Well-Tempered Cello, Op. 38
Songs and Dances, Op. 84
Ode for Cello and Piano (1919)
Alexander Ivashkin, cello, Geoffrey Tozer, piano (1999)   CHANDOS CHAN 9770

Three Cello Sonatas (Op. 29; Op. 30, No. 1; Op. 30, No. 2)
Ode; Suite for cello solo, Op. 76
Songs and Dances, Op. 84
Alexander Rudin, cello, Victor Ginsburg, piano (2007)   Vista Vera VVCD-00124

Sonata No. 1 for Cello and Piano, Op. 29
Simca Heled, cello, Jonathan Zak, piano (1986)
(w/ Rodrigo Siciliana, Ries Sonata, Bazelaire Suite, Breval, Mendelssohn, Weber, Rimsky-Korsakov)
                                              CLASSICO 153 (Formerly InSync C 4154)

Sonata No. 3 for Cello and Piano, Op. 30, No. 2
Yuri Semenov, cello, Ksenia Stegman, piano (2006)
(w/ Rubinstein, Gretchaninov)   MELODIYA MELCD1000970

Ode for Cello and Piano (1919)
Wolfgang Lehner, Cello, Madeleine Stucki, Piano (2001)
(In *Russian Soul*, w/Hovhanesian, Rebikov, Karjinsky, Tchaikovsky, Akimenko, Gliere, Sokolow, Arensky, Cui, Rachmaninoff,
Harsanyi)   GALL1001

Ode for Cello and Piano (1919)
Gaspar Cassado, cello, Michael Raucheisen, piano
(w/ Cassado, Granados, Debussy, Handel, Mendelssohn, Tchaikovsky, Liszt, Dvořak, Bruch, Glazunov, Saint-Saëns, Popper)
                                              DANTE LYS 184

Songs and Dances, Op. 84: No. 2, Tatar Dance (2007)
(In *Miniatures and Folklore*, w/Moskowski, Wieniawski, Albeniz, Dinicu, Prokofiev, Gabrielli, Glazunov, Stutschewsky, Ben-
Haim, Scriabin, Tsintsadze, Mendelssohn, Popper, Faure, Tchaikovsky, Duport, Ibert, Cassado, Bloch, Piatti, Brahms, Kreisler)
Gavriel Lipkind, cello
Alexandra Lubchansky, piano   Berlin Classics 1614 (2 CDs)

Sonata Sportive for Bassoon and Piano, Op. 63
(In *Revolution for Bassoon*, w/ Gliere, Rathaus, Casadesus, Bizet, Massenet, Fučik, Elgar, W. Lloyd Weber, Rota, G.
Gould, Foote)
Junko Kundo, bassoon, Mitsutaka Shiraishi, piano   Hänssler Classic HAN 98502

Duo for Violin and Cello, Op. 49
Eleonora Turovsky, violin, Yuli Turovsky, cello (1986)
(w/ Stravinsky, Glière, Prokofiev)   CHANDOS CHAN 8652

Sonatine for ThreeTimpani and Piano, Op. 58
Duo Vivace: Albrecht Volz, Andreas Baumann (2000) (In *Pictures for Piano and Percussion*,
w/ Tanner, B. Hummel, Desportes, Green)   AUDITE 95433

Andante for Tuba and Piano, Op. 64
Blair Bollinger, bass trombone, Hugh Sung, piano (1998)
(In *Fancy Free*, w/ Fetter, Spillman, Lassen, Vilette,
Ibert, Tomasi, Smith)   D'NOTE DND 1033

Piano Trio, Op. 34
Odeon Trio (1986)
(w/ Taneyev Trio)   PRO ARTE CDD 303

Trio for 3 Flutes, Op. 59
Duo for 2 Flutes, Op 108
Prelude for 2 Flutes, Op. 24, No. 3
Etude (1927)
Bent Larsen, Henrik Svitzer, et. al. (1999)
(In *The Russian Flute*, w/Cui, Gretchaninov)   CLASSICO 258

Trio for 3 Flutes, Op. 59
Flutention Flute Trio (1997)
(w/ Boismortier, Mozart, Devienne)   CLASSICO 199

Ten Bagatelles, Op. 5, arr. four guitars
Take Four Guitar Quartet (2002)
(w/ Bach, Purcell, Britten, Pujol,
Vuong-Thatch, Mosca, Gershwin, Puccini)   ARS MUSICI AM13162

String Quartet No. 2, Op. 40
New World Quartet (1978)
(w/ Surinach, Hindemith, Bloch,
Stravinsky, Rosza, Korngold)   VOXBOX2 CDX 5071

Quintet for Winds, Op. 107
Cumberland Wind Quintet (1997)
(*In Shadows and Dreams*, w/Baumann,
Dollarhide, Hoover, Jager)   CENTAUR CRC 2335

Quintet for Winds, Op. 107
Prague National Theater Wind Quintet (2000)
(w/ quintets by Rubinstein, Ippolitov-Ivanov, Tansman)   DYNAMIC 296

LP RECORDINGS

ORCHESTRAL MUSIC

Symphony No. 2, Op. 77
  Louisville Orchestra,
  Robert Whitney, conductor (1964)
                                        Louisville LS-645
                                        RCA Gold Seal,
                                        GL 25059

Symphony No. 4, Op. 91
  Nürnberg Symphony,
  Rato Tschupp, conductor (1974)
                                        Colosseum SM 551

Symphonic Prayer, Op. 93
  Nlirnberg Symphony,
  Glinter Neidlinger, conductor (1972)
                                        Colosseum SM 543

Suite for Orchestra, Op. 87
  Louisville Orchestra,
  Robert Whitney, conductor (1955)
                                        Louisville LOU 545-2

Suite for Orchestra, Op. 87
  (identified as "from the ballet *The Abyss*")
  Nürnberg Symphony,
  Othmar M. F. Maga, conductor
                                        Colosseum SM 560

Serenade for String Orchestra, Op. 97
  Munich Chamber Orchestra,
  Hans Stadlmeir, conductor (1975)
                                        Impromptu SM 191506;
                                        MHS 3752

Georgiana Suite, Op. 92
  Frankenland State Orchestra,
  George Barati, conductor (1961)
                                        Lyricord LL 103
                                        SESAC C 2001/02

Festmusik from *Die Hochzeit der Sobeide*, Op. 45a
  Bochum Symphony,
  Othmar M. F. Maga, conductor (1977)
                                        Impromptu SM 191510

Russian Dances, Op. 50
  Nünberg Symphony,
  Zsolt Deaky, conductor (1978)
                                        Colosseum SM 578

Symphonic March, Op. 80
  Rhineland Philharmonic,
  Klaus Peter Seibel, conductor (1976)
                                        RBM 3052

Symphonic March, Op. 80
  (arranged for symphonic band)
  Gardiens de la Paix Band,
  Desiré Dondeyne, conductor (1977)
                                        Disques Serp MC 7040

Fanfare for Brass and Percussion
  Locke Brass Consort (1976)
                                        Unicorn RHS 339

                                        Denotes reissue

CONCERTED MUSIC:

Piano Concertos No. 2, Op. 26
  Composer, piano
  Louisville Orchestra,
  Robert Whitney, conductor (1961)
Louisville LOU-615
RCA Gold Seal GL 25059

Piano Concertos No. 2, Op. 26; No. 5, Op. 96
  Composer, piano
  Bavarian State Radio Orchestra,
  Rafael Kubelik, conductor (1968)
Deutsche Grammophon
139379

Piano Concerto No. 5, Op. 96
  Weng Gi In, piano
  Rhineland Philharmonic,
  Pierre Stoll conductor (1973)
RBM 3016

Bagatelles for Piano and Orchestra, Op. 5
  Margrit Weber, piano
  Berlin Radio Symphony Orchestra,
  Ferenc Fricsay, conductor (1961)
Deutsche Grammophon
138710
Heliodor 87938

Bagatelles for Piano and String Orchestra, Op. 5
  Jürgen Meyer-Josten, piano
  Württemberg Chamber Orchestra,
  Jürg Farber, conductor (1973)
Turnabout TVS-S 34545

Bagatelles for Piano and String Orchestra, Op. 5
  Michelle Roy, piano
  Nünberg Symphony Orchestra,
  Michel Maynaud, conductor
Colosseum SM 802

Triple Concertino for Violin, Cello, Piano and Orchestra, Op. 47
  Göbel-Trio, Berlin
  Nürnberger Symphoniker,
  Uwe Mund, conductor (1978)
THOROPHON MTH 230

Concerto for Harmonica and Orchestra, Op. 86
  John Sebastian, Harmonica
  Stuttgart Radio Orchestra,
  Hans Schwieger, conductor (1959)
Heliodor HS 25064

PIANO MUSIC

Nocturne, Op. 2, No. 1
    Composer (1954)
      (w/ Sonatine, Bagatelles. etc.).....................................Music Library MLR 7043

Sonatine Romantique, Op. 4
    Composer (1954)
      (w/Bagatelles, Arabesques etc.) ....Music Library MLR 7043
    Bennett Lerner (1985)
      (w/Concert Etudes, Opivochki etc.)................................. ETCETERA ETC 1033

Bagatelles, Op. 5
    Composer (1954)
        (w/Sonatine, Arabesques etc.) . . . . .Music Library MLR 7043
    Composer (1968)
        (w/Sonata No. 1, Nostalgic Preludes etc.) . . . . EMI CVC 2124
    Robert Howat (1979)
        (w/Expressions, Preludes Op. 85 etc.) . . . . .Orion ORS 79329
    Maria Kalamkarian
        (w/Sonata No. 2) . . . . .German Columbia SMC 80 970
    Helmut Roloff (1959) . . . . Deutsche Grammophon 32 229
                                                                                     (45 rpm)
    John Ranck (1959) . . . . Zodiac LPZ 1002
                                                       International Piano Library IPA 2002

Eight Preludes, Op. 9
    Monique Haas (1984)
        (w/Sonata No. 2, Voeux etc.) . . . . Aulos Aul 53573

Four Arabesques, Op. 11
    Composer (1954)
        (w/Bagatelles, Sonatine etc.) . . . . .Music Library MLR 7043
    Bennett Lerner (1985)
        (w/Etudes Op. 52, Opivochki etc.). . . . . ETCETERA ETC 1033

Sonata No. 1, Op. 22
    Composer (1968)
        (w/Bagatelles, Nostalgic Preludes etc.). . . . . EMI CVC 2124

Four Nostalgic Preludes, Op. 23
    Composer (1968)
        (w/Bagatelles, Sonata No. 1 etc.) . . . . EMI CVC 2124

Voeux, Op. 39b
    Monique Haas (1984)
        (w/Sonata No. 2, Eight Preludes etc.) . . . . Aulos Aul 53573

Five Chinese Concert Etudes, Op. 52
    Bennett Lerner (1985)
        (w/Arabesques, Opivochki etc.) . . . . ETCETERA ETC 1033

Etude, Op. 56, No. 7
    Composer (1968)
        (w/Bagatelles, Sonata No. 1 etc.) . . . . EMI CVC 2124

Chant et Refrain, Op. 66
    Bennett Lerner (1985)
        (w/Etudes Op. 52, Opivochki etc.). . . . . ETCETERA ETC 1033

Showcase, Op. 75
    Robert Howat (1959) . . . . .Music Library MLR 7098

Expressions, Op. 81
    Robert Howat (1956)
        (w/Preludes, Op. 85). . . . . Music Library MLR 7072

    Robert Howat (1979)
        (w/Bagatelles, Preludes, etc.) . . . . .Orion ORS 78329
    Composer (No. 9)(1968)
        (w/Bagatelles, Sonata No. 1 etc.) . . . . EMI CVC 2124

Five Songs Without Words, Op. 82
    Robert Howat (4) (1979)
        (w/Bagatelles, Preludes, etc.) . . . . .Orion ORS 78329

Twelve Preludes, Op. 85
    Robert Howat (1956) (w/Expressions) . . . . .Music Library MLR 7072
    Robert Howat (4) (1979)
        (w/Bagatelles, Preludes, etc.) . . . . .Orion ORS 78329

Eight Pieces, Op. 88
    Monique Haas (1984)
        (w/Sonata No. 2, Eight Preludes etc.) . . . . Aulos Aul 53573
    Bennett Lerner (1985)
        (w/Etudes, Op. 52, Sonatine etc.). . . . . ETCETERA ETC 1033
    Thérèse Dussaut (1974 . . . . .Arion ARN 38262
                                                        Musical Heritage Society 3617

    Composer (Nos. 4, 8) (1968)
        (w/Bagatelles, Sonata No. 1 etc.) . . . . EMI CVC 2124

Sonata No. 2, Op. 94
    Monique Haas (1984)
        (w/Eight Preludes, Op. 9, Voeux etc.). . . . . Aulos Aul 53573
    Maria Kalamkarian
        (w/Bagatelles). . . . . .German Columbia SMC 80 970

Opivochki, [Op. 109]
    Bennett Lerner (6) (1985)
        (w/Etudes, Op. 52, Sonatine etc.). . . . . ETCETERA ETC 1033

FOR OTHER SOLO INSTRUMENTS
Suite for Harpsichord, Op. 100
    Antoinette Vischer (1967) (2 mvmts.) . . . . Wergo S34 60028

Processional and Recessional for Organ (1962)
    Herbert Manfred Hoffmann. . . . . .De Camera Magna SM 932 58

Suite for Solo Cello, Op. 76
    Paul Tortelier (1969)
        (w/Piano Quintet, Duo, Trio, etc.). . . . . .HMV CSD 3226
    Ken Yasuda (1975) . . . . Columbia (Japan) (UDI 4) 40x-9022-ND
                                                         Denon OX-7076-ND

Caprices Diatoniques for Celtic Harp (1973)
    Denise Megevand (1974) . . . . Arion 382 45
    Helga Stork (Nos. 3, 4)(1984). . . . . .Colosseum Col 9002

Partita for Accordion (1961)

Milan Blaha (1968). . . . . Supraphon 0 11 0238
Joseph Macerollo (1970)
    w/Tzigane for Accordion (1966) . . . . Kaibala

CHAMBER MUSIC
Sonata for Violin and Piano, Op. 14
    Yehudi Menuhin, violin, Composer, piano (1972)

    . . . . BBC Records REGL 409

    Michael Appleman, violin, Diane Huling, piano (1986)

    . . . . Vox Altera (audio cassette)

Sonata No. 1 for Cello and Piano, Op. 29
    S. Heled, cello, J. Zak, piano (1986). . . . . (cassette) INSYNC C4154
    Esther Nyffenegger, cello, Annette Weisbrod, piano (1983)
        (w/Sonata No. 3, Preludes). . . . . De Camera Magna SM 93718

Sonata No. 3 for Cello and Piano, Op. 30, No. 2
    Esther Nyffenegger, cello, Annette Weisbrod, piano (1983)
        (w/Sonata No. 1, Preludes). . . . . De Camera Magna SM 93718

Sonatine Sportive for Saxophone and Piano, Op. 63
    Paul Brodie, saxophone, George Brough, piano

    . . . . Golden Crest RE 7028

    Ed Bogaard, saxophone, Ton Hartsuiker, piano (1982)

    . . . . Telefunken 6. 42841 AZ

    Daniel Deffayet, saxophone, Jacqueline Bussol, piano (1967)

    . . . . Fidelio 34001

    Marcel Mule, saxophone, Marthe Lenom, piano (1955)

    . . . . London/Decca

Twelve Preludes for Cello and Piano, Op. 38
    Esther Nyffenegger, cello, Annette Weisbrod, piano (1983)
        (w/Sonatas Nos. 1, 3). . . . . De Camera Magna SM 93718
    Seymour Barab, cello, William Masselos, piano (Nos. 5, 7) (1950)

    . . . . Paradox

Ode for Cello and Piano (1919)
    Janos Starker, cello. . . . . Columbia (England) CX 1700
    Gaspar Cassado, cello (1935). . . . . Polydor (78 rpm)

Andante for Tuba and Piano, Op. 64
    Mel Culbertson, tuba, Michael Krist, piano (1978)
        (w/Brass Quintet, Op. 105) . . . . RCA RL 303 21

Duo for Violin and Cello, Op. 49
    Yon Pascal Tortelier, violin, Paul Tortelier, cello (1969)
        (w/Quintet, Trio, etc.) . . . . EMI Pathé-Marconi 2C 063-10912
                                            HMV CSD 3225

Trio for Violin, Cello and Piano, Op. 34
    Composer, piano, Y. P. Tortelier, violin, P. Tortelier, cello (1969)
        (w/Quintet, Duo, etc.) . . . . EMI Pathé-Marconi 2C 063-10912
                                            HMV CSD 3225

Göbel Trio. . . . . De Camera Magna SM 92112
Odeon Trio (1978) . . . . RCA RL 303 24; Pro Arte PAL 1052
Pro Musica Trio (1955). . . . . .Pro Musica PMT 201
Western Arts Trio (1979) . . . . .Laurel Record LR 109

Flute Trio, Op. 59
    Rehm, Daschler, Dold, flutes (1971) . . . . Corona SM 30 001

Flute Quartet, Op. 60
    Roger Bourdin Quartet (1970) . . . . Arion 30 A 071
                                           Musical Heritage Society 3072
    Ensemble Quattro Flauti (1980). . . . . SV F667.317
    Kulhau Quartet (1982) . . . . Telefunken 6.42708 AZ

String Quartet No. 2, Op. 40
    Y. & P. Tortelier, Groupe Instrumental de Paris (1969)
        (w/Quintet, Duo, etc.) . . . . EMI Pathé-Marconi 2C 063-10912
                                                      HMV CSD 3225
    New World Quartet (1978). . . . . .ox SVBX 5109

Quintet for Piano and Strings, Op. 44
    Composer, Y. & P. Tortelier, Groupe Instrumental de Paris (1969)
        (w/Duo, Trio, etc.) . . . . EMI Pathé-Marconi 2C 063-10912
                                                       HMV CSD 3225

Brass Quintet, Op. 105
    Annapolis Brass Quintet. . . . . .Crystal S 207
    John Taber, Rodney Miller, trumpets, Adrian van Woudenbert, horn, John Moore, trombone, Mel Culbertson, tuba
        (1978) (w/Andante, Op. 64) . . . . RCA RL 303 21

VOCAL MUSIC
Haltes, Op. 17
    Nicolai Gedda, tenor, Composer, piano (1973)
        (w/Seven Songs, Op. 71) . . . . .EMI Pathé Marconi 2C 065 14028

Seven Songs on Chinese Poems, Op. 71
    Nicolai Gedda, tenor, Composer, piano (1973)
        (w/Haltes, Op. 17) . . . . .EMI Pathé Marconi 2C 065 14028
    Yi Kwe Sze, bass, Brooks Smith, piano (2) (1966)
        (w/Chinese Folksongs). . . . . rmac 6517

Seven Chinese Folksongs, Op. 95
    Yi Kwe Sze, bass, Brooks Smith, piano (2) (1966)
        (w/Songs on Chinese Poems). . . . . rmac 6517

Cantata, *Vom Spaß und Ernst*, Op. 98
    Anton Diakov, bass, Annet Weisbrod, piano (3 excerpts)
    . . . . Pick 70 119

❀   ❀   ❀

TCHEREPNIN'S RECORDED PERFORMANCES

COMMERCIAL RELEASES

Music by Tcherepnin
CONCERTOS
Piano Concerto No. 2, Op. 26 . . . . LOUISVILLE
    Composer, Piano   LOU-615 (1961)
    Robert Whitney, Louisville Orchestra   RCA Gold SealGL 25059

Piano Concerto No. 2, Op. 26 . . . . DEUTSCHE GRAMMOPHON
Piano Concerto No. 5, Op. 96   139379 (1968)
    Composer, Piano   CD 435-157-2
    Rafael Kubelik, Bavarian Radio Orchestra
(in Rafael Kubelik rare recordings, 8 CD box w/Beethoven,
Mozart, Hartmann, Martinon, Schoenberg, etc.)   DG 4775838 (2006)

SOLO PIANO MUSIC
Eight Bagatelles . . . . ELECTROLA 78rpm
(from Ten Bagatelles, Op. 5, Nos. 1-3; 5-9)   G.DB 4440 (1935)

Ten Bagatelles, Op. 5 . . . . .MUSIC LIBRARY
                                                  ** MLR 7043 (1954)

Ten Bagatelles, Op. 5   ## EMI CVC 2124 (1968)
                  ##CD: EMI 9 07256 2 (two discs, w/chamber music, songs)

Chanson pour la Chérie, Op. 27, No. 2 . . . . ELECTROLA
Hommage à la Chine, Op. 52, No. 3   78rpm (1935)
                                  Japanese Victor release VE 1003

Sonatine Romantique, Op. 4 . . . . .MUSIC LIBRARY
Four Arabesques, Op. 11   ** MLR 7043 (1954)
Nocturne, Op. 2, No. 1

Piano Sonata No. 1, Op. 22 . . . . ## EMI CVC 2124 (1968)
Four Nostalgic Preludes, Op. 23   ##CD:EMI 9 07256 2 (two discs,
Etude, Op. 56, No. 7   w/chamber music, songs)
Expression, Op. 81, No. 9
Impromptu, Op. 88, No. 4
Burlesque, Op. 88, No. 8

PIANO ROLLS
from *Petite Suite*, Op. 6 (three movements) . . . . AMPICO (1926)

CHAMBER MUSIC
Sonata for Violin and Piano, Op. 14 . . . . BBC RECORDS
Yehudi Menuhin, violin; Composer, piano   BEGL 409 (1972)

Denotes reissue . . . . ** Denotes coupling
                                               ## Denotes coupling

Quintet for Piano and Strings, Op. 44 . . . . EMI Pathé-Marconi
Trio for Violin, Cello and Piano, Op. 34   C 063 10912 (1969)
    Composer, piano, Y. P. Tortelier, violin,   HMV CSD 3225
    P. Tortelier, cello, Groupe Instrumental de Paris   ##CD:EMI 9 07256 2
(w/String Quartet, No. 2, Duo for Violin and Cello   (two discs
Suite for Solo Cello)   w/piano music, songs)

SONGS
Haltes, Op. 17 . . . . EMI Pathé-Marconi
Seven Songs on Chinese Poems, Op. 71   2C 065 14028
    Nicolai Gedda, Tenor, Composer, Piano   (1973)
(also including songs by Nicolai Tcherepnin ##CD:EMI 9 07256 2)

Music by Other Composers
Kiyose: Springtime at the Hills . . . . JVC 78 rpm (1936)
Matsudaira: Prelude in D major
Koh: Sketch, Op. 3A
Ota: Trafic (*sic*) Sign

Balakirev: Songs . . . . EMI Pathé-Marconi
    Boris Christoff, bass, Tcherepnin, piano   2C 063-10149 (1967)
(Also contains orchestral songs by   CD Reissue in
Balakirev, conducted by Georges Tzipine)   CZS 7 67496 2 (5 CDs)

Borodin: Songs . . . . EMI Pathé-Marconi
    Boris Christoff, bass, Tcherepnin, piano   2C 063-10147 (1966)
(Also contains orchestral songs by Borodin,   ⊠ CD Reissue in
conducted by Georges Tzipine)   CZS 7 67496 2 (5 CDs)

PIANO ROLLS
Rubinstein: Nocturne in F . . . . AMPICO (1926)
(transcribed by Tcherepnin)

UNPUBLISHED RECORDINGS FOR BROADCAST
Music by Tcherepnin

As Pianist
Sonata No. 1, Op. 22 . . . . Columbia University (1965)
Sonata No. 2, Op. 92
Prelude, Op. 85, No. 9

As Conductor
Symphony No. 1, Op. 42 (1970) . . . . BBC Symphony Orchestra
Symphony No. 2, Op. 77 (1968?) . . . . Munich Philharmonic
Divertimento, Op. 90 (1968) . . . . BBC Northern Symphony Orchestra
Symphony No. 4, Op. 91 . . . . BBC Symphony Orchestra

❀   ❀   ❀   ❀   ❀   ❀

A SELECTED BIBLIOGRAPHY
WRITINGS ABOUT ALEXANDER TCHEREPNIN

I. Books

Arias, Enrique Albert: **Alexander Tcherepnin-A Bio-Bibliography**, Greenwood Press, Westport, Ct., 1989.

Chang, Chi-Jen: **Alexander Tcherepnin, His Influence on Modern Chinese Music**, Dissertation for Dr. of Ed. Degree, Teachers College, Columbia Univ., New York, 1983.

Cooley, Christopher: **TheEvolution of the Nine-Step Scale in the Chamber Music of Alexander Tcherepnin**. DMA dissertation, Manhattan School of Music, 2004.

Korabelnikova, Liudmila: **Alexander Tcherepnin: Dolgoe Stranstve**, Iazyki russki kultury, Moscow, 1999.

Korabelnikova, Liudmila: **Alexander Tcherepnin: The Saga of a Russian Émigré Composer**, Indiana University Press, Bloomington and Indianapolis, 2008.

Troncin, Dominique: **l'Oeuvre pour piano seul d'Alexandre Tcherépnine** (in French), Dissertation, Universite de Paris IV, Sorbonne: 1985.

Wang, T.: **Alexander Tcherepnin's** *Five Concert Studies*: **an homage to Chinese musical styles, instruments and traditions**, DMA Dissertation, University of Arizona, 1999.

Wrenn, M. **The Solo Piano Music of Alexander Tcherepnin: a performance analysis of three representative works**, DMA Dissertation, University of Kentucky, 1998.

Wuellner, Guy S.: **The Complete Piano Music of Alexander Tcherepnin: An Essay Together with a Comprehensive Project in Piano Performance**. DMA dissertation. School of Music, University of Iowa, 1974.

Veenstra, Kimberly Anne: **The Nine-Step Scale of Alexander Tcherepnin: Its Conception, Its Properties, and Its Use**, PhD dissertation, Ohio State University, 2009

Yashirin, Svetlana: **A Manifestation of Apollonian Ecumenism in Selected Piano Works of Alexander Tcherepnin (1899-1977)**, DMA dissertation, University of Nebraska, 2006.

❋ ❋ ❋

Music of the Tcherepnins, (London: Boosey & Hawkes, 1969).

II. Periodicals

Abbott, William, ed.: "Alexander Tcherepnin, Conference Headliner," *Badger Notes* (Winter 1960), River Falls, Wis.

Arias, Enrique Albert: "Tcherepnin's *Sonatine Romantique*," *Clavier* 31, No. 10, 1992, Evanston, Ill.

Arias, Enrique Albert: "*Vom Spass und Ernst*: Alexander Tcherepnin's last major vocal compoosition." *Singing* 62, Jan-Feb 2006

Asklund, Gunnar: "A Conference with Alexander Tcherepnin," *Etude* LXVI/12 (Dec. 1948), Philadelphia.

Aubry, Françoise: "Alexandre Tcherepnine" (in French), *Musique et Concerts* No. 19, (Sept.-Oct. 1985), Paris.

BIBLIOGRAPHY

Belaieff, Victor: "Alexander Tcherepnin and Contemporary Music" (in Russian), *Sovremannaja Muzika* No. 11 (1925), Moscow.

Bienvenu, Lily: "Alexandre Tcherepnine-Paul Tortelier" (in French), *Le Guide du Concert et du Disque* (March 15, 1969).

Bryant, Celia Mae: "Teaching a Contemporary Masterwork, Tcherepnin's Etude Op. 56, No. 7," *Clavier* V/1 (Jan. 1966), Evanston, Ill.

_________________: "Teaching One of the Tcherepnin Piano Pieces,": *Clavier* XIII/1 (Jan, 1974), Evanston Ill.

_________________: "The Joy of the Chase: A Lesson on a Piece by Alexander Tcherepnin," *Clavier* X/1 (Jan. 1971), Evanston, Ill.

Clark, Frances: "A Visit with Alexander Tcherepnin," *Clavier* VII/2 (March 1968), Evanston, Ill.

_________________: "Alexander Tcherepnin Chinese Bagatelles, Op. 51, No.3," *Piano Quarterly Newsletter*, No. 13 (Fall, 1955).

_________________: "Questions and Answers," *Clavier* (Dec. 1987). Evanston, Ill.

Daniel, Oliver, "Alexander Tcherepnin," *BMI The Many Worlds of Music* (Nov. 1964), New York.

Delaney, Donald P.: "Pro Musica Hosts Russian Composer," *Magazine of the Times Advertiser* (May 13, 1973), Trenton, New Jersey.

Dunn, Robert: "Piano Footnotes: An Analytic Interpretation Lesson on A. Tcherepnin's Song Without Words, No. 4," *Clavier* III/2 (March 1964), Evanston, Ill.

Freedman, Guy & A. Tcherepnin: "Spanning the Generations: An Interview," *Music Journal* XXXIV (Sept. 1976), New York.

Goldsmith, Harris: "Record Review of Tcherepnin Piano Music played by Bennet Lerner," *Keynote Magazine* Vol 10, No. 11 (Jan. 1987), New York.

Goss, Louise L.: "A Tribute to Alexander Tcherepnin," *Clavier* XVII/6 (Sept. 1978), Evanston, Ill.

Katigbak, Adelaida: "A Conversation with A. Tcherepnin," *The Piano Quarterly* LXII (Winter 1967), New York.

Khaimovsky, G. S.: "Alexander Tcherepnin Speaks" (in Russian), *Sovietskaya Musika* (Aug. 1967), Moscow.

Klay, Walter: "Der Komponist Alexander Tcherepnin" (in German), *TV, Radio Zeitung Programm 7* (February 1973), Basel.

Layton, Robert: "Alexander Tcherepnin," *The Listener* 89/2293 (March 1973), London.

_________________: "Alexander Tcherepnin at 75," *Tempo* No. 108 (March 1974).

McLachlan, Murray: "Around the World in 80 Years." *Piano* 11:32 May-June 2003

Mihalovici, Marcel: "Adieu à Alexandre Tcherepnine" (in French) *Adam Magazine*, (1978), London.

Mitsukuri, Shutuki: "Alexander Tcherepnin" (in Japanese), *Music Review* III/3 (Jan. 1933), Tokyo.

Miura, Atsushi: "Alexander Tcherepnin in Moscow" (in Japanese), *The Ongaku-Geijutzu* (Jan. 1968), Tokyo.

Orga, Ates: "Alexander Tcherepnin" *Records & Recordings*, Vol 20, No.12 (Sept. 1977), London.

Osborne, S.: "Tcherepnin's Teaching Pieces" *Clavier* 39, December 1998

Ramey, Phillip: "Remembering Tcherepnin," *Chicago Magazine* XXVIII/9 (Sept. 1979).

________________: "Alexander Tcherepnin at 70," *New York Philharmonic Program Book* (Jan. 30, 1969) and, in German, *Verlagsnachrichten* Nr. 5 (July 1969), Boosey & Hawkes, Bonn.

Reich, Willi: "Alexander Tcherepnin," *Chesterian* XIII/102 (April-May 1932), London.

________________: "Alexander Tscherepnin" (in German), *der Auftakt* Heft 11/12 (1931), Prague.

________________: "Alexander Tscherepnin zum 60. Geburtstag" (in German), *Melos* (1959), Mainz.

Sargeant, Winthrop: "The Audience, Venice," *The New Yorker* (Oct. 6, 1956), New York.

Slonimsky, Nicolas: "Alexander Tcherepnin Septuagenarian," *Tempo* Nr.87 (Winter 1968/69), London.

Smith, Monica: "Dynasty Developing," *Records & Recording* (May, 1970), London.

Smith, Patrick J.: "Alexander Tcherepnin, Today is the Golden Age...," *High Fidelity/Musical America* (June 1969).

Snook, Paul: "Tcherepnin: Triple Concerto," *Fanfare Magazine* (Sept.-Oct. 1982).

Tcherepnin, Ming: "Tcherepnin's Chinese Bagatelles: A Master Lesson," *Clavier* (Sept. 1983), Evanston, Ill.

Tischer, Gerhardt: "Alexander Tscherepnin" (in German), *Deutscher Musikzeitung Nr. 12* (1933), Cologne.

Truscott, Harold: "A Note on Tcherepnin's Fourth Symphony," *Tempo* No. 57 (1961), London.

Ussachevsky, Vladimir: "Alexander Tcherepnin," *Proceedings of the American Academy and Institute of Arts and Letters* II/29 (May 1978).

Wallerstein, Gerry: "Happy Birthday to Alexander Tcherepnin," *Clavier* XIII (Jan. 1974), Evanston, Ill.

Weidinger, Hildegard: "Alexander Tscherepnin" (in German), *Musik aus Amerika* Heft 54 (Aug. 1962), Vienna.

Wimbush, Roger "Here and There," *The Gramophone* (July 1969), London.

Wuellner, Guy S.: "A Chinese Mikrokosmos," *College Music Symposium*, Journal of the College Music Society, Vol. 25 (1985), Madison, Wi.

________________: "Alexander Tcherepnin, 1899-1977," *The Piano Quarterly* (Winter 1977-1978).

________________: "Alexander Tcherepnin's Bagatelles, Op. 5: A Comparison of Editions," *The Piano Quarterly* (Fall 1977).

________________: "The Cello and Piano Works of Alexander Tcherepnin," *The American String Teacher* (Autumn 1977), Lawrenceville, N. J.

________________: "The Piano Concertos of Alexander Tcherepnin, Part I," *The American Music Teacher* (June-July 1978).

________________: "The Piano Concertos of Alexander Tcherepnin, Part II," *The American Music Teacher* (Sept.-Oct. 1978).

________________: "The Songs of Alexander Tcherepnin," *The NATS Bulletin* (Dec. 1978).

________________: "The Theory of Interpoint," *The American Music Teacher* (Jan. 1978).

BIBLIOGRAPHY

_______________: "The Piano Etudes of Alexander Tcherepnin. *J ALS* 35 (Jan-Jun 1994)

Zimdars, Richard: "8 Pieces for Piano, Op. 88 by Alexander Tcherepnin," *Clavier* XXIV/2 (Feb. 1985), Evanston, Ill.

❊ ❊ ❊

"The Piano Quarterly's 40 Best," *The Piano Quarterly* No. 139.

"Les Tcherepnine" (in French), *Bulletin d'Information* Nr. 24 (Paris: Boosey & Hawkes, 1967).

"Tcherepnin's Diamond Jubilee,": *Pan Pipes* LXVI/2 (March 1974).

III. Newspapers

Action, Charles: "Russian Conducts R. T. E. S. O.," *The Irish Times* March 9, 1970.

Aprahamian, Felix, "Love from Lucerne," *The Sunday Times* (London), Sept. 3, 1978.

Belliard, Maxime: "Concerts et Recitals" (in French), *Le Nouveau Journal*, March 3, 1969

Belt, Byron: "Tcherepnin Calls Music His Religion," *Long Island Press*, May 10, 1970.

Blyth, Alan: "Tcherepnin's 79 Years of Music," *The Times* (London), June 20, 1969.

Borowski, Felix: "Tcherepnin Premieres Symphony," *Chicago Sun-Times*, March 21, 1952.

Buckley, Charles: "Tcherepnin Triumphs as Composer, Pianist," *Chicago Herald-American*, March 21, 1952.

Chissel, Joan: "BBC SO/Davis Festive Hall/Radio 3", *The Times* (London), March 15, 1973.

Durgin Cyrus: "Boston Symphony Orchestra-New Tcherepnin Symphony," *Boston Daily Globe*, Dec. 6, 1958.

Dettmer, Roger: "Tcherepnin Plays Self-Survey Recital," *Chicago's American*, May 4, 1960.

Ericson, Raymond, "Alexander Tcherepnin," *The New York Times*, Oct. 1, 1977.

_______________: "Music for Cello and Piano by Alexander Tcherepnin," *The New York Times*, Feb. 16, 1971.

Eschrich, Klaus-Henning: "Reviews on the Opera, The Marriage by Mussorgsky-Tcherepnin" (in German) *N. Wilhelmshavener Zeitung*, March 24, 1984.

Eyer, Ronald: "Contemporary Old Master," *New York Herald Tribune* Feb. 4, 1962.

Feder, Edgard: "Tcherepnine" (in French) *France-Amérique* (New York) March 11, 1971.

Frankenstein, Alfred: "Alexander Tcherepnin in Interesting Concert," *The San Francisco Chronicle*, Aug. 10, 1955.

_______________: "Russian's Works Well Played-Tcherepnin, Blinder in Recital," *The San Francisco Chronicle*, Aug. 24, 1955.

Greenfield, Edward: "BSO/Davis," *The Guardian* (London), March 15, 1973.

_______________: "White Citizen," *The Guardian* (London) June 10, 1974.

Helm, Everett: "Alexander Tcherepnin; Eine Neuausgabe von Willi Reich Monographie," *Neue Zuricher Zeitung* (Zurich) Jan. 21, 1974.

Henahan, Don: "Chicago Composers Honored," *Chicago Daily News*, Dec. 31, 1958.

Henderson, Robert: "Novel Effect of Tcherepnin 1st Symphony," *The Daily Telegraph* (London), March 15, 1973. Hohohan, John: "At 71 the Way-Out Composer!" *Sunday Independent* (Dublin), March 8, 1970.

Kamp, Richard: "Schwierige einsame Leute, Opern von Mihalovici und Mussorgski/Tscherepnin in Oldenburg" (in German), *N. Wilhelmshavener Zeitung*, March 30, 1984.

Loppert, Max: "Cherepnin's First Symphony," *The Financial Times* (London), March 15, 1973.

Loveland, Kenneth: "Lucerne Celebrates Some Anniversaries," *The Times* (London), Aug. 30, 1978.

Marsh, Robert C. "Discovery of Tcherepnin," *Chicago Sun-Times*, May 5, 1960.

_______________: "Tcherepnin's Back-With Fine Symphony," *Chicago Sun-Times*, Feb. 22, 1959.

Morin, Raymond: "Music Shed Concerts Finish 3rd Series," *Telegram* (Worcester, Ma.), Aug. 3, 1959.

Pascal, Claude: "The Tcherepnin Dynasty," *Le Figaro* (Paris), Aug. 30, 1978.

Neubauer, Simon: "Zwitterwesen der Opernbuhne, 'krapp' von Mihalovici und 'Die Heirat' von Mussorgskij/Tscherepnin in Oldenburg" (in German), *Weser-Kurier*, March 3, 1984.

Pleasants, Henry: "Tcherepnin Carries Years Lightly," *International Herald Tribune* (Paris), June 13, 1974.

Reich, Willi: "Alexander Tcherepnin Dies," *Neue Zuricher Zeitung* (Zurich), Oct. 1977.

Rhein, John von: "The Memories, Melodies of Music's Giant Linger On," *Chicago Tribune* (Chicago), Jan. 21, 1979.

Rogers, Harold, "Tcherepnin Symphony in Premiere," *Christian Science Monitor* (Boston), Dec. 6, 1958.

Stevens, David: "Music in Lucerne, Sound Portrait of Tcherepnins." *International Herald Tribune* (Paris), September 2-3, 1978.

Taylor, Robert: "Symphony Concert," *Boston Herald*, Dec. 4, 1958.

Tircuit, Heuwell: "The Trend for Man is Up," *San Francisco Chronicle*, Dec. 24, 1969.

Wallerstein, Gerry: "Citizen of the World Comes to Bucks County," *Philadelphia Inquirer*, May 13, 1973.

Woodward, Ian, "Alexander Tcherepnin's Broad Musical Heritage," *The Christian Science Monitor* (London), March 7, 1970.

_______________: "Childbirth at Seventy," *The Guardian* (London), Aug. 15, 1969.

"Alexander Tcherepnin," *The Daily Telegraph* (London), Oct. 1, 1977.

"An Interview with Tcherepnin," *The Peiping Chronicle* (Peiping, China) May 27, 1934.

"Obituary: Alexander Tcherepnin," *The Times* (London), Oct. 3, 1977.

"Tcherepnin Sets New Task for Young Chinese Composers," *The Peiping Chronicle* (Peiping, China), Dec. 5, 1934.

IV. Books and Periodicals in Chinese

Chang, Chi-Jen: "Alexander Tcherepnin and the Modern Chinese Music," *Ming Po Monthly* XIV/9 (Sept. 1979), Hongkong;
also in **Music, Men, Ideas** (Taiwan: Times Cultural Publications, 1985);
and **Western Music Reference Materials** V. 6 (1980), Central Conservatory of China, Beijing.

Cheng, Bi-Juan: **A Study on Four Piano Pieces of Tcherepnin with Chinese Musical Idiom.** M. M. Thesis, Taiwan Teachers College, Taipei, June 1984.

Gao, Ting-tzi: "Souvenirs of Musician Tcherepnin's China Sojourn," *Beijing Arts* (March, 1981), Beijing.

He, Luting: "Remembering Mr. Tcherepnin," from the special edition commemorating the 5th anniversary of Tcherepnin's death, *Music and Audiophile* (Sept. 1982), Hongkong.

Hsiao, Yiu Mei: "Alexander Tscherepnin," *Music Magazine* I/3 (July 1934), Shanghai.

Jiang, Dingxian: "In Memory of A. Tcherepnin," *Journal of the Central Conservatory of Music* (Quarterly) 4/1982, Beijing.

Liu, Xiu-an: "Remembrances of Russian Composer Tcherepnin," from the special edition commemorating the 5th anniversary of Tcherepnin's death, *Music and Audiophile* (Sept. 1982), Hongkong.

_______________: "Tcherepnin is leaving China," *Music Education* V/4 (1937), Jiangxi. Ouyang, Mei-Lun: "Tcherepnin: The Man and His Music," *The Art of Music* 4/1982, Shanghai.

Wen, Loong-Hsing: "Tcherepnin Memorial Concert," *Tradition and Recreation* (Sept.-Dec. 1984), Taiwan.

Xiao, Yu: "Alexander Tcherepnin's Works of Chinese Musical Idiom," *Music and Audiophile* I/9 (Sept. 1982), Hongkong.

Zhou, Wenzhong: "Tcherepnin's Contributions in Music," *The Art of Music* 4/1982, Shanghai.

Zhou, Xiaoyen: "Fond Remembrances of a Great Musician who Passionately Loved China." Ibid.

❈   ❈   ❈

Other Sources

Blume, F. ed.: **Die Musik in Geschichte und Gegenwart** (2nd Edition, Kassel; Barenreiter, 1994).

Calvocoressi, M. D.: "Tcherepnin Nicolas Nicolaievitch & Alexander Nicolaievitch," **Cobbett's Cyclopedic Survey of Chamber Music**, 2nd. Ed., 2v. ed. (London; Oxford Univ. Press, 1963).

Ewen, David: **Composers Since 1900** (New York; H. W. Wilson, 1969).

Hinson, G. Maurice: **Guide to the Pianists' Repertoire** (Supplement), Bloomington; Indiana University Press, 1980).

Machlis, Joseph: **Introduction to Contemporary Music** (2nd Edition), (New York; W. W. Norton, 1979).

Norris, Geoffrey, ed.: **The Concise Oxford Dictionary of Music**, (London; Oxford, 1980).

Pavlenova, V. P.: "Alexander Tcherepnin" (in Russian), **Musical Encyclopedia** Vol. 6, (Moscow; 1983).

Riemann, Hugo: **Musik-Lexicon** (Mainz; Schott, 1959).

Rostand, Claude: **Larousse Dictionary of Contemporary Music** (Paris; Larousse, 1970).

Sadie, Stanley, ed.: **The New Grove Dictionary of Music and Musicians**, 2nd Edition (London; Macmillin Pub., 2001).

Slonimsky, Nicolas: "Alexander Tcherepnin," **Baker's Biographical Dictionary of Musicians**, 8th Ed. (New York, Schirmer Books, 1992).

Stuckenschmidt, H. H.: **Twentieth Century Music**, translated from German by Richard Deveson (London; George Weidenfeld & Nicolson Ltd., 1969).

Thomson, Virgil: **American Music Since 1910** (New York; H. R. and Winston, 1970).

Vinton, John, ed. **Dictionary of Contemporary Music**, "Alexander Tcherepnin" by Phillip Ramey (New York; E. P. Dutton, 1974).

❊　❊　❊

Encyclopaedia Britannica (Chicago; Encyclopaedia Britannica, 2007).

"Alexander Tcherepnin," **Britannica Book of Music** (New York, Doubleday/Britannica Books, 1980)

Who's Who in the World, "Alexander Tcherepnin," p. 893, (Chicago, 1971)

❊　❊　❊　❊　❊　❊

INDEX[1]

PART I: COMPOSITIONS BY ALEXANDER TCHEREPNIN

---

[1]Catalogue entries (pp. 353ff) are not indexed.

PART II: WORKS BY OTHER COMPOSERS

PART III: GENERAL INDEX

A

❈ ❈ ❈ ❈ ❈ ❈

BACK COVER

As a birthday card for his first wife Louisine in 1931, Tcherepnin laboriously created this thematic catalogue of the works he had composed during the course of their relationship. The inmost of the 36 nested circles encloses the date 14 XI 1931. Lines radiating outward from it intersect with the lines of the surrounding circles to create a grid for the letters of various inscriptions and the notes of the themes

The four circles immediately surrounding the center contain birthday wishes and endearments penned letter-by-letter within the grid lines:

2. Tous voeux de bonheur 3. Eternel devo[u]ement 4. Toute toute tendresse 5. Tout amour tout amour

The catalogue itself occupies circles 6 through 30, and reads radially from "out" to "in" rather than circularly. Circles 10 through 6 give the titles of eleven instrumental scores, the names of nineteen operatic characters, and the names of five characters and the setting from the never performed (and possibly never finished) ballet Sodom's Miracle. (Thirty-six names in all). Lined up with these titles and names in circles 30 through 11 are thirty-six musical themes associated with them. Gridlines serve as staves; filled-in spaces are musical notes, appropriately stemmed.

Circles 35 through 31 contain birthday wishes in English, French, German and Russian, penned left to right (no longer radially) five letters per line into the 36 five-square-by-five-square arrays that abut the 36 musical themes (some of the wishes continue through two or three arrays). These wishes, lined up with the character themes, read:

Heureux anniversaire heureu[x] (KOLYA); Alle zusammen gesund und fröhlich (ONUFRY)

Сохрани нас боF bcex b месте (EUDOXIA)

God keep us all together

Maudinka et Toukeshka souhaitent a Tetienka tout le bien au monde Modinka et Tuteneschka (GRIGORI; SOBEIDE; KAUFMNN)

The birds of Islip great (sic) you (BARAM)

Du bist die ehrlichste von Allen (GANEM); Tu es la meilleure de tous, chérie (GÜLISTANE)

Jede von dieser Musik ist dank dir entstanden und strebt zu dir (BUDDA; ST. THERESE)

Dans la musique te chanter ma petite bien aimée mon inspiration (BOXER; MÄDCHEN)

Чтобы боF нас храни bcex b месте и Yтобы да си и здоровья (ZWERG; SCHALNASSAR)

May God keep us all together and give us strength and health

Hallo hallo hallo all the greetings in Englisch (sic) hallo hallo (GÄRTNER; SCHMU)

Allons mains en main et chaque nouvelle année plus réussit (LOTH; MRS LOT)

Möge jedes Jahr neue Freude sein (MISS LOT)

Чтобы бы о мноFо радости и сYастья b наступаюуем нobom Fоду (BOTEN; REX SOD)

Lots of joy and happiness in the coming new year

All the best for you my darling (SODOM)

Que Dieu te donne tout le bien (STUDENT); Gib dir Gott alles Gute und Liebe (KAMMERKONZERT)

Все сYастье b предстояу (sic) Fоду (TRIO) (Предстояуем)

All happiness in the coming year

Alles gute in kommenden Jahr (ROMANCE); Heureux anniversaire souhaite (VOEUX); All best wishes of happiness (BIRD)

Uюбоbь здоровье сYастье храни тебя боF и сbятой Нико ай (BIRDS; SYMPHONY)

Love health happiness may God and Saint Nicholas bless you and keep you

Gluck gesundheit liebe Gluck (QUINTET); Heureuse année toute bonheur (QUARTET)

Many happy returns happy year (MAGNA)

Glückliches Jahr liebe Glück (KONZERT [No. 3])

СYастье здоровье б аFоно уYие) (OL-OL)

Happiness health and well-being

The outer rim (circle no. 36) repeats the date November 14, 1931 in French, English and Russian.